Dating the Old Testament

Dating the Old Testament

Craig Davis

Printed in the United States of America by
RJ Communications
51 East 42nd Street, Suite 1202,
New York, NY 10017

ISBN-13: 978-0-9795062-0-8
ISBN-10: 0-9795062-0-4

Cover Design by RJ Communications

Front Cover Photo: Qumran in the Judean Desert, where the Dead Sea
Scrolls were found. Photo from www.istockphoto.com

www.datingtheoldtestament.com

CONTENTS

CHAPTER 1

Introduction

1.1 Purpose and Scope

The purpose of this book is to establish when the books of the Bible were written. It will not attempt to establish dates with great precision, but rather will place each book in the proper time period in Old Testament history.

To achieve the purpose of this book, we will look closely at internal biblical evidence. This will involve some exercise in literary criticism and also biblical exegesis. We will need to look at the Hebrew language and at the historical setting for the Old Testament. We will in some cases review archeological data and other writings from the ancient Middle East. However, this is not a book about those important topics (archeology, Bible commentary, literary criticism, etc.). They are only introduced in so far as they are necessary to address the question of when the books of the Old Testament were written.

1.2 Methodology and Assumptions

One of the difficulties in writing a book like this is that orthodox Jews and Christians understand the Bible to be inspired by God, while secular readers understand the Bible to be of human origin only. I am a Christian, but I have written this book predominately from a critical perspective, looking at the Bible as a human book. For Christians, this is actually not in conflict with divine inspiration. Christians believe that God worked through human beings and normal human processes to produce the Bible; He did not write it Himself in heaven (like the Moslems believe about the Koran) or hand it to a man on gold tablets (like the Mormons believe about the Book of Mormon). To date the Bible within human history, therefore, we will look at the origin of the Bible from the human side. However, although this book will approach the Bible from the standpoint of its human origins, we will not use anti-supernaturalism as a presupposition in reasoning. By anti-supernaturalism we mean a worldview that rules out *a priori* any possibility of historical divine intervention, prophecy, or real miracles in the Bible. This presupposition can come into play when dating Old Testament passages, and some readers may be uncomfortable setting it aside. For example, the 26th chapter of Leviticus discusses the threat of exile if Israel is disobedient, and Israel really was exiled to Babylon in 586 B.C. An anti-supernatural presupposition would rule out the possibility of divine prophecy and therefore would not allow Leviticus 26 to be dated before 586 B.C. no matter how strong the evidence for an earlier date. This book will not use such presuppositions.

We should acknowledge that we are greatly separated in time, language and culture from the texts we will examine. We should also understand that in many cases the evidence available to date a text is limited, and that our misunderstanding of the evidence might in some cases mislead us. These thoughts should caution us to proceed with humility.

Finally, I am by profession an engineer, and this affects the way I organize and present the facts in this book. This book is structured with a numeric outline much like a technical document, which is the way I am most accustomed to writing. Also, because numbers usually represent hard facts, this book uses numbers wherever possible. To best determine the truth, I wanted to bring to bear as many facts as possible.

1.3 Authorship

For biblical passages, the subjects of date of writing and authorship are closely linked, for obvious reasons. If we know the author of a book, we can usually know the date of writing as well. In this book, we will in some cases attempt to identify the author. In general, however, we will avoid the subject of authorship unless it can help to determine the date of writing. There are two reasons for doing this.

First, there are cases where considerable evidence can be marshaled for a particular date of writing, but only limited evidence can be offered for the author being person X as opposed to person Y, or even to some person unknown to us today. For example, Joshua is traditionally considered to be the author of the book of Joshua, writing before 1200 B.C. But this is primarily based on tradition; not much else can be said for authorship by Joshua as opposed to authorship by one of his close personal assistants, or even by a contemporary like Phinehas the priest. On the other hand, authorship by anyone in Joshua's generation would date the book before 1200 B.C., while the main competing theory has the book of Joshua not being completed until after 600 B.C. The difference between 1200 B.C. and 600 B.C. is very great, with different political, religious, language and cultural environments in place. Quite a bit can be said as to whether Joshua, or any book, reflects a 1200 B.C. background or a 600 B.C. background.

Second, when specific details of authorship are dropped, conclusions about dates can be altered. Consider as an example a quote from Num 12:3: "Now the man Moses was very humble, more than any man who was on the face of the earth." One theory about this verse is that Moses is the author, writing prior to 1200 B.C., and a second theory is that this verse was written by an unknown figure about 750 B.C. Without considering any context or other related evidence, one would by default favor the latter date, simply because it is difficult to imagine the most humble man on earth writing that he was the most humble man on earth. However, if we drop the subject of authorship and consider only the matter of date of writing, the picture changes substantially. If the pen was in the hand of a close aide who knew and loved Moses, and felt that Moses was being greatly wronged in the story of Numbers 12, the verse describing Moses' humility becomes more appropriate, and a person who knew Moses personally would be more likely to write Num 12:3 than a person who lived 500 years later.

1.4 Oral Tradition

This book does not address the topic of oral tradition in any detail. Oral tradition can be defined as the process of recounting a story over many years by word of mouth, with the story being changed or adapted to the culture over a period of time. Although it is possible for a story to be conveyed orally in exactly the manner it was originally told (this is especially true with regard to songs), this category of oral tradition is not meaningful in dating a book. An oral tradition that preserves a story perfectly is essentially the same as a story being written by the original story teller. On the other hand, an oral tradition that changes over time will generally carry the marks of the later time in which it is written down.

1.5 Alternate Viewpoints

Much has been written on the subject of the authorship and dates of the books of the Bible. For purposes of brevity, in most cases this book makes little or no mention of the viewpoints that differ with its own. An exception is made in the case of the authorship and date of the Hexateuch (Genesis – Joshua), because the prevailing theory of Hexateuch sources has, over the last 100 years, been used as a framework which frowns over the entire Old Testament. This prevailing theory, the Documentary Hypothesis, is discussed in some depth in chapter 3. Additionally, alternate theories on the date of Isaiah and Daniel will be discussed, because in those two cases also a strong consensus has developed, and that consensus is mostly unrelated to the Documentary Hypothesis.

1.6 Conventions

The following conventions are used throughout this book.

1. Hebrew Bibles are divided into three sections: the Law (Torah), the Prophets and the Writings. This is a theological arrangement of books which was present in antiquity, and is the one recognized in the New Testament (Luke 24:27, 24:44, etc.), as opposed to the more topical arrangement found in modern English Bibles. This grouping and order of books is shown below:

Law	Prophets	Writings
Genesis	Joshua	Psalms
Exodus	Judges	Job
Leviticus	Samuel	Proverbs
Numbers	Kings	Ruth
Deuteronomy	Isaiah	Song of Solomon
	Jeremiah	Ecclesiastes
	Ezekiel	Lamentations
	Hosea	Esther
	Joel	Daniel
	Amos	Ezra
	Obadiah	Nehemiah
	Jonah	Chronicles
	Micah	
	Nahum	
	Habakkuk	
	Zephaniah	
	Haggai	
	Zechariah	
	Malachi	

In this arrangement, the historical books Joshua – Kings are called former prophets, while Isaiah – Malachi are called latter prophets, with the exception of Daniel and Lamentations, which are grouped in the Writings. In this book, we will use this threefold division of the Old Testament.

2. "Torah," the Hebrew word for law, is used to describe the first five books of the Bible: Genesis, Exodus, Leviticus, Numbers and Deuteronomy. "Torah" is used rather than the other common term, "Pentateuch." "Pentateuch" is an extra-biblical word used to denote the first five books of the Bible, while "Torah" is a word used within the Bible, a fact that is occasionally meaningful in our study.[1]

3. Dates are given using the traditional Christian terminology B.C. and A.D.

4. English language quotes are from the 1995 edition of the New American Standard Bible (NASB) unless otherwise noted. The NASB is used because it is a highly literal modern translation well suited for the purposes of this book. In places where the verse numbering is different between Hebrew and English, the English translation verse number is used, except for those cases where the Hebrew wording is explicitly discussed, in which case the Hebrew verse number is placed in parenthesis, as in Ps 68:19 (Heb 68:20).

5. Because the Hebrew names for God are sometimes a factor in the subject of date and authorship of books in the Bible, "YHWH" is occasionally spelled out as the name of God, which is translated LORD (with all capital letters) in most English language Bibles. "Elohim" and "El" are occasionally spelled out rather than the English translation "God."

6. Hebrew language transliterations are my own attempt at a phonetic pronunciation.

---

[1] When the Hebrew word "torah" is found within the Bible, it sometimes refers exclusively and definitively to the first five books of the Bible, but many times the reference is to law in a more general sense. Trying to identify which meaning is intended can be thought-provoking.

CHAPTER 2

Absolute and Relative Dating

There are quite a few tables and dates in this chapter. It is not necessary to study them closely at this time, since we are not breaking any new ground with these tables or dates. At this point, we are just establishing the chronological framework that existed in the Old Testament period. In subsequent chapters, we will begin to place the books of the Old Testament into this chronological framework.

To determine when the books of the Bible were written we will use both absolute and relative dating techniques. Absolute dating means assigning a specific time to an event. In this book, that will mean assigning a year or a range of years to an event, such as the writing of a book of the Bible. Relative dating is the process of determining the order in which events occurred. Often it will be possible to determine that event A happened before event B, even though we cannot be sure of the specific year in which A occurred – we can only know it was sometime before B. We can usually use absolute and relative dating techniques together to reach conclusions on dates. For example, based on multiple references to other leaders in the region, we can know that Zerubbabel was governor in Judah beginning in about 525 B.C. That is an absolute date – not because we are absolutely certain it was 525 instead of 524 or 526, but because we can assign a year to it and be confident that we are at least very close. 1 Chron 3:19-21 lists Zerubbabel, his son and two of his grandsons. This tells us that the earliest possible date for the writing of this passage in 1 Chronicles is not until after Zerubbabel's grandchildren were born. It tells us nothing about the latest possible date for the passage. This is an example of relative dating.

2.1 Absolute Dating

2.1.1 Establishing a Timeline

The following events are used as a foundation for discussions on dates in this book:

> 165 B.C. – Judas Maccabeus captures Jerusalem
>
> 333 B.C. – Greek Conquest of the Persian Empire
>
> 538 B.C. – Persian Conquest of the Babylonian Empire
>
> 586 B.C. – Babylonian Conquest of Judah and Jerusalem
>
> 721 B.C. – Assyrian Conquest of the Northern Kingdom of
>   Israel

We can start with these dates because scholars across the board agree on the historical nature of the five events listed above, and with the exception of the Assyrian conquest, they also agree to within one year on the dates. Working from these dates and using the biblical record from 1 and 2 Kings, Table 2-1 can be built.

Table 2-1 Kings of Israel and Judah

Kings of Israel (Northern Kingdom)			Kings of Judah (Southern Kingdom)		
Name	Date of Reign B.C.	Years	Name	Date of Reign B.C.	Years
Jeroboam I	931-910	22	Rehoboam	931-913	17
Nadab	910-909	2	Abijah	913-911	3
Baasha	909-886	24	Asa	911-870	41
Elah	886-885	2			
Zimri	885	7 days			
Omri	885-874	12			
Ahab	874-853	22	Jehoshaphat	873-848	25
Ahaziah	853-852	2			
Jehoram	852-841	12	Jehoram	848-841	8
Jehu	841-814	28	Ahaziah	841	1
			Athaliah	841-835	6
Jehoahaz	814-798	17	Jehoash	835-796	40
Jehoash	798-782	16	Amaziah	796-757	29

Table 2-1 Kings of Israel and Judah (continued)

Kings of Israel (Northern Kingdom)			Kings of Judah (Southern Kingdom)		
Name	Date of Reign B.C.	Years	Name	Date of Reign B.C.	Years
Jeroboam II	793-753	41	Azariah	792-740	52
Zechariah	753-752	6 months			
Shallum	752	1 month			
Menahem	752-742	10			
Pekahiah	742-740	2			
Pekah	752-731	20	Jotham	750-732	16
Hoshea	731-722	9	Ahaz	735-716	16
			Hezekiah	716-687	29
			Manasseh	697-643	55
			Amon	643-641	2
			Josiah	641-609	31
			Jehoahaz	609	3 months
			Jehoiakim	609-598	11
			Jehoiachin	598-597	3 months
			Zedekiah	597-586	11

Table 2-1 is not completely without problems. In particular, some reigns overlap due to co-regencies (a custom started by David with Solomon in 1 Kgs 1:28-53, as a good tactic to avoid succession struggles). However, the cross-checking between the two kingdoms, combined with external checks which can be made for a number of the kings, gives good confidence that Table 2-1 is essentially correct. We are not breaking new ground here - this table, or something very close to it, is reproduced in many books on Old Testament history.

After the Babylonian exile, we can construct a time frame for key leaders in the province of Judah shown in Table 2-2.

Table 2-2 Post-Exilic Leaders in Judah[1]

Leader	Years B.C.	Biblical References Used for Dating
Sheshbazzar	539-?	Ezra 1:1, 1:8; 5:14, 5:16
Zerubbabel	525-?	Hag 1:1, Ezra 2:2, etc.
Elnathan		
Yehoezer		
Ahzai		
Ezra	458?-428	Ezra 7:1-8, 4:7
Nehemiah	445-425	Particularly Neh 2:1
Bahohi (Bagoas)	407	

In general, we can have good confidence in the accuracy of the dates of key events in the first millennium B.C., but we have limited confidence in the dates of key events earlier than the first millennium B.C. The reason for having good confidence in the dates in the first millennium B.C. can be illustrated by looking first at Table 2-1. The table shows two parallel king lists, and the Bible's record always cross-references the dates of the reign of each king from one kingdom to the date of the reign of the king in the other kingdom. For example, 1 Kgs 15:1-2 says "In the eighteenth year of the reign of Jeroboam son of Nebat, Abijah became king of Judah, and he reigned in Jerusalem three years." The top of Table 2-1 shows Jeroboam in the left column and Abijah in the right column, and a comparison will show that Abijah's reign beginning in Jeroboam's 18th year. In the first millennium B.C., we also have good records outside of the Bible, in particular the dynasties in Egypt, Assyria and Babylon, with associated chronologies. In addition to having multiple chronologies, we also have multiple historical records describing events and interactions between the people spanning across the chronologies. For exam-

---

[1] Extra-Biblical names based on archeology, cited in Yamauichi, *Persia and the Bible*, p. 265

ple, Assyrian records and the Bible both describe the Assyrian king Sennacherib's campaign against Judah when Hezekiah was king.[2] Looking at Table 2-4, the Partial Assyrian King List, and comparing it to the Judean king list in Table 2.1 we see that Hezekiah and Sennacherib reigned at the same time with an overlap of 17 years. This gives us good confidence in the chronology of both the Assyrian list and the biblical Judah/Israel list. Tables 2-3, 2-4, 2-5 and 2-6 also show several of the other more prominent documented interactions between kingdoms. For dating biblical events, the earliest record we have of an interaction between kingdoms is Pharaoh Shishak's invasion of Israel when Rehoboam, son of Solomon, is king in Judah, in a campaign mentioned in 1 Kgs 14:25-26. Shishak's campaign is also described on an Egyptian relief in the temple of Amun at Karnuk.[3] The relief lists Israelite cities captured, though not including Jerusalem. The list of kings of Judah shows Rehoboam reigning from 931 to 913 and the Egyptian king list in Table 2-3 shows Shoshenq I (Shishak) reigning from 945 to 924. This means we have two independent witnesses that are in agreement on the time of Shishak's reign, and the Judean king list from the Bible is consistent with the Egyptian chronology.

Aside from the king lists included here, we have further help in establishing a historical timeline from other sources. Among the most prominent of these are the Black Obelisk of Shalmaneser III, which contains an image of King Jehu of Israel, the Mesha inscription[4] of Moab, which mentions King Omri of Israel, and the Tel Dan Stele[5] set up by King Hazael of Syria, which mentions King Jehoram of Israel and King Ahaziah of Judah, of the "house of David."

---

[2] Rogerson, *Chronicle of the Old Testament Kings*, p. 141
[3] Rogerson, *Chronicle of the Old Testament Kings*, p. 95
[4] Rogerson, *Chronicle of the Old Testament Kings*, p. 102
[5] Rogerson, *Chronicle of the Old Testament Kings*, p. 8

Black Obelisk of Shalmaneser III. This close-up of the second panel is labeled as showing "Jehu, son of Omri" paying tribute to Shalmaneser in 841 B.C.

Table 2-3 Partial Egyptian King List

King	Years B.C.	Biblical References
Rameses I	1295-1294?	Israelite slaves built a city named Rameses (Exod 1:11)
Seti I	1294-1279?	
Rameses II	1279-1213?	
Merneptah	1213-1203?	Merneptah Stele mentions Israel
Shoshenq I (Shishak)	945-924	1 Kgs 11:40, 14:25, 2 Chron 12:2-9
Nekau II (Neco)	610-595	2 Kgs 23:29-35, 2 Chron 35:20-22, 36:4, Jer. 46:2

Table 2-3 Partial Egyptian King List (continued)

King	Years B.C.	Biblical Reference
Osorkon (So)	735-712	2 Kgs 17:4
Apries (Hophra)	589-570	Jer 44:30

Table 2-4 Partial Assyrian King List

King	Years B.C.	Biblical Reference
Shalmaneser III	858–824 B.C.	Black Obelisk references Jehu, King of Israel[6]
Shamshi-Adad V	823–811 B.C.	
Adad-nirari III	810–783 B.C.	
Shalmaneser IV	782–773 B.C.	
Ashur-dan III	772–755 B.C.	
Ashur-nirari V	754–745 B.C.	
Tiglath-pileser III	745–727 B.C.	2 Kgs 15:29, 16:7, 16:10, 1 Chron 5:6, 5:26, 2 Chron 28:20
Shalmaneser V	726–722 B.C.	2 Kgs 17:3, 18:9
Sargon II	721–705 B.C.	Isa 20:1, Sargon's Nimrod Prism IV.25-41 names Pekah and Hoshea[7]
Sennacherib	704–681 B.C.	2 Kgs 18:13, 19:16, 19:20, 19:36, 2 Chron 32:1-2, 32:9-10, 32:22, Isa 36:1, 37:17, 37:21, 37:37
Esarhaddon	680–669 B.C.	2 Kgs 19:37; Isa 37:38; Ezra 4:2
Ashurbanipal	668–627 B.C.	
Ashur-etel-ilani	626–623 B.C.	
Sin-shar-ishkun	622–612 B.C.	

[6] Rogerson, *Chronicle of the Old Testament Kings*, p. 111
[7] Rogerson, *Chronicle of the Old Testament Kings*, p. 141

Table 2-5 Partial Babylonian King List

King	Years B.C.	Biblical Reference
Marduk-apla-iddina II	721–710	Isaiah 39:1, 2 Kgs 20:12
Shamash-shum-ukin	667–648	
Nabopolassar	625–605	
Nebuchadnezzar II	604–562	2 Kgs 24:1 etc., 2 Chron 36:6 etc., Dan 1:1 etc., Ezra 1:7 etc., Neh 7:6, Esth 2:6, Jer 21:2 etc., Ezek 29:19 etc.
Amel-Marduk	561–560	2 Kgs 25:27, Jer 52:31
Neriglissar	559–556	
Labashi-Marduk	556	
Nabonidus	555–539	

Table 2-6 Partial Persian King List

King	Years B.C.	Biblical Reference
Cyrus II the Great	559–530	2 Chron 36:22-23, Isa 44:28, 45:1, Ezra 4:3, etc.
Cambyses II	530–522	
Darius I	521–486	Ezra 4:5, 4:24
Xerxes (Ahasuerus)	486–465	Esth 1:1
Artaxerxes I	465–424	Neh 2:1
Darius II	423–405	Neh 12:22
Artaxerxes II	405–359	
Artaxerxes III	358–338	
Artaxerxes IV	338–336	
Darius III	336–330	

Prior to the time of King Rehoboam of Judah, reaching back into the second millennium B.C., the picture becomes more difficult on all points. From the Mesopotamian region the lights go out, as the older Assyrian and Babylonian dynasties do not record any interaction so far southwest as the land of Israel. Egyptian pharaohs did not record their defeats, so finding a direct Egyptian record to anything like the exodus is a hopeless cause. To further cloud the subject, some Egyptologists disagree on how to interpret the Egyptian king list in the second millennium B.C.[8]. The one clearly documented interaction we have from an Egyptian source that can help a little is the Merneptah Stele, an Egyptian record describing the Palestinian campaign of Pharaoh Merneptah. A line near the end says "Israel is laid waste, her seed [grain] is no more." Based on the Egyptian king list (using the conventional chronology), this would have been between 1213 and 1203 B.C. The Merneptah Stele does not mention any cities in the hill country of Israel, so the Egyptian campaign probably only came into tangential contact with the Israelites, but this record is still significant because it is the earliest extra-Biblical reference to Israel. However, the date range of 1213-1203 serves only to establish that an Israelite settlement in Canaan began before that time, which is no great revelation, since the latest suggested date for an exodus is in the early 13th century B.C.

To establish a biblical chronology in the second millennium B.C., we are left with basically the biblical record alone. We will first use the biblical record to establish a provisional timeline, and then explain why it can only be provisional, until better analysis or more evidence is discovered to modify it or firm it up. 1 Kgs 6:1 gives a time span of 480 years from the exodus until the founding of the temple in the fourth year of Solomon's reign. Since Solomon

---

[8] An issue described in, for instance, *A Test of Time*, by David Rohl. Rohl's chronology of Egypt differs from the conventional chronology by hundreds of years due to overlapping of the 21st and 22nd dynasties. Also challenging the standard chronology are Donavan Courville, *The Exodus Problem and its Ramifications*, Immanuel Velikovsky, *Rameses II and His Time, A Volume in the Ages of Chaos Series*, and others. In this book, we use the conventional chronology of Egypt.

was Rehoboam's father and he reigned 40 years, apparently dying in 931 B.C., his reign would have begun in 970 B.C., and his fourth year would be 966 B.C. This would put the exodus 480 years earlier at 1446 B.C. Between Solomon's reign and the exodus we have a 40 year reign of David, an unclear length of time for the reign of Saul, some time for the leadership of Samuel, several hundred years for the period of the judges, some period before that for the time of Joshua, and 40 years for the Israelites wandering in the wilderness. A chronology of the judges is shown in Table 2-7. The grand total of 410 years in Table 2-7 is a little too much to fit within our 480 year window and still leave room for David, Saul, Samuel, Joshua and the wilderness period. Since the judges seemed to act in a largely regional or tribal context rather than a national context, it is reasonable to believe that the judges overlapped in time, leaving the period described in the book of Judges somewhat less than the 410 years in the table 2-7. Jephthah, the eighth judge in the list, states in Judg 11:26 that Israel has been living east of the Jordan for 300 years, a figure in general agreement with the 480 year span given in 1 Kgs 6:1, especially if a modest amount of overlap is assumed in the chronology of the judges.

Table 2-7 Chronology for the Judges

Foreign Power	Years Oppressed	Judge	Years of rule	Years of rest	Reference in Judges
Cushan-Rishathaim	8				3:8
		Othniel		40	3:11
Eglon	18				3:14
		Ehud		80	3:30
Jabin	20				4:3
		Deborah		40	5:31
Midian	7				6:1
		Gideon		40	8:28
		Abimelech	3		9:22
		Tola	23		10:2
		Jair	22		10:3
Ammon	18				10:8
		Jephthah	6		12:7
		Ibzan	7		12:9
		Elon	10		12:11
		Abdon	8		12:14
Philistines	40				13:1
		Samson	20		16:31
Totals	111		99	200	

Grand Total: 410 years

Table 2-8 then shows a provisional chronology from the exodus to Solomon.

Table 2-8 Provisional Chronology from Moses to Solomon

Event	Date B.C.
Exodus under Moses	1446
Entrance to Canaan	1406
Death of Joshua	1386
Death of Joshua's elders	1366
12 Judges from the book of Judges	1366-1070
Samuel	1070-1020
Saul's reign	1040-1008
David's reign	1008-968
Solomon's reign	970-931

Having established a provisional timeline from Moses to Solomon, we now in fairness need to point out the numerous reasons why precise dates in this era are uncertain. The problems are listed below:

1. We have already indicated that certain elements in the timeline are not dated in the Bible, so we have had to settle for estimates. Undated elements include the length of time David and Solomon were co-regents, the length of Saul's reign, the length of Samuel's judgeship, the length of Joshua's life after entering Canaan and the length of his companions' administration before the cycle of the judges begins (Judg 2:7).

2. No significant extra-biblical references are available to cross-check this chronology.

3. The book of Exodus does not name the pharaoh in Egypt, so we cannot cross-reference to an Egyptian king list.

4. Most of the genealogies in the Bible seem too short to get 400 years in between the exodus and David. Ruth 4:18-22 is typical, allowing only five or six generations between the exodus and David. In some cases the Bible's genealo-

gies may be open – not always tracing directly from father to son, but skipping some generations. Moses' genealogy in Exod 6:16-20 has Moses only four generations down from Levi, but his contemporaries Bezalel and Elishama (Num 1:10) have longer genealogies. Bezalel is seven generations down from Jacob (1 Chron 2:1, 2:4, 2:5, 2:9 and 2:18-21), and Elishama is nine generations down (1 Chron 7:22-27). 1 Chron 7:22-27 also seems to put Joshua 11 generations down from Ephraim. The longer genealogies, as in 1 Chronicles 7, seem more likely, but the shorter genealogies are more frequent (Josh 7:1, for another example).

5.   The biblical king list prior to King Rehoboam of Judah is now a single list with a united monarchy, so our ladder to the past is now only a single pole.

6.   Some writers suggest that the period of 480 years in 1 Kgs 6:1 is figurative, representing 12 generations of 40 years each.

2.1.2 Dates of Writing of Other Early Texts

Several ancient sources outside of the Old Testament are repeatedly referenced in this book, and it is necessary at this point to establish their dates of writing.

1.   Ugaritic texts, sometimes called the Ras Shamra tablets, are from the city of Ugarit in Syria, which was destroyed around 1180 B.C. All Ugaritic texts are written in cuneiform on tablets and are thought to date from 1400-1200 B.C. Ugaritic is a Semitic language similar to Hebrew, and can provide some insight into the early Hebrew language. The Ugaritic texts also provide background on the Canaanite religions.

2.   The Wisdom of Jesus Ben Sirach, also called Ecclesiasticus or Ben Sirach, was written about 185 B.C. Ben Sirach is present in Catholic Bibles as part of the apocrypha. While most apocryphal books are preserved only in Greek, most

of Ben Sirach has been preserved in its original Hebrew form. Ben Sirach was written after the death of the high priest Simon in 196 B.C. (Sir 50:1), but before the power struggle of Simon's successors in 175 B.C. and before the activities of the Maccabean period. In the prologue to the Greek translation of Ben Sirach, the translator says he came to Egypt in 132 B.C., and that he is the grandson of the author. This is consistent with a date range for Ben Sirach between 196-175 B.C. Ben Sirach is useful for dating purposes because it helps show the form of the Hebrew language around 185 B.C., and because it is one of the earliest apocryphal books.

3. Most of the other apocryphal books present in the Catholic Bible were written during the Maccabean period of 165 to 63 A.D. This book references 1 Maccabees, written between 135 and 63 B.C., and 2 Maccabees, written about 40 B.C.

4. The Septuagint is a Greek translation of the Old Testament, including the apocrypha, made between 250 B.C. and 0 A.D. The exact date of translation is disputed, but some of the older books of the Old Testament are thought to have been translated at the earlier end of this range, while other books were translated later.

5. Targums are Aramaic explanations of the Old Testament. The dates of the earliest Targums are disputed, but some of them definitely originated before the time of Christ.

6. Many of the Dead Sea Scrolls were written in Qumran when the settlement there was inhabited, from 168 B.C. to 68 A.D. Some scrolls were carried to Qumran, allowing for a few of them to be older than the community. None are more recent than 68 A.D. The Dead Sea Scrolls include the oldest existing biblical manuscripts.

7. The books of the New Testament were written in the first century A.D. The differences of opinion on the dating of New Testament texts are very important, making the dif-

ference between eyewitness and non-eyewitness testimony. However, for purposes of this book, the understanding that the New Testament is the work of first century A.D. Jews is sufficient, and disputes of 30-40 years do not matter. The New Testament was written in Greek.

8. Flavius Josephus was a Jewish historian who wrote extensively toward the end of the first century A.D. Josephus wrote in Greek also.

9. The Peshitta is a translation of the Old Testament into Syriac, an eastern Aramaic language, in the first two centuries A.D.

10. The Jewish Talmud was written to codify the Torah. The first portion of the Talmud to be written was the Mishna, around 200 A.D. The Mishna is a larger body of work than the Old Testament and shows the form of early post-biblical Hebrew, as well as describing some Jewish traditional thinking on the development of the Old Testament.

11. The Vulgate is a Latin translation of the Bible produced by Jerome by about 400 A.D.

2.1.3 Identifying the Oldest Biblical Manuscripts

It is axiomatic that a book cannot be written later than its earliest copy, so identification of the oldest biblical manuscripts is an initial step in dating the books of the Old Testament. With a few isolated exceptions, the oldest biblical manuscripts are the Dead Sea Scrolls.

The Dead Sea Scrolls were discovered in eleven caves from 1947-1956 near the Qumran ruins by the northwest shore of the Dead Sea. The archeological remains from the Jewish community at Qumran date from 140 B.C. to 68 A.D. The Jewish-Roman war of 66-70 A.D. ended the Jewish presence at Qumran, with the scrolls likely remaining undisturbed from 68 A.D. until their discovery in 1947. The archeological remains at Qumran have been dated using the following methods: (1) carbon-14 dating, (2) comparison of pottery and (3) coins. The scrolls at Qumran have been dated by the following techniques: (1) Paleography – the study of the way letters were written by ancient scribes, (2) Accelerator Mass Spectrometry, a refined form of Carbon-14 dating and (3) internal references.[9] Some of the biblical Dead Sea Scrolls have been given dates as old as 250 B.C. (those would have originated elsewhere and been brought to Qumran), and none are newer than the end of the Qumran community in 68 A.D.

The Dead Sea Scrolls collection of about 800 manuscripts contains 202 identified biblical scrolls.[10] This doesn't mean there are 202 complete biblical books from start to finish; it means there were once 202 books and we now have what is left of them. In the case of the "Great Isaiah Scroll" found in cave 1, it really is the entire book of Isaiah from the first to the last verse. In other cases, we have only a small fragment or two of a scroll. Usually, it is something in between those two extremes. In this book, when we reference a Dead Sea Scroll, we will identify it by the number officially assigned to it for research and reference purposes. For example, the Isaiah scroll mentioned above is 1QIsa[a]. Most Dead Sea Scrolls will be referenced by their number; for example, scroll 4Q104 is a scroll containing portions of Ruth.

In addition to knowing that a book cannot be written later than its copy in the Dead Sea Scrolls, we can usually go further with our conclusions. For example, if there is a Dead Sea Scroll commentary on a biblical book, we can conclude that the biblical book had to be written some time before the commentary, allowing enough time for the biblical book to be accepted as an authoritative text. How much time does that require? There a judgment will be subjective. We will deal in some cases with issues like this later in this book.

---

[9] VanderKam, *The Dead Sea Scrolls Today*, pp. 16-23
[10] VanderKam, *The Dead Sea Scrolls Today*, p. 30

Identification of the oldest Old Testament texts can affect the discussion of the date of the writing of the books in one of three ways. The first way involves a few cases where identification of the oldest manuscripts has direct bearing on the dating of certain Old Testament books – an idea we will develop later. The second way involves additional cases in which current disputes about dates are not affected, but the discovery of the Dead Sea Scrolls altered the parameters of the debate in the past. For example, before the discovery of the Dead Sea Scrolls, many writers assigned some of the Psalms to the Maccabean period. This idea became untenable based on the Dead Sea Scrolls' evidence, since some Psalms Dead Sea Scrolls were dated at essentially the same time as the Maccabees. Third, for most books the oldest manuscripts play no role in determining the time when the book was written. An example would be the book of Ruth – scholars disagree on whether it was written in 1000 B.C., 400 B.C., or somewhere in between. The Dead Sea Scroll manuscript of Ruth dated around 50 B.C. cannot be used to address the question. Nevertheless, we have chosen in this book to list the oldest manuscript for every book in the Old Testament, for completeness sake.

2.2 Relative Dating
2.2.1 Relative Dating Principles
Before looking at any biblical text in detail, let us establish some principles about how information flows from older times and older texts to newer texts, and how information from more recent times can get into older texts. The logic of these principles should be readily apparent.

First, we will define and illustrate a principle on how more recent information gets into older texts. When a culture has a very old document, a more modern reader will find that certain things about that old document may be hard to understand. Therefore, certain modifications to the old text may be made to help the more modern reader understand it. If the old text references geography which is unknown to a modern audience, the copier may update the geographic references. For example, if we had an old text which said "The Philistines settled as far north as Qasile," we might update it to say "The Philistines settled as far north as Tel Aviv," since Tel Aviv is built over the ancient settlement of Qasile. Both statements are identical in meaning, but since almost no one has heard of Qasile, that reference is not useful for the modern reader. Therefore, we say "The Philistines settled as far north as Tel Aviv," but we don't mean that Tel Aviv existed in the time of the Philistines. This has clearly happened in the Torah. Gen 14:14 says Abraham pursued his relative's captors northward "as far as Dan"[11]. The city of Dan was named after Dan, the great-grandson of Abraham, so it would not have been in existence by that name when Abraham made his pursuit. However, for the later Israelite readers, Dan was a well-known location marking the northern-most outpost of the land of Israel, so the passage would be under-standable once "Dan" was inserted. Likewise, in an old text, the grammar may be archaic, so a more modern copier might update the grammar. Certain other steps might be taken to update an older text, in the interest of ensuring that a modern audience can understand it. For example, modern readers of Shakespeare's *Hamlet* may read from a version which has explanatory margin notes or footnotes. This sort of information flow of newer informa-tion finding its way into older text is, however, restricted, because some types of modern information will never get into an older text. For example, certain modern vocabulary, like the word "telephone," will never find its way into *Hamlet*, since they didn't have telephones in Hamlet's time. Likewise, modern issues and concerns unknown at the time of the ancient document will not find their way into the older document: no concerns about nuclear proliferation will ever get back into *Hamlet*. Thus, information

---

[11] Not all writers agree that Genesis 14 was written before the Dan tribe settled in the north. The principle should still be understandable even if the example is disputed.

flow from newer times into older texts is possible, but tends to be restricted in scope. Therefore, to return to a biblical example, if the Torah was written before the division of Israel into a northern and southern kingdom, we should find in the Torah no hint of concerns related to the divided Kingdom of Israel and Judah.

Several other factors can further restrict the flow of information from later times into older texts. The *Hamlet* example is useful as an illustration because it is poetry. It is usually not possible to update poetry without ruining some aspect of the poem. Therefore, we read *Hamlet* in the archaic grammar in which it was originally written – the grammar has not been updated even though it is difficult for a modern reader. Likewise, Hebrew poetry and songs are present throughout the Bible, and these often show evidence of more archaic grammar than the surrounding prose. Modern writers often assume that a passage consisting of archaic poetry is an older work inserted into a newer text. In some cases, this may be what happened, but it is also possible that the poem is the true marker of the antiquity of the entire text, but the language of the surrounding prose has been updated. Also, Old Testament documents eventually took on a special status as holy texts, a status which deterred scribes from changing the text even when they felt it was difficult to understand or even when it looked wrong. The Masoretes, the Hebrew scribes who produced the text we have today, formalized this tendency by developing a system for leaving difficult passages unchanged in the text (the "kethiv") and noting in the margin how they felt the passage should be read (the "qire").

At this time, we may need to deal with two potential objections to this principle. The first objection is that in some cases it may be suggested that an old text has been updated with a great deal of much newer information, resulting in essentially a new text. For example, there is a suggestion that the old original book of Isaiah consisting of most of Isaiah 1-39 has been updated with newer passages written entirely in the exilic and post-exilic period. This certainly could have happened in theory and our principle should not rule it out as an impossible occurrence. The objection is understood; we will not use the principle in a way that would rule that possibility out *a priori*. The second objection deals with the role of prophecy, in the sense of foretelling the future. The presence of a passage which is clearly intended to be prophetic will not, for our purposes, be considered as new information getting into an older text. We will not assume that a fulfilled prophecy was written after the fact - that would be an anti-supernatural assumption.

Second, let us describe how information can flow forward in time. If a culture has an old document available, newer texts can and will draw information from the old document. This forward information flow would be especially heavy when the text is central to a culture's history, religion and legal background, as theoretically could have been the case with the Torah and ancient Israel. Therefore, if the Torah is older than the rest of the Old Testament, we should expect to find repeated references to it; the newer prophets and writings would draw information from the older Torah.

Although almost all the information in an old document has the potential to flow into newer documents, in practice only a limited amount of information will do this. For example, although the language from Shakespeare's Hamlet may be archaic, we still use "thee" and "thou" some – this usage is limited. A biblical example is the phrase "gathered to his people," used to describe death in the Torah 10 times. It is used once more shortly afterward, slightly modified, in Judg 2:10, then not used again until they read the book of the law in Josiah's time, prompting the prophetess Huldah to echo this phrase in 2 Kgs 22:20 and 2 Chron 34:28. Other information flow will be rarer still. Old issues prominent in an old document that have vanished in a more modern time will not usually find their way into the more modern documents. Using the Hamlet example, we can say that we don't write much any more about problems in the royal family of Denmark. In a biblical example, the giants (sons of Anak, or Anakim) were a big issue at the time of the initial approach to the land of Canaan (mentioned 18 times up through Judg 1:20 – "we were like grasshoppers in our eyes" - Num 13: 33), but they are never brought up again in the prophets or writings.

These principles are useful in determining the relative dating of different passages and Old Testament books. These principles help us put the books in the proper order. They do not by themselves allow us to put a date on a book. For that kind of absolute dating, other techniques are required.

2.2.2 Linguistics

The Hebrew language did not remain static during the development of the Old Testament, but changed over time, as all living languages do. With caution, we can apply linguistic principles to determine which writings are earlier and which writings are later. Caution is needed for four reasons. First, there is very little Hebrew language material available from the time of the Bible other than what is present in the Bible. In particular, all the extra-biblical Hebrew writings that have been preserved from before the exile equal no more than a few pages of biblical text. This makes it hard to date Biblical Hebrew, because so little non-biblical Hebrew is available for comparison. Second, it is possible in theory that some biblical writers may have archaized; that is, for reasons of formality, used language older than the normal language in use at their time. Third, as we have already mentioned, there is evidence that for a while the scribes who copied the scriptures took steps to bring the language of the text up to date. This has had the effect of masking some of the archaic elements of the language which may have originally been present in the older books, but have now been lost. This effect can most clearly be seen in the area of spelling, but may also be present in other areas of the language. Fourth, the very fact that the books of the Old

Testament have been dated the way they have has driven an understanding of how the Hebrew language developed over time. Since we believe many of these books have been dated incorrectly by most modern writers, this has lead in some areas to an incorrect understanding of how the language developed. This is a significant enough issue that we have proceeded to develop our own limited description of how Hebrew developed in the biblical period, which we have included in this book as Appendix B.

In certain cases, we will compare the linguistic of the books in the Bible with the extra-Biblical Dead Sea Scrolls. These are scrolls like the Damascus Document, Jubilees, the Copper Scroll, commentaries on books of the Bible, etc. that number almost 600 scrolls. These extra-Biblical Dead Sea Scrolls provide information on what Hebrew and Aramaic linguistics were like in the Maccabean and Roman periods (167 B.C. and later).

CHAPTER 3

Dating the Torah

The first five books of the Bible, Genesis, Exodus, Leviticus, Numbers and Deuteronomy, are commonly called the books of the law. They are sometimes called the books of Moses, the Law of Moses, the Torah (Hebrew for law), or the Pentateuch. The first book of the Torah, Genesis, deals with the creation of the world and selected stories of its early history, then focuses on the patriarchs of the nation of Israel: Abraham, Isaac, Jacob and his twelve sons, chiefly Joseph. It ends with the death of Joseph in Egypt. Genesis covers a period in excess of 2000 years in time. The geographic setting of Genesis ranges over most of the Middle East, from Egypt in the South to the Ararat Mountains in Turkey. Exodus covers a period of over 200 years, but focuses on the last few years in which God uses Moses to lead the Israelites out of Egypt to receive the law in the wilderness, at Mount Sinai. Leviticus deals with a period of only a few days, all at Mount Sinai, where God speaks to the people about laws governing everything from sacrifices to personal holiness to mold removal. Numbers covers a period of about 40 years in which the Israelites wander through the wilderness, at times dealing with internal and external opposition and also receiving more laws. The name, "Numbers," comes from two censuses taken at the beginning and end of the 40 year period. Most of Deuteronomy covers a one day address given by Moses at the end of his life, in which he recounts a second time for the people the laws God gave them, and binds them to live in covenant with God and His law. The entire book takes place on the east side of the Jordan River across from Jericho, and ends with the death of Moses.

3.1 Brief History of Viewpoints

3.1.1 Traditional View

The traditional understanding of the Torah's origin is that it was written by Moses during Israel's time in the wilderness, sometime in the 15th-13th century B.C. Mosaic authorship was affirmed in the Old Testament prophets and writings, and later in the Apocrypha and the New Testament. Early Jewish and Christian writers recognized Moses as author of the Torah. This traditional understanding of the Torah as a unified whole with Moses as its author was not seriously challenged until the 19th century A.D.

Within the overall understanding of Mosaic authorship of the Torah there has been variation. Orthodox Judaism has generally understood that every word of the Torah was given to Moses by God. Other writers consider certain passages to be added later, such as Deuteronomy 34, the last chapter of the Torah that describes Moses' death. There has also been disagreement about whether the Torah as we have it today is essentially identical to what Moses wrote, or whether the language and geographical references were updated by scribes up through the period of the Babylonian exile.

3.1.2 Documentary Hypothesis

In 1753, the French scholar Jean Astruc wrote *Conjectures on the Original Documents that Moses Appears to Have Used in Comprising the Book of Genesis*. Astruc separated Genesis into two sources, "Elohist" and "Jehovist," based on the divine names for God, Elohim and YHWH (A German transliteration of the consonants in "YHWH" and the vowels in "Adonai" produce "Jehovah"). In Germany in 1805, W.M.L. DeWette proposed that the book of Deuteronomy was not written by the same author as Genesis – Numbers. These ideas were further developed by Herman Hupfeld and the teaching of Karl Graf. The development of the Documentary Hypothesis climaxed in 1878, when the German theology professor and historian Julius Wellhausen published *Prolegomena to the History of Ancient Israel,* a comprehensive work describing all of Old Testament history and using more than 5000 scripture references. Wellhausen's arguments persuaded much of the establishment of his day. Noteworthy converts included William Gesenius, and making the jump to the English speaking world, English cleric Samuel Driver, along with Americans Francis Brown and Charles Briggs. Gesenius' Hebrew Grammar and The Brown-Driver-Briggs Hebrew-English lexicon are still standard works used today.

**Julius Wellhausen, 1844-1918, who
Popularized the Documentary Hypothesis**

The Documentary Hypothesis as espoused by Wellhausen divides the Torah into four primary sources:

J = Jehovist, written about 850 B.C.

E = Elohist, written about 750 B.C.

D = Most of Deuteronomy, written about 621 B.C. during Josiah's reform

P = Priestly, written 500-450 B.C.

Wellhausen believed J and E came together sometime before D, and he also recognized Leviticus 17-26 (the "Holiness Code") as a separate and possibly older source within P. Finally, a redactor, or editor, combined the disparate sources into the unified whole. The Torah as we have it today was published by Ezra in 444 B.C. The book of Joshua was the product of these same sources, giving rise to the term "Hexateuch" to describe the first six books of the Bible. Appendix A provides a table of Genesis – Joshua broken down into sources as suggested by the Documentary Hypothesis. All the scripture references in this book that attribute a scripture to a source (J, E, D or P) use the breakdown in Appendix A.

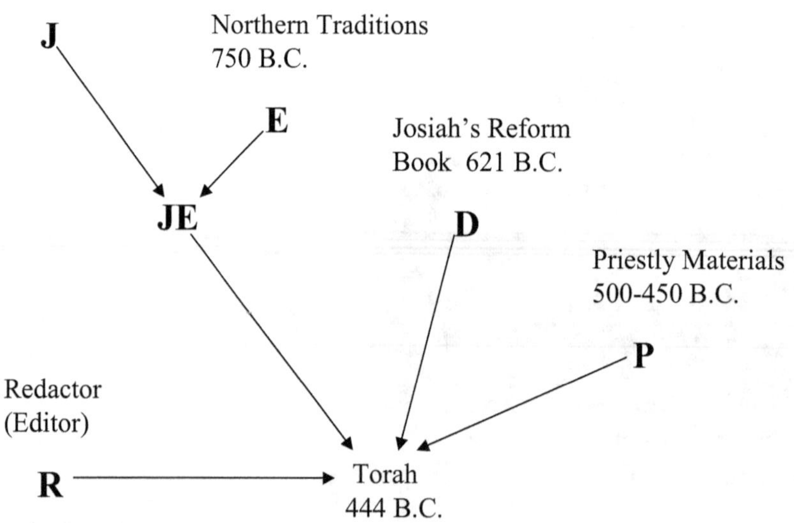

Figure 3-1 Development of the Torah
According to the Documentary Hypothesis

3.1.3 20th Century Variants

The 20th century saw numerous variations offered on the standard Documentary Hypothesis. These included moving the date of J down to the Babylonian exile[1], or back in time to Solomon's court in 950 B.C.[2]. Richard Friedman proposed moving the composition of P before the exile to the reign of Hezekiah, before D.[3] Other writers have suggested two Deuteronomic sources D1 and D2 (an idea currently widely accepted), or multiple Jehovist sources.[4] Oral tradition study has led to the idea that some or all sources existed in oral form for an extended period of time before they were written down. Archeology has not been entirely supportive of Wellhausen's conclusions, and in the minds of some scholars the modern Documentary Hypothesis is in a "state of crisis."[5] However, no suitable idea has been widely accepted to replace it. Despite the many attacks leveled at the Documentary Hypothesis, it remains today the most commonly used explanation of the origin of the Torah. The acceptance of the Documentary Hypothesis extends across secular, Jewish and Christian circles, and it is taught in all but the most religiously conservative colleges and seminaries.

Although many variants to Wellhausen's model of the Documentary Hypothesis have been offered, none have been able to gain wide acceptance over time. Each variant has different strengths and weaknesses, and in this book we cannot address them all. The model of Friedman, moving the P source back in time before the exile, avoids some of the difficulties of Well-

---

[1] As in Blenkinsopp, *The Pentateuch, An Introduction to the First Five Books of the Bible*

[2] Von Rad, *Genesis, A Commentary*, p. 25

[3] Friedman, *Who Wrote the Bible*, p. 188

[4] As in Simpson, "The Growth of the Hexateuch", p. 185, *The Interpreter's Bible Commentary*

[5] Blenkinsopp, *The Pentateuch, An Introduction to the First Five Books of the Bible*, p. 19

hausen's model. However, the earlier date for P means dropping the argument that Ezekiel was a transitional figure in the development of priestly law (an important point for some source critics), and Wellhausen's model is still the one predominately taught today. As Friedman puts it, "To this day, if you want to disagree, you disagree with Wellhausen. If you want to pose a new model, you compare its merits with those of Wellhausen's model."[6] Therefore, in this chapter, we will disagree with Wellhausen.

In some circles, rejection of the Documentary Hypothesis has been coupled with the introduction of the Tablet Theory of Genesis, first popularized by Percy Wiseman, 1888-1948, in *New Discoveries in Babylonia about Genesis*. The Tablet Theory recognizes 11 sources, or tablets, for Genesis, each set apart by the phrase "These are the generations (Hebrew "toledot") of ..." (KJV). The 11 sources were written by the individual named in the phrase, and later compiled by Moses to form Genesis as we have it today. The thinking behind the Tablet Theory has been influential enough that some modern translations use "account" as the translation for "toledot," producing the formula "This is the account of ..." to separate each source.

3.2 Unity or Division

Before addressing the question of when the books of the Torah were written, we need to understand whether these books were written by a single hand (Moses or another single hand), or by different sources as alleged by the Documentary Hypothesis. In this chapter, we will demonstrate that the evidence indicates the Torah is the work of a single author. We will first address some of the more prominent arguments offered in favor of the Documentary Hypothesis, then we will introduce a case for the overall unity of the Torah.

---

[6] Friedman, *Who Wrote the Bible*, p. 26

3.2.1 Arguments for Sources
3.2.1.1 Divine Names

The Old Testament makes careful use of divine names. The most common names are "Elohim" (אלהים), translated as "God" in English Bibles, and "YHWH" (יהוה), translated as LORD with all capital letters in most English Bibles. "El," a shortened form of Elohim, is sometimes used in conjunction with other words as a more descriptive title: El Shaddai, El Elyon, El the God of Israel, etc. "Elohim" has to be understood in context because it is also used to refer to false gods, or "other gods." YHWH is also combined with other words to vary the name, as in "YHWH Yireh" (The LORD who sees, or who will provide) and later in the Bible "YHWH Tsavaot" (LORD of Hosts).

Source critics view the use of these names as an indicator of the source of the text. This is usually the first argument offered for the Documentary Hypothesis and the argument that gives the sources their names. Therefore, passages that use "YHWH" are assigned to the "J" source, and passages that use "Elohim" are assigned to the "E" source or the "P" (Priestly) source. P allows the use of YHWH after Exod 6:3 and E allows the use of YHWH after Exod 3:14. Problems with this approach are immediately apparent: Elohim occurs often in J passages (many times together with YHWH in Genesis 2-3, and exclusively in Gen 3:1, 3:3, 3:5, 31:50, 33:5, 33:11 and others). YHWH occurs in the "E" passages of Gen 21:33, 22:11, 22:14 and 28:21, and in the "P" passages of Gen 5:29, 17:1 and 21:1. To address these problems, the critics appeal to the later work of an editor, or redactor (sometimes referred to as "R"). This redactor is frequently used to cover flaws in the theory.

Efforts to separate sources by divine names can lead to extreme and unwarranted conclusions. For example, to keep YHWH out of E, Friedman assigns Gen 22:11-15 and part of 22:16 to the redactor, leading to the incredible conclusion that in the E source Abraham actually did sacrifice his son Isaac. He then supports this by saying Isaac does not again appear in E[7], though without considering E passages like Exod 3:6 "I am the God of your fathers, the God of Abraham, the God of Isaac, and the God of Jacob." One can only wonder how Jacob got there without Isaac.

Furthermore, the source critics have a dilemma in explaining names in the Torah. There are no names in the Torah based on the name YHWH[8], neither names of people nor places. These Yahwistic (YHWH-based) names became so prominent later that the majority of the kings of Judah and about one third of all male Jews had Yahwistic names. The Documentary Hypothesis can explain why there are no Yahwistic names in P or E (the name wasn't revealed until the time of Moses), but in Genesis through Numbers there are 195 names in J, a source that uses YHWH right from the beginning, and none of them are Yahwistic either. There is a better explanation for this, and we will get to it later.

The field of textual criticism has also not been helpful to the Documentary Hypothesis in this area of names of God. The breakdown of sources by names used by proponents of the Documentary Hypothesis is based on the Hebrew Masoretic Text. This is not a bad choice. If we had to pick only one Old Testament text to use, it would be the Masoretic Text – the text used in synagogues today, and the text on which almost all Bible translations are based. However, it would be a mistake to think that the Masoretic Text always reflects the original text.[9] The field of textual criticism attempts, among other things, to identify what the original text was. Since we have other sources besides the Masoretic Text, we can compare them. Table 3-1 below shows a list of instances in which the divine name used in another major text differs from the Masoretic Text in a fashion not in keeping

---

[7] Friedman, *The Bible with Sources Revealed*, p. 65

[8] The Yahwistic name Joshua is an exception, but he was born "Hoshea" and had his name changed (Num 13:16).

[9] This is generally considered to be a truism. See Emanuel Tov, *Textual Criticism of the Hebrew Bible,* p.11, for a discussion.

with the Documentary Hypothesis.[10] For translations, such as the Septuagint, this assumes a reverse translation back to Hebrew.

Table 3-1 Textual Differences in Names for God

Reference	Name in Masoretic Text	Name in Other Text	Other Text Source
Gen 4:6, 4:15, 4:26, 5:29, 6:3, 6:5, 6:8, 7:5, 7:16, 8:21, 10:9, 11:9b	YHWH	YHWH Elohim	Septuagint ("kurios" translated from YHWH)
Gen 4:1, 4:4, 4:9, 12:17, 13:14, 15:6, 15:7, 16:5, 18:1, 30:27, 38:7, 38:10, Exod 4:1[11], 4:11, 4:30, 4:31, 5:21, 8:29-30 (8:25-26 Hebrew), 9:5, 10:18, 13:21, 14:13, 14:31c, 15:1, 19:18, 19:21,	YHWH	Elohim	Septuagint ("theos" translated from Elohim)

[10] The Septuagint used is Alfred Rahlf's 1979 Edition, Deutsche Bibelgesellschaft, Stuttgart Germany. The Samaritan Pentateuch used is the 1918 version published by August von Gall. In most cases, the references to the Septuagint, Samaritan Pentateuch and the Vulgate in Table 3-1 can also be derived from the textual apparatus of the *Biblia Hebraica Stuttgartensia*.

[11] Some Source Critics allow J to use Elohim in direct speech, as in Exod 4:1 and 5:21

Reference	Name in Masoretic Text	Name in Other Text	Other Text Source
19:23, 19:24, 24:2, 24:11			
Gen 7:1	YHWH	Elohim	Elohim in Samaritan Pentateuch and Syriac, YHWH Elohim in Septuagint
Gen 2:4, 2:5, 2:7, 2:9, 2:19, 2:21, 3:22, Exod 3:18	YHWH Elohim	Elohim	Septuagint
Gen 19:29a, 21:2, 21:4, Exod 3:4b	Elohim	YHWH	Septuagint
Gen 7:9	Elohim	YHWH	Samaritan Pentateuch, Vulgate
Gen 28:4, 31:7, 31:16, Exod 3:4a	Elohim	YHWH	Samaritan Pentateuch
Gen 6:12, 6:22, 8:15, 9:12, 28:20	Elohim	YHWH Elohim	Septuagint
Gen 20:4	Adonai	YHWH	Some Hebrew manuscripts
Gen 43:28	None	Elohim	Samaritan Pentateuch and Septuagint
Gen 31:44	None	Elohim	Septuagint
Exod 19:22b	None	Elohim	Some Septuagint manuscripts

To be completely clear about this table, we are not alleging that the Masoretic Text reading is the wrong one in all of these cases;

in general it is the best text, and on specific instances we can probably never be certain which reading is original. However, every alternate reading in Table 3-1 would, if it were the original text, need to be listed as another exception to the Documentary Hypothesis rules for divine names. By contrast, in all the exceptions already listed in the second paragraph of this section, there are no textual issues; all the main sources agree on the reading. Also, we can be confident that the Septuagint translator in particular did not take liberties with his work; the Septuagint version of the Torah usually stays so close to the Hebrew original that the Greek reading is awkward. Instead, the Septuagint translator was looking at a different Hebrew text than the Masoretic text. There is a certain irony here in that the source critics almost need to defend the inerrancy of the Masoretic text in this area.

The problem this presents for the Documentary Hypothesis can be set forth in logical terms as follows. A particular old text (the Masoretic Text) is used to construct a theory (the Documentary Hypothesis), but the text still presents several difficulties for the theory. If the theory is true, and other old texts exist, then examination of those texts may be expected to remove some of the difficulties. However, with this theory, examination of other old texts (Septuagint, Samaritan Pentateuch) shows the opposite to be true. All the difficulties remain; none are removed, and a substantial list of additional difficulties is introduced. This implies that the theory is not true.

The choice to separate sources by divine names should also be suspect in light of the fact that every prophetic book in the Bible, including all 12 Minor Prophets, uses both YHWH and Elohim. It is only in the Torah that source critics try to pry the text apart with this criterion.

We will discuss divine names again later, but for now we should just say that a better understanding of the use of divine names is described by Umberto Cassuto[12] and others; that the variation in choice of names is not accidental, but intentional, by decision. Elohim and YHWH are not completely interchangeable in Biblical Hebrew. Elohim is a title rather than a name. Elohim is used to describe God when He is viewed as transcendent, or as a judge, or when a more global nature of God is in view. YHWH is a personal name and is used when God is personally, intimately involved with men. YHWH walks, talks, eats and bargains with men (as in Genesis 18). YHWH is also used when an Israelite character of God is in view. For example: Exod 7:1: "Then YHWH said to Moses, 'see, I make you as Elohim to Pharaoh.'" To Moses – YHWH, to Pharaoh: Elohim. An additional example is in Gen 9:26-27, where Noah blesses Shem (the line of Israel) with YHWH and Japheth with Elohim. This usage of YHWH and Elohim is not limited to the Torah, but continues through the Old Testament. The prophets to Israel routinely use YHWH. YHWH speaks to Jonah, but the people of Nineveh believe Elohim. In Daniel, written from Babylon, Elohim is used throughout and YHWH not at all, except in Daniel 9, at which time YHWH is used repeatedly as Daniel turns and prays for Jerusalem and Judah. The usage of divine names in the Torah is consistent with the rest of scripture, following consistent language guidelines. It should not be used as a criterion for separation of sources.

3.2.1.2 Unique Vocabulary within Sources

In addition to YHWH and Elohim, the Documentary Hypothesis alleges that certain other words and names are unique to each source. The general response to this suggestion is that the Bible writers, like most everyone else, use multiple names and words for the same thing. For example, a home in New York City could be located in "New York City," "Manhattan," "the Big Apple," or "back east," depending on the context and writer's choice. In the

---

[12] Umberto Cassuto, *The Documentary Hypothesis*, Lectures 2 and 3, pp. 15ff

Bible, a different name is often used for the same person or place even within the same sentence: "God spoke to *Israel* in visions of the night and said, '*Jacob, Jacob.*'" (Gen 46:2). Also, in the Documentary Hypothesis, there is a tendency to pull certain names into certain sources. This leads to circular reasoning something like this:

1. Most references to YHWH are assigned to J,
2. Since J has most of the YHWH references while E and P do not
3. J must be a separate source from E and P.

Clearly this is not a logical argument. Let us also note that there are numerous cases of people or places in the Bible where two names are given for the same person or place, and usually sources are not an issue. The list below shows a few of these:

1. Abram — Abraham
2. Sarai — Sarah
3. Jacob — Israel
4. Jethro — Reuel
5. Joshua — Hoshea
6. Gideon — Jerubbaal
7. Eshbaal — Ishbosheth
8. Joseph — Zaphenath-Paneah
9. Daniel — Belteshazzar
10. Hananiah — Shadrach
11. Mishael — Meshach
12. Azariah — Abednego
13. Azariah — Uzziah
14. Luz — Bethel
15. Beersheba — Sheba
16. Kiriath Arba — Hebron
17. Mount Hermon — Sirion, Senir
18. Jerusalem — Zion, Ariel, Jebus, Salem
19. Babylon — Shishak, Chaldea, Shinar
20. Solomon — Jedidiah

21. Sinai	Horeb
22. Ephrath	Bethlehem
23. Galeed	Jegar Sahadutha, Mizpah

We should keep in mind that multiple different languages were involved in the ancient Middle East, and in many cases names will be different in different languages. Nevertheless, let us consider some of the more common examples given to support the Documentary Hypothesis. Keep in mind that the word counts used in the following examples are low in number, weakening the argument in any case.

3.2.1.2.1 Name of Laban's Home Town

Source critics suggest that only P uses "Paddan-aram" as the name of Laban's home. P includes 10 references to Paddan-aram. J calls it Haran three times in one conversation, and P also calls it Haran in Gen 12:5. Haran is the grandfather of Laban in both P and J. Apparently Laban is homeless (or his home is nameless) in E, though he lives in the "land of the sons of the east" (Gen 29:1). However to get all the Paddan-aram's into P, the Documentary Hypothesis splits Gen 31:18 into two parts, taking only the second half into P. Then it splits Gen 33:18 into three parts, taking only the middle phrase, "when he came to Paddan-aram": "Now Jacob came safely to the city of Shechem, which is in the land of Canaan, when he came from Paddan-aram, and camped before the city." The Documentary Hypothesis has no flexibility to select a larger section in Genesis 31 because other P guidelines require it to exclude the household idols in 31:19, and it cannot take a larger section in Genesis 33 because P must exclude the altar in Gen 33:20. These two verse fragments are the only sections assigned to P in a five chapter stretch from Genesis 30 through 34. J and E are left with no mention of the place from which Jacob returned.

3.2.1.2.2 Sinai/Horeb

Sinai and Horeb are two different names for the mountain where God gave the law to Moses. The Documentary Hypothesis suggests that Horeb is used by E and D, while Sinai is used by J and P. Sinai is used in the Torah 30 times: 13 times in Exodus, 4 in Leviticus, 12 in Numbers and 1 in Deuteronomy. Horeb is used 12 times in the Torah: 3 times in Exodus and 9 times in Deuteronomy. Both names are mentioned in the prophets and the writings.

Several problems with the theory are apparent. First, the Documentary Hypothesis again has to make small cuts in the narrative to pull Horeb into E in Exod 17:6 and 33:6. The cuts in the narrative in Exodus 17 leave J with the people thirsting for water but not getting any. Second, the cut in Exod 33:6 serves no purpose but to pull Horeb into E, then the E account is left dangling all the way until Numbers 10. Third, Sinai is used in Deut 33:2, a passage source critics do not assign to J or P.

There is no agreement on the modern geographical location of Mount Sinai/Horeb, though many suggestions have been made. It has been suggested that Horeb and Sinai are separate peaks, that Horeb is a peak in the Sinai range, and that Sinai is a peak in the Horeb range; a detailed study of the topic is beyond the scope of this book. We can note that the words are used differently. When Sinai is used, the Torah says "Mount Sinai" or "wilderness of Sinai" 28 out of 30 times. The exceptions are Exod 16:1, which has other geographical references, and Deut 33:2, which is part of a song. When Horeb is used, it stands alone 11 out of 12 times. Only in Exod 33:6 does it say "Mount Horeb." "Wilderness of Horeb" does not appear.

3.2.1.2.3 Jethro/Reuel

The name of the father-in-law of Moses is Reuel in Exod 2:18 and Num 10:29. In Exod 3:1, 4:18 and 18:1-12 his name is Jethro. The totals are 2 Reuels and 10 Jethros, with the Jethro passages assigned to E and the Reuel passages assigned to J. In passages assigned to both sources he is called a priest of Midian, and his daughter Zipporah and Moses' son Gershom are named. We cannot be certain why there are two different names, but it is worth noting that when Reuel is used it is in relation to his children (daughters in Exodus 2, his son Hobab in Numbers 10). When Jethro is used, it is in relationship to Moses.

3.2.1.2.4 Ishmaelites/Midianites

Joseph is sold to "Ishmaelites" in Gen 37:25-27 and 39:1, passages assigned to J. However, in the first half of Gen 37:28, they are described as "Midianites" in a passage assigned to E. This is another case where the Documentary Hypothesis splits off half a verse in order to get the right vocabulary word into the desired source. The last part of 28 has to revert back to J to avoid the non-sequitur of Joseph never making it to Egypt in J. That there is a connection between Midianites and Ishmaelites is apparent from Judg 8:24 when the Midianites Gideon is fighting are called Ishmaelites.

3.2.1.2.5 Jacob/Israel

The Abingdon Bible Commentary suggests that after the birth of Benjamin, J calls Jacob by the name "Israel," while E continues with the name "Jacob."[13] This suggested argument is a good example of how misleading it is to offer a vocabulary-based argument without also providing a complete breakdown of sources. Based on the Appendix A breakdown, after the birth of Benjamin (why the birth of Benjamin is used as a marker is another question not addressed), J uses "Israel" 19 times, but E also uses Israel 10 times. P uses Israel once and unassigned passages use Israel 5 times. J uses "Jacob" 4 times, E uses Jacob 16 times, P uses it 17 times and unassigned passages use it 3 times. What this is all supposed to prove is anybody's guess.

---

[13] Eiselen, Frederick Carl, "The Pentateuch – Its Origin and Development", article in *The Abingdon Bible Commentary*, pp. 139-140

It should be clear that after Jacob is given the new name Israel, both "Jacob" and "Israel" continue to be used interchangeably, and this is true in all sources. In fact, three verses use both names in the same verse (Gen 46:2, 49:2 and 49:24). This is different from what happens with Abraham, who when his name is changed from "Abram" to "Abraham" (in P only), is never again called "Abram" in any source.

3.2.1.2.6 Additional Vocabulary Arguments

In addition to the proper names cited above, the source critics make claims for unique vocabulary differences within sources. The reader will realize that in some cases this will be a natural outgrowth of the way the sources are divided. For example, since almost all references to the tabernacle are placed in P, the vocabulary word for "tabernacle" will show up almost entirely in P. Likewise, since all the building instructions are in P, most all references to cubits, curtains, acacia wood and any fixtures associated with the tabernacle will only appear in P. This is obviously no argument for multiple sources.

Sometimes, vocabulary-based arguments rob the text of intended meaning. As an example, there are two words translated as "maid" or "maidservant" in the Bible: "shifkah" (שפחה) and "amah" (אמה). Some source critics have suggested that only E knows the word "amah," and they have divided the passages accordingly.[14] This ignores the subtle difference of meaning in the two words. A "shifkah" is a maidservant with no standing, value, or importance, while an "amah" has a measure of status and worth. Sarah says to Abraham, "Please go in to my shifkah [Hagar], perhaps I will obtain children through her" (Gen 16:2). Later when Hagar has a child, Ishmael, Sarah is jealous and says "drive out this amah [Hagar] and her son" (Gen 21:10). Why does Sarah upgrade Hagar from "shifkah" to "amah?" The answer is

---

[14] As in Jacobs, "Elohist", in *Jewish Encyclopedia*, 1906 version

obvious – Hagar has become the mother of the master's oldest son – she is now important, with real standing. The use of these words can be verified by comparing these passages to the book of Ruth. In Ruth 2:13, when Ruth first meets Boaz and is somewhat intimidated, she calls herself a "shifkah." Later, in a different situation she essentially proposes marriage to him, and wanting to describe herself as a person of worth, she presents herself as an "amah" in Ruth 3:9. The lesson here is that the Documentary Hypothesis, by splitting sources up based on vocabulary, often does violence to the subtler meaning of the biblical text.

Vocabulary based studies are sometimes used to suggest modifications to the Documentary Hypothesis. Blenkinsopp, for example, uses vocabulary to suggest an exilic date for the narratives of Gen 2-4.[15] This would seem to conflict with the reading of Hos 6:7, a pre-exilic prophet, discussed in 3.2.2.4.4, even without combining the J and P sources.

Some source critics prefer to leave certain passages unassigned (such as Genesis 34), because to assign them to any given source would lead to breaking the "rules" of vocabulary, message, or style for that source. Yet in order to make a valid argument based on vocabulary breakdown, one which withstands the test of logic, the theory must first be fully defined, with every scripture from Genesis through Joshua assigned to some source, even if that source is the "editor." Making an argument based on a few words that look unique in a few chapters, without fully defining the theory to see if it can stand against opposing evidence, is insufficient. Only with a fully defined theory can an argument based on vocabulary within sources be examined on its merit.

In general, vocabulary-based arguments using words that appear a low number of times are of limited value, since depending on which words are selected, they can be used to prove almost any point. This is especially true with the Documentary Hypothe-

---

[15] Blenkinsopp, *The Pentateuch*, p. 65

sis, since vocabulary is one of the criteria used to separate the sources in the first place.

3.2.1.3 Altars and Sacrifices

The source critics have suggested that the different sources have radically different perspectives on altars and sacrifices. This view can be summarized as follows: J and E allow anyone to build altars and offer sacrifices, D condemns this practice, and P prescribes a central altar associated with a central sanctuary, with only priests descended from Aaron performing sacrifices. Wellhausen extends this idea into a historical model in which early Israel practiced freedom to build altars and offer sacrifices, this practice later being abolished by Josiah, then formalized into the full priestly sacrificial system after the exile.

Because sacrificial practices have been extinct in Judaism and Christianity for almost 2000 years, we may have difficulty grasping the complex set of taboos which surrounded the use of altars and sacrifices in ancient Israel. Let us attempt to summarize the system, including on each point verses in Moses' Deuteronomy address, verses which should all be assigned to D.

1. All altars associated with foreign gods and/or Canaanite practices are to be destroyed (Exod 34:12-14, Deut 7:5, 12:2-4).

2. Simple stone altars can be made by anyone, with sacrifices offered on such altars. These altars must be made with uncut stones – no tools, no stairs, and certainly they must not be accompanied by idols or Asherah poles. Such altars can in most cases be made by one person in a few minutes time (Exod 20:24-26, Deut 16:21-22 and 27:5-7). This practice finds its fulfillment in the patriarchs (Gen 22:9, 33:20, etc.), by Moses after the exodus (Exod 24:4), in the time of Joshua (Josh 8:30-31), in the time of the judges (Judg 6:25-26 and 13:16-20), under Samuel (1 Sam 7:17), in the united kingdom period (1 Sam 14:35 and 2 Sam 24:25) and in the

divided kingdom period (1 Kgs 18:30-32 and Isa 19:19). The use of informal altars dwindles during Hezekiah's reforms and the conquest of Samaria (2 Kgs 18:22) and dies out after Josiah's reforms and the conquest of Judah. Even in the more "priestly" history of Chronicles, written after P, David offers up a burnt offering in 1 Chron 21:26 on an altar not associated with the tabernacle.

3. A major central altar is constructed with the tabernacle: bronze, square, with four horns at the corners for tying sacrifices on it (Exod 27:1 and throughout Leviticus and Numbers, see also Deut 12:5-6). Only the priests can offer sacrifices on this altar (2 Chron 26:16-19), though they may do so on behalf of someone else. This is the main altar of which there must be no imitation. This main altar is present in the time of the judges (1 Sam 2:28, 2:33) and in the united monarchy period before the temple is built (1 Kgs 1:50, 2:28). When Solomon builds the temple, he overlays the central altar with gold (1 Kgs 6:20-22). Attempts to imitate the central altar almost lead to civil war in Josh 22:10-29, and are condemned as the preeminent sin in Northern Israel in the divided kingdom period (1 Kgs 12:26-33 and Amos 3:14), a sin that for political reasons no northern king is willing to undo. Kings of Judah are also evaluated on their willingness to destroy "high places" (1 Kgs 14:23, 15:14, 22:43 and all subsequent kings), where sacred pillars, images and altars that might compete with the central altar stood.

The summary above fits well with the teaching of the Torah, without requiring any division of sources, and is consistent with the biblical record of the history of Israel.

3.2.1.4 Priests and Levites

Source critics suggest that D has a different theology of the priesthood than P. In D, the whole tribe of Levi are considered priests (Deut 17:9, 17:18; 18:1, 21:5, 24:8 and 27:9), while in P only the sons of Aaron are priests and the Levites are helpers to the priests.

First, we should note that even in D Aaron's son Eleazar becomes a priest of unique importance when Aaron dies (Deut 10:6). The Documentary Hypothesis argument leans heavily on the phrase "Levitical priests" in Deuteronomy. However, "Levitical priests" occurs also in 2 Chron 23:18 and 30:27 (also in Jer 33:18, 33:21, Ezek 43:19 and 44:15). 2 Chronicles is a late book, written long after it was established that the priestly line came from Aaron. In particular, 2 Chron 5:5 has "Levitical priests" carrying the Ark of the Covenant, a job assigned to Levites who are not Aaron's descendants (Num 3:31, 1 Chron 15:2, along with Deut 31:9, 31:25). Therefore, we should understand that the terms "priests," "Levites," and "Levitical priests" sometime overlap in meaning, and Deuteronomy is not giving a unique theology of the priesthood.

We can note here a further difficulty in the Documentary Hypothesis viewpoint that Deuteronomy was a product of Josiah's reform. Josiah went further than any previous king in concentrating all worship in Jerusalem. This strengthened the priests, the descendants of Aaron who served at the temple, at the expense of the other Levites. Yet it is Deuteronomy more than any other book that emphasizes that all Levites are priests.

3.2.1.5 Canaanites

Gen 12:6 says when Abram reached Shechem that "the Canaanite was then in the land." Gen 13:7 says when Abram and Lot were in Bethel "the Canaanite and the Perizzite were dwelling then in the land." Source critics have suggested that this indicates these passages were written much later when Canaanites were no longer in the land. This is probably the wrong way to read those verses. For one thing, Canaanites remained as a minority in the land throughout the biblical period. They were there at the time of

Solomon, about 950 B.C. (1 Kgs 9:16), they were there at the time of Ezra, about 450 B.C. (Ezra 9:1), and some were still there at the time of Jesus (Matt 15:22). The correct way to read these verses is not "the Canaanites don't live here any more but they did back then"; rather, the verses should be read to mean "back when Abram first entered the land, the Canaanites were already living there."

3.2.1.6 Across the Jordan

Source critics have suggested that the phrase "across the Jordan," used in Deut 1:1, 1:5, 4:41, 4:46, 4:47 and 4:49, to apply to the east side of the Jordan, implies that the writer is west of the Jordan (in the land of Israel rather than the wilderness). This has been used as an argument for a late date for Deuteronomy.

First, this can hardly be used as an argument for a late date, since within three months of Moses' speech in Deuteronomy the Israelites are in Gilgal, which is west of the Jordan (Deut 1:3 and Josh 4:19). It can only be an argument that Deuteronomy was not put in its final form in the two month, nine day interval between the speech and the crossing of the Jordan. Note also that all the "across the Jordan" references are accompanied by an additional geographical reference to avoid any confusion on the part of the reader. Finally, we observe that in Moses' speech given east of the Jordan, he makes a reference to "across the Jordan" in Deut 11:30, and in that instance he is talking about mountains Ebal and Gerizim on the *west* side of the Jordan. Therefore, the only "across the Jordan" reference used in a direct speech places the speaker and the people on the east side of it and not in the land of Israel.

3.2.1.7 Style Differences

Source critics suggest that the different sources show major differences in style, with J and E being lively and colorful, P being dry, and D being hortatory and prophetic. This is another case of circular reasoning. D is naturally going to be hortatory in nature;

almost all of D consists of Moses' final address to the people. Leaders say hortatory things at times like that. All of the genealogies and technical data are assigned to P. Of course, passages with genealogies and technical data are going to be dry. There are several genealogies assigned to J (Gen 4:16-22 and 10:8-19), and they are also dry. P has a few narratives, and they are also lively, like the P portion of the flood story.

When P does tell a narrative, some of the supposedly unique features of P disappear. For example, Source critics have mentioned that P gives numbers with the smaller unit first in Hebrew (Methuselah was 9 + 60 + 900, Gen 5:27), while J gives the larger number first (YHWH will not destroy Sodom if He finds 40 + 5 in it, Gen 18:28). Umberto Cassuto points out that this is actually a feature of the Hebrew language and not a function of sources.[16] When precision is important to the author, the smaller number goes first (5 and 40). In a narrative, precision is not usually important, and the larger number goes first. When P has a narrative with numbers, P also puts the larger number first ("Abram was 90 and 9 years old..." Gen 17:1).

Comparison with other ancient Middle Eastern literature shows that the Torah is not unique in having a mix of different styles of literature. To give one example, the biography of the Egyptian general Uni, dated to about 2300 B.C., contains flowing narrative (like J and E) when his campaigns are described, stereotyped refrains to indicate recognition by Pharaoh and to list accomplishments (like P), as well as a victory hymn.[17] This work was carved in stone at the request of Uni, and so there is no chance of any integration of multiple sources.

---

[16] Cassuto, *The Documentary Hypothesis*, lecture 4, pp. 52ff

[17] Patterson, *Introduction to the Old Testament*, p. 526, citing Kitchen, *Notes on Some Problems in the Book of Daniel*, p. 349

3.2.1.8 Repetition on a Small Scale

The Documentary Hypothesis uses repetition as an argument for multiple sources – the argument being that one source says something, which must then also be said in another source. However, we should recognize that a unified text can contain repetition. Repetition is a common part of Hebrew writing style, especially in poetry, but also in narrative. The flood story provides an example that illustrates the point well. Table 3-2 below shows Gen 7:17b-21 from the alleged P source next to the parallel Gen 7:17a and 22-23 from the alleged J source.

Table 3-2 Flood Story Repetition

"P" Source	"J" Source
[17b] and as the waters increased they lifted the ark high above the earth. [18]The waters rose and increased greatly on the earth, and the ark floated on the surface of the water. [19] They rose greatly on the earth, and all the high mountains under the entire heavens were covered. [20] The waters rose and covered the mountains to a depth of more than twenty feet. [21] Every living thing that moved on the earth perished-birds, livestock, wild animals, all the creatures that swarm over the earth, and all mankind.	[17a] For forty days the flood kept coming on the earth, [22] Everything on dry land that had the breath of life in its nostrils died. [23] Every living thing on the face of the earth was wiped out; men and animals and the creatures that move along the ground and the birds of the air were wiped from the earth. Only Noah was left, and those with him in the ark.

The repetition is apparent. However, the repetition is more pronounced within the sources than across the sources. The water rises in verse 17, 18, again in 19 and again in 20, all of which are assigned to P. The animals die in verse 22 and again in verse 23, both of which are assigned to J. Repetition cannot be used to divide these sources; if it could, then verses 18-23 could in theory be split into as many as six different sources. The reader should also note that the repetition is not completely identical; like other examples of biblical parallelism, each repeated element serves to advance the meaning.

Let us consider a second biblical narrative for comparison. Daniel 3 tells the story of the three Hebrew youths and the fiery furnace. Although questions abound on the authorship of Daniel, chapter 3 is understood to be the work of a single author. Here the repetition is also clear from Table 3-3, which shows selected verses from Daniel 3.

Table 3-3 Repetition in Daniel

[2] He then summoned the satraps, prefects, governors, advisers, treasurers, judges, magistrates and all the other provincial officials to come to the dedication of the image he had set up.	[3] So the satraps, prefects, governors, advisers, treasurers, judges, magistrates and all the other provincial officials assembled for the dedication of the image that King Nebuchad-nezzar had set up, and they stood before it.
[5] As soon as you hear the sound of the horn, flute, zither, lyre, harp, pipes and all kinds of music, you must fall down and worship the image of gold that King Nebuchadnezzar has set up. [6] Whoever does not fall down and worship will imme-	[7] Therefore, as soon as they heard the sound of the horn, flute, zither, lyre, harp and all kinds of music, all the peoples, nations and men of every language fell down and wor-shiped the image of gold that King Nebuchadnezzar had set

diately be thrown into a blazing furnace."	up.
[8] At this time some astrologers came forward and denounced the Jews. [9] They said to King Nebuchadnezzar, "O king, live forever! [10] You have issued a decree, O king, that everyone who hears the sound of the horn, flute, zither, lyre, harp, pipes and all kinds of music must fall down and worship the image of gold, [11] and that whoever does not fall down and worship will be thrown into a blazing furnace.	[14] and Nebuchadnezzar said to them, "Is it true, Shadrach, Meshach and Abed-nego, that you do not serve my gods or worship the image of gold I have set up? [15] Now when you hear the sound of the horn, flute, zither, lyre, harp, pipes and all kinds of music, if you are ready to fall down and worship the image I made, very good. But if you do not worship it, you will be thrown immediately into a blazing furnace. Then what god will be able to rescue you from my hand?"

In this story from Daniel, the repetition is so pronounced that it seems awkward on the ear of a modern English speaker, but there is no hint of multiple sources at work in this story. These two examples are not remarkable or unusual, but rather are typical of biblical narratives. We should understand, therefore, that repetition is part of the literary style of the Torah, as well as the rest of the Bible.

3.2.1.9 Repetition of Accounts

Aside from the repetition we find in the Torah that occurs on a small verse to verse scale, the Documentary Hypothesis suggests that repetition of entire accounts is an argument for multiple sources. To a modern reader this may seem to be one of the more persuasive arguments for multiple sources, but it is in this area that modern intuition fails us: the type of repetition found in the

Torah is actually an argument for a single author. We do not have stories that are repeated, but rather different stories with repeated themes and motifs. The stories are told in such a way as to emphasize the repetition; this is part of the literary technique of ancient Hebrew; it was what the ear of the listener would await. Nevertheless, let us evaluate the more prominent of these repeated stories.

3.2.1.9.1 Creation

The poster child example of multiple sources offered by the Documentary Hypothesis is the division of Genesis 1-3 into two separate creation accounts, with the break occurring in the middle of Gen 2:4. The first creation account of Genesis 1 is assigned to P, because of its precise, orderly nature and the use of Elohim as the name for God. The second creation account beginning in Gen 2:4b is assigned to J because of the use of the name YHWH and because of the anthropomorphic nature of His actions. This doublet is actually in a different category from the others. In other cases, we may have two different events that have similarities, but it is clear that there cannot have been two creations.

In analyzing the passage from a Documentary Hypothesis perspective, the problems rush in quickly. The second creation account has very little creating in it – there is no mention of the creation of the heaven, earth, light, darkness, sun, moon, stars, sea, dry land, or fish. All God creates in the second account is one man and one woman, trees in a garden He has planted, and enough animals for Adam to name in one day before he falls asleep. The Genesis 2 account, assigned to J, does not use YHWH alone, but always together with Elohim, "LORD God" in English. While the Ten Commandments in Exodus are assigned to either E or some other early source, they are dependent on the Genesis 1 account of P (see Exod 20:11, speaking of creation in six days), an impossibility given that E was purportedly written 300 years before P. Both passages share the rare feature of God speaking in the plural (Gen

1:26, 3:22, see also 11:7). Genesis 1-3 was not treated as two accounts in antiquity; in Matt 19:4-5 Jesus quoted from both accounts together.

A better explanation of Genesis 1-3 is that the first section is told from a cosmic, or God's eye viewpoint. The second section deals with the creation as experienced by one man, Adam. The personal name YHWH is used, because in this section YHWH deals personally with man. YHWH is combined with Elohim, because in this first introduction of His name the author needs to emphasize YHWH = Elohim the Creator of the universe, a connection not necessarily clear to an ancient Middle-Eastern audience. YHWH is dropped from the name by the serpent during his temptation in Gen 3:1-5. This is also intentional on the part of the serpent, as he wants to disconnect man from his relationship with God. The use of divine names is not an artifact of separate sources, but it is rather deeply intentional, adding to the meaning of the story. Genesis 1-3 further establishes that YHWH Elohim the Creator is also the Lawgiver and Judge. This concept, which seems natural to a western mind, was alien to most of the ancient world - the pagan gods were not the source of morality; their own behavior was often immoral. This idea that the Creator is also the Lawgiver is largely lost if Genesis 1-3 is split into separate accounts. The concept of Elohim as creator and YHWH as lawgiver as described in Gen 1-3 is echoed in Psalm 19: "The heavens are telling of the glory of Elohim" (Ps 19:1)…"The law of YHWH is perfect" (Ps 19:7).

3.2.1.9.2 Covenant with Abraham/Promise of Isaac

Source critics suggest that the multiple passages in which God makes promises to Abraham constitute evidence for multiple sources. The correct response to this suggestion is that God's promises to Abraham are the unifying theme of the Abraham narrative, not an argument for separate sources.

The Abraham narrative begins (Gen 12:1-3) and ends (Gen 22:17) with God's promise.[18] After Genesis 12, each subsequent promise expands and further develops the theme. The promise is repeated in Gen 12:7 after Abram gets to Canaan, specifying that this is the land of promise. The promise in Gen 13:14-17 is for land and numerous offspring. The promise in Genesis 15 specifies an heir, a son, and for the first time is put in the form of a covenant (Gen 15:18). Note also how this chapter begins with the comforting "Do not be afraid, Abram, I am your shield" (Gen 15:1). The reason Abram needs this assurance is due to his warlike action in Genesis 14, an action that could provoke powerful enemies. The Documentary Hypothesis loses this connection by assigning Genesis 15 to J and Genesis 14 to a different source. After the birth of Ishmael, the covenant is further developed in Genesis 17 with name changes for Abraham and Sarah, the introduction of circumcision and the stipulation that the promised son would not be Ishmael, but would rather be born from Abraham's wife Sarah. In Genesis 18, nine years later, God makes a personal visit, informing Abraham and 90 year old Sarah that their son would be born next year. This laughable prospect provides the eventual name for the child (Isaac = laughter). Therefore, we can see seven different instances (the number seven probably not being a coincidence) when God blesses and makes promises to Abraham. Each instance occurs at a different time and for a different reason to add to the story:

1. God gives a command with a promise. Abraham obeys (Gen 12:1-3).
2. Abraham arrives in Canaan. God promises him this land (Gen 12:7).
3. There is a famine, and Lot has just chosen the best land. Will the promise still be fulfilled? Yes – Gen 13:14-17.

---

[18] See section 3.2.3.1 on the Abraham narrative chiasm

4. Abraham gets involved in a dangerous war. Will the promise still be fulfilled? Yes – Genesis 15.
5. Abraham has a son, but not by his wife. Is this the way the promise will be fulfilled? No – Genesis 17.
6. Sarah is now 90 years old. Surely the promise can no longer be fulfilled, can it? It can – Genesis 18.
7. After the promised son is miraculously born, God tells Abraham to sacrifice him. Will the promise now be broken? It will not – Gen 22:17.

3.2.1.9.3 My Wife is My Sister

There are three accounts in Genesis in which one of the patriarchs says that his wife is his sister. In Gen 12:10-20, Abram says this about Sarai in Egypt. In Genesis 20, Abraham says this about Sarah in Gerar, and in Genesis 26 Isaac says this about Rebekah in Gerar. Once again, these are separate stories, each with a unique purpose.

The Gen 12:10-20 story, assigned to J, takes place shortly after Abram's arrival in Canaan. This story foreshadows the later experience of the nation Israel; it is a microcosm of the exodus story before the exodus really happens. First there is a famine, leading to the journey to Egypt. Sarah is taken (like Israel is later enslaved), then God sends plagues on Pharaoh, who finally lets the Hebrews go. This is an example of another type of repetition – the larger story (the exodus) is a later repetition of this earlier, smaller event.

The Genesis 20 story, assigned to E, is in a different location (Gerar) with a different king (Abimelech). Sarah is once again taken, but the king does not touch her. Perhaps this is because Sarah is not described in this story as being a beautiful woman (she is supposedly past her child-bearing years). In this story the king confronts Abraham and asks for an explanation. Abraham's answer includes an interesting fact we hadn't heard before – that Sarah is actually his half-sister.

The Genesis 26 story, assigned to J, is back in Gerar with either the same Abimelech or an heir by the same name, but this time Isaac is the one who passes off his wife Rebekah as his sister, no doubt following the dubious example of his parents. Unlike the other stories, Rebekah is not taken into the foreign court, despite Isaac being there "a long time" (Gen 26:8). Abimelech sees Isaac caressing Rebekah and the ruse is exposed.

Because the Genesis 12 and Genesis 26 stories are both allocated to J, only the Genesis 20 account can generally be used as an argument for sources. However, it is in that story that Abraham says he and Sarah pull this stunt "everywhere they go," implying clearly that they have done it before, as back in Genesis 12.

There are many repeated elements in the stories of the patriarchs, some of which are shown in Table 3-4 below. These should be understood as intentional themes, not as a haphazard product of disparate sources.

Table 3-4 – Repeated Elements in Patriarchal Stories

Abraham	Isaac	Jacob
Barren wife	Barren wife	Barren wife
Receive God's promise	Receive God's promise	Receive God's promise
Two prominent sons	Two prominent sons	
Preference for the younger son	Preference for the younger son	Preference for the younger son(s)
Famine problems	Famine problems	Famine problems
Build altar in Shechem		Build altar in Shechem
Travel from Shechem to Bethel		Travel from Shechem to Bethel
Build altar in Bethel		Build altar in Bethel

Table 3-4 – Repeated Elements in Patriarchal Stories (continued)

Abraham	Isaac	Jacob
	Long distance (Haran) wife	Long distance (Haran) wives
Wife-sister ruse	Wife-sister ruse	
Child from maid-servant		Children from maidservants

3.2.1.9.4 Reasons for Jacob to go to Laban

Gen 27:1-45, assigned to J or E (or split between both according to some source critics), tells how Rebekah and Jacob trick Isaac, who has now gone blind, into blessing Jacob as the firstborn instead of Esau. Esau is so upset about this that he thinks about killing Jacob. Rebekah tells Jacob to go to Haran to visit her brother Laban until Esau cools off. In Gen 27:46 – 28:9, assigned to P, Rebekah tells Isaac how unhappy she is about Esau's wives, who are local women (Hittites – see Gen 26:34-35), prompting Isaac to send Jacob off to Laban. Source critics suggest that these are two different sources giving different reasons for Jacob's trip.

The correct reading of this passage is that it is one continuous story. Rebekah, having manipulated her son in Gen 27:8-13, knows how to manipulate her husband as well, which is what she does in Gen 27:46. Also, notice how Gen 28:7, assigned to P, says "Jacob obeyed his father *and his mother*" by leaving. Jacob's mother only told him to leave back in Gen 27:43-35, in the alleged J section of the story. Note also the chiasm pattern in this story shown in section 3.2.3.1 below.

3.2.1.9.5 Manna and Quails

The Documentary Hypothesis assigns most of Exodus 16 to P and assigns Numbers 11 to J/E, both of which contain stories dealing with manna and quail. A quick look is sufficient to reveal that these are different stories, not two accounts of the same story, and that the Numbers 11 story is dependent on the Exodus 16 story.

Manna is given for the first time in Exodus 16, with full instructions on when to gather it, along with special provisions for the Sabbath day. The quails are a one time event in Exodus 16, but the manna continues throughout the 40 year wilderness experience. The second account starts in Num 11:4 with the people again grumbling, but this time it is because they are tired of eating nothing but manna. Since the later story is dependent on an earlier story, the two stories cannot be placed in separate sources. The story continues with Moses approaching God and showing symptoms of burnout, so God has 70 elders selected to help him. God promises the people that they will eat meat until they are sick of it (Num 11:19-20) and a plague breaks out when they do.

3.2.1.9.6 Water from a Rock

The Exod 17:2-7 and Num 20:2-13 accounts are a suggested doublet. The place is the same (wilderness of Sin), the complaint is the same (no water) and the initial result is the same (Moses strikes the rock and water comes out). However, the Numbers account is dependent on events that had occurred between the two stories. Part of the peoples' complaint is "If only we had died when our brothers fell dead before the LORD!" in Num 20:3, referring to the previous several chapters' events. The Numbers account also is subtly dependent on the Exodus account. In the Exodus account, God tells Moses to strike the rock. He obeys and water comes out. In the Numbers account, the story starts the same but then diverges. God tells Moses to *speak* to the rock. Moses instead *strikes* the rock. Why would he strike it? Why would he expect that to accomplish anything? Because he remembered what happened earlier – he was part of the first story and was trying to produce an encore. God ends up displeased with his disobedience, and Moses suffers the consequence of not being allowed to enter the Promised Land.

3.2.1.9.7 Ten Commandments

The Documentary Hypothesis suggests that there are three different versions of the Ten Commandments: the first in Exod 20:1-17 from either E or an unknown source, the second in Exod 34:10-26 from J and the third in Deut 5:6-21 from D.

To explain this, first we should understand that the Deut 5:6-21 passage is simply a retelling of the story of Exodus 19 and 20. The commandments match almost word for word except for the rationale behind the Sabbath command. Moses is speaking in Deuteronomy 5 and recounting the events of Exodus 19 and 20. The fact that Moses recounted something that happened earlier does not imply evidence for different sources. The Exodus 34 passage is also not a separate source describing the same event as Exodus 20. Exodus 34 happens after the golden calf incident, which prompted an angry Moses to break the tablets he had received earlier. Exod 34:1 and 34:4 indicate that this time Moses is bringing new tablets to replace the ones broken earlier. Therefore, it is clear that Exodus 20 is one story, Exodus 34 is the story of a second event that happened later, and Deuteronomy 5 is a recounting by Moses of the Exodus 19-20 story.

The only real problem that remains is that the commandments given in Exodus 34 are dramatically different from the ones in Exodus 20 and Deuteronomy 5. Exod 34:10-26 lists a series of commands (apparently a few more than ten), only three of which correspond to the Exodus 20 list, and even on those the wording is much different. Moses is told to "write these words" in Exod 34:27. Exod 34:28 then says: "Moses was there with the LORD forty days and forty nights without eating bread or drinking water. And he wrote on the tablets the words of the covenant-the Ten Commandments." The answer to the problem is that God wrote the words in Exodus 20, then rewrote them in Exod 34:1b, when He says, "Chisel out two stone tablets like the first ones, and I will write on them the words that were on the first tablets, which you broke." Then Moses wrote the words in Exod 34:10-26 (different words). This interpretation is confirmed by Deut 10:1-5, where Moses describes making a second set of tablets and says "The LORD wrote on these tablets what he had written before, the Ten Commandments." Note how Appendix A leaves Exod 34:1b absent from all sources. The Documentary Hypothesis doesn't like Exod 34:1b because it tends to resolve this problem.

3.2.1.9.8 Naming of Beersheba

Abraham gives a name to Beersheba ("well of the oath") in Gen 21:31, then Isaac similarly names the same place in Gen 26:33. The Documentary Hypothesis suggests that these are parallel accounts in different sources, with the Abraham account assigned to E and the Isaac account assigned to J.

First, let us notice that Beersheba is mentioned in both E and J before it is named (Gen 21:14 –E, Gen 21:32-33 and 26:33 – J, also Gen 22:19). This is in keeping with the scribal practice that allows newer geographic names to get into older documents in order to make them understandable to the reader. Geographically, Beersheba is important, because all the patriarchs spend time there.

Second, in order to get the Beersheba naming of Gen 21:31 into E, the Documentary Hypothesis has to perform fine surgery, snipping it away from the surrounding J passages of Gen 21:28-30 and 32-33.

Third, in Gen 26:33, Isaac did not actually choose the name Beersheba, but just "Sheba" ("oath"), a name which is echoed in Josh 19:2. Since different people at different times gave different names to a place, this can hardly be called an evidence for multiple sources.

3.2.1.9.9 Naming of Bethel

The Documentary Hypothesis suggests that Bethel was named twice, first in Gen 28:19 in J, then in Gen 35:15 by either E or P. The short answer to this is that Bethel was indeed named twice by Jacob, and undoubtedly had to be named yet again by his descendants in Joshua's time. The fact that a young man passing through a place (which is what Jacob was in Genesis 28) decides to give that place a new name doesn't mean the new name will appear on the next edition of a map. When Jacob returns many years later to Bethel in Genesis 35, the naming is more permanent because this time he can pass it on to his large family. His descendants retained this memory and brought it with them when they re-entered Canaan in Joshua's time.

3.2.1.9.10 Korah, Dathan and Abiram

The rebellion of Korah, Dathan and Abiram in Numbers 16 is one of several stories that the Documentary Hypothesis attempts to pry apart into two stories (the flood story and the burning bush story are other examples). The Documentary Hypothesis assigns the rebellion of Korah to P and the rebellion of Dathan and Abiram to J. The P account thus serves to show the superiority of Aaronic priests over other Levites, represented by Korah, while the J account upholds Moses' authority and makes the Reubenites, represented by Dathan and Abiram, look bad. The source critics point to Deut 11:6, which mentions Dathan and Abiram but not Korah, to bolster their case.

First, we should notice that the story will not come apart easily. Three verses (Num 16:1, 16:24 and 16:27) mention Korah, Dathan and Abiram, all three together, and these must either be split apart or assigned to the redactor. Num 26:8-11 looks back on the event and again names all three so it also has to be assigned to the redactor. Second, it should not be surprising when any rebellion occurs to find that there is more than one reason for it. Most wars have multiple causes, which are often so tangled that historians do not agree on the primary cause of a conflict. The rebellion against Moses is a similar situation. Korah, Dathan and Abiram all have complaints against Moses, though not the same ones. Third, notice that the Documentary Hypothesis has to deviate from its usual guideline of having Moses and Aaron work together in P, since Moses acts alone in Num 16:4 and 16:8, and Moses alone hears from God in 16:23. The P account also has to deviate from its usual picture of God, who gets very angry (16:45) in the aftermath of the incident. The P account does not make explicitly clear that Korah gets killed at the end of the story. Moses chooses not to mention Korah in Deuteronomy perhaps because it is painful to him; Korah was a Levite, from his own tribe.

It is also realistic to assume that in any rebellion against Moses, the rebels (Dathan and Abiram) felt the need to have the support of some Levites (Korah), as Levites had assumed a role of religious leadership in Israel. To seek religious backing for political actions is fully in accord with human nature.

Psalm 106 is also instructive on this story. This is a late psalm, either exilic or post-exilic (106:47), so the fact that the author knows P (based on 106:30) says nothing about the date of P. Yet note that like Deuteronomy the Psalm mentions only Dathan and Abiram (106:17), not Korah, though it knows the whole story, as is clear from 106:16.

3.2.1.10 Convergence of Evidence

Friedman argues that the strongest evidence establishing the Documentary Hypothesis is that multiple lines of evidence converge. The duplicate accounts overlay with unique vocabulary, selected divine names, etc.[19]

We have already seen how the individual lines of evidence are unreliable. We believe the convergence argument is also overstated and tends to be based on circular reasoning, because numerous passages are assigned to a given source for one reason only. To use the beginning of the Abraham story as an example, Genesis 12-13 is assigned to J with the exception of 12:4b-5, 13:6 and 13:11b-12a, which are assigned to P. The first two of those passages are assigned to P for one reason only – they deal with

---

[19] Friedman, *The Bible with Sources Revealed*, p. 27

possessions and property, a favorite topic for P. There is no convergence here; they do not use any divine names or other features distinctive to P. Removing the P verses from the larger J passage tends to make the J passage read worse rather than better, the opposite of what would be expected if the P verses were really a foreign entity. However, leaving the verses in the J passage would mean we now have discussion of property and possessions in J, which would then detract from the vocabulary based arguments stating that these words are unique to P. This would then lead to less "convergence" in other passages. This same type thing occurs with many other passages: a passage is assigned to a source for one reason only, or removed from a source, or assigned to the redactor because it exhibits one characteristic of an allegedly different source. When the one-reason cases are set aside, the uniqueness of each source diminishes and the argument for convergence diminishes as well.

Still, a core issue remains that must be addressed. This is best illustrated by an example. Genesis 15 (J) and Genesis 17 (P) are a suggested doublet describing God's covenant with Abram. Different though the two stories may be, let us assume for a moment that this really is a case of two different sources describing essentially the same thing. Without making any unreasonable cuts in these accounts, we still count nine occurrences of YHWH and no occurrences of Elohim in the J account of Genesis 15, as opposed to one occurrence of YHWH with eleven occurrences of Elohim in Genesis 17. Thus the argument for convergence: not only is there a doublet, but each part of the doublet uses different names for God; two independent lines of evidence converge. Friedman lists 31 suggested doublets in the Torah dealing with either stories or laws, with independent lines of evidence for each.[20]

---

[20] Friedman, *The Bible with Sources Revealed*, pp. 28-30

This calls for logical thinking. If there are exactly 31 possible doublets in the Torah and all are supported by multiple independent lines of evidence, it would constitute a strong argument for the Documentary Hypothesis. The flaw in this argument is that there are not exactly 31 possible doublets, instead, there are many more. Consider the account of Joseph's dreams. Gen 37:5-8 is dream #1, which Joseph tells to his brothers, and Gen 37:9-11 is a similar dream #2, which Joseph tells to his brothers and his father. Both dreams are assigned to E; there are no independent lines of evidence suggesting different sources. However, this is a true doublet. If Joseph had said in Gen 37:5 "YHWH spoke to me in a dream" and in Gen 37:9 "Elohim spoke to me in a dream," then this doublet would certainly have been added to the source critics' list. Many such doublets exist in the Torah, with no independent lines of evidence to justify splitting them into sources. Some of these are listed below:

1. Joseph has two dreams and tells his brothers (Gen 37:5-11), both in E.
2. Joseph listens to two dreams in prison: one from the baker, one from the butler (Genesis 40), both in E.
3. Pharaoh has two dreams (Gen 41:1-7), both in E.
4. Adam names his wife "woman" (Gen 2:23) and names his wife "Eve" (Gen 3:20), both in J.
5. The matriarch is barren (Sarah in Genesis 16, 18 and 21, Rebekah in 25:21 and Rachel in 29:31/30:1-2): Sarah is in P and J, Rebekah and Rachel are both in J.
6. Joseph's brothers make two trips to Egypt (Genesis 42 and 43). Elements of both trips are in both J and E.
7. Judah's two sons killed by YHWH (Gen 38:7-10), both in J.
8. Isaac has twins (Gen 25:24-26) and Judah has twins (Gen 38:27-30), both with unusual stories of childbirth: Jacob's hand is on Esau's heel, Zerah's hand comes out first and is marked with a scarlet ribbon, but Perez is born first. Both stories are in J.

9. The younger son is chosen – Isaac, Jacob, Judah, Joseph, Ephraim, Moses and Eleazar. This theme is in multiple sources.

10. Saving the righteous from destruction (Noah, Lot, in Genesis 6-8 and 19). Noah's story is in J and P, Lot's is in J.

11. Famine leading to travel, leading to "my wife is my sister" stories of Gen 12:10-20 and 26:1-11, both in J.

12. Meeting a wife-to-be at the well (Gen 24:11-25, 29:1-14 and Exod 2:15-21), all three in J.

13. Wife offers maidservant as second wife (Gen 16:1-3, 30:3-5 and 30:9-10). The sources are mixed.

14. Esau sells his birthright to Jacob (Gen 25:29-34); Jacob steals Esau's blessing (Genesis 27). Both stories are in J.

15. Conflict with Abimelech about wells (Gen 21:25-30 and 26:15-31). Both stories are in J (although source critics do not all agree, Friedman assigns the first to E).

16. The list of who went to Egypt (Gen 46:8-27 and Exod 1:1-5) is present twice, both times in P.

17. Build a lamp stand (Exod 25:31-40 and 37:17-24), both in P.

18. Build the Ark of the Covenant (Exod 25:10-22 and 37:1-9), both in P.

19. Passover instructions (Exod 12:1-13, Lev 23:5-7 and Num 9:1-14), all in P.

20. Do not eat blood (Gen 9:4, Lev 7:26-27, 17:10-16 and 19:26), twice in P and twice in the Holiness Code.

21. Do not give your offspring to Molech (Lev 18:21 and 20:1-5), both in Holiness Code.

22. Yahweh will scatter you (Deut 4:26-28 and 28:64), both in D2.

23. Do not worship other gods (Deut 5:7, 6:14, 7:4, 8:19, 11:16, etc.), all in D1.

24. Death penalty for worshipping other gods (Deut 13:1-16 and 17:1-7), both in D1.

The list above is only a start, and if laws are fully included, a much larger list of possible doublets could be constructed. For example, we can certainly imagine that if the sacrifice laws in Leviticus 1-6 showed more variety than they do, the source critics might say something like "J only recognized burnt offerings and E peace offerings, but P adds grain, guilt and sin offerings." Furthermore, if all examples of parallel repetition are included (such as the repetition within each source in the flood story as shown in Table 3-2, above), the number of possible doublets reaches an enormous level.

Clear repetition occurs outside the Torah with stories in the Torah as well. Judg 19:20-24, where the evil men of the city surround the house of a traveling Levite, wanting to molest him, is unmistakably a parallel to the events of Sodom in Gen 19:2-8.

The conclusion is that there are so many passages in the Torah that are potential doublets that it is a statistical certainty that many of them will show collaborative evidence for sources, regardless of whether or not such sources exist. This is not a convergence of evidence for the Documentary Hypothesis so much as it is the natural consequence of an author who used different terminology in different situations. Note that various kinds of repetition are so common in the Torah that there are also repeated ideas that do not seem to be doublets – for example, issues related to Joseph's coat (Gen 37:3, 37:23 and 37:31-32 compared with 39:12-13, 39:15 and 39:18), or a man not recognizing the woman with whom he sleeps (Gen 19:30-38, 29:24-25 and 38:16).

Garrett concludes, "The use of doublets and repetition as evidence for multiple documents in Genesis is perhaps of all the arguments the most persuasive for the modern student, while in fact being the most spurious and abused piece of evidence…It is an entirely modern reading of the text and ignores ancient rhetorical concepts. In an ancient text, there is no stronger indication that only a single document is present than parallel accounts. Doublets, that is, two separate stories that closely parallel one another, are the very stuff of ancient narrative."[21]

3.2.2 Issues with the Documentary Hypothesis

Having addressed some of the main arguments offered in favor of the Documentary Hypothesis, we will now point out some of the difficulties with the theory.

3.2.2.1 Analytical Problems with P

The premise behind P is that it was written during the post-exilic period, about 500-450 B.C. The author of P codified the role of priests and Levites, with special emphasis on the sacrificial system and the tabernacle. The author wished to establish that priests and Levites were given a central role from the beginning, with centralized worship first at the tabernacle and then at the temple. P emphasizes the supremacy of the priests, the descendants of Aaron, over other Levites. Only priests were allowed to perform sacrifices. P is careful to exclude all references to the patriarchs or anyone else performing a sacrifice. P is also responsible for most of the genealogies, references to wealth, and anything that reflects a numbered, ordered, account. Wellhausen believed the tabernacle never existed, and that its description in P was retroactively modeled on the temple.[22] The considerable description of the tabernacle, along with the related rules for sacrifices and regulations for priests and Levites were only invented in the post-exilic period.

3.2.2.1.1 Pious Fraud

If the Documentary Hypothesis is correct, then the passages assigned to P are a pious fraud. There never was a tabernacle, nor a high priest, nor a well-regulated sacrificial system, nor a signifi-

---

[21] Garrett, *Rethinking Genesis*, pp. 19-20
[22] Wellhausen, *Prolegomena to the History of Ancient Israel*, p. 36ff

cant role for worship by Levites prior to the Babylonian exile. These ideas were developed only during and after the exile by priests who wanted to formalize and centralize their role in Israelite worship. To do this, they fabricated the history of these things and inserted it in their record of their people's history. Some devout churchmen who have embraced the Documentary Hypothesis shrink from the obvious conclusion that this reduces much of the Old Testament to a lie, but Wellhausen did not. He at least faced the brutal logical conclusion of his theory: "It is not the case that the Jews had any profound respect for their ancient history; rather they condemned the whole earlier development, and allowed only the Mosaic time along with its Davidic reflex to stand; in other words, not history, but the ideal. The theocratic ideal was from the exile onward the center of all thought and effort, and it annihilated the sense for objective truth, all regard and interest for the actual facts as they had been handed down. It is well known that there never have been more audacious history-makers than the Rabbins. But Chronicles affords evidence sufficient that this evil propensity goes back to a very early time, its root the dominating influence of the Law, being the root of Judaism itself."[23] It should be eye-opening to realize that, along with the anti-Semitic overtones present in this statement, Wellhausen believed that the writing of P stemmed from an "evil propensity."

3.2.2.1.2 Sequence Problems

Source critics suggest that the primary history of Israel, running from the book of Judges through 2 Kings, was written before P. As a result, information unique to P (such as the tabernacle) should be absent from the primary history. When something from P does appear (such as a mention of the tabernacle, or tent of meeting, as in 1 Kgs 8:4) it is condemned as a later interpolation or an editorial

---

[23] Wellhausen, *Prolegomena to the History of Ancient Israel*, p. 161

revision. There is no good way for anyone to either prove or disprove that such interpolations occurred, they are simply used as a deus ex machina to explain places where the Documentary Hypothesis doesn't work. The only reasonable way to respond to claims of such interpolations is to pile up a high stack of examples of P information present in the primary history and other early texts, in the hope that readers will recognize the weakness of the Documentary Hypothesis position in this area. Therefore, we offer the following list:

1. In Judg 8:27, Gideon uses gold to make an "ephod," a priestly garment introduced only in P (Exodus 39, etc). Others to use or wear an ephod are Micah (Judg 17:5), Samuel (1 Sam 2:18), other priests (1 Sam 2:28), Ahijah (1 Sam 14:3), 85 priests (1 Sam 22:18), Abiathar (1 Sam 23:6) and David (2 Sam 6:14). Hosea, an early writing prophet, mentions the ephod in Hos 3:4.

2. In Judg 13:5-7 and 16:7, Samson is described as a Nazirite. The rules for Nazirites are given only in P, in Numbers 6. Amos, one of the early writing prophets, also mentions Nazirites in Amos 2:11-12.

3. 1 Samuel 1-3 is clearly set at the tabernacle. Notice in particular 1 Sam 1:24 "house of YHWH" and 1 Sam 2:22 "tent of meeting" (using the Hebrew [אהל מועד] wording from P). "Temple of YHWH" is used in 1 Sam 3:3 and "house of YHWH" is in 1 Sam 3:15. This passage also refers to the portion of food reserved for the priests (1 Sam 2:13-15, dependent on Lev 7:29-34) and God's establishment of a hereditary priesthood (1 Sam 2:30).

4. The Ark of the Covenant in 1 Sam 4:4 reflects the design of Exod 25:10-22, with cherubim. This is also true in 2 Sam 6:2.

5. In 1 Sam 14:32-33, the people sin by eating meat with the blood, something forbidden by Lev 17:10 and other P or Holiness Code passages.

6. In 1 Sam 20:26, Saul thinks David may be absent from a banquet because he is ceremonially unclean. The idea of being unclean is based on the P instruction in Leviticus and Numbers.

7. In 1 Sam 21:4-6, David eats the "bread of the presence," defined in the P/Holiness Code passage of Lev 24:5-9.

8. In 1 Sam 28:6, The LORD does not answer Saul by "urim." Urim is introduced in the P passages of Exod 28:30, Lev 8:8 and Num 27:21.

9. In 2 Sam 7:6, God says He has been in a tent, a tabernacle, since the exodus.

10. The anointing oil "from the tent" in 1 Kgs 1:39 is apparently from the anointing oil associated with the tabernacle, described in P (Exod 30:23-32).

11. In 1 Kgs 1:50, Adonijah flees to the altar and grabs its horns. Joab does the same in 1 Kgs 2:28-30, where the altar is described as being in the tent of YHWH. This is clearly the central altar described in P (Exod 29:12, Lev 4:25, etc.).

12. 1 Kgs 8:4 mentions the tabernacle and its furnishings.

13. Jeroboam's feast (1 Kgs 12:32-33) mimics the date for the Feast of Tabernacles described in P/Holiness Code (Lev 23:34): "like the feast which is in Judah" (eighth month and fifteenth day vs. the seventh month and fifteenth day).

14. Naboth refuses to sell his vineyard in 1 Kgs 21:3 based on inheritance laws from P (Num 36:7).

15. In 2 Kgs 19:15 and Isa 37:16, Hezekiah's mention of God dwelling above the cherubim indicates that he knows the architecture of the Ark of the Covenant and how God speaks between the cherubim, as described in the P passage of Exod 25:18-22.

16. In 2 Kgs 22:4, 22:8 and 23:4, Hilkiah is described as the "high priest," a term introduced only in P (Num 35:25, 35:28).

17. Isaiah, a pre-exilic prophet, uses the words "formless" and "void" (Hebrew "tohu" and "bohu" [בהו and תהו]) in Isa 34:11, echoing the P creation story in Gen 1:2. Isaiah also alludes to the P creation story in Isa 42:5, 45:12, 45:18 and 65:17.

18. Jeremiah, a pre-exile/exilic prophet, also talks about the earth being "formless and void" (Jer 4:23) echoing the P creation story in Gen 1:2.

19. Jeremiah's land purchase in Jeremiah 32 reflects the P/Holiness Code laws of land redemption (Lev 25:25).

20. Jer 17:26 lists many of the offerings described in P (Leviticus 1-7).

21. Amos 4:5 mentions the people offering thank offerings with leaven, a practice sanctioned in Lev 7:13. Also, the peace offerings of Amos 5:22 reflect Lev 7:11-15.

22. Ezek 22:26 quotes from Lev 10:10, about distinguishing "between the holy and the profane, and between the unclean and the clean."

23. The Ten Commandments rationale in Exod 20:11, "for in six days the LORD God made the heavens and the earth…" reflects the P creation account of Genesis 1. The Ten Commandments account in Exodus 20 is sometimes assigned to E and sometimes to an older independent source, yet it is dependent on P information.

24. Deut 16:13 instructs the people to celebrate the Feast of Booths (sometimes called the Feast of Tabernacles), but doesn't explain the significance of the booths. The significance of the booths is described in Lev 23:34-43. Also, Hos 12:9 alludes to the feast of booths.

25. Deut 23:10 looks to be dependent on cleanliness laws in P.

26. Deut 24:8 looks to be dependent on the numerous laws in P (Leviticus 13-14) relating to how to handle skin diseases.

27. The morning and evening sacrifices from P (Num 28:3-4) are reflected in 1 Kgs 18:29, 2 Kgs 3:20 and 2 Kgs 16:15.

28. In Deut 4:41-43, Moses sets up three cities of refuge east of the Jordan. This is not well explained in D, because the concept of cities of refuge has already been explained thoroughly in P (Num 35:6-34).

29. Finally, in Kings, there is an echo of a story in the Torah.[24] Jeroboam I makes two golden calves (1 Kgs 12:28), echoing Aaron's sin in Exodus 32. Jeroboam's son Abijah dies as a child (1 Kgs 14:1-17) and his other son Nadab is murdered (1 Kgs 15:25-28). Just as Jeroboam's sin echoes Aaron's, the names of his children who die echo Aaron's sons Nadab and Abihu, who die in Leviticus 10 (notice the slight difference though – Abihu is not a Yahwistic name, Abijah is. No one born before the exodus is given a Yahwistic name). The fact that the historian in Kings chooses to record this account in such a way implies that he was familiar with the story of Aaron and his sons, and that Aaron's account was written before 1 Kings. Since the story of Nadab and Abihu is in P, the sequence is not consistent with the Documentary Hypothesis. We can be confident that the Torah account was written first, since Aaron's sin in creating the golden calf is in E, while the Nadab and Elihu story is in P. Only if the stories are put together do they accurately match the Jeroboam account.

This should not be viewed as a complete list of all possible sequence errors in the Bible dealing with alleged P text. We could, for example, offer examples in the Psalms where the psalmist knew P. Source critics may in those cases dismiss the psalms as being later in time than we think they are. We have only listed selected examples coming from texts that are widely agreed to pre-date P.

There are also issues related to relevance of the laws in P.

---

[24] This discussion is taken from Damrosch, article on Leviticus, in *The Literary Guide to the Bible*, p. 71

1. P provides laws about making war and taking spoils – laws that would be irrelevant in a post-exilic era when Judah was a province of Persia. Also, taking female captives as wives (Num 31:18), in addition to being irrelevant, would conflict with the struggle of Ezra and Nehemiah against mixed marriages in the post-exilic period.

2. Laws related to Urim and Thummim would be irrelevant, as they were not used in the post-exilic period (Neh 7:64-66).

3. P spends considerable time describing the construction of the Ark of the Covenant and the cherubim, items not present in the second (rebuilt) temple.

4. The leprosy laws (Leviticus 13) would be unworkable in a post-exilic period. A Jew living in Babylon or other far off country could hardly be expected to travel to Jerusalem to be inspected by a priest.

5. P contains many details about land allotments to the northern tribes. Num 32:33-38 touches on this first, and the subject is expanded in P passages of Joshua in Joshua 19-21. These land allotments would be irrelevant by the proposed date of writing of P, since the northern tribes had ceased to exist and most of the land listed was not under Jewish control.

3.2.2.1.3 Laws about Non-existent Features

Aside from the issue that P spends a great deal of time describing things, such as the tabernacle, that critics say never existed, there is the problem of continuing laws related to those items. For example, the instruction is clear that all sacrifices must be done at the tabernacle (Lev 17:3-5). However, the tabernacle dropped out of prominence when the temple was built, and was certainly destroyed by the time of the exile (Lam 2:6). Friedman, who supports the Documentary Hypothesis but dates P before the exile, puts the problem well: "Why would a priest write a law code that said that sacrifices can only be offered at a place that did not exist any more?"[25] Exod 25:22 states that God would speak to Israel from the Ark of the Covenant, from "between the two cherubim." Why would a priest say this is where God speaks, when he didn't know where the ark was or what had happened to it? Exod 28:30 says Aaron shall wear a breastplate containing Urim and Thummim, with which he "shall carry the judgment of the sons of Israel over his heart before the LORD *continually*." Urim and Thummim were not used by the second temple priests. Why would a priest write a law for himself which he would not be able to keep?

3.2.2.1.4 Dietary Laws

Archeology speaks in an interesting way to attest to the antiquity of some of the P passages. All the dietary laws in the Torah come from passages assigned to P. Perhaps most prominently, Lev 11:7 forbids eating pork. In twelfth century B.C. Canaan, pig bones are found in the archeological refuse of some places but not in others. They are frequently found in Philistine dominated areas of southwest Canaan and they are found in Ammonite areas east of the Jordan. However, they are absent in the central highland settlements where Jews were concentrated. Iron Age 1 settlements there seem to show a diet that included sheep, goats and perhaps a kind of deer, but no pigs.[26] The implication is that the Jews were obeying the Leviticus 11 dietary laws 700 years before the alleged date for P.

3.2.2.1.5 Calendar

Most of the references to months in the Bible are done by number: first month, second month, etc. The modern Jewish calendar uses a set of names for months that were adopted from the Babylonian

---

[25] Friedman, *Who Wrote the Bible?*, p. 186
[26] Kitchen, *On the Reliability of the Old Testament*, p. 230

names, names the Jews picked up in exile. In the indisputably post-exilic books of Ezra, Nehemiah, Esther and Zechariah, the Babylonian adopted names (Adar, Chislev, Nisan, Elul, Tebeth, Sivan and Shebat) occasionally begin to appear along with the month number (Ezra 6:15, etc.). This begins early in the post-exilic period in the book of Zechariah (520-518 B.C.), in Zech 1:7, before the alleged writing of P. There are 17 occurrences of the adopted month names in the Old Testament. However, the P passages never use the post-exilic names, always relying on only the month number. The pre-exilic names (Aviv/Abib, Ziv, Ethanim, Bul) occur seven times in the Old Testament, including Exod 13:4 (J), 23:15, 34:18 (J) and Deut 16:1 (D).

3.2.2.1.6 Silver Amulets

In 1979, two small silver amulets were found in a burial cave in a hillside known as Ketef Hinnom, west of the Old City of Jerusalem. [27] The amulets were embedded in pottery and other material from the sixth and seventh centuries B.C. The handwriting on the amulets contains the Priestly Blessing of Num 6:24-26, written in Paleo-Hebrew script in the archaic fashion. The amulets date to around 600 B.C., making them the oldest biblical passage yet found. They are now kept at the Israel Museum in Jerusalem. The 600 B.C. date is at least 100 years before the P source (which contains this passage) was purportedly written, and significantly, it is before rather than after the exile.

3.2.2.2 Analytical Problems with D

The premise behind D is that it was written about 621 B.C., during Josiah's reform. The D source constitutes basically the book of Deuteronomy, and this was the "book of the law" discovered by Hilkiah the priest during the reign of Josiah (2 Kgs 22:8). The Deuteronomy 12 passage about centralized worship is used to

---

[27] New York Times 9/28/2004 by John Noble Wilford

justify Josiah's crusade against the high places (2 Kgs 23:8-19). Many source critics suggest two Deuteronomic sources D1 and D2, with the second making additions in the early exilic period.

3.2.2.2.1 Pious Fraud

The problem with this 621 B.C. date for D is that, in a similar fashion as P, it makes Deuteronomy a pious fraud; the book was written and then "discovered" immediately afterward. It masquerades as the teaching of Moses, but is really the project of someone hundreds of years later who wanted to concentrate spiritual authority in Jerusalem. It is then used to revise all of Israel's history from Joshua through Kings (the "Deuteronomic history"), condemning almost every king in the list for not removing the high places, based on a rule which had only just been invented. Much of the Old Testament history is indeed written from the theological perspective of Deuteronomy, but this was because Deuteronomy was a foundational book written at the beginning of Israel's history, not because it was written at the end to explain history. In the New Testament, Deuteronomy is quoted 51 times, including three times by Jesus during His temptation. The possibility that such a foundational biblical work is based on deception should be indigestible, at least to believers.

A skeptic should also ask: how likely is it that such a fraud could be successful? It would have to fool the king, the priests, the people, Jeremiah, the prophetess Huldah and the author of Kings. The project of writing such a book is analogous to someone writing a book today named "The Prophecies of Joan of Arc," hiding it in a Paris monastery, then discovering it and passing it off as authentic, then persuading people to modify their religion because of it.

3.2.2.2.2 Identity of the "Book of the Law"

The Documentary Hypothesis holds that the "book of the law" discovered in Josiah's reform was D, consisting of all or most of

Deuteronomy (2 Kgs 22:8). While many modifications to the Documentary Hypothesis have been proposed, this identification of the book of the law has served as an anchor to date D in almost every variation of the theory. Even writers who reject the Documentary Hypothesis assert that the discovered book was "probably all or part of Deuteronomy"[28]. This idea is based primarily on the fact that Josiah's reform emphasized the destruction of all religious shrines (high places) outside of Jerusalem, a crusade supported by the text of Deuteronomy 12.

However, this very central idea, that the discovered book was Deuteronomy, is open to serious question. As part of Josiah's reform, the king reads from this book to the people in 2 Kgs 23:2, a reading described as from "the book of the covenant," a phrase echoed again in 2 Kgs 23:21. The only reference in the Torah to the "book of the covenant" is not in Deuteronomy, but in Exod 24:7. Also, when the "book of the law" is used elsewhere, there is no indication that it is limited to Deuteronomy. In Nehemiah 8 it almost surely refers to the whole Torah. Furthermore, the Chronicles account of Josiah's reform (2 Chronicles 34) has him purging the high places *before* the book of the law is found. Also, the Chronicles account of Josiah's Passover, after the book is found, has details (2 Chron 35:10-14) which are based on rules from Leviticus. Finally, the author of Kings repeatedly evaluates each king of Judah on whether or not he removes the high places, or "bamot," (במות), and the fact that Josiah is brave enough to do so is considered central to his reform, yet the high places are not mentioned by name in Deuteronomy 12, nor anywhere in Deuteronomy in the sense of a place of false worship. Nonetheless, 2 Kgs 23:25, "with all his heart and all his soul and all his might," is clearly an echo of Deut 6:5, so Deuteronomy has to be part of the picture. The best fit for the circumstances is to assume that the

---

[28] Bill T. Arnold and Bryan E. Beyer, *Encountering the Old Testament*, p. 245

"book of the law" was essentially the whole Torah, including Deuteronomy.

Wellhausen makes a big point over a single Hebrew preposition, comparing 2 Kgs 22:10, where Shaphan "read the book" (ויקראהו) to the king, with 2 Chron 34:18, where Shaphan "read *out of* the book" (ויקרא בו), suggesting that the reason for the difference is the author of Kings is thinking about reading the whole book of Deuteronomy, while the Chronicler cannot imagine anyone reading the whole Torah to the king.[29] However, "read out of" is a normal way of saying "read" in Hebrew, and does not necessarily mean either a whole or a subset of the book is intended. A counter-example is in Jer 36:14, where the same Hebrew terminology is used in reference to reading a scroll, and the entire scroll is in view.

3.2.2.2.3 Relationship between Deuteronomy and Jeremiah

Source critics point to a close connection between Jeremiah and Deuteronomy, using this as evidence that Deuteronomy was composed in Jeremiah's time. Friedman even identifies Jeremiah as the author of both D1 and D2, but writing at two different times.[30] Some similarities are certainly there; Jeremiah knew the law. But the similarities between Deuteronomy and Jeremiah are due to the fact that Jeremiah is dependant on Deuteronomy, not that they came from the same author. The differences between Jeremiah and Deuteronomy are significant. Deuteronomy has laws against Ammon and Moab (Deut 23:3-4) and in favor of Edom (Deut 23:7-8). Jeremiah says just the reverse, promising restoration for Moab and Ammon (Jer 48:47 and 49:6), but not Edom (Jer 49:17-18). Jeremiah uses the formulation "declares YHWH" 165 times, which is more than once per page on any Bible. This formula is not used at all in Deuteronomy, and appears

---

[29] Wellhausen, *Prolegomena to the History of Ancient Israel*, p. 202
[30] Friedman, *Who Wrote the Bible*, p. 111

only once anywhere in the Torah (Gen 22:18). The overall perspective of Jeremiah is different from that of Deuteronomy. In Deuteronomy, a covenant is established, and the people can choose to keep it or not. In Jeremiah, the perspective is that there was a covenant, but now it has been broken.

3.2.2.2.4 Deuteronomy Before the Prophets

Notice the similarity between the beginning of Isaiah and Deut 32:1.

Isaiah 1:2a	Deut 32:1

"Listen, O heavens, and hear, O earth;
  For the LORD speaks,"
	"Give ear, O heavens, and let me speak;
	  And let the earth hear the words of my mouth."

This similarity is unlikely to be a coincidence; either Isaiah is echoing Deuteronomy or vice-versa. The date of Isaiah 1 is not in real dispute; it was written in the late eighth century B.C., nearly 100 years before the discovery of the book of the law in Josiah's reform (621 B.C.). Let us demonstrate why Isaiah is likely to be borrowing from Deuteronomy.

The book of Deuteronomy is written much in the form of an ancient Middle Eastern suzerainty treaty, with YHWH being the ruler and Israel being the vassal (for more on this treaty form, see section 3.3.8). One element always present in such treaties is a list of witnesses, which would usually be a long list of pagan gods. Of course, pagan gods are not acceptable in Deuteronomy, so a substitute is made: heaven and earth are the witnesses: "I call heaven and earth to witness against you today..." (Deut 4:26), "I call heaven and earth to witness against you today, that I have set before you life and death, the blessing and the curse. So choose life in order that you may live, you and your descendants..." (Deut 30:19), "Assemble to me all the elders of your tribes and your officers, that I may speak these words in their hearing and call the heavens and the earth to witness against them" (Deut 31:28). Now we come to Isaiah, the first book of the latter prophets to appear in the Bible. Has Israel been faithful to YHWH? The prophets say no, but the first thing they must do, the very first thing, is to call the witnesses. When Isaiah says "Listen, O heavens, and hear, O earth," he is calling the witnesses from Deuteronomy.

This should demonstrate that Deuteronomy was written not just before Isaiah, but long before. Time would be needed for Deuteronomy to be accepted as the law of YHWH, then more time would be needed to allow for a sustained period of rebellion for the treaty to be considered broken.

There are other examples showing that the early prophets, the ones living before the time of Josiah, already knew Deuteronomy:

1. Micah, a contemporary of Isaiah's also may have referenced Deuteronomy. Mic 6:8, "He has showed you, O man, what is good. And what does the LORD require of you? To act justly and to love mercy and to walk humbly with your God," seems to echo Deut 10:12: "And now, O Israel, what does the LORD your God ask of you but to fear the LORD your God, to walk in all his ways, to love him, to serve the LORD your God with all your heart and with all your soul."

2. Hosea 5:10 echoes the Deut 19:14 law regarding removing landmarks.

3. Hosea 2:8 and 2:22 pick up the phrase from Deut 7:13, 11:14, 12:17, 14:23, 18:4 and 28:51, "grain, new wine and oil."

4. Amos 8:5 reflects knowledge about the laws concerning uneven weights and measures in Deut 25:13-15.

5. Verbal parallels exist between Hos 1:9 and Deut 32:21, "not God" and "not people."

6. Amos 4:4, about bringing a tithe every three days, seems to be a sarcastic reference to the laws of Deut 14:28 and 26:12 about bringing a tithe every three years.

7. Further parallels can be seen in Isaiah, such as between Deut 32:39, "I, even I, am He," and Isa 43:10-11, 43:25 and 51:12.[31]

We should add that in general the older prophets, the ones who preceded Josiah's reform, were familiar with a law or "Torah," mentioning it in Hos 4:6, 8:1, 8:12, Amos 2:4, Mic 4:2, Isa 1:10, 2:3, 5:24, 8:16 and 8:20.

3.2.2.2.5 Irrelevant History and Law

Source critics suggest that Deuteronomy was written in Josiah's time to address specific concerns of that time, and in particular, to support his reforms. However, the historical background given in Deuteronomy is largely irrelevant to Josiah's time. The first three chapters of Deuteronomy give an extensive review of wilderness wanderings, battles and land allocations to northern tribes east of the Jordan. This kind of historical information is also sprinkled throughout chapters 5-11. What would any of this have to do with the southern Kingdom of Judah more than 500 years later? In a similar manner, some of the laws in Deuteronomy would be obsolete by Josiah's time. These include injunctions to destroy the seven nations in the land of Canaan (Deut 20:16-18) and the Amalekites (Deut 25:17-19), as well as laws about setting up cities of refuge (Deuteronomy 19).

The Deuteronomy laws concerning kings do not fit Josiah's time either. Why emphasize that the king must be a native citizen (Deut 17:15), when a Davidic king had been ruling for almost 400 years? Why warn that the king should not cause the people to return to Egypt (Deut 17:16)? The people in Moses day frequently

---

[31] Section 4.2.1 discusses reasons for dating Isaiah 40-66 before Josiah.

brought up the idea of returning to Egypt, but it was obsolete in Josiah's day.

The passages of Deut 13:1-5 and 17:2-7 stipulate the death penalty for anyone who is found to have worshipped foreign gods, or any god other than Yahweh. This would be an unrealistic penalty in Josiah's time. Coming after the reign of Manasseh and Amon, probably most of the people in the country would have to be executed.

Perhaps the worst of these instructions, from a Documentary Hypothesis standpoint, is Deut 27:4-7, where not only are the people instructed to set up an altar on a high place (exactly the kind of thing Josiah was busy destroying), but they are commanded to sacrifice on it. Then to top it off, the high place is on Mount Ebal, a mountain in northern Israel (Samaria).

3.2.2.3 Premise of J and E

The premise behind J is that it is a source from the Southern Kingdom of Judah that uses primarily YHWH as the name for God. YHWH in J is very anthropomorphic, walking, talking, arguing, and even eating and wrestling with man. J is generally dated as the oldest of the sources at around 850 B.C., though different scholars have proposed a range spanning from 950 to 550 B.C. A creative separate reading of the J texts has been rendered by Bloom and Rosenberg, in *The Book of J*, in which they identified the author of J as a woman in King Rehoboam's court, due to the high profile of women and their sympathetic treatment in J passages (see specifically the treatment of Tamar in Genesis 38).[32]

The premise behind E is that it is a source from the northern Kingdom of Israel (though many of the E stories are set in the south) that uses primarily Elohim for God prior to Exod 3:14. God is more aloof in E than in J, speaking from heaven or in dreams rather than walking with man on earth. E was written about 750

---

[32] Bloom and Rosenberg, *The Book of J*, introduction

B.C., before the fall of Samaria to the Assyrians in 721 B.C. E was fused with J sometime after the fall of Samaria but before the development of D. Scholars often refer to passages as belonging to JE because of the difficulty of distinguishing between the sources. In addition, E has usually been the smallest of the main sources and, as Blenkinsopp says, there is "not much enthusiasm for retaining it."[33] Friedman, on the other hand, expands the scope of E beyond that of most source critics, and even identifies him specifically as a Levite from Shiloh.[34]

Because J and E are the earliest sources, older than the prophets, we cannot do as we did with P and D, using the prophets' dependency on J/E passages as an argument against them. Most source critics agree that J and E are old; they just differ significantly on the date. Any Psalm written by David or his contemporaries (about 1000 B.C.) would precede J and E (as well as D and P), and some of those psalms do show a knowledge of J and E passages. For example, David's Psalm 68 is usually acknowledged to be an old Psalm, and 68:8, with Mount Sinai shaking, seems to indicate a knowledge of J (Exod 19:18). However, the Psalms are usually not easy to date because they are short and therefore offer little internal evidence for when they were written. Source critics will not recognize the validity of the attributions of the psalms (not agreeing that "a Psalm of David" was written by David), so we will not rely on this line of argument.

We can point out that in Gen 12:6, the oak tree near Shechem is in J. In Gen 35:4 the oak tree near Shechem is in E. This is apparently the same tree. Would two different authors writing in different countries 100 years apart mention the same oak tree?

---

[33] Blenkinsopp, *The Pentateuch, An Introduction to the First Five Books of the Bible*, p. 26

[34] Friedman, *Who Wrote the Bible*, pp. 72ff

3.2.2.4 Analytical Problems with JEDP
3.2.2.4.1 Absence of Archeological Evidence

No ancient biblical texts have been discovered that show the separation of sources into JEDP as described by the Documentary Hypothesis, and we do have multiple texts in which to look for them. We have the Septuagint, which comes from a different textual strain as our primary Masoretic text, but no sources are to be found in the Septuagint. We have the Samaritan Pentateuch, representing perhaps a textual strain closer to the Septuagint than the Masoretic text, but no sources are there either. Similarly, we have nothing in the Targums, an early Aramaic paraphrase, or the Vulgate, the early Latin translation of the Bible. Most noteworthy are the Dead Sea Scrolls, which contain partial scrolls from all books of the Torah, including 15 scrolls from Genesis, 17 from Exodus, 13 from Leviticus, 8 from Numbers and 29 from Deuteronomy. There are also commentaries and other Dead Sea Scrolls that reference the Torah. None of these scrolls reflect a division of the Torah into sources. The earliest of these scrolls has been dated at 250 B.C., and none are newer than the Roman-Judean war in 68 A.D. Also, no ancient commentaries or other references to sources have been discovered.

Discovery of a reliable ancient manuscript reflecting source divisions as proposed by the Documentary Hypothesis would provide strong evidence for the theory, but no such ancient manuscripts have been found.

3.2.2.4.2 Samaritan Pentateuch

The ancient Samaritans have since before the time of Christ maintained a separate copy of the Torah. This text, commonly called the Samaritan Pentateuch, is still used by the small Samaritan community living today. An ancient scroll, called the Nablus roll, contains a notation that it was copied by "Abishua son of

Phinehas, son of Eleazar son of Aaron."[35] If this inscription was genuine, it would quickly settle all our questions as to the date of the Torah, but it is generally agreed that the inscription has to be a forgery, probably of the 12th or 13th century A.D., if for no other reason than that the type script used is probably too late.

There is still some question as to when the Samaritan Pentateuch diverged from the Masoretic text. One theory is that this occurred immediately after the Assyrian conquest of the northern Kingdom of Israel, when a priest returned from Assyria to teach the people resettled in northern Israel (2 Kgs 17:27-28). This would be around 720 B.C., and if true, it would also falsify the Documentary Hypothesis, being 100 years too soon for D and 200 years too soon for P. This idea receives some support from Ezra 4:2, in which the Samaritans, speaking to Zerubbabel, ask to help with building the temple, and claim that they have not sacrificed to God since the days of Esarhaddon, king of Assyria (680-669 B.C.). However, it is also possible that the Samaritans got their version of the Torah sometime in the post-exilic period. Therefore, the existence of the Samaritan Pentateuch in and of itself is not a convincing argument against the Documentary Hypothesis.

However, there is still an important point to be made. The Samaritan Pentateuch is a "pentateuch" instead of a "hexateuch," as the Documentary Hypothesis proposes. The book of Joshua is not included in the Samaritan Pentateuch[36], despite favorable elements for Samaritans in Joshua, such as the ceremony on Mounts Ebal and Gerizim (Josh 8:30-34), the prominent position of city of Shechem (Josh 17:7, 20:7, 21:21, 24:1, 24:25 and 24:32) and the fact that Joshua, as an Ephraimite, would have been a natural hero to the community of northern Israel. The Samaritans recog-

---

[35] Tov, *Textual Criticism of the Hebrew Bible*, p. 82

[36] There is a Samaritan book about Joshua, but it is a different book from the one in the Bible.

nized from antiquity the unity of the Torah as it exists today and excluded other books from it.[37]

3.2.2.4.3 Micah's Meditations

In Micah 6-7, Micah offers an indictment of the nation not unlike that of his contemporary Isaiah in Isaiah 1. Instead of calling heaven and earth as witnesses, Micah calls the mountains and the hills (Mic 6:1-2). As Micah pleads the case he reflects on history, mentioning Moses, Aaron and Miriam with the exodus (6:4), then Balak and Balaam (6:5), and the journey from Shittim to Gilgal (6:5), Gilgal being the Israelite base camp in the book of Joshua. Later, he mentions the northern Israelite kings Omri and Ahab (6:16), both prominent kings but well in his past. He meditates further (7:14-15) on how in the still more recent past Israel used to eat peacefully in Bashan and Gilead (but no more, those territories are lost), and ends with a remembrance of God's love for and promise to Jacob and Abraham (7:20). The pertinent point for our purposes is that Micah's reflection deals with the entire Torah, particularly in 6:4-8. 6:4 deals with stories from Exodus about Moses, Aaron and Miriam. 6:5 deals with the Balaam story in Num 22. Then 6:6-7 contemplate the sacrificial offerings described in Leviticus, while 6:8 ends with a conclusion worthy of Deuteronomy. Note the similar wording of Mic 6:8 and Deut 10:12 – "what does the LORD require of you." Compare also Mic 6:11 with Lev 19:36 and Mic 6:15 with Deut 28:38-40. Micah can be reliably dated nearly 100 years before the proposed date for D and 200 years before P. See section 4.2.9 for more on dating the book of Micah.

---

[37] Along these same lines, the Sadducees, a political/religious faction that emerged in the Maccabean period prior to 100 B.C., accepted a unified Torah but excluded Joshua.

3.2.2.4.4 Adam

Hos 6:7 says "But they like Adam have transgressed the covenant: there have they dealt treacherously against me." The identification of Adam is important in this verse. The Hebrew word "adam" can also mean mankind in general, but in this verse the meaning seems to point in particular to Adam. Almost all modern translations use "Adam." The reason this is significant is that Hosea is one of the earliest writing prophets, perhaps even the first. The context of the passage, complaining about the sins of Ephraim (Hos 6:4) and Gilead (Hos 6:8), dates the passage to before the fall of the northern Kingdom of Israel in 721 B.C. At first glance this may not look like a problem for the Documentary Hypothesis, since the passages of Gen 2-4 which talk about Adam are assigned to J, and J is usually dated before Hosea. However, the Hebrew usage in Gen 2-4 reveals something that is lost in an English translation. All references in Hebrew in Gen 2-4 to Adam use a definite article (Hebrew "ha'adam" [האדם]), which is best translated not as a proper name, "Adam," but simply as "the man." It is not until Gen 5:1 that "Adam" is used as a name, without the definite article in Hebrew. Most modern translations have gone back over and filled in the name "Adam" for all references to "the man" in Gen 2-4. The most literal translations (such as the American Standard Version, New American Standard Bible and Young's Literal Translation) do not use "Adam" until Gen 5:1. Note that the Gen 5:1 passage is in P, a source supposedly not written until 500-450 B.C. Furthermore, Adam doesn't "transgress the covenant" in P; that only happens in J. Therefore, for Hosea to write what he did, he not only has to have both the J and P sources available, but they have to be together like they are in the Torah today.

3.2.2.4.5 Presuppositions – Anti-Supernaturalism and the Evolution of Religion

Wellhausen says "in the course of a casual visit in Gottingen in the summer of 1867, I learned through Ritschl that Karl Heinrich Graf placed the Law later than the Prophets, and, almost without knowing his reasons for the hypothesis, I was prepared to accept it."[38] Why would Wellhausen accept this viewpoint without any evidence? If Wellhausen was like most people, he did so because it was entirely consistent with his presuppositions. Wellhausen, although a Lutheran, held to an anti-supernatural view of the Old Testament and to an evolutionary understanding of the development of religion. These two presuppositions were fundamental to the development of the Documentary Hypothesis and remain essential to it.

Underlying any discussion of the origin of the Torah is the issue of whether or not the Bible is a supernatural book, a book inspired by God. In this book, we are approaching the Bible as a human book and trying to avoid issues dealing with its supernatural character. However, this cannot be done completely. An individual's religious outlook will certainly affect one's viewpoint on the Bible. The Documentary Hypothesis has near its root an anti-supernatural presupposition regarding the Torah. The crux of the problem for some source critics is that the Torah clearly predicts several things about Israel's future, most prominently the exile, as in Leviticus 26 (P or Holiness Code) and Deuteronomy 28 (D). It also alludes to the fact that Israel would have kings (Gen 17:6, 35:11 - P), and that they would come from the tribe of Judah (Gen 49:10 - J). An individual who excludes ahead of time any possibility of divine prophecy has no recourse but to date major portions of both D and P after the exile. However, a presupposition like this can block out the truth; one who insists on such a

---

[38] Wellhausen, *Prolegomena to the History of Ancient Israel*, p. 3

position before examining the evidence will not be able to follow the evidence if it leads in a direction incompatible with the pre-supposition.

The second presupposition underlying the Documentary Hypothesis is the idea of the evolutionary development of relig-ion, with polytheism evolving in ancient Israel into henotheism (worship of one god without denying the existence of other gods) and then finally into monotheism. This idea found fertile soil in the late 19th century, when the newly proposed Darwinian evolu-tion became wildly popular, and efforts were made to extend the theory to fields outside of biology. No one bothered to explain why polytheism should evolve into monotheism in Israel - no such evolution took place in any other religion in the world. Furthermore, no one questioned why such extensive evolution should be observable entirely within the time period of the Old Testament. Nevertheless, the idea of the evolution of religion is commonly used by critics to date books in the Old Testament. Passages that express strong monotheism must by this reasoning be late, along with passages that show a high degree of structure (like the P passages), as well as passages with detailed laws.

Without doubt, the faith and practice of the people of Israel changed over time during the Old Testament period. However, the evolution of religion concept adopted by the critics was not an idea drawn from the text of the Bible, nor was it an idea drawn from archeology. It was simply an overarching dogma through which the Bible was interpreted. Archeology has not been suppor-tive of this philosophy:

1. No images of YHWH have been found in the land of Is-rael[39]

---

[39] Outside of Israel, in the northeastern Sinai site of Kuntillet 'Ajrud, a possible image of YHWH represented as a bull and dated around 800 B.C. was found. The point still remains, as multiple statues of less influential Canaanite gods, such as Baal and Asherah, have been found within the land of Israel.

2. The Ugaritic tablets, representing another religion in the second millennium B.C., contain detailed sacrificial laws, like Leviticus.[40]

3. The Ebla tablets, which predate the Torah by many years, have an abstract creation verse reminiscent of the Genesis 1 account:

> "Lord of heaven and earth:
>
> The earth was not, you created it,
>
> The light of day was not, you created it,
>
> The morning light you had not [yet] made exist."[41]

(We should not overstate the case; Ebla was still a polytheistic society). The Ebla texts also tallied detailed lists of the numbers of sacrifices and offerings to be performed by the royal family to certain gods. These included grain, beer and oil offerings, along with animal offerings of sheep and oxen.[42]

4. The Code of Hammurabi, which predates the earliest possible date for the Torah by several hundred years, is a highly detailed legal code.

The importance of the presupposition of the evolution of religion and the damage it has done to modern biblical scholarship cannot be overemphasized. The entire edifice of Old Testament dating used by the critics is based on this presupposition. It led the source critics to conclude that passages with pronounced monotheism, or a high moral code, or a well-structured law system must necessarily be given a late date. This led to the Torah being dated essentially after the prophets rather than before the prophets. Then there was the ripple effect; passages in the prophets or Psalms, or even passages in the historical books that seem dependent on the Torah must be given an even later date. This in

---

[40] McDowell, *The New Evidence that Demands a Verdict*, p. 425, 428

[41] Pettinato, *The Archives of Ebla, An Empire Inscribed in Clay*, p. 244

[42] Mitchell Dahood, "Ebla, Ugarit and the Bible". Included in Pettinato, *The Archives of Ebla, an Empire Inscribed in Clay*, p. 253-256

many cases is not possible without assuming wholesale post-exilic interpolations and revisions, greatly altering books from their original form. Having thus chronologically reordered most of the Old Testament, the critics will then be further misled by placing the linguistics and remaining doctrinal topics, etc., in their newly established (wrong) places in time, leading to still further wrong conclusions. Having begun with error, the process feeds on itself relentlessly.

3.2.2.4.6 How to Ruin a Good Story #1

The story of Joseph in Genesis 37-50 is one of the most beautiful and moving stories in the Bible. Joseph, the privileged youth, is envied and betrayed by his own brothers, who with callous cruelty sell him as a slave. He is taken to Egypt, where his superior conduct and ability raise him to the highest place in his master's household. His integrity costs him, as he is falsely accused by his master's lustful wife, resulting in an unjust imprisonment. Still, his excellent conduct allows him to rise in the ranks of the prisoners, until a chance encounter gives him the opportunity to correctly interpret the dreams of two of Pharaoh's officials, one of whom returns to Pharaoh's service and temporarily forgets Joseph. Joseph's big chance finally arrives when Pharaoh has a dream that only Joseph can interpret. Pleased and impressed, Pharaoh not only releases Joseph, but appoints him as Prime Minister of Egypt. When the terrible famine foretold by Joseph's understanding of Pharaoh's dream occurs, his brothers travel from Canaan to Egypt to buy food from Joseph, but do not recognize him. After a series of tests convince Joseph that his brothers have reformed, a poignant reunion is affected. Joseph says of his brother's conduct, "you meant evil against me, but God meant it for good." (Gen 50:20).

What happens when the Documentary Hypothesis gets a hold of this story? P has very little of the story, giving no explanation why Joseph enters Pharaoh's service and no reason why Jacob and family move to Egypt. P has only a bare outline, bringing in the list of Joseph's family in Genesis 46 but not much else. In Exodus 1 in P, the Egyptians turn on the Israelites without explanation. All efforts to divide Genesis 37 between J and E sources result in a total mess. P takes Gen 37:1-2 and because E likes dreams it takes Gen 37:5-11. Gen 37:3-4 and 37:12-20 are assigned to "J or E." The reason for indecision is if they are assigned to E, the following J passage in Gen 37:21 makes no sense. On the other hand, if they are assigned to J, the E passages beginning in 37:22 make no sense. The non-sequiturs continue throughout the story. E finds Joseph in prison in Genesis 40 for no reason, but in time to hear more dreams. J, having landed Joseph in prison in Genesis 39, suddenly has him standing before Pharaoh for an unknown reason in Gen 41:29, or if the Gen 41:29-44 passage is assigned to E, then J goes straight from Joseph being in prison to having Pharaoh offer him a wife in Gen 41:45. It is in fact impossible to make any sense out of the Joseph story using only the J or E source. Yet the Documentary Hypothesis would have us believe that from these incoherent scarred scraps, some editor was able to weave one of the greatest short stories in world literature. This stretches credulity past the breaking point. Of course, source critics will argue that the editor excluded material from J and E as well, and that those sources, if we had the originals, would be more coherent than the remnants we have today. Well, perhaps - but that is an argument based on no evidence. The critics are in effect saying "Once upon a time, the Joseph story was formed from a source named J, a source for which there is no manuscript evidence. Of course, J as we perceive it today doesn't make sense, but it would if we had the original J." Let the reader decide if this is a logical argument.

3.2.2.4.7 How to Ruin a Good Story #2

The account of the 10 plagues on Egypt in Exodus 7-12 is a coherent story that flows well from start to finish. Egypt's stubborn Pharaoh refuses to let Israel go and is exposed to a trial of increasingly severe plagues, until a climactic tenth plague results in the death of all of Egypt's firstborn sons. This leads simultaneously to the establishment of the Israelite Passover commemoration and the exodus from Egypt. The plagues have an element of contest between YHWH and the gods of Egypt (Exod 7:10-12 and 12:12). The reader may also notice some natural progression in the plagues – if the Nile river water went bad, might the frogs leave the river bank?

We can also see elements of a pattern in the plagues, as shown in the Table 3-5 below.[43]

Table 3-5 Patterns in the Plagues

Plague #	Forewarning	Timing	Command Where	Stretch Out Hand/Rod
1	Yes	In the morning	Station self	Yes
2	Yes	None	Go to Pharaoh	Yes
3	No	None	None	Yes
4	Yes	In the morning	Station self	No
5	Yes	None	Go to Pharaoh	No
6	No	None	None	No
7	Yes	In the morning	Station self	Yes
8	Yes	None	Go to Pharaoh	Yes
9	No	None	None	Yes
10	Yes	None	None	No

---

[43] Adapted from Kitchen, *On the Reliability of the Old Testament*, p. 253

Now let us consider what happens when the Documentary Hypothesis gets a hold of this story. P can record only 5 of the 10 plagues: water to blood, frogs, gnats, boils and death of the firstborn. The cattle plague in Exod 9:1-7 is not assigned to any source for some reason. J fares a little better with 6 of the 10 plagues: water to blood, frogs, flies, hail, locusts and death of the firstborn. Hapless E has only 4 plagues: water to blood, hail, locusts and darkness. E does get to hold the staff of Moses most of the time, though not when Moses uses it to split the sea in Exod 14:16. In fact, E doesn't get to have a Passover account or even an exodus account at all – E jumps straight from warning about the final plague, to a description of the exodus route, to the people grumbling in the wilderness about no water in Exodus 17.

This is a second example of how the Documentary Hypothesis transforms one great story into three poor story scraps that have no structure or flow, and often don't even make sense.

3.2.2.4.8 Discontinuities

As we discovered above, the J, E and P accounts do not by them-selves tend to tell a continuous story. Here is a partial list of additional discontinuities in each source, besides those mentioned above:

1. Ishmael is promised in J (Gen 16:11) but never born.
2. Abram is renamed to Abraham only in P (Gen 17:5), but his new name is picked up in J and E also.
3. Isaac grows up in E (Gen 21:8) but was not born.
4. Jacob and Esau are not mentioned being born in P, but "Isaac was 60 years old when she gave birth to them" (Gen 25:26).
5. In Gen 28:11-12, Jacob has a dream in E with no context.
6. Jacob tricks his father Isaac in Genesis 27 (usually assigned to J), but he is tricked by Laban into marrying Leah in E (Gen 29:15-25). This ruins the poetic justice aspect of the story.

7. Jacob doesn't get married in J, but starts having children by Leah and Rachel in Gen 29:31.

8. In Gen 32:13b-23, Jacob worries about appeasing Esau in E, but he only tricked him in J.

9. The Dinah incident in Genesis 34 in J or E is dependent on the circumcision covenant, which was only introduced in P. Also, see Exod 4:24-26 in J, dependent on the circumcision covenant.

10. Jacob dies only in P, but Joseph weeps and has him embalmed in J in Genesis 50. His brothers worry about it in E in Gen 50:15-21.

11. Moses has grown up in J in Exod 2:11, but was only born in E. He is abruptly introduced in P in Exod 6:2.

12. Moses is told to take the staff with which to perform signs in Exod 4:17 in E, but the signs were given in J.

13. J includes the golden calf incident in Exod 32:7-12, but there is no punishment or consequence in J.

14. In Numbers 13 and 14 in JE, Joshua is excluded from the good spies (only Caleb is good in J), but he ends up leading Israel into Canaan.

3.2.2.4.9 History as Presented By the Documentary Hypothesis

The Documentary Hypothesis completely retells the history of ancient Israel. A few polytheistic nomads settle in Canaan, maybe or maybe not after a previous stay in Egypt. They eventually settle on worshipping one god in a free and easy way, without extensive religious or civil regulations. They grow into two nations, which maybe were once one nation but then again maybe not. The two nations develop alternate parallel histories (J and E) of their tribal ancestry. When northern Israel falls, Judah takes over the story. To centralize their national capital as a religious focal point as well, Josiah's scribes forge the book of Deuteronomy (D), putting their new legal code in the mouth of the ancient figure, Moses. During the exile, this D perspective is used to rewrite the nation's history

(Joshua through Kings). After the exile, lying priests (P) take the forgery further, inventing a non-existent tabernacle and placing a full range of religious and legal rituals in the mouth of the ancient Moses. The P perspective is then used as the overarching one to pull the whole story together chronologically and into a continuous whole.

This is the picture of ancient Israel as described by the Documentary Hypothesis. But this picture is not the story the Bible tells at all. There are thousands of scripture verses, passages and entire books that contradict this story. To account for this negative evidence the Documentary Hypothesis must introduce the roles of the Editor and Interpolator.

3.2.2.4.10 The Editor/Interpolator

The Documentary Hypothesis leans heavily on the role of multiple editors and interpolators. The first editor fused together the J and E accounts, a second editor mixed in D and a third editor restructured the whole under the framework of P. All of the editors had the unusual characteristic of tolerating contradictory accounts, merging them cleverly in such a way as to minimize or eliminate the contradictions. These editors covered their tracks so carefully that nobody was able to discover them for thousands of years. The editing process was supplemented by interpolators who sprinkled the history books with interpolations of other legal matters like Nazirite vows, ritual uncleanness, taboos about sacrifice and the like, along with numerous allusions to a history that didn't really happen.

The problem with this editor/interpolator tandem is that it serves primarily as a mechanism to dismiss problems with the Documentary Hypothesis. Any of the numerous passages that conflict with the Documentary Hypothesis are simply assigned to the work of a later editor or interpolator. This is the death of scholarship – there is no point offering scriptural evidence against the Documentary Hypothesis if it will constantly be waved away as an editorial gloss or later interpretation. And it must be waved away. If Num 16:1, 16:24 and 16:27 are not editorial glosses, then the breakout of Numbers 16 into J and P sources is false. If 1 Kgs 8:4 is not an interpolation, Wellhausen's entire framework falls to the ground. It is at this point, on the role of the editor and interpolator, that the Documentary Hypothesis seems to move away from true scholarship, becoming dogma, a belief to be tenaciously held regardless of the data.

3.2.3 Evidence of Literary Unity

Before we deal further with the date of the Torah, we will present two additional lines of evidence for the literary unity of the Torah, without regard to when it was written.

3.2.3.1 Literary Patterns

It is common practice to break down scripture passages into outlines, but we should realize that outlines are a western invention and were generally not in the mind of the Bible authors when they wrote. However, certain structures were intentionally used by Bible authors. These include acrostics (Psalm 119, Prov 31:10-31, Lamentations 1-4 and others), parallelism and chiasms. If it could be demonstrated that these structures were imposed by an author in a passage that supposedly spans multiple sources, that would be an argument for a unified text and a single author. Although in theory a final editor could impose some limited structure on a compilation of sources, a complex pattern that spans sources would render any theory of multiple sources unlikely.

A chiasm is a structure that reverses and ends back where it starts. In the Bible, a small chiasm is usually lost in translation because it depends on the order of the words in Hebrew. An example is Gen 2:23:

A	To this	לזאת
B	she will be called	יקרא
C	woman	אשה
D	because	כי
C′	from man	מאיש
B′	she was taken	לקחה
A′	this	זאת

This example verse is entirely within the proposed J source, and so it does not bear on the issue of single or multiple sources. The following short example does span sources; in fact, it spans the first break between sources that is proposed by the Documentary Hypothesis and also the Tablet Theory (Gen 2:4):

A	the heaven	השמים
B	and the earth	והארץ
C	in the creating of them	בהבראם
D	in the day	ביום
C′	of YHWH Elohim making	עשות יהוה אלהים
B′	earth	ארץ
A′	and heaven	ושמים

This chiasm is short and not quite perfect, because the words YHWH Elohim in the second half of the chiasm do not have a match in the first. So it raises the question: is this chiasm intentional or coincidental? The phrase "earth and heaven" gives a clue that it is intentional. "Heaven and earth" is a common phrase in the Bible, occurring 31 times in some form. However, the reverse "earth and heaven" is rare, and elsewhere just used to indicate something "between earth and heaven" (1 Chron 21:16, Ezek 8:3 and Zech 5:9). The rarity of the phrase implies that it was inverted intentionally to form the chiasm. Also, the contrasting verbs (creating/making) are both infinitive constructs without the preposition "to" (Hebrew "ל"), a form that accounts for less than 5% of the verbs in the Old Testament.

Gen 6:8-9 is another short chiasm that spans sources:

A Noah   ונח
B   found favor   מצא חן
C   in the eyes of YHWH   בעיני יהוה
D   These are the generations of Noah   אלה תולדת נח
E   Noah was a righteous man   נח איש צדיק
E'   perfect he was   תמים היה
D'   in his generations   בדרתיו
C'   with God   את־האלהים
B'   walked   התהלך
A' Noah   נח־

The Documentary Hypothesis assigns "Noah found favor in the eyes of YHWH" to J and the rest of this passage to P, thus breaking the chiasm.

A much longer chiasm dealing with the flood story from Gen 6:10-9:19 is shown below.[44] Notice that this long chiasm starts immediately after the one in the previous example ends.

A Noah (6:10a)
B Shem, Ham and Japheth (6:10b)
C   Ark to be built (6:14-16)
D   Flood announced (6:17)
E   Covenant with Noah (6:18-20)
F   Food in the Ark (6:21)
G   Command to enter the Ark (7:1-3)
H   7 days waiting for flood (7:4-5)
I   7 days waiting for flood (7:7-10)
J   Entry to ark (7:11-15)

---

[44] This example is taken from Kikawada, *Before Abraham Was*, p. 104

K   Yahweh shuts Noah in (7:16)
L   40 days flood (7:17a)
M   Waters increase (7:17b-18)
N   Mountains covered (7:18-20)
O   150 days waters prevail (7:21-24)
P   God Remembers Noah (8:1)
O'   150 days waters abate (8:3)
N'   Mountain tops become visible (8:4-5)
M'   Waters abate (8:6)
L'   40 days (end of) (8:6a)
K'   Noah opens window of ark (8:6b)
J'   Raven and dove leave ark (8:7-9)
I'   7 days waiting for waters to subside (8:10-11)
H'   7 days waiting for waters to subside (8:12-13)
G'   Command to leave the ark (8:15-17)
F'   Food outside the ark (9:1-4)
E'   Covenant with all flesh (9:8-10)
D'   No flood in future (9:11-17)
C'   Ark (9:18a)
B'   Shem, Ham, Japheth (9:18b)
A'   Noah (9:19)

The significance of this chiasm is that it gives evidence for a single
coherent design of the entire flood story, unlike the Documentary
Hypothesis, which proposes that in this passage there are 24
switches back and forth between the P and J source (see Appendix
A for a breakdown). Particularly striking and unlikely to be
coincidental is the chiasm in numbers of days: 7-7-40-150-150-40-
7-7.

A still longer chiasm in Genesis can be seen in the overall
structure of the stories about the life of Abraham:

A Genealogy of Terah (11:27-32)
B God promises to bless and multiply Abram (12:1-3)

C   Abraham obeys God (12:4-9)
D   Sarai in foreign palace; ordeal ends in peace and success;
        Lot parts (12:10-13.18)
E   Abram comes to the rescue of Sodom and Lot (14:1-24)
F   Covenant with Abram; Annunciation of Ishmael
            (15:1-16:16)
F'   Covenant with Abraham; Annunciation of Isaac
            (17:1-18:15)
E'   Abram comes to the rescue of Sodom and Lot (18:16-19:38)
D'   Sarah in foreign palace; ordeal ends in peace and success;
        Ishmael parts (20:1-21:34)
C'   Abraham obeys God (22:1-14)
B' God promises to bless and multiply Abraham (22:15-19)
A' Genealogy of Nahor (22:20-24)

This chiasm gives evidence for a single design of the story of
Abraham, a story which in the Documentary Hypothesis encom-
passes multiple passages switching between J, E and P sources.

The following chiasm in Genesis 27-28 tells the story of Isaac's
blessing and birthright, spanning J/E and P sources.[45]

A Isaac and the son of the blessing/birthright – Esau (27:1-5)
B   Rebekah sends Jacob onstage (27:6-17)
C   Jacob appears before Isaac, receives blessing (27:18-29)
C'   Esau appears before Isaac, receives anti-blessing (27:30-40)
B'   Rebekah sends Jacob offstage (27:41-45)
A' Isaac and the son of the blessing/birthright –Jacob (27:46-28:5)

Additional examples could be provided, but the conclusion
should already be clear. The literary structure of multiple passages in the Torah shows evidence for a single author. Furthermore, the presence of these structures might give us reason to

---

[45] Fokkelman, *The Literary Guide to the Bible*, essay on Genesis, p. 46

believe that the author was very skillful and sophisticated in the way he arranged his material.

3.2.3.2 Literary Themes

The Torah, like much of the Bible, is a highly heterogeneous document. Long narrative prose passages are interspersed with short and sometimes medium length poems and songs, lists, genealogies, speeches and extended legal codes. The prose sections are sometimes tense and compact, as in the near sacrifice of Isaac in Genesis 22, and sometimes long and relaxed, as in the arrangement of a wife for Isaac in Genesis 24. The heterogeneous nature of the Torah does not argue for multiple sources; individual authors often use multiple types of literature in one work. A better standard to use to evaluate whether the Torah consists of single or multiple sources is that of literary themes. Multiple common themes are developed throughout the Torah which span all the proposed sources. Some of these themes are described below, not necessarily in order of importance.

1. Fertility – This theme is introduced in the creation story in Gen 1:28, "Be fruitful and multiply," repeated after the flood in Gen 9:1 and again to Jacob in Gen 35:11 (see also Gen 1:22, 8:17 and 9:7). The name of Eve, the mother of all living, adds to the theme (Gen 3:20). Almost the entire account of Abraham deals with the tension over whether or not he would have any children. He receives the promise of descendants "as the stars of the heavens and as the sand which is on the seashore" (Gen 22:17, 12:2, 15:5; see also Exod 32:13, Deut 1:10, 10:22 and 28:62), yet remains childless into old age. Three matriarchs, Sarah, Rebekah and Rachel are all barren and God has to intervene to give them children (Gen 21:1, 25:21 and 30:22-23). Lot's daughters (Gen 19:31-38) resort to subterfuge to obtain children, along with Tamar (Gen 38:14-20). Judgment falls when procreation is corrupted (Gen 6:2-6) or interrupted (Gen

38:9-10). Pharaoh attempts to interfere in the process, but is thwarted first by two midwifes and later by his own daughter (Exod 1:7-2:10). The process reaches its zenith with the stupendous numbers of Israelites counted in the censuses of Numbers 1 and 26.

2. Preference for the younger child – In violation of the custom of the time (Gen 29:26), the tenor of its own law (Deut 21:17) and the desire of the patriarchs (Gen 17:18, 25:28 and 48:18), the Torah shows a continual selection of the younger child instead of the older. The pattern begins when Adam's line is preserved through Seth rather than Cain or Abel. Isaac is favored over Ishmael, Jacob over Esau, Joseph over his brothers and Ephraim over Manasseh. Among the women, Rachel is desired over Leah. Less prominently, Judah is favored over the older sons of Leah, Judah's sons Perez and Zerah are favored over the older Er and Onan and Moses is called ahead of his older siblings Aaron and Miriam. For the priesthood, Eleazar is chosen after his brothers Nadab and Abihu sin.

3. Progressive revelation of God through names – God is introduced as Elohim in Genesis 1. YHWH is tied to Elohim in Genesis 2-4 and men begin to call on the name of YHWH in Gen 4:26. Melchizedek appears as a priest of El Elyon (God Most High) in Gen 14:18-20, and then Abram ties YHWH to El Elyon in Gen 14:22. Hagar, fleeing from Sarah, is confronted by "El Rai" (God who sees me) in Gen 16:13. El Shaddai (Almighty God) is introduced in Gen 17:1. Gen 18:25 calls God "the Judge of all the earth." Gen 22:14 names the location of Isaac's binding "YHWH Yireh" (The LORD will provide). In Gen 24:3, Abraham's servant swears by "YHWH Elohe of heaven and earth." In Gen 28:13-14 Jacob encounters "YHWH Elohe of your father Abraham and your father Isaac," who he later calls the "Fear of Isaac" (Gen 31:42). Jacob is renamed Israel (strives

with God) and names the place of his struggle "Peniel" (face of God). He names his altar "El Elohe Israel" (God the God of Israel) and the place of his first encounter with God "Bethel" (house of God). The revelation of names climaxes in Exodus where "the God of your fathers, the God of Abraham, the God of Isaac, and the God of Jacob" (Exod 3:6) reveals His name as "I Am Who I Am" in Exod 3:14. After the Exodus, God is commonly referred to with some variant of "YWHH your God who brought you out of the land of Egypt, out of the house of slavery" (Exod 20:2).

4. God takes the initiative – This theme is not limited to the Torah; it is also pervasive in the Prophets and the New Testament. (It is not a major theme in the Writings, which mostly deal with man's response to God). The theme of God taking the initiative is listed here primarily because it stands in such contrast to the "gradual evolution of monotheism" belief that underpinned the source critics who developed the Documentary Hypothesis. The Torah does not tell a story of man reaching out for God. Instead, God is the one who acts: God sends the flood but saves Noah; God destroys Sodom but saves Lot. God chooses Abraham, Isaac and Jacob. He tells Jacob where to go and when. God calls Moses and drags him, unwilling, into his service. God plagues Egypt, brings Israel out and gives them His law amid signs and wonders. When His pillar of cloud/fire moves, the people move, and when it stops, they stop. At all points it is God who is primarily driving the storyline.

These four themes are pervasive in the Torah and span across all its literary types as well as its proposed sources. This is evidence for the unity of the work and for a single guiding hand as its author.

3.2.4 Conclusion

We believe the evidence shows the Torah is essentially a literary unity rather than a composite of sources as described by the Documentary Hypothesis. The Documentary Hypothesis makes important claims about the date of writing for the alleged sources of the Torah. We have concluded that the sources are not real, and therefore the dates have no grounding in reality either. Furthermore, some of the evidence offered against the Documentary Hypothesis so far, such as the idea that the Torah preceded the prophets, points to an overall early date for the writing of the Torah. In the next section, we will attempt to determine how early it was.

3.3 Dating the Torah
3.3.1 Authorship

The traditional understanding of the Torah has always been that it was a unified composition with Moses as its author. Mosaic authorship of the Torah implies a date of writing during the exodus generation. The tradition of Mosaic authorship is based on internal evidence and statements by later writers.

3.3.1.1 Internal Statements

Several passages in the Torah mention that it was Moses who wrote down at least a portion of the text. These are:

1. Exod 24:4-8, referring to chapters 21-23: "Moses wrote down all the words of the LORD."
2. Exod 34:27 referring to Exod 34:10-26: "Then the LORD said to Moses, 'Write down these words, for in accordance with these words I have made a covenant with you and with Israel.'"
3. Num 33:2 referring to chapter 33: "Moses recorded their starting places according to their journeys by the command of the LORD,"

4. Deut 31:9, referring probably to an earlier portion of Deuteronomy, "So Moses wrote this law and gave it to the priests, the sons of Levi who carried the Ark of the Covenant of the LORD, and to all the elders of Israel."

5. Deut 31:22, referring to chapter 32: "So Moses wrote this song the same day, and taught it to the sons of Israel."

6. Deut 31:24-26, referring probably to an earlier portion of Deuteronomy: "It came about, when Moses finished writing the words of this law in a book until they were complete, that Moses commanded the Levites who carried the Ark of the Covenant of the LORD, saying, "Take this book of the law and place it beside the Ark of the Covenant of the LORD your God, that it may remain there as a witness against you."

3.3.1.2 Old Testament Statements

Scripture passages beginning immediately after the death of Moses attribute the entire law to him. This attribution of the law to Moses continues throughout the Old Testament. The whole Torah is often treated as one book, even when more than one of the five books is clearly in view. Old Testament references to what "Moses said" or "Moses commanded" are too numerous to reference, but some of the more specific passages are:

1. Josh 1:7-8 "Only be strong and very courageous; be careful to do according to all the law which Moses My servant commanded you; do not turn from it to the right or to the left, so that you may have success wherever you go. This book of the law shall not depart from your mouth, but you shall meditate on it day and night, so that you may be careful to do according to all that is written in it; for then you will make your way prosperous, and then you will have success."

2. Josh 8:31-32 "…just as Moses the servant of the LORD had commanded the sons of Israel, as it is written in the book

of the law of Moses, an altar of uncut stones on which no man had wielded an iron tool; and they offered burnt offerings on it to the LORD, and sacrificed peace offerings. He wrote there on the stones a copy of the law of Moses, which he had written, in the presence of the sons of Israel."

3. 1 Kgs 2:3 "Keep the charge of the LORD your God, to walk in His ways, to keep His statutes, His commandments, His ordinances, and His testimonies, according to what is written in the Law of Moses, that you may succeed in all that you do and wherever you turn,"

4. 2 Kgs 14:6 "But the sons of the slayers he did not put to death, according to what is written in the book of the Law of Moses, as the LORD commanded, saying, 'The fathers shall not be put to death for the sons, nor the sons be put to death for the fathers; but each shall be put to death for his own sin.'" (The quote is from Deut 24:16)

5. 2 Chron 23:18 "Moreover, Jehoiada placed the offices of the house of the LORD under the authority of the Levitical priests, whom David had assigned over the house of the LORD, to offer the burnt offerings of the LORD, as it is written in the law of Moses--with rejoicing and singing according to the order of David."

6. Ezra 3:2 "Then Jeshua the son of Jozadak and his brothers the priests, and Zerubbabel the son of Shealtiel and his brothers arose and built the altar of the God of Israel to offer burnt offerings on it, as it is written in the law of Moses, the man of God."

7. Neh 8:1 "And all the people gathered as one man at the square which was in front of the Water Gate, and they asked Ezra the scribe to bring the book of the law of Moses which the LORD had given to Israel."

8. Dan 9:13 "As it is written in the law of Moses, all this calamity has come on us; yet we have not sought the favor of

the LORD our God by turning from our iniquity and giving attention to Your truth."

9. Mal 4:4 "Remember the law of Moses My servant, even the statutes and ordinances which I commanded him in Horeb for all Israel."

See also Josh 23:6, 2 Kgs 23:25, 2 Chron 35:12 and Ezra 6:18.

3.3.1.3 New Testament Statements

In the New Testament, Jesus and the Apostles recognized Moses as the writer of the Torah. New Testament passages involving the Pharisees and Sadducees make it clear that they also recognized Moses as the lawgiver:

1. Matt 8:4: "And Jesus said to him, 'See that you tell no one; but go, show yourself to the priest and present the offering that Moses commanded, as a testimony to them.'" The reference is to Leviticus 14. A parallel passage is in Mark 1:44.

2. Matt 19:8: "He said to them, 'Because of your hardness of heart Moses permitted you to divorce your wives; but from the beginning it has not been this way.'" The reference is to Deut 24:1-4. A parallel passage is in Mark 10.

3. Mark 7:10 "For Moses said, 'Honor your father and your mother'; and, 'He who speaks evil of father or mother is to be put to death." The reference is to Exod 20:12; 21:17 and Deut 5:16

4. Mark 12:26 "But Jesus said to them, 'But regarding the fact that the dead rise again, have you not read in the book of Moses, in the passage about the burning bush, how God spoke to him, saying, 'I am the God of Abraham, and the God of Isaac, and the God of Jacob?'" A parallel passage is in Luke 20:37.

5. Luke 16:29-31 "But Abraham said, 'They have Moses and the Prophets; let them hear them.' But he said, 'No, father Abraham, but if someone goes to them from the dead, they will repent!' "But he said to him, 'If they do not listen to

Moses and the Prophets, they will not be persuaded even if someone rises from the dead.'"

6. Luke 24:27 "Then beginning with Moses and with all the prophets, He explained to them the things concerning Himself in all the Scriptures."

7. Luke 24:44 "Now He said to them, 'These are My words which I spoke to you while I was still with you, that all things which are written about Me in the Law of Moses and the Prophets and the Psalms must be fulfilled.'"

8. John 1:17 "For the Law was given through Moses; grace and truth were realized through Jesus Christ."

9. John 5:46 "For if you believed Moses, you would believe Me, for he wrote about Me."

10. John 7:19 "Did not Moses give you the Law, and yet none of you carries out the Law?"

11. John 7:22 "For this reason Moses has given you circumcision (not because it is from Moses, but from the fathers), and on the Sabbath you circumcise a man. If a man receives circumcision on the Sabbath so that the Law of Moses will not be broken, are you angry with Me because I made an entire man well on the Sabbath?"

11. Rom 10:5 "For Moses writes that the man who practices the righteousness which is based on law shall live by that righteousness."

12. 1 Cor 9:9 "For it is written in the Law of Moses, 'You shall not muzzle the ox while he is threshing.'" The reference is to Deuteronomy 25:4.

3.3.1.4 Traditional Statements

Ancient tradition outside the scriptures also ascribes the Torah to Moses. Notables include:

1. Philo, Jewish philosopher theologian born about 20 A.D.: "But I will...tell the story of Moses as I have learned it, both from the sacred books, the wonderful monuments of

his wisdom which he has left behind him, and from some of the elders of the nation." (Philo, WP, 279)

2. Flavius Josephus, born 37 A.D.: "For we have not an innumerable multitude of books among us, disagreeing from and contradicting one another (as the Greeks have), but only 22 books [our present 39], which are justly believed to be divine; and of them, five belong to Moses, which contains his laws, and the tradition of the origin of mankind till his death."[46]

3. Babylonian Talmud, Mishna (Pirqe Aboth I, 1), a Jewish commentary on the law written about 200 A.D.: "Moses received the Law on Sinai and delivered it to Joshua; Joshua in turn handed it down to the Elders (not to the seventy Elders of Moses' time but to the later Elders who have ruled Israel, and each of them delivered it to his successor); from the Elders it descended to the prophets (beginning with Eli and Samuel), and each of them delivered it to his successors until it reached the men of the Great Assembly."

4. Early Christian church fathers ascribing the Torah to Moses include[47]:
   1. Melito, Bishop of Sardi (175 AD)
   2. Cyril of Jerusalem (348-386 AD)
   3. Hilary (366 AD)
   4. Rufinus (410 AD)
   5. Augustine (430 AD)

3.3.2 Geography

The Torah shows signs of a desert setting with an Egyptian background, as opposed to a setting in the land of Israel. This

---

[46] Flavius Josephus, *Against Appion* (1:8)
[47] List from McDowell, *The New Evidence that Demands a Verdict*, p. 459

indicates that it was written before the Jewish nation settled in Israel.

The author of the Torah is familiar with the land of Egypt. He is familiar with the reeds in the Nile (Exod 2:3) and knows that it would be safe to put a child in a basket in that river (the Jordan River flows too quickly and would be dangerous). He knows of places like Rameses and Succoth (Exod 12:37), Etham (Exod 13:20), Pi-Hahiroth, Migdol and Baal-zephon (Exod 14:2).

The author feels a need to explain things in Canaan with reference to things in Egypt. When describing a portion of the land of Canaan, the plain of the Jordan, he says it is "like the land of Egypt as you go to Zoar" (Gen 13:10). This kind of statement would be meaningless to a later Israelite living in Israel, who probably wouldn't know anything about Zoar. It would, however, be meaningful to people who had lived in Egypt all their life and recently left. Similarly, describing Hebron, the author states: "Now Hebron was built seven years before Zoan in Egypt," another meaningless statement for a native born Israelite, but useful for someone who had lived in Egypt.

The phrase "land of Canaan" is used 51 times in the Torah, 34 of those occurrences being in Genesis. The phrase passes out of use in the Bible soon afterward. "Land of Canaan" is an improbable phrase to describe the land of Israel to Israelites living in Israel; it has a connotation of a foreign land. Some passages seem to emphasize this: "Now Jacob came safely to the city of Shechem, which is in the land of Canaan" (Gen 33:18). "Sarah died in Kiriath-arba (that is, Hebron) in the land of Canaan" (Gen 23:2). Shechem and Hebron are among the most prominent cities in Israel, yet these verses seem to need to explain where they are. Consider how Gen 23:2 would read if it were rewritten in 21st century terms: "His wife died in Chicago, in the country of the United States." A sentence like that would not be written by an American, but it could be written by someone not living in the

United States. Likewise, the Gen 23:2 and 33:18 passages are best understood as being written outside of the land of Canaan.

The wilderness geography in the Torah is often very detailed, especially in Numbers 33, a passage listing 51 places, but also even in short passages like Deut 1:1-2. Canaanite geography by contrast is more general. Canaanite geography is often described with reference to border features rather than interior features, as is fitting for a people on the outside looking in (Mountains of Amorites, Lebanon, etc.).

The list of animals in Leviticus 21 and Deuteronomy 14 includes ostriches, wild ox/antelope and the ibex, animals that are native to the Sinai Peninsula but not Israel. None of the animals in these chapters are peculiar to Israel. The acacia tree, used for building the tabernacle, is native to Egypt and Sinai but not Israel. Acacia wood is mentioned 28 times in Torah and four times in the rest of the Bible (none of those times referring to trees then in the land of Israel).

3.3.3 Nomadic Setting

The Torah does not address people living in cities or people living in an agrarian lifestyle, like the Israelites after they entered the land of Canaan. Instead, it is written to people in "the camp" (מחנה). "The camp" is addressed in all the alleged sources (examples: J – Exod 33:7, E – Exod 19:16, D – Deut 23:10-12, P – Num 3:38, Holiness Code – Lev 17:3). "The camp" implies a nomadic rather than a settled group. After the book of Joshua, "the camp" is used, with a few exceptions, to describe an army camp. After Joshua, Israel no longer dwells in a camp; they live in the cities, villages and agricultural settlements in the land of Israel.

The camp setting governs the narrative of the exodus. The pillar of cloud/fire moves before the camp (Exod 14:19). Stories happen inside, outside and at the edge of the camp (Exod 32:17, 32:19, 32:26 and 32:27). There are detailed instructions for how to camp (Numbers 2) and how to march out (Num 10:14-36). The instructions given for making the tabernacle, the ark, the altar and associated furnishings in Exodus 25-30 make detailed provisions for these things to be mobile – they are built with rings through which poles can be inserted, allowing them to be carried.

The laws given in the Torah are clear if applied to a camp lifestyle, but their application to an agricultural settlement requires some interpretation. For example, there are numerous references to things that must be done "outside the camp," but what would "outside the camp" mean in an agricultural settlement? Outside the home? Outside the farm? (That might put a person on his neighbor's farm.) Lev 17:1-4 requires all animal killing to be done at the tabernacle – an idea which is workable in a camp setting but unthinkable after Israel had settled "from Dan to Beersheba." Even the law about eating in "the place YHWH chooses" (Jerusalem) envisions the citizen returning to his "tent," rather than his "house" (Deut 16:7). The camp setting for the laws in the Torah gives evidence that it was written when the Israelites were camped in the wilderness, before their entry into the land of Canaan. It is unlikely that a later settled people would create their religious law and direct it toward a nomadic people.

3.3.4 Eyewitness Character of the Exodus

Certain portions of the narrative in the Torah have an eyewitness quality to them. This includes Exod 15:27, which lists the number of fountains (12) and palm trees (70). Num 11:7-8 describes the taste of manna and how the people would cook it. Also, the repeated instruction to remember certain things has an eyewitness quality: "Remember you were a slave" (Exod 13:3, 5:15, 15:15, 16:12, 24:18 and 24:22), "remember what the LORD your God did to Pharaoh" (Deut 7:18), "remember that the LORD your God led you all the way these 40 years" (Deut 8:2), "Remember! Do not forget how you provoked the LORD your God to wrath in the wilderness" (Deut 9:7), "Remember the day you came out of the land of Egypt all the days of your life" (Deut 16:3), "Remember what the LORD your God did to Miriam on the way…" (Deut 24:9) and "Remember what the Amalekite did to you on the way" (Deut 25:17).

3.3.5 Egyptian Background

There are numerous elements of the Torah that point to an Egyptian background. These elements are supportive of a date close to the time of the exodus from Egypt. Some of these are listed below:

1. No Pharaoh is named in the Torah, neither the Pharaoh Joseph knew, nor the Pharaoh Joseph did not know (Exod 1:8), nor the Pharaoh of the exodus. Unfortunate though this is for historians, it was in keeping with the custom of the New Kingdom Egyptian official language at that time, which was to refer to the king simply as Pharaoh, without connecting the name.[48] In later biblical passages, when the Israelites are no longer in Egypt and no longer following Egyptian customs, the Pharaoh sometimes is named (1 Kgs 14:25 – Pharaoh Shishak, 2 Kgs 17:4 – So, King of Egypt, 2 Kgs 23:29 - Pharaoh Neco, Jer 44:30 - Pharaoh Hophra).

2. Deut 17:16 warns that any anticipated king must not cause the people to return to Egypt. This ceased to be an issue almost as soon as the generation of the exodus died off.

3. The diet mentioned in Num 11:5: "We remember the fish which we used to eat free in Egypt, the cucumbers and the melons and the leeks and the onions and the garlic" matches closely with what Herodotus (writing about 450 B.C.) says about Egyptian diet: "On the pyramid it is declared in Egyptian writing how much was spent on radishes and onions and leeks for the workmen."[49]

4. Gen 43:32 says: "So they served him by himself, and them by themselves, and the Egyptians who ate with him by

---

[48] Archer, *A Survey of Old Testament Introduction*, p. 105
[49] Herodotus, *An Account of Egypt*, Project Gutenberg e-text

themselves, because the Egyptians could not eat bread with the Hebrews, for that is loathsome to the Egyptians." This seems an unlikely comment from a later Israelite writer.

5. The statement in Gen 46:34 that shepherds were loathsome to the Egyptians is supported historically by the absence of sheep on Egyptian reliefs. Cattle, on the other hand, are common on Egyptian reliefs. Note also that Pharaoh's dream in Gen 41:1-4 involved cattle rather than sheep.

6. The murmuring motif in the wilderness usually involved Egypt, actually beginning in Egypt (Exod 5:21). "Is it because there were no graves in Egypt that you have taken us away to die in the wilderness?" (Exod 14:11).

7. Jacob and Joseph were both embalmed (Gen 50:2 and 50:26). Embalming was an Egyptian custom, not practiced in Israel.

8. Num 13:22 dates the founding of Hebron to the founding of the Egyptian city of Zoan. This points to an early date of writing, because for later Israelites, Hebron would have been well-known and Zoan virtually unknown.

9. The author was familiar with Egyptian irrigation and felt it was necessary to explain that Canaan, unlike Egypt, relied on rain (Deut 11:10-11).

10. The author was familiar with how Egyptians made bricks from mud and straw (Exod 5:6-12), a practice still sometimes used in Egypt today.

11. Gen 47:26 states that Joseph's 20 percent land tax for Pharaoh is a law in Egypt "to this day." "This day" is the day of the writer, and could comfortably apply to the exodus generation, which would be familiar with Egyptian tax law. The later Kingdom of Israel would be less likely to be familiar with Egyptian laws.

12. A puzzling aspect of the Exodus story is that in Exod 1:8-10, the Pharaoh is concerned about the numbers of the Is-

raelites at the time of Moses birth. Then 80 years later, with the Israelites surely more numerous than before, this no longer seems to be an issue. The explanation is possibly to be found in the fact that Egypt was ruled from 1674-1567 by the Hyksos, a non-native people who founded the 15th dynasty in Egypt.[50] Coming from a minority ruling class, the statement "the people of the sons of Israel are more and mightier than we" is entirely understandable. This subtle knowledge of Egyptian political history is not likely to be the sort of thing that would be understood by an Israelite writer from a later time.

3.3.5.1 Plagues on Egypt

The plagues on Egypt were understood by the biblical writer to be a judgment on the gods of Egypt: "against all the gods of Egypt I will execute judgments" (Exod 12:12), and "The LORD had also executed judgments on their gods." (Num 33:4). The plagues can be accounted for as follows:[51]

1. Nile turns to blood (Exod 7:15-25) – This addresses the Nile god Hapi. Egyptian writings spoke of Hapi as the one who kept Egypt alive.

2. Frogs (Exod 8:1-6) – This addresses the Egyptian goddess Hekhet, who was depicted as a human female with a frog's head.

3-4. Both the third and fourth plagues involve flying insects (Exod 8:16-24) – These plagues may address Kheprer, the Egyptian self-generated god of resurrection, who is depicted as a flying beetle.

---

[50] As a reminder, we are not confident in the strict accuracy of dates in the 2nd millennium B.C. However, it is well established that the Hyksos, a non-Egyptian race of people, did rule Egypt for some time during this period.

[51] This list of Egyptian gods is taken from Currid, *Ancient Egypt and the Old Testament*, pp. 109-113

5. The plague on Egyptian livestock (Exod 9:1-7) – There were multiple Egyptian bull cults including gods named Apis, Buchis and Mneuis, and bulls were sometimes understood as the embodiment of the major Egyptian gods Ptah and Ra.

6. The boils plague (Exod 9:8-12) – This could address the goddess Sekhmet, a lion-headed deity of plagues, who was believed to be able to bring about or prevent epidemics and pestilence.

7. Hail (Exod 9:13-35) – This could have addressed the Egyptian heavenly deities, Nut, Shu and Tefnut.

8. Locusts (Exod 10:1-20) – This might have been addressed to the minor Egyptian god Senehem, who protected Egypt from ravages of pests.

9. Darkness (Exod 10:21-29) – This plague certainly addressed the main Egyptian god Amon-Re, sometimes called Ra, the sun-god. The Hebrew word for evil or harm is "ra'ah" (רעה), a similar sounding word to Ra the sun-god, and it is possible that the author of the Torah used a play on words in passages such as Exod 10:10, 32:22, Num 20:5 and Deut 9:18.

10. The tenth plague, the death of the firstborn (Exod 11:1-10, 12:29-30) – This plague would be addressed to Pharaoh himself as a god of Egypt and against his succession. Additionally, Exod 11:7, "But against any of the sons of Israel a dog will not even bark," could be a reference to Anubis, the Egyptian god of the dead and embalming, who would have no power over the Israelites during the plague. Anubis was depicted as a dog in Egyptian religion.

In addition to the plagues, the contest of rods to snakes (Exod 7:8-12) addresses Egyptian deification of snakes. Egyptians feared the serpent because of his power and danger, but also looked to him for protection. The Egyptian serpent goddess Uraeus personified the cobra and was a goddess of Lower Egypt. Wadjet was a serpent goddess, who along with Nekhbet, was understood to give Pharaoh the power to control all Egypt.[52] The two goddesses were represented on the front of Pharaoh's crown as an enraged cobra. It should be noted that the identification of Pharaoh with serpents was understood also in a later biblical text (Ezek 29:3).

3.3.5.2 Anti-Egyptian Theology

"Choose life" (Deut 30:19). Portions of the theology of the Torah are anti-Egyptian, in that the Egyptian culture placed great emphasis on death, while the Torah emphasizes life. The Egyptians employed sophisticated embalming practices, mummies, and massive pyramids for dead kings. An important religious text in ancient Egypt was titled "The Book of the Dead." Egyptians commonly wrote letters to dead relatives asking for help in ordinary matters.[53] By contrast, the Torah is careful to ensure that no one knows where Moses was buried – so there was no temptation to go through any Egyptian-inspired tomb commemoration or death ritual. In a type of regulation unusual to the world's religions, the Torah bans priests from contact with dead bodies (Lev 21:11), a regulation that also applies to Nazirites (Num 6:6). For anyone, contact with a dead body rendered them ceremonially unclean (Num 19:11). The Torah separates meat (death) from milk[54] (life) in Exod 23:19, 34:26 and Deut 14:21, and menstruation (death) from intercourse (life) in Lev 20:18. Eating food with blood is strictly forbidden, because "the life of the flesh is in the blood" (Lev 17:10-11). The Torah forbids making "any cuts in your body for the dead" (Lev 19:28, see also Deut 14:1), and food was not to

---

[52] For a more detailed description of serpent theology and Egypt, see Currid, *Ancient Egypt and the Old Testament*, pp. 82-94.

[53] Currid, *Ancient Egypt and the Old Testament*, p. 222

[54] The prohibition against boiling a goat in its mother's milk may also have been a reaction to non-Egyptian pagan practices. Archer, *A Survey of the Old Testament Introduction*, p. 163 states that the Ras Shamra tablets allow boiling a goat in its mother's milk as being an acceptable sacrifice to a god. The majority of the Ras Shamra tablets are dated to about 1375 B.C.

be given to the dead (Deut 26:14). Anyone who conducts a séance to call someone up from the dead is to be put to death (Deut 18:11). Finally, in an unusual omission for a lengthy religious text, the Torah is silent on the subject of life after death.

A second area in which the Torah is anti-Egyptian can be found in the curious wording of the creation story, where God made "two great lights" (Gen 1:16), but the light source, the sun, "the greater light to govern the day," is not named. In fact, light is created in Gen 1:3, before the sun. This de-emphasis on the sun contrasts with the Egyptian worship of Ra, the sun god. Deuteronomy twice warns the people not to worship the sun (4:19 and 17:2-5).

By contrast, the Torah contains no specific warnings against Baal worship. General warnings against following other gods are provided, but the Baal worship which was popular in Canaan and became such a religious scourge in Israel for hundreds of years, beginning with Judges and not ending completely until after Jeremiah, is not mentioned.

3.3.6 Biography of Moses

The biographical background of Moses is full of details unlikely to be invented by a writer in the Israelite kingdom period. Moses, the great hero of the Jewish faith, apparently has an Egyptian name (Exod 2:10). The wife of Moses is not Jewish, but rather a Midianite (Exod 2:16 and 2:21). The burial place of Moses is not in the land of Israel, but on a mountain in the territory of Moab (Deut 34:5-6). These facts argue more for the historicity of the story of Moses in the Torah than the date of the Torah, but historicity and date go together somewhat when the facts are not flattering. A story told many hundreds of years after the fact is likely to avoid the less palatable elements.

3.3.7 Political Background

The political background of the Torah is the second millennium B.C., and no significant reflection of later times is present. To consider the nation-states involved, there is no mention in the Torah, even as a prophesy, about the split between the northern Kingdom of Israel and the southern Kingdom of Judah. This split, after it happened, dominated the political landscape of the Old Testament. Working backwards from the great empires that would eventually rule all or part of Israel, there are no mentions of Persia or Greece and five total mentions of Babylon (Babel) and Assyria. On the other hand, there is quite a lot of attention given to the Amorites (72 mentions), the Canaanites (63 mentions), the Hittites (38 mentions), the Jebusites (36 mentions), the Hivites (23 mentions), the Perizzites, (19 mentions), the Anakim (18 mentions) and the Girgashites (7 mentions), most of whom drop out of sight during the time of the Kingdom of Israel. It could truly be said that the Torah is more concerned about giants (sons of Anak or Anakim) than about giant military empires.

During the first millennium B.C., Israel and Judah were ruled by kings, then later by governors under foreign kings. The Torah has nothing to say about governors. It gives brief advice in Deut 17:14-20 dealing with future kings, and as one might expect with advice given far ahead of time, almost all of it is either unnecessary (king must not be a foreigner, king must not cause the people to return to Egypt), or gets ignored (king must not have many wives, many horses, silver or gold). There is a great deal of law dealing with what judges should do (Exod 21:22, 22:8, Num 25:5, Deut 1:16, 16:18, 17:12, 19:17, etc.), and even more about what priests should do. In a similar manner, Leviticus 4 has rules governing the sins of the priests, the people and the "chief" (4:22), but not the king.

3.3.8 Deuteronomy as a Treaty

The book of Deuteronomy consists almost entirely of the final address of Moses to the people of Israel. There are many ways Moses could have chosen to structure his final words, but the structure he apparently chose is similar to that of a suzerainty treaty – a contract between two unequal parties. This treaty form was usually used between two kings or two nations, one a master and the other a vassal. In the case of Deuteronomy, the LORD is the master and Israel is the vassal. Second millennium B.C. Hittite suzerainty treaties took the following structure:

1. Preamble
2. Historical Background
3. Treaty Stipulations
4. Invocation of Witnesses
5. Deposition of Written Copy of the Treaty
6. Curses and Blessings.

Deuteronomy contains all of these elements, in essentially the same order. Table 3-6 shows a side by side comparison between a second millennium B.C. Hittite treaty and the book of Deuteronomy, extracting selected text from each.

Table 3-6 Deuteronomy Treaty Structure

Treaty between Mursili and Duppi-Tesub[55]	Deuteronomy
Preamble B i.1 Thus says My Majesty, Mursili, Great King, king of the Hatti …	*Preamble* 1:1-5 These are the words which Moses spoke to all Israel across the Jordan in the wilderness…

---

[55] Itamar Singer in Hallo, *The Context of Scripture*, Vol. II, pp. 96ff

Treaty between Mursili and Duppi-Tesub[55]	Deuteronomy
Historical Background B. i.3 Duppi-Tesub! Your grandfather Azira submitted to my father. When it came about that the kings of Nuhhasse and the king of Kinza became hostile, Azira did not become hostile. When my father fought his enemies, Azira likewise fought them. Just as Azira protected my father, my father protected Azira together with his land…	*Historical Background* 1:6-3:29 The LORD our God spoke to us at Horeb, saying, 'You have stayed long enough at this mountain. Turn and set your journey, and go to the hill country of the Amorites, and to all their neighbors in the Arabah, in the hill country and in the lowland…
Stipulations D. ii.10 …Whoever is My Majesty's enemy shall be your enemy, and whoever is My Majesty's friend shall be your friend… A ii.46 If someone should bring up before you, Duppi-Tesub, evil words about the king or about the land of Hatti, you shall not conceal it from the king… A iii.30 If a fugitive enters your land in flight, seize him and extradite him…	*Stipulations* 4:1-26:19 Now, O Israel, listen to the statutes and the judgments which I am teaching you to perform, so that you may live and go in and take possession of the land which the LORD, the God of your fathers, is giving you…
Invocation of the Witnesses D iii.5 Behold, let the thousand gods stand by for this oath! Let	*Invocation of the Witnesses* 30:19 I call heaven and earth to witness against you today, that

Treaty between Mursili and Duppi-Tesub[55]	Deuteronomy
them observe And listen! Sun-god of Heaven, Sun-goddess of Arinna, Storm-god of Heaven, Storm-god of Hatti, Seri and Huri…. *A iv.4-20* …mountains, rivers, springs, great sea, heaven and earth, winds, clouds. Let them be witnesses to this treaty and to the oath!	I have set before you life and death, the blessing and the curse…31:28 Assemble to me all the elders of your tribes and your officers, that I may speak these words in their hearing and call the heavens and the earth to witness against them.
Written Copy *A iv.21* All the words of the treaty and the oath which are written on this tablet	*Written Copy* 31:9 So Moses wrote this law and gave it to the priests, the sons of Levi who carried the Ark of the Covenant of the LORD, and to all the elders of Israel.
Curses and Blessings *A iv.21-32* If Duppi-Tesub does not keep these words of the treaty and the oath, then let these oath gods destroy Duppi-Tesub together with his head, his wife, his son, his grandson, his house, his land and together with his possessions. But if Duppi-Tesub observes these words of the treaty and the oath that are written on this tablet, let these oath gods protect Duppi-Tesub together with his head, his wife, his son,	*Curses and Blessings* 28:2-14 All these blessings will come upon you and overtake you if you obey the LORD your God: "Blessed shall you be in the city, and blessed shall you be in the country… 28:15-68 But it shall come about, if you do not obey the LORD your God, to observe to do all His commandments and His statutes with which I charge you today, that all these curses will come upon you and overtake you: Cursed shall you

Treaty between Mursili and Duppi-Tesub[55]	Deuteronomy
his grandson, his city, his land, your house, your subjects, and together with your possessions!	be in the city, and cursed shall you be in the country…

The similarity between Deuteronomy and second millennium treaties provides evidence that Deuteronomy was written in the second millennium B.C., not later. It has been suggested that Deuteronomy is similar to first millennium B.C. treaties as well, but first millennium B.C. suzerainty treaties did not contain a historical background in the second section, as is present in the second millennium B.C. treaties and in Deuteronomy 1:6-3:29. Here is a list of treaties from the second millennium B.C., all of which contain a historical background section:

1. Suzerainty Treaty between Suppiluliuma and Aziru – Hittite treaty mid 14th to late 13th century B.C.[56]
2. Suzerainty Treaty between Tudhaliya and Sausgamuwa - Hittite treaty mid 14th to late 13th century B.C.[57]
3. Suzerainty Treaty between Tudhaliya IV with Kurunta of Tarhuntassa - Hittite treaty mid 14th to late 13th century B.C.[58]
4. Abbael's Gift of the City of Alalakh – Old Babylonian period (2000-1595 B.C.)[59]
5. The Laws of Hammurabi (1792-1750 B.C.), though not generally considered to be a treaty, are also put in the second millennium B.C. treaty format, with a historical background at the beginning and blessings and cursings at the end.[60] The Sumerian Laws of Ur-Namma (2112-2095 B.C.)

---

[56] Hallo, *The Context of Scripture*, Vol. II, pp. 93-95
[57] Hallo, *The Context of Scripture*, Vol. II, pp. 98-100
[58] Hallo, *The Context of Scripture*, Vol. II, pp. 100-106
[59] Hallo, *The Context of Scripture*, Vol. II, pp. 329
[60] Hallo, *The Context of Scripture*, Vol. II, pp. 335-353

and Laws of Lippit Ishtar (2017-1985 B.C.) also have historical background sections.[61]

Here is a list of treaties from the first millennium B.C., none of which contain a historical background section like Deuteronomy:

1. Treaty between Ashur-nirari V and Mati'ilu of Arpad (about 750 B.C.)
2. Treaty between Esarhaddon and Baal of Tyre (about 675 B.C.)
3. Esarhaddon Vassal Treaties (multiple treaties – about 675 B.C.)

M.G. Kline concludes: "…Now that the form critical data compel the recognition of the antiquity not merely of this or that element within Deuteronomy but of the Deuteronomic treaty in its integrity, any persistent insistence on a final edition of the book around the seventh century B.C. can be nothing more than a vestigial hypothesis, no longer performing a significant function in Old Testament criticism."[62]

3.3.9 Genesis

We must now turn to the unique position of Genesis within the Torah. Unlike the rest of the Torah, neither Moses nor anyone else in the exodus generation were eyewitnesses to the events in Genesis. Genesis is in a separate category from the other four books, because of its long time duration and earlier, different setting.

3.3.9.1 Antiquity of Genesis

The antiquity of the customs of the patriarchs in Genesis suggests that the book could not have been written in the kingdom period, or even during the exodus, unless some earlier source was used.

---

[61] Hallo, The Context of Scripture, Vol. II, pp. 408-413

[62] Patterson, *Introduction to the Old Testament*, pp. 649-650, citing M.G. Kline, Treaty of the Great King, p. 13ff

The following list shows archaic customs from Genesis which are never practiced by later Israelites:

1. The custom of the wife suggesting that the husband marry her maidservant, with the understanding (which never quite seemed to work out) that the children would be credited to the wife (Gen 16:2, 30:3-4 and 30:9). Although this custom was never practiced by later Israelites, it is supported by the Code of Hammurabi, laws 144-146: "If a man take a wife and this woman give her husband a maidservant, and she bear him children, but this man wishes to take another wife, this shall not be permitted to him; he shall not take a second wife." "If a man take a wife, and she bear him no children, and he intend to take another wife: if he take this second wife, and bring her into the house, this second wife shall not be allowed equality with his wife." "If a man take a wife and she give this man a maid-servant as wife and she bear him children, and then this maid assume equality with the wife: because she has borne him children her master shall not sell her for money, but he may keep her as a slave, reckoning her among the maid-servants."[63] The Code of Hammurabi was a Mesopotamian law code of the 18th century B.C., near to the time of the Genesis patriarchs.

2. The custom of taking an oath by swearing with the hand under the thigh (24:2-3, 24:9 and 47:29).

3. The ruse, attempted three different times to try to avoid harm, of a patriarch claiming that his wife was his sister (Gen 12:13, 20:2 and 26:7).

4. Some custom, perhaps not well understood today, attributing extreme importance to possession of household idols, even in a household that primarily worshipped YHWH. The importance was great enough that Rachel stole them

---

[63] Translated by L. W. King, 1910

(31:19), Laban's anger climaxed with the issue of the stolen gods (31:30), and Jacob pronounced a death penalty on whoever took them (31:32).

5. Abraham apparently adopted Eliezer of Damascus, a servant, to be his legal heir (Gen 15:2), only to be displaced by the birth of Ishmael and Isaac. The Nuzi tablets, dated to the 15th century B.C., show support for this custom.[64]

6. The legitimacy of selling one's birthright, as done by Esau (Gen 25:29-34), is also supported by the Nuzi Tablets.[65]

The fact that the customs of the patriarchs do not fit well within the Kingdom of Israel period hints at a date of writing not in that period, but earlier and closer in time to the events.

In addition to the customs of the patriarchs, the following verses point to an ancient setting for the stories in Genesis:

1. The long life spans of the patriarchs are associated only with antiquity and are not related to any heroic nature on the part of the characters. Later great heroes like David and Solomon lived normal life spans.

2. When Abraham gave Lot his choice of land, Lot looked toward the Jordan valley as far south as Sodom and observed that it was "well watered everywhere" (13:10). Anyone who has been to Israel will wonder what he could have been thinking – the land chosen by Lot is harsh desert, or at least it is now. The original author of 13:10 or a later scribe felt the need to insert "this was before the LORD destroyed Sodom and Gomorrah."

3. The story of the near sacrifice of Isaac in Genesis 22 would be unthinkable in a later Israelite setting, because human sacrifice was strictly forbidden by the law.

4. Abraham's marriage to Sarah, his half-sister (Gen 20:12), would have been considered incestuous by the time the

---

[64] Archer, *A Survey of the Old Testament Introduction*, p. 160
[65] Archer, *A Survey of the Old Testament Introduction*, pp. 160-161

law was given (Lev 18:9), but there is no hint of condemnation of this by the author of Genesis. In fact the opposite occurs, as Abraham and Sarah are uniquely blessed.

The following verses show additional internal evidence of antiquity in terms of when the text was first written:

1. Gen 10:19 sounds like it predates the destruction of Sodom: "The territory of the Canaanite extended from Sidon as you go toward Gerar, as far as Gaza; as you go toward Sodom and Gomorrah." If Moses was the first writer of these words, he would be giving directions based on cities that ceased to exist hundreds of years earlier. (The Documentary Hypothesis would be giving directions based on cities that ceased to exist a thousand years earlier).

2. The phrases "land of the south" (Gen 20:1, 24:62) and "east land" (Gen 25:6) seem to envision lands that are not part of a nation-state, a situation existing in 2000 B.C. but not in 1000 B.C.

3. Archaic names, not used in the later Kingdom of Israel, are sometimes used for well-known geographic locations. Sometimes the text includes what may be later additions that bring the name up to date, and sometimes it does not. Examples are Luz for Bethel (Gen 28:19, 35:6 and 48:3), Bela for Zoar (14:2 and 14:8), Valley of Siddim for the Salt Sea (14:3), En-mishpat for Kadesh (14:7), Hobah for a location north of Damascus (14:15) and Kiriath-arba for Hebron (23:2 and 35:27).

4. Some of the passages in Genesis show evidence for antiquity just based on their obscurity. Noah's ark lands on the mountains of Ararat (Gen 8:4), a painfully far distance from the land of Israel and even farther from Egypt. Gen 2:10-14 describes a geographic setting for Eden in which one river divides into four (a setting that does not match any known location). One of the river branches irrigates

the land of Havilah (an unknown place), where there is gold, and "the gold of that land is good" (2:12). The wording is strange. What is good about the gold? Is there somewhere where the gold is bad?

3.3.9.2 The Genesis Tablets

Moses was separated in time from the patriarchs by several hundred years at a minimum, and from the earlier stories in Genesis by a period far longer still. Yet we have seen that the Genesis accounts accurately reflect the culture and times of the patriarchs. How can this be explained?

The Tablet Theory of Genesis first suggested by Percy Wiseman makes a genuine effort to explain the appearance of antiquity in Genesis. Wiseman states: "The book of Genesis was originally written on tablets in the ancient script of the time by the patriarchs who were intimately concerned with the events related, and whose names are clearly stated. Moreover, Moses, the compiler and editor of the book, as we now have it, plainly directs attention to the source of his information."[66]

The Tablet Theory suggests that the text of Genesis 1:1 – 37:2 was originally written on clay tablets, in what was a common Mesopotamian practice, and that the tablets were similar to other Mesopotamian cuneiform clay tablets that have been discovered by archeologists. These clay tablets usually end with a colophon, an inscription with a name or title identifying the tablet. Wiseman suggests that the colophons have been largely retained in Genesis in the phrase "These are the generations of…"(KJV) in Gen 2:4, 5:1, 6:9, 10:1, 11:10, 11:27, 25:12, 25:19, 36:1 and 37:2. The Hebrew word "toledot" (תולדות), translated as "generations" in the KJV (translated as "account" in the NIV and NASB) has long been recognized as a key word, and in fact the Greek translation of it, "geneseos" is the source of the name, "Genesis." "Toledot" is

---

[66] Wiseman, *Ancient Records and the Structure of Genesis*, p. 20

derived from the root word "yalad" (ילד), which means to bear a child. This word is clearly connected to a genealogy in Ruth 4:18 and in 1 Chron 1:29. Therefore, most scholars have historically tied "These are the generations of..." to the genealogy of the individual named. However, that interpretation is weakened by the fact that in Gen 2:4, 6:9, 25:19 and 37:2, no genealogy either precedes or follows the verse. The source critics would like to say that the generations formula goes with the P source and precedes a genealogy, but in Gen 2:4, it comes at the end of the alleged P creation account, rather than the beginning. Wiseman's case is strengthened by the slight variation in wording in 5:1, "This is the *book of the* generations of Adam," and the wording in the Septuagint in 2:4, "This is the *book of the* Generations of the heavens and the earth," implying that those sections were once independent books. Wiseman's theory divides Genesis into 11 tablets as follows:

Tablet	Starting Verse	Ending Verse	Owner or Writer
1	Gen 1:1	Gen 2:4a	God Himself (?)
2	Gen 2:4b	Gen 5:1a	Adam
3	Gen 5:1b	Gen 6:9a	Noah
4	Gen 6:9b	Gen 10:1	Shem, Ham & Japheth
5	Gen 10:1b	Gen 11:10a	Shem
6	Gen 11:10b	Gen 11:27a	Terah
7	Gen 11:27b	Gen 25:19a	Isaac
8	Gen 25:12	Gen 25:18	Ishmael, through Isaac
9	Gen 25:19b	Gen 37:2a	Jacob
10	Gen 36:1	Gen 36:43	Esau, through Jacob
11	Gen 37:2b	Exod 1:6	Jacob's 12 sons

The last section of Genesis, after 37:2, is primarily the story of Joseph. This story was recorded in Egypt, where writing was done not on clay tablets but on papyrus. Therefore, the Joseph story has no colophon, and is not considered a tablet like the other stories.

Some Mesopotamian tablets include a date of writing. In Gen 11:26, Terah may be dating his tablet as being written when he was 70 years old. The last three Genesis tablets appear to date themselves by the location of the patriarch at the time of writing. Note that these lines stand in close proximity to the end of each tablet:

25:11 "And Isaac lived in Beer-lahai-roi"

36:8　"And Esau lived in the hill country of Seir"

37:1　"And Jacob lived in the land where his father had sojourned, the land of Canaan."

Cuneiform Tablet of one of the Amarna Letters, circa 1400 B.C.

Wiseman also observed that for collections involving multiple tablets there were also "catch-lines" to connect a tablet to its predecessor and successor. Note how the proposed catch-lines for the Genesis tablets shown below again stand in close proximity to the beginning or ending of each tablet. The catch Lines are:

1:1	"God created the heavens and the earth"
2:4	"The LORD God made earth and heaven"
2:4	"when they were created"
5:2	"when they were created"
6:10	"Shem, Ham and Japheth"
10:1	"Shem, Ham and Japheth"
10:1	"after the flood"
10:32	"after the flood"
11:10	"after the flood"
11:26	"Abram, Nahor and Haran"
11:27	"Abram, Nahor and Haran"
25:12	"Abraham's son"
25:19	"Abraham's son"
36:1	"Esau is Edom"
36:8	"Esau is Edom"
36:9	"father of the Edomites"
36:43	"father of the Edomites"

Tablets 8 and 10, the Ishmael and Esau tablets, differ from the others in that they give a brief account of people who are outside the chosen line. Therefore, the Ishmael tablet is preserved because he gave the account to his brother, Isaac, and the Esau account is preserved through his brother Jacob. In each case, the non-chosen line (Ishmael and Esau) has its account included after two brothers bury their father – Isaac and Ishmael bury Abraham in Gen 25:9, and Jacob and Esau bury Isaac in Gen 35:29. Also, in the tablets of the non-chosen line, the toledot statement comes first, unlike all the other accounts. Here we suggest that the Esau Tablet 10 actually consists of two tablets. The first tablet includes Gen 36:1-8, given to Jacob by Esau, perhaps at their father's funeral

(Gen 35:29). The second tablet brings Esau's descendants farther down in time, includes Gen 36:9-43a, and was inserted into the account by the Israelites some time later. This is the reason for the two catch-lines ("Esau is Edom" and "father of the Edomites") instead of one in the Esau account

The final compiler of Genesis produced a unified book rather than a series of tablets. He also probably performed something of a translation (as we will discuss later) as he did his work. Still, the outline of the tablets seems to have survived mostly intact, as figure 3-2 shows.

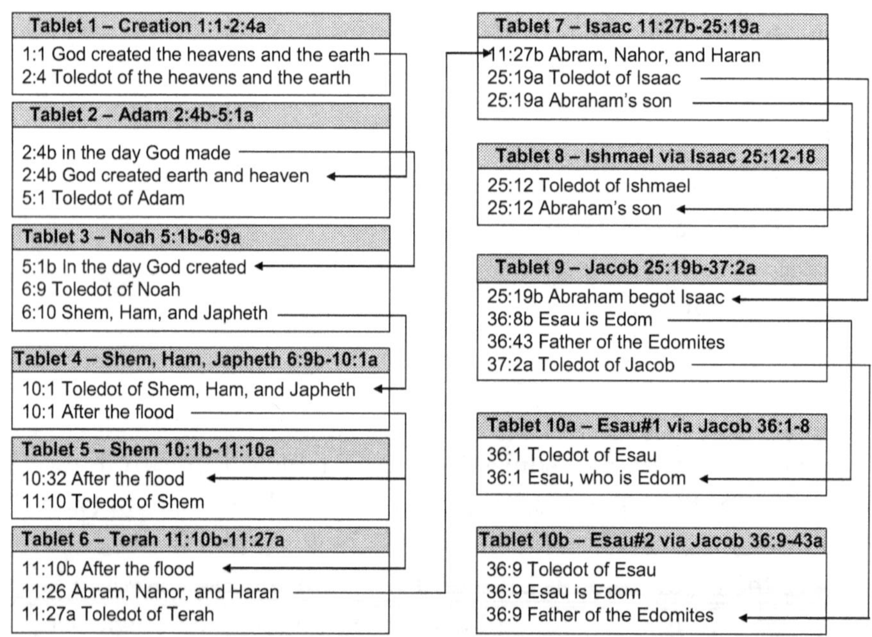

Figure 3-2 The Genesis Tablets

Certain imperfections with the Tablet Theory are readily apparent. The tablets, as shown in Figure 3-2, are not connected in a consistent manner: the catch-lines are sometimes at the beginning and sometimes at the end. In tablets 6 and 8, assigned to individuals outside the chosen line (Ishmael and Esau), the "toledot" statement is at the beginning of the tablet rather than the end. There also may be vestiges of additional tablets in Genesis: the "after the flood" catch-line appears three times rather than two, and "the years of the life of Sarah" in Gen 23:1a and 23:1b reads suspiciously like a catch-line separating two tablets.

Further support for the Tablet Theory comes from several additional facts:

1. In no instance is an event described that could not have been known by the person assigned to the tablet.

2. In all instances, the history of events in a tablet ceases before the death of the person assigned to the tablet.

3. Within the ten tablets of Genesis, the beginning of each tablet is usually followed by a brief repetition of a prominent feature of the preceding section. For example, Tablet 2 has Gen 2:7, repeating the creation of man. Tablet 3 has Gen 5:1b-2, looking back on the first two tablets dealing with the creation of man and the name Adam (mankind). Tablet 4 has 6:11-12, reiterating the wickedness of man found in Tablet 3, and so on.

4. Abraham, the most prominent figure in Genesis, does not have a tablet. This fact indicates that the toledot structure is something other than a breakdown based simply on a list of the main figures in the book.

5. The law at Mount Sinai is initially given written on "tablets" (Exod 24:12, 31:18 and 32:15-16), with writing on both sides, as in the Mesopotamian custom. Although these are stone tablets and not clay tablets, they are still breakable when thrown (32:19), so they must have been similar in composition to the Mesopotamian tablets.

6. The way the books of the Torah are divided is itself not unlike the way the Mesopotamian tablets are divided. The Hebrew names are taken from the first line in each book, as follows:

a. Genesis – בראשית "In the Beginning" (from Gen 1:1)
b. Exodus – ואלה שמות "These are the names" (from Exod 1:1)
c. Leviticus – ויקרא "And He called" (from Lev 1:1)
d. Numbers – במדבר "In the wilderness" (Num 1:1)
e. Deuteronomy – אלה הדברים "These are the words" (Deut 1:1)

The books also show a tendency to connect by repetition the beginning of a new book with the ending of a previous book. Exod 1:1-5 lists the names of the people who went to Egypt, a summarized repeat of Gen 46:8-27. Leviticus ends "These are the commandments which the LORD commanded Moses for the sons of Israel at Mount Sinai" (Lev 27:34) and Numbers begins, "Then the LORD spoke to Moses in the wilderness of Sinai" (Num 1:1). Numbers ends "These are the commandments and the ordinances which the LORD commanded to the sons of Israel through Moses in the plains of Moab by the Jordan opposite Jericho" (Num 36:13), and Deuteronomy begins "These are the words which Moses spoke to all Israel across the Jordan in the wilderness" (Deut 1:1). The connection between Exodus-Leviticus is weaker, with God speaking from the tabernacle (Lev 1:1) after His glory filled it in Exod 40:34-38.

It is not necessary to think that the content of Genesis 1-37 was the full extent of historical material available to the compiler of Genesis. There are hints that other material was available and he left it out. For example, Gen 48:22 seems to be a reference to a story left out – Jacob fighting the Amorites at Shechem (The book of Jubilees 34:5-9 mentions the same thing). Also, Gen 49:31 mentions the death and burial of Rebekah and Leah, events not described in narrative, even though the death of Rebekah's nurse is mentioned in the narrative of Gen 35:8.

Christians may be interested to know that although the New Testament mentions Moses 79 times, it does not attribute author-

from one pen. And we can draw another conclusion which is perhaps even more provocative.

3.3.9.2.2 Genesis and the Divine Name

Let us consider something else *not* found in the Torah: Yahwistic names. A Yahwistic name is a name using part of the divine name YHWH. In general, the names translated into English that end in "jah" (Elijah, Abijah, etc.), or "iah" (Isaiah, Jeremiah, etc) or begin with "Jeho" (Jehoshaphat, Jehoiachin, etc.) are Yahwistic names. In the time of the kings, more than one third of the male Hebrews have Yahwistic names. The reason these names do not appear in the Torah is given in Exod 3:13-15 and 6:2-3: the name YHWH was not used before the time of Moses. These verses are shown below with the Hebrew names for God plugged in.

Exodus 3:13-15

> "[13]Then Moses said to God, "Behold, I am going to the sons of Israel, and I will say to them, 'The God of your fathers has sent me to you.' Now they may say to me, 'What is His name?' What shall I say to them?"
>
> [14]God said to Moses, "I AM WHO I AM"; and He said, "Thus you shall say to the sons of Israel, 'I AM has sent me to you.'"
>
> [15]God, furthermore, said to Moses, "Thus you shall say to the sons of Israel, 'YHWH, the God of your fathers, the God of Abraham, the God of Isaac, and the God of Jacob, has sent me to you ' This is My name forever, and this is My memorial-name to all generations."

The name YHWH means "He is" – it is a third person rendering of "I am."

Exodus 6:2-3:

> ²God spoke further to Moses and said to him, "I am YHWH;
> ³and I appeared to Abraham, Isaac, and Jacob, as El Shaddai, but by My name, YHWH, I did not make Myself known to them."

Until God spoke to Moses, the name YHWH was unknown to the Hebrews. Actually, there is one Yahwistic name in the Torah: Joshua ("Yehoshua") the son of Nun. However, he was not born with that name. He was born "Hoshea" and Moses changed his name to Joshua (Num 13:16), after the events of Exodus 3 and 6. No one born prior to the exodus was given a Yahwistic name. The Documentary Hypothesis leans heavily on Exodus 3:13-15 and Exodus 6:2-3, the former assigned to E and the latter to P, to explain why YHWH does not appear in E or P passages in Genesis.[70] We have already seen that this does not entirely work – there are a few mentions of YHWH in E and P. The Documentary Hypothesis also has no good explanation for the personal names, because there are 195 names in J, which does use YHWH from the beginning, and none of those names are Yahwistic either. Perhaps the most puzzling example of all is Ishmael; he seems to have the *wrong* name. Gen 16:11 says:

> "The angel of YHWH said to her further,
>
> "Behold, you are with child,

---

[70] The Documentary Hypothesis approach to these verses is also unsound. It loses the context of the Exodus 6 passage by assigning Exod 5:5-6:1 to J. In Exodus 5, Moses' initial approach to Pharaoh goes badly and the Israelite slaves get an increased workload. This explains why the Israelites are unreceptive to Moses' message in Exod 6:9 and why Moses himself is reluctant to return to Pharaoh in Exod 6:12. In the Exodus 3-4 passage, splitting the burning bush story into separate J and E sources leads to non-sequiturs in both accounts. To list a few, God calls to Moses from the midst of "the bush" in E (Exod 3:4) – but E hasn't identified any bush, and in fact the bush is not burning in E (The Documentary Hypothesis has to split Exod 3:4 into two sources, since it contains both YHWH and Elohim). Later, Moses is instructed in E (4:17-18) to take "this rod" with which to do "the signs", but the rod and the signs were only introduced in J.

And you will bear a son;
And you shall call his name Ishmael,
Because YHWH has given heed to your affliction."
But Ishmael doesn't mean "YHWH has given heed." It might mean "El has given heed," or "Elohim has given heed," or it could even be "man from Elohim." It is definitely an "El" name – if it was Yahwistic it would be "Ishmayah." The difficulty in this passage only compounds in verse 13 when the names are mixed yet again: "Then she called the name of YHWH who spoke to her, "You are a God who sees" ('El roi', not 'YHWH roi'). The Torah has numerous "El" names, but no Yahwistic names. The implication is clear: YHWH was not in the text of the Genesis tablets used by the author of the Torah. Instead, he saw another name there, and replaced it with YHWH in his translation.

What name for God was used on the Genesis tablets? The answer is given to us in Exod 6:3: El Shaddai. The translator chose not to translate every occurrence; he left it in once each for Abraham, Isaac and Jacob (Gen 17:1, 28:3 and 35:11), each time in a passage where the name is very important. He then used it three more times, twice in the Joseph story (Gen 43:14 and 48:3), then concluded with Exod 6:3, "I appeared to Abraham, Isaac, and Jacob, as El Shaddai, but by My name, YHWH, I did not make Myself known to them." Every occurrence of El Shaddai is in direct speech; it is never used by the narrator. Also, we do have in the Torah, in addition to the many "El" names, three "Shaddai" names – Shedeur (Num 1:5), Zurishaddai (Num 1:6) and Ammishaddai (Num 1:12), implying that Jews born before the exodus did name their children after El Shaddai – just never after YHWH. In addition to translating El Shaddai as YHWH, it is also possible that to suit his purposes, the translator may have in some cases also substituted YHWH for Elohim.

The situation is understandable in light of the revelation God gave to Moses using the new name, YHWH. The author needed to translate Genesis for his generation, and wanted to establish the connection between the God of the patriarchs (El Shaddai) and the God of the exodus (YHWH). This connection is clear enough in the narrative for the exodus story, but the author felt it was important to also make the connection there in the divine names used in Genesis.

To further support the idea that the Genesis tablets were translated with YHWH substituted for El Shaddai, we should consider one other Old Testament text that we believe is a later translation of a patriarchal age original – the speeches in the book of Job. The translator of Job did not follow the convention of the translator of Genesis, but left "Shaddai" alone. It is usually translated into English as "The Almighty," appearing 31 times in the speeches in Job, as opposed to YHWH appearing only once. Shaddai appears later in the direct speech of Balaam (Num 24:4, 24:16) and Naomi (Ruth 1:20-21), both of whom spent time outside the Hebrew-speaking Israelite culture. The full extent of other biblical references to Shaddai outside of the Torah, Ruth and Job are Ps 68:14, 91:1, Isa 13:6 = Joel 1:15, Ezek 1:24 and 10:5.

We should note that Giovanni Pettinato's translation of the Ebla tablets may indicate the existence of Yahwistic names in Ebla, north of Canaan and long before the exodus.[71] Pettinato's translation and interpretation of these names are still controversial among scholars. If these are in fact Yahwistic names, it would not necessarily falsify this theory explaining the revelation of divine names in Genesis, since the Ebla culture was somewhat removed from Israel. However, if inscriptions identified such names among the Hebrew people before Moses, this theory would be falsified.

3.3.10 Antiquity of Interpolations

A few verses in the Torah appear to not have come from the original author, and yet the nature of these interpolations is such that they also appear old, predating the Kingdom of Israel. As a

---

[71] Giovanni Pettinato, *The Archives of Ebla, An Empire Inscribed in Clay*, p. 248-249

cautionary note, it is always speculative to suggest that particular verses are interpolations, especially when there is no manuscript evidence for it. However, the following passages do seem to be reasonable candidates:

1. Genesis 36 deals with the descendants of Esau, and part of the chapter, verses 31-39, appears to bring the list of kings of Edom down in time past the patriarchs to about the time of Saul or David (Gen 36:31). This is a normal kind of addition – much like when a person has an old family genealogy, and he chooses to keep it up to date with more recent additions to the family. However, this interpolation still does not get out of the second millennium B.C. – it stops around the time of David.

2. Deut 3:9 interrupts Moses' address when he mentions Mount Hermon to say "(Sidonians call Hermon Sirion, and the Amorites call it Senir)." This interpolation looks ancient. For one thing, the later Israelites would not care what anyone else called Mount Hermon; it is the mountain near their own northern border. What the few scattered Amorites that remained, or the modest city of Sidon called it would be unimportant. For another thing, if a major regional power in Lebanon was to be named, it would have been Tyre rather than Sidon, since by the time of David Tyre was more powerful than Sidon and also closer to Mount Hermon. It was only in the period of the Judges and before that Sidon was preeminent. Therefore, if this verse is an interpolation, it dates back before the time of David, back into the second millennium B.C.

3. Deut 3:13b-14 is a second verse dealing with geography in the same passage that looks like an interpolation: "(concerning all Bashan, it is called the land of Rephaim. Jair the son of Manasseh took all the region of Argob as far as the border of the Geshurites and the Maacathites, and called it, that is, Bashan, after his own name, Havvoth-jair, as it is to

this day)." In this case, the suggestion that this verse is an interpolation seems more certain, primarily because of its connection to Judg 10:4. Yet the time of the interpolation still looks early. The area of Bashan passed out of control of the southern Kingdom of Judah as soon as the division of the kingdom in 931 B.C., and the other peoples named also seem to have passed out of existence before the end of the second millennium B.C.

4. Deuteronomy 34, describing the death of Moses, is likely to have been written some time after Moses, due especially to the phrases "no man knows his burial place to this day" in 34:6 and "since that time no prophet has risen in Israel like Moses" in 34:10. This passage would have been written after the migration of the Dan tribe northward, based on 34:1 (meaning this passage was not written by Joshua, as some have suggested), but prior to the time of the divided monarchy, based on the mention of Naphtali, Ephraim and Manasseh in 34:2.

5. Finally, we should consider the situation of the Philistines. It is understood that the Philistines migrated from the area of the Aegean Sea to the coastal area of Israel in about 1190 B.C. This is generally consistent with the biblical record, as the Philistines are not listed as one of the seven people groups in the land of Canaan, when those groups are repeatedly listed in the Torah (Canaanites, Amorites, Perizzites, Hittites, Hivites, Girgashites and Jebusites). The Philistines are also mostly absent in the story of the conquest of Canaan in the book of Joshua. They only make a significant appearance beginning in Judges, at a time consistent with the secular historical record. However, "Philistines" are mentioned ten times in the Torah (Gen 10:14, 21:32, 21:34, 26:1, 26:8, 26:14, 26:15, 26:18, Exod 13:17, 23:31). The phrase in Gen 10:14 might be considered a normal interpolation, added because the Philistines be-

came important. Most of the other passages all deal with geography, which would be best explained to the people in the Israelite kingdom period with reference to the Philistines. The outlier passage is Genesis 26, which calls Abimelech the king of the Philistines, and refers to his people as Philistines. It is possible that some Philistines may have migrated to the land of Canaan early, and these may be the people encountered by Isaac. However, this seems unlikely, since there is no other historical record of such a migration, and "Abimelech" is a Semitic, rather than an Indo-European name (The Philistines were an Indo-European people). On the other hand, a Canaanite could be named Abimelech. Probably, Genesis 26 is a story that was updated to use the name "Philistines" to describe the people who lived in the land that later became Philistia.

There are two points to make here. First, the Torah we have today is not exactly in the form used by the original author. Interpolations to bring the language and the geography up to date have been made. In a few cases, minor additions have been made to complete a story or record, as in the story of Jair in Deut 3:13-14 and the Edomite king list in Genesis 36. The second point here is that the interpolations are old – from the time of David or older. Therefore, the original text must be older still.

3.3.11 Linguistic Analysis
3.3.11.1 Phrasing and Vocabulary

Exclusion of common words, phrases, or ideas can also be used to show a single or unique authorship. It would not be surprising, if the Torah was written before the prophets and the writings, to find that many vocabulary words and figures of speech from these later periods are absent in the Torah. This is in fact the case, as the examples below demonstrate.

1. The phrases "Lord of Hosts" or "God of Hosts" is pervasive in the Old Testament, used 272 times in 16 different

books beginning in 1 Sam 1:3. However, this common phrase is absent in the Torah. Source critics claim a close connection between Jeremiah and Deuteronomy, yet Jeremiah has "LORD of Hosts" 80 times and Deuteronomy none. Also not used as a name for God in the Torah is "Holy One" or "Holy One of Israel," a formula used 48 times, mostly in Isaiah, but also in Jeremiah, Ezekiel, Daniel, Hosea, Habakkuk, 2 Kings, Job, Psalms and Proverbs.

2. Jerusalem is named 667 times in the Old Testament beginning in Josh 10:1. It is not mentioned by name in the Torah. Other locations in the land of Israel are named in the Torah, including Shechem, Bethel, Bethlehem, Hebron and Beersheba, the last three all in the territory of Judah, like Jerusalem. This is explained by the fact that when the Torah was written, Jerusalem was not an important city. However, this obvious explanation is not consistent with the Documentary Hypothesis, which has all four sources of the Torah being written after Jerusalem had become the capital, and after the temple had been built there. The issue is sharpest with regard to Deuteronomy, a book the source critics allege was written with the purpose of concentrating all worship in Jerusalem. Yet even though Deuteronomy mentions Samaritan high places (Mount Ebal and Mount Gerizim), it does not mention Jerusalem. Likewise, "Zion," which is often substituted for Jerusalem and used 154 times, is not found in the Torah.

3. The oath "as YHWH lives" or "as your soul lives" is used 49 times in the Bible, beginning in Judg 8:19, but not in the Torah. Also, the occasional oath form "YHWH do so to me and more also," used 7 times (Ruth 1:17, 1 Kgs 19:2, etc.), is not in the Torah. Oaths are taken in the Torah, but the only form associated seems to be the archaic "put your hand under my thigh" and swear form (Gen 24:2 and 47:29).

4. The phrase "declares the LORD" appears 332 times in the prophets, but only once in the Torah (Gen 22:16). Interestingly, it also only occurs once in the writings, in 2 Chron 34:27, quoting 2 Kgs 22:19.

5. As was discussed in section 3.3.9.2.2 above, there are about 200 Yahwistic names in the Bible, but none in the Torah or Joshua except Joshua, who was Hoshea before he had his name changed.

The absence of common words and phrases in the Torah is a more severe problem for theories of multiple sources than for theories of a single author, because their omission cannot be attributed to the quirks of one author. All the sources omit them. The problem is not alleviated by changing the dividing points between sources, and adding additional sources only makes it worse – even more sources would then be deviating from standard language usage. The only way to get rid of the problem is to get rid of the later sources altogether. This is both an argument against the Documentary Hypothesis and an argument for an early date for the Torah.

3.3.11.2 Relationship to Other Languages

The Hebrew language used in the Torah and throughout the Bible is from the Semitic family of languages. It is most closely related to other Canaanite languages, such as Phoenician or Moabite, and not quite so closely related to early Semitic languages used in Mesopotamia, such as Akkadian and Aramaic. Biblical Hebrew is largely unrelated to the language of the Persians, who ruled Judah in the later biblical period. The Egyptian language of the period of Pharaohs belongs to the same larger group of languages as Hebrew (the Afro-Asiatic group) but Egyptian does not fall under the sub-group of languages regarded as Semitic family.[72]

---

[72] In modern Egypt, Arabic is spoken. Arabic and Hebrew are in the same Semitic language family. The Egyptian language of the time of the Pharaohs was a different language.

A certain amount can be learned about the dating of the Torah by comparing the Hebrew of the Torah to the other Semitic languages of the biblical period. However, more can be learned by comparing Hebrew to the non-Semitic languages of Persian and Egyptian. The reason is that if the Hebrew of the Torah shows influence from a non-Semitic language, it says something about the history of the language and the environment in which it was written. Consequently, some of the best linguistic markers for dating the books of the Old Testament are the presence or absence of loan-words from non-Semitic languages. These loan-words point to cultural interactions and events which can often be dated.

3.3.11.2.1 Absence of Persian Influence in the Torah

The first non-Semitic language to discuss is Persian. There was virtually no interaction between Israel and Persia prior to the Persian conquest of Babylon in 538 B.C. After that, Judah became a province of the Persian Empire. Consequently, we find no Persian loan-words in Hebrew texts written before 538 B.C. After that, a number of Persian loan-words appear in post-exilic books, 35 of which are listed in Table B-1 of Appendix B. There are no Persian words or names in the Torah, and Persia is not mentioned in the Genesis 10 table of nations. In fact, there are no undisputed Persian words in the entire primary history (Genesis through Kings). This is evidence that none of the primary history was written during the Persian period (after 538 B.C.).

3.3.11.2.2 Egyptian-Influenced Linguistics

The second non-Semitic language to discuss is Egyptian. If the story of the captivity in Egypt is true and the Torah was written in the exodus generation, Biblical Hebrew would likely show evidence of being influenced by Egyptian as it was spoken in the second millennium B.C.

In 1933, Abraham S. Yahuda wrote *The Language of the Pentateuch in its Relation to Egyptian,* in which he alleged that an Egyptian background thoroughly colored the language and customs of the Pentateuch. This idea was entirely opposed to the Documentary Hypothesis, but Yahuda was confident: "This conception may not be readily accepted. But the path here indicated will eventually be followed, even if it takes a longer time than could be anticipated."[73] It is clear that if the Torah was written by the exodus generation, then much of its background must be Egyptian. Most of the examples in this section are taken from Yahuda's work. For purposes of brevity, we have omitted most of Yahuda's discussion, as well as his Egyptian text references, and have generally cited only one biblical passage for each word.

Some of the most common Hebrew words that have Semitic language roots appear to have been modified and come to their current form through the influence of Egyptian. These are described below:

1. "Mitzraim" (מצרים), the name for Egypt, is a dual form word in Hebrew, indicating that there are two entities in view. It has long been recognized that this dual form reflects the division of Egypt into upper and lower Egypt. The Egyptians themselves used a word meaning "two lands" or "twin land." All Semitic languages have single, plural and dual forms for nouns, but Hebrew is the only Canaanite dialect that uses a dual form word for Egypt. The Amarna tablets, showing Canaanite correspondence with Egypt, use "mitzri mitzari," a similar, but singular form. This is evidence that "Mitzraim" entered the Hebrew language through Egyptian influence on a Semitic root word during the time of Israel's stay in Egypt.[74] In a related matter, Pharaoh is referred to in the plural (probably actually the dual, since the consonants are the same) in Gen 40:1, when the chief butler and baker sinned against

---

[73] Yahuda, *The Language of the Pentateuch in its Relation to Egyptian*, p. xxxviii
[74] Yahuda, *The Language of the Pentateuch in its Relation to Egyptian*, pp. 25ff

"their lords" the king of Egypt (English translations by ne-
cessity make it singular). The same plural/dual form appears in Gen 42:30, 42:33 and 44:8, applied to Joseph as the
Prime Minister of Egypt. In ancient Egyptian texts, Pharaoh is referred to in dual form, since he was lord of the
"two lands," so the author of the Torah may have adopted
this usage.[75]

2. "Shamayim" (שמים), the word for heaven, is also a dual
    form word in Hebrew, often leaving translators unsure
    whether to use "heaven" or "heavens." While other Se-
    mitic languages have a close cognate word for heaven, He-
    brew is the only language in which it is in dual form. The
    dual conception was familiar to the Egyptians, who envi-
    sioned two heavens, one stretching over the world of the
    living, and a second heaven over the world of the dead.
    "Shamayim," therefore, is likely an original Semitic lan-
    guage word that developed its current Hebrew form dur-
    ing the time of Israel's stay in Egypt.[76]

3. Additional Hebrew words that are sometimes in plural
    form due to Egyptian influence are "chaim" (חיים) for
    "life," and "damim" (דמים), for "blood."[77]

Additional Hebrew vocabulary that apparently is based on
Egyptian includes the following:

1. "Teva" (תבה), the word for ark, is from the Egyptian word
    ḏb3.t meaning box, coffer, or chest. This word is used for
    both Noah's ark and the ark in which baby Moses was
    placed. In both these passages, "teva" is used rather than
    the Canaanite/Hebrew word for boat, "aniyah," (אניה)
    which appears elsewhere in scripture.[78] "Teva" occurs 28

[75] Yahuda, *The Language of the Pentateuch in its Reslation to Egyptian*, p. 14

[76] Yahuda, *The Language of the Pentateuch in its Relation to Egyptian*, pp. 123ff

[77] Yahuda, *The Language of the Pentateuch in its Relation to Egyptian*, p. 194

[78] Yahuda, *The Language of the Pentateuch in its Relation to Egyptian*, p. 205

times in the Bible, only in the Torah, and it appears in passages assigned to both P and J.

2. "Yeor" (יאר), translated as the Nile river, is from the Egyptian *'io'r*.[79] In Biblical Hebrew this word came to mean a great river in general as opposed to a specific name, and was therefore used to also designate the Tigris River in Dan 12:5-7.

3. "Toehva" (תועבה), the word for abomination, is a formation of the Egyptian word *w'b* (ועב).[80]

4. "Hithmahmeah" (התמהמה), the word for "to linger," occurring in Gen 19:16, 43:10 and Exod 12:39, is derived from the Egyptian *myh* (מהא or מהה).[81]

5. "Matsot" (מצות), the word for unleavened bread, is from the Egyptian *ms.t* or *mswt* (feminine), for a sort of bread or cake.[82]

6. "Shesh" (שש), translated "linen" in Gen 41:42 then used 34 more times in the Torah and four times afterward, is a type of Egyptian linen.[83]

7. "Khamushim" (חמשים), for "ranks" in Exod 13:18 and "khashim" (חשים) for "armed" in Num 32:17 are derived from the Egyptian *hmś* (חמש), a word denoting a type of lance or harpoon.[84]

8. "Ephah" (איפה), a grain measure, is from the Egyptian *ip.t*.[85] Other weights and measures derived from Egyptian

---

[79] Brown, Driver and Briggs, *Hebrew and English Lexicon of the Old Testament*, p. 384

[80] Yahuda, *The Language of the Pentateuch in its Relation to Egyptian*, p. 95

[81] Yahuda, *The Language of the Pentateuch in its Relation to Egyptian*, p. 94

[82] Yahuda, *The Language of the Pentateuch in its Relation to Egyptian*, p. 95

[83] Brown, Driver and Briggs, *Hebrew and English Lexicon of the Old Testament*, p. 1059

[84] Yahuda, *The Language of the Pentateuch in its Relation to Egyptian*, p. 96

[85] Yahuda, *The Language of the Pentateuch in its Relation to Egyptian*, p. 271

include zeret (זרת), meaning a span, and "hin" (הין), a liquid measure.[86]

9. "Gome" (גמא), for reeds or papyrus, is understandably an Egyptian loan-word.[87]

10. "Tene" (טנא), for "basket," in Deut 28:17 is from the Egyptian *dny*.[88]

11. "Qemakh" (קמח), for flour or meal in Gen 18:6, is an Egyptian loan-word.[89]

12. "Misheret" (משארת), for "kneading bowl," also used in Deut 28:17, is from the Egyptian *ḫ3r* , also pronounced *š3r* (שאר).[90]

13. "Khemet" (חמת), for "skin of water" in Gen 21:14, is the Egyptian *ḫn.t* for "hide, skin."[91]

14. "Geshem" (גשם), for "rain" in Gen 7:12, is from the Egyptian *gsm*.[92] Note that in addition to this Egyptian loan-word, Hebrew retains a Semitic language word for rain, "matar" (מטר). In later biblical texts, "Geshem" seems to be used for stronger storms while "matar" is used for ordinary rain, though the usage overlaps.

15. "Eytan" (איתן), a word not well understood, used for "normal state" in Exod 14:27, "the sea returned to its normal state," is perhaps from the Egyptian *itn* (אתן), meaning "soil" or "ground." This would render the translation, "the sea returned to its ground."[93]

Egyptian idioms are present in the Torah. An English speaking reader will recognize some of these examples, but not others, as some of the idioms have been translated literally into English

---

[86] Archer, *A Survey of the Old Testament Introduction*, pp. 102-103

[87] Archer, *A Survey of the Old Testament Introduction*, pp. 102-103

[88] Yahuda, *The Language of the Pentateuch in its Relation to Egyptian*, p. 97

[89] Archer, *A Survey of the Old Testament Introduction*, pp. 102-103

[90] Yahuda, *The Language of the Pentateuch in its Relation to Egyptian*, p. 97

[91] Yahuda, *The Language of the Pentateuch in its Relation to Egyptian*, p. 271

[92] Yahuda, *The Language of the Pentateuch in its Relation to Egyptian*, p. 213

[93] Yahuda, *The Language of the Pentateuch in its Relation to Egyptian*, p. 98

while others have been interpreted. The following list contains Egyptian idioms used in the Bible:

1. "Kiss" (נשק) as a synonym for "eat" in Gen 41:40.[94]

2. "Vigorous" (חיות) in Exod 1:19, describing Hebrew women giving birth, is from the Egyptian word ʿw.t, a designation for small cattle, like goats, who give birth quickly. The Hebrew midwives are (falsely) conveying to Pharaoh a contemptuous description of Hebrew women, thereby protecting both themselves and the children.[95]

3. "You have made us odious" or literally "stink" (הבאשתם את ראתנו) in Exod 5:21 is an Egyptian idiom for libel, accuse, or insinuate.[96]

4. "Voices of God" (קולות אלהים), an Egyptian idiom for thunder, appears in Exod 9:28.[97]

5. "Lift up your head" (ישא פרעה את ראשך), used in Gen 40:13 to describe the restoration of Pharaoh's imprisoned butler, is an Egyptian idiom for awakening the dead to life.[98]

6. Gen 48:10 says the eyes of Jacob "were heavy" (כבדו), an Egyptian idiom meaning weak or dim.[99]

7. Exod 10:5 says the locusts would be so thick that they would cover "the surface of the ground" (עין הארץ), literally, the "eye" of the ground. The "eye of the ground" was actually an Egyptian idiom for the sun, so the biblical phrase may mean that the locusts would be so thick that they would block out the sun. This interpretation is

---

[94] Yahuda, *The Language of the Pentateuch in its Relation to Egyptian*, p. 7

[95] Yahuda, *The Language of the Pentateuch in its Relation to Egyptian*, p. 53

[96] Yahuda, *The Language of the Pentateuch in its Relation to Egyptian*, p. 58

[97] Yahuda, *The Language of the Pentateuch in its Relation to Egyptian*, p. 59

[98] Yahuda, *The Language of the Pentateuch in its Relation to Egyptian*, p. 61

[99] Yahuda, *The Language of the Pentateuch in its Relation to Egyptian*, p. 62

strengthened by Exod 10:15, which says that when the locusts came, the land "was darkened."[100]

8. "Mouth" (פי) is an Egyptian idiom for command, a usage reflected in Gen 41:40 and 45:21.[101]

9. The phrases "strong hand" (יד חזקה) and "outstretched arm" (זרוע נטויה), used repeatedly in the Torah, are common Egyptian expressions of strength.[102]

10. When the Egyptian magicians cannot replicate the lice plague, they say, "This is the finger of God" (אצבע אלהים) in Exod 8:19. "The finger of" followed by the name of an Egyptian god was current in Egyptian magical texts.[103]

11. The two words used in the exodus narrative to describe the condition of Pharaoh's heart, "heavy" (כבד), as in Exod 9:7, and "strong" (חזק), as in Exod 7:13, (both "heavy" and "strong" are usually translated as "hardened") are Egyptian idioms. A "heavy heart" means to be stubborn, and a "strong heart," means to be arrogant.[104]

12. The phrase "on this very day" in Exod 12:17, 12:41 and 12:51 has the unusual word "bone" (עצם) in it, translated as "very" or "same." This metaphorical use of "bone" is also present in Egyptian.[105]

13. "Bone of my bones" (עצם מעצמי), from Gen 2:23, has an analogous Egyptian usage.[106]

14. The Biblical simile "as the sand of the sea" (כחול הים), meaning "very many," was common in Egyptian.[107]

---

[100] Yahuda, *The Language of the Pentateuch in its Relation to Egyptian*, p. 62

[101] Yahuda, *The Language of the Pentateuch in its Relation to Egyptian*, p. 64

[102] Yahuda, *The Language of the Pentateuch in its Relation to Egyptian*, p. 66

[103] Yahuda, *The Language of the Pentateuch in its Relation to Egyptian*, p. 66

[104] Yahuda, *The Language of the Pentateuch in its Relation to Egyptian*, p. 68

[105] Yahuda, *The Language of the Pentateuch in its Relation to Egyptian*, p. 70

[106] Yahuda, *The Language of the Pentateuch in its Relation to Egyptian*, p. 277

[107] Yahuda, *The Language of the Pentateuch in its Relation to Egyptian*, p. 76

15. "Living soul" (נפש חיה) or "living creature," as in Gen 1:24, was present in Egyptian, with חיה applying to animals, like the Bible but unlike other Semitic languages.[108]

16. In the flood story, God says "I will blot out man whom I have created" (Gen 6:7, see also Gen 7:4). An Egyptian text preserved in two papyri from the 19th dynasty (1295-1187 B.C.) has the god Atum saying "I will however, blot out everything that I have made." Noteworthy is the common use of "blot out" (מחה), meaning "annihilate, destroy," in both stories.[109]

17. Gen 4:11 says the earth "opened its mouth" (פצתה את פיה) to receive Abel's blood. This picture of the earth opening its mouth has parallels in several Egyptian texts.[110]

The Torah uses Egyptian titles, manners and customs of speech:

1. In Gen 47:9, Jacob appears before Pharaoh and when asked how old he was, says "The years of my sojourning are one hundred and thirty; few and unpleasant have been the years of my life, nor have they attained the years that my fathers lived during the days of their sojourning." This reflects good Egyptian court etiquette, as Jacob, who was certainly much older than Pharaoh, has to assure Pharaoh that his years are "few," since the Egyptians understood Pharaoh to be an immortal endowed with millions of years.[111]

2. In Gen 45:8, the relatively young man Joseph describes himself as a "father to Pharaoh." "Father" was a common Egyptian priestly title, and Pharaoh had given Joseph the daughter of the Priest of On as wife (Gen 41:45).[112]

---

[108] Yahuda, *The Language of the Pentateuch in its Relation to Egyptian*, pp. 138ff

[109] Yahuda, *The Language of the Pentateuch in its Relation to Egyptian*, p. 211

[110] Yahuda, *The Language of the Pentateuch in its Relation to Egyptian*, p. 277

[111] Yahuda, *The Language of the Pentateuch in its Relation to Egyptian*, p. 17

[112] Yahuda, *The Language of the Pentateuch in its Relation to Egyptian*, p. 23

3. In Gen 43:16, 44:1 and 44:4, there is a man described as being the "house steward," with the Hebrew wording "the one who was over the house" (אשר על הבית). This is an Egyptian designation for a high administrative officer.[113]

4. "Sar" (שר) is a word found in both Egyptian and Semitic languages, but in other Semitic languages it means "prince." In Hebrew it is used to mean either a prince or any higher official or dignitary (Gen 39:1, 40:2, etc.). This reflects the Egyptian usage of the word rather than the usage prevalent in Akkadian.[114]

5. In Gen 40:3, the "jail" is literally the "house of Sohar" (בית הסהר). "Sohar" appears in Egyptian New Kingdom inscriptions as the name of a fortress where corrupt officials and notorious criminals were consigned.[115]

6. In the last plague, all the firstborn would die, from the firstborn of Pharaoh to the firstborn of the "slave girl who is behind the millstones" (השפחה אשר אחר הרחים) (Exod 11:5). This phrase appears literally in an Egyptian text, The Wisdom of Ptahhotep.[116]

Certain language features and practices picked up from Egypt remained with the Israelites for some time. More than 400 inscribed stone weights have been found, mostly in Judah, from the eighth and seventh centuries B.C. Shekel weights occur with the values 1, 2, 4, 8, 12, 16, 24 and 40, with the majority carrying a symbol for shekel, followed by a numeral in a system derived from Egyptian hieratic.[117]

Moving in the other direction, certain Canaanite/Hebrew words were picked up by the Egyptian language and used in the New Kingdom period (1550-1070 B.C.). Three of these Canaanite

---

[113] Yahuda, *The Language of the Pentateuch in its Relation to Egyptian*, p. 30

[114] Yahuda, *The Language of the Pentateuch in its Relation to Egyptian*, p. 35

[115] Yahuda, *The Language of the Pentateuch in its Relation to Egyptian*, p. 38

[116] Yahuda, *The Language of the Pentateuch in its Relation to Egyptian*, p. 83

[117] Alan Millard, in Hallo, Ed., *The Context of Scripture*, Vol. II, p. 209

loan-words to Egyptian also appear in the patriarchal stories in Genesis:

1. "Khanikim" (חניכים) is used for "trained men" in Gen 14:14, the only occurrence of this word in the Bible. In Egyptian New Kingdom texts, this word *hnk* appears with the meaning of "confederate, supporter, ally" of a chief leader, and is frequently used to refer to Canaanite or Syrian enemies of Egypt. This is the same meaning as in Genesis 14.

2. "Na'arim" (נערים) is translated as "young men" (the soldiers) in the same story in Gen 14:24. "Na'arim" is a common word in Hebrew, but it usually means "youths," and only in the Genesis 14 passage is it used to apply to soldiers. In Egyptian New Kingdom texts, "na'arim" is used to apply to Asiatic or Canaanite warriors.

3. "Beraka" (ברכה) is translated as "gift" in Gen 33:11. "Berakah" is a common word, but would normally be translated as "blessing," and only here and in a few other older passages does it bear the connotation of "gift." New Kingdom Egyptian also uses "beraka" for gift.[118]

Biblical Hebrew and the Canaanite languages are closely related and could be called dialects of the same language. However, these words give an indication that Biblical Hebrew picked up some Canaanite words from a time period prior to the exodus, and these words were used with their old meanings at the time of the writing of the Torah. We know what the meanings of these words were during the patriarchal period because of the Egyptian texts. "Khanikim" disappears from later use, while "na'arim" and "beraka" in later use mean something different from their initial use in the patriarchal stories.

Finally, there are many Egyptian names in the Torah, giving evidence of its origin in the exodus generation. Some of the

---

[118] Yahuda, *The Language of the Pentateuch in its Relation to Egyptian*, pp. 290ff

Egyptian names are given to Jews. Egyptian names in the Torah include Potipherah, Potiphar, Zaphenath-paneah, Asenath, On, Rameses, Pithom, Moses, Hophni, Phinehas, Putiel and Merari.

In conclusion, it appears that Biblical Hebrew was significantly influenced by the Egyptian language. Furthermore, the Egyptian influence is concentrated most heavily in the Torah, as all the examples in this section involve words or idioms present in the Torah. Some of these words and idioms remained in the Hebrew language throughout later periods, while others seem to have dropped from use. This is evidence that the Torah was largely a product of the exodus generation.

3.3.11.2.3 Pre-Egyptian Linguistics

Some of the names and words used early in Genesis show evidence of a linguistic influence that precedes the period of the exodus. This is best demonstrated by comparing certain Hebrew words to the Akkadian language. These words include:

1. "Hiddekel" (חדקל), the name for the Tigris River used in Gen 2:14, apparently entered the Hebrew language from the early Akkadian form "idiklat," since that is closer to the Hebrew than the later Assyrian form "diklat," and the later Persian word "Tigra."[119]

2. "Casdim" (כשדים) for Chaldeans, first appearing in Gen 11:28, apparently entered the Hebrew language before the 'sd' sound changed to 'ld', a change that took place in the time frame 2000-1500 B.C. when the Sumerian language yielded to Akkadian.[120]

3. "Tehom" (תהום), translated as "the deep" in Gen 1:2, 7:11 and 8:2, is from the Akkadian *tamtum*, the word used in the corresponding Akkadian flood and creation stories.

---

[119] Yahuda, *The Language of the Pentateuch in its Relation to Egyptian*, p. 288
[120] Yahuda, *The Language of the Pentateuch in its Relation to Egyptian*, p. 289

This word is peculiar to Hebrew and Akkadian to the exclusion of the other Semitic languages.[121]

4. "Gopher" (גפר), the type of wood used for Noah's ark in Gen 6:14, is from the Akkadian *giparru*, a kind of tree or reed. Likewise, "kopher" (כפר), for "pitch" in Gen 6:14 is from the Akkadian *kupru*, meaning bitumen.[122]

5. "Barzel" (ברזל), the word for iron in Gen 4:22 etc., is from the Akkadian *parzillu*.[123]

6. "Sepher" (ספר), the word for book, is from the Akkadian word *shipru* or *shapiru*[124]

Names showing Akkadian influence include:
1. Abram, from the Akkadian *Abarama*
2. Nahor, from the Akkadian *Naḫiri* or *Naḫirau*
3. Terah, from the first part of some Akkadian names, such as *Tarḫu-nazi* and *Tarḫu-undaraba*
4. Haran (Gen 11:32) from the Akkadian *Ḫarranu*
5. Serug (Gen 11:21), from the Akkadian *Sarugi*[125]

The most influential language in the ancient Middle East prior to Akkadian was Sumerian. Names showing Sumerian influence include:
1. Lamech, from the Sumerian *Lumgu*[126]
2. Ur (of the Chaldeans) from the Sumerian *uru*, meaning city[127]

One case in which a Genesis story has been widely compared to an Akkadian text is the comparison of the Genesis flood story to the Akkadian Gilgamesh Epic, a Mesopotamian creation and flood story. In both stories, a divine being sets out to destroy humanity

---

[121] Yahuda, *The Language of the Pentateuch in its Relation to Egyptian*, p. 106

[122] Yahuda, *The Language of the Pentateuch in its Relation to Egyptian*, p. 113

[123] Yahuda, *The Language of the Pentateuch in its Relation to Egyptian*, p. 118

[124] Yahuda, *The Language of the Pentateuch in its Relation to Egyptian*, p. 118

[125] Yahuda, *The Language of the Pentateuch in its Relation to Egyptian*, pp. 287ff

[126] Yahuda, *The Language of the Pentateuch in its Relation to Egyptian*, p. 287

[127] Yahuda, *The Language of the Pentateuch in its Relation to Egyptian*, p. 288

by means of a flood, but one man is saved by building a ship and floating it out. A similar Akkadian flood story also occurs in the Atrahasis Epic. Both the Atrahasis and Gilgamesh stories were likely written before Abraham came to Canaan, and numerous parallels can be drawn between the stories, implying a single common origin for these stories. However, although the stories are obviously related and a few linguistic connections exist (as in "gopher" wood described above), linguistic features on the whole in the Genesis creation/flood stories do not match Akkadian.[128] The reason can be understood: Although the Genesis flood story may have originally been written in Akkadian, most linguistic similarities were washed out when it was translated into an Egyptian-influenced Hebrew.

3.3.11.3 Antiquity of the Hebrew

Several words and word forms used in the Torah appear to be archaic, appearing only in older biblical passages. In the examples below, we point out that in addition to being archaic, some of these words span the alleged Documentary Hypothesis sources. These words include:

1. The Hebrew third person feminine singular pronoun "hie" (היא), translated "she" or "her" when referring to people and "it" or "that" when referring to a feminine gender object, is used 541 times in the Bible. However, it is used only 11 times in the Torah. Instead, the Torah usually lets the third person masculine pronoun "hue" (הוא) serve double duty as both masculine and feminine. This is sufficiently different from known Hebrew language usage that the Masoretes provide a "qire" vowel reading of הִוא (a dot is under the first letter, representing a vowel) to distinguish between feminine and masculine pronouns.[129] This irregu-

---

[128] Yahuda, *The Language of the Pentateuch in its Relation to Egyptian*, pp. 106ff
[129] A "qire" reading is an indication that the word should be read differently from what is written, and usually is in the form of a marginal note.

lar (הוּא) usage is found 53 times in Genesis, 11 times in Exodus, 46 times in Leviticus, 24 times in Numbers, 34 times in Deuteronomy, and nowhere else in the Bible. Broken down by sources, it appears 33 times in J, 12 times in E, 33 times in D, 55 times in P, 20 times in the Holiness Code and 12 times in passages that are unassigned or given to the redactor. The usage immediately switches beginning in Joshua, where "hie" is used 31 times. According to the Documentary Hypothesis this would mean that all the sources used "hue" up through Deuteronomy, then they all switched to "hie" simultaneously beginning in Joshua.[130] For reasons explained in Appendix B, we believe this is not so much an argument for a very early date for the Torah, but it is a good argument against the Documentary Hypothesis and in favor of the literary unity of the Torah.

2. "Ha'el" (האל), meaning "these" with a definite article, is used only in the Torah, instead of the usual "ha'eleh" (האלה), which is also used in the Torah and elsewhere in the Bible. "Ha'el" appears in Gen 19:8, 19:25, 26:3, 26:4, Lev 18:27, Deut 4:42, 7:22 and 19:11.

---

[130] Continuing on the lines of third person singular gender, the Torah uses the word "na'ar" (נער) 20 times for young woman, instead of "na'arah" (נערה) which is used just once in the Torah (Deut. 22:19), but 63 times elsewhere in the Bible. Also, the use of the Hebrew "-h" instead of "-w" for third masculine singular suffixes is reflected in unique usage in the Torah, such as "ahaloh" (אהלה) for "his" tent four times, but only early in Genesis. The "-h" suffix usage apparently occurs again in Gen 49:10-11, "Shiloh", and "'irah" for "his donkey". Going the opposite way is Gen 38:2, where "shemo" has to be translated "her name" instead of the usual "his name". However, we are not offering these examples as evidence of the antiquity of the Torah, since the usage of vowel suffixes shown in these examples is found in Hebrew inscriptions from as late as the Lachish letters of 587 B.C. It appears that the scribes who copied the Bible were more conservative in their efforts to copy the Torah than in their work on other books. They preserved this archaic feature in the Torah, but updated the language in the other books.

3. The Torah shows a preference for listing Abraham, Isaac and Jacob all together, while the prophets and writings tend to list only Jacob. Beginning in Exodus, after all three patriarchs are dead, the three are listed together 15 times in the Torah, while Jacob is listed alone 13 times. In the prophets and writings, the three patriarchs are listed together eight times, with Jacob listed alone 145 times. The Abraham, Isaac and Jacob group is found in J, E, P, D and the Holiness Code. With a unified Torah, this is easy to explain – the author wants to emphasize that the God of the exodus, the Lawgiver, is the same as the God of the nation's patriarchs. With the Documentary Hypothesis assumption that the sources were written much later during the time of the prophets, that explanation is weaker. In the prophets and writings, Jacob is usually listed alone because his sons become the nation of Israel, while Isaac and Abraham had other children who are outside of Israel.

4. The Torah uses the dual form of the noun to say two cubits (Exod 25:10, 25:17, 25:23, 37:1, 37:6, 37:10, 30:2), two years (Gen 11:10, 45:6), two weeks (Lev 12:5), two days (Exod 16:29, Num 9:22, 11:19), two times (Gen 27:36, 41:32, 43:10, Num 20:11), and two kinds (Lev 19:19, Deut 22:9). This usage of the dual begins to drop out of Hebrew prior to the exile in favor of the "two + plural" form (1 Sam 13:1, etc). This is described further in Appendix B, section B.3.4.

5. In Gen 11:30 "walad" (ולד) is used instead of the usual yeled (ילד) for child. This is the only appearance of "walad" in the Bible. This is probably reflective of a larger shift from "waw" to "yodh" that took place early in Hebrew, as also the usual "diyn" (דין) for "strive" is "dun" (דון) in Gen 6:3, and the name of Eve (חוה) is supposed to mean "life" (חיה) based on Gen 3:20.

6. In Gen 24:65 and 37:19, "hallazeh" (הלזה) is used as a demonstrative pronoun (translated "this" or "that"), a usage not seen after Genesis.

7. The scapegoat in Lev 16:10 and 16:26 is in Hebrew the goat "to azazel" (לעזאזל). The meaning of "azazel" is obscure, probably because it was an archaic word which passed out of use. A longer discussion on the azazel goat is in section 6.1.

8. Gen 37:25 uses "lot" (לט) for "myrrh," rather than the word "mor" (מר) which is used in all biblical passages after the Torah.

9. "Kesev" (כשב), the word for lamb, and "kisbah" (כשבה), for ewe lamb, are used 14 times in the Torah, appearing in J/E (Gen 30:32-40), P (Lev 3:7) and D (Deut 14:4). These words do not appear outside the Torah. The more common word for lamb with transposed consonants "keves" (כבש) appears 115 times in the Bible, both in the Torah and elsewhere.

10. "Tsakhaq" (צחק) is the only word for laugh in the Torah, appearing 11 times including passages in J (Gen 18:13), E (Gen 21:9) and P (Gen 17:17). This form does not disappear completely, perhaps because it was used to form the name of Isaac, and it appears twice more outside the Torah, in Judg 16:25 and Ezek 23:32. The later form of the word for laugh, "sakhaq" (שחק), appears 52 times, all outside the Torah.

11. "Mabbul" (מבול), the word used to describe the flood of Noah, occurs 12 times in the Torah and once in Ps 29:10. "Mabbul" occurs in both P and J.

12. "Sheretz" (שרץ), the word for swarming things, occurs 15 times in the Bible, all in the Torah. It appears in P, D, and the Holiness Code section of Leviticus.

13. "Tsur" (צור), meaning rock but used as a designation for God, occurs in the Bible primarily in older poetry. It occurs

eight times in Moses' song in Deuteronomy 32. Four Israelite names use "tsur" as part of their name in the Torah: Elizur (Num 1:5), Zurishaddai (Num 1:6), Pedahzur (Num 1:10) and Zuriel (Num 3:35). The phenomenon of "tsur" names among Israelites does not occur after the second millennium B.C. Apparently, "tsur" was also used as a designation for deity in the Midianite culture, as it appears in Midianite names (Num 25:15, 31:8 and Josh 13:21).

14. The older word for kingdom, "mamlakah" (ממלכה), is used 9 times in the Torah. The later word, "malkut" (מלכות), occurs only in Num 24:7, in Balaam's prophecy – a special case because Balaam's prophecy probably comes from the mouth of a non-Hebrew speaker. "Mamlakah" appears in all Documentary Hypothesis sources (the P appearances are in Joshua 13).

15. The Torah follows the guidelines of older Biblical Hebrew in the use of the pronouns "ani" and "anoki." The 127 occurrences of "anoki" are an indicator of age (the companion "ani" occurs 153 times). Source critics have noted that "anoki" is rare in passages attributed to P, but this is due to frequent use of a few formulaic expressions that always use "ani" in any source, particularly "ani YHWH" ("I am the LORD"). There are no instances in the Torah where "ani" is followed by an adjective, a feature common in Late Biblical Hebrew (for example, "I was naked" in Gen 3:10 uses "anoki," whereas "I am dark, but lovely" in the later Song 1:5 uses "ani").

16. There are some words in the Torah that the translators of the Septuagint didn't know how to translate, and they therefore just transliterated them. These include: "erabon" (ערבון) for pledge in Gen 38:17-18 and "kivrat" (כברת) for "a distance" in Gen 48:7. This implies that the language of the Torah was sometimes too old for the translators of the Septuagint, who worked around 250 B.C., to handle.

17. Torah Hebrew frequently uses anthropomorphisms applied to God. God walks (Gen 3:8, Lev 26:12 and Deut 23:14 [23:15 Heb]), smells (Gen 8:21 and Lev 26:31) and has a hand, face and back (Exod 33:22-23). Such anthropomorphisms are avoided in later writings (compare the later Ezek 37:27 with Lev 26:11-12).

3.3.11.4 Early Poems

There are several long poems in the Torah: the Blessing of Jacob in Genesis 49, the Song of Moses in Exodus 15, the Oracles of Balaam in Numbers 23-24, the Song of Moses in Deuteronomy 32 and the Blessing of Moses in Deuteronomy 33. These poems exhibit early linguistic features beyond what is evident in the prose portions of the Torah and should be understood to reflect, to a certain extent, Early Biblical Hebrew rather than Classical Biblical Hebrew. Some of the common features of Classical Biblical Hebrew, such as definite articles, direct object markers and the relative pronoun "asher" are rare or nonexistent in these early poems. These poems are generously filled with rare vocabulary which is probably archaic. Other early features in these poems include:

1. The use of imperfect form verbs for what appear to be completed past tense references (Exod 15:5, 15:7, 15:12, Deut 32:8, 32:10, 32:13, 32:16-17, 32:38, etc.), a feature common in early poetry, rare in other poetry, and nonexistent in prose.

2. Deut 32:13 and 33:29 use the term "high places" (במות) in a positive sense, as opposed to later writings which use it in an entirely negative sense as a place of corrupted worship.

3. An early relative pronoun "zu" (זו), apparently meaning "this" people, is in Exod 15:13 and 15:16. "Zu" occurs 14 times in the OT, primarily in old poetry, and does not occur in any indisputably exilic or post-exilic text.

4. Use of the older "mo" (מו) suffixes to indicate third person plural (Deut 32:27, 32:32, 32:35, 32:38, 33:2 and 33:29)

5. The use of "Rock" (צור) as a designation for God (Deut 32:4, 32:15, 32:18, 32:31 and 32:37)

6. Deut 32:7 uses a feminine plural for "days," whereas in later Biblical Hebrew this is a masculine noun.

7. Deut 32:15 and 32:17 use the mostly older name for God, "Eloah," apparently a singular form of Elohim (v17).

8. Gen 49:25, Num 24:4 and 24:16 all use "Shaddai" for God, and Deut 32:17 is the only passage in the Bible that makes a plural form of "Shaddai."

It has been an almost unchallenged tenant of modern critical study of the Bible that early poetry is encased in much later prose accounts. Due to linguistics, source critics often acknowledge the antiquity of some or all of Genesis 49, Exodus 15 and Deuteronomy 32, considering them to be older than the surrounding prose text. The thinking, then, is that either the final compiler of the Torah, or one of the sources, was aware of these poems from either an ancient oral or written tradition, and used them to supplement his account.

Although this is plausible in theory, a person not already indoctrinated with this idea might be suspicious of it. It certainly is not a pattern that is always true. The latter prophets frequently mix prose and poetry, and both are usually dated at the same time. When we read Tolkien, no one would think that the poetry embedded inside the narrative is older than the narrative around it, despite linguistic differences more pronounced than those in the Bible. In works outside of the Bible that combine both poetry and prose, it is not normal to date the poetry older than the prose. An equally reasonable assumption is that the early poetry represents the real antiquity of the text, and that the prose has been somewhat updated by the scribes, masking out the most archaic features. The scribes would not update the poetry as much, since changing poetry in such a manner detracts from its style. Also, if a poem is a popular song, any changes to it would likely be rejected by the community.

3.3.3.5 Spelling

The trend in the Hebrew language was to use more vowel letters as time progressed; early Hebrew used few to no vowel letters, while later Hebrew used many. Spelling in the Torah is by far the oldest in the Bible (See Table B-2 in Appendix B). The usefulness of this spelling data is limited, since no biblical passage, including even the earliest poems, reflects a spelling pattern earlier than about 600 B.C. – the pre-exilic scribes apparently were in the habit of updating spelling when they copied the scriptures. However, spelling can be used to help distinguish between pre-exilic and post-exilic writings, as the later writings use more vowel letters. The P source is purportedly well into the post-exilic period, but Anderson and Forbes conclude based on their study of Hebrew spelling, "…the P source shows no marked tendency to post-exilic practice. If anything, P is more conservative than the others and quite out of line with post-exilic compositions."[131]

3.4 Oldest Texts

A silver amulet with Numbers 6:24-26, mentioned in section 3.2.2.1.4, has been dated to 600 B.C. Other than that, the oldest texts of the Torah are from the Dead Sea Scrolls. They are distributed as follows:

    Genesis - 15 scrolls
    Exodus – 17 scrolls
    Leviticus – 13 scrolls
    Numbers – 8 scrolls
    Deuteronomy – 29 scrolls

The Dead Sea Scrolls include fragments of a Targum (Aramaic translation) of Leviticus (scroll 4Q156) dated to the second century B.C., 21 tefillin (phylacteries) containing short Torah passages (4Q128-148) and eight mezuzot (parchments for the doorpost of a

---

[131] Anderson and Forbes, *Spelling in the Hebrew Bible*, pp. 190-191

house) with short Torah passages (4Q149-155 and 8Q4). The Dead Sea Scrolls also include commentaries and works based on the Torah. These include the Genesis Apocryphon (1QapGen, 1Q20, 4Q537 and 4Q538) and numerous works related to various characters in the Torah. There is a Greek language paraphrase on Exodus (4Q127) and on the Torah (4Q364-367). Books of the Torah are treated as authorities by numerous extra-biblical Dead Sea Scrolls.

3.5 Conclusion

The Torah was written largely by the generation involved in the exodus from Egypt, around 1400 B.C. For Genesis 1-37, earlier written source material was used, in a language somewhat different from the Hebrew found in the rest of the Old Testament. For this reason, the Hebrew text of Genesis 1-37 as we have it today can be regarded as a translation. Minor revisions of the Torah were made up until about the time of the David.

CHAPTER 4

Dating the Prophets

4.1 Former Prophets

The former prophets consist of the books of Joshua, Judges, 1 and 2 Samuel and 1 and 2 Kings. They describe Israel's history from the conquest of Canaan up through the Babylonian captivity, a period stretching from about 1406 to shortly after 586 B.C. 1 and 2 Samuel were originally one book, and 1 and 2 Kings were also originally one book.

Source critics connect Joshua with the Torah, using the same J, E, D and P sources, producing a "hexateuch." However, there is no critical consensus on the authorship of Judges through Kings. Some source critics detect traces of J, E, D and P in these books too, but this idea is not widely accepted. The only point on which there is general agreement is that all these books view Israel's history through the lens of Deuteronomy. The traditional viewpoint assigns authorship of the former prophets to Joshua, Samuel and other individuals near in time to the events being described. The traditional viewpoint notes the emphasis of the authority of prophets over the nation and its rulers – hence the term, "former prophets."

The former prophets record events in mostly chronological order. However, the transition between books is not seamless. Judges recapitulates some of the events in Joshua. Samuel starts near the end of the period of the judges, but is not connected anywhere to the sequence of the judges. On the other hand, the transition from Samuel to Kings is smooth, perhaps reflecting the influence of a single hand in the final compilation of those books. The former prophets are selective in the events they record, sometimes omitting events which did not fit their spiritual purpose. For instance, they do not record the major earthquake in the days of King Uzziah (Amos 1:1 and Zech 14:5), or how it came to be that Shiloh, the early home of the tabernacle, was abandoned or destroyed (Ps 78:60, Jer 7:12-14 and 26:6-9).

4.1.1 Joshua

The book of Joshua is set immediately after the death of Moses and covers a period of less than one generation. It describes the crossing of the Jordan River by the Israelites, a series of successful military campaigns led by Joshua, an allotment of land to each of the tribes of Israel, and a reaffirmation of the covenant with the LORD.

The traditional viewpoint on the origin of Joshua is that it was written by Joshua himself, during his lifetime, with a short epilogue added after his death (Josh 24:29-33). The idea that Joshua is the author finds some internal support from Josh 24:25-26, "So Joshua made a covenant with the people that day, and made for them a statute and an ordinance in Shechem. And Joshua wrote these words in the book of the law of God; and he took a large stone and set it up there under the oak that was by the sanctuary of the LORD." Several later biblical passages mention Joshua, but shed little further light on the date or authorship of the book. In the other early history books, Joshua figures prominently in Judges 1-2 and gets one mention in 1 Kgs 16:34, indicating that the authors of those books were familiar with him.

The Talmud states that Joshua wrote the book of Joshua, except for Josh 24:29-33, which was added by the priests Eleazar and Phinehas.[1]

Most source critics attribute authorship of Joshua to the same sources (J, E, D and P) that they believe are present in the Torah. The arguments already offered against the Documentary Hypothesis in the Torah largely apply also to Joshua. Furthermore, Joshua was understood from antiquity to be a separate work from

---

[1] Baba Bathra 15a

the Torah; Joshua was never included with it. Unlike the Torah, which is full of laws, no laws are codified in Joshua, showing Joshua to be a different type of work than the Torah.

4.1.1.1 Internal Evidence

The following passages in Joshua describe circumstances continuing "to this day," that is, the day the passage was written:

4:9 standing stones remain in the Jordan River

5:9 location is named Gilgal

6:25 Rahab still alive

7:26 heap of stones remains over Achan's grave

8:28 Ai desolate

8:29 heap of stones remains over the king of Ai's grave

9:27 Gibeonites hew wood and draw water

13:13 Geshurites and Maacathites remain

14:14 Hebron belongs to Caleb

15:63 Jebusites in Jerusalem

16:10 Canaanites in Gezer

Several of these passages are instructive, and point to an early date. Josh 9:27 has the Gibeonites doing menial service for the altar of the LORD, a situation that could not have continued past the time of Saul at the latest, based on 2 Sam 21:1. This dates the passage before 1000 B.C. Josh 15:63 says Jebusites live at Jerusalem, probably indicating that the book was written before David conquered Jerusalem and made it his capital. This also dates the book prior to 1000 B.C. The statement in 16:10 that the Canaanites live in Gezer requires a date before Pharaoh killed all the Canaanites there and gave it to Solomon as a dowry when Solomon married Pharaoh's daughter (1 Kgs 9:16). The two verses arguing most specifically for an early date are 14:14 and 16:25, which intimate that Caleb and Rahab, respectively, are still alive. This would make the writing of the book a contemporary record of the events it describes. Even the less specific verses about stones remaining in a place generally favor an earlier date, since the meaning of a pile of stones is not something likely to be recalled for hundreds of years.

Other political references point in a subtle way to an early date. Sidon is still supreme in Lebanon (Josh 11:8, 13:4-6 and 19:28), and the inhabitants of Lebanon are considered enemies. By the time of David and afterward, Tyre had passed Sidon in importance in Lebanon and was on such friendly terms with Israel that they helped build Solomon's temple. The political structure of Canaan, with 32 kings west of the Jordan, reflects the tiny city-state structure present in Joshua's day – not later. The Philistines receive only a passing mention in Josh 13:2-3; they obviously are not a major menace yet, as they would become as early as the time of the judges. Still, mention of the Philistines is problematic, as most historians date their arrival in Canaan to about 1190 B.C., based on their interaction with the Egyptian 19th dynasty. This would be after the time of Joshua, and 13:2-3 shows no sign of being a later addition or an update to a geographical reference. As we indicated in chapter 2, a very accurate chronology of events in the second millennium B.C. is somewhat beyond our grasp, so we will allow the difficulty to stand for now.

Progress in occupying and settling the land is discussed almost not at all in Joshua, a fact that is often lost to the modern reader due to the triumphant tone of the book. When the Israelites cross the Jordan River, they set up a base camp at Gilgal (4:19). The book continues throughout to describe a camp setting for Israel rather than a setting of a settled people. After the battle of Jericho, they destroy Jericho and do not occupy it, but return to the camp at Gilgal. Likewise, they destroy Ai, with no occupation (8:28) and return to Gilgal. Even after the major victories in chapters 10-12, the Israelites still are based in Gilgal (14:6), with an allocation of the land not performed until after completion of the military campaign. As is the case in some modern wars, the initial military victory proves to be accomplished more easily than the occupation that follows. This is nowhere more clear than in the case with the tribe of Dan, which is allocated land in central Israel (19:40-48). As time went on, the Dan tribe was not able to settle the area, and they moved instead to the far north of the country (Judges 18). However, the book of Joshua leaves the Dan tribe in the "wrong" place, knowing nothing about their future migration. This points to a date for the book of Joshua prior to the Dan migration that occurred in the period of the Judges. Gilgal remains prominent in Israel's history up through the time of Hosea (Hos 4:15, 9:15 and 12:11) and Amos (4:4 and 5:5), then disappears from the scene, probably as a result of the Assyrian conquest of the northern Kingdom of Israel.[2]

The book of Joshua contains old Canaanite place names with later better-known names sometimes placed alongside in a parenthetical manner. These include Baalah / Kiriath-jearim (15:9), Mount Jearim / Chesalon (15:10), Kiriath-arba / Hebron (15:13), Kiriath-hezron / Hazor (15:25), Kiriath-sannah / Debir (15:49), Kiriath-baal / Kiriath-jearim (15:60) and "the Jebusite" / Jerusalem (15:8, 18:28). It is unlikely that an Israelite writer from the kingdom period onward would refer to Jerusalem by an old Canaanite name, as occurs in 15:8 and 18:28. These names point to an early date for the book, with later geographical names inserted by scribes in the copying process, to make the text understandable.

In Josh 5:6, the narrator makes a one-time slip from a third person perspective to first person, mentioning the land the LORD would give "to us."[3] This first person reference supports the idea that the words were written by someone who participated in the events. Joshua himself is a reasonable candidate for authorship of the book, since he would be knowledgeable of almost all the events described in the book, and some events (Josh 5:13-15) relate

---

[2] It is possible (but by no means certain) that more than one city in Israel was named Gilgal

[3] Actually, this occurs also in 5:1 also in the "kethiv" (the written text), where it reads "we crossed over" the Jordan. The "qire" (the Masoretic scribe's margin note) modifies this to read "they crossed over".

only to him. There is no clear evidence of the use of extra sources in Joshua. The book of Joshua does make mention of the "book of Jashar" in Josh 10:13 (see also 2 Sam 1:18), but there is no indication it was used as a source for Joshua.

Some writers have felt it necessary to move the writing of Joshua well down in time, distant from the events described, due to the sweeping success and idealism present in much of the book. However, other ancient Middle Eastern war reports written by the victors immediately after their campaigns show similar records of sweeping successes, and, like Joshua, attribute the successes to the involvement of their gods. Numerous examples exist, ranging from Egyptian inscriptions such as the Merneptah Stele from the 13th century B.C., which gives a lengthy list of victories, to the Moabite record of victory over Israel in the Mesha Stele in the ninth century B.C., which gives credit to the Moabite god Chemosh. It would not be unusual in an ancient Middle Eastern culture to find that Israel had written a contemporary record, the book of Joshua, to celebrate their entry into Canaan. On the contrary, it would be unusual if they had not.

One passage that could be used to support a later date in the divided kingdom time frame is Josh 11:21-22, "Then Joshua came at that time and cut off the Anakim from the hill country, from Hebron, from Debir, from Anab and from all the hill country of Judah and from all the hill country of Israel. Joshua utterly destroyed them with their cities. There were no Anakim left in the land of the sons of Israel; only in Gaza, in Gath, and in Ashdod some remained." The use of the words "Judah" and "Israel" in the same verse usually points to a divided kingdom viewpoint. It is possible, however, that this verse is an exception to the rule. The verse focuses on the tribe of Judah, since most of the Anakim were inside territory allotted to Judah. It then expands to the rest of Israel, since a few of the Anakim might be outside Judah's territory but within Israel's territory. The next verse says that the only remaining Anakim were outside all of Israel's territory. The passage starts from a central point (Judah's territory) and expands outward, so it could understand Judah to be a subset of Israel, as it was in Joshua's period, rather than a counterpart to it as it became later.

The Josh 13:30 mention of Jair appears to be a later insertion based on Judg 10:3-4. This same mention of Jair is also inserted into Num 32:41. The mention of Othniel in Josh 15:17 is not necessarily a later insertion. Othniel is Israel's first judge (Judg 3:9), who delivered Israel after 8 years of oppression (Judg 3:8). The time frame is small enough for the same Othniel to capture Kiriath-sepher (Josh 15:16-17) as a younger man and then to serve as the first judge some years later. The account of the death of Joshua and Eleazar along with the reburial of Joseph (Josh 24:29-33) appears to be a later addition used to give the book a fitting ending.

4.1.1.2 External Dependencies – Inputs

Although we have argued that Joshua is separate from the Torah, Joshua is clearly dependent on it, and is written in such a way as to make a smooth transition from the end of Deuteronomy to the beginning of Joshua. Especially noteworthy is the charge in Deuteronomy 31, given three times, to be "strong and courageous" (Deut 31:6, 31:7 and 31:23). This charge is repeated in Joshua 1 four times (Josh 1:6, 1:7, 1:9, 1:18 and then again in 10:25). The author of Joshua had the material from Deuteronomy available to him. Joshua references "the book of the law" in Josh 1:8, 8:31, 8:34 and 23:6. The renewal of the covenant on Mount Ebal described in Josh 8:31-35 is based on the command of Deut 27:4-8, but more than just Deuteronomy is in view, as the phrase in Josh 8:31, "an altar of uncut stones on which no man had wielded an iron tool," is dependent on Exod 20:25, "If you make an altar of stone for Me, you shall not build it of cut stones, for if you wield your tool on it, you will profane it." Josh 17:3-4, dealing with the daughters of Zelophehad, completes a story that started in Num 27:1-11.

4.1.1.3 External Dependencies - Outputs

The passage in Judg 1:12-15 about Caleb's inheritance is taken from Josh 15:16-19, and Judg 2:6-9, about the death of Joshua, is a repeat of Josh 24:28-31. Later books show knowledge of the stories of Joshua, but do not tend to quote from it. Examples include David knowing about the Gibeonites in Joshua 9 (2 Sam 21:1), Micah knowing about Israel's crossing to Gilgal (Mic 6:5), and most specifically, the author of Kings knowing about Joshua's curse on Jericho (Josh 6:26 and 1 Kgs 16:34).

4.1.1.4 Linguistic Analysis

The linguistic features in Joshua support an early date for the book, although Joshua does not show the many archaic characteristics that are present in the Torah. The use of הוא as a third person singular feminine pronoun, occurring 168 times in the Torah, does not occur at all in Joshua, which instead uses היא all 31 times when such a pronoun is needed. This usage continues throughout the rest of the Bible. Joshua has a much different spelling pattern than any book in the Torah, as evidenced by Table B-2 in Appendix B.

The expression מזה, literally "from this," is used to mean "here" in 4:3. This expression is common in pre-exilic texts but does not make it into post-exilic texts, which instead use מקום.

Like the Torah, there are no Yahwistic names in Joshua. Some of the names of Canaanite kings, such as Adoni-zedek ("my lord is righteous" in 10:1), make good sense in Hebrew, showing the close relationship between the Hebrew language and the language of the Canaanites.

There are no Persian or Greek words in Joshua. The early pronoun "anoki" is used seven times. The older form of the word for kingdom, "mamlakah," is used five times, while its later variant "malkut" is not used. "Ehdah" (עדה), a mostly pre-exilic word meaning "congregation," is in 9:15, 9:18, 18:1, 22:12 and 22:16-20. "Zulah" (זולה), meaning "except" in 11:13, appears almost exclusively in pre-exilic texts.

4.1.1.5 Oldest Texts

The oldest texts of Joshua are two Dead Sea Scrolls: 4Q47 and 4Q48. Portions of eight chapters are represented. In addition, a copy of Joshua was found at Masada dated from 169-93 B.C. by mass spectrometer radiocarbon dating.[4] It is a paraphrase of Joshua 23-24. The Dead Sea Scrolls also contain two copies of the Apocryphon of Joshua, an extra-biblical work related to Joshua (4Q378-379) and the Testimonia (4Q175 lines 21-23), an extra-biblical work that references Joshua as authoritative.

4.1.1.6 Conclusion

The book of Joshua was written in large part close to the time of the events it records, placing the book at about 1385 B.C. Certain additions were made later, including the account of Joshua's death in 24:29-33 and the mention of Jair in Josh 13:30.

4.1.2 Judges

The book of Judges is set immediately after the death of Joshua and covers a period of several hundred years. It describes a repeating downward spiral in which the Israelites first depart from following YHWH, then they are oppressed by a foreign power, they cry out to YHWH, they are delivered by a judge, and then they have rest for a while. Twelve judges are named but only five are described in any detail. Judges ends with two depressing stories about the northern migration of the tribe of Dan and a civil war between the tribe of Benjamin and the other tribes.

---

[4] VanderKam, *The Dead Sea Scrolls Today*, p.18

Some conservative traditions have held Samuel to be the author of Judges, placing the writing in the eleventh century B.C. Other source critics have pulled the date of writing all the way down to the Babylonian exile, after 586 B.C.

We believe there are three sections of the book, which can be dated to different periods. These sections can be divided as follows:

Section 1 – Judg 1:1-2:5
Section 2 – Judg 2:6-chapter 16
Section 3 – Judges chapters 17-21.

Although there is a possibility that these three sections came from different sources, we should clarify that the use of these sources is in no way similar to the alleged use of sources in the Torah, an idea which we have rejected. The sections/sources in Judges are not woven together like a tapestry or scrambled like an omelet, but laid naturally end to end to form a complete book. The books of Samuel and Kings will make similar use of sources.

4.1.2.1 Internal Evidence
4.1.2.1.1 Third Section of Judges

We will deal with the third and last section of the book first, since the author of the third section was responsible for putting the book into its essentially final form, and arranged the first two sections to meet his purposes. This section of Judges contains two stories, the first describing events leading to the migration of the Dan tribe to the north (Judges 17-18), and the second describing events leading to a civil war that almost wiped out the tribe of Benjamin (Judges 19-21).

In the third section of the book, the author of Judges uses the phrase "in those days" seven times (17:6, 18:1 twice, 19:1, 20:27-28 and 21:25). This phrase occurs only in the third of the three sections of the book. Each time he uses this phrase he is drawing an implicit comparison between "those days" and "this day" – the author's day. The comparison can be summarized as follows:

Verses	Those Days	This Day
17:6	No king in Israel, lawlessness	King in Israel
18:1	No king in Israel	King in Israel
18:1	Dan tribe not settled	Dan settled in the north
19:1	No king in Israel	King in Israel
20:27	Ark at Bethel	Ark not at Bethel
20:28	Phinehas is high priest	Phinehas is not high priest
21:25	No king in Israel, lawlessness	King in Israel

These verses imply that the author's day is during the time of the united monarchy, when there is a king in the land, a situation the author believes is better than the situation of the Judges. This is not the perspective of Samuel (1 Sam 8:6-22), so this is an argument against the traditional view that Samuel is the author of Judges. The story of the Dan tribe's migration argues in favor of the united monarchy date rather than the divided monarchy, since Dan went with the northern tribes. Also arguing in favor of a united monarchy date is the terminology "king in Israel" as opposed to "in Judah." The phrase "everyone did what was right in his own eyes" (17:6 and 21:25) contrasts better with Solomon's rule than David's or Saul's, since government control peaked under Solomon. The stories in the third section of Judges are revolting in nature, with little redeeming value. This is intentional on the part of the author, as he intends to paint the time of the Judges as a dark age in Israel's history, compared with the more enlightened period of the monarchy.

Judg 18:30 uses a phrase about the Dan tribe's priests continuing "until the day of the captivity of the land." Some writers have suggested that this phrase points to a composition after the Assyrian captivity in 722 B.C. Out of context, this suggestion would have merit, but the pro-monarchy viewpoint of the story (17:6, 18:1) points to an earlier date. The next verse, 18:31, speaks of the time period in which the tabernacle was at Shiloh. Shiloh was eventually destroyed, apparently by the Philistines, so "captivity of the land" probably refers to an earlier experience, such as the Philistine period of dominance. For that matter, a one letter change would alter "captivity of the land" to "captivity of the ark," which would indicate that the events of 1 Samuel 4-5 are in view.

The third section of Judges does not follow the second section chronologically. Phinehas, the son of Eleazar and grandson of Aaron, is still the high priest (20:28), so the events of Judges 19-21 are not more than one generation removed from the entry into the land of Canaan.

4.1.2.1.2 Second Section of Judges

The second section of Judges consists of Judg 2:6 through chapter 16. This is the section that gives the book its name, as all the judges appear in this section. The author of the third section of Judges apparently shaped this section of Judges as well (though he likely was not the one who first penned these stories), since in the story of every major judge he includes some element that is grotesque and revolting (King Eglon's fat covering Ehud's knife hilt after he was stabbed, Jael driving a tent peg through Sisera's head while he slept, Jephthah sacrificing his daughter, etc.). This is in keeping with the desire of the author to depict the era of the judges as a dark age in Israel's history. This section of Judges is the first scripture passage to mention the "Baals" (2:11, 3:7, 8:33, 10:6 and 10:10) and is also the first text to give an indication that Canaanite idolatry would be a chronic temptation for the pre-exilic Israelites.

Nevertheless, the second section of Judges stands on its own as a literary unity, apart from the rest of the book. Judg 2:6 could be considered as a starting point for the book and used as a transition from the end of Joshua. The second section in its entirety has an *inclusio* format, meaning that there is a center (Gideon makes an

Ephod in Judg 8:22-28), and on either side of the center the same types of things happen:

1. Shamgar kills Philistines with an ox goad (3:31), Samson kills Philistines with a donkey's jawbone (15:15-17)
2. Transjordan oppression from the descendants of Lot (3:12-14 and 10:6-9)
3. A military leader gets killed by a woman (4:21 and 9:53)
4. Fighting with a tower (8:17 and 9:46-49)
5. Ephraimites harshly complain about not being called to the fight (8:1 and 12:1)

This second section of Judges includes chronological information adding up to 410 years (see Table 2.7 for a Judges chronology). Although some of the careers of judges may have overlapped, the indication is still that the middle section was written no earlier than what is essentially the end of the time of the judges. The Philistines are well entrenched by the time of the last major judge, Samson, and conflict with the Philistines continues into the book of Samuel.

The Song of Deborah in Judges 5 is an old song included in this section of Judges, probably written at the time of the event. In this song, the LORD comes from Mt. Seir, not from his temple, in 5:4. The song lists eight tribes of Israel, leaving out Levi and the too far south tribes of Judah and Simeon, while making the curious substitution of Machir, the son of Manasseh, for his father. The Dan tribe in 5:17 is in "ships," apparently still on the southern coast of Israel, before they migrated to the far north. It is possible that Judges 5 was written during a time of rebellion against Egyptian dominion over Canaan. In Judg 5:2, "leaders led" (בפרע פרעות) could be read in Hebrew as "when Pharaoh led," and the name of the Canaanite army commander Sisera could reflect the Egyptian sun god Ra. Egypt did dominate Canaan for part of the second millennium B.C., but the evidence is probably too limited to say whether or not this was one of those times.

Judges 5 is a rare case in that scholars of most every persuasion agree that it has a very early date of writing, in the second millennium B.C. For some critics, this makes the Song of Deborah the earliest Biblical text.

4.1.2.1.3 First Section of Judges

The first section of Judges, from 1:1 – 2:5, appears to be older than the rest of the book. The author of Judges uses the phrase "to this day" in narration six times, with "this day" being the day when the author writes:

    1:21 Jebusites and Benjamin live together in Jerusalem

    1:26 City named Luz (named after the captured Bethel) in the land of the Hittites

    6:24 Gideon's altar still in Ophrah of the Abiezrites

    10:4 thirty cities in Gilead called Havvoth-Jair

    15:19 En Hakkore in Lehi

    18:12 Mahane Dan west of Kiriath-jearim

Most of these passages do not help much, but the first two, which are in the first section of Judges, are instructive. The description of Jebusites and Benjamin living together at Jerusalem in 1:21 sounds like it was written before David captured the city and made it his capital. The Hittite empire collapsed in the late 13th century B.C.,[5] so the reference in 1:26 to the land of the Hittites looks like it was written before then.

Judg 1:18-19 gives an additional dating clue with its description of what the tribe of Judah was and was not able to accomplish. Judah was unable to drive out the people of the plains, yet they took Gaza, Ashkelon and Ekron – three cities soon to be associated with the powerful Philistines. The probable reason for this unexpected result is that the military campaign of Judah mentioned in Judges 1 predates the arrival of the Philistines, who migrated into the coastal area from Asia Minor around 1180 B.C. The Philistines

---

[5] Scarre and Fagan, *Ancient Civilizations*, p. 222

tried to move further southwest into Egypt, but were defeated by Pharaoh Rameses III (1182-1151 B.C.).[6] Judg 1:29, which allows the Canaanites to dwell in Gezer, presupposes a time before Pharaoh gifted Gezer to Solomon as a bridal dowry (1 Kgs 9:16).

Some parts of Judges 1 read like eyewitness accounts, such as the Judg 1:6-7 account about cutting off the thumbs and toes of Adoni-bezek, and Adoni-bezek's following confession that he had done the same thing to 70 other kings.

We can note also that Judg 1:1 begins after the death of Joshua, while the second section begins (Judg 2:6) with Joshua still alive. Therefore, we have multiple lines of evidence to indicate that the first section of Judges, from 1:1-2:5, is separate from the latter two sections, and looks to have been written earlier than those sections.

4.1.2.1.4 Internal Evidence Summary

We therefore have internal evidence, based on the third section of the book, that Judges was completed during the united monarchy period and probably the reign of Solomon (970-931 B.C.). The second section of Judges, from 2:6 – chapter 16, was collated by the author of the third section as well. However, the first section of Judges, from 1:1-2:5, looks older by more than 200 years, and is not significantly connected to the rest of the book, so we can conclude that the author probably used that older material without alteration. The author was already familiar with the text of Joshua - Judg 2:6 repeats the end of Joshua (Josh 24:28) and picks up the story from there.

4.1.2.2 External Dependencies – Inputs

Judg 19:20-24 is unmistakably connected to the events of Sodom in Gen 19:2-8. The Genesis passage should be understood to have been written first, as the author of Judges is using the parallel to

---

[6] Rogerson, *Chronicle of the Old Testament Kings*, p. 60

say "We became as bad as Sodom." Likewise, the battle sequence in Judg 20:29-35 matches the sequence in Joshua's battle against Ai in Joshua 8. Jephthah's speech in Judg 11:15-27 reflects a thorough knowledge of the history described in Numbers 20-21. Writers of all persuasions recognize that Judges reflects the "Deuteronomic principle," that obedience to God leads to blessing and disobedience leads to punishment. This principle is reflected in the repeated cycle of punishment and rescue which is found in the large central section of Judges. The passage in Judg 1:12-15 about Caleb's inheritance is repeated almost exactly from Josh 15:16-19. Likewise, Judg 2:6-9, about the death of Joshua, is a repeat of Josh 24:28-31. Therefore, Judges should be understood to have been written in the order it appears in the Bible, after the Torah and after Joshua.

4.1.2.3 External Dependencies - Outputs

The stories in Judges are known to later Israelite characters. In 1 Sam 12:9-12, Samuel recalls multiple stories from Judges. Joab mentions the death of Abimelech (2 Sam 11:21 citing Judg 9:50-54). In fairness, the fact that these stories are known does not prove that the book was written at that time, since stories can be handed down without a literary connection. Isaiah similarly knows the story of Gideon, as is shown in Isa 10:26. The author of Psalm 83:9-11, a Psalm ascribed to Asaph, gives a list of villains from Judges: Midian, Sisera, Jabin, Oreb, Zeeb, Zebah and Zalmunna. The literary connection is stronger here, by virtue of the fact that the psalmist matched the order of appearance and spelling from Judges on all of those names.

4.1.2.4 Linguistic Analysis

There are no Persian or Greek words in Judges. The early pronoun "anoki" is used eleven times. The expression מזה, literally "from this," is used to mean "here" in 6:18. This expression is common in pre-exilic texts but does not make it into post-exilic texts, which instead use מקום. "Ehdah" (עדה), a mostly pre-exilic word meaning "congregation," is in Judg 20:1, 21:10, 21:13 and 21:16.

There are three occurrences in Judges of the short form of the relative pronoun (5:7, 7:12 and 8:26), with 5:7 occurring in the Song of Deborah. The relative pronoun shows up heavily in Late Biblical Hebrew, thus creating an unusual distribution in time: it occurs occasionally in very early texts and heavily in very late texts, but almost not at all in between.

Micah (מיכיהו) in Judg 17:1 is the first person in the Bible to be born with a Yahwistic name. Yahwistic names are names using Yahweh as part of a personal name, and by the kingdom era, more than one third of all male names in Israel are Yahwistic names.

Judges introduces the oath form "as the LORD lives" (Judg 8:19) which eventually appears 35 times in the Bible, along with four occurrences of a similar "as your soul lives." This oath form extends as far in time as Jeremiah, and does not appear in exilic or post-exilic texts.

Judges uses "makar" (מכר), usually translated as "sold," to mean give into the power of an enemy (2:14, 3:8, 4:2 and 10:7), without having anything to do with money. This is an Early Biblical Hebrew feature, found also in Deut 32:30. Later usage of this word always involves money.

Judg 2:10 uses "gathered to their fathers" as a euphemism for death. This is an early expression found only once afterward (2 Kgs 22:20), yet it is still probably later than the similar "gathered to his people" phrase used in the Torah.

The linguistic features of Judges 5, the Song of Deborah, are characteristic of Early Biblical Hebrew. It uses imperfect tense verbs to describe past actions, as in 5:26, "she reached out" (תשלחנה), and avoids the Classical Biblical Hebrew use of waw + imperfect verbs. Judges 5 is also generously sprinkled with rare and archaic vocabulary.

The original spelling of "laugh," צחק, is used throughout the Torah and only twice afterward. One of those instances is in Judg

16:25 (mocking Samson), a verse which uses both the original spelling and also the later spelling, שחק.

Finally, Biblical Hebrew expresses the term "men of," as in "men of Sodom" (Gen 13:13) with the construct form of the plural noun "anshay" (אנשי). However, when the phrase is the very common "men of Israel" or "men of Judah," the form is "ish Yisrael" (איש שראל) or "ish Yehudah" (איש יהודה), as in Judg 7:8, 15:10, etc. This is irregular, because "ish" (איש) is singular, but it is used to mean "men." This mixed usage, with איש used for "men of Israel/Judah" and אנשי used for "men of" practically everywhere else (including cities within Israel) is consistent across different books of the Bible regardless of their date of writing. It is therefore interesting to see the irregular usage (איש) also in Judg 7:24, 8:1 and 12:1 applied to "men of Ephraim." This implies that at the time of writing, "men of Ephraim" was as common a phrase as "men of Israel" and "men of Judah." This would be unlikely to be true after the kingdom divided, and therefore supports a date for Judges prior to that time.

4.1.2.5 Oldest Texts

The oldest texts of Judges are three Dead Sea Scrolls: 1Q6, 4Q49 and 4Q50. Portions of five chapters are represented.

4.1.2.6 Conclusion

Judges was completed in the period of the united monarchy, probably under the reign of Solomon, in about 950 B.C. Older written material was used, including the book's beginning (1-2:5) and the Song of Deborah (chapter 5).

In Judg 8:14, Gideon captured a young man at random from the city of Succoth and asked for the names of its leaders. The young man *wrote down* the names of 77 city leaders. This minor aspect of the story of Gideon testifies to the literacy of the age, which may have been beyond what modern writers normally assume. The considerable library of Ugaritic material discovered at Ras

Shamra, just north of Israel, also comes from the period of the judges. It should not be considered a surprise to realize that much of the Old Testament was written in the second millennium B.C.

4.1.3 First and Second Samuel

These two books describe the history of Israel from the end of the time of the judges through the kingship of David, a period from about 1050-970 B.C. The two books in their current form were originally one book, with the division into two not occurring until the Septuagint was translated around 200-100 B.C. The Greek text is longer than the Hebrew text and so the book was divided into two scrolls. The Hebrew version was not divided in two until the middle ages.

The Babylonian Talmud states that Samuel is the author of the book, which was later completed by Gad the Seer and Nathan the prophet.[7] However, Samuel dies (1 Sam 25:1) less than half way through the combined book of 1-2 Samuel, so Samuel cannot be considered the author in the same manner as Joshua for the book of Joshua, or Moses for the Torah.

4.1.3.1 Internal Evidence
4.1.3.1.1 Sources in Samuel

Some source critics attempt to track the J, E, D and P sources into Samuel (an approach we have already rejected). Others have tried to split Samuel into pro and anti-monarchy sources, while still others attribute most of the book to a court historian from Solomon's time, or attribute the entire book to a Deuteronomic historian writing during the Babylonian exile. No critical consensus exists on the subject. In the effort to locate sources for the book of Samuel, perhaps inadequate attention has been given to what the Bible itself says about written sources of information for this period of time. 1 Chron 29:29 says "Now the acts of King David, from first to last, are written in the chronicles of Samuel the seer,

---

[7] Baba Bathra 15a

in the chronicles of Nathan the prophet and in the chronicles of Gad the seer." We believe most of Samuel can be attributed to these three sources, with the understanding that a later writer compiled them together into the book of Samuel as we have it today.

The "chronicles of Samuel the seer" are likely 1 Samuel 1-7. This source begins with the stories around Samuel's birth and childhood. It should be understood to end by 1 Sam 7:17, because all problems have been solved: the Philistines have been defeated and "did not come anymore within the border of Israel" (although they will again just a few chapters later), Israel's territory has been recovered, and the Ark of the Covenant returned to Israelite territory. After these happy events, 1 Sam 7:15-17 all but says "the end." 1 Sam 10:25 indicates that Samuel made written records, so it is plausible that Samuel himself is the source for the first part of the book.

The "chronicles of Nathan the prophet" pick up in 1 Samuel 8 with Samuel being old and his sons dishonest. The "chronicles of Nathan the prophet" contain all the epic stories about Saul and David, continuing probably through 2 Samuel 20. 2 Sam 20:23-26, which lists David's cabinet ministers, appears to be another passage that concludes a book. Certain aspects of this section, such as the description of the food in 1 Sam 30:12, have the ring of an eyewitness account. A clue as to the reality of separate sources can be found in the way Nathan himself is named. Nathan is mentioned ten times in 2 Samuel 7 and 2 Samuel 12. The first time he is designated as "Nathan the prophet" (2 Sam 7:2) and the other nine times he is designated as just "Nathan." In the later account of 1 Kings 1, he is designated as "Nathan the prophet" nine times.

Usage of the "chronicles of Gad the seer" may be limited to just 2 Samuel 24, where Gad is mentioned five times. This chapter looks like it comes after David's story was supposed to end, but this is intentional on the part of the final compiler of Samuel and

Kings – it serves to bridge from Samuel to Kings with the purchase of the land Solomon will use to build the temple.

One additional source may be in view: that of Jehoshaphat the son of Ahilud, David's "recorder" (2 Sam 20:24). Ancient Middle Eastern kings routinely employed a recorder who kept court records. These records are repeatedly mentioned in the book of Kings as "the book of the chronicles of the kings of Israel" and "the book of the chronicles of the kings of Judah." It is likely that some of David's records, recorded by Jehoshaphat, were included in Samuel. The list of David's mighty men in 2 Sam 23:8-39 looks like the work of a recorder, along with possibly 2 Sam 23:1-7, "David's last words."

The poetry in Samuel probably came from still additional sources. Hannah's song of thanks in 1 Samuel 2 gives something of a theme for the entire work in 1 Sam 2:8-10. 2 Sam 1:18 says David's dirge for Saul and Jonathan in 2 Sam 1:19-27 is in the "Book of Jashar" (translated as "book of the just"). 1 Samuel 22 is a lengthy psalm which essentially repeats Psalm 18. A close analysis, however, shows that the two passages (Psalm 18 and 1 Samuel 22) have numerous minor differences. See Appendix B, section B.1.1.1 for a closer comparison of Psalm 18 and 1 Samuel 22.

4.1.3.1.2 Final Compilation of Samuel

An important "then and now" verse is the parenthetical comment in 1 Sam 9:9: "(Formerly in Israel, when a man went to inquire of God, he used to say, 'Come, and let us go to the seer'; for he who is called a prophet now was formerly called a seer.)" This verse was apparently inserted into Nathan's account by the final compiler. The word "seer" was still occasionally in use in the late eighth century B.C. It was used in Isa 29:10, 30:10, Amos 7:12 and Mic 3:7, all quotes from eighth century B.C. prophets. After that time, "prophet" is used instead of "seer," 152 times in the writing prophets Isaiah through Malachi. This fact supports the idea that the final compiler of Samuel worked much later than his original sources. For reasons we will explain later, we believe that he worked during the reign of Josiah (641-609 B.C.).

To further help identify the final date of writing, we can reference the verses in Samuel that say "to this day" (the day of the author). These verses are listed below:

1 Sam 5:5	Priests of Dagon do not tread on the threshold of Dagon in Ashdod
1 Sam 6:18	Large stone in the field of Joshua the Beth-shemite
1 Sam 27:6	Ziklag has belonged to the kings of Judah
1 Sam 30:24-25	Statute in Israel that spoils of battle shared with those who stay with the baggage
2 Sam 6:8	Place is called Perez-uzzah
2 Sam 18:18	Pillar called Absalom's monument

The temple of Dagon in Ashdod (1 Sam 5:5) was not destroyed until the Maccabean period, long after any proposed date for the book, so this verse is not a help. 1 Sam 30:24-25 implies that the author's time is still in a period where Israel can go to war, indicating a pre-exilic date. The verse in this list that is most useful in establishing a date is 1 Sam 27:6. It seems to date Samuel in the divided monarchy period, due to the phrase "kings of *Judah*" (not Israel). Since it says "kings" (plural), it would not be at the beginning of the divided kingdom period under Rehoboam, the first king, but sometime after him. 1 Sam 3:1, "a word from the LORD was rare in those days," also sounds like it was written when the prophetic movement was in full bloom, a characteristic feature of the divided monarchy period.

The book of 2 Samuel ends in chapter 24 with the account of David's census, the resulting judgment and the purchase of the threshing floor of Araunah the Jebusite. This site will be used to build Solomon's temple. The fact that the book ends this way is instructive. A seemingly more appropriate ending would have been David's "last words" in 2 Sam 23:1-7, or perhaps his concluding psalm in 2 Samuel 22. Most appropriate of all would be to end the book with the account of David's death, as was done for Moses in Deuteronomy and for Joshua in the book of Joshua, but David's death is not recorded until 1 Kings 2. The explanation for the chosen ending is that the author did not intend 2 Samuel 24 to be a final ending – he intended it to lead into his next account, the book of 1-2 Kings. The "to be continued" nature of the ending of Samuel and the seamless transition from Samuel to Kings leads to the conclusion that the individual who put Samuel into its final form is the same individual who is responsible for most of Kings. This is not an individual who knows about the Babylonian exile. In fact, 2 Sam 7:12-16, describing God's eternal covenant with David, is a difficult passage for anyone to explain in light of the exile. As we will see in our discussion of Kings, the author of most of Kings wrote during the reign of Josiah – only the ending of 2 Kings was added later. This gives us an indication that Samuel also was put in its final form during the reign of Josiah (641-609 B.C.).

4.1.3.2 External Dependencies - Inputs

The book of Samuel is dependent on the Torah and Judges. In 1 Sam 12:7-11, Samuel recounts the history of Israel, mentioning specifically Sisera, Jerubbaal and Jephthah. A literary, as opposed to just an oral dependence, is likely due to the unusual term "sold" in 1 Sam 12:9, a term used in Judges to describe God giving Israel into the hands of their enemies.

4.1.3.3 External Dependencies – Outputs

The dependency of Chronicles on Samuel and Kings is well known. The Table 4-1 below lists passages in Samuel which are used by Chronicles. In many cases, the passages from Samuel are quoted verbatim.

Table 4-1 Samuel and Chronicles Parallel Passages

1 Sam 31:1-13	1 Chron 10:1-12
2 Sam 5:1-10	1 Chron 11:1-9
2 Sam 5:11-25	1 Chron 14:1-17
2 Sam 6:1-11	1 Chron 13:5-14
2 Sam 6:12-16	1 Chron15:25-29
2 Sam 6:17-19	1 Chron 16:1-3
2 Sam 7:1-29	1 Chron 17:1-27
2 Sam 8:1-8	1 Chron 18:1-17
2 Sam 10:1-19	1 Chron 19:1-19
2 Sam 11:1	1 Chron 20:1
2 Sam 12:30-31	1 Chron 20:2-3
2 Sam 23:8-29	1 Chron 11:11-41
2 Sam 24:1-25	1 Chron 21:1-26

The table below shows a typical passage.

2 Samuel 8	1 Chronicles 18
1 Now after this it came about that David defeated the Philistines and subdued them; and David took control of the chief city from the hand of the Philistines.	1 Now after this it came about that David defeated the Philistines and subdued them and took Gath and its towns from the hand of the Philistines.
2 He defeated Moab, and measured them with the line, making them lie down on the ground; and he measured two lines to put to death and one full line to keep alive And the Moabites became servants to David, bringing tribute.	2 He defeated Moab, and the Moabites became servants to David, bringing tribute.

3 Then David defeated Hadadezer, the son of Rehob king of Zobah, as he went to restore his rule at the River.	3 David also defeated Hadadezer king of Zobah as far as Hamath, as he went to establish his rule to the Euphrates River.
4 David captured from him 1,700 horsemen and 20,000 foot soldiers; and David hamstrung the chariot horses, but reserved enough of them for 100 chariots.	4 David took from him 1,000 chariots and 7,000 horsemen and 20,000 foot soldiers, and David hamstrung all the chariot horses, but reserved enough of them for 100 chariots.

The dependency is obvious. Chronicles occasionally has more details, as in this passage it names Gath, Hamath and the Euphrates River. Chronicles often omits the more negative stories, or negative aspects of the same story, as in killing Moabite captives in v2. Sometimes the two books will report different numbers, as in the horsemen of v4.[8]

Other than Chronicles, it is difficult to determine which biblical texts are dependent on Samuel, for multiple reasons. First, as we have shown, Samuel in its final form uses multiple much older sources, and it will not be possible to distinguish between whether a text is using the source (for example, "the chronicles of Nathan the prophet") or the final book of Samuel. Second, almost all subsequent biblical texts mention David. The biography of David is almost entirely from Samuel, but the tradition associated with David was so prominent that he could readily be mentioned by any number of individuals who never read Samuel. Certainly King Hazael of Syria, in the ninth century B.C., never read the book of Samuel, yet he set up the Tel Dan Stele describing his victory over Ahaziah the son of Jehoram of the "house of David."

---

[8] The Masoretic Text has different numbers of horsemen in this passage, but the Septuagint has the same number, 7000, in both Samuel and Chronicles.

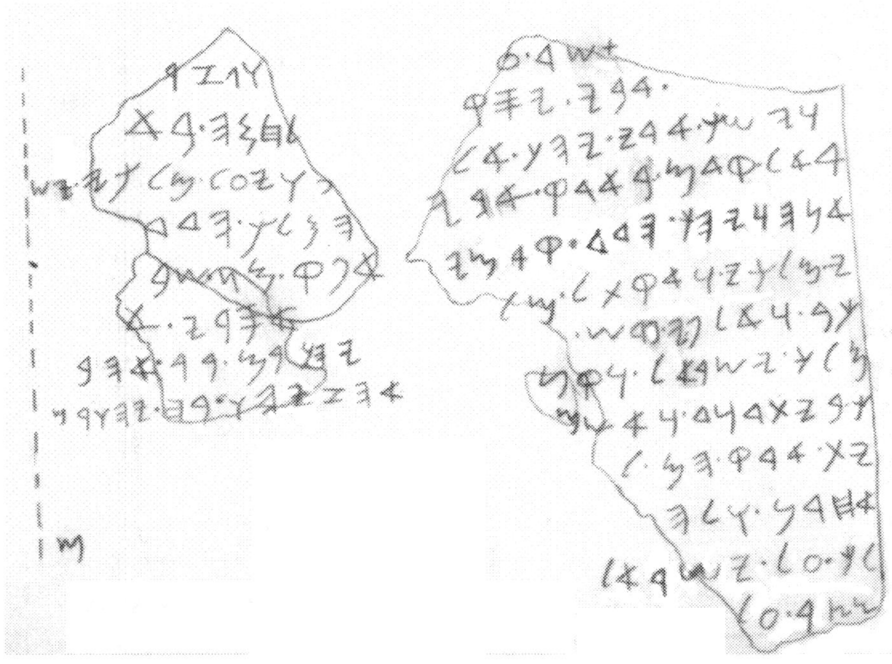

**Figure 4-1 Drawing of the Tel Dan Stele,
which mentions the "House of David"[9]**

The headings in Psalms 3, 18, 30, 51, 52, 54, 56, 57, 59, 60, 63 and 142 mention events in David's life recorded in Samuel. However, the headings for Psalms 7 and 34 seem to mention events in David's life not recorded in Samuel.

More meaningful are texts that mention characters from Samuel other than David. These include Ps 99:6 and Jer 15:1, which both name Samuel along with Moses. Isa 10:29 mentions Gibeah of Saul. The fact that Gibeah was Saul's home town (1 Sam 10:26 and 11:4) is relatively obscure, so Isaiah may have had the text of Samuel (or, as we have mentioned, "the chronicles of Nathan the prophet") available to him by 700 B.C.

---

[9] Drawing is by Schreiber for Wikipedia, May 14 2005

In the prayer of Hannah, 1 Sam 2:8 matches Ps 113:7-8. Psalm 113 is a late psalm and is probably the borrower. Psalm 18 matches 1 Samuel 22, but both are early, apparently tracing to an original song of David. The Psalm 18 version of the song looks a little older from a linguistics perspective, but this is probably due to scribal influence (See the discussion in Appendix B, section B.1.1.1).

4.1.3.4 Linguistic Analysis

The linguistic evidence from Samuel is consistent with a pre-exilic date for the book. There are no Persian or Greek words in Samuel. The early pronoun "anoki" is used 42 times. The older word for kingdom, "mamlakah," is used 12 times as opposed to one occurrence of the newer form "malkut." "Zulah" (זולה), meaning "except" in 1 Sam 21:10 and 2 Sam 7:22, appears almost exclusively in pre-exilic texts. The designation of God as "Rock" multiple times in the poems of 1 Samuel 2 and 22 is a metaphor prominent only in earlier texts. David's name is spelled in the short form דוד all 575 times it appears in Samuel, as opposed to the later form דויד that was used after the exile. Table B-2 in Appendix B shows that Samuel has a lower percentage of long "o" vowel letters than any book outside the Torah, Kings and Ruth.

The grammar of Samuel is not as early as the Torah. Instead of using the dual form for years, Samuel uses the "two + plural" form to mean two years in 1 Sam 13:1 and 2 Sam 2:10. Likewise, Samuel uses the "two + plural" form rather than the dual form to mean two days in 2 Sam 1:1. Samuel does use the dual form for "two times" in 1 Sam 18:11. The expression "mizeh...mizeh" (מזה...מזה), meaning "here and there" (1 Sam 2:13), is exclusive to pre-exilic texts.

God "walks" (usually translated "moves about") in 2 Sam 7:6, but not in the parallel later passage of 1 Chron 17:5. God "smells" in 1 Sam 26:19. [10] Such anthropomorphisms applied to God are a mark of earlier Hebrew. God also "repents" (usually translated "was grieved") in 1 Sam 15:35, another characteristic of earlier passages (as in Gen 6:6).

The "Song of the Bow" in 2 Sam 1:19-27 is a dirge composed by David to mourn the death of Saul and Jonathan. Similar dirges are present in Amos 5:1-3, Lamentations 1-4, Ezek 19:1-14, 26:17-18, 27:3-10, 27:28-32 and 27:34-36. These later dirges all use a "limping meter," in which the latter part of each line is shorter than the first part of the line. This limping meter is not present in 2 Sam 1:19-27, perhaps indicating that it was composed before it became customary to put dirges into the "limping meter." Likewise, the short dirge David composed for Abner in 2 Sam 3:33-34 does not use the limping meter. Also, the dirge for Saul and Jonathan contains an imperfect tense verb in 2 Sam 1:22 to refer to a completed past event (תשוב = "returned"), a feature characteristic of early Hebrew poetry before 750 B.C. 2 Samuel 22, which matches Psalms 18, shows similar marks of Early Biblical Hebrew. There are numerous instances of imperfect tense verbs to refer to completed past events, as in 2 Sam 22:14, 22:16, etc. The dirge of 2 Samuel 1 and the song in 2 Samuel 22 both use the term "high places" (במות) in a positive sense (2 Sam 1:19, 1:25, 22:34, as well as 1 Sam 9:13-14) while later writings use it in an entirely negative sense as a place of corrupted worship.

The author of Samuel and Kings treats personal names with "baal" as part of the name as a vulgarity, and alters all such names to say "bosheth," meaning "the shameful thing." Ish-bosheth (2 Sam 2:8) is substituted for Eshbaal (1 Chron 8:33), Mephibosheth (2 Sam 4:4) for Meribaal (1 Chron 8:34) and Jerubbesheth (2 Sam 11:21) for Jerubbaal (Judg 9:1). The substitutions are instructive in several ways. First, Judges allows "baal" names and Samuel does

---

[10] Most English translations of 1 Sam 26:19 say "'accept' an offering". The Hebrew word is ירח, meaning smell.

not. This implies that the final compiler of Samuel and the author of Judges are not the same person, contrary to some theories that the entire primary history of Judges to Kings was the work of one Deuteronomic historian. Second, "Mephibosheth" appears in 2 Sam 21:7-8, which is outside the "chronicles of Nathan" section we have proposed, implying that the name changing was not the work of that source, but the work of the final compiler of Samuel. If Samuel was compiled during the reign of Josiah, this would make sense, because at that time there was a sharp backlash against the Baal worship revived by Josiah's father, Manasseh (2 Kgs 23:4-5). Finally, it is instructive that Chronicles, a later history than Samuel/Kings, preserves the more original "baal" names. This implies that the author of Chronicles was using more material than just Samuel and Kings for his information – he may have had access to the older sources mentioned in 1 Chron 29:29.

"LORD of Hosts," a designation for God used 229 times in the Bible, is introduced for the first time in 1 Sam 1:3. "Zion," a designation for Jerusalem used 167 times in the Bible, is introduced for the first time in 2 Sam 5:7.

4.1.3.5 Oldest Texts

The oldest texts of Samuel are four Dead Sea Scrolls: 1Q7, 4Q51, 4Q52 and 4Q53. Most of the chapters in Samuel are represented, particularly by 4Q51, which is very extensive. Scroll 4Q52 is dated to the third century B.C., making it the oldest or second oldest Dead Sea Scroll, and therefore perhaps the oldest biblical scroll in existence.[11] Also, the Psalms scroll 11Q5 contains the last words of David from 2 Samuel 23:1-7a. The Dead Sea Scrolls also contain extra-biblical works related to Samuel (4Q160 and 6Q9), and the Florilegium (4Q174), part of which deals with the promise of an eternal dynasty for David in 2 Samuel 7.

---

[11] VanderKam, *The Dead Sea Scrolls Today*, p. 129

4.1.3.6 Conclusion

Samuel was written in its final form during the reign of Josiah, between 641 and 609 B.C. The author used much older sources, dating to the time of David around 1000 B.C.

4.1.4 First and Second Kings

Just like Samuel, the two books of kings in their current form were originally one book, with the division into two not occurring until the Septuagint was translated. The Greek text is longer than the Hebrew text and so the book was divided into two scrolls. The Hebrew version was not divided in two until the middle ages. The history contains a mostly terse summary of each king of Israel and Judah, but is expanded greatly by epic accounts of Solomon, Elijah, Elisha, and to a lesser extent Hezekiah and Josiah.

4.1.4.1 Internal Evidence

The Talmud identifies Jeremiah as the author of Kings,[12] a view shared by some modern writers, including Richard Friedman. It is only fair to state that with respect to the writing of Kings, we have drawn somewhat from the ideas of Friedman (though not with regard to Jeremiah being the author), with whom we differed so sharply on the Torah.

Kings is almost unique among the Old Testament historical books in that it is immediately clear when it was finished – it was during the Babylonian exile. Writers of all persuasions agree on this (with a few rare exceptions). The book describes the destruction of Jerusalem in 586 B.C. It then describes a minor event that takes place in 561 or 560 B.C.: the release of Jehoiachin from prison by the Babylonian King Evil-Merodach (the Amel-Marduk of Table 2-5). In doing this, the author has brought the story up to date. The book then ends, with no hint or foreshadowing of the extraordinary events of 538 B.C.: the conquest of Babylon by

---

[12] Baba Bathra 15A

Persia and the end of the exile. We can be confident, then, that the book of 1-2 Kings was completed in the narrow window between 562 and 538 B.C. We will call the person who completed the book Judean Prophet #2. His role in finishing Kings is roughly analogous to the second Deuteronomist recognized by some critics, but we will not use that terminology, because it incorrectly implies authorship of part of the Torah. This Judean Prophet #2 wrote 2 Kings 24-25, and perhaps back as far as 2 Kgs 23:26, but no further. The major portion of Kings is the work of his predecessor, Judean Prophet #1.

Judean Prophet #1 lived during the reign of Josiah (641-609 B.C.). He had access to the court records of the kings of Israel and the kings of Judah, and used them to form the backbone of his work. These court records are called "The Book of the Acts of Solomon" (1 Kgs 11:41), "The Book of the Chronicles of the Kings of Israel" (1 Kgs 14:19 and 17 more times) and "The Book of the Chronicles of The Kings of Judah" (1 Kgs 14:29 and 14 more times). "The Book of the Chronicles of the Kings of Israel" includes every king of Israel except for the last one, Hoshea, who was king when Israel fell to Assyria. Likewise, every king in Judah is mentioned in the "Book of the Chronicles of the Kings of Judah" except for the short-lived Ahaziah, the queen regnant Athaliah and the last two kings, Jehoiachin and Zedekiah. Judean Prophet #1 compared the Judean kings, either favorably or unfavorably, to David (1 Kgs 15:3, 15:11, etc.), and evaluated them on the basis of whether or not they removed the "high places" (1 Kgs 15:14, 22:43, etc.). Judean Prophet #2, by comparison, ignores these subjects in his evaluation of the last kings of Judah. Judean Prophet #1 includes a reference to his king, Josiah, all the way back at the beginning of the divided kingdom (1 Kgs 13:2). Besides the court records, he uses at least three additional sources:

1. Isaiah is used to fill out the account of Hezekiah's time. 2 Kgs 18:13-20:21 closely follows Isaiah 36-39. On our convic-

tion that the Isaiah passage came first and Kings made use of it, see section 4.2.1.2.12.

2. A northern Israeli source we will call "Northern Prophet" provided the accounts of Elijah, Elisha, and the destruction of the Baal cult (1 Kgs 17:1 through 2 Kgs 10:33).

3. The seamless transition from Samuel to Kings implies that Judean Prophet #1 was also the compiler of the writings of 1 and 2 Samuel. He would also have used records from the court historian of Solomon's time, who may have collected the stories of Samuel, Saul, David and Solomon (1 and 2 Samuel up through perhaps 1 Kings 10).

The following passages in Kings describe circumstances continuing "to this day," that is, the day the passage was written:

1 Kgs 8:8	Poles holding the Ark of the Covenant are in the inner sanctuary
1 Kgs 9:13	Galilee cities are called Cabul
1 Kgs 9:20-21	Solomon made the Canaanites forced laborers
1 Kgs 10:12	Almug trees
1 Kgs 12:19	Israel in rebellion against house of David
2 Kgs 2:22	Waters of Jericho purified
2 Kgs 8:22	Edom in revolt against Judah
2 Kgs 10:27	House of Baal a latrine
2 Kgs 14:7	City named Joktheel
2 Kgs 16:6	Edomites/Arameans live in Elath
2 Kgs 17:34	Samaritans follow earlier customs and don't fear the LORD
2 Kgs 17:41	Samaritans practice syncretic religion

Several of these "to this day" references point to a pre-exilic composition, and none are inconsistent with a writing at the time of Josiah. 1 Kgs 8:8 indicates that the Ark of the Covenant is in the temple, requiring a date before the destruction of the temple in 586 B.C. Both Israel (1 Kgs 12:19) and Edom (2 Kgs 8:22) are in rebellion against Judah and the House of David, requiring the existence of Judah and the monarchy. The Samaritan references (2 Kgs 17:34 and 17:41) require a time period well after the fall of the northern Kingdom of Israel in 722 B.C.

4.1.4.2 External Dependencies – Inputs

The author of Kings knows the Torah. Elijah's 40 day trip to Sinai echoes the exodus story, and the story about Elijah's death and his heir, Elisha, splitting the Jordan River echoes Moses' death and Joshua's crossing the Jordan. The list in Section 3.2.2.1.2 includes some additional instances in which the author of Kings demonstrates knowledge of the Torah.

The warnings of exile that appear in Kings do not imply knowledge of the Babylonian exile as an event that has already happened. These warnings (as in 1 Kgs 9:4-7 and 2 Kgs 22:16-17) are general in nature, and largely repeat what was already written in Deuteronomy (as in Deut 29:24-28).

The author of Kings knows the story of Joshua's curse on Jericho (Josh 6:26, 1 Kgs 16:34). He also knows and uses the book of Isaiah, as described in section 4.2.1.2.12.

4.1.4.3 External Dependencies - Outputs

Jeremiah chapter 52 was apparently borrowed from 2 Kings 24:18-25:30. The formula used to introduce Zedekiah in Jer 52:1 is the same formula used throughout the book of Kings,[13] so without being certain as to the author of Kings, we should still assign the priority on this passage to the book of Kings.

Chronicles is dependent to a certain extent on the entire primary history (Genesis – Kings), but relies more heavily on either Kings or the sources for Kings more than all the other books combined. Chronicles sometimes paraphrases stories from Kings,

---

[13] The formula used throughout the book of Kings is, with minor variations: "<king's name> was <number> years old when he became king, and he reigned <number> years in Jerusalem. His mother's name was <name> the daughter of <name>."

as with Solomon's prayer for wisdom (1 Kgs 3:6-9, 2 Chron 1:8-10) and sometimes quotes Kings verbatim. The Table 4-2 below provides a lengthy list of passages in Kings which are used by Chronicles. It excludes the passages both have in common with Isaiah.

Table 4-2 Kings and Chronicles Parallel Passages

1 Kgs 2:11	1 Chron 29:27
1 Kgs 3:4	2 Chron 1:3
1 Kgs 3:5-13	2 Chron 1:7-12
1 Kgs 5:2-5	2 Chron 2:3-4
1 Kgs 5:6	2 Chron 2:8
1 Kgs 5:7-8	2 Chron 2:11-12
1 Kgs 5:9	2 Chron 2:16
1 Kgs 5:15	2 Chron 2:18
1 Kgs 6:1-3	2 Chron 3:1-4
1 Kgs 6:20-21	2 Chron 3:8-9
1 Kgs 6:23-27	2 Chron 3:10-13
1 Kgs 7:21	2 Chron 3:17
1 Kgs 7:23-26	2 Chron 4:1-5
1 Kgs 7:38-39	2 Chron 4:6-7
1 Kgs 7:40-51	2 Chron 4:11-5:1
1 Kgs 8:1-66	2 Chron 5:2-14; 6:1-42; 7:1-10
1 Kgs 9:1-11	2 Chron 7:11-22; 8:1-2
1 Kgs 9:17-25	2 Chron 8:5-13
1 Kgs 9:26-28	2 Chron 8:17-18
1 Kgs 10:1-27	2 Chron 9:1-27
1 Kgs 10:28-29	2 Chron 1:16-17
1 Kgs 11:41-43	2 Chron 9:29-31
1 Kgs 12:1-19	2 Chron 10:1-19
1 Kgs 12:21-24	2 Chron 11:1-4
1 Kgs 14:21-22	2 Chron 12:13-14

1 Kgs 14:25	2 Chron 12:2
1 Kgs 14:26-28	2 Chron 12:9-11
1 Kgs 14:29-31	2 Chron 12:15-16
1 Kgs 15:1-2	2 Chron 13:1-2
1 Kgs 15:7-8	2 Chron 13:22-14:1
1 Kgs 15:11-12	2 Chron 14:2-3
1 Kgs 15:13-15	2 Chron 15:16-18
1 Kgs 15:17-18	2 Chron 16:1-2
1 Kgs 15:19-22	2 Chron 16:3-6
1 Kgs 15:23-24	2 Chron 16:11-13
1 Kgs 22:1-35	2 Chron 18:1-34
1 Kgs 22:42-50	2 Chron 20:31-21:1
2 Kgs 8:17-23	2 Chron 21:5-10
2 Kgs 8:26-29	2 Chron 22:2-6
2 Kgs 11:1-21	2 Chron 22:10-24:1
2 Kgs 12:1-14	2 Chron 24:2-14
2 Kgs 12:17-21	2 Chron 24:23-26
2 Kgs 14:1-6	2 Chron 25:1-4
2 Kgs 14:7	2 Chron 25:11
2 Kgs 14:8-14	2 Chron 25:17-24
2 Kgs 14:17-22	2 Chron 25:25-26:2
2 Kgs 15:2-3	2 Chron 26:3-4
2 Kgs 15:5-7	2 Chron 26:21-23
2 Kgs 15:32-35	2 Chron 27:1-2
2 Kgs 15:36-38	2 Chron 27:7-9
2 Kgs 16:2-6	2 Chron 28:1-6
2 Kgs 16:7	2 Chron 28:16
2 Kgs 16:8	2 Chron 28:21
2 Kgs 16:19-20	2 Chron 28:26-27
2 Kgs 18:1-3	2 Chron 29:1-2
2 Kgs 20:20-21	2 Chron 32:32-33
2 Kgs 21:1-9	2 Chron 33:1-10
2 Kgs 21:17	2 Chron 33:18

2 Kgs 21:18-24	2 Chron 33:20-25
2 Kgs 22:1-2	2 Chron 34:1-2
2 Kgs 22:3-20	2 Chron 34:8-28
2 Kgs 23:1-4	2 Chron 34:29-33
2 Kgs 23:6-10	2 Chron 34:3-7
2 Kgs 23:21	2 Chron 35:1
2 Kgs 23:22-23	2 Chron 35:18-19
2 Kgs 23:29-30a	2 Chron 35:20-24
2 Kgs 23:30b-31	2 Chron 36:1-2
2 Kgs 23:33-34	2 Chron 36:3-4
2 Kgs 23:36	2 Chron 36:5
2 Kgs 24:1	2 Chron 36:6
2 Kgs 24:5	2 Chron 36:8
2 Kgs 24:8-10	2 Chron 36:9-10a
2 Kgs 24:17-20	2 Chron 36:10b-13
2 Kgs 25:1	2 Chron 36:17
2 Kgs 25:13-14	2 Chron 36:18-19
2 Kgs 25:18-19	2 Chron 36:20-21

4.1.4.4 Linguistic Analysis

Because Kings and Chronicles have so many parallel passages, a comparison of the linguistics between the earlier book, Kings, and the later book, Chronicles, is instructive in showing the differences between Classical and Late Biblical Hebrew. Because Classical Biblical Hebrew is the norm, these differences are not described here, but in the section on Chronicles in 5.12.3.

There are no Persian or Greek words in Kings. The early pronoun "anoki" is used seven times, along with the companion "ani," used 39 times. The older word for kingdom, "mamlakah" is used 13 times as opposed to one occurrence of the later word "malkut." "Zulah" (זולה), meaning "except" in 1 Kgs 3:18, 12:20 and 2 Kgs 24:14, appears almost exclusively in pre-exilic texts.

Some unusual forms appear in the section of the book dealing with Elijah, Elisha, and the destruction of the Baal cult. This is probably a reflection of a northern Israelite dialect in which this section of Kings was originally written. An Aramaic second person singular suffix, "ki" (כי) occurs four times in 2 Kgs 4:2-7. This is the only appearance of this suffix in the Bible outside of four late psalms and Jer 11:15. אתי is used for "you" (feminine) in 2 Kgs 4:16 and 4:23, instead of the usual אתנה. הנכה for "behold, you" is an unusual form in 2 Kgs 7:2, as is הלז for "this" in 2 Kgs 4:25.

Kings looks to be in a transitional phase for dual form words, as it uses a dual form for "two years" (1 Kgs 15:25, 1 Kgs 16:8 and 2 Kgs 15:23), "two times" (1 Kgs 11:9), "two talents" (1 Kgs 16:24, 2 Kgs 5:23) and two measures" (2 Kgs 7:1, 7:16 and 7:18). However, the last "two years" reference in Kings uses the later "two + plural" form in 2 Kgs 21:19.

Kings uses the older month names: Ziv – second month (1 Kgs 6:1), Bul – eighth month (1 Kgs 6:38) and Ethanim – seventh month (1 Kgs 8:2). Ziv, Bul and Ethanim are known from the Phoenician language, making it likely that this early Hebrew calendar reflected Canaanite month names. Later biblical texts use the modern Jewish calendar month names, which were borrowed from the Babylonian names.

The expression "mizeh" (מזה), literally "from this," is used to mean "here" in 1 Kgs 17:3. This expression is common in pre-exilic texts but does not make it into post-exilic texts, which instead use מקום. Similarly, the expression "mizeh...mizeh" (מזה...מזה), meaning "here and there" (1 Kgs 10:19-20), is exclusive to pre-exilic texts.

Kings has one of the oldest spelling patterns in the Bible outside the Torah, as shown in Table B-2 in Appendix B. Kings spells David's name using the early short form דוד 93 times, and the later long form דויד 3 times.

4.1.4.5 Oldest Texts

The oldest texts of Kings are two Dead Sea Scrolls: 4Q54 and 5Q2. Portions of only three chapters are represented. In addition, scroll 4Q382 paraphrases part of Kings.

4.1.4.6 Conclusion

Kings was placed in its final form during the Babylonian exile between 560 and 540 B.C. However, the bulk of the work, all but the last 2-3 chapters, was compiled during the reign of Josiah, after the period of Josiah's reform. This requires a date between 641 and 609 B.C. The Judean prophet who compiled Kings also compiled Samuel, using for both his books multiple older sources written near the time of the events they describe. For the book of Kings, these sources include at a minimum (1) The Book of the Acts of Solomon, (2) The Book of the Chronicles of the Kings of Israel, (3) The Book of the Chronicles of the Kings of Judah, (4) The Elijah/Elisha stories from the hand of a northern prophet, and (5) Isaiah.

4.2 Latter Prophets

The Major Prophets (Isaiah, Jeremiah and Ezekiel) are in chronological order, and some effort may also have been made to put the Minor Prophets in chronological order. The number of the prophets has some significance, with three Major Prophets and twelve Minor Prophets matching the pattern of three patriarchs (Abraham, Isaac and Jacob) and twelve sons of Jacob.[14] It is possible that a desire to meet this pattern figured into the way books were grouped in the Old Testament canon (Daniel is not counted among the prophets, but Jonah is).

---

[14] In the New Testament this pattern is also apparent, with three inner disciples and twelve total disciples of Jesus.

4.2.1 Isaiah

Isaiah the son of Amoz was married, the father of two sons and a resident of Jerusalem in the eighth century B.C. As the first of the major writing prophets, his career can be reliably dated to span the period of at least 740 to 700 B.C. Isa 1:1 introduces the book of Isaiah and places his ministry during the reign of Uzziah, Jotham, Ahaz and Hezekiah, kings of Judah. 2 Kings 19-20, 2 Chronicles 32 and 2 Chron 26:22 provide external testimony to Isaiah. The first part of the book of Isaiah begins when king Uzziah (Azariah) dies in 740 B.C., and continues through a time of crisis between Judah and an alliance of the northern Kingdom of Israel with Syria. Both Syria and Israel were effectively destroyed by an Assyrian invasion in 721 B.C. Isaiah 36-39 is set during the later Assyrian invasion of Judah by Sennacherib in 701 B.C. Isaiah records as history the death of Sennacherib in 681 B.C. and his replacement by Esarhaddon (Isa 37:38), so the book could not have been placed in its final form before then.

Although the date of Isaiah's life is not in doubt, the unity of the book is disputed. The traditional understanding is that the entire book of Isaiah was written by Isaiah during his lifetime. The modern critical understanding of Isaiah splits the book into three parts: part 1 consisting of chapters 1-39 and written predominately by Isaiah, chapters 40-55 written by an anonymous author during the Babylonian exile ("Deutero-Isaiah" or Second Isaiah) about 540 B.C., and chapters 56-66 written in the postexilic period, about 500 B.C., again by an anonymous author ("Trito-Isaiah" or Third Isaiah). In the earlier part of the 20th century, the trend was toward even a more fragmented and later date for portions of Isaiah. For example, in 1910, Prof R.H. Kennett of Cambridge, in his Schweich Lectures, said Isaiah was written at five different times, with chapters 11-12, 19, 24-27, 29-30, 32-35, 42, 49-66 and portions of 1-2, 4, 8-10, 16-18, 23, 41, 44-45 and 48 written during the Maccabean period of 167-140 B.C.[15] To squelch this trend came Qumran scroll 1QIsa[a] , dated from 125-100 B.C. and containing every verse from Isaiah 1:1 to 66:24. Critics today have retreated back to the understanding of a Deutero-Isaiah writing from exile and a Trito-Isaiah early enough in the post-exilic period to stay out of range of any evidence from Qumran. We will demonstrate that in fact the entire book of Isaiah is essentially from a single author, Isaiah the son of Amoz, and that it was completed by the early seventh century B.C.

4.2.1.1 The Case for the Division of Isaiah

It is apparent even at a glance that the subject, the tone of the book, and to an extent even the style of Isaiah changes at the beginning of chapter 40. The first part of the book is largely a book of judgment, the second part is a book of comfort. The first part of Isaiah mixes prose and poetry, the second part is more heavily poetic. Assyria figures prominently in the first part (mentioned 43 times), while the second part mentions Assyrians only once (52:4). There are biographical passages mentioning Isaiah in the first part of the book (1:1, 2:1, 7:3, 13:1, 20:2 and ten times in chapters 37-39), but no such passages in the second part.

Chapters 40-66 do not read as though they are addressing the Kingdom of Judah as it existed in Isaiah's time. Jerusalem is described as being physically ruined (44:26, 58:12, 61:4, 63:18 and 64:10-11). An imminent *return* is predicted (41:9), and that return will not be related to Assyria but will be from *Babylon* (48:20). The gods specifically mocked are Babylonian gods (46:1). The community is in need of comfort and assurance that their time of suffering has come to an end (40:1-2). These passages seem to apply most directly to an Israelite community in exile in Babylon.

The most significant argument for a later date for Isaiah 40-66, and the one which will be conclusive for any secular critic, is the

---

[15] Article on Isaiah, *International Standard Bible Encyclopedia,* 1915 edition

mention by name in Isa 44:28 and 45:1 of Cyrus, along with the statement that he will allow Jerusalem to be rebuilt. Cyrus, king of Persia, conquered Babylon in 538 B.C. and issued a proclamation ending Judah's exile (2 Chron 36:22-23). The Cyrus passage in Isaiah 44-45 is prophetic in nature, but to suggest that Isaiah would call someone by name more than 100 years before he was born requires a belief in divine prophecy (although it is not without parallel that a Bible prophet should name someone not yet born - Isaiah does the same thing earlier with Immanuel in Isa 7:14, and Ezekiel names Gog in Ezek 38:1, 38:3, etc.). Even for believers, the specificity of the prophecy so far in the future is sometimes seen as a stretch. As Driver puts it: "The prophet speaks always, in the first instance, to his own contemporaries," not "to generations yet unborn."[16]

Cyrus the Great, King of Persia

These arguments, combined with lesser arguments based on style and theological content, have settled the case among most

---

[16] Driver, *Introduction to the Literature of the Old Testament*, p.237

scholars, so that a date of about 540 B.C. for the second part of Isaiah is now an accepted conclusion, with some writers going further and dividing the second portion of Isaiah again, to form a first, second and third Isaiah. However, a close analysis of the text indicates that proponents of a single author for the entire book of Isaiah have the better case.

4.2.1.2 The Case for the Unity of Isaiah
4.2.1.2.1 Testimony of Antiquity

The testimony of antiquity supports the unity of the book of Isaiah. Ben Sirach, writing about 200 B.C., says: "For Hezekiah did what was pleasing to the Lord, and he held strongly to the ways of David his father, which Isaiah the prophet commanded, who was great and faithful in his vision. In his days the sun went backward, and he lengthened the life of the king. By the spirit of might he saw the last things, and comforted those who mourned in Zion. He revealed what was to occur to the end of time, and the hidden things before they came to pass" (Sir 48:25-28 RSV). The verses tie the Isaiah of Hezekiah's time to the words of comfort and prediction found in the second part of the book.

The New Testament quotes frequently from Isaiah. Table 4-3 below lists nine New Testament passages naming Isaiah as the author of the first part of the book and ten New Testament passages naming Isaiah as the author of the second part of the book.

Table 4-3 New Testament References to Isaiah

Isaiah Passage	New Testament Passage	Speaker
Isa 1:9	Rom 9:29	Paul
Isa 6:9	Matt 13:14-15, Mark 4:12, Luke 8:10	Jesus
Isa 6:9-10	John 12:39-41	John
Isa 6:9-10	Acts 28:25-27	Paul

Isaiah Passage	New Testament Passage	Speaker
Isa 9:1-2	Matt 4:14-16	Matthew
Isa 10:22-23	Rom 9:27-28	Paul
Isa 11:10	Rom 15:12	Paul
Isa 29:13	Matt 15:7-9, Mark 7:6-7	Jesus
Isa 40:3	Matt 3:3	Matthew
Isa 40:3	Mark 1:1-3	Mark
Isa 40:3	John 1:23	John the Baptist
Isa 40:3-5	Luke 3:4-6	Luke
Isa 42:1-4	Matt 12:17-21	Matthew
Isa 53:1	John 12:37-38	John
Isa 53:1	Rom 10:16	Paul
Isa 53:4	Matt 8:17	Matthew
Isa 53:7-8	Acts 8:28-33	Luke
Isa 61:1-2	Luke 4:17-19	Luke
Isa 65:1-2	Rom 10:20-21	Paul

Josephus, writing about 93 A.D., indicates that King Cyrus of Persia was shown the prophecy with his name in it, and this motivated his proclamation. Josephus says "This was known to Cyrus by his reading the book which Isaiah left behind him of his prophecies, for this prophet said that God had spoken thus to him in a secret vision…this was foretold by Isaiah 140 years before the temple was demolished. Accordingly, when Cyrus read this, and admired the divine power, an earnest desire and ambition seized upon him to fulfill what was so written."[17] Skeptics may question the historical value of Josephus' account, but regardless of that historical value, Josephus makes it clear that the ancients understood very well and accepted as true the idea that Isaiah wrote

[17] Flavius Josephus, *Antiquities of the Jews*, Book 11 Chapter 1 paragraph 1.

about events in the distant future – this is not a new discovery of modern critics.

4.2.1.2.2 Geography

The land of Israel is mostly very rugged, with steep, rocky hills, valleys, caves and even mountains, though none of the mountains are very high. The land around Babylon is an alluvial plain, flat, smooth, watered by the Tigris and Euphrates rivers. In other words, the geography of the two countries is different. With this in mind, we should consider the geographical setting of the writing of Isaiah 40-66. An Israelite, as opposed to a Babylonian setting is immediately clear (Isa 40:3-4):

> "A voice is calling,
>> "Clear the way for the LORD in the wilderness;
>> Make smooth in the desert a highway for our God.
> [4]"Let every valley be lifted up,
>> And every mountain and hill be made low;
>> And let the rough ground become a plain,
>> And the rugged terrain a broad valley..."

This is Israeli geography. The geographical references to mountains and hills continue (40:9, 40:12; 41:15, 41:18, etc.). Isa 41:19 provides a list of trees native to Israel: cedar, acacia, myrtle, olive, juniper, box tree and cypress. References to Israel's neighbor Lebanon are in 40:16. It seems unlikely that a prophet writing nearly 50 years into the exile would use numerous geographical references with which only the oldest among his target audience could identify.

A few source critics acknowledge this problem, and allow that Deutero-Isaiah was writing from the land of Israel. Bernhard Duhm, who popularized the view that there were three Isaiahs, says of Deutero-Isaiah, "He certainly did not live in Babylonia."[18] However, this admission gives away half the game, for now we

---

[18] Seitz, *Zion's Final Destiny*, p. 8

have the man who is supposedly the prophet to the Babylonian exiles not living in exile.

4.2.1.2.3 Temple and Sacrifices

Isaiah 40-66 includes references to sacrifices not relevant to a community in exile. These include:

"Even Lebanon is not enough to burn,
    Nor its beasts enough for a burnt offering." (40:16),
"You have not brought to Me the sheep of your burnt offerings,
    Nor have you honored Me with your sacrifices
    I have not burdened you with offerings,
    Nor wearied you with incense.
  You have bought Me not sweet cane with money,
    Nor have you filled Me with the fat of your sacrifices;
    Rather you have burdened Me with your sins,
    You have wearied Me with your iniquities." (43:23-24)

These verses indicate that the hearers are in the habit of performing sacrifices. This was not possible during the Babylonian exile, but it was possible when Isaiah wrote.

More passages in Isaiah 56-66 mention the Temple and sacrifices (56:5-7, 60:7 and 66:3). Some critics explain these away by use of a third Isaiah writing after the exile, when the temple is rebuilt. However, "second Isaiah" (43:28) also mentions "princes of the sanctuary," implying that a Temple existed at that time also.

4.2.1.2.4 Canaanite Idolatry

Polemic messages against idol worship are a unifying theme throughout both parts of Isaiah (1:29, 2:8, 10:10-11, 17:8, 19:1, 19:3, 21:9, 30:22, 31:7, 40:19, 41:29, 42:8, 42:17, 44:9, 44:15, 45:16, 46:6-7, 48:5, 57:5, 65:2-4, 66:3 and 66:17). Canaanite idol worship, which was a huge spiritual problem for the pre-exilic community, became largely a dead issue during and after the exile. With the exception of 47:13 and the specific references to Babylonian idols in 46:1, the idolatry in the second part of the book appears to be of the Canaanite variety. Certainly passages like "Who inflame yourselves among the oaks, under every luxuriant tree, who slaughter the children in the ravines, under the clefts of the crags?" (57:5) are unmistakably addressing Canaanite and not Babylonian idolatry. This implies that at the time the second part of Isaiah was written, Canaanite idolatry was a serious concern. This state of affairs was true during the time of Isaiah the son of Amoz, but not true during or after the exile.

4.2.1.2.5 Isaiah's Children and Friends

Isaiah 7-8 is set during a time of political crisis for the Kingdom of Judah. Judah is under pressure from an alliance between Syria and the northern Kingdom of Israel. Isaiah's message at this time is that these two kingdoms are not a concern; they will soon be conquered by Assyria. It is at this time that Isaiah's wife gives birth to their second son. Isaiah names this child Maher-shalal-hash-baz (Isa 8:3 - the longest name in the Bible), which means "swift is the booty, speedy is the prey." The explanation for the name is given in Isa 8:4 – before the boy is even old enough to talk, the wealth and spoil of Syria and Israel will be carried away by the Assyrians. This story, along with the name of Isaiah's second son, provides a setting just before the fall of the northern Kingdom of Israel to Assyria in 722 B.C.

Now let us consider the beginning of this story in Isa 7:1-3. Going to meet the king of Judah with God's message are Isaiah and his first son, Shear-jashub. Shear-jashub means "a remnant will return." The reason for this name is not given, but there is a clear allusion to the return of the people, not just spiritually to God, but also a physical return to Jerusalem. The "remnant" are the ones who will return from the Babylon captivity, a common theme in scripture and a message Isaiah preaches in both the first and second parts of his book (10:20-22, 11:11, 11:16, 46:3 and 48:20). The wording of Isa 10:21 actually begins with the name of Isaiah's first son, "A remnant will return." The critics are misleading when they say Isaiah the son of Amoz would not speak to future generations, since he addresses them with something as basic as the name of his first son. The names of Isaiah's children are not accidental; see Isa 8:18: "Behold, I and the children whom the LORD has given me are for signs and wonders in Israel from the LORD of hosts."

Finally, Isa 62:4, in the second part of the book, would have unique personal meaning for Isaiah's king, Hezekiah. This verse says: "It will no longer be said to you, "Forsaken," Nor to your land will it any longer be said, "Desolate"; But you will be called, "My delight is in her," And your land, "Married"; For the LORD delights in you, And to Him your land will be married." The Hebrew word for "my delight is in her" in this verse is "Hephzibah." Hephzibah was the name of Hezekiah's *wife* (2 Kgs 21:1).

4.2.1.2.6 Setting of the First Part of Isaiah

There are additional passages in the *first* part of Isaiah that address the captivity and exile as an already accomplished fact (1:7-9, 5:13, 14:1-4 and 35:1-10) and others which point forward to it (3:24-26, 5:5-6, 6:11-13, 24:11-12, 27:3 and 32:13-18). Although Babylon is mentioned four times in the second part of the book, it is mentioned nine times in the first part. Since we have already seen how the second part of Isaiah in different ways and certain points addresses a people not in exile, as Harrison puts it, "The supposedly divergent historical standpoints of the two main sections of the prophecy as isolated by critical study are certainly by no means as different as has been imagined."[19]

4.2.1.2.7 Setting of the Second Part of Isaiah

The location of the speaker in the second part of Isaiah is in Israel, not Babylon. Consider: "...for your sake I have sent to Babylon..." (43:14). The speaker, God in this case, "sends" to Babylon because

---

[19] Patterson, *Introduction to the Old Testament*, p. 778

He is not there. Additional verses speak of Babylon as somewhere else, not where the speaker is: "Calling a bird of prey from the east, the man of My purpose from a far country" (46:11), and "Depart, depart, go out from there, touch nothing unclean" (52:11).

In the second part of Isaiah, the cities of Judah are addressed as if they are still standing (40:9). Also, the walls are standing (62:6) – walls that will be torn down by the Babylonians and not rebuilt until the time of Nehemiah around 445 B.C, a date probably too late for even a third Isaiah.

4.2.1.2.8 An End and a Beginning

If we were to think that the work of a new prophet begins in chapter 40, multiple problems immediately leap out. First, this new prophet is anonymous, unlike all the other writing prophets.[20] Not only is the new prophet anonymous in the text of the book, but there seems to be no recollection or remembrance of him anywhere. Zechariah and Haggai wrote shorter books just a few years later and they are well documented (Zech 1:1, Hag 1:1, Ezra 5:1, 6:14, Psalms 145 and 146 in the Septuagint). We are faced with the unlikely scenario in which a great prophet's name and memory are lost, but his writing preserved. Furthermore, his writing was not attached to the work of his contemporaries, like Zechariah or Haggai, or to recently completed works which dealt extensively with the exile, like Jeremiah or Ezekiel, but instead his writing attached itself to the 150-200 year old work of Isaiah. This would be roughly analogous to a contemporary writing about the American south attaching itself to *Uncle Tom's Cabin*, without anyone commenting on it.

Second, consider the way chapter 40 begins: "Comfort, o comfort my people." This seems to be the wrong way for a

---

[20] No prophets are anonymous with the possible (but not certain) exception of Malachi. Malachi's name means "my messenger", and some have suggested that this is not a proper name, but rather a title.

prophet to begin. No prophet begins a book with a message of comfort. Prophets invariably begin either with a message of judgment, or a call to repentance.

Finally, we should back up some and consider how the first part of the book ends. Isaiah 36-37 has the story of the spectacular deliverance of Jerusalem from the Assyrian army, but this is not the end. The end occurs after Hezekiah gets sick, recovers, greets the Babylonian envoys and shows them around. Isaiah indicates this might not have been a good idea because Babylon will eventually take all the things he showed, and Hezekiah says, well "at least there will be peace and truth in my days." This would seem to be a strange and anticlimactic way to end a book. Also, though the timing is close, chapters 38-39 apparently occur chronologically before the destruction of the Assyrian army in chapter 37, so this portion of Isaiah is not strictly chronological (to build a chronology, see 36:1, 38:1, 38:5-6 and 2 Kgs 18:2). The reason for the current order of the book is that 39:5-8 provide Isaiah's way of introducing the Babylonian exile, which hasn't yet happened, before he addresses the future exiles in chapter 40.

4.2.1.2.9 Unity of Isaiah Demonstrated by Literary Construction
Critics allege the change in style that begins in chapter 40 is evidence for a different author. However, any author can change certain aspects of his style when he changes the subject, and if it fits his purposes. Isaiah does change style in some ways, but we shall demonstrate that in numerous ways, both parts of the book show unmistakable evidence that they came from the same mind. Let us consider some of the aspects of Isaiah's literary style.

First, Isaiah has the habit of stringing together rhetorical questions, as in "Who hath heard such a thing? Who hath seen such things? Shall the earth be made to bring forth in one day? Or shall a nation be born at once?" (66:8). This is done in both the first and second portions of the book (1:11-12, 5:4, 10:3, 10:8-11, 28:9, 28:24, 40:12-14, 40:21, 40:28, 41:2-4, etc.).

Second, Isaiah commonly uses perfect tense verbs for prophetic future events. In English this has the effect of speaking of future events in the past tense, as in "Therefore my people are gone into captivity, because they have no knowledge" (5:13 KJV) and "Surely he hath borne our griefs, and carried our sorrows" (53:4 KJV). This occurs in 5:13, 9:1-7, 10:28-31, 53:1-12 and 66:7-8, to list a few examples.

Third, Isaiah is fond of using an emphatic duplication of words – something he does in both parts of the book:

2:7-8	"Their land has been filled with... Their land has been filled with... Their land has been filled with..."
2:12-16	"upon all... upon all... upon all... upon all... upon all... upon all... upon all... upon all..."
3:24	"instead of... instead of... instead of... instead of ... instead of..."
6:3	"Holy, holy, holy"
8:9	"Gird yourselves, yet be shattered; gird yourselves, yet be shattered,"
11:2	"spirit of...spirit of...spirit of...spirit of..."
15:1	"Surely in a night Ar of Moab is devastated and ruined; Surely in a night Kir of Moab is devastated and ruined."
21:9	"fallen, fallen"
21:11	"Watchman, how far gone is the night? Watchman, how far gone is the night?"
24:16	"Woe to me, woe to me"
28:10	"Order on order, order on order, line on line, line on line, a little here, a little there." (also in 28:13)
29:1	"Woe Ariel, Ariel"
38:19	"The living, the living"
40:1	"Comfort, comfort"
40:7-8	The grass withers, the flower fades...The grass withers, the flower fades

40:24	"scarcely have...scarcely have...scarcely has..."
41:26	"surely there was...surely there was...surely there was..."
43:11	"I, I"
43:25	"I, I"
48:15	"I, I"
51:12	"I, I"
51:9, 52:1	"awake, awake"
51:9-10	"Was it not you who...Was it not you who..."
51:17	"Rouse yourself! Rouse yourself!"
52:11	"depart, depart"
55:13	"instead of... instead of... "
57:14	"build up, build up"
57:19	"peace, peace"
60:17	"instead of... instead of... instead of... instead of ..."
61:3	"instead of... instead of... "
62:10	"build up, build up"
65:1	"Here am I, here am I"
65:13-14	"Behold, my servants will...but you will be... Behold, my servants will...but you will be... Behold, my servants will...but you will be... Behold, my servants will...but you will be..."

Although other passages in the Bible use similar repetition, nowhere else is this done so frequently or with such a marked effect as in Isaiah.[21] These are just three examples of a literary style which remains the same in both parts of the book.

In 1954, Rachel Margalioth wrote the Hebrew book *Echad Hayah Yeshayahu* (Isaiah was One), which was translated into English in 1964 as *The Indivisible Isaiah*. This book demonstrates by literary style that the second portion of Isaiah was written by the same

---

[21] Jeremiah, for example, uses repetition less, and when he does, he usually puts it in the mouth of those he is criticizing, as in Jer 6:14 and 7:4.

author as the first portion of Isaiah. In this area Mrs. Margalioth produced an exhaustive amount of evidence, and most of what we will cite below is a subset of examples taken directly from her book. Most of these examples can be understood using an English language Bible. We have frequently provided the Hebrew text for these examples, because some translations use different wording in different places, while the Hebrew does not vary. If the number of examples provided seems excessive, this is because the idea of a unified Isaiah flies into the teeth of entrenched scholarship, and we do not wish to cut the evidence short.

4.2.1.2.9.1 Designations of God

Isaiah uses a variety of designations for God which are rare or unique in the Old Testament. They are found in both portions of the book.

1. "Holy One of Israel" (קדוש ישראל). This phrase is used 12 times in the first part of Isaiah and 13 times in the second part (1:4, 5:19, 5:24, 10:20, 12:6, 17:7, 29:19, 30:11, 30:12, 31:1, 37:23, 41:14, 41:16, 41:20, 43:3, 43:14, 45:11, 47:4, 48:17, 49:7, 54:5, 55:5, 60:9, 60:14). This phrase is used only four additional times in the Bible, one of those being 2 Kgs 19:22, a passage involving Isaiah. Isaiah's choice of words may have been influenced by his experience in Isa 6:3, with the heavenly beings calling "holy, holy, holy."

2. "His Holy One" (קדושו), referring to God with a third person inflection, is in 10:17 and 49:7, but not found elsewhere in scripture.

3. "Lofty and exalted one" (רם ונשא) is in 6:1 and 57:15, but not found elsewhere in scripture. (33:10 and 52:13 are slight variations)

4. "Mighty One" (אביר) is in 1:24, 10:13, 49:26 and 60:16, but not found elsewhere in the prophets.

5. Designation of God as "light" (אור) is in 10:17, 60:1 and 60:19, and found elsewhere in the Old Testament only in Micah 7:8 (Micah being a contemporary of Isaiah).

6. Designation of God as "your salvation" (ישעך) is in 17:10 and 62:11, but not found elsewhere in the Old Testament.

7. Designation of God as "Creator," using the Hebrew word "yotzer" (יוצר) with inflections, is in 22:11, 27:11, 43:1, 44:2, 44:24, 45:9, 45:11, 49:5 and 64:7, but not found elsewhere in scripture. Jeremiah develops this idea in Jeremiah 18, but does not apply the name "yotzer" to God.

8. Designation of God as "Maker," using the Hebrew word "asah" (עשה) with inflections, is in 17:7, 22:11, 27:11, 29:16, 44:2, 51:13 and 54:5, but not found elsewhere in scripture except Hos 8:14. Without inflections it is present elsewhere, as in Ps 124:8.

9. "Rock" (צור) is used as a designation of God in Isa 17:10, 30:29, 44:8 and 51:1, but not elsewhere in the prophets except for the early poetry in 1 Samuel 2 and 22. "Rock" is a common designation of God in early poetry, but this usage had mostly ceased by the time of the prophets.

10. "Righteous One" (צדיק) is used for God in 24:16 and 53:11, with Prov 21:12 being the only other occurrence of this term in scripture.[22]

4.2.1.2.9.2 Designations of the People of Israel

Isaiah uses a collection of unique metaphors, both positive and negative, to describe Israel. These appear in both portions of the book.

1. "Blind" (עור or עורים), used as a metaphor for spiritual blindness, is in 29:18, 35:5, 42:7, 42:16, 42:18, 42:19, 43:8 and 56:10, but not found elsewhere in the Old Testament.

---

[22] The reference in Isa 53:11 is to the Suffering Servant, accepted by Christians as a reference to Christ

2. "Deaf" (חרש or חרשים), used as a metaphor for people who are unable to hear God's word, is used in 29:18, 35:5, 42:18, 42:19 and 43:8, but not found elsewhere in scripture. Isaiah's use of blind and deaf in a spiritual sense is tied to his initial vision in 6:9-10:

   "He said, "Go, and tell this people:
      'Keep on listening, but do not perceive;
      Keep on looking, but do not understand.'
     "Render the hearts of this people insensitive,
     Their ears dull,
     And their eyes dim,
     Otherwise they might see with their eyes,
     Hear with their ears,
     Understand with their hearts,
     And return and be healed."

3. "Offspring" (זרע), used in a derogatory sense for Israel, is in 1:4, 57:3 and 57:4, but not found elsewhere in scripture. In each section, "offspring" is used in apposition with "sons."

4. "Those who forsake the LORD" (עזבי יהוה) is in 1:28 and 65:11, but not found elsewhere in scripture.

5. "The ransomed of the LORD" (פדויי יהוה) is in 35:10 and 51:11, but not found elsewhere in scripture.

6. "The work of my hands" (מעשה ידי) is in 29:23 and 60:21, but not found elsewhere in scripture. Assyria is also called "The work of my hands" in 19:25. Similar variations are in 45:11 and 64:7.

7. "Sons" (בנים) who were "reared" (גדל) are in 1:2 and 51:18, but not found elsewhere in scripture.

8. Israel is designated as the "vineyard of the LORD" (כרם יהוה) in 5:7 and "planting of the LORD" (מטע יהוה) in 61:3, but there is no similar use elsewhere in the Old Testament.

9. "Poor" (singular or plural of עני), used in the sense of de-
    scribing all the people of Israel as opposed to the economic
    sense of the word, is in 14:32, 26:6, 41:17 and 49:13, but not
    found elsewhere in the prophets.
10. "Needy" (אביונים), again used to describe all the people, is
    in 14:30, 25:4 and 41:17, but not elsewhere in the prophets.
11. Compare "and He will gather the dispersed of Israel"
    (11:12) with "who gathers the dispersed of Israel" (56:8).
12. Compare also 28:5, "In that day the LORD of hosts will be-
    come a beautiful crown and a glorious diadem to the rem-
    nant of His people," with 62:3: "You will also be a crown
    of beauty in the hand of the LORD, and a royal diadem in
    the hand of your God."

4.2.1.2.9.3 Formulas of Address

Isaiah uses multiple unique forms address. These include:

1. "Will say the LORD" (יאמר יהוה). This formula of address
    is most unusual and is lost in translations, which must
    necessarily render it "says the LORD," using an English
    past tense, as is a common formula of address in the other
    prophets. Isaiah uses this phrase, "will say the LORD" or
    "will say your God," with a Hebrew imperfect tense (usu-
    ally translated into English as a future tense, though that is
    not an exact match), rather than the more common perfect
    tense. This is found in 1:11, 1:18, 33:10, 40:1, 40:25, 41:21
    and 66:9, but not found elsewhere in the prophets.
2. "For the mouth of the LORD has spoken" (כי פי יהוה דבר)
    is in 1:20, 40:5 and 58:14, but not found elsewhere in scrip-
    ture.
3. A "voice saying" (קול אמר), is in 6:8 and 40:6, but not
    found elsewhere in scripture.
4. A "voice calling" (קול קורא) is in 6:4 and 40:3, but not
    found elsewhere in scripture.

5. "And now the LORD speaks" (ועתה יהוה דבר) is in 16:14, "and now the LORD says" (ועתה אמר יהוה) is in 49:5, but neither appears elsewhere in scripture.

6. "Hear the word of the LORD, you…" (שמעו דבר יהוה) is in 1:10, 28:14 and 66:5, but not elsewhere in the prophets.

7. "Listening listen" (שמעו שמוע), usually translated something like "keep on listening," is in 6:9 and 55:2, but not found elsewhere in the prophets.

8. "Come near" and "hear" (קרבו and שמע) in the same phrase are in 34:1 and 48:16, but not found elsewhere in the prophets.

9. "Give ear," "attend" and "hear" (הקשב, האזינו and שמע) in the same phrase are in 28:23 and 42:23, but not found elsewhere in scripture.

10. "I have declared" (הגדתי), to confirm a prophecy, is in 21:10, 43:12, 44:8 and 48:3, but not found elsewhere in scripture

4.2.1.2.9.4 Zion and Jerusalem

Isaiah addresses Jerusalem in multiple unique ways. These include:

1. Isaiah mentions "Zion" and "Jerusalem" together in parallelism more than all the other prophets put together (2:3, 4:3, 4:4, 10:12, 10:32, 24:23, 30:19, 31:9, 33:20, 37:22, 37:32, 40:9, 41:27, 52:1, 52:2, 62:1 and 64:9 [Heb 64:10]).

2. Jerusalem is addressed in second person with the phrase "you will be called" (יקרא לך or לך יקרא) in 1:26, 58:12 and 62:4 and 62:12, but nowhere else in scripture. Similar variations are in 42:6, 47:5, 60:14 and 61:6.

3. A prophecy of "no weeping" and no "voice of crying" in Jerusalem is in 30:19 and 65:19, but not found elsewhere in scripture.

4. Jerusalem is asked to "cry aloud" and "sing" in 12:6 and 54:1, but nowhere else in scripture.

5. "Zion" is called "my people" in 10:24 and 51:16, but no-where else in scripture.

6. God "reigns" in Zion in 24:23 and 52:7, wording not found else in the prophets.

7. "Tent" (אהל) and "stakes" (יתדות) are used in reference to Zion in 33:20 and 54:2, but nowhere else in scripture.

4.2.1.2.9.5 Ingathering of the Exiles

Each major prophet discusses the return of Jewish exiles to Israel, with distinctive terminology. Jeremiah says they will return from the countries "where I have driven them" (Jer 16:15, 23:3, 23:8, 29:14 and 32:37), while Ezekiel says they will be gathered from "where you have been scattered" (Ezek 11:17, 20:34, 20:41, 28:25 and 29:13). Isaiah also uses special terminology, with more variation, to discuss the return of the Jewish exiles to Israel, and this terminology is present in both portions of the book.

1. "And the ransomed of the LORD shall return, and come with singing unto Zion, and everlasting joy shall be on their heads; they shall obtain gladness and joy, and sorrow and sighing shall flee away" from 35:10 is repeated with only one letter difference in 51:11. "Everlasting joy" (שמחת עולם), a phrase that appears only in Isaiah, is also in 61:7.

2. "Gather" the "dispersed of Israel" (קבץ with נדקי ישראל) is in 11:12 and 56:8, but not found elsewhere in scripture.

3. "Raise up an ensign" for "the nations" (נשא נס לגוים) is in 11:12 and 49:22, but not found elsewhere in scripture. The same words are found with different application in 5:26.

4. The revival of "wilderness," used in parallel with "desert" (ערבה and מדבר), is in 35:1, 35:6, 40:3, 41:19 and 51:3, but not found elsewhere in scripture.

5. "Parched land"…"springs of water" (שרב...מבועי מים) is in 35:7 and 49:10, but not found elsewhere in scripture. 46:18 has a similar wording.

6. Isaiah speaks of laying down a "highway" (מסלול or מסלה)
    for the convenience of the returning exiles in 11:16, 35:8,
    40:3 and 62:10, but no similar use of this word is found in
    scripture. A highway or highways in general also appear
    in 7:3, 19:23, 33:8, 36:2, 49:11 and 59:7.
7. The exiles return to "the holy mountain, Jerusalem"
    (הר הקדש ירושלם) in 27:13 and 66:20, a phrase not used
    elsewhere in scripture (Dan 9:16 uses it in reverse order).

4.2.1.2.9.6 Messages of Consolation

The following examples all occur in messages of consolation.

1. "They will plant vineyards and eat the fruit"
    (ונטעו כרמים ואכול פרים) is in 37:30 and 65:21, but not
    found elsewhere in scripture.
2. "The glory of Lebanon" (כבוד הלבנון) comes to Israel in
    35:2 and 60:13. This phrase is not found elsewhere in the
    Bible.
3. The "Eyes of the blind" are "opened" (using Hebrew
    words עינים, עור and פקח) in 35:5 and 42:7. This phrase is
    not found elsewhere in the Old Testament.
4. People and roads are "called holiness" (קרא ל הקדש) in
    35:8 and 62:12, while inanimate objects, the city and trees,
    are "called righteousness" (קרא ל הצדק) in 1:26 and 61:3.
    There is no similar use elsewhere in scripture.
5. "Growth" and "fruit of the earth" (with Hebrew words
    צמח, פרה and ארץ) are used metaphorically to express sal-
    vation in 4:2 and 45:8, but nowhere else in scripture.
6. "Peace" (שלום) and "righteousness" (צדקה) are together in
    9:7 (Heb 9:6), 32:17, 48:18, 54:13-14 and 60:17, but nowhere
    else in the prophets.
7. The use of "moment" (רגע) in the context of the reduction
    of the duration of evil is in 26:20, 54:7 and 54:8, but not
    elsewhere in the prophets.

8. The LORD will "hear" (שמע) and "answer" (ענה), the words together in parallel in 30:19 and 65:24, but not elsewhere in the prophets.

9. "I shall guard" (נצר), with the LORD as the subject, is in 27:3, 42:6 and 49:8, but not found elsewhere in scripture.

10. "Walls" (חומות) and "salvation" (ישועה) are together in 26:1 and 60:18, but are not found together elsewhere in scripture.

11. "Walls" (חומות) and "gates" (שערים) are in 26:1-2, 60:10-11 and 60:18 as objects of consolation. Elsewhere in scripture they are together only in a derogatory context (Jer 1:15 and Ezek 26:10). Extending the idea, opening the gates for the benefit of the nation or nations (using Hebrew words פתח שערים גוי and בוא) in 26:2 and 60:11 is also unique in scripture.

12. "Eating" the "good" is connected to "hearing" (Hebrew words אכל טוב and שמע) in 1:19 and 55:2, but nowhere else in scripture.

13. Compare also 35:6 "For waters will break forth in the wilderness and streams in the Arabah" with 41:18, "I will make the wilderness a pool of water and the dry land fountains of water."

4.2.1.2.9.7 Expressions of Joy and Gladness

The following examples are taken from passages which express joy and gladness.

1. "They shall sing" (using the Hebrew root word רון or רנן) is in 24:14, 42:11, 52:8 and 65:14, but not found elsewhere in the prophets.

2. "Break forth into singing" (פצח רנה) is in 14:7, 44:23, 49:13, 54:1 and 55:12, but not found elsewhere in scripture.

3. "Lift up the voice" (קול with נשא) and "sing" is in 24:14 and 52:18, but not found elsewhere in scripture.

4. "Cry aloud" (צהלי) and "sing" is in 12:6 and 54:1, but not found elsewhere in scripture.

5. "Sing…for," as a command with a reason, is in 26:19 and 52:9, but not found elsewhere in the prophets.

6. "Sing" a "song" (using שיר and שירה) is in 5:1, 26:1 and 42:10, but not found elsewhere in the prophets.

7. "Rejoicing" (משוש without inflections) is in 8:6, 24:8 (twice), 24:11, 32:13, 32:14, 60:15, 62:5, 65:18 and 66:10, but only otherwise in the prophets in Ezek 24:25.

8. "Gladness and joy" (ששון ושמחה) is in 22:13, 35:10, 51:3 and 51:11, but not found elsewhere in the prophets.

9. "Everlasting joy" (שמחת עולם) is in 35:10, 51:11 and 61:7, but nowhere else in scripture.

4.2.1.2.9.8 Universal Millennium

Isaiah speaks of a universal millennium in which all nations dwell in peace and follow the law of God. These passages are in both portions of the book.

1. "The wolf and the lamb [are together]…and the lion will eat straw like the ox…they will not hurt or destroy in all My holy mountain," is in 11:6-9 and 65:25, but nowhere else in scripture.

2. "For out of…shall go forth the law," (using the Hebrew words תורה and יצא) is in 2:3 and 51:4, but not elsewhere in scripture, except that Micah 4:1-3 is a copy of Isaiah 2:2-4.

3. "The Spirit" (רוח) of the LORD is "upon him" (עליו) in 11:2 and 42:1, an idea not found elsewhere in scripture concerning the future.

4. "He will judge" (שפט) "the nations" (גוים) is in 2:4 and 42:1. The idea of judging the nations in the sense of bringing justice (not punishment) to them is not found elsewhere in the prophets.

5.   God's "house" (בית) and his "mountain" (הר) are places of pilgrimage for "people" (עמים) in 2:3 and 56:7, but nowhere else in scripture.

6.   "They shall see" (ראה) "the glory of the LORD" (כבוד יהוה) in 35:2 and 40:5, a formulation not found elsewhere in scripture. A similar formulation is in 66:18.

7.   "Fear" (ירא) and "glory" (כבוד) are used together in a promise for the future in 25:3 and 59:19, but not elsewhere in the prophets. They are together with a different usage in Mal 1:6.

8.   They "shall lift up" (נשא) and "sing" (רנן) and "glorify the LORD" in the "isles" (איים) of the "sea" (הים) in 24:14-15 and 42:10-12.

4.2.1.2.9.9 Words of Admonition

The following examples are taken from passages with words of admonition.

1.   "Gardens" (גנות) are described as places of idol worship in 1:29, 65:3 and 66:17, but nowhere else in scripture.

2.   "Terebinths" (אלים) are described as places of idol worship in 1:29 and 57:5, but nowhere else in scripture.

3.   "They shall be ashamed" (יבשו) of their "desires" (Hebrew root חמד), in which the desires are idols, is in 1:29 and 44:9, but nowhere else in scripture.

4.   "Burnt offerings" (עולות) and "fat" (חלב) are together in 1:11 and 43:23-24 in words of admonition to the people, a formulation unique in the prophets.

5.   "Meal offerings" (מנחה) and "iniquity" (און) are together in 1:13 and 66:3, but nowhere else in scripture.

6.   "I take no pleasure" (לא חפצתי), with God as the subject reprimanding the people, is in 1:11, 65:12 and 66:4, but nowhere else in scripture.

7. "Your hands are full of blood" is in 1:15, and "your hands are defiled with blood" is in 59:3, formulations not found elsewhere in scripture.

8. "They refused" (לא אבו) to "hear the teaching" (שמעו תורה) is in 30:9 and 42:24.

9. "You have not remembered" (לא זכרת) with God as the direct object, is in 17:10 and 57:11, but not found elsewhere in scripture.

10. A variation of "Shall the clay say to its creator?" (יצר אמר ליוצרו) is in 29:16 and 45:9, but not found elsewhere in scripture.

11. A reprimand in parallelism for drinking "wine" (יין) and "strong drink" (שכר) is found in 5:11, 24:9, 28:7, 29:9 and 56:12, but not elsewhere in scripture. The passages in 29:9-10 and 56:10-12 are also both associated with blindness and slumber.

12. Carousers drinking wine and boasting about "tomorrow" (מחר) are in 22:13 and 56:12, but not elsewhere in the Old Testament.

13. "Ears" (אזן) which do not "hear" (שמע) are in 6:9-10 and 48:8, but not elsewhere in the prophets.

14. "That we may know" (ונדעה) is in 5:19, 41:23 and 41:26, in each case challenging a deity to reveal its power. This is not found elsewhere in scripture.

4.2.1.2.9.10 Words of Chastisement

Most of the following phrases are in passages of chastisement.

1. "Sit to the ground" (ישיבה לארץ) is in 3:26 and 47:1. This is unique among the prophets.

2. "And behold, darkness" (והנה חשך) is in 5:30 and 59:9, but nowhere else in scripture.

3. "None will pass" (אין עובר) is in 34:10 and 60:15, but not elsewhere in scripture.

4. "They shall not rise" (בל יקומו) is in 14:21, 26:14 and 43:17, but nowhere else in the prophetic writings. It is found in Ps 140:11. The usage is unusual due to the older poetic negation (בל) rather than the more common negation (לא). There are eight other occurrences of "not rise" in the Bible (2 Sam 22:39, Job 14:12, 25:3, Ps 41:8 [Heb 41:9], Jer 51:64, Amos 5:2, 8:14 and Nah 1:9), and all use לא rather than בל.

5. "Vain" (הבל) and "vanity" (ריק) are together in 30:7 and 49:4, but nowhere else in scripture.

6. "Fade as a leaf" (using נבל and עלה) is used as a simile in 34:4 and 64:5, but nowhere else in scripture.

7. "To moan as a dove" (using הגה and יונה) is in 38:14 and 59:11, but nowhere else in scripture.

8. "Drunken, but not with wine" (using שכר and יין) is in 29:9 and 51:21, but nowhere else in scripture.

9. "Be for a burning fire" (using היה, לשרפה and אש) is in 9:4 and 64:10, but not elsewhere in scripture. Compare also 1:7 with 64:9-10.

10. "Fire" and "your adversaries" (צריך) are in 26:11 and 64:1, but nowhere else in scripture.

11. "Chaff" (מץ), "mountains" (הרים) and "wind" (רוח) are together in 17:13 and 41:15-16, but nowhere else in scripture.

12. "Behold…He will come…and his…wheels/chariots like a whirlwind" are in 5:26-28 and 66:15, but nowhere else in scripture.

13. "For behold, the LORD…The LORD…with His sword" (using כי הנה יהוה and בחרבו) is in 26:21-27:1 and 66:15-16, but nowhere else in scripture.

14. "The voice of the LORD" (קל יהוה) brings evil to an enemy in 30:31 and 66:6, but nowhere else in scripture.

15. "The voice the uproar" (קל שאון) is in 13:4 and 66:6, but nowhere else in scripture.

16. "The LORD," "anger" (אף), and "flame of fire" (להב אש) are in 30:30 and 66:15, but nowhere else in scripture. A similar passage is in 29:6.

17. "I have brought down" (ואוריד) is in 10:13 and 63:6, but nowhere else in scripture.

18. "Hungry" (רעב), "drinks" (שתה) and "faint" (יעף) are together in 29:8 and 44:12, but nowhere else in scripture.

19. Compare also 1:15 "Yes, even though you multiply prayers, I will not listen; your hands are covered with blood," with 59:2-3, "And your sins have hidden His face from you so that He does not hear. For your hands are defiled with blood."

4.2.1.2.9.11 Thesis and Antithesis

Several prophets express praise and blessing by converting their own previous derogatory phrases, or vice versa. For example, Hosea first says: "I will no longer have mercy," and "you are not my people" (Hos 1:6 and 1:9), then converts his terminology, saying: "say to your brothers: 'my people' and to your sisters 'mercy is shown'" (Hos 2:1). Jeremiah converts his terminology several times, as in saying, "Behold, what I have built I am about to tear down, and what I have planted I am about to uproot" (Jer 45:4), and conversely saying "then I will build you up and not tear you down, and I will plant you and not uproot you" (Jer 42:10). Jeremiah also warns three times that "the voice of joy and the voice of gladness, the voice of the bridegroom and the voice of the bride" would be removed (Jer 7:34, 16:9 and 25:10), then using identical wording says they will be restored in Jer 33:11. Mrs. Margalioth likens this to a mother promising her son a trumpet if he is good, then threatening not to buy the trumpet if he misbehaves.[23] Isaiah does this also, as in "Sons I have reared and brought up" (Isa 1:2), then "I have neither brought up young men

---

[23] Margalioth, *The Indivisible Isaiah*, p. 39

nor reared virgins" (Isa 23:4). This is one of a number of examples in which both the thesis and antithesis are present in the first part of Isaiah. The table below shows examples where the thesis and antithesis are in different portions of the book.

First Part of Isaiah (1-39)	**Second Part of Isaiah (40-66)**
…instead of sweet perfume there will be putrefaction; instead of a belt, a rope; instead of well-set hair, a plucked-out scalp; instead of fine clothes, a donning of sackcloth; and branding instead of beauty. (3:24)	Instead of bronze I will bring gold, and instead of iron I will bring silver, and instead of wood, bronze, and instead of stones, iron. (60:17)
For you will be like … a garden that has no water. (1:30)	And you will be like a watered garden (58:11)
And the land is utterly desolate…and the forsaken places are many in the midst of the land. (6:11-12)	It will no longer be said to you, "Forsaken," nor to your land will it any longer be said, "Desolate"; (62:4)
Sharon is like a desert plain (33:9)	Sharon will be a pasture land for flocks (65:10)
Therefore their Maker will not have compassion on them. (27:11)	He will have compassion on him (55:7)
Therefore the Lord does not take pleasure in their young men, nor does He have pity on their orphans or their widows; (9:17)	For the LORD has comforted His people and will have compassion on His afflicted. (49:13)

First Part of Isaiah (1-39)	Second Part of Isaiah (40-66)
Who say, "…let Him hasten His work, that we may see it; and let the purpose of the Holy One of Israel draw near and come to pass, that we may know it!" (5:19)	That they may see and recognize…that the hand of the LORD has done this, and the Holy One of Israel has created it. (41:20)
Shall the potter be considered as equal with the clay, that what is made would say to its maker, "He did not make me"; (29:16)	We are the clay, and You our potter; and all of us are the work of Your hand. (64:8)
The people who walk in darkness will see a great light; those who live in a dark land, the light will shine on them. (9:2)	We hope for light, but behold, darkness, for brightness, but we walk in gloom. (59:9)
And have put your trust in oppression and guile, and have relied on them (30:12)	Let him trust in the name of the LORD and rely on his God (50:10)
Then justice will dwell in the wilderness and righteousness will abide in the fertile field. (32:16)	Justice is turned back, and righteousness stands far away; (59:14)
Also righteousness will be the belt about His loins, and faithfulness the belt about His waist. (11:5)	No one sues righteously and no one pleads honestly (59:4)
For you have forgotten the God of your salvation and have not remembered the rock of your refuge. (17:10)	But you will forget the shame of your youth, and the reproach of your widowhood you will remember no more. (54:4)
And the ears of the deaf will be unstopped. (35:5)	Even from long ago your ear has not been open (48:8)

First Part of Isaiah (1-39)	Second Part of Isaiah (40-66)
As the pregnant woman approaches the time to give birth, she writhes and cries out in her labor pains, thus were we before You, O LORD. We were pregnant, we writhed in labor, we gave birth, as it seems, only to wind. (26:17-18)	Before she travailed, she brought forth; before her pain came, she gave birth to a boy. Who has heard such a thing? Who has seen such things? Can a land be born in one day? Can a nation be brought forth all at once? As soon as Zion travailed, she also brought forth her sons. (66:7-8)
Children have come to birth, and there is no strength to deliver. (37:3)	Shall I bring to the point of birth and not give delivery?" (66:9)
'Keep on listening, but do not perceive; Keep on looking, but do not understand.' (6:9)	Do you not know? Have you not heard? Has it not been declared to you from the beginning? Have you not understood from the foundations of the earth? (40:21)

The following tables of thesis and antithesis involve in the first column prophecies concerning Tyre, Sidon, Babylon and Assyria. They are converted in the second column to prophecies concerning Israel.

First Part of Isaiah (1-39)	Second Part of Isaiah (40-66)
I have neither travailed nor given birth (23:4)	As soon as Zion travailed, she also brought forth her sons. (66:8)
But pelican and hedgehog will possess it, and owl and raven will dwell in it; (34:11)	Even My chosen ones shall inherit it, and My servants will dwell there. (65:9)

First Part of Isaiah (1-39)	Second Part of Isaiah (40-66)
Its smoke will go up forever, from generation to generation it will be desolate; none will pass through it forever and ever. (34:10)	Whereas you have been forsaken and hated with no one passing through, I will make you an everlasting pride, a joy from generation to generation. (60:15)
Lift up a standard on the bare hill, raise your voice to them (13:2)	Get yourself up on a high mountain, O Zion, bearer of good news, lift up your voice mightily, (40:9)
and will cut off from Babylon name and survivors (14:22)	I will give them an everlasting name which will not be cut off. (56:5)
The sun will be dark when it rises and the moon will not shed its light. (13:10)	No longer will you have the sun for light by day, nor for brightness will the moon give you light (60:19)
No one in it is weary or stumbles (5:27)	Though youths grow weary and tired, and vigorous young men stumble badly, (40:30)
Nor is the belt at its waist undone, nor its sandal strap broken.(5:27)	To loosen the bonds of wickedness, to undo the bands of the yoke, (58:6)
His breath is like an overflowing torrent...to shake the nations (30:28)	I extend peace to her like a river, and the glory of the nations like an overflowing stream; (66:12)
And the light of Israel will become a fire and his Holy One a flame, and it will burn and devour (10:17)	When you walk through the fire, you will not be scorched, nor will the flame burn you. (43:2)

First Part of Isaiah (1-39)	Second Part of Isaiah (40-66)
They will be gathered together like prisoners in the dungeon and will be confined in prison; (24:22)	To bring out prisoners from the dungeon And those who dwell in darkness from the prison. (42:7)

4.2.1.2.9.12 Word Combinations

1. The following word combinations are unique in the Bible, but present in both parts of Isaiah:

A. "Portion" (חלק) … "lot" (גורל) – 17:14 and 57:6

B. "Regard" (שאה) … "look" (ראה) – 17:7, 17:8 and 41:23

C. "Bruised reed" (קנה רציץ) – 36:6 and 42:3 (2 Ki 18:21 = Isa 36:6)

D. "The grass withers" (יבש חציר) – 15:6, 40:7 and 40:8 (Quoted in the New Testament)

E. "The flower fades" (ציץ נבל) – 28:1, 40:7 and 40:8 (Quoted in the New Testament)

E. "Water courses" (יבלי מים) – 30:25 and 44:4

F. "Crevices of the crags" (סעיפי הסלעים) – 2:21 and 57:5

G. "The way of justice" (אורח משפט) - 26:8 and 40:14

H. "Looked for justice" (קוה משפט) – 5:7 and 59:11

I. "To whom will you…" (על מי + verb second person plural imperfect) – 10:3 and 57:4

J. "Continually" (תמיד) … "daytime" (יומם) … "night" (לילה) – 21:8 and 60:11

K. "Exalted" (רום) … "lifted up" (נשא) – 33:10 and 52:13

L. "Widened" (הרחיב) … "mouth" (פי) – 5:14 and 57:4

M. "And He will give" (ונתן) … "seed" (זרע) … "and bread" (לחם) – 30:23 and 55:10

N. "And it will be a sign … to the LORD" (לאות, ליהוה and והיה) - 19:20 and 55:13. There are other passages where there is a sign for the people (Exod 12:13), but not for the LORD.

O. "And who can turn it back?" (ומי ישיבנה), referring to the hand of the LORD - 14:27 and 43:13

P. "I made it…I fashioned it" (using עשה and יצר in first person) - 37:26, 43:7 and 46:11. Note that 37:26 and 46:11 also use a form of the phrase "I bring to pass."

Q. "As…so shall it be" (כאשר…כן יהיה), where "as" is followed by a simile - 29:8 and 55:10-11

R. "To turn as sheep every man to…" (using פנה, כצאן and איש) - 13:14 and 53:6

S. "Generation" (דור) … "land of the living" (ארץ החיים) - 38:11-12 and 53:8

2. The following word combinations are unique in the prophets (Joshua – Kings being included as prophets with Isaiah – Malachi), but present in both parts of Isaiah:

A. "Man" (אנוש) … "man" (אדם) – 13:12, 51:12 and 56:2

B. "Nations" (גוים) … "peoples" (לאומים) – 34:1 and 43:9

C. "Wisdom and knowledge" (חכמע ודעת) – 33:6 and 47:10

D. "Stock" (גזע) … "Root" (שרש) – 11:1 and 40:24

E. The idea of "forever" is expressed a number of different ways in Hebrew. Isaiah alone among the prophets uses the phrase (עדי עד) for forever in 26:4 and 65:18.

F. "A day of vengeance" (יום נקם) - 34:8, 61:2 and 63:4

4.2.1.2.9.13 Vocabulary Words

1. The following Hebrew words are unique in the Bible, but present in both parts of Isaiah:

A. "Thorn" (נעצוץ) – 7:19 and 55:13

B. "Infants" (תעלולים) – 3:4 and 66:4

C. "Afflicted" (עניה) – 10:30, 51:21 and 54:11

D. "Pleasure" (ענג) – 13:22 and 58:13

E. Imperative of "come" (אתיו) replacing the usual (באו) – 21:12, 56:9 and 56:12

F. "As a tent" (כאהל) – 38:12 and 40:22

G. "As wool" – (כצמר) – 1:18 and 51:8

H. "Terrible" (עריץ) as a noun rather than an adjective – 29:20 and 49:25

I. "Thirst" (צמא) as a noun rather than an adjective – 21:14, 29:8, 32:6, 44:3 and 55:1

J. "And His Spirit" (ורוחו) – 30:28, 34:16 and 48:16

K. "Your cry" (זעק with pronominal suffix) – 30:19 and 57:13

L. "Look" (imperative of חזה) – 33:20 and 48:6

M. "For my own sake" (למעני) – 37:35, 43:25 and 48:11

N. "They shall help" (יעזרו) – 30:7 and 41:6

O. "You were honored" (נכבדת) – 26:15 and 43:4

P. "You have kindled" (בערתם) – 3:14 and 50:11

Q. "You shall scatter them" (תזרם) – 30:22 and 41:16

R. "For profit" (להועיל) – 30:5 and 48:17

S. "Shall be lowered" (ישפלו) – 10:33 and 40:4

T. "Swallowed up" (מבלעים) – 9:15 and 49:19

2. The following Hebrew words are unique in the prophets (Joshua – Kings being included as prophets with Isaiah – Malachi), but present in both parts of Isaiah:

A. "Rush" (אגמון) – 9:13, 19:15 and 58:5

B. "Branch" (נצר) – 11:1, 14:19 and 60:21

C. "Offspring" (צאצאים) – 22:24, 34:1, 42:5, 44:3, 48:19, 61:9 and 65:23

D. "Eggs" (ביצים) – 10:14 and 59:5

E. "Bruises" (חבורה) – 1:6 and 53:5

F. "Basilisk" (צפעוני) – 11:8 and 59:5

G. "Viper" (אפעה) – 30:6 and 59:5

H. "Rahab" (רחב) – 30:7 and 51:9

I. "Way" (אורה, replacing the usual דרך) – 2:3, 3:12, 26:7, 26:8, 30:11, 33:8, 40:14 and 41:3

J. "Threshing-sledge" (חרוץ) – 28:27 and 41:15

K. "Uprightness" (מישרים) – 26:7, 33:15 and 45:19

L. "Darkness" (מחשך instead of the usual חשך) – 29:15 and 42:16

M. "Willows" (ערבים) – 15:7 and 44:4

N. "Righteousness" (צדקות in plural) – 33:15 and 45:24

O. "Broken up" (מוט) – 24:19, 40:20, 41:7 and 54:10

P. "Driven" (נדף) – 19:7 and 41:2

Q. "At your presence" (מפניך) – 26:17, 63:19, 64:1 and 64:2

R. "My salvation" (ישועתי) – 12:2, 49:6 and 56:1

S. "For fuel" (לבער) – 5:5, 6:13 and 44:15

T. "Are higher" (גבהו) – 3:16 and 55:9

U. "He will be exalted" (ירום) – 30:18 and 52:13

V. "Meditate" (חגה as a transitive verb) - 33:18 and 59:3

3. The following Hebrew words occur in both parts of Isaiah, and are otherwise rare in the prophets (as specified below):

A. "Grass" (חציר) – 15:6, 37:27, 40:6, 40:7, 40:8, 44:4 and 51:12 (also 1 Kgs 18:5). Notice the man = grass formulation in 37:27, 40:6, 40:7 and 51:12

B. "Man" (אנוש replacing the usual איש) – 8:1, 13:7, 13:12, 24:6, 33:8, 51:7, 51:12 and 56:2 (also Jer 20:10)

C. "Cloud" (עב) – 14:14, 18:4, 19:1, 25:5, 44:22 and 60:8 (also 1 Kgs 18:44)

D. "Peoples" (לאמים used to mean gentiles, instead of the usual גוים) – 17:12, 17:13, 34:1, 41:1, 43:4, 43:9, 49:1, 55:4 and 60:2 (also Hab 2:13 = Jer 51:58).

E. "Chaos/formless/nothingness/desolation" (תהו) – 24:10, 29:21, 34:11, 40:17, 40:23, 41:29, 44:9, 45:18 and 49:4 (also 1 Sam 12:21 and Jer 4:23).

F. "For them" (למו replacing the usual להם) – 16:4, 23:1, 26:14, 26:16, 30:5, 35:8, 48:21 and 53:8 (Hab 2:7)

G. "Zulah" (זולה), meaning "except" - 26:13, 45:5, 45:21 and 64:3

H. "Not" (בל replacing the usual Hebrew negations לא and אל) – 14:21, 26:10, 26:11, 26:14, 26:18, 33:20, 33:21, 33:23, 33:24, 35:9, 40:24, 43:17, 44:8, 44:9. This word is common in early Psalms and in Job, but occurs in the prophets only in Hosea, another early prophet (Hos 7:2 and 9:16). Note the unusual usage "not...not...not" in 33:20, 40:24 and 44:9, a formulation with no parallel in scripture.

4.2.1.2.10 Interpolations

We should note that critics not only divide Isaiah beginning in chapter 40; they also ascribe various passages in the first part of Isaiah to later interpolators or to the second or third Isaiah. Driver, who saw two Isaiahs and not three, excludes from the original Isaiah 13:1-14:23, 21:1-10, chapters 24-27 and 34-36.[24] Schokel excludes from the original Isaiah chapters 24-27, most of 13-14, 31-33 and the second half of 11, while considering 2:2-5 and 11:1-9 doubtful.[25] It is beyond our scope to deal with all the various proposed interpolations in the first part of Isaiah. The literary parallels above cover most of these passages, and Mrs. Margalioth has similar lists for some of these passages within the first part of Isaiah, using examples like those shown above.[26] Isa 13:1 states that this message came from Isaiah the son of Amoz. See also section 4.2.2.3 on Jeremiah's dependencies on Isaiah 13 and 14.

4.2.1.2.11 External Dependencies

There are instances in which later prophets show dependence on Isaiah. It is not unusual in the Bible for two prophetic passages in different books to be so similar that we can conclusively say one was dependent on the other, or both were dependent on the same previous source. However, it is usually difficult to determine which passage is original and which passage is the borrower. In the case of Isaiah, we can find two examples where we can say the second part of Isaiah was original and a later, but still pre-exilic prophet was the borrower.

Consider first Zeph 2:15 and Isa 47:8.

---

[24] Driver, *An Introduction to the Literature of the Old Testament*, p. 204-246

[25] Schokel, essay on Isaiah, from *Literary Guide to the Bible*, p. 166

[26] Margalioth, *The Indivisible Isaiah*, p. 22-30

Isaiah 47:8a	Zephaniah 2:15a
Now, then, hear this, you sensual one, Who dwells securely, Who says in your heart, 'I am, and there is no one besides me	This is the exultant city Which dwells securely, Who says in her heart, "I am, and there is no one besides me"

Isaiah is original and Zephaniah is the borrower. We can know this because the language and imagery is typical to Isaiah throughout his book (Isa 45:5, 45:6, 45:18 and especially 47:10 for "I am," then 32:9 and 32:11 for criticism of women who think they are secure), but not typical for Zephaniah. Zephaniah wrote during Josiah's reign (Zeph 1:1), before the exile. His quote from the second part of Isaiah gives evidence that all of Isaiah was written before Zephaniah, and not during the exile.

A second strong connection appears between Nahum 1:15 and Isa 52:7.

Isaiah 52:7	Nahum 1:15
How lovely on the mountains Are the feet of him who brings good news, Who announces peace And brings good news of happiness, Who announces salvation, And says to Zion, "Your God reigns!"	Behold, on the mountains the feet of him who brings good news, Who announces peace! Celebrate your feasts, O Judah; Pay your vows For never again will the wicked one pass through you; He is cut off completely.

Again, the language is typical to Isaiah and not Nahum. Isaiah has "good news" in 40:9, 41:27, 60:6 and 61:1, and "peace" 21 times, while the LORD reigns in Zion also in 24:23. Nahum has none of these ideas in other verses. On the contrary, Nahum 1:15 is disconnected from the rest of the context of the book of Nahum, which is otherwise a prophecy dealing with Nineveh. Therefore, Nahum is the borrower. Nahum was written before the fall of Nineveh in 609 B.C., and his quote from the second part of Isaiah gives evidence that all of Isaiah was written before Nahum, and not during the exile.

In Jeremiah's prophecy against Babylon in Jeremiah 50-51, Jeremiah begins to sound like Isaiah. These chapters retain the marks and historical setting of Jeremiah, but it is clear that he has been reading an Isaiah scroll and is freely using Isaiah's thoughts and phrases, particularly those of Isaiah's prophecy against Babylon in Isaiah 13-14. Isaiah 13-14, by contrast, does not sound like Jeremiah, so we can conclude that Isaiah 13-14 came first and Jeremiah is the borrower. Isaiah's influence in Jeremiah 50-51 can be seen as follows:

1. Jer 50:29 and 51:5 use the divine title "Holy One of Israel." This is the only usage of this title in the prophets outside of Isaiah, who uses it 25 times in his book and once (Isaiah speaking) in 2 Kgs 19:22.

2. Jeremiah begins to use repetition in a manner reminiscent of Isaiah (Jer 50:35-37 and 51:20-23).

3. "Stir up the Medes" (Isa 13:17) corresponds to "arouse the spirit of the kings of the Medes" (Jer 51:11).

4. "Instruments of indignation" (כלי זעמו) are in Isa 13:5 and Jer 50:25.

5. "Desert creatures" and "ostriches" will live there, and it will never be inhabited (Isa 13:20-21, Jer 50:39).

6. The cruelty of Babylon's enemies is described in Isa 13:18 and Jer 50:42.

7. "Lift up a signal" (שאו נס) is in Isa 13:2 and Jer 51:12 and 51:27.

8. Babylon aspired to "ascend to heaven" in Isa 14:13 and Jer 51:53.

9. לאמים is used for "peoples" in Jer 51:58, a wording common in Isaiah and otherwise only in the identical verse in Hab 2:13.
10. "Stretches out the heavens" is in Jer 51:15, a wording that is common in Isaiah.
11. "They will each turn to his own people, and each one flee to his own land." Is in Isa 13:14 and Jer 50:16.

Given our understanding that all of Isaiah preceded any of Jeremiah, we would also suggest that Jer 31:35, "…Who stirs up the sea so that its waves roar; The LORD of hosts is His name," is borrowed from Isa 51:15.

Isaiah 13:6 closely parallels Joel 1:15.

Isaiah 13:6	Joel 1:15
Wail, for the day of the LORD is near! It will come as destruction from the Almighty.	Alas for the day! For the day of the LORD is near, and it will come as destruction from the Almighty.

Taken in isolation, it is not clear which verse comes first. Isaiah's verse fits into the context better, but "The Day of the LORD" is a phrase appearing elsewhere in Joel, but not in Isaiah. In both books, this is the only use of Almighty ("Shaddai") as a designation for God. Most likely, the idea of the "Day of the LORD" was a commonly spoken formula, as it is used in many prophets, often with the idea that it is "near." Based on our other criteria for dating Isaiah and Joel, we believe the Isaiah verse came first. A second dependency appears between Isaiah 2:4 (Isa 2:4 = Mic 4:3) and Joel 3:10.

Isaiah 2:4	Joel 3:10
And they will hammer their swords into plowshares and their spears into pruning hooks	Beat your plowshares into swords And your pruning hooks into spears;

Because Joel reverses the idea of Isaiah and Micah, creating weapons instead of destroying them, Joel is likely the borrower. It is unlikely that both Isaiah and Micah would take Joel's phrase and reverse it the same way.

4.2.1.2.12 Parallels with Kings and Chronicles

Isaiah 36-39 closely parallels 2 Kings 18:13-20:21. For the most part, these passages are duplicated verbatim, so closely that we can be certain that one was essentially copied from the other. In such cases, one rule of thumb says that the shorter version is original, later copiers being more likely to expand on a subject than to delete material. By this rule, Isaiah is original. The 2 Kings passage adds the events in 2 Kgs 18:14-16, and expands slightly on Isaiah's passage in 2 Kgs 18:17, 18:26, 18:32, 18:34, 19:20, 19:35 and 20:4-6. The author of 2 Kings makes one major deletion, leaving out the entire prayer of Hezekiah from Isa 38:9-20. Other than that, the Isaiah passage is never fuller than the Kings account by more than one word per verse.

Linguistic evidence also points to the Isaiah passage being original. The phrase "Holy One of Israel" in Isa 37:23 and 2 Kgs 19:22, is, as we have seen, common to Isaiah, but this is its only appearance in Genesis through Kings. Other passages which sound like Isaiah are "Have you not heard?" (Isa 37:26/2 Kgs 19:25 - see Isa 40:21), "The zeal of the LORD will perform this" (Isa 37:32/2 Kgs 19:31 – see Isa 9:7), "bruised reed" (Isa 36:6/2 Kgs 18:21 – see Isa 42:3) and "children have come to birth and there is no strength to deliver" (Isa 37:3/2 Kgs 19:3 – see Isa 26:17-18 and 66:9). Furthermore, "pen" (פֶּן), meaning "lest," is a word used mostly in early texts. Note that while Isa 36:18 has it, the duplicate 2 Kgs 18:32 substitutes "ki" (כי). The passage in 2 Kgs 18:14-16, which is not present in Isaiah, spells the name of king Hezekiah "חזקיה," as opposed to the longer form "חזקיהו" used throughout Isaiah and in most of the rest of the Kings passage. This indicates that 2 Kgs 18:14-16 is most likely an addition from a separate source (perhaps the court records of the Kings of Judah mentioned so many times in Kings).

Finally, the history in Joshua through Kings tends to follow a pattern: disobedience leads to trouble, obedience leads to deliverance. To follow this pattern, the chapters in Isaiah should follow the sequence 38-39-36-37, rather than their existing sequence. The existing sequence for the story is appropriate for the book of Isaiah, because it ends up pointing to Babylon, but it is not in keeping with the "Deuteronomic" pattern of Kings.

Therefore, the textual criticism rule of thumb, the linguistic evidence and the sequence of the story all point to the Isaiah passage being original, with the author of 2 Kings copying from Isaiah to construct his narrative. This is consistent with our dating of Isaiah at about 680 B.C., with most of 2 Kings coming about 60 years later.

The parallel passage in 2 Chronicles 32 is much abbreviated compared to Isaiah and Kings, such that it is not possible to determine which text the Chronicles author was using. Chronicles is a post-exilic book, and in all probability the author of Chronicles had both Isaiah and Kings before him as he did his work.

4.2.1.2.13 Parallels with Micah

The prophet Micah was a contemporary of Isaiah, and parallels between Isaiah and Micah are clear, especially with the essentially duplicated Isa 2:2-4 and Mic 4:1-3. However, parallels between Isaiah and Micah continue into the second part of Isaiah also. These include Isa 41:15-16 with Mic 4:13, Isa 48:2 with Mic 3:11, Isa

49:23 with Mic 7:17, Isa 52:12 with Mic 2:13, and Isa 58:1 with Mic 3:8.

4.2.1.2.14 Predictive Elements

The book of Isaiah contains numerous predictions, from the birth of children (7:14) to the fall of Israel and Syria (8:4, etc.), the coming of the Messiah (9:1-7, etc.), the failure of the Assyrian invasion (37:33-35) and more. Furthermore, the predictions are not mere sideshows to Isaiah, but rather a central part of his message. He brags about them (42:9 and 45:21), reminds his hearers of them (43:9, 43:12 and 48:3-7), keeps a record of them (8:16 and 30:8) and challenges other gods to do the same (41:21-23 and 44:7-8), mocking their failure to do so (44:25). It is in this context that the prophecy about Cyrus is given. The LORD in His address to Cyrus says twice: "I have called you by name...though you have not known me" (45:3-5). The critics are right in thinking that the naming of Cyrus is important evidence. Isaiah apparently thought so too.

4.2.1.2.15 Final Compilation of Isaiah

The first narrative section of Isaiah (chapters 6-8) is written in first person, while the second narrative section (chapters 36-39) is written in third person. In addition, several passages are introduced as coming from Isaiah, but with the wording in third person (1:1, 2:1 and 13:1). Isaiah began his career in 740 B.C., so he would have been rather old to record the death of Sennacherib in 680 (37:38), though this is by no means impossible. These facts raise the possibility that the book of Isaiah was placed in its final form by some of Isaiah's follower's, based on a lifetime's collection of his writings. This should not detract from the essential understanding of Isaiah as the author of the entire book. Even the second narrative passage of 36-39 shows the trademark literary style of Isaiah. Compare, for example: "The zeal of the LORD of hosts will accomplish this" (9:7 and 37:32).

4.2.1.3 Linguistic Analysis

The linguistic evidence in Isaiah is consistent with a date of 700 B.C. Isaiah has no Greek or Persian words, although he uses an exceptionally large vocabulary of 2186 words (Ezekiel has a 1535 word vocabulary, Jeremiah has 1653 and Psalms has 2170). Although we do not think Aramaisms are an especially good indication for dating Biblical Hebrew, it is still worth mentioning that Isaiah contains no obvious Aramaisms in any part of the book. The older pronoun "anoki" is used 20 times, with 16 of those occurrences in the second part of the book. The older word for kingdom, "mamlakah" is used fourteen times (twice in the second part of the book), while the later "malkut" is absent. The early relative pronoun "zu" (זו) is present in 42:24 and 43:21. "Zu" occurs 14 times in the Old Testament, but is not present in any indisputably exilic or post-exilic text. The archaic negation "bal" is common throughout the book. The older word for "spoil, booty" (בז) is in 42:22 (later usage is בזה). The early word for "way, path" (ארח) is in 2:3, 3:12, 26:7-8, 30:11, 33:8, 40:14 and 41:3. The adverb of time, "bterem" (בטרם), in 42:9, 48:5 and 66:7, appears almost exclusively in pre-exilic texts. "Zulah" (זולה), meaning "except" in 26:13, 45:5, 45:21 and 64:3, appears almost exclusively in pre-exilic texts. The early poetic pronominal suffix "mo" (מו), used to identify third person plural forms, is attached to prepositions in 16:4, 30:5, 35:8 and 48:21. The later, more standard form of this suffix is "hem" (הם) or "am" (ם). David's name is spelled with the earlier form דוד in all occurrences in the book, including the one occurrence in the second half (55:3). Critics who support the idea of a second Isaiah admit that their linguistic arguments are not strong, as Hurvitz states: "the language of second Isaiah is well anchored in Classical Biblical Hebrew and the imprints of Late Biblical Hebrew are quite scanty."[27]

Against the evidence already presented, it would seem difficult to make a linguistic case for a late dating of Isaiah 40-66, but it has been tried. Examples of some of the arguments include:

1. The word מערב is used to mean "west" in Isa 43:5, 45:6 and 59:19. This word appears elsewhere seven times in the post-exilic book of Chronicles and in the mostly late Psalms 75, 103, and 107 (though we have dated Psalm 75 early), while the earlier word, ימה, appears in Classical Biblical Hebrew, including Isa 11:14 and 24:14. It has been suggested that this use of a Late Biblical Hebrew word is evidence for a late date for the latter part of Isaiah. This argument is weakened by the fact that מערב appears in the Ugaritic language 500 years before Isaiah, meaning "sunset." Furthermore, the argument is insensitive to the poetry in these passages. In each of the passages 43:5, 45:6 and 59:19 (but not 11:14 or 24:14), מערב is used in parallel with מזרח, meaning "east." In these passages, both words are prefixed with an additional מ, meaning "from." The result is strong alliteration in the pronunciation of "mimizrakh" (ממזרח) in parallel with "mima'arav" (ממערב). This is superior to "mimizrakh" in parallel with "miyam" (מים). Isaiah likely had both words available to him, and he made his choice for poetic as opposed to chronological reasons.

2. The word עולמים is used for "forever" in Isa 26:4, 45:17 and 51:9. עולמים is a plural form of the much more common עולם, and only appears elsewhere in 1 Kgs 8:13 (= 2 Chron 6:2), Ps 61:4 [Heb 61:5], Ps 77:5 [Heb 77:6], Ps 77:7 [Heb 77:8], Ps 145:13, Dan 9:24 and Ecc 1:10. The weakness of

---

[27] Ehrensvard, "Linguistic Dating of Biblical Texts", in Young, *Biblical Hebrew Studies in Chronology and Typology*, p. 175

this argument is apparent in the fact that 1 Kgs 8:13 would not appear to be a late text, and a late date for Psalms 61 and 77 is debatable (we have dated those two psalms early). Furthermore, the argument also requires moving Isaiah 26 to the second part of Isaiah, a choice with which not all advocates of a second Isaiah would agree. The best explanation for the use of this word again lies in literary and poetic reasons. All three occurrences of עולמים in Isaiah are in parallel, when two different words meaning "forever" are required. When no parallel word is required, Isaiah uses the more common עולם, even in the second part of the book (Isa 9:6, 40:8, 40:28, etc.).

3. It has been suggested that the word כאחד, meaning "together," is in Isa 65:25 and only otherwise in post-exilic texts Ecc 11:6, 2 Chron 5:13, Ezra 2:64, 3:9 and 6:20. The suggestion is immediately suspect, as כאחד appears in other early passages, such as Gen 49:16, where a translation of "together" is also possible, if not usual. Isa 65:25, speaking of incompatible animals coexisting together, can be contrasted with a similar passage in Isa 11:6-7 which uses another word for together, יחדו. The second part of Isaiah also uses this other word for together (יחדו) 17 times, including three times in the "third" section, Isa 60:13, 65:7 and 66:17. The author had both words available to him. The explanation for the use of כאחד is likely again to be for poetic reasons. כאחד is actually a combination of two words: כ for "like/as" and אחד for "one." The verse can be literally read: "The wolf and the lamb will graze as one, and the lion will eat straw like the ox." The second part of the verse, the parallel phrase, also employs the attached preposition כ to form "like the ox." Although this phrase is present in 11:7 also, it is not in parallel with the phrase using יחדו for together. The use of כאחד improves the poetry.

4.2.1.4 Oldest Texts

The oldest texts of Isaiah are 21 Dead Sea Scrolls. Scroll 1QIsaᵃ, the Great Isaiah Scroll, contains every verse of the book. Perhaps more significant for dating purposes is scroll 1Q8, or 1QIsaᵇ, a proto-Masoretic text containing portions of 44 chapters of Isaiah and dating to 150 B.C. In addition, six Dead Sea Scrolls are commentaries on Isaiah.

4.2.1.5 Conclusion

Isaiah 1-66 was placed in its final form by about 680 B.C. or shortly afterwards, and is all the work of Isaiah, the son of Amoz. The book was not written all at the same time; some portions were written earlier and other portions written later in Isaiah's life.

4.2.1.6 Isaiah Addendum - Isaiah's Role in the Publication of Other Texts

Isaiah may have played a significant role in the collection of older Old Testament material. There are several lines of evidence indicating that this may be the case. First of all, there are several points to make about Isaiah personally:

1. Isaiah was a uniquely talented writer. While many prophets could preach, Isaiah could also write, not just in the sense that he was literate, but in the sense that he could create a masterpiece. Isaiah uses a larger vocabulary than any other book in the Old Testament. He mixes prose and poetry, includes literary structures like chiasms, and retains a unique writing style.

2. Isaiah was the only writing prophet who was indisputably a "court prophet," that is, a prophet who worked for the king and prophesied in his court. Although court prophets were common (1 Kgs 22:6), their loyalty to the king could be thought to compromise their integrity, and all the other writing prophets were apparently outsiders. Isaiah, however, worked for the king of Judah and seemed to be espe-

cially close to Hezekiah, with whom he apparently collaborated for the entirety of Hezekiah's 29 year reign. As a court prophet, Isaiah had ready access to royal documents and archives present in the capital, Jerusalem. Prov 25:1 mentions a role for the "men of Hezekiah" in collating the book of Proverbs, and it is likely that Isaiah, Hezekiah's main prophet and most talented writer, played a role in that project.

3. Circulating in the upper class in Jerusalem makes it likely that Isaiah spoke Aramaic as well as Hebrew, a skill not shared by most Jews of the day (2 Kgs 18:26).

Isaiah and Hezekiah also lived in a unique period of Israel's history, in that they were prominent in the southern Kingdom of Judah at the time that the northern Kingdom of Israel fell. The only way for a northern writing to make it into the canon of scripture, therefore, was to "emigrate" south, and this would need to have happened during the time of Hezekiah and Isaiah. This apparently did happen in the case of the northern prophets Hosea and Jonah and the southern prophet to the north, Amos. All three of these prophets prophesied shortly before Isaiah, but their life spans overlapped his and he may have helped collate their work. Note how Hos 1:1 gives a list of kings of Judah (Uzziah, Jotham, Ahaz and Hezekiah) that exactly matches Isa 1:1, even though Hosea was not a prophet to Judah but to the north, and despite the fact that the written body of his prophecy was apparently completed before the time of Hezekiah. Isaiah may also have helped collate the northern Israelite material now found in Kings related to Elijah, Elisha, and the destruction of the Baal cult.

There were no writing prophets from either the north or the south whose lives clearly ended before the time of Isaiah, although prophets were active in Israel for more than 300 years before him. On the other hand, at least four other writing prophets lived during his time (Hosea, Amos, Jonah and Micah).

4.2.2 Jeremiah

Jeremiah is the longest book in the Bible. Jeremiah was a prophet of priestly descent who warned of the coming Babylonian exile.

4.2.2.1 Internal Evidence

Jeremiah's prophecy begins in the 13th year of Josiah (Jer 1:2) in 629 B.C., when Jeremiah considered himself to be "a youth" (1:6). His work continues past the Babylonian destruction of Jerusalem in 586 B.C., when Jeremiah is carried against his will down to Egypt (Jer 43:1-7).

Jeremiah is full of biographical information providing a setting shortly before and just after the exile. Specific date information related to three of the last four Judean kings, Josiah, Jehoiakim and Zedekiah is present in 1:2, 25:1, 25:3, 28:1, 32:1, 36:1, 36:9, 39:2, 45:1 and 46:2. These passages also make it clear that the events in Jeremiah are not recorded in chronological order; the book skips around in time. Numerous additional individuals are mentioned throughout the book to further cement our understanding of the setting of the book. Although most of Jeremiah's life and career are before the destruction of Jerusalem in 586 B.C., chapters 40-44 describe events occurring immediately after 586 B.C.

With the book of Jeremiah we have a uniquely complex textual situation. It is clear from the numerous historical references in the book that Jeremiah is not written in anything close to chronological order, and its structure has been considered a puzzle. Also, the differences between the Septuagint and the Masoretic Text are much greater in Jeremiah than in any other biblical book. These differences are such that they are not a matter of translation; the scribe who performed the translation was clearly working from a different Hebrew text. The Septuagint is shorter, with about 60 full verses missing, plus a number of words and phrases. In addition, the order of the books is altered, with chapters 46-51 placed after chapter 25, and other minor changes. Two of the Dead Sea Scroll texts of Jeremiah support the Septuagint version.[28]

Fortunately, we have more biographical information on the people involved in the book of Jeremiah than any other book, and this helps to explain the textual situation. Jeremiah worked with a scribe, Baruch the son of Neriah (Jer 36:4), for much of his life. Jeremiah would dictate and Baruch would write his message. In Jeremiah 36, Baruch read a scroll of Jeremiah's words in the temple. Word found its way to an unrepentant king Jehoiakim, who cut it up and burned it. This scroll would not be the book of Jeremiah in the form we have it today, though it may have contained much of the same material. Afterward, Jeremiah and Baruch collaborated to rewrite the scroll with additional material (Jer 36:27-32). This would also not be the book of Jeremiah that we have today – this was only the mid-point of his career. Jeremiah and Baruch continue to work together through the reign of Zedekiah (Jeremiah 32). In chapter 29, Jeremiah sends a letter from Jerusalem to the first group of exiles to Babylon, a letter which we can assume was widely circulated, since it apparently had the approval of the king of Babylon (29:3). After the destruction of Jerusalem and the assassination of Nebuchadnezzar's hand-picked governor Gedaliah, Jeremiah is taken against his will to Egypt, with Baruch still with him (Jeremiah 43). There, at some point, the two of them finish their writing.

Now we can consider what happened to the text of Jeremiah. Although his message was never well received, Jeremiah grew to be very prominent toward the end of his life, and he was known to both the kings of Judah and Babylon. The exile, the destruction of Jerusalem and the temple, and the execution of King Zedekiah's sons proved Jeremiah's warnings to be stunningly accurate. His message of judgment had been mixed with hope (Jeremiah 31), and his writings therefore seemed to attain a scriptural status with

---

[28] Tov, *Textual Criticism of the Hebrew Bible*, p. 320

unprecedented speed (2 Chron 35:25, 36:12, 36:21-22, Ezra 1:1, Dan 9:2, Zech 1:6 and 7:7). In fact, it is possible that parts of Jeremiah were essentially treated as scripture by the exiled Jews in Babylon while Jeremiah was still alive and writing in Egypt. After the exile then, multiple different manuscripts of the words of Jeremiah were in circulation, some produced in Babylon, some in Egypt and maybe some in Israel. As a result, major textual variants of Jeremiah remained when the Septuagint was translated and the Dead Sea Scrolls were copied. It is possible that the post-exilic prophet Zechariah even included Jeremiah texts in chapters 9-14 of his book (see section 4.2.15 on Zechariah), a view that would be supported by Matt 27:9-10.

One of the primary roles of textual criticism is to determine the most likely original text, but in the case of Jeremiah this would seem to be impossible – no text by itself was exclusively the original. By the year 500 B.C., the circulated texts of Jeremiah most probably included a Babylonian version, an Egyptian version, and possibly an Israelite version, and all these truly reflected the words of Jeremiah. Therefore, we will not attempt to distinguish whether the Masoretic Text version or the Septuagint version of Jeremiah is superior – they are both likely to be correct and even "original," in their own way.

4.2.2.2 External Dependencies - Inputs

Jeremiah chapter 52 was apparently borrowed from 2 Kgs 24:18-25:30, although some writers have credited Jeremiah himself with being the author of Kings (which would give a different twist to the idea of borrowing). The formula used to introduce Zedekiah in Jer 52:1 is the same formula used throughout the book of Kings,[29] so without being certain as to the author of Kings, we

---

[29] The formula used throughout the book of Kings is, with minor variations: "<king's name> was <number> years old when he became king, and he reigned <number> years in Jerusalem. His mother's name was <name> the daughter of <name>"

should still assign the priority on this passage to the book of Kings. This chapter's description of the destruction of Jerusalem is still a fitting way to end the book of Jeremiah, since the thrust of his career pointed toward that event. The idea that Jeremiah 52 is an appendage is further supported by Jer 51:64, "Thus far are the words of Jeremiah," perhaps indicating that what follows (chapter 52) are not the words of Jeremiah.

Jer 26:18 is an unusual case where one prophetic book explicitly cites another by name. In this verse, Micah of Moresheth is named and Mic 3:12 is quoted. Micah was written 80-100 years before this event.

As described in section 4.2.1.2.11, Jeremiah 50-51 is dependent on Isaiah 13-14. Although the Jeremiah 50-51 passage is not clearly dated, Isaiah was born a little less than 100 years before Jeremiah, and the two passages are probably separated by nearly that amount of time. One verse in this passage, Jer 51:58, shows further the influence of Hab 2:13:

Habakkuk 2:13	Jeremiah 51:58
Is it not indeed from the LORD of hosts that peoples toil for fire, and nations grow weary for nothing?	Thus says the LORD of hosts, "The broad wall of Babylon will be completely razed and her high gates will be set on fire; so the peoples will toil for nothing, and the nations become exhausted only for fire."

The influence is more striking in Hebrew than in English because of the irregular word choice of לאמים for "nations" instead of the usual גוים. לאמים is only used elsewhere in the prophets in Isaiah. Habakkuk was a contemporary of Jeremiah and context provides no clear clue as to which text was written first. Since Jeremiah was apparently meditating on other scripture (particularly Isaiah) when he wrote this passage, it seems more likely that Habakkuk was written first.

The phrase in Jer 14:10, "He will remember their iniquity and call their sins to account" appears to be dependent on Hos 8:13 and 9:9. Jer 16:19, which says, "O LORD, my strength and my fortress, my refuge…" seems to reflect wording common in the Davidic Psalms. Jer 6:25, 20:10, 46:5 and 49:29 all use the phrase "terror on every side," apparently picked up from Ps 31:13.

Jeremiah is familiar with the Torah, including those elements source critics assign to P, the priestly source. Jer 4:23 unmistakably echoes Gen 1:2, describing the earth as "formless and void," a phrase which appears only in these two instances in the Bible. God says in Jer 6:19 that the people have rejected "my Torah." Jeremiah knows (and is unimpressed with) the priestly sacrifices and offerings (17:26). Jer 7:23, looking back to the exodus, quotes loosely from Exod 19:5, Lev 26:12 and Deut 6:3. Jer 34:14 cites the law regarding release of Hebrew slaves in the seventh year (Exod 21:2 and Deut 15:12). Jer 48:45-46, part of an oracle against Moab, is clearly dependent on Num 21:28-29. Jeremiah is familiar with the work of Moses and Samuel (Jer 15:1), Hezekiah and Micah (Jer 26:19), and also some of the more obscure information in Kings (Jer 41:9 compare 1 Kgs 15:17-22).

Jer 20:14-15 reflects the same idea as Job 3:3-6, though with different wording.

4.2.2.3 External Dependencies - Outputs

The similarities between Jer 49:7-22 and Obadiah are sharp, as the table below shows:

Jeremiah 49	Obadiah
(14) I have heard a message from the LORD, and an envoy is sent among the nations, saying, "Gather yourselves together and	(1) …We have heard a report from the LORD, and an envoy has been sent among the nations saying, "Arise and let

come against her, and rise up for battle!"	us go against her for battle"--
(16) …The arrogance of your heart has deceived you, O you who live in the clefts of the rock, who occupy the height of the hill, though you make your nest as high as an eagle's, I will bring you down from there," declares the LORD.	(3) The arrogance of your heart has deceived you, you who live in the clefts of the rock, in the loftiness of your dwelling place, who say in your heart, 'Who will bring me down to earth?'
(9) If grape gatherers came to you, would they not leave gleanings? If thieves came by night, they would destroy only until they had enough.	(5) If thieves came to you, if robbers by night-- O how you will be ruined!-- Would they not steal only until they had enough? If grape gatherers came to you, would they not leave some gleanings?

There are additional looser connections between the two texts not shown in the table. In this case, we assign the priority to Jeremiah. His series of oracles against foreign nations (Jer 46-51) begin with a date in the fourth year of Jehoiakim, 605 B.C., before the fall of Jerusalem (Jer 45:1). Obadiah reflects a perspective shortly after the fall of Jerusalem (see section 4.2.7). The time difference is apparent in the two passages, as Jeremiah gives no reason for the judgment on Edom, while Obadiah does give a reason – the un-neighborly behavior of the Edomites when the Babylonians sacked Jerusalem in 586 B.C. (Obad 10-14). Jeremiah's silence about Edom's behavior is telling, since Jewish resentment over this matter was extreme (Ps 137:7, Lam 4:21-22, Ezek 25:12-14, 35:1-15 and Mal 1:2-4), and is an additional clue that Jeremiah 49 was first written before the exile.

Jeremiah's prophecy about the exile lasting 70 years (25:12 and 29:10) is picked up by Daniel (Dan 9:2) and Zechariah (Zech 1:12

and 7:5) and is also probably the prophecy the chronicler has in mind in 2 Chron 36:21-22.

Jer 31:29-30 contains a proverb that is quoted exactly by Ezekiel (Ezek 18:2-3), "The fathers have eaten sour grapes and the children's teeth are set on edge." This is not, however, a certain case of one prophet borrowing from the other. A common saying or formulaic statement like this proverb could be so widely used that both prophets used it completely independently. In a similar category is Jer 33:11, "...Give thanks to the LORD of hosts, For the LORD is good, for His lovingkindness is everlasting." This saying is widely used elsewhere (1 Chron 16:34, 2 Chron 5:13, 7:3, Ezra 3:11, Ps 100:5, 106:1, 107:1, 118:1 and 136:1). Ps 1:1-3 may be related to Jer 17:7-8, but the similarity is limited.

4.2.2.4 Linguistic Analysis

The linguistic features of Jeremiah are consistent with a date around 600 B.C. The early pronoun "anoki" is used 28 times, along with the companion "ani," used 41 times. The earlier word for kingdom, "mamlakah," is used three times, while the later word, "malkut," is not used. Jeremiah is the last biblical writer chronologically to make frequent use of "pen" (פן), meaning "lest," using the word seven times (1:17, 4:4, etc.). "Ehdah" (עדה), a mostly pre-exilic word meaning "congregation," is in 30:20. Jer 28:3 and 28:11 use a dual form noun for "two years," a characteristic of earlier writings.

Jer 10:11 is entirely in Aramaic – the only Aramaic in the entire book. No clear explanation for this feature is known.

The spelling in Jeremiah is the oldest of the latter prophets in the Bible; older than either Isaiah or Ezekiel. See Table B-2 in Appendix B for reference.

4.2.2.5 Oldest Texts

The oldest texts of Jeremiah are six Dead Sea Scrolls: 2Q13, 4Q70, 4Q71, 4Q72, 4Q72a and 4Q72b. Portions of 34 chapters are repre-

sented. The Dead Sea Scrolls also include four copies of an extra-
biblical work related to Jeremiah, the Apocryphon of Jeremiah.

**Clay seal of Baruch, son of Neriah, Jeremiah's
scribe. The inscription reads: "[belonging] to
Berekhyahu, the son of Neriyahu, the scribe."**

4.2.2.6 Conclusion

The book of Jeremiah was compiled from material written by
Jeremiah through his scribe Baruch at multiple points during his
lifetime. These writings spanned the reign of Josiah through
Zedekiah, from 629 to 586 B.C. Jeremiah 40-44 was written after
the fall of Jerusalem, probably between 586 and about 580 B.C.
The existence of numerous scrolls containing Jeremiah's writing
probably posed a challenge in the effort to gather all his material
into a single book, and this may not have been completed until
after the exile, in the late sixth century B.C. Variants remained, as
is evidenced by the differences in the Masoretic Text and Septuagint versions of Jeremiah. Jeremiah 52 was taken from 2 Kings and
appended to the end of the book to establish the full vindication of
Jeremiah's prophecy and provide a fitting conclusion to the book.

4.2.3 Ezekiel

Ezekiel was one of the early captives taken to Babylon with Jehoiachin, before the destruction of Jerusalem and the temple. The book of Ezekiel is marked by spectacular visions and a redemptive look at Israel's future.

4.2.3.1 Internal Evidence

The date of the book of Ezekiel is not widely disputed. Ezekiel uses the exile of King Jehoiachin in 597 B.C., ten years before the destruction of Jerusalem, as his time reference, dating his passages from that point. The book of Ezekiel begins in the fifth year of the Babylonian exile of King Jehoiachin (Ezek 1:2), 593 B.C., and continues until the 27th year (29:17), or 570 B.C. Most of the oracles in Ezekiel 1:1-33:21 are near to but preceding the fall of Jerusalem in 586 B.C., based on the time references in 1:2, 24:1, 26:1, 29:1, 31:1, 32:1 and 32:17. As a result, these oracles frequently address the situation back in Israel, even though Ezekiel himself is in Babylon. The short passage in 29:17-21 is much later, in about 570 B.C., based on the time reference in 29:17. After Ezekiel learns about Jerusalem's fall in 33:21, the prophet has only a few more words of judgment, then his message takes a turn towards hope for the future. Ezekiel's vision of a future temple in chapters 40-48 is dated to about 573 B.C., based on the time reference in 40:1.

The unity of Ezekiel is supported by the repetition throughout the book of certain unique or nearly unique phrases, such as "the hand of the LORD" being "upon me" (seven times) and "son of man" as God's way of addressing Ezekiel (93 times). Ezekiel also repeats the phrase, "will know that I am the LORD" 63 times out of 77 overall occurrences in the Bible, and he addresses God as "sovereign LORD" (Hebrew "adonai YHWH") 217 times. Although oracles from different times are present in the book, Ezekiel has the appearance of a book which was written from beginning to end rather than a loose compilation of his writings.

Ezekiel does not borrow or quote much from earlier biblical books, but he does show knowledge of the prior existence of both the Torah and prophets (7:26), understanding that it was the priest's responsibility to teach the Torah. He mentions the Garden of Eden (28:13 and 31:8-9). Ezek 22:10-11 condemns people for breaking laws found in the Holiness Code (Lev 18:8 and 18:15). He accuses the people five times (20:16, 20:21, 20:24, 22:8 and 23:38) of having "profaned my Sabbaths," using language from Exod 31:14. He repeats the familiar Torah phrase "land flowing with milk and honey" (20:6). Ezek 22:26 quotes from Lev 10:10, dealing with the need to make a distinction between "the holy and the common, the clean and the unclean." Ezekiel occasionally echoes Isaiah, when he speaks of spiritual blindness and deafness (12:2 compare Isa 6:9-10, 29:18, 35:5, 42:18, 42:19 and 43:8), or his designation of God as "Holy One in Israel" (39:7). Ezekiel echoes his older contemporary Jeremiah when he says in Ezek 13:10 and 13:16 "peace, when there is no peace" (see Jer 6:14 and 8:11), and warns of sword and famine in 5:17, 6:11-12, 7:15 and 14:21 (compare Jer 5:12, 11:22, etc. - 28 times in Jeremiah).

Source Critics point to a relationship between Ezekiel and the P source of Genesis-Joshua, saying that the order of writing was (1) J (2) E (3) D (4) Ezekiel (5) Holiness Code (6) P. We believe this understanding is incorrect. Ezekiel's interest in priestly matters is due to the fact that he is a priest (Ezek 1:3). However, Ezekiel's vision of the temple and the land allocations in chapters 40-48 are idealistic, looking to a future not realized by the exiles who returned from Babylon. Ezekiel's temple was never built; it matches neither the first nor the second temple. Likewise, Ezekiel's division of the land among the tribes is also idealistic; by comparison, the division described in Joshua (purportedly written by P) is specific, realistic, and matches what is known of the history of Israel. It would seem strange to suggest that Ezekiel's highly idealistic vision during the exile would inspire priests writing after the exile to write a highly realistic account of what happened before the exile.

4.2.3.2 Linguistic Analysis

Ezekiel, written during the exile, stands at a transitional point in linguistic terms, with elements of both Classical Biblical Hebrew and Late Biblical Hebrew. The linguistic features of Ezekiel support an exilic date for the book.

In most ways, the linguistic characteristics of Ezekiel are not strikingly different from the earlier Major Prophets, Isaiah and Jeremiah. However, some Late Biblical Hebrew elements begin to creep in. Examples include:

1. Earlier books say "two cubits" by using the dual form אמתים, but Ezekiel uses the later "two + plural" form שתים אמות (40:9, 41:3, 41:22 and 43:14).

2. Ezekiel uses the later piel stem of קום to mean "raise up, establish" (13:6), where the earlier usage requires the hiphil stem for this meaning.

3. Ezekiel uses the late מקדש for sanctuary rather than the earlier קדש (48:11).

Examples where Ezekiel shows both early and late features include:

1. In describing the holiness of God, the early books all use the niphal stem of קדש, while the later books use the hithpael stem. Only Ezekiel uses both forms (20:41 and 36:23).

2. Classical Biblical Hebrew uses רבוע for "square," while later Hebrew uses מרבע., and Ezekiel uses both the early and late forms (41:21 and 43:16 are early, 40:47 and 45:2 are late).

3. The third person masculine singular form of the verb חיה, "to live," appears in Ezekiel in both the early חי (20:11) and the late form חיה (18:23).

4. Ezekiel uses both the early שש and the later בוץ for "linen" (16:10 and 27:16).

The early pronoun "anoki" is used only once[30] in Ezekiel, while the companion "ani" is used 159 times. Seven of the occurrences of "ani" come after the word "behold" (הנה): Ezek 6:3, 34:11, 34:20, 37:5, 37:12, 37:19 and 37:21. This usage is contrary to the practice of earlier Hebrew, which requires "anoki" after "behold." This may be an indication that it was during Ezekiel's time, the time of the exile, that usage of the pronoun "anoki" began to fade. בטרם, meaning "before" in a temporal sense, is not found in post-exilic writings, and it latest appearance is in Ezek 16:57.

Ezekiel includes several lamentations that use the limping meter (Ezek 19:1-7, 26:17-18 and 32:2).[31] This literary device was introduced by the time of Amos (Amos 5:1-3 – 750 B.C.) and was popular in Ezekiel's time, as it is also used throughout Lamentations 1-4. The earlier word for kingdom, "mamlakah," is used three times in Ezekiel, while the later "malkut" is not used.

The spelling in Ezekiel is not as old as the primary history (Genesis through Kings) or Jeremiah, but slightly older than Isaiah, the Minor Prophets and most of the Writings. See Table B-2 in Appendix B for reference. Ezekiel's transitional nature can again be shown by the spelling of David's name: the early short form דוד is used three times and the later long form דויד once.

4.2.3.3 Oldest Texts

The oldest copies of Ezekiel are six Dead Sea Scrolls (1Q9, 3Q1, 4Q73, 4Q74, 4Q75 and 11Q4) containing portions of nine chapters, and one scroll found at Masada. The Dead Sea Scrolls also include an extra-biblical work related to Ezekiel (4Q384 and 4Q391).

4.2.3.4 Conclusion

Ezekiel was written during the Babylonian exile, shortly after 570 B.C.

---

[30] Even this one use in Ezek 36:28 is in question, as not all manuscripts have it.

[31] The "limping meter" is a poetic form in which the second part of the line is shorter than the first part, usually with a three word/two word division.

4.2.4 Introduction to the Minor Prophets

It is common today to think of the Minor Prophets as consisting of twelve independent books: the book of Hosea, the book of Joel, the book of Amos, and so on. This thinking is mostly correct, as these men were historical figures prophesying independently of one another. However, it is important to realize that from antiquity, all the Minor Prophets have been collated together in one scroll. The Dead Sea Scrolls include seven Minor Prophets scrolls, not independent scrolls for each prophet. Around 185 B.C., Ben Sirach referred to Isaiah, Jeremiah and Ezekiel, then to the Minor Prophets as "the twelve" (Sir 49:10). The Minor Prophets were counted in the Hebrew canon as one book rather than twelve.

The fact that the Minor Prophets were treated as one book from antiquity has several implications in addressing their date of writing. For one thing, spelling patterns are similar, and generally late, across all twelve Minor Prophets. The eighth century B.C. prophets, Hosea, Amos and Jonah, show the same spelling practice as the later prophets Haggai and Zechariah. This is almost certainly due to the activity of the scribes who copied the Minor Prophets scroll as a whole and imposed their standard of spelling on it (for more on spelling, see Appendix B section B.3.16).

4.2.5 Hosea

Hosea is the first of two prophetic books addressed to the northern Kingdom of Israel (Amos is the second). Its beginning is set during the reign of Jeroboam II of Israel (793-753 B.C.). Hosea's family life is used as a metaphor for God's relationship with Israel.

Portions of Hosea's work must be dated before the death of Jeroboam II in 753 B.C., due to the absence of mention of any other northern king in 1:1, and also due to the statement "I will punish the house of Jehu for the bloodshed of Jezreel" (1:4), a statement that looks forward to the end of Jeroboam's kingship and its replacement by a non-relative, not from Jehu's line. This occurred when Jeroboam's son was assassinated after only a six month reign (2 Kgs 15:8-12). Political references to Egypt and Assyria are a little too vague to be helpful (Hos 5:13, 7:11, 9:6, 10:6 and 12:1), but may refer to Israel's diplomatic activities shortly after Jeroboam II. 2 Kgs 15:19 describes Menahem's bid to win over Tiglath-pileser of Assyria in 738 B.C., and 2 Kgs 16:7 describes King Ahaz of Judah's attempt to do the same in 734 B.C. In any case, Hosea would not have written anything after the Assyrian king Tiglath-pileser deported residents of Gilead (2 Kgs 15:29), because that region is considered Israelite (Hos 5:1, 6:8 and 12:11) by Hosea. This deportation occurred during the reign of Pekah (752-731). Therefore, 731 B.C. is the latest possible date for Hosea.

The date of 731 B.C. requires us then to explain the first verse of the book, which dates Hosea "during the reigns of Uzziah, Jotham, Ahaz and Hezekiah, kings of Judah, and during the reign of Jeroboam son of Joash king of Israel." It would be unusual for a northern prophet to date his message by kings in Judah, and the last of those kings, Hezekiah (716-687), is too late for the book. The explanation probably lies in the fact that the northern kingdom was permanently destroyed; any northern writings that made it into scripture did so via refugee immigration into Hezekiah's kingdom after the fall of Samaria. Hosea's prophecy therefore begins in Hos 1:2; Hos 1:1 is an introductory verse supplied by Judean scribes in Hezekiah's time.

The storyline of Hosea's family and the use of the word "Ephraim" to describe northern Israel (34 times beginning in 4:17, more than all the other prophets combined), argues in favor of the unity of the book.

Hosea knows the law. He accuses Israel of forgetting the Torah in 4:6, and of rebelling against it in 8:1. In 8:12, he is clear about the fact that the Torah has been written down – Hosea is not appealing to just a traditional oral law or set of customs. In 4:2 he lists sins forbidden by the Torah. Since Hosea mentions the Valley of Achor in the context of coming up from Egypt (Hos 2:15), he probably has in mind the story in Joshua (Josh 7:26) in which the valley got its name. Hos 13:10-11 shows the prophet's familiarity with the book of Samuel, in which the people asked for a king (1 Sam 8:5-6). This is the extent of it; Hosea knows the history of Israel through the book of Samuel, and does not show knowledge of any of the other books in the Bible. This is consistent with what would be expected from an 8th century B.C. prophet in the northern Kingdom of Israel.

Since Hosea preceded Isaiah by a few years, it is possible that Isaiah quotes from him in Isa 43:11 and 45:21:

Hosea 13:4	Isaiah 43:11	Isaiah 45:21
Yet I have been the LORD your God Since the land of Egypt; and you were not to know any god except Me, for there is no savior besides Me.	I, even I, am the LORD, and there is no savior besides Me.	…And there is no other God besides Me, A righteous God and a Savior; There is none except Me.

4.2.5.1 Linguistic Analysis

The linguistic features in Hosea are consistent with an eighth century B.C. date. The early pronoun "anoki" is used four times. The older word for kingdom, "mamlakah," is used instead of one of the newer forms. The early relative pronoun "zo," meaning "this," is present in 7:16, and the old poetic negation "bal" is in 7:2 and 9:16. "Ehdah" (עדה), a pre-exilic word meaning "congregation," is in 7:12. "Zulah" (זולה), meaning "except" in 13:4, appears almost entirely in pre-exilic texts. Hos 6:2 uses the early dual form (יָמַיִם) for "two days."

The spelling is relatively homogenous among all the Minor Prophets, probably because the scroll of Minor Prophets was copied and maintained as a single scroll of 12.[32] Therefore, spelling cannot be used with confidence to distinguish between dates for the Minor Prophets. Still, David's name is spelled in the older form דוד in 3:5.

4.2.5.2 Oldest Texts

There are fragments of seven Minor Prophets scrolls among the Dead Sea Scrolls, three of which (4Q78, 4Q79 and 4Q82) contain portions of Hosea. In addition, scrolls 4Q166 and 4Q167 are a commentary on Hosea.

4.2.5.3 Conclusion

Hosea was written before 731 B.C. Some of Hosea's oracles date from the reign of Jeroboam II of Israel, probably around 760 B.C.

4.2.6 Joel

Joel is one of the most difficult books in the Bible to date. Joel is named as the son of Pethuel, but beyond that, nothing is known about him. His prophecy is not directly connected to any king. Suggested dates for the book range from the ninth century B.C., which would be very early, to the late pre-exilic period, to the early post-exilic period, and as far down as the fourth century B.C.

The prophecy cannot be earlier than Jehoshaphat (873-848) due to mention of "The valley of Jehoshaphat" in 3:2 and 3:12, and some would connect Joel to the reign of Joash shortly afterward (835-796). The placement of this book in the canon, early in the sequence of Minor Prophets, supports this idea. Tyre, Sidon, Philistines, Egypt, Edom, Sabeans and Greeks are mentioned in the book, some of which (excluding the Greeks) were prominent enemies early in Israel's history, an argument used by supporters of an early date for the book. Some have suggested that Joel 2:1-11 looks forward to the Babylonian attack on Jerusalem, thus arguing

---

[32] Anderson and Forbes, *Spelling in the Hebrew Bible*, p. 315-316

for a late pre-exilic date, just before the Babylonian captivity. However, this passage is better understood as a continuing description of the locust invasion of chapter 1. Arguing against a very early date is the reference to a northern army (2:20), a problem more associated with the Assyrians and Babylonians. This interpretation would essentially equate Joel's "Day of the LORD" with the Babylonian campaign against Jerusalem.

We believe the internal evidence is more in favor of a post-exilic date. The phrases in Joel 3:1, "bring back the captives of Judah and Jerusalem," and "scattered among the nations" in 3:2 sound post-exilic. The reference to Greeks in 3:6 also favors a post-exilic date, but it is not evidence that the book was written after Alexander the Great (333 B.C.) – Ezekiel, writing about 570 B.C. makes a similar passing mention of Greece (Ezek 27:19 – the Hebrew word "Javan" means Greece). Greece had occasional involvement with the Middle East from antiquity. The comment about Edom's behavior in 3:19 also sounds post-exilic. Jerusalem seems to have a wall (Joel 2:9), which would mean the book comes after the work of Nehemiah in 445 B.C. Arguing from silence we can note that there is no mention of a king or a kingdom, nor is there any condemnation of idolatry or worship at high places. There is no mention of Assyrians, Syrians, or Babylonians. This implies a state of affairs existing after the exile. Joel also addresses the elders and priests (1:2 and 1:13-14), not the king or princes. This implies a state of affairs after the exile, when there is no king. The mention of Sidon in 3:4 indicates that the book had to be completed before 345 B.C., when Sidon was destroyed.

Joel knows the Torah, as he makes reference to the Garden of Eden (2:3). There are numerous connections between Joel and the other prophets, and although in most cases the direction of the borrowing is not clear in isolation, the fact that there exists such a density of connections in Joel implies that Joel is a late writer and that he quoted other prophets. Connections include Joel 1:15 and 2:1 with Ezek 30:2-3, Isa 13:6 and 13:9, Joel 3:16 with Jer 25:30 and

Amos 1:2, Joel 3:2 with Isa 66:18, Joel 2:32 with Isa 37:32 and Joel 3:18 with Amos 9:13. Also, Joel 3:10 inverts the "swords into plowshares" and "spears into pruning hooks" formula of Isa 2:4 and Mic 4:3. Perhaps most instructive is the match of Jonah 4:2 with Joel 2:13, "gracious and compassionate, slow to anger, abounding in lovingkindness, relenting of evil," and Jonah 3:9 with Joel 2:14, "Who knows whether He will not turn and relent." Both books use these words well in their context, and in the case of "gracious and compassionate...," this appears to be a widely used saying (see Exod 34:6, Ps 86:15, Ps 103:8 and 145:8). We would favor the idea that Jonah is original and Joel is the borrower, because "Who knows, God may turn and relent" in Jonah comes from the lips of a non-Israelite who would not be familiar with Joel's prophecy, and he certainly did not get those words from Jonah - Jonah not wanting God to relent. Also, the use of "God," rather than Yahweh – the LORD, coming from a non-Israelite has a feel of originality in Jonah. These dependencies tend to date Joel after all the other prophets.

4.2.6.1 Linguistic Analysis

Linguistic evidence does not give a clear picture of the date of the book. Joel mostly avoids late vocabulary, and there are no Persian words in the book, but there are a few hints that point to a late date of writing. Joel 1:17 uses ותיהם as a feminine plural with pronominal suffix on the words "their clods," and this is a predominately late form, the earlier form being ותם. Joel uses "ani" three times as a first person singular pronoun rather than the earlier form "anoki." This includes Joel 3:10 (Heb 4:10), "I am strong," or "I am a mighty man," a type of construction where earlier passages usually prefer "anoki" (Gen 27:11, 1 Sam 30:13, etc., but see also 2 Kgs 1:10 for a contrary example). Early vocabulary includes "orakh" (ארח) for "way, path" in 2:7. Altogether, these linguistic arguments are little more than hints, and the linguistic features of Joel overall do not provide a strong argument for any date.

4.2.6.2 Oldest Texts
There are fragments of seven Minor Prophets scrolls in the Dead Sea Scrolls, two of which (4Q78 and 4Q82) contain portions of Joel.

4.2.6.3 Conclusion
Joel is probably post-exilic, written after the work of Nehemiah in rebuilding the wall of Jerusalem in 445 B.C., making Joel the last of the writing prophets in the Bible. Because Joel shows only a few traits of Late Biblical Hebrew, we cannot date it too much later than that, and will settle on a date between 445 and 400 B.C. This is a tentative conclusion.

4.2.7 Amos
Amos is the second of two prophetic books addressed to the northern Kingdom of Israel (Hosea is the first). Amos 1:1 sets the book during the reign of Uzziah in Judah (792-740 B.C.) and Jeroboam II in Israel (793-753 B.C.), "two years before the earthquake." Yigal Yadin dates the earthquake at around 760 B.C. based on destruction debris in the excavations at Hazor.[33] Amos' message is an appeal to spiritual and social justice.

The depiction of Israel resting in wealth and comfort suggests a date after the success of Jeroboam II in recapturing territory described in 2 Kgs 14:25. Israel is wealthy and at ease (Amos 6:1-5), its religious ritual carefully maintained (4:4-5, 5:21-23, 7:13 and 8:14), and the people confident because of their military success (6:13). Because Amos sees Israel at its high point, while Hosea sees it in decay, Amos is probably written before Hosea, and is therefore the earliest of the writing prophets.

---

[33] Yadin, "Excavations at Hazor", 1964, *The Biblical Archeologist Reader 2*, edited by David Noel Freedman and Edward F. Campbell Jr., Garden City NY, Doubleday

Amos is familiar with David (6:5 and 9:11), as well as the earlier rulers of Syria, Ben-hadad and Hazael (1:4). Amos 5:25 mentions the 40 years in the wilderness described in the Torah, and Amos 7:4 references the "great deep" of Gen 7:11. Amos 9:2-4 may be a rare case where a prophet borrows from a Psalm (Ps 139:8-10), but the wording is not precise enough to be definitive.

Amos uses the title "LORD God of Hosts" seven times out of the 33 occurrences in the Bible. This phrase was introduced in David's time (1000 B.C. – 2 Sam 5:10 and seven times in Psalms) and ended with Jeremiah (580 B.C – seven times in Jeremiah). Amos is comfortably in the middle of this date range.

Several passages in Joel are dependent on Amos. Without a larger context, these dependencies could go in either direction, but we have placed Amos first based on the discussion on the date of Joel in section 4.2.5.

Amos 9:13 – Joel 3:18

Amos 9:13	Joel 3:18
Behold, days are coming… When the mountains will drip sweet wine And all the hills will be dissolved.	And in that day The mountains will drip with sweet wine, And the hills will flow with milk,

Amos 1:2 - Joel 3:16.

Amos 1:2	Joel 3:16
He said, "The LORD roars from Zion And from Jerusalem He utters His voice…	The LORD roars from Zion And utters His voice from Jerusalem…

4.2.7.1 Linguistic Analysis

The linguistics features in Amos are consistent with an eighth century B.C. date. The archaic pronoun "anoki" is used eight times. The earlier word for kingdom, "mamlakah" is used once, with the later companion "malkut" is not used. David's name is spelled in the later long form דויד in 6:5 and 9:11. This is due to the fact that all the Minor Prophets were managed as one scroll, and the spelling pattern became relatively late in the entire scroll due to the work of the scribes who copied the scroll. The anthropomorphism of God smelling is present in Amos 5:22 (Hebrew ירח sometimes translated as "accept" literally means "smell"). Amos uses the term "high places" (במות) in a positive sense (4:13), while later writers use it in an entirely negative sense as a place of corrupted worship.

Amos is apparently the first individual to write a lamentation using the "limping meter" (5:1-3), a poetic device used later in Ezekiel and Lamentations.

4.2.7.2 Oldest Texts

There are fragments of seven Minor Prophets scrolls in the Dead Sea Scrolls, two of which (4Q78 and 4Q82) contain portions of Amos.

4.2.7.3 Conclusion

Amos was written between 781 and 753 B.C. If the earthquake of Amos 1:1 was in 760 B.C., then Amos was written in 762 B.C., making Amos the first of the latter prophets to be written.

4.2.8 Obadiah

Obadiah, the shortest book in the Old Testament, contains a message of judgment against Edom. The book includes no personal information about Obadiah, nor is the book set in the reign of any king to help us with a date. We must therefore infer the date of the book from the contents of the prophecy in it. Obad 10-14 blames Edom for hostile conduct when Jerusalem was sacked. This event probably reflects the Babylonian conquest in 586 B.C. Edom's behavior at this time evoked tremendous resentment in

Israel, as reflected in Ps 137:7, Lam 4:21-22, Ezek 25:12-14, 35:1-15 and Mal 1:2-4. Thus, Obadiah should be dated shortly after the fall of Jerusalem in 586 B.C., when the memories of Edom's role were still vivid.

There is, however, a different tradition hinted at by the placement of Obadiah early in the list of Minor Prophets. This tradition places Edom's un-neighborly behavior during the reign of Jehoram (852-841), when Edom gained independence from Judah (2 Kgs 8:20-22 and 2 Chron 21:8-10). 2 Chron 21:16-17 records a Philistine and Arab attack on Jerusalem, and Edom may have shown hostility at this time. The mention of the Philistine plain in Obad 19 strengthens this theory, and such an early date opens up the possibility that this Obadiah is the man who talked with Elijah in 1 Kings 18. However, the Obadiah of 1 Kings 18 is not designated as a prophet, and his position in the northern Kingdom of Israel, rather than the southern Kingdom of Judah, argues against this idea. Further, Obad 19 presupposes the elimination of the northern kingdom, since Benjamin (from Judah) will possess Gilead (in the north). Finally, the magnitude of the disaster described in Obad 10-14 matches the events of 586 B.C. better than the Philistine/Arab attack of Jehoram's time, an event not significant enough for the author of Kings to mention.

Obadiah was a contemporary of Jeremiah, and borrowed from Jer 49:7-22 for some of his message (see section 4.2.2.3).

A connection may exist between Obadiah and Joel involving Obad 10 and Joel 3:19, Obad 11 and Joel 3:3, and Obad 15 and Joel 1:15, 2:1, 3:4, 3:7 and 3:14.

4.2.8.1 Linguistic Analysis

Obadiah is representative of Classical Biblical Hebrew, with no distinctive early or late marks.

4.2.8.2 Oldest Texts

There are fragments of seven Minor Prophets scrolls in the Dead Sea Scrolls, one of which (4Q82) contains portions of Obadiah.

4.2.8.3 Conclusion

Obadiah was written shortly after the fall of Jerusalem, perhaps about 585 B.C.

4.2.9 Jonah

The book of Jonah is a short story set during the reign of Jeroboam II of Israel (793-753 B.C.). Unlike the other prophets, Jonah is called to deliver a message not to Israel, but to the Assyrian city of Nineveh. The theme of the book is God's concern for a gentile kingdom.

The traditional view of the book of Jonah is that the book was written by Jonah himself, giving the book an early date in the eighth century B.C. Jonah is mentioned in 2 Kgs 14:25 and identified as "Jonah the son of Amittai, the prophet, who was of Gath-hepher." This makes Jonah a prophet from the northern Kingdom of Israel, from the land allotted to the tribe of Zebulun.

One critical view of the book of Jonah assigns its writing to a late date in the post-exilic period, around 450 B.C. The book is seen, along with Ruth, as a protest against the policies of Ezra and Nehemiah. Ezra and Nehemiah forbade mixed marriages (Jews with gentiles) and restricted foreign involvement in the activities in Jerusalem. In the book of Jonah, God's concern for the gentile city of Nineveh stands in contrast to the post-exilic exclusion of gentiles from the congregation of Jews.

Jonah's position in the Minor Prophets (fifth out of twelve in the Hebrew Bible) indicates a traditional belief in an early date. In the apocrypha, Jonah is mentioned in Tobit 14:4 and 14:8, while Ben Sirach 49:10 mentions the "twelve prophets," a count of

Minor Prophets which has to include Jonah to get to twelve.[34] In the New Testament, Jesus mentions Jonah in Matt 12:39-41 (Luke 11:29-32 is a parallel passage) and Matt 16:4. These verses can be used to argue for the historicity of Jonah, but they do not directly address the date of its writing. However, an early date and historicity tend to go together, while a late date often implies that a story is not historical, but was developed to teach a lesson.

The fact that Jonah is a prophet from northern Israel rather than Judah poses problems (though different ones) for both early and late dates. Jonah's prayer refers to the temple (2:4 and 2:7), a reference that might be unusual for a northern prophet during the reign of Jeroboam II, since the Jerusalem temple is most likely the one in view, though God's heavenly temple (as in Ps 11:4 and Isa 6:1) is possible. For a late, post-exilic date, using a northern prophet (a Samaritan) would hardly seem to be the best choice to represent the Jewish people in a message about religious inclusiveness.

4.2.9.1 Literary Considerations

Jonah is a short story with a compact point – God has compassion on the gentiles and so should you. Two other biblical books are short stories: Ruth and Esther. Esther is post-exilic and the date of Ruth is disputed.

A late date for Jonah might suggest (but does not demand) that Jonah is an allegory. There are other allegories in the Bible, but they are usually easy to spot (Ecc 12:2-6, Ezek 37:1-10, etc.). There are other parables in the Bible (Judg 9:8-15, 2 Sam 12:1-4, etc.), but they tend to be short and again, easy to spot. If Jonah is an allegory, it is by far the longest and most complex allegory in the Bible. Also, it is not clear what chapter 2 of Jonah would contribute to an allegory. Finally, if Jonah is a post-exilic allegory it

---

[34] Tobit was written perhaps in the third century B.C. and is present in the Dead Sea Scrolls in Aramaic and Hebrew. Ben Sirach was written near 185 B.C.

would be subversive in nature, and would have difficulty being accepted as a canonical book counted among the prophets. Literary considerations do not favor a late date for Jonah.

4.2.9.2 Theological Considerations

The perspective of Jonah 3:10, "When God saw their deeds, that they turned from their wicked way, then God relented concerning the calamity which He had declared He would bring upon them. And He did not do it," reflects an early theological perspective. God intended to cause a "calamity" in Nineveh. Amos, another prophet during the reign of Jeroboam, says "If a calamity occurs in a city has not the LORD done it?" (Amos 3:6) In post-exilic writings, God allows calamities to occur, but does not cause them directly (compare the earlier 2 Sam 24:1 to the post-exilic 1 Chron 21:1). The idea that God changed his mind in verse 10 compares well with Torah passages such as God being sorry he made man (Gen 6:6) and God intending to destroy Israel, but getting talked out of it by Moses (Exod 32:14). God does not change His mind in post-exilic writings.

Concern for gentile kingdoms appears more prominently in other eighth century B.C. writings (Isa 2:2-4, Mic 4:1-3 and Amos 1:3-2:3) than in post-exilic texts.

The critique of idols in the prayer of Jonah 2:7 suggests a pre-exilic date, since idols had ceased to become an issue for the post-exilic Jewish community.

4.2.9.3 Political Considerations

Jonah is set during the reign of Jeroboam II, when Assyrian pressure had not yet begun to impinge on Israel. We know from the Black Obelisk of Shalmaneser that Jehu, King of Israel, and Shalmaneser III, king of Assyria, previously had some sort of alliance or vassal relationship. [35] In this political context, a mission

---

[35] Kitchen, *On the Reliability of the Old Testament*, p. 27

trip is conceivable. After the Assyrian conquest of Israel in 721 B.C. and the Assyrian war with Hezekiah, it would seem less likely that a Jewish author would write favorably about the Assyrians. The political environment favors an early date for the book of Jonah.

4.2.9.4 Historical and Geographical Considerations

The geographic place names in Jonah do not help to determine a date. Joppa and Tarshish are both recognized as port cities before the suggested early date for Jonah and after the suggested late date. Nineveh was an ancient city in Assyria long before Jonah, with palaces and temples, though it did not become the Assyrian capitol until the reign of Sennacherib (704-681 B.C.).

An ancient Assyrian inscription indicates that the city of Calah, Assyria, which was not as large as Nineveh, had 69,574 inhabitants in 879 B.C.[36] This would mean the Jonah 4:11 population of Nineveh (120,000), 100 years later is in the right ballpark. Jonah left Nineveh and watched it from the east (4:5). Nineveh was located on the east bank of the Tigris River, with hills east of the city. This would give Jonah a good vantage point to view the city, as well as an early view of any enemy army, which would need to approach Nineveh from his side of the river. These points of accuracy would seem unlikely in a post-exilic allegory.

4.2.9.5 External Dependencies - Outputs

As discussed in the section 4.2.6 on Joel, Jonah 4:2 matches Joel 2:13, "gracious and compassionate, slow to anger, abounding in lovingkindness, relenting of evil," and Jonah 3:9 is close to Joel 2:14, "Who knows whether He will not turn and relent," with evidence that Jonah is original and Joel is the borrower.

---

[36] Wycliffe Bible Encyclopedia, p. 1208

4.2.9.6 Linguistic Analysis

There is a noted Aramaic idiom in Jonah, "beshelmi" (בשלמי), "on whose account," in 1:7 along with "besheli", (בשלי) "on account of me" in 1:12. As explained in section 2.2.2.2, a small number of Aramaisms proves little. In this case, the Aramaism is actually understandable, since Jonah is on a ship with gentile sailors who were probably speaking Aramaic. The sailors spoke the words in verse 7, and when the lot fell on Jonah, they spoke to him with the more Hebraic form of the same idiom in 1:8 "ba'asher lemi" (באשר למי).

There are no Persian words in Jonah. The early pronoun "anoki" is used twice. These facts favor the idea that Jonah was written before the exile, rather than the post-exilic Persian period.

4.2.9.7 Oldest Texts

There are seven scrolls of Minor Prophets among the Dead Sea Scrolls, three of which (4Q76, 4Q81 and 4Q82) contain portions of Jonah.

4.2.9.8 Conclusion

The theological, political, geographical and linguistics evidence favors an early date for the book of Jonah. Literary considerations are at least neutral. Jonah was probably written during the reign of Jeroboam II, before Assyrian pressure significantly affected Israel, around 760 B.C.

4.2.10 Micah

Micah was a contemporary of Isaiah. Mic 1:1 dates itself from the time of the Judean kings Jotham, Ahaz and Hezekiah. Hezekiah died in 687 B.C., so we can expect the book was completed by this time. In addition, with Micah we have the unique mention of his name in Jer 26:18, along with a precise quote of Mic 3:12. The Jeremiah passage is from the beginning of the reign of Jehoiakim, in 609 B.C., so the quotation is of a passage written at least 80-100 years earlier. Micah seems to be written before Hezekiah's re-forms, due to the mention of the high places (1:5), and before the destruction of Samaria (1:6). Israel's primary foreign enemy in Micah's account is Assyria (5:5-7 and 7:12). The negative reference to Northern Israelite kings Ahab and Omri (6:16) implies a date before the fall of Northern Israel. Mic 6:7 may be a reference to Hezekiah's huge sacrifice in 2 Chron 29:32-33.

Micah 6-7 reflects a meditation on Israel's history and on the Torah, as described in section 3.2.3.5.2.

Micah was a contemporary of Isaiah, and Mic 4:1-3 essentially duplicates Isa 2:2-4.

Isaiah 2:2-4	Micah 4:1-3
[2]Now it will come about that in the last days the mountain of the house of the LORD will be established as the chief of the mountains, and will be raised above the hills; and all the nations will stream to it.	[1]And it will come about in the last days that the mountain of the house of the LORD will be established as the chief of the mountains. It will be raised above the hills, and the peoples will stream to it.
[3]And many peoples will come and say, "Come, let us go up to the mountain of the LORD, to the house of the God of Jacob; that He may teach us concerning His ways and that we may walk in His paths." For the law will go forth from Zion and the word of the LORD from Jerusalem.	[2]Many nations will come and say, "Come and let us go up to the mountain of the LORD and to the house of the God of Jacob, that He may teach us about His ways and that we may walk in His paths" for from Zion will go forth the law, even the word of the LORD from Jerusalem.
[4]And He will judge between the nations, and will render decisions for many peoples; and they will hammer their	[3]And He will judge between many peoples and render decisions for mighty, distant nations; then they will hammer

swords into plowshares and their spears into pruning hooks; nation will not lift up sword against nation, and never again will they learn war.	their swords into plowshares and their spears into pruning hooks; nation will not lift up sword against nation, and never again will they train for war.

Mic 4:4 concludes the oracle by stating "for the mouth of the LORD of Hosts has spoken," wording suspiciously similar to Isaiah (Isa 1:20, 40:5 and 58:14), implying that Isaiah is original. Mic 4:10 speaks of the Babylonian exile, but does so in a foretelling manner, before the event occurred.

Mic 1:10, "Tell it not in Gath" echoes David's Song of the Bow in 2 Sam 1:20.

4.2.10.1 Linguistic Analysis

There are no Persian words in Micah. The early pronoun "anoki" is used once, in 3:8. The earlier word for kingdom, "Mamlakah" is used in 4:8. The early word "orakh" (אֹרַח) for "way, path" is in 4:2.

4.2.10.2 Oldest Texts

There are seven scrolls of Minor Prophets among the Dead Sea Scrolls, two of which (4Q81 and 4Q82) contain portions of Micah. There is also a Dead Sea Scroll Micah commentary (1Q14).

4.2.10.3 Conclusion

Micah was written during Hezekiah's reign, before the fall of Samaria. This is a narrow time window of 728-722 B.C.

4.2.11 Nahum

The book of Nahum is set during the time of the Assyrian empire. It describes God's impending judgment on Assyria and its capitol, Nineveh.

The date of the writing of the book of Nahum is not seriously disputed. Nah 3:8-10 refers to the capture of Thebes by the Assyrians under Ashurbanipal, a well-known historical event dated in 664 B.C. The book condemns Nineveh and predicts its destruction, another well-known event that occurred in 612 B.C. Therefore, the book was written somewhere in the time frame 664-612 B.C. The prophet's depiction of Nineveh makes it sound as if the Assyrians are in an advanced state of decline and their destruction is imminent. This would favor a date closer to the end of the range than the beginning.

Nah 1:3 reflects the Torah (Exod 34:6-7). Ezekiel (Ezek 24:6 and 24:9) may have picked up Nahum's phrase "woe to the bloody city" (Nah 3:1).

Nah 1:15 is dependent on Isa 52:7. Reasons for the priority of Isaiah on this passage are described in section 4.2.1.2.11.

Isaiah 52:7a	Nahum 1:15a

How lovely on the mountains
    Are the feet of him who
brings good news,
    Who announces peace
	Behold, on the mountains the
	feet of him who brings good
	news,
	Who announces peace!

4.2.11.1 Linguistic Analysis

Nahum is representative of Classical Biblical Hebrew, with few early or late marks. The dual form noun is used to say "two times" in Nah 1:9, a practice which is rare in late writings. The older word for kingdom, "mamlakah," is used in 3:5.

4.2.11.2 Oldest Texts

There are seven scrolls of Minor Prophets among the Dead Sea Scrolls, one of which (4Q82) contains portions of Nahum. The Dead Sea Scrolls also include a commentary on Nahum (4Q169).

4.2.11.3 Conclusion

Nahum was written between 664 and 612 B.C., and probably closer to the end of that range than the beginning.

4.2.12 Habakkuk

The book of Habakkuk is set shortly before the Babylonian exile, though it is not tied to a particular king's reign. Habakkuk questions God first about why the sins of Judah are seemingly ignored, and then about why God would judge Judah through an even more sinful nation (Babylon). The topic discussed clearly dates the book shortly before Babylonian pressure came to bear on Judah, around 600 B.C. Since Habakkuk has such a low estimation of the spiritual condition of the nation (1:2-4), the writing is likely to be after Josiah's death, since Josiah led significant reforms, with the situation deteriorating afterward. This would squeeze the writing of the book into a very small time window: 609-600 B.C.

There exists a textual question dealing with chapter 3, the prayer of Habakkuk. It has been suggested that this chapter was originally a separate poem not connected with the work of the prophet. This is a rare case in which there exists textual evidence for such a claim. The Dead Sea Scroll Habakkuk commentary (1QpHab) addresses only the first two chapters of the book. The scribe clearly left blank space after the second chapter. This textual argument is less than conclusive, though, since the scroll in question is not a copy of Habakkuk but a commentary, and the third chapter could have been beyond the purpose of the commentator.

With such a short book as Habakkuk, we cannot know enough about Habakkuk's writing style to say whether chapter 3 is typical of that style. It does show some of the same gentle alliteration as in the first two chapters (1:5, 1:6, 1:8, 2:3, 2:9, 3:2 and 3:6). Rather than being a later addition to the book, it is more likely that Habakkuk 3 is an older psalm/prayer used by Habakkuk in response to the revelation he received in chapters 1-2. Hab 3:3 says God comes form Teman/Mt Paran rather than Mount Zion (as in Deut 33:2 rather than Ps 20:2, 110:2, etc.). The enemies of 3:7, Cushan and Midian, ceased to be enemies after the period of the judges (Cushan may be associated with the evil king Cushan-rishathaim of Judg 3:8).

The prayer in chapter 3 can be considered Habakkuk's response to what he heard in the first two chapters: "I have heard the report about You and I fear" (3:2). The statement of faith in 3:17-18 indicates the prophet will continue to rejoice in God regardless of how bad things get due to the Babylonians.

Since Habakkuk 3 is a musical prayer, perhaps it is not surprising that this is one of the few places where a prophet is clearly influenced by a psalm. Habakkuk 3 has a number of connections with Psalm 18. Most striking is Hab 3:19 with Ps 18:33.

Psalm 18:33	Habakkuk 3:19
He makes my feet like hinds' feet, and sets me upon my high places.	...and He has made my feet like hinds' feet, and makes me walk on my high places.

The connections are sharper in Hebrew than in English, such as the irregular spelling "Eloah" (אלוה) for God rather than Elohim, in Hab 3:3 and Ps 18:31 (Heb 18:32).

See section 4.2.2.2 for a discussion of the relationship between Hab 2:13 and Jer 51:58.

4.2.12.1 Linguistic Analysis

The linguistic features of Habakkuk are consistent with a pre-exilic date. The early pronoun "zu," meaning "this," appears in 1:11.

Habakkuk's prayer in chapter 3 shows numerous connections with Early Biblical Hebrew. The word "Selah" in 3:3, 3:9 and 3:13, which is usually not translated in English Bibles, and the fact that the psalm has musical instructions in 3:1 are features of the older psalms in the book of Psalms. Early vocabulary includes "omer" (אמר) for "speech, word" in 3:9, "makhatz" (מחץ) for "strike" in 3:13, and "Eloah" for God in 3:3. There may be some uncertainty as to whether verses 3-15 should be rendered in past or present tense, but the use of perfect and imperfect verbs together and often in parallel matches early poetry's use to describe past tense events. The imperfect verbs (3:3, 3:4, 3:5, 3:7, 3:9, 3:10 and 3:12) used in this manner imply a date of ultimate origin prior to the prophetic period, prior to 750 B.C. Hab 3:19 uses the term "high places" (במות) in a positive sense, as opposed to other writings in the prophets, which use it in a negative sense as a place of corrupted worship.

4.2.12.2 Oldest Texts

There are seven scrolls of Minor Prophets among the Dead Sea Scrolls, one of which (4Q82) contains portions of Habakkuk. The Dead Sea Scrolls also include a substantial commentary on Habakkuk chapters 1-2 (1QpHab).

4.2.12.3 Conclusion

Habakkuk was written between 609 and 600 B.C. The prayer of Habakkuk in chapter 3 is drawn from much earlier material.

4.2.13 Zephaniah

The date of Zephaniah is not widely disputed. Zephaniah is set during the reign of Josiah (641-609 B.C.). The prophet is identified as a descendant of King Hezekiah four generations down (Zeph 1:1). Zephaniah predicts the destruction of Nineveh (2:13), an event that occurred in 612 B.C. This would set Zephaniah's date between about 641-621 B.C. Zephaniah's depiction of the idolatrous state of worship in Judah (1:4-6) and complacent attitude (1:12) may imply that the book was written before the beginning of Josiah's reforms. On the other hand, punishment of the "king's sons" (1:8) could refer to Josiah's sons and if so would make the prophecy literally true if applied to his sons Jehoahaz, Jehoiakim, Jehoiachin and Zedekiah. Condemnation of the king's sons implies they were old enough for moral accountability, requiring a date later in Josiah's reign, since Josiah was only eight years old when he became king. Alternatively, "king's sons" could mean more generally "royal family," or even the sons of a previous king, in which case it would give us no clue for a date. The evidence from 1:8 is inconclusive.

4.2.13.1 Linguistic Analysis

The oath form in 2:9, "'as I live', declares YHWH," is consistent with literature of that period (Jer 22:24 and 46:18). The older word for kingdom, "mamlakot," is in 3:8.

4.2.13.2 Oldest Texts

There are seven scrolls of Minor Prophets among the Dead Sea Scrolls, three of which (4Q77, 4Q78 and 4Q82) contain portions of Zephaniah.

4.2.13.3 Conclusion

Zephaniah was written between 641 and 612 B.C. This makes Zephaniah an early contemporary of Jeremiah and Habakkuk.

4.2.14 Haggai

The book of Haggai is set in the early post-exilic period during the leadership of Zerubbabel (after 525 B.C.). Haggai exhorts the people to complete work on the rebuilt temple. The date of Haggai is not widely disputed, and according to Archer, he "enjoys the unusual status of being uncontested by all critics of every persuasion"[37]. He writes in the second year of Darius 1 of

---

[37] Archer, *A Survey of the Old Testament Introduction*, p. 407

Persia (520 B.C.), before the Temple has been completely rebuilt. His messages are dated in the first day of the sixth month (1:1), the twenty-first day of the seventh month (2:1), and the 24th day of the ninth (2:10 and 2:20) month (probably August 29, October 17 and December 18) of the second year of King Darius, during the governorship of Zerubbabel and the high priesthood of Joshua son of Jehozadak.

Haggai knows the Torah, including the cleanliness laws (2:12-14) associated with the priests, and he connects the priests with the law in 2:11. Like most post-exilic books set in Israel, Haggai makes mention of the governor (1:1) and the high priest (2:4), who fill the leadership role previously occupied by a king. Haggai is mentioned in Ezra, a book written later, in Ezra 5:1 and 6:14.

4.2.14.1 Linguistic Analysis

Haggai uses the older word for kingdom, "mamlakot," twice in 2:22. Haggai does show the beginning of a trend in Late Biblical Hebrew to use participles where earlier language would have been more likely to use finite verbs, as in 2:6, "and I will shake" (ואני מרעיש).

4.2.14.2 Oldest Texts

There are seven scrolls of Minor Prophets among the Dead Sea Scrolls, two of which (4Q77 and 4Q80) contain portions of Haggai.

4.2.14.3 Conclusion

Haggai was written in 520 B.C.

4.2.15 Zechariah

The scroll of Minor Prophets is generally understood to consist of exactly twelve prophets, the last two being Zechariah and Malachi. However, there is another way to look at the Minor Prophets scroll. It can be divided into eleven prophets, ending with Zechariah 1-8, followed by three "oracles." For purposes of dating

Zechariah and Malachi, the eleven prophets plus three oracles structure looks to be more helpful. A unique phrase, not appearing elsewhere in the Bible, appears in Zech 9:1, Zech 12:1 and Mal 1:1: "The oracle of the word of the LORD" (משא דבר יהוה). It is significant that all three of these occurrences come at the end of the Minor Prophets scroll, though spanning two books. The first two oracles are anonymous, and the third (Mal 1:1) is assigned to Malachi. Arguably, the third could be considered anonymous too, since "Malachi" means "my messenger," and it may not be a proper name.[38] In this book, we will treat it as a proper name. We believe that the oracles of Zechariah 9-11, Zechariah 12-14 and Malachi 1-4 are three independent texts. The Zechariah oracles are not fundamentally connected with Zechariah 1-8, and the Malachi oracle may contain two different sources. Before we deal with the oracles, we will first address the prophet Zechariah himself.

4.2.15.1 Zechariah 1-8

Zechariah is dated in the second to the fourth year of Darius 1 (Zech 1:1, 1:7 and 7:1) and the governorship of Zerubbabel. This would be a narrow range of 520-518 B.C. This makes Zechariah a contemporary of Haggai, and both prophets identify the high priest at that time as "Joshua the son of Jehozadak" (Zech 6:11 and Hag 1:1). The recent freshness of the return from Babylon can be felt in verses like 6:10, identifying three returning men as "the captives." Zechariah is mentioned along with Haggai by Ezra, a book written later, in Ezra 5:1 and 6:14. These straightforward indicators all appear in Zechariah 1-8, and can be used with confidence to date Zechariah 1-8 in the immediate post-exilic period.

Zechariah mentions the "former prophets" in 1:4, 7:7 and 7:12, probably with Jeremiah chiefly in mind, since he mentions

---

[38] The Septuagint reads "his messenger" – not a proper name. Also, "Malachi" occurs again in Mal 3:1, and it is translated there as "my messenger".

Jeremiah's 70 years prophecy (Jer 25:11-12 and 29:10) in 1:12 and 7:7, and since Zech 1:4 seems to be dependent on wording in Jeremiah (Jer 18:11 etc.). The phrase in Zech 2:8, "apple of the eye," may be dependent on Ps 17:8.

4.2.15.2 Oracles of Zechariah 9-14

The issue with the date of Zechariah involves chapters 9-14, which appear to be disconnected from the rest of the book. Some writers have suggested that chapters 9-14 are later additions to Zechariah. However, the bulk of the evidence indicates the reverse; these chapters are *older* than the rest of the book. 9:10, 10:7 and 11:14 talk about the northern Kingdom of Israel, or Ephraim, as if it still exists, a situation prior to 722 B.C. Assyria, destroyed in 612 B.C., is mentioned in 10:10-11. The idols of 13:2 and idols and diviners of 10:2 point to a pre-exilic period, since Canaanite idolatry was a dead issue after the exile. The phrase "house of David" (12:7, 12:8, 12:10, 12:12 and 13:1) refers to the monarchy in Jerusalem, also pointing to a pre-exilic text. Further helping to date the passage is the fact that a standing temple is assumed in Zech 9:8, 11:13 and 14:21 (it was only in work during the timeframe of Zechariah 1-8 and Haggai). Chapter 12 deals with Judah, and Zech 12:11 may allude to Josiah's death at Megiddo, during the time of Jeremiah. Also, the statement, "you will flee just as you fled before the earthquake in the days of Uzziah king of Judah (14:5)," seems to imply a memory fresher than the 250 years between this earthquake and Zechariah's time. The mention of Greece in 9:13 is not an argument for a late date, since Greece was known to Israel in pre-exilic times (Ezek 27:19, in the early exile, names Greece also). The oracle of Zechariah 9-11 mentions twelve other foreign entities, and Greece is just part of the laundry list.

The differences between Zechariah 1-8 and the oracles of 9-14 include:

1. The phrase, "Thus says YHWH" is in Zech 1:3, 1:4, 1:14, 1:16, 1:17; 2:8; 3:7, 6:12; 8:2, 8:3, 8:4, 8:6, 8:7, 8:9, 8:14, 8:19,

      8:20 and 8:23, but only the oracles in 11:4. The 11:4 phrase differs from all the others, being the only one that says "Thus says YHWH my God."

2. The phrase, "The word of YHWH came to" is in Zech 1:1, 1:7; 4:8, 7:1, 7:4, 7:8, 8:1 and 8:18, but not in the oracles of chapters 9-14.

3. Zechariah is mentioned by name four times in chapters 1-8, but not in chapters 9-14.

4. Other personal names are in chapters 1-8, but none in chapters 9-14.

On the other side of the ledger is one striking similarity between Zechariah 1-8 and 9-14, the uncommon phrase "go to and fro" (מעבר ומשב) in 7:14 and 9:8.

The New Testament book of Matthew provides a clue as to the author of the oracles of Zechariah 9-14. Matt 27:9-10 quotes Zech 11:12-13 and says these words came from *Jeremiah*. It is instructive to compare the passages:

Matthew 27:9-10	Zech 11:12-13 (MT)
And they took the thirty pieces of silver, the price of the one whose price had been set by the sons of Israel; and they gave them for the potter's field, as the Lord directed me.	So they weighed out thirty shekels of silver as my wages. Then the LORD said to me, "Throw it to the potter, that magnificent price at which I was valued by them." So I took the thirty shekels of silver and threw them to the potter in the house of the LORD.

Although the connection is obvious, it is clear that Matthew is not quoting from either the Masoretic Text or the Septuagint, which matches the Masoretic Text on this passage. Matthew's mention of Jeremiah has historically been considered either his mistake or a later scribe's error, but given the fact that the prophet's name and the text both differ from what we have in the Old Testament today, we might consider the possibility that Matthew had a different text that connected this passage to Jeremiah.[39]

The following is a list of similarities between Jeremiah and Zechariah 9-14.

Phrase or Subject	Zechariah	Jeremiah
Damascus and Hamath	9:1-2	49:23
Tower of Hananel	14:10	31:38
Corner gate	14:10	31:38
Benjamin's gate (only elsewhere in Ezek 48:32)	14:10	37:13
Gather them to…Gilead	10:10	50:19
Fire on Lebanon's cedars	11:1	22:6-7
House of David	12:7-8, 12:10, 12:12 and 13:1	21:12
Inhabitants of Jerusalem	12:5-8, 12:10 and 13:1	4:4 and 15 more times
False dreams	10:2	23:32
Diviners lying	10:2	27:9
Shepherds as (bad) national leaders	10:2-3	50:6, etc.
Shepherds wail	11:3	25:34-36
Woe to the shepherds	11:17	23:1
No light from heaven	14:6	4:23
Stretching the heavens	12:1	51:15
Foundations of the earth	12:1	31:37
Young lions roar, leading to ruin	11:3	2:15
I will not pity them	11:6	13:14

---

[39] Matthew's Old Testament quotations seem to come from a mix of texts. Matt 1:23 is from the Septuagint, Matt 2:15 from the Masoretic Text, Matt 2:23 from neither. The subject is beyond the scope of this book.

Phrase or Subject	Zechariah	Jeremiah
What is to die, let it die	11:9	15:2
Potter	11:13	18:1-6
Mourn for an only son	12:10	6:26
Punishment on prophets	13:2-3	23:34
Prophesy falsely	13:3	23:25
They will be as they were before	10:8	30:20
They will call and I will answer	13:9	29:12-13

The list above is a long list for a short passage. By comparison, Zechariah 1-8 has fewer connections to Jeremiah, and some of those he credits to the "former prophets" (1:4 and 7:7), perhaps indicating that Zechariah had read a Jeremiah scroll and was using some of his ideas.

The biggest issue with dating Zechariah 9-11 at the time of Jeremiah is not that it is too early, but that in some places it looks to be not early enough. References to "Ephraim" and "Joseph" (9:10, 9:13 and 10:6-7) could realistically be considered a product of the divided kingdom era (before 722 B.C.). However, Jeremiah in his own book occasionally speaks like this also (Jer 31:9 and 31:18-20). Jeremiah's life was still long after the earthquake of Uzziah's time (Zech 14:5).

Zech 9:10b looks to be dependent on Ps 72:8, "And His dominion shall be from sea to sea, and from the river to the ends of the earth." Psalm 72 is attributed to Solomon, so it would have been written before any of the prophets.

4.2.15.3 Linguistic Analysis

Zechariah 1-8 frequently uses participle verbs to reflect present tense, a feature present in all ages of Biblical Hebrew but more frequent in the latter books. Zech 1:7 uses the Babylonian month name "Shebat," and 7:1 uses the month name "Chislev." These later names are used only after the Babylonian exile. The early pronoun "anoki" is used five times in Zechariah, with all the occurrences in the latter portion of the book (11:6, 11:16, 12:2 and 13:5 [twice]), supporting the idea of a pre-exilic date for the oracles of chapters 9-14.

4.2.15.4 Oldest Texts
There are seven scrolls of Minor Prophets among the Dead Sea Scrolls, three of which (4Q76, 4Q80 and 4Q82) contain portions of Zechariah.

4.2.15.5 Conclusion
Zechariah chapters 1-8 were written between 520 and 518 B.C. The oracles of Zechariah 9-11 and 12-14 are two separate unattached messages written earlier, probably by Jeremiah. The oracles address a state of affairs prior to the exile, so the dates for both should be between 620 and 586.

The life of Jeremiah in particular made it likely that many of his writings may not have made it into the book that carries his name (see section 4.2.2). It is not strange to think that the prophet Zechariah, writing perhaps 50 years after Jeremiah's death, would have picked up some unattached writings of Jeremiah and included them in his own message to Judah. Alternatively, it is also possible that this action was taken not by Zechariah, but by the anonymous individual who first pulled together all of the Minor Prophets into one scroll.

4.2.16 Malachi
The book of Malachi is named based on Mal 1:1, "The burden of the word of the LORD to Israel by Malachi." Malachi may be a personal name, but since most prophets are identified by the name of their father also, and "Malachi" can be read here as "my messenger" in Hebrew, some writers suggest that Malachi was not a historical person. Because the style of most of Malachi is quite unique, not matching any other prophet or Old Testament book, we will retain the tradition of calling the author by the name

"Malachi." We have tentatively divided Malachi into two different sources, with Malachi chapters 1-2 and 3:7-15 assigned to the historical prophet we will call Malachi.

Malachi wrote in the post-exilic period, though a precise date is difficult to ascertain. The temple has been rebuilt (1:10 and 3:1), requiring a date after 515 B.C. Judah has a governor (1:8) who is probably not Nehemiah since Nehemiah declined gifts (Neh 5:14-18) like those described in Mal 1:8. Malachi's concern over inter-marriage with foreign women (2:11) matches well with Ezra (Ezra 9:2, 10:3 and 10:16-44) and Nehemiah (Neh 10:30), and his concern about funding the temple (3:8-12) also matches the time of Nehemiah (Neh 10:32-39). Religious rituals have been in progress for some time, because people are growing weary of them (1:13). Some of these problems were corrected by Nehemiah in 444 B.C., so the best date for Malachi would be 500-450 B.C. Mal 1:3-5 presupposes the destruction of the nation of Edom, which happened during the time of the Babylonian Empire, before the return from exile.

Malachi's question and answer style (1:2-3, 1:6-8, 1:9-10, etc.) is unique among the prophets.

A second, older source appears to be present in Mal 3:1-6 and 3:16-4:6, and this source bears a striking resemblance to Isaiah. This source may have been included by Malachi in his own work, or it may have been folded in by the individual who pulled together all of the Minor Prophets into one scroll. We will refer to this source as Malachi-Isaiah. This is the first of several texts outside the book of Isaiah that we believe can ultimately be traced to Isaiah.

Once again, a clue to the author is found in a New Testament book. Mark 1:2-3 says, "As it is written in Isaiah the prophet...," then quotes from Mal 3:1 followed by Isa 40:3.[40] Some have

---

[40] The Greek Textus Receptus from which the King James Version was translated does not name Isaiah here. The Nestle-Aland Greek New Testament (Fourth Revised Edition), from which most modern translations are made, puts the

suggested that Mark chose to name only the latter of his sources, while others have suggested an error on the part of Mark or a later scribe. It is instructive to compare all the texts using Mal 3:1:

Mark 1:2	Matt 11:10	Luke 7:27	Mal 3:1 (Hebrew MT)	Mal 3:1 (Septuagint)
Behold, I send my messenger ahead of you, who will prepare your way	Behold, I send my messenger ahead of you, who will prepare your way before you	Behold, I send my messenger ahead of you, who will prepare your way before you	Behold, I send my messenger, and he will prepare a way before me	Behold, I send forth my messenger, and he will survey the way before me.
Ιδου αποστελλω τον αγγελον μου προ προσωπου σου ος κατασκευασει την οδον σου	ιδου εγω αποστελλω τον αγγελον μου προ προσωπου σου ος κατασκευασει την οδον σου εμπροσθεν σου	ιδου εγω αποστελλω τον αγγελον μου προ προσωπου σου ος κατασκευασει την οδον σου εμπροσθεν σου	הנני שלח מלאכי ופנה־דרך לפני	ιδου εγω εξαποστελλω τον αγγελον μου και επιβλεψεται οδον προ προσωπου μου

Mark 1:2, Matt 11:10 and Luke 7:27 agree closely with each other, less with the MT, and still less with the Septuagint. Although the

reading naming Isaiah in its "A" category, meaning that the committee that produced this Greek New Testament believes the text mentioning Isaiah is certain.

connection is obvious, it is clear that Mark is not quoting from either the Masoretic Text or the Septuagint. Given the fact that the prophet's name and the text both differ from what we have in the Old Testament today, we might consider the possibility that Mark had a different text that connected this passage to Isaiah.[41]

Malachi-Isaiah has a Messianic tone matching that of Isaiah, the most Messianic of the prophets. The following table shows some of the topical and linguistic similarities between Malachi and Isaiah.

Phrase or Subject	Malachi	Isaiah
My messenger whom I send (only occurrence in the Old Testament)	3:1	42:19
Clear the way (done by the messenger – Hebrew פנה דרך). This appears also in Isa 62:10. These are the only occurrences of this phrase in the Old Testament.	3:1	40:3
Cleansing fire (using צרף)	3:2	1:25 and 41:7
Concept of the righteous being recorded in a book (using כתב)	3:16	4:3
Evildoers are chaff, burned up	4:1	5:24
Strike the land	4:6	11:4

There is a limited amount of text to use for analysis, yet some connection to Isaiah can be seen.

It appears that Joel quotes from Malachi, as Mal 4:5b matches Joel 2:31b, "before the coming of the great and terrible day of the LORD."

---

[41] Matthew's Old Testament quotations seem to come from a mix of texts. Matt 1:23 is from the Septuagint, Matt 2:15 from the Masoretic Text, Matt 2:23 from neither. A detailed treatment of the subject is beyond the scope of this book.

4.2.16.1 Linguistic Analysis

Mal 1:6 (twice) and 1:14 use the pronoun "ani" in the construction "I am a Father," "I am a Master" and "I am a great King." In earlier Hebrew, "anoki" would have been preferred in these phrases (see Appendix B, section B.3.7). The absence of "anoki" here is a feature of Late Biblical Hebrew.

On the other hand, the early pronoun "anoki" does appear in 4:5 (Heb 3:23). An earlier word, "pen" (פן), meaning "lest" appears in 4:6 (Heb 3:24). These features hint at a pre-exilic text for the Malachi-Isaiah portion of Malachi.

4.2.16.2 Oldest Texts

There are seven scrolls of Minor Prophets among the Dead Sea Scrolls, two of which (4Q76 and 4Q78) contain portions of Malachi.

4.2.16.3 Conclusion

Malachi was written between 500 and 450 B.C., after the temple had been rebuilt, but before the reforms of Nehemiah. Malachi 3:1-6 and 3:16 – 4:6 likely are drawn from earlier material and quite possibly from Isaiah, allowing a date range of 740-680 B.C. for these passages.

CHAPTER 5

Dating the Writings

5.1 Psalms

Dating the book of Psalms is different from dating any of the other books evaluated so far, because unlike all the previous books, Psalms presents itself as an anthology, a collection of works from writers of different times. Therefore, we have provided a table that dates each Psalm individually. Some Psalms contain strong evidence that can be used to determine a date of writing, while in many cases a Psalm gives few if any clues as to when it was written. For this reason, we have included along with our proposed date for each Psalm a probability ranking on a scale of 1-10 (1 = lowest probability and 10 = highest probability) that the proposed date is close to correct. For example, the table entry for Psalm 137 reads: 586 (9), a date of 586 B.C. with a very high probability that this date is close to correct. Psalm 98 shows 700 (3), a proposed date of 700 B.C., but with low confidence in the accuracy of that date.

5.1.1 Authorship Attributions

Many of the Psalms include a header which contains an attribution of authorship. Authorship of the Psalms is attributed as follows:

1. David (73 total) – Psalms 3-9, 11-32, 34-41, 51-65, 68-70, 86, 101, 103, 108-110, 122, 124, 131, 133 and 138-145
2. Asaph (12 total) – Psalms 50 and 73-83
3. Sons of Korah (11 total) – Psalms 42, 44-49, 84-85 and 87-88
4. Solomon – Psalms 72 and 127
5. Heman the Ezrahite – Psalm 88 (along with the sons of Korah)
6. Ethan the Ezrahite – Psalm 89

    7.   Moses – Psalm 90

    8.   Anonymous[1] – Psalms 1-2, 10, 33, 43, 66-67, 71, 91-100, 102, 104-107, 111-121, 123, 125-126, 128-130, 132, 134-137 and 146-150

David lived from about 1038 to 968 B.C., so this provides a date range for Psalms attributed to him. Solomon, the son of David, reigned from 970-931 B.C., providing a date range for Psalms 72 and 127. Ethan the Ezrahite and Heman the Ezrahite are Solomon's contemporaries according to 1 Kgs 4:31 and 1 Chron 15:19.

1 Chron 6:39 and 15:19 identify Asaph as a singer in David's time. However, over 500 years later, Ezra 3:10 mentions "the Levites, the sons of Asaph" in connection with temple music, and it is not certain if this Asaph is the same as David's contemporary. Additionally, there was a "recorder" named Asaph in Hezekiah's time, around 700 B.C. (2 Kgs 18:37). Because of the uncertainty of the identification of Asaph, we have not chosen to use his name as an aid in dating the Psalms attributed to him. More problematic is the fact that the Psalms of Asaph seem to come from several different time periods, so we appear to not be dealing with a single author.

The "sons of Korah" are apparently descendants of Korah the Levite who rebelled against Moses. "Sons" can extend down to any period in history, and with the sons of Korah this is hinted at in Num 26:11. They are named as a group as early as the time of David (1 Chron 26:19) and are still present at the time of Jehoshaphat, 873-848 B.C. (2 Chron 20:18-19), with no indication of a termination of their work. Therefore, "sons of Korah" will also not be a useful attribution for assigning a date.

To date the individual Psalms, the first question we must address is whether or not to take the authorship attributions seriously. Since almost half of the Psalms are attributed to David,

---

[1] Psalm 2 is anonymous in the Old Testament, but Acts 4:25 attributes it to David. Likewise, Hebrews 4:7 attributes Psalm 95 to David. The Septuagint also attributes some of the anonymous Psalms to various authors.

these Psalms would all date to the tenth century B.C. if the attributions are correct. This would mean these Psalms were written before any of the prophets.

The viewpoint of antiquity is that the attributions are historical. In the New Testament, Jesus (Matt 22:43, Mark 12:36 and Luke 20:42 quoting Ps 110:1), Peter (Acts 1:16 referencing Ps 41:9, Acts 2:25 quoting Ps 16:8-11) and Paul (Rom 4:6 quoting Ps 32:1-2 and Rom 11:9 quoting Ps 69:22-23) all speak of David being the author of Psalms attributed to him. The statement of Jesus (Matt 22:43) is particularly striking, because the point Jesus is making is invalid if David is not the author of Psalm 110. 2 Maccabees alludes to David's authorship of some Psalms (2 Macc 2:13), and the Mishna also teaches Davidic authorship of the Psalms.[2]

David's life provides the historical background for a number of the Psalms, as shown in the list below.

1 Sam 19:11	Psalm 59
1 Sam 21:10-15	Psalm 56
1 Sam 21:10-22:2	Psalm 34
1 Sam 22:9	Psalm 52
1 Sam 23:15-23	Psalm 54
1 Sam 24 or 22:1-2	Psalm 57
1 Sam 24 or 22:1-2	Psalm 142
2 Sam 8:3, 8:13 and 1 Chron 18:9-12	Psalm 60
2 Sam 11-12	Psalm 51
2 Sam 15-18	Psalm 3
2 Sam 22:5	Psalm 63
2 Sam 22	Psalm 18
1 Chron 21:1-22:1	Psalm 30

[2] Baba Bathra 14b

However, not all the information in the Psalm headings comes from the books of Samuel, Kings and Chronicles – in Psalm 7 "Cush" is unknown, and in Psalm 34 "Abimelech" is used instead of Achish, though the heading seems to refer to the Achish of 1 Sam 21:10-15. The heading of Psalm 60 contains details not present in Samuel. Likewise, the heading of Psalm 30, "A Song at the Dedication of the House," would have been unnatural if it was based only on the text of the Psalm, which mentions nothing about the temple or any other house.

It is possible that none of the headings came from the original authors' pens, yet they still show signs of antiquity. Some were old enough so as to be not understood by the Septuagint translators. For example "to the choir director" in many Psalms is translated by the Septuagint as "to the end," "to the lilies" in Psalm 80 is translated as something like "to those who change," and "to the maidens" in Psalm 46 is translated as "to hide."[3] Also, the spelling of David's name in the attributions is in the older short form "דוד." Since all indisputably post-exilic books of the Bible spell David's name in the long form "דויד" (279 out of 279 times), this suggests that the headings containing David's name may be pre-exilic.

David's reputation as a musician is well established independent of the Psalms. He first comes to the attention of Saul due to his musical ability (1 Sam 16:17-23). He composed a song of mourning for Saul and Jonathan (2 Sam 1:17-27), a lament for Abner (2 Sam 3:33-34), and his last words are a poem (2 Sam 23:1-7). In addition, David's Psalm in 2 Samuel 22 is a copy of Psalm 18. Chronicles says David appointed music leaders (1 Chronicles 25) and includes a poem by David in 1 Chron 29:10-15. Another early witness is Amos, who makes a backhanded reference to David as a musician in Amos 6:5.

---

[3] The Septuagint combines Psalm 9-10 into one, leaving most of the Psalm numbers one less than in the Masoretic Text and English translations. The Septuagint also joins Psalms 114-115, but splits both 116 and 147 in two.

There are no obvious anachronisms in the Davidic Psalms. This implies that the attributions were not written in the sense of dedicating the Psalm to David, or writing in the spirit of David. If that had been the case, then some of the clearly late Psalms would have been attributed to him. With 73 out of 150 Psalms attributed to David, it would be statistically likely that some of the late Psalms would be included, but they are not. No Psalms which reference the Babylonian exile (like 137), nor the return from exile (like 107 or 126) are assigned to David. It might be suggested that the mention of the temple would be an anachronism, since the temple was built by David's son, Solomon, after David's death. Yet this is not necessarily so, since the temple was in David's heart and head (2 Sam 7:1-5) and David made provision for it before he died (1 Chron 29:1-9). Furthermore, some of David's temple references are in future tense (Ps 68:29), and a number of others seem to refer to God's temple in heaven rather than in Jerusalem (as in Ps 11:4, 18:6, etc.). Finally, even the tabernacle that preceded the Temple was sometimes described as a temple (1 Sam 1:9 and 3:3).

For these reasons, we will give the benefit of the doubt to the authorship named in the headings. Each Psalm attributed to David is dated to some period in his life. When additional evidence supports Davidic authorship, we have increased the probability ranking for the suggested date. There are a few cases where the internal evidence weighs against Davidic authorship in Psalms attributed to him, and for those cases we have reduced the probability ranking.

Some words, phrases and ideas recur regularly in Davidic Psalms, and these lend support to the idea of Davidic authorship. The occurrence of these phrases in anonymous Psalms has in a few cases led us to also date those Psalms to David's time, as with Psalm 71. Some Davidic phrases along with a ratio of their occurrences in Davidic versus Non-Davidic Psalms are shown below:

1. "Be gracious to me": 15-2, and also from David's mouth in 2 Sam 12:22 (18 total occurrences in the Bible)
2. "Deliver me": 15-2
3. "Sheol": 10-5
4. "Bones": 11-2
5. "Enemies" or "enemy": 57-21
6. "Rescue me" or "rescue my soul": 8-3
7. "My rock": 9-3, also in David's mouth in 2 Sam 22:2
8. "My fortress": 4-2
9. "My salvation": 12-5
10. "My deliverer": 4-0
11. Davidic Psalms typically end with an expression of faith, even when they are cries for help.
12. Davidic Psalms are usually at least partially in first person singular voice.
13. Davidic Psalms 6, 7, 12, 16, 21-23, 25, 27, 28, 30, 34, 40 and 41 all share the trait of changing the mode of address right at the center of the Psalm, from either addressing God as second person "You" to mentioning God in the third person, or vice versa. Psalm 23 is one example: "*He* guides me in the paths of righteousness for *His* name's sake. [Switch from third to second person] Even though I walk through the valley of the shadow of death, I fear no evil, for *You* are with me."

5.1.2 The Five Books of Psalms

The book of Psalms as we have it today was originally five books, divided as follows:

Book 1 - Psalms 1-41 or 2-41[4]

Book 2 - Psalms 42-72

Book 3 - Psalms 73-89

---

[4] Psalm 1 is probably an introduction to the entire book of Psalms rather than a part of book 1.

Book 4 - Psalms 90-106

Book 5 - Psalms 107-150

The fivefold division of Psalms may be intended to parallel the five books of the Torah. Each book closes with a doxology or the words "amen and amen." The different books show some marked distinctions.

	Book 1	Book 2	Book 3	Book 4	Book 5
	1-41	42-72	73-89	90-106	107-150
Use of "YHWH"	278	32	44	105	236
Use of "Elohim"[5]	15	165	46	6	10
Musical Instructions	7	10	5	0	0
Use of "Selah"	17	30	20	0	4
Psalms of David	37	18	1	2	15
Acrostic Psalms	4	0	0	0	4
"Hallelujah"	0	0	0	5	25
Use of "shin" as relative pronoun	0	0	0	0	17
Songs of Ascents	0	0	0	0	15
Psalms of Haggai or Zechariah[6]	0	0	0	0	6

---

[5] The word counts include attributions and the doxology at the end of the book. Word counts for YHWH do not include the short form "Yah". Word counts for Elohim (God) include all instances of the Hebrew אלהים, regardless of whether it is discussing the true God or false gods. Elohim with pronominal suffixes ("my God", or "our God") takes a slightly different form and is not included in this count.

[6] In the Masoretic Text and English translations, no Psalms are attributed to Haggai or Zechariah. This row is a count of these attributions in the Septuagint, Vulgate and Peshitta.

The evidence is clear that there are distinctions between the five books within Psalms. These distinctions have something to say about their date of writing and also about the date of the compilation of each book. We believe the evidence points to a different completion date, or what we will call a "publication date," for each of the five books. Furthermore, the books are sequenced based on their publication date, with Book 1 published first and Book 5 published last. Books 1 and 2 are pre-exilic publications, and books 3-5 are post-exilic publications. All five books contain some early Psalms, but only books 3-5 contain late Psalms. At times, Psalms from the later books will draw from texts of Psalms in the earlier books.

5.1.3 Additional Guidelines for Dating the Psalms

Aside from the authorship attributions, it is usually difficult to date individual Psalms based on internal or linguistic evidence, because they tend to be very short. Often there will not be more than a weak and inconclusive clue or two to help us. Still, several additional rules of thumb can be applied. The Psalms that speak of an Israelite king (2, 18, 20, 21, 33, 45, 48, 63, 72, 89 and 110) should be assumed to be pre-exilic, since there were no Israelite kings between 586 and 140 B.C. The existence of pre-exilic Psalms of worship is attested by Ps 137:3-4, Amos 5:23 and Isa 30:29. The Psalms of Ascents appear to be a post-exilic collection used for pilgrimage festivals at the second temple. One of these Psalms (126) is clearly post-exilic, and a few others give clues that they are post-exilic, so we will date most of this collection to the post-exilic period around 500 B.C. The Psalms that say "hallelujah" (הללו־יה) (102, 104-106, 111-113, 115-117, 135 and 146-150) are assumed to be post-exilic, since this phrase does not appear in any early text, including any Psalm attributed to David or one of his contemporaries. Note that all the Ascents Psalms and the hallelujah Psalms appear in the latter portion of the book of Psalms, which is the latest portion of the book to find canonical form.

5.1.4 Psalms Book 1

The Psalms in Book 1 consist primarily of Psalms of David, with all Psalms showing some sign of antiquity. Psalm 1 appears to be not part of Book 1, but an introduction to the entire book of Psalms.

Psalms 9-10, 25, 34 and 37 are all acrostic Psalms; that is, each verse or phrase begins with a different letter, starting with the first letter of the Hebrew alphabet and ending with the last. However, all of the acrostics in these Book 1 Psalms are abnormal in that they are not letter perfect; certain letters in the sequence seem to be missing or misplaced. These abnormalities are actually an argument for the antiquity of these Psalms. The Hebrew alphabet at the time of David may have used a different alphabetical order than that used later in the Old Testament and modern period (see Appendix B section B.3.2 for a discussion of the older alphabetical order and a discussion of the acrostic Psalm 34). The different alphabetical order combined with the activity of the scribes who copied the Psalms created a situation in which the original acrostics for these Psalms have apparently been altered slightly. By contrast, the acrostics Psalms written later (111, 112 and 119) remain as letter perfect acrostics. The acrostic Psalm 145 is a special case that will be discussed later.

Psalm	Date B.C.	Attri-bution	Discussion
1	440 (2)	None	This Psalm gives few clues as to its date of writing. Unlike almost all other Psalms in book 1, it is not attributed to David. The suggested date is primarily based on the premise that this Psalm is not part of book 1, but rather is an introduction to the entire book of Psalms, and as such was written near

Psalm	Date B.C.	Attri-bution	Discussion
			the end of the period of biblical Psalms. The use of multiple definite articles and four occurrences of the relative pronoun "asher" (אשר) in this Psalm are in any case not consistent with very early poetry.
2	1000 (7)	None	This Psalm is not attributed to David, but it is likely to be from the time of David anyway. The Psalm is certain of the political and military strength of the Israelite king. Kings of gentiles are ruled by kings in Zion and fruitlessly wish to break free. This setting is applicable only in the united monarchy period of David and Solomon. Linguistically, the Psalm has the "mo" (מו) pronominal suffix in v3 and v5, a feature not present in later poetry. "Pen" (פן), meaning "lest" in v12, appears almost exclusively in earlier texts. The word "bar" (בר) in v12 could be an Aramaism for "son," if that translation is correct – it could also be translated "in purity." Even if the translation is "son," the Aramaism doesn't point to a late date, as it comes in direct address to non-Hebrew speak-ing, possibly Aramaic speaking peoples.
3	980 (6)	David	The attribution indicates the Psalm was written during Absalom's revolt, about 980 B.C. The shield of v3 is an example of the military imagery common in Davidic Psalms. The mention of ene-

Psalm	Date B.C.	Attri-bution	Discussion
			mies in v1 and 6 is the first of many appearances in the Psalms showing David's frequent preoccupation with his enemies.
4	1000 (5)	David	This Davidic Psalm seems to take ideas from the priestly blessing of Num 6:24-26, though it does not use the same wording. The ideas of the LORD lifting up one's countenance in v6, being gracious in v2 and providing peace in v8 all echo the priestly blessing.
5	990 (6)	David	David's preoccupation with his enemies is evident in v8-10. Older grammar is reflected in the "mo" suffixes of v10-11 (Heb 11-12). Early vocabulary includes "omer" (אמר) for "speech, word" in v1 (Heb v2).
6	1000 (7)	David	David's preoccupation with his enemies is reflected in v8 and 10. Phrasing common to David includes "bones" (v2), "be gracious to me" (v2) and "my supplication" (v9).
7	980 (7)	David	The attribution of this Psalm mentions an event in David's life that is not clearly described in the books of 1 or 2 Samuel, since Cush the Benjaminite is an unknown figure (perhaps connected to Shimei? - 2 Sam 16:5). This argues for the antiquity of the attribution – it was not based on information available to us today. David's preoccupation with his enemies and the military imagery in

Psalm	Date B.C.	Attribution	Discussion
			v10, 12 and 13 are consistent with other Davidic Psalms. Davidic phrasing includes "deliver me" (v1).
8	1000 (6)	David	Despite this being a Psalm of nearly pure praise, the author still mentions enemies (v2), as is typical in Davidic Psalms. The wording in v5 about making man "a little lower than Elohim" is unlikely to be a late phrase, as it would later be considered irreverent. Early vocabulary includes "enosh" (אנוש) for "man" (v4 [Heb v5]).
9	980 (7)	David	Psalms 9 and 10 are one Psalm in the Septuagint. Also, Psalms 9-10 together form an acrostic in Hebrew, making it nearly certain that these two Psalms were originally combined. The fact that the acrostic is not letter perfect (the fourth and 12th to 17th letters of the Hebrew alphabet are not represented) is actually a mark of antiquity. It indicates that the language of the Psalm may have been updated in such a manner as to spoil the acrostic. The triumphant nature of this Psalm matches the Davidic period, and the reference to Zion (9:11) requires a date near the end of that period. David's preoccupation with his enemies surfaces in 9:3 and following. The early pronoun "zu" (זו) is in (9:15[Heb 9:16] and 10:2). Davidic phrasing includes "be gracious to me"

Psalm	Date B.C.	Attribution	Discussion
			(9:13). Early vocabulary includes the negation "bal" (בל) in 10:4, 10:11, 10:15 and 10:18, "enosh" (אנוש) for "men" in 9:19-20 (Heb 9:20-21) and 10:18, and "selah" (9:16 and 9:20).
10	980 (7)	David (continued from Psalm 9)	See the discussion on Psalm 9.
11	1000 (5)	David	David's preoccupation with his enemies is apparent in the verses addressing the wicked (v2, 5 and 6), although in this Psalm his concern is less personal than usual.
12	1000 (6)	David	David's preoccupation with his enemies is again apparent in only a general sense in this Psalm. The early relative pronoun "zu" is present in v7 (Heb v8).
13	1000 (6)	David	This Davidic Psalm shows his typical concern over his enemies (v4). "Pen" (פן), meaning "lest," in v3 (Heb v4) appears almost exclusively in earlier texts.
14	990 (3)	David	This Psalm is a near duplicate of Psalm 53, with Psalm 53 substituting Elohim for all four occurrences of YHWH. The last verse sounds exilic, and presents evidence contrary to the attribution to David. Still, there is no mention of foreigners or foreign lands, unlike the

Psalm	Date B.C.	Attri-bution	Discussion
			other exilic or post-exilic Psalms that refer to the captivity of the people (Ps 126, 137, 79, 106:47 and 107:2-3), so the captivity of v7 may refer to something other than the Babylonian exile.
15	990 (7)	David	The author asks in v1 about who may dwell in the LORD's tabernacle or "tent," rather than the LORD's temple. The tent is on Mount Zion. This points to a time after David made Jerusalem his capitol, but before the temple was built.
16	1000 (6)	David	Early "bal" negatives are present in v2, 4 and 8, and the early "orakh" (ארח) for "way, path" is in v11.
17	1000 (7)	David	David's preoccupation with his enemies is evident in v9-13. The early "bal" negative appears twice in v3. The early relative pronoun "zu" is in v9, and a "mo" suffix is in v10. Davidic phrasing includes "shadow of your wings" (v8).
18	980 (9)	David	This can be identified as a Davidic Psalm with more confidence than any other Psalm. This Psalm is the same as David's Psalm in 2 Samuel 22. Verses 43-45, about foreigners obeying the author in fear and trembling, could hardly be referring to someone other than David. David's preoccupation with his enemies is evident in v3, 17, 37, 40 and 48. The identification of the author as a military man in verses 34-35 and 39

Psalm	Date B.C.	Attri-bution	Discussion
			fits David. The cherub in v10 points to a pre-exilic period, since cherubim were present on the Ark of the Covenant and in the first temple, but not in the second temple. The term "high places" (במת) is used in a favorable sense in v33 (Heb v34), just as it is in David's elegy for Saul and Jonathan (2 Sam 1:19 and 1:25). In the prophetic period, the term "high places" is uniformly negative (except in Hab 3:19 where this verse is quoted), so this Psalm must have preceded the prophetic period. Imperfect verbs are routinely used to describe past events (v4, 6, etc. [Heb v5, 7, etc.]), a feature of early poetry. Davidic phrasing includes "my deliverer" (v2) and "my rock" (v2 and 46). The designation of God as "rock" (v2, 31 and 46) is a metaphor prominent only in earlier texts. Early vocabulary includes "zulah" (זולה) in v31 (Heb v32).
19	1000 (6)	David	The date is based primarily on the attribution. The Psalm gives few further clues as to its date of writing, although if the first part of the Psalm has a Canaanite connection, as some suppose, that would argue for its antiquity. Early vocabulary includes "orakh" (ארח) for "way, path" in v5 (Heb v6) and "omer" (אמר) for "speech, word" in v2 and 14 (Heb v3 and 15).

Psalm	Date B.C.	Attri-bution	Discussion
20	1000 (6)	David	The reference to God's "anointed" (v6) refers to an Israelite king, making the Psalm pre-exilic.
21	980 (7)	David	This royal Psalm is identified with David. David's preoccupation with his enemies is evident in vv8-12. "Bal" negatives are present in v2, 7 and 11 (Heb v3, 8 and 12). Davidic phrasing includes the "length of days" (ארך ימים) wording for eternal life in v4 (Heb v5), matching Psalm 23:6. Early "mo" suffixes are in v9, 10 and 12 [Heb v10, 11 and 13]. Early vocabulary includes "selah" in v2.
22	1000 (6)	David	"Bashan" in v12 points to a united monarchy time frame, since Bashan was lost to Judah upon the division of the kingdom. The older "anoki" in v6 (Heb v7) helps rule out a late date.
23	1000 (7)	David	The shepherd motif in this Psalm may reflect David's childhood background. David's preoccupation with his enemies appears in v5. David also was an individual who was anointed (v5). Davidic phrasing includes the "length of days" (ארך ימים) wording for eternal life in v6.
24	1000 (7)	David	Earlier vocabulary includes "selah" in v6 and 10. The use of an imperfect tense verb to describe past action in v2 is characteristic of Hebrew poetry before 750 B.C.

Psalm	Date B.C.	Attri-bution	Discussion
25	1000 (7)	David	David's preoccupation with his enemies is evident in vv2-3 and 19. Davidic phrasing includes "be gracious to me" (v16) and "deliver me" (v20). This is an imperfect acrostic Psalm in that there is no verse beginning with the letter "waw," yet there is one extra verse on the end of the Psalm that is not part of the acrostic. This is likely a sign of antiquity, as is explained in the alphabet section in Appendix B.3. Early vocabulary includes "orakh" (ארח) for "way, path" in v4.
26	1000 (6)	David	Davidic phrasing includes "be gracious to me" (v11).
27	1000 (8)	David	The "tent" tabernacle in vv5-6 suggests a time when the tabernacle was still standing. David's preoccupation with his enemies is evident in vv2-3, 6 and 11-12. Davidic phrasing includes "be gracious to me" (v7) and "deliver me" (v12).
28	1000 (7)	David	The word for inner sanctuary (דביר) in v2 is used uniquely for the pre-exilic sanctuary. Davidic phrasing includes "my supplication" in v2 and 6. An early "mo" suffix is in v8. Early language includes the designation of God as a "Rock," and "pen" (פן), meaning "lest" in v1.
29	1000 (7)	David	Some writers think this is the oldest Psalm. Sirion, the old Sidonian name for

Psalm	Date B.C.	Attribution	Discussion
			Mount Hermon, is in v6. This is the only Psalm that mentions Noah's flood (v10). The identification of YHWH's voice with thunder and lightning has led to the suggestion that this Psalm has been adapted from a Canaanite hymn to Baal, or conversely that this Psalm is an intentional polemic against Baal worship. Either case is an argument for the antiquity of the Psalm.
30	1000 (6)	David	Davidic phrasing includes "be gracious to me" (v10). A "bal" negative is in v6 (Heb v7).
31	1000 (7)	David	Davidic phrasing includes "be gracious to me" (v9), "my supplication" (v22) and "deliver me" (v1, 15). An early "zu" relative pronoun is in v4 (Heb v5). Early language includes the designation of God as a "Rock" (v2). "Terror on every side" (v13) is apparently used by Jer 6:25.
32	980 (7)	David	Early vocabulary includes "selah" (v4-5 and 7). Davidic vocabulary includes "bones" (v3). Early particles include a "bal" negation (v9) and a "zu" relative pronoun (v8). The need for forgiveness described in this Psalm is a subject that would have been close to David's heart.
33	1000 (3)	None	V10, 16 and especially 12 carry a tone indicating that they were written in the kingdom period. This Psalm is not attributed to David, and it is written in

Psalm	Date B.C.	Attri-bution	Discussion
			the first person plural voice, a feature not typical of David. We have dated it to the time of David based primarily on its position within the other book 1 Psalms.
34	1000 (7)	David	Davidic vocabulary includes "bones" (v20). This Psalm is an alphabetical acrostic. The sense of the Psalm may be improved slightly by altering the order of the verses to conform to the Hebrew alphabetical order as it existed in the tenth century B.C. (see Appendix B, section B.3.2). This would involve switching v15 and 16 (Heb v16 and 17), for example. This is a mark of antiquity, as the current Hebrew alphabetical order was well established later in the Old Testament period.
35	1000 (7)	David	This Psalm reflects David's preoccupation with enemies throughout. The description of the author's behavior (v13-14) seems to fit David's loyalty to Saul, and supports Davidic authorship. Familiar Davidic vocabulary includes "bones" (v10), "aha aha" (v21), "pursue" (v3 and 6) and "salvation" (v3). An older "mo" suffix is present in v16.
36	1000 (6)	David	Verse 5 is essentially replicated in two other Davidic Psalms (57:10 and 108:4). Davidic phrasing includes "shadow of your wings" (v7).
37	975	David	If David is the author, this Psalm was

Psalm	Date B.C.	Attri-bution	Discussion
	(5)		written when he was old (v25). The Psalm reads more like a series of proverbs than most Psalms and contains few clues as to its date. The acrostic pattern of the Psalm does show an irregularity on the *pe-ayin* transition (missing the *ayin*), perhaps showing evidence that an older alphabet was in use when the Psalm was written (see Appendix B, section B.3.2). However, the evidence is not as clear as on Psalm 34.
38	1000 (7)	David	The sufferings of the Psalmist here are similar to Psalms 22 and 39. Davidic vocabulary includes "bones" (v3) and "salvation" (v22). David's preoccupation with his enemies is evident in v12, 19 and 20. "Pen" (פֶּן), meaning "lest" (v16 [Heb v17]) appears almost exclusively in earlier texts.
39	1000 (6)	David	Similarities with Psalm 38 are present in tone and phrasing, as in v9 and 38:13, "I do not open my mouth." The early pronoun "anoki" is in v12 (Heb v13). Davidic phrasing includes "deliver me" (v8).
40	1000 (6)	David	David's preoccupation with his enemies is apparent in vv14-15. Archer sees a connection to a Ugaritic hymn in v13 (with Ugaritic using El instead of YHWH).[7] Ugaritic predates David, so

---

[7] Archer, *A Survey of the Old Testament Introduction*, p. 403

Psalm	Date B.C.	Attri-bution	Discussion
			such a connection implies antiquity. Verses 13-17 are essentially replicated in Ps 70:1-5. Davidic phrasing includes "my deliverer" (v17), "deliver me" (v13) and "aha, aha" (v15).
41	1000 (6)	David	David's preoccupation with his enemies is apparent throughout this Psalm. Davidic vocabulary includes "be gracious to me" in v4 and 10. V13 probably does not belong to this Psalm, but is rather the benediction for the entire Book 1 section of Psalms.

5.1.5 Psalms Book 2

Book 2 differs sharply from Book 1 in that Elohim is used as a designation for God 165 times, as opposed to just 15 times in Book 1. The use of YHWH decreases from 278 times to 32 times. The use of Elohim in this section is at least partly due to the activity of the scribes who copied the book. In some cases, the original writing was YHWH, with a later scribe changing the reading to Elohim. This can be seen most clearly from verses that have been duplicated from Book 1 with YHWH changed to Elohim, as in 14:2 = 53:2. Also, there are certain readings such as "O God [Elohim], You are my God [Elohim]" (63:1), that sound as if the first Elohim was originally YHWH. It is difficult to say when these changes were made, but it was likely early, when Book 1 and Book 2 were treated separately, because no YHWH to Elohim change is apparent in Book 1. Ps 72:20, which ends Book 2, says that "the prayers of David the son of Jesse are ended," and may indicate that all of chapters 2-72 are an old collection.

Beginning with Book 2, we have noted that there exist linguistic similarities between some of these Psalms and the book of Isaiah.

While this does not necessarily mean that Isaiah himself wrote these Psalms, it does give some evidence that these Psalms came from the same environment as Isaiah – the royal court of the southern Kingdom of Judah, around 700 B.C.

Psalm	Date B.C.	Attribution	Discussion
42	975 (6)	Sons of Korah	Psalm 42 and 43 were probably originally one combined song, since the meter matches, a series of questions is present in both, and 42:5 is used as a refrain in 42:11 and 43:5. The reference to the Hermon mountain range in far northern Israel favors a united monarchy date, since this area was lost to Judah when the kingdoms split. The Psalm sounds similar to Davidic Psalms, except that this Psalm begins the heavy use of "Elohim" in place of "YHWH," a tendency that continues throughout Book 2. Early language includes the designation of God as a "Rock" (v9)
43	975 (6)		See the discussion on Psalm 42.
44	700 (6)	Sons of Korah	The situation in this Psalm seems to best fit the time of Hezekiah. The Psalm should not be considered exilic or post-exilic because Israel still has armies (v9). Yet, the present distress described in the Psalm includes the people being scattered among the nations (v11). This occurs at a time when the author believes the people have been loyal to God (v20-21). The situation could fit the

Psalm	Date B.C.	Attri-bution	Discussion
			Assyrian invasion of Judah, which followed the captivity of northern Israel and also resulted in the loss of many cities in Judah (Isa 36:1). "Selah" in v8 goes with mostly older Psalms. The wording of this Psalm shows some affinity to Isaiah, including the use of jackals in v19 (Isa 13:22, 34:13, 35:7 and 43:20), "sheep to slaughter" in v22 (Isa 22:13 and 53:7), and the word "leum-mim" (לאמים) for people in v2 (Heb v3), which appears nine times in Isaiah. The use of an imperfect tense verb to describe past action in v2 (Heb v3) is usually a characteristic of early Hebrew poetry before 750 B.C. Early vocabulary includes "orakh" (ארח) for "way, path" in v18 (Heb v19).
45	950 (5)	Sons of Korah	This Psalm seems to best fit the reign of Solomon, celebrating one of his marriages. The united monarchy's alliance with Tyre (v12) is still intact, and the gold from Ophir (v9) matches the time of Solomon (1 Kgs 9:28). An older "mo" suffix is present in v16 (Heb v17). Contrary evidence is in v6 (Heb v7), where "malkut," a usually late word for "kingdom," appears.
46	700 (3)	Sons of Korah	This Psalm is assigned near to the time of the Assyrian invasion of Judah during Hezekiah's reign, based mainly on the tone of the Psalm and its proximity to

Psalm	Date B.C.	Attri-bution	Discussion
			other Psalms that seem to be from that time. Also, the phrase "God of Jacob" (v7, 11) occurs in the prophets only in Isa 2:3 = Mic 4:2, prophets living at this time. Early vocabulary usage includes "anoki" for "I" in v10 (Heb v11), "mam-lakot" for "kingdom" in v6 (Heb v7), a "bal" negation in v6 (Heb v7) and "selah" in v3 and 11.
47	700 (3)	Sons of Korah	This Psalm gives few clues as to its date. The triumphant tone might point to any number of successful or celebratory occasions. A date of 700 B.C. is possible, since the defeat of the Assyrians at the time of Hezekiah was one such occasion. There are weak connections to Isaiah, such as the fivefold repetition "sing praises…" in v6-7, a feature similar to Isaiah's style (see section 4.2.1.2.8), and the use of "leummim" (לאמים) for "people" (v3 [Heb v4]). This Psalm also is in proximity to others of the same date. "Selah" is an early vocabulary term in v4.
48	700 (4)	Sons of Korah	This Psalm mentions Judah without Israel (v11), favoring a date after the united monarchy. The events of v4-6 could reflect the failed Assyrian inva-sion near 700 B.C. Verbal connections to Isaiah include "Mount Zion" (v2, 11, also 8 times in Isaiah) and "ships of Tarshish" (v7, also 4 times in

Psalm	Date B.C.	Attri-bution	Discussion
			Isaiah)."Selah" is an early vocabulary term in v8.
49	700 (2)	Sons of Korah	This Psalm gives few clues as to its date. Verbal connections to Isaiah include "inhabitants of the world" (v1 and 4 times in Isaiah). An early "mo" suffix is in v11 (Heb v12) and a "bal" negation in v12 (Heb v13). "Selah" is an early vocabulary term in v13 and 15.
50	700 (2)	Asaph	This Psalm gives few clues as to its date. The attribution to Asaph separates it from the preceding collection of the sons of Korah. We have placed it at the time of Hezekiah based on its proximity to the preceding Psalms and a few connections in the theme and wording to Psalms 96-99. Early vocabulary includes "anoki" for "I" in v7, "selah" in v6, "Eloah" (אלוה) for God and "pen" (פן) for "lest" in v22. V6a matches Ps 97:6.
51	1000 (7)	David	The specific setting described in the attribution for this Psalm argues for Davidic authorship. Davidic vocabulary includes "be gracious to me" (v1), "bones" (v8) and "deliver me" (v14).
52	1015 (6)	David	This Psalm has a specific attribution dating it to David before he became king. Early vocabulary includes "selah" in v3 and 5.
53	990 (3)	David	This Psalm is a near duplicate of Psalm 14, with this Psalm substituting Elohim for all four occurrences of YHWH. The

Psalm	Date B.C.	Attribution	Discussion
			last verse sounds exilic, and presents evidence contrary to the attribution to David. Still, there is no mention of foreigners or foreign lands, unlike the other exilic or post-exilic Psalms that refer to the captivity of the people (Ps 126, 137, 79, 106:47 and 107:2-3), so the captivity of v6 may refer to something other than the Babylonian exile.
54	1015 (6)	David	This Psalm has a specific attribution dating it to David before he became king. David's preoccupation with his enemies is present throughout the Psalm. Early vocabulary includes "selah" (v3).
55	1000 (6)	David	David's preoccupation with his enemies is evident throughout this Psalm. Early vocabulary includes "selah" (v7 and 19) and "enosh" (אנוש) for "men" (v13 [Heb v14]). Davidic phrasing includes "my supplication" (v1).
56	1015 (6)	David	This Psalm has a specific attribution dating it to David before he became king. David's preoccupation with his enemies is evident throughout the Psalm. Davidic phrasing includes "be gracious to me" (v1). Early vocabulary includes "enosh" (אנוש) for "men" (v1 [Heb v2]).
57	1015 (6)	David	This Psalm has a specific attribution dating it to David before he became king. Davidic vocabulary includes "be

Psalm	Date B.C.	Attri-bution	Discussion
			gracious to me" (v1). Early vocabulary includes "selah" (v3 and 6). Davidic phrasing includes "shadow of your wings" (v1). V5 and 11 match Ps 108:5, and v9-10 matches Ps 108:3-4. Psalm 108 is also a Davidic Psalm.
58	1000 (5)	David	An early "mo" pronominal suffix is in v6 (Heb v7) and a "bal" negation is in v8 (Heb v9).
59	1015 (8)	David	This Psalm has a specific attribution dating it to David before he became king. Furthermore, the author's description of his situation within the Psalm (v2-7) closely matches David's experience. An air of firsthand authenticity is present as the author describes how his hunters "belch" (v7), "growl" (v14) and "howl" (v15). Davidic vocabulary includes "my stronghold" (v9, 16 and 17). Early "mo" pronominal suffixes are present in v11-13 (Heb v12-14). "Pen" (פֶּן), meaning "lest," in v11 (Heb v12) and "selah" (v13) appear almost exclusively in earlier texts. Davidic phrasing includes "deliver me" (v1-2).
60	1000 (8)	David	The geographic and tribal references (Shechem, Gilead, Manasseh, Ephraim and Judah) in vv6-8 point to a united monarchy date. The military background, with enemies of Edom, Moab and Philistia (v8-9) match David's wars. Early vocabulary includes "selah" (v4).

Psalm	Date B.C.	Attri-bution	Discussion
			Verses 5-12 are repeated in 108:6-13.
61	1000 (6)	David	The Psalm gives few clues as to its date, other than the attribution. The author does appear to be a king (v6-7). Early vocabulary includes "selah" (v4).
62	1000 (7)	David	Early vocabulary includes "selah" (v4 and 8), the designation of God as a "Rock" (v2, 6 and 7), and the relative pronoun "zu" (v11 [Heb v12]). Davidic vocabulary includes "my stronghold" (v2 and 6).
63	1000 (5)	David	The attribution seems to indicate a time before David became king, yet the author's seeming identification of himself as king (v11) supports a date after he became king. David's preoccupation with his enemies is evident in vv9-10. Davidic phrasing includes "shadow of your wings" (v7). Late vocabulary includes "shavakh" (שבח) for "praise" in v3 (Heb v4).
64	1000 (6)	David	David's preoccupation with his enemies is evident throughout the Psalm. The early "mo" suffix is present in v5 and 8 (Heb v6 and 9).
65	985 (5)	David	This Psalm gives essentially no clues as to its date other than the attribution to David.
66	700 (2)	None	This Psalm gives evidence of antiquity but few clues as to its precise date. It does not seem Davidic, because it lacks Davidic phrasing and David does not

Psalm	Date B.C.	Attri-bution	Discussion
			typically include a historical review, as appears in v6. "Shout joyfully to God, all the earth" (v1) is repeated in Ps 98:4 and 100:1, both of which also are anonymous. The 700 B.C. date is based on this Psalm's position in book 2, which has other Psalms of that era, and its tenuous connection to the Psalm 93, 96-100 group of that era. The use of two imperfect tense verbs to describe past action in v6 is usually a characteristic of early Hebrew poetry before 750 B.C. Early vocabulary includes "enosh" (אנוש) for "men" (v12).
67	700 (2)	None	This Psalm gives few clues as to its date. The universal tone of the poem, as opposed to an Israel-centered tone, would be consistent with some of the writing around 700 B.C. Early vocabulary includes "selah" (v1 and 4). V1 draws wording from the priestly blessing of Num 6:24-26.
68	980 (8)	David	This Psalm has more indications of antiquity than any other Psalm. The list of tribes in v27, combining the southern tribes of Benjamin and Judah with the northern tribes of Zebulun and Naphtali, supports a united monarchy date. The envoys coming from Egypt and Ethiopia in v31 indicate a time when Israel was strong, and such interaction with Egypt and Ethiopia did take place

Psalm	Date B.C.	Attribution	Discussion
			during Solomon's reign. The mountains of Bashan (v15) on the Golan Heights, with Mount Hermon and Zalmon (v14), were lost to Judah during the divided kingdom, so their mention supports an earlier date. V8 reflects knowledge of the events of Exod 19:18, and vv7-8 seem to echo the Song of Deborah in Judg 5:4-5. The description of God as a Being who "rides" through the desert or heaven (v4 and 33) echoes some descriptions of Baal found in Ugaritic texts. Early vocabulary includes "Shaddai" as a name for God (v14 [Heb v15]), the relative pronoun "zu" (v28 [Heb v29]), "mamlakot" for kingdoms (v32 [Heb v33]), "selah" (v7, 19 and 32), "makhatz" (מחץ) for "strike" in v23 (Heb v24) and "omer" (אמר) for "speech, word" in v11 (Heb v12). This Psalm has by some measures more rare vocabulary than any other Psalm, with 11 words that are "hapex logomena," appearing only once in the Bible. Imperfect tense verbs are used to describe past tense events in v9-10 (Heb v10-11), a feature of Early Biblical Hebrew poetry. The Psalm does not sound specifically Davidic, and we have placed it at the end of David's reign when plans for a temple were in place (v29).
69	1010	David	David's preoccupation with his enemies

Psalm	Date B.C.	Attribution	Discussion
	(4)		is evident in v4 and 18-28. That the writer is a prominent person is evident from v12. V35, mentioning Judah only, is contrary evidence that could be construed to point to a divided kingdom date or later. This could be because Judah was David's tribe and for a time he reigned only over Judah. Davidic phrasing includes "deliver me" (v14).
70	1000 (6)	David	This Psalm is a repeat of Psalm 40:13-17, with several substitutions of Elohim for YHWH. See the discussion on Psalm 40.
71	980 (6)	None	This Psalm appears to be a Davidic Psalm, though it lacks an attribution to him in the Masoretic Text. The Septuagint attributes it to David. The author plays the harp and lyre (v22), hobbies which match David. David's preoccupation with his enemies is evident in vv10-13. Davidic phrasing includes "deliver me" (v2). The author is well known (v7) and followed God from his youth (v5, 17). The designation of God as a "Rock" (v3) is characteristic of early poetry.
72	950 (7)	Solomon	The reference to the Israelite king ruling "from sea to sea and from the river to the ends of the earth" (v8) fits Solomon's reign, as well as the gifts received from Sheba and others (v9-11, 15). Verses 19b-20, beginning with "amen and amen," should be understood as an ending to all of book 2 rather than this particular

Psalm	Date B.C.	Attri- bution	Discussion
			Psalm.

5.1.6 Psalms Book 3

The first eleven Psalms in Book 3 are attributed to Asaph. Efforts to find common themes in the Asaph Psalms are unconvincing. Some suggested common themes are that in the Asaph Psalms God is *judge* (50, 75, 76 and 82), He speaks (50, 75, 81 and 82), He is a shepherd (74:1, 77:20, 78:52, 79:13 and 80:1) and is often called "El" (God) or "Elyon" (Most High). These Psalms mention Joseph or Ephraim (77:15, 80:1 and 81:4-5). However, these ideas are present in other Psalms as well, and their level of concentration in the Asaph Psalms is unremarkable. Based on other factors in these Psalms, we have reached the problematic viewpoint that the Asaph Psalms do not all come from the same individual nor from the same time. One characteristic all the Asaph Psalms have in common is the preference for Elohim as a divine name instead of YHWH. This is a continuation of the practice in Book 2, and was likely a feature of the activity of the scribes (Ps 80:7 and 80:14 say "God of Hosts" rather than the common "LORD of Hosts") who copied the book rather than a characteristic of the author. The preference for Elohim in the Asaph Psalms of Book 3 is not so pronounced as in Book 2.

Within Book 3, there appears to have been an effort to group Psalms topically, putting side by side Psalms like 79 and 80, which both contain prayers for restoration in times of difficulty.

Psalm	Date B.C.	Attri- bution	Discussion
73	1000 (2)	Asaph	This Psalm shows signs of antiquity, but gives few clues as to its specific date. There is a sanctuary (v17), precluding the possibility of an exilic date. Older

Psalm	Date B.C.	Attri-bution	Discussion
			grammar includes "mo" pronominal suffixes (v5-7). Older vocabulary includes "Rock" as a designation for God in v26, "she'er" (שאר) for "flesh" in v26, "enosh" (אנוש) for "men" (v5) and "ak" (אך) for "surely" in v1 and 13.
74	580 (8)	Asaph	The distress described in this Psalm is clearly set in the Babylonian exile, most specifically shown by v7 "They have burned your sanctuary to the ground." This therefore becomes the first exilic Psalm, and establishes the principle that Psalms attributed to Asaph are not necessarily to be considered as written by the recorder Asaph of Hezekiah's time (2 Kgs 18:18) or the singer Asaph of David's time (1 Chron 16:5-7). A few traces of antiquity remain in this Psalm, including "Ehdah" (עדה), a mostly pre-exilic word meaning "congregation" in v2, and one imperfect verb that appears to be acting as past tense in v14.
75	1000 (2)	Asaph	There are signs of antiquity in the Psalm, but few clues as to its specific date. We place it at the time of David primarily on the basis of the musical note in the attribution: "Al-tashkheth," or "do not destroy." This melody was used for Davidic Psalms 57, 58 and 59. Early vocabulary includes "selah" and "anoki" in v3 (Heb v4) and "ak" (אך), meaning "surely" in v8 (Heb v9).

Psalm	Date B.C.	Attribution	Discussion
76	700 (4)	Asaph	This Psalm could be understood to fit the situation in Hezekiah's time after the failed Assyrian invasion (v3 and 5). The mention of Judah before Israel in v1 favors the post-divided kingdom period. Early vocabulary includes "selah" (v3 and 9).
77	1000 (4)	Asaph	The attribution mentioning "Jeduthun" is also present in Davidic Psalms 62 and 77. The mention of Joseph without Judah in v15 hints at a united monarchy date. The use of three imperfect tense verbs to describe past action in vv16-17 (Heb vv17-18) is characteristic of early Hebrew poetry before 750 B.C.
78	700 (6)	Asaph	This Psalm has a lengthy history of Israel up through David. However, the hostility to the northern tribe of Ephraim (vv9-11 and 67-68) favors a date either in the divided monarchy period, or after the fall of the northern Kingdom of Israel. The time of Hezekiah's reign may be a good candidate. The negative reference to high places (v58, compare 2 Kgs 18:4) fits this period, and the designation of God as "Holy One of Israel" (v41) is almost exclusive to Isaiah, who lived at this time. "Zoan" in Egypt (v12 and 43) is also mentioned in Isa 19:11, 19:13 and 30:4, but only two other times in scripture. Older vocabulary includes "Rock" as a designation

Psalm	Date B.C.	Attri-bution	Discussion
			for God (35) and "she'er" (שאר) for flesh in v20. The Psalm is early enough to preserve some tradition of the destruction of Shiloh (v60), a subject not covered in the primary history of Judges and Samuel. The heavy usage of waw + imperfect verbs to recount past tense events, mixed with instances of the earlier usage of imperfect verbs for past events (v15, 20, 26, 29, 36, 44, 45, 50, 58, 64 and 72), supports a date in the transitional time period between Early Biblical Hebrew and Classical Biblical Hebrew.
79	580 (8)	Asaph	This Psalm is a lament over the destruction of Jerusalem in 586 B.C. Jerusalem is in ruins and the temple defiled (v1), many are dead (vv2-3) and the land has been laid waste (v7). VV6-7 match Jer 10:25. The older word for kingdom, "mamlakah" is in v6.
80	1000 (7)	Asaph	This Psalm, though set in a difficult period, still favors a united monarchy date. The mention of northern tribes of Ephraim and Manasseh along with Benjamin and Joseph (v1-2), but without Judah, supports a date before the division of the kingdom. The description of God above the cherubim (v1) has the Ark of the Covenant in view, indicating a pre-exilic date. Israel's branches recently reached "the river"

Psalm	Date B.C.	Attribution	Discussion
			(v11), meaning the Euphrates, a maximum only briefly touched in the united monarchy period. The melody mentioned in the attribution, "shoshannim," meaning "lilies," is also present in Psalm 45 and Davidic Psalm 69. The use of three imperfect tense verbs to describe past action in v8 and 11 (Heb v9 and 12) is characteristic of early Hebrew poetry before 750 B.C. An older "mo" suffix is present in v5 (Heb v6).
81	1000 (6)	Asaph	The mention of Joseph in v5 hints at a united monarchy date. Early vocabulary includes "selah" (v7) and "anoki" for "I" in v10 (Heb v11). Verse 10 is essentially quoting Exod 20:1. V6-7 and 12 (Heb vv7-8 and 13) show the early use of imperfect verbs describing past tense action.
82	700 (2)	Asaph	This Psalm gives few clues as to its date. The universal tone (v8) does match other writings from the time of Hezekiah and Isaiah (the book of Isaiah, Psalm 67, 96-98, etc.). Early vocabulary includes "selah" (v2).
83	700 (6)	Asaph	The list of enemies includes Assyria (v8), requiring a date before the fall of Assyria in 612 B.C., and Philistia (v7), requiring a date before Nebuchadnezzar's conquest a few years later. Tyre, an ally in David's time, is now an enemy, requiring a date after 900 B.C. Early

Psalm	Date B.C.	Attribution	Discussion
			vocabulary includes "selah" (v8). Early "mo" suffixes are present in v11 and 13 (Heb v12 and 14).
84	700 (2)	Sons of Korah	This Psalm has few clues as to its date. The theme of pilgrimage to Zion rules out an exilic date. The absence of a definite article on phrases like "blessed be the man" (v5 and 12 [Heb v6 and 13]) makes this Psalm look older than other Psalms with similar wording (for example, Ps 1:1). Early vocabulary includes "selah" (v4 and 8).
85	500 (6)	Sons of Korah	The first two verses, with the phrase "restored the captivity of Jacob," indicate this is a post-exilic Psalm. The absence of any late grammar, combined with early vocabulary such as "selah," points to an early post-exilic date. VV2-4 (Heb vv3-5) have six perfect tense and no imperfect tense verbs describing past tense action, a formula consistent with Classical rather than Early Biblical Hebrew.
86	1000 (6)	David	David's preoccupation with his enemies is evident in v14. Echoes of Exodus are in v8 (compare Exod 15:11), v5 and v15 (compare Exod 34:6). Davidic vocabulary includes "be gracious to me" (v3 and 16) and "my supplication" (v6)
87	680 (2)	Sons of Korah	This Psalm is difficult to date due to conflicting lines of evidence. It looks to be dependent on Isa 30:7, due to the

Psalm	Date B.C.	Attribution	Discussion
			unusual mention of Rahab as a place-name for Egypt (v4). The mention of Babylon and Philistia in v4 in a semi-positive sense is unusual and implies a time before Babylonian pressure increased on Judah and before Philistia was conquered. This would be between 700-610 B.C. However, the Hebrew phrase "ish and ish" (איש ואיש) in v5, meaning this one and that one, is elsewhere a post-exilic usage (See Esth 1:22, Ezra 10:14, Neh 13:24, 1 Chron 26:13, 28:14-15, 2 Chron 8:14, 11:12 and 19:5). Early vocabulary includes "selah" (v3).
88	950 (2)	Sons of Korah and Heman the Ezra-hite	This Psalm has an unusual double attribution, to both Heman and the sons of Korah. Early vocabulary includes Selah in v7 and 10. V15 (Heb v16) may favor a later date, with "ani" used as a first person pronoun with an adjective (where in early usage "anoki" is expected) – on the other hand, "ani" may be used here because it rhymes in Hebrew with the adjacent word "ahni," for afflicted. The suggested date is based on the attribution and not much else.
89	950/ 700 (5)	Ethan the Ezra-hite	This Psalm looks to have originally been written in Solomon's time, as the attribution would suggest. V12 mentions northern Israeli locations Tabor

Psalm	Date B.C.	Attri-bution	Discussion
			and Hermon, supporting a united monarchy date. VV3-4 reference the covenant with David. The original composition only appears to reach to about verse 37, after which the mood turns down. The Psalm may have been adapted to the low point of the time of the Assyrian invasion of Judah, around 700 B.C. The connections between this Psalm and Isaiah suggest this. V10 mentions Rahab (also in Isa 30:7, 51:9, Ps 87:4, Job 9:13 and 26:12). "Holy One of Israel" is in v18 (a phrase appearing 25 times in Isaiah). Righteousness and justice are in parallel (v14 and eleven times in Isaiah), and lovingkindness and faithfulness are in parallel four times (v2, 24, 33, 49, also in Isa 16:5). Older "mo" suffixes are in v17 (Heb v18). Early vocabulary includes the designation of God as a "Rock" (v26).

5.1.7 Psalms Book 4

Chronicles provides a good clue as to the date of publication of Book 4. The passage in 1 Chron 16:8-36 repeats first Ps 105:1-15, then Ps 96:1-13, then finally Ps 106:1 and 106:47-48. Of most significance for dating purposes is that Psalms 106:48, quoted in Chronicles, is apparently not an intrinsic part of Ps 106, but is rather the doxology that closes all of Book 4 of the Psalms. This means that the chronicler had the entire Psalms Book 4 before him as he did his work. This theory is further supported by the fact that the chronicler copied from three Psalms (96, 105 and 106) and all three are in Book 4. With Chronicles written near 400 B.C., this implies that Book 4 was completed before that time.

Quite a few phrases are shared between Psalm 93 and Psalms 96-100, and as a group they seem to have some dependence on Isaiah. Since these Psalms offer few other clues as to their date, we have tentatively placed them all at the time of Isaiah. The triple repetition in 93:3, "the floods...the floods...the floods..." is a feature of Isaiah's style (see section 4.2.1.2.8), and this is repeated in 96:1-2, "Sing to the LORD...sing to the LORD...sing to the LORD...," then again in 96:7-8, "Ascribe to the LORD...ascribe to the LORD...ascribe to the LORD...". This type of repetition is not unknown in other Psalms (see Psalms 13 and 29 for similar cases), but it is uncommon. Isaiah is the only prophet to use "loving-kindness" and "faithfulness" in parallel (Isa 16:5), as in 98:3 and 100:5. Isaiah uses "enthroned above the cherubim" (Isa 37:16 and Ps 99:1). "Holy arm" is only found in Isa 52:10 and Ps 98:1). Ps 98:4 and Isa 44:23 are similar, while Ps 98:3b and Isa 52:10b both say "all the ends of the earth may see the salvation of our God." Isaiah is also the only one outside Psalms who mentions islands (Isa 11:11, 40:15, 42:10 and 49:1), as in Ps 97:1. These Psalms all use Classical Biblical Hebrew, with virtually no marks of either early or late dates, with only Psalm 99 providing any internal evidence not related to linguistics. These Psalms show some connection to Psalm 47, which we also date to the time of Isaiah.

Psalm 103 is the first of a group of Psalms we have marked as "reworked" from the time of David. The idea here is that there existed a Davidic original, but that original Psalm was rewritten in Late Biblical Hebrew to produce the Psalm that we have today. Psalm 104 may reflect a different type of rework – an older core Psalm, consisting of verses 2-34, remains intact, but has been expanded by the first and last verse (v1 and 35).

None of the Psalms in Book 4 or Book 5 have musical instructions.

Psalm	Date B.C.	Attribution	Discussion
90	1400 (5)	Moses	The attribution of this Psalm to Moses marks it as the oldest Psalm. The tone of the poem fits the wilderness wandering experience. Like the song of Exodus 15, this Psalm has no definite articles, no direct object pointers, and no use of the relative pronoun "asher," any of which would tend to mark the Psalm as a later work if they were present. Early vocabulary includes "bterem" (בטרם) for "before" (v2) and "enosh" (אנוש) for "men" (v3).
91	1000 (4)	None	This Psalm gives few clues as to its date. Older vocabulary includes "Shaddai" (v1), "pen" (פן) for "lest" (v12) and "anoki" for I (v15). The military imagery and personal nature of trust in the LORD are characteristics of Davidic Psalms, and this Psalm is attributed to David in the Septuagint.
92	990 (2)	None	The personal nature of this psalm and the concern over enemies (v11) match Davidic psalms. However, the initial waw + imperfect verbs in vv10-11 (Heb vv11-12) argue against an early date. Older vocabulary includes "Rock" as a designation for God (v15).
93	700 (4)	None	The triple repetition "the floods have lifted up" is similar to the style of Isaiah. Early vocabulary includes a "bal" negation in v1, in a phrase repeated in 96:10 and 1 Chron 16:30. The phrase,

Psalm	Date B.C.	Attri-bution	Discussion
			"The LORD reigns" (v1) also tends to tie this Psalm in with Psalms 96-99 (96:10, 97:1 and 99:1).
94	700 (2)	None	The Psalm gives few clues as to its date. "Rock" as a designation for God (v22) favors an early date.
95	1000 (2)	None	The Psalm gives few clues as to its date. "Rock" as a designation for God (v1) favors an early date. The New Testament (Hebrews 4:7) and the Septuagint attribute this Psalm to David.
96	700 (3)	None	The Psalm gives few clues as to its date. It is attributed to David in the Septuagint. Much of this Psalm is repeated in 1 Chron 16:23-33. An older "bal" negation is in v10, a verse partially repeated from 93:1.
97	700 (3)	None	The mention of Zion and Judah (not Israel) in v8 could match the Judah alone period of history. The use of "hodu" (הודו) (v12) rather than "hallel" as a call to praise/thanks supports a pre-exilic date. V6a matches Ps 50:6a.
98	700 (3)	None	This Psalm gives few clues as to its date. The linguistic evidence shows no early or late marks. "Holy arm" in v1 matches Isa 52:10, and v3b matches Isa 52:10b. "Shout joyfully to God, all the earth" (v1) is repeated in Ps 66:1 and 100:1, and v9 is repeated from 96:13.
99	700 (4)	None	The reference to cherubim (v1) implies the Ark of the Covenant is still in place,

Psalm	Date B.C.	Attri-bution	Discussion
			along with temple worship (v9). V4 may be interpreted to apply to an Israelite king. "The LORD reigns" in v1 repeats the introduction to Psalms 93 and 97.
100	700 (2)	None	This Psalm gives few clues as to its date. The linguistic evidence shows no early or late marks. "Shout joyfully to God, all the earth" (v1) is repeated in Ps 98:4 and 66:1. "We are His people and the sheep of His pasture" (v3) may be drawn from 95:7.
101	1000 (6)	David	The author has real political power (v8), supporting Davidic authorship. The short lines and three word/two word meter in this Psalm are similar to Ps 19:7-10.
102	700 (2)	None	This is one of the most difficult Psalms to date. Reading v16 as "When the LORD builds up Zion" could be read to support an exilic or post-exilic date, but this understanding is not mandatory. Some of the ideas and vocabulary look Davidic ("bones" in v3 and 5, concern about enemies in v8), and this Psalm is sandwiched between two other Psalms of David. However, the theology about Zion, which became part of Israel only in the middle of David's life, looks to be too far advanced in time for this to be a Davidic psalm. Some of the wording sounds like Isaiah, as in v26, "They [heavens and earth] will perish, but You

Psalm	Date B.C.	Attribution	Discussion
			will endure" (compare Isa 51:6). The pelican and owl of v6 are also mentioned in Isa 34:11. The Psalm exhibits Classical Biblical Hebrew linguistics. The older word for kingdom, "mamlakah" is in v22 (Heb v23).
103	980/ 500 (5)	David	This Davidic Psalm is written in Late Biblical Hebrew. This implies that this may have been an earlier work by David which was substantially revised in a later period. Psalms 104, 122, 124, 131, 133, 144 and 145 are also in this category. The most pronounced late linguistic marker is the "ki" (כי) suffix, an Aramaic grammatical feature, on second person singular nouns in v3, 4 and 5. Late vocabulary includes the later word for kingdom, "malkut," in v19. Early vocabulary includes "enosh" (אנוש) for "man" (v15)
104	1000 /500 (2)	None	The first and last verses of this Psalm tie it to Psalm 103 by the phrase "Bless the LORD O my soul" (as in 103:1, 103:2 and 103:22), but the core of this Psalm exhibits earlier linguistics, not showing signs of rework. It is possible that the core of the Psalm consists of verses 2-34, with the first and last verses added late. The "hallelujah" in the last verse (v35) is elsewhere limited to post-exilic Psalms. Internal linguistic evidence for the core of the psalm supports an earlier date.

Psalm	Date B.C.	Attri-bution	Discussion
			Imperfect verbs are repeatedly used in vv5-8 for past tense actions, supporting a date prior to 750 B.C. "Bal" (v5 and 9) is used as a negation, and "anoki" is used for "I" in v34. Early vocabulary includes "enosh" (אנוש) for "men" (v15).
105	520 (4)	None	This Psalm reviews Israel's history up through the conquest of Canaan. The fact that this extensive historical review is silent on the matter of Israelite kings hints at a date of writing when Israelite kings did not exist, thus a post-exilic date. Verses 1-15 match 1 Chron 16:8-22 almost exactly. The usage, 22 times, of waw + imperfect verbs to recount past tense events is representative of Classical Biblical Hebrew as opposed to early Hebrew. However, one outlier exists in v40, where an imperfect verb is used to say "he satisfied them." The "hallelu-jah" in v45 also fits with other post-exilic Psalms. The older word for kingdom, "mamlakah," is in v13.
106	500 (7)	None	V47, "gather us from the nations," coming on the heels of the distress described in v35-46, marks the Psalm as either exilic or post-exilic. The opening and closing "hallelujah" tie this Psalm to the previous two. V1 and 47 - 48 are reflected in 1 Chron 16:34-36. The usage, 54 times, of waw-consecutive verbs to recount past tense events matches

Psalm	Date B.C.	Attri-bution	Discussion
			Classical Biblical Hebrew as opposed to early Hebrew. Giving contrary evidence, four imperfect verbs acting as past tense in v12 and 17-19 may hint at an earlier tradition embedded in this later Psalm. The choice of the word "ahmad" (עמד) in v30 for "rose up" matches Late Biblical Hebrew – earlier usage would be "qum" (קום). Late vocabulary includes "shavakh" (שבח) for "praise" (v47). Both Psalms 105 and 106 use the unusual "land of Ham" to mean Egypt (105:23, 105:27 and 106:22).

5.1.8 Psalms Book 5

The decision to conclude Book 4 with Psalm 106 and begin Book 5 with Psalm 107 was apparently arbitrary, perhaps based on a desire to have 17 Psalms in both books 3 and 4 (17 being associated with the name YHWH). Beginning with Psalm 103, many of the Psalms begin to show a myriad of verbal characteristics that are absent in the earlier part of Psalms and either absent or rare in the Bible as a whole. Some of these are listed below, along with the Psalms that have these characteristics.

1. Use of hallelujah (הללויה): 104, 105, 106, 111-113, 115-117, 135 and 146-150
2. Use of "shin" (ש), as an attached relative pronoun: 122, 123, 124, 129, 133, 135, 137, 144 and 146
3. Use of the Aramaic second person pronominal suffix, "ki" (כי): 103, 116, 135 and 137
4. Unique wording of "Maker of heaven and earth" (עשה שמים וארץ): 115, 121, 124, 134 and 146
5. Reference to "house of Aaron": 115, 118 and 135

Within this portion of the Psalms, the following sub-collections can be observed:

1. Psalms of ascent (120-134). This collection appears to be diverse in date of writing.
2. The first hallelujah collection (111-113 and 115-117). This collection shows heavy dependence on earlier Psalms and other scriptures. It appears to be entirely post-exilic.
3. The second hallelujah collection (146-150). This collection also appears to be entirely post-exilic.

Two factors combine to pull the dates of these Psalms to a mostly early post-exilic time frame. First, Psalm 137 can be dated with high confidence to the exile itself. The intense bitterness directed toward Babylon in this Psalm requires an exilic date between 586 and 538 B.C. Yet this Psalm has two elements from the list above, the "shin" pronoun and the Aramaic "ki" suffix. This indicates that neither of these features should be regarded as especially late. Second, as noted in the introduction to Book 4 in section 5.1.7, 1 Chron 16:8-36 quotes from Psalms 96, 105 and 106, including the doxology that ends Book 4. Since the Book 4 / Book 5 division seems arbitrary, this implies that the chronicler had a complete Book 4 and 5 available when he wrote.

Psalm	Date B.C.	Attri-bution	Discussion
107	500 (9)	None	This Psalm is clearly post-exilic, with vv2-3 addressed to the Israelites redeemed and gathered from the nations. It may be that this Psalm was intended as an introductory Psalm to the post-exilic Book 5. V40 speaks of princes with contempt, implying they are foreign, and the Israelite royal line is not ruling. V1 connects this Psalm with the previous Psalm (106:1). V40a matches Job

Psalm	Date B.C.	Attribution	Discussion
			12:21a, and v35 is dependent on Isa 41:18. Early vocabulary includes "omer" (אמר) for "speech, word" in v11.
108	1000 (7)	David	This Psalm is a composite of two earlier Davidic Psalms, 57:7-11 and 60:5-12. The mention of Gilead, Manasseh, Ephraim and Philistines suggests a united monarchy date.
109	1000 (6)	David	David's preoccupation with his enemies is present throughout the Psalm. Older vocabulary includes "anoki" (v22). The heading "to the choir director" is a mark of antiquity. Davidic phrasing includes "deliver me" in v21.
110	1000 (6)	David	Identifying this as a Messianic Psalm, based on v1 and 5, as opposed to addressing an historical Israelite king, leaves us with no real clues as to the date of writing, other than the attribution to David. Old vocabulary includes "makhatz" (מחץ) for "strike/shatter" in v5 and 6.
111	500 (5)	None	Psalms 111-113 and 115-117 appear to be a collection and are dated together. All three begin and/or end with "halle-lujah." This Psalm seems to show many dependencies on earlier Psalms and on wisdom literature. Examples include v1 on Ps 138:1, v2 on Ps 92:5, v5 on Ps 105:8, v10 on Job 28:28 and Prov 1:7, etc. The fact that this Psalm is a perfect acrostic in the modern alphabetical

Psalm	Date B.C.	Attribution	Discussion
			order argues against an early date (see the discussion on the Hebrew alphabet in Appendix B.3.2). This psalm is attributed to Haggai in the Vulgate
112	500 (6)	None	This Psalm is similar to Psalm 1. It also shows many dependencies on other Psalms, as in v1 on 128:1, v5 on 37:26, v6 on 15:5 and 55:22, v8 on 54:7, and v10 on 35:16 and 37:12. Usage of the qal stem of "ka'as" (כעס), meaning "be angry," in v10 is unique to Late Biblical Hebrew. The fact that this Psalm is a perfect acrostic in the modern alphabetical order argues against an early date (see the discussion on the Hebrew alphabet in Appendix B.3.2).
113	500 (5)	None	This Psalm again shows dependencies on earlier scriptures, as in vv7-9 on the prayer of Hannah, especially 1 Sam 2:8, v5 on Exod 15:11, v4 on Ps 57:11, v2 on Dan 2:20, and v1 on 135:1.
114	900 (4)	None	This Psalm is much older than the collection surrounding it (111-113 and 115-117). The use of imperfect verb tenses to describe past actions in v3, 5 and 6 is characteristic of Hebrew poetry prior to 750 B.C. A predominately early word for God, "Eloah," appears in v7. The description of Judah as God's sanctuary in v2 suggests a date when the first temple is standing.
115	500	None	This Psalm mentions the "house of

Psalm	Date B.C.	Attri- bution	Discussion
	(7)		Israel" (v12) and the "house of Aaron" (v10, 12). There is no mention of the "house of David," implying that this is a post-exilic Psalm with no Davidic king present. Idols are happily mocked – they seem not to be a problem for Israel, and this also supports a post-exilic setting. V2 matches Ps 79:10, v3 is similar to Ps 135:6 and Dan 4:35, and v8 matches 135:18. The phrase, "Maker of heaven and earth" (v15) ties this Psalm in with other Book 5 Psalms (121:2, 124:8, 134:3 and 146:6)
116	500 (6)	None	This Psalm was written when the temple was standing in Jerusalem (v19) – probably the second temple. V3 is dependent on Ps 18:4, and vv17-18 on Ps 50:14. V7 has a "ki" Aramaic suffix, although v16 has the more common "ka" Hebrew suffix.
117	500 (5)	None	This short Psalm is dated based on the use of "hallelujah" and its proximity to the previous hallelujah Psalms. Late vocabulary includes שבח (v1).
118	440 (8)	None	"House of Aaron" (v3) without a corresponding "house of David" sounds post-exilic. The negative view of princes (v9) indicates a post-exilic period with gentile princes. The hostility of sur-rounding nations (vv10-12) matches the time of Nehemiah. Also, the often quoted vv22-23, "the stone the builders

Psalm	Date B.C.	Attribution	Discussion
			rejected has become the head of the corner," sounds like the joy of the community returned from exile. V14 quotes from Exod 15:2. V1 matches Ps 106:1, 107:1 and 1 Chron 16:34 (these all may trace originally to Jer 33:11). The repetition in this Psalm (vv8-9, 15-16, etc.) is reminiscent of Isaiah and establishes a separate style from the previous "hallelujah" Psalms.
119	550 (3)	None	Dating this Psalm is difficult. Though it is very long, it provides virtually no clues as to a political or a religious setting. An argument from silence can say that the absence of any religious references to Jerusalem or to sacrifices implies an exilic setting. Each verse attempts to include some reference to the law. Such high reverence and love for the law is difficult to find in pre-exilic times. The reference to kings in v46 sounds as if these are gentile kings, which would date the Psalm after the fall of Jerusalem. Yet some of the linguistic evidence points to an early date. Early vocabulary includes "orakh" (ארח) for "way, path" in v15, 101 and 104, and "anoki" in v19, 141 and 162. The particle "na" (v76 and 108) is more prominent in early than late writings. An early "bal" negation is in v121 and a "mo" suffix is in v165. On the other

Psalm	Date B.C.	Attri-bution	Discussion
			hand, some of the linguistic evidence points to a late date. In v63, the usage of "ani" equated with "companion" matches Late Biblical Hebrew, as "anoki" would be expected earlier. Late vocabulary includes שלט (v133) for "have dominion". The fact that this Psalm is a perfect acrostic in the modern alphabetical order argues against an early date (see the discussion on the Hebrew alphabet in Appendix B.3.2). This mixture of linguistic evidence points to a transitional period in Hebrew, as in the time of Ezekiel, the time of the exile.
120	500 (5)	None	The author speaks with the voice of a Jew in the Diaspora, away from Jerusalem. This first Psalm of Ascents sets the stage for a pilgrimage to Jerusalem described in the subsequent Psalms. The connection suggests a post-exilic date.
121	500 (4)	None	There is no setting for this Psalm, except that it is a Psalm of Ascents looking forward to a pilgrimage to Jerusalem. The phrase, "Maker of heaven and earth" (v2) ties this Psalm in with other Book 5 Psalms (115:15, 124:8, 134:3 and 146:6).
122	980/ 500 (4)	David	Some Septuagint manuscripts do not assign Psalm 122 to David. The phrase "house of David" in v5 sounds like a pre-exilic but post-David phrase.

Psalm	Date B.C.	Attribution	Discussion
			Thrones and palaces in Jerusalem sound pre-exilic, and the idea of *multiple* tribes going up to Jerusalem (v4) does seem to fit with a united monarchy period more than any other. In v4 we have the first appearance in Psalms of an attached Hebrew "shin" particle (שׁ) used as a relative pronoun. The early spelling of David is used in the attribution, but the later spelling is used in v5. The evidence on this Psalm is mixed, so we date it tentatively to the latter part of David's reign, based on the attribution and the mention of multiple tribes, with a later rework in the post-exilic period
123	550 (5)	None	Psalm 123 is dated to the exile due to God being enthroned in heaven (v1 – but not Zion), and because the Psalmist sees the community as being "greatly filled with contempt" (v3). An attached "shin" particle is in v2.
124	980/ 500 (3)	David	Psalm 124 is attributed to David and leaves no significant evidence for dating. The existence of three "shin" particles implies that this Psalm was reworked in the post-exilic period into its current form. VV3-5 and 7 have 7 perfect tense verbs and no imperfects, a ratio representative of Classical rather than Early Biblical Hebrew. The phrase, "maker of heaven and earth" (v8) ties this Psalm in with other Book 5 Psalms

Psalm	Date B.C.	Attri-bution	Discussion
			(115:15, 121:2, 134:3 and 146:6)
125	520 (4)	None	This Psalm's perspective on the immovability of Mt Zion and God's protection of his people there could fit with a pre-exilic time, perhaps after the failed Assyrian invasion. However, it is assigned to Haggai in the Peshitta, an early Aramaic translation, and it is unlikely (though not impossible) that a tradition of later authorship would develop over an earlier text. The Hebrew for "upright in heart" in v4 (לישרים בלבותם) is not an expected form and probably late, as the earlier Psalms which have the same meaning use a construct form (7:10 [Heb 7:11], 11:2, 32:11, 36:10 [Heb 36:11] and 94:15). Earlier passages that say "cannot be moved" (v1) use "bal" (בל) instead of "lo" (לא) as a negation (Ps 10:6, 46:5 [Heb 46:6], 93:1, 96:10, Prov 12:3).
126	520 (9)	None	This short Psalm can be dated with high confidence. The reference to a return from captivity (v1) while knowing that the exile is still a reality for many (v4) places this Psalm in the early post-exilic period. This Psalm is also assigned to Haggai in the Peshitta.
127	950 (5)	Solomon	This Psalm is attributed to Solomon and leaves virtually no additional evidence for dating.
128	520	None	This Psalm looks to be connected to

Psalm	Date B.C.	Attribution	Discussion
	(3)		Psalm 125 due to the repeated blessing, "Peace be upon Israel" (125:5 and128:6) and the use of Zion and Jerusalem together (125:1-2 and 128:5)
129	500 (3)	None	This Psalm gives few clues as to its date. Psalms 129-131 seem to be connected, as they all contain exhortations directed to Israel. "Shin" relative pronouns appear in v6 and 7.
130	500 (2)	None	This Psalm gives few clues as to its date. The address to "Israel" alone (not Judah) in v7 argues against a divided kingdom or Judah-alone pre-exilic date.
131	980/ 500 (2)	David	This short Psalm is dated to the time of David based solely on the attribution. We are also assigning this Psalm to the collection of reworked Psalms due to this Psalm's association with Psalms 129 and 130. Notice the phrase "O Israel hope in the LORD" in 131:3 and 130:7.
132	700 (6)	None	This Psalm is clearly post-Davidic, due to the prayer asking the LORD to remember David (v1 and following). It is also clearly pre-exilic, with the emphasis on the Davidic covenant and the mention of the Ark of the Covenant in v8 (the ark disappears during the exile). The older short spelling of David's name is used throughout the Psalm. The early relative pronoun "zo" (זו) appears in v12. The phrase "Mighty One of Jacob" from v2 and 5 is also in

Psalm	Date B.C.	Attri-bution	Discussion
			Isa 49:26 and 60:16 (and Gen 49:24).
133	980/ 500 (6)	David	This is one of the Psalms that we put in the category of Davidic/reworked. The reference to Mount Hermon in v3 supports the idea that the Psalm originated with David, since Hermon was lost to the Davidic monarchy as early as the time of Rehoboam (931 B.C.). The two "shin" relative pronouns in v2 and 3 are evidence of later language.
134	500 (3)	None	This short Psalm gives few clues as to its date of writing. The phrase, "Maker of heaven and earth" (v3) ties this Psalm in with other Book 5 Psalms (115:15, 121:2, 124:8 and 146:6)
135	500 (7)	None	This Psalm is dated to the post-exilic period, primarily due to the references to "house of Israel," "house of Aaron," and "house of Levi" in vv19-20, without mentioning the "house of David." This indicates that the priestly office is in effect at the time of writing, but the royal office was not. V2 indicates that there is a standing temple. The fact that idols are a problem for other nations but seemingly not for Israel (v15-18) also fits the post-exilic period. The use of "hallelujah" (v1, 3 and 21), the "shin" relative pronoun (v8 and 10) and the Aramaic "ki" pronominal suffix (v9) support a post-exilic date. The earlier word for kingdom, "mamlakot" is used in v11.

Psalm	Date B.C.	Attri-bution	Discussion
136	440 (5)	None	This Psalm is dated near the time of Nehemiah based on verbal parallels with Chronicles, Nehemiah and Ezra. The most important of these is the title "God of Heaven" in v26, which was popular in the Persian era (2 Chron 36:23, Ezra 1:2, 5:11 and Neh 1:4). An attached "shin" relative pronoun is in v23.
137	586 (9)	None	This Psalm can be dated to the early exile with high confidence. "By the rivers of Babylon, There we sat down and wept, When we remembered Zion…For there our captors demanded of us songs…" (v1, 3) reflects the grief of the captives taken to Babylon. The freshness of the trauma is evident from verses 8-9, cursing Babylon: "How blessed will be the one who seizes and dashes your little ones against the rock." This is probably an emotional response by eyewitnesses to the murder of King Zedekiah's little children by the Babylonians in 2 Kgs 25:7. Psalm 137 is attributed to David in the Septuagint, but this must be wrong. Verse 6 has an Aramaic style "ki" suffix and verses 8-9 have "shin" relative pronouns.
138	1000 (6)	David	Psalms 138-145 are a Davidic collection. In Psalms 144-145, some evidence of reworking of the language is present. Psalms 138-143 seem to have earlier

Psalm	Date B.C.	Attri-bution	Discussion
			Hebrew and show no signs of rework. David's frequent preoccupation with his enemies appears in this Psalm in v7. The use of an imperfect tense verb to describe past action in v3 is characteristic of early Hebrew poetry before 750 B.C. Early vocabulary includes "omer" (אמר) for "speech, word" in v4.
139	1000 (7)	David	This Davidic Psalm says "to the choir director," a feature of the older Psalms. There are no marks of Late Biblical Hebrew in this Psalm. Some older vocabulary is present, as in "Eloah" for God in v19, "orakh" (ארח) for "way, path" in v3, and "ak" for "surely" in v11. David's frequent preoccupation with his enemies shows up in vv19-22, a passage perhaps more striking than usual because it deviates from the theme of the rest of the Psalm. The use of two imperfect tense verbs to describe past action in v13 and 16 is characteristic of early Hebrew poetry before 750 B.C.
140	1015 (7)	David	This Davidic Psalm says "to the choir director," a feature of the older Psalms. The entire Psalm reflects David's frequent preoccupation with his enemies. Since he seems to count himself among the poor and needy, the Psalm was probably written before he became king. Early features include "bal" as a

Psalm	Date B.C.	Attri-bution	Discussion
			negation in v10 and 11 (Heb v11 and 12), "selah" after v4, 6 and 9, "ak" for "surely" in v13 (Heb v14), and the "mo" pronominal suffix in v3 and 9 (Heb v4 and 10). Davidic phrasing includes "my supplication" (v6).
141	1000 (7)	David	This Davidic Psalm reflects David's frequent preoccupation with his enemies in vv9-10. The older pronoun "anoki" is in v10 and "bal" is used as a negation in v4. Davidic vocabulary includes "bones" (v7).
142	1015 (7)	David	This Davidic Psalm gives its time of writing in the attribution, "when he was in the cave." This would be before David was king, while he was hiding from Saul either in the cave of Adullam (1 Sam 22:1) or En Gedi (1 Sam 24:1-7). The identification of the Psalm as a "maskil" may also be an early mark. The early relative pronoun "zu" is in v3 (Heb v4). Early vocabulary also includes "orakh" (ארח) for "way, path" in v3 (Heb v4). Davidic phrasing includes "deliver me" (v6).
143	1000 (7)	David	This is the last Davidic Psalm that does not show signs of rework. The early relative pronoun "zu" in v8, the "selah" after v6 and the absence of late features make the language of this Psalm look early. David's frequent preoccupation with his enemies is evident in v3 and 12.

Psalm	Date B.C.	Attribution	Discussion
			Davidic phrasing includes "my supplication" (v1) and "deliver me" (v9).
144	1000 /500 (6)	David	This is a Davidic/reworked Psalm. The author is both a warrior (v1) and a musician (v9), a description that fits David. The author believes that kings need salvation in v10, a verse in which he names himself (using the early spelling for David). V3 repeats a phrase from Ps 8:4, an earlier Davidic Psalm. The extent of the rework may be limited to the addition of vv12-15, where the tone changes, to a Davidic original. A "shin" relative pronoun is in v15. Davidic phrasing includes "my deliverer" (v2), "my stronghold" (v2) and "deliver me" (v7, 11). Older language includes the designation of God as a "Rock" (v1) and "enosh" (אנוש) for "men" (v3).
145	1000 /500 (4)	David	This is a Davidic/reworked Psalm. Like many Davidic Psalms, the mode of address is changed during the Psalm from addressing God in second person (v1-16) to referring to Him in third person (v17-21), although in this case the change is not made right at the center of the Psalm. The late word for kingdom, "malkut," appears in v11, 12 and 13. An ancient element may be present in v13, as Ugaritic texts pre-dating David also use the phrase "Thy

Psalm	Date B.C.	Attri-bution	Discussion
			kingdom is everlasting, thy power to all generations."[8] Late vocabulary includes "shavakh" (שבח) for "praise" (v4). This is an acrostic Psalm, which is perfect except for the missing "nun" verse. This verse appears in a Dead Sea Scroll, and has now been inserted in some modern translations.
146	500 (7)	None	Psalms 146-150 are treated as a group of post-exilic Psalms composed at about the same time. Their anonymity, their placement together in the book, the repeated use of "hallelujah" along with many other occurrences of the verb "hallel" (praise) ties these five Psalms together. None of these Psalms assume any pre-exilic feature, such as an Israelite king or an Ark of the Covenant. Psalms 146-148 are attributed by the Septuagint and the Peshitta to the post-exilic prophets Haggai and Zechariah. Psalm 146:3, "put not your trust in princes," strikes a post-exilic tone. "Shin" relative particles appear in v3 and v5. The phrase, "maker of heaven and earth" (v6) ties this Psalm in with other Book 5 Psalms (115:15, 121:2, 124:8 and 134:3)
147	500 (7)	None	Verse 2, which talks about building Jerusalem and gathering the dispersed

---

[8] Archer, *A Survey of the Old Testament Introduction*, p. 430

Psalm	Date B.C.	Attri-bution	Discussion
			of Israel, marks this Psalm as post-exilic. See also the discussion on Psalm 146. Late vocabulary includes "shavakh" (שבח) for "praise" in v4 and perhaps also "kinnes" (כנס) for "gather" in v2. Early vocabulary includes a "bal" negation (v20). This Psalm is attributed to Haggai and Zechariah in the Septuagint and the Peshitta.
148	500 (7)	None	See the discussion on Psalm 146. This Psalm is attributed to Haggai and Zechariah in the Septuagint and the Peshitta.
149	500 (7)	None	See the discussion on Psalm 146.
150	500 (7)	None	See the discussion on Psalm 146. This Psalm may be considered as a benediction or doxology to conclude either Book 5 of the Psalms, or perhaps to conclude the entire book of Psalms.

5.1.9 Linguistic Analysis

The linguistic evidence in Psalms varies from one Psalm to another and is described in the tables above.

5.1.10 Oldest Texts

The oldest manuscripts of Psalms are 36 Dead Sea Scrolls. Most of the book is represented, and many of the Psalms are represented multiple times. The Dead Sea Scrolls also include a commentary on Psalm 37 (4Q171 and 4Q173). Some Psalms texts from the Dead Sea Scrolls include non-Biblical Psalms, and occasionally the order of Psalms is different from the modern canonical order.

The discovery of the Dead Sea Scrolls altered the critical viewpoint on dating the Psalms. Before 1948, scholars were inclined to date some Psalms (74, 79, 83 and a number of others) as late as the Maccabean period, in the second century B.C. This viewpoint was not limited to liberal critics, but included Bible commentaries and some major church figures such as John Calvin, who attributed 44, 74 and 79 to the Maccabean period.[9] However, the Dead Sea Scrolls included many Psalms scrolls, and in most cases the Psalms had already been placed in their modern order.[10] This showed that a complete book of Psalms was already in wide circulation in the Maccabean period. As a result, modern writers tend to push the latest Psalms back in time to the Persian period (538-332 B.C.) or shortly afterward.

5.1.11 Conclusion

The entire collection of Psalms was completed before the book of Chronicles was written, before 400 B.C. The first two books of Psalms, consisting of Psalms 2-72, are a pre-exilic collection. The last three books are a post-exilic collection that contains both early and late Psalms. Psalm 1 is probably a late psalm used as an introduction to the entire book of Psalms.

5.2 Job

The book of Job addresses philosophical questions related to God's sovereignty and why good people suffer. Job is given a generally ancient setting, but it is not directly coupled with a particular time or place.

---

[9] International Standard Bible Encyclopedia, 1915 version, article on Psalms

[10] In most cases, the Dead Sea Scrolls place the Psalms in their modern order, but not always. In particular, the largest recovered Psalms scroll, 11Q5, has most of the Psalms from 101 to 150, but in a somewhat jumbled order, and it also includes several unknown Psalms and a Psalm from the last chapter of Ben Sirach.

Job is difficult to date because the author is anonymous, there are no unambiguous references to other biblical people or events, and the theme of the book does not uniquely address any particular period in history. The Talmud assigns authorship of Job to Moses, making the book as early as the Torah.[11] Some Christian writers, noting the patriarchal setting of Job, date the book even earlier than Moses, making it the oldest book in the Bible. At the other extreme, some modern writers have followed the trend toward dating as much as possible as late as possible, and place Job in the post-exilic period around 400 B.C. Another common conjecture has it written at the time of Solomon, near 950 B.C., as that age is associated with biblical wisdom literature.

5.2.1 Origin of the Book of Job

With caution, we suggest four things about the origin of the book of Job:

1. There existed an early text of Job not written in Hebrew
2. Job in its current form was translated into Hebrew around the time of Hezekiah
3. The translator was Isaiah.
4. The introduction and conclusion to Job (chapters 1-2 and 42:7-17) are in a somewhat different category from the rest of the book.

We will support each of these suggestions in turn.

5.2.1.1 Early Text of Job

The setting for the book of Job is ancient, and located in the general vicinity of what would become the land of Edom. This conclusion is more certain than any conclusion we can make about the date the book was written. The land of Uz (Job 1:1) was apparently located in ancient Edom or Arabia, and Job's friend

---

[11] Baba Bathra 15a

Eliphaz was from Teman (Job 2:11), a few miles east of Petra in Edom. Evidence of an ancient setting includes:

1. Job lived 140 years after his suffering (42:16), a lifespan reached only by the patriarchs.
2. Job's practice of offering burnt offerings (1:5) for his family is inconsistent with later laws for sacrifices.
3. The "qesitta" (קשיטה) as a piece of money suggests an early date (Job 42:11, Josh 24:32 and Gen 33:19).
4. Job makes no reference to any event in Israel's history.

Other features pointing to an unusual setting for Job also should probably be understood to indicate an older setting. These include:

1. Repeated references to snow (6:16, 9:30, 24:19, 37:6 and 38:22) and ice (6:16, 37:10 and 38:29-30) seem strange based on later/modern weather patterns in Edom.
2. The animals behemoth (40:15-24) and leviathan (41:1-34) do not match any later known animals of Edom or Israel. The usual identification of behemoth as a hippopotamus should be rejected, since a hippo does not have a tail like a cedar tree (40:17). Efforts to identify leviathan as a crocodile fail for numerous reasons, especially because leviathan is a fire-breather (41:18-21), more akin to the idea of a dragon (see Isa 27:1) than any modern reptile. In any case, hippos and crocodiles are not native to Edom.
3. A note in the Septuagint says Job is Jobab of Gen 36:33, five generations down from Abraham. It is difficult to know how seriously to take this, other than to note that the setting is correct.

An ancient setting by itself does not always require an ancient original date of writing, but it would be a first necessary requirement. However, the way the book of Job treats the material supports an early date of writing. In particular, since the book treats as praiseworthy Job's sacrificial practices – practices that would be considered wrong at a later date – the book was probably written when these practices were thought to be a good thing.

5.2.1.2 Book of Job as a Translation

The book of Job shows several marks of being a translation:

1. Job is distinctively non-Israelite in nature, saying nothing about the land of Israel, the people and history of Israel, or the religious practices in Israel. The names of Job and his friends are not Israelite names. This, along with the Edomite setting, hints at a non-Israelite origin for the book. If the book's origin was not within Israel, the original language would likely not be Hebrew.

2. The translator of Job faced the same question as the translator of Genesis 1-36 (see 3.3.9.2.2) in dealing with the name of God, but he dealt with it differently. While the translator of Genesis 1-36 liberally substituted YHWH for "Shaddai" or "El Shaddai," the translator of Job chose not to translate this name. As a result, "Shaddai," usually translated as "the Almighty" in English, is used as a name for God 31 times in the book of Job. All of these occurrences are in the direct speech of the characters, beginning in chapter 3. After the introduction in chapters 1-2, YHWH appears only twice in direct speech in Job. "Shaddai" occurs only 17 times elsewhere in the Bible, and where it does, it often has a non-Israelite origin (Num 24:4, 24:16, Ruth 1:20-21, etc.).

3. The translator also left intact the title "Eloah" (אלוה), translated as "God," 41 times. Eloah is probably a singular form of Elohim, the normal word for God, which has a plural form in Hebrew although it is usually singular in meaning.

To address the date of the translation of Job, let us begin by showing that the evidence works against the idea of a late post-exilic date. This evidence includes:

1. One of the Dead Sea Scrolls of Job, scroll 4Q101, is written in the angular paleo-Hebrew script, a phenomenon found elsewhere in the Dead Sea Scrolls only on a few Torah scrolls. The more modern square Hebrew script was introduced around the time of the exile, and the preservation of the older script in some scrolls argues for recognition by the copier of the antiquity of the text. It is also unlikely (though not impossible) that any book written originally in the modern script, as some of the later books may have been, would be copied back into the older script.

2. Ezekiel 14:14 and 14:20 mention Job, Daniel and Noah as examples of righteous men. This implies that Ezekiel was familiar with at least a tradition about Job, if not the written book of Job. Ezekiel wrote early in the exile.

3. Although the identification of Job is not certain, he is apparently an Edomite, or at least a man living in the land later called Edom. Israelite resentment and disgust with Edom rose to great heights after the exile due to the Edomite conduct during the destruction of Jerusalem (Ps 137:7, Lam 4:21-22 and Obadiah), making an Edomite hero unlikely.

4. The linguistic evidence points to a period of writing before the exile (see 5.2.4, below).

At the same time, some aspects of Job point to a time of writing later than the patriarchal period. These include:

1. Unlike the Torah, Job does not show marks of Egyptian influence, either in internal evidence or language. It also does not show many of the early language features of the Torah listed in section 3.3.11. This makes it unlikely that Job was written by Moses, or any Israelite of the exodus generation.

2. The Chaldeans (1:17) are not mentioned as a people having contact with Israel or Edom until the time of Isaiah (ex-

cepting the geographical clarification in Genesis about "Ur of the Chaldeans").

5.2.1.3 Isaiah as the Translator of Job

The facts above indicate that to date the Hebrew version of the book of Job, we are left with a situation where we must abandon both ends of the Old Testament period, and look for a date closer to the middle. The time of Hezekiah and Isaiah is consistent with this evidence.

Isaiah, living at the time of Hezekiah, could have participated in the effort to collect and publish wisdom literature which apparently took place in that day (Prov 25:1). A considerable body of material was likely published about this time, including Proverbs, stories of the northern Israelite prophets Elijah, Elisha, Hosea, Amos and Jonah, along with the southern prophet Micah and of course, Isaiah. Isaiah would have taken the story of the ancient Edomite patriarch, Job, and translated it into Hebrew for the Judean reader. The publication of Job at this time seems plausible. This theory is consistent with the ancient setting and not quite so ancient linguistic aspects of the book.

We can show that a number of parallels exist between Isaiah and Job in the area of phrasing. The following phrases appear in both Job and Isaiah:

1. "The hand of the LORD has done this" (Job 12:9 and Isa 41:20)
2. "Who will contend with me?" (Job 13:19 and Isa 50:8)
3. "Conceive mischief and bring forth iniquity" (Job 15:35 and Isa 59:4)
4. "Offspring and posterity" (Job 18:19 and Isa 14:22)
5. "Honorable man" – the Hebrew wording is unique and unusual (נשוא פנים) (Job 22:8 and Isa 3:3, 9:14)

We can draw the following additional parallels between Isaiah and Job:

1. Both books show a tendency to ask strings of rhetorical questions. Job is full of them, and they also occur commonly in Isaiah, as in Isa 10:8-11, 40:12-14, 40:21, etc.

2. Both books use a broad vocabulary. Job uses five different words for gold. Six different words for traps are in 18:8-10 and five words for lion in 4:10-11. By comparison, Isaiah uses the broadest vocabulary of any book in the Bible, a vocabulary of 2186 words.

3. Job and Isaiah are the only books in the Bible to use the word "kabir" (כביר), meaning "great" (Job 8:2, 15:10, 31:25, 34:17, 34:24, 36:5, Isa 10:13, 16:14, 17:12 and 28:2).

4. Job uses "enosh" (אנוש) for "man" 18 times (4:17, 5:17 etc.) instead of the usual "ish" (איש). Isaiah uses "enosh" nine times (8:1, 51:7, etc.). This word is used elsewhere in the Bible 15 times: in Deut 32:26, 2 Chron 14:10, Jer 20:10 and a number of mostly early Psalms.

5. "Eloah" is used for God (41 times in Job, also in Isa 44:8, Deut 32:15, Prov 30:5 and four times in Psalms)

6. "Shaddai" is used as a name for God, usually translated as "the Almighty," 31 times in Job and only 16 times elsewhere, including Isa 13:6.

7. The description of God as "Maker" occurs five times in Job, eight times in Isaiah, and ten other times in the Bible.

8. "Redeemer" is used 14 times in Isaiah as a title for God. It also appears in Job 19:25. Whether or not Job 19:25 refers to God is an argued point.

9. "Holy One" is used as a name for God (Job 6:10, "Holy One" appears 29 times in Isaiah)

10. Chaldeans (Job 1:17 and seven times in Isaiah)

11. Sabeans (Job 1:15 and Isa 45:14)

12. Water evaporates, rivers parched and dry (Job 14:11 and Isa 19:5)

13. Drunken man staggers (Job 12:25 and Isa 19:14)

14. Hidden treasures (Job 3:21, Prov 2:4 and Isa 45:3)

15. Breath of the LORD destroys (Job 4:9 and Isa 11:4)
16. Descendants and offspring like grass (Job 5:25 and Isa 44:3-4)
17. Earth shakes/trembles out of its place (Job 9:6 and Isa 13:13)
18. Sun and stars dark (Job 9:7 and Isa 13:10)
19. Saying to God "What are you doing" (Job 9:12 and Isa 45:9)
20. God acting "like a lion" (Job 10:16 and Isa 38:13)
21. Man like a flower that withers (Job 14:2 and Isa 40:6-8)
22. Driven into darkness (Job 18:18 and Isa 8:22)
23. Teaching God? (Job 21:22 and Isa 40:14)
24. Worms cover them (Job 21:26 and Isa 14:11)
25. Spitting at the face (Job 30:10 and Isa 50:6)
26. Hide in the dust (Job 40:13 and Isa 2:10)

The matching list of animals in the two books is also interesting:

1. Rahab as a sea monster (Job 9:13, 26:12 and Isa 30:7, 51:9)
2. Leviathan (Job 41:1, Isa 27:1 also Ps 74:14 and 104:26)
3. Wild donkey (Job 6:5, 11:12, 24:5, 39:5 and Isa 32:14)
4. Young lion (Job 4:10, 38:39, Isa 5:29, 11:6 and 31:4)
5. Cobra (Job 20:14, 20:16 and Isa 11:8)
6. Raven (Job 38:41 and Isa 34:11)
7. Wild ox (Job 39:9-10 and Isa 34:7)
8. Ostrich (Job 30:29, 39:13, Isa 13:21, 34:13 and 43:20)
9. Hawk (Job 39:26 and Isa 34:15)
10. Spider's web (Job 8:14, 27:18 and Isa 59:5)

At this point, two objections could legitimately be raised. First, how can we know that the author of Job was not an individual who wrote later than Isaiah and copied Isaiah's phrasing? This question cannot be answered with absolute authority, but several points can be made. Job does not make extensive use of phrasing from any other prophet or from the Torah. It would be strange for the language of a late writing to attach itself to Isaiah only. Second, at least one major element of Isaiah's style, emphatic duplication (see 4.2.1.2.8), is completely absent in Job. It would be unusual for a later work to attach itself to Isaiah's style in numerous minor details, while staying completely independent of it in such a major area. The reason Isaiah's emphatic duplication is not found in Job is probably because Isaiah is not the author of Job; he is just the translator. A translator can be expected to produce the same vocabulary that he uses himself, but his capacity to impose his own style on the translation is limited.

The second objection is a more plausible one. How can we be sure that Isaiah was a translator of Job, rather than just a reader who borrowed phrases from Job? To address this question, we note that the phrasing in Isaiah is closer to Job than the Torah, although Isaiah knows the Torah. Isaiah occasionally uses distinctive Torah phrases,[12] the Torah was important to Isaiah (Isa 2:3, 5:24, 8:20, etc.), and certainly more important for the people of Israel than the book of Job. Since Isaiah knew both the Torah and Job, and considered the Torah the more important of the two, it would be strange to find that his language more closely matched Job – unless he himself was responsible for the language of Job. It is also plausible that Isaiah's experience translating Job had an effect on his choice of words and phrases in his own book.

5.2.1.4 Introduction and Conclusion of Job

Job 1-2 and 42:7-17 provide a narrative frame for the book of Job. Differences between this frame and the body of the book are apparent. The frame is prose and the body is poetry. Different names for God are used. We have provided some evidence that the central body of Job is a translation of an older text. However, the narrative frame does not show major marks of being such a translation. We can note that Job's three daughters (42:14) have names which are not common Hebrew names, and whether or not they are of Hebrew origin is debatable. The frame fits the body of

---

[12] As in Isa 34:11 using the rare phrasing תהו and בהו from Gen 1:2 ("formless and void")

the story, though, and it would be rash to try to separate the two in time without compelling evidence. It is possible that the frame is a narrative retelling of the Job story rather than a translation of an early text. Some of the evidences for antiquity are in the frame (Job's long life span and the practice of sacrifice by a non-priest). The frame is written in Classical Biblical Hebrew, and should probably be dated along with the rest of the book.

5.2.2 External Dependencies

Several passages in Psalms may be dependent on Job.

Job	Psalms
7:17 What is man that You magnify him, And that You are concerned about him?	8:4 What is man that You take thought of him, And the son of man that You care for him?
12:21 He pours contempt on nobles (שופך בוז על־נדיבים)	107:40 He pours contempt upon princes (שופך בוז על־נדיבים)

Proverbs 9:10 (see also Prov 1:7) may actually borrow twice from Job, using phrases from two different sources, first the phrase "Holy One" from Job 6:10, and then more tellingly:

Job 28:28 … the fear of the Lord, that is wisdom; And to depart from evil is under-standing.	Prov 9:10 The fear of the LORD is the beginning of wisdom, And the knowledge of the Holy One is understanding.

Note that we will date Proverbs 1-9 to the time of Hezekiah and Isaiah.

Heman the Ezrahite, the author mentioned in the inscription of Psalm 88, had 14 sons and 3 daughters, matching Job (1 Chron 25:5), and Psalm 88 is a lament similar to parts of Job. This is an interesting fact, but it probably does not lead anywhere.

5.2.3 Linguistic Analysis

There are no Persian words in Job. The older pronoun "anoki" is used eight times (its counterpart "ani" is used 27 times). The older poetic negation "bal" is used once, in 41:15, and the early particle "lbilti" (לבלתי) is in 42:8. "Pen" (פן), meaning "lest" (36:18), appears almost exclusively in earlier texts. Other early vocabulary includes "orakh" (ארח) for "way, path" in 8:13, 13:27, 19:8, 22:15, 30:12, 33:11 and 34:11, "yareakh" (ירח) for "month" in 3:6, 7:3, 29:2 and 39:2 and "omer" (אמר) for "speech, word," in 6:26, 20:29, 22:22, 32:12, 32:14, 33:3 and 34:7.

The older "mo" pronominal suffix appears on a noun in 27:23. While it is unusual for this suffix to appear on a noun in a text written this late (700 B.C.), its usage allows the verse to rhyme. This is an illustration of how an author can alter the linguistics to fit his purpose and should serve as a cautionary note against using a single piece of linguistic evidence as an absolute chronological marker. The "mo" suffix is attached to prepositions in 6:16, 15:28, 16:4, 20:23, 29:21, 29:22, 30:2 and 30:5. This usage of "mo" attached to prepositions is not surprising, since Isaiah does the same thing (Isa 16:4, 30:5, 35:8 and 48:21).

The poetry in Job sometimes makes use of imperfect verbs to designate non-repeated past tense events, as in Job 4:12-16, 10:10-11 and 15:7. This is a characteristic of Early Biblical Hebrew, and is not present in Isaiah. Other early Semitic languages, such as Ugaritic and the language of the Amarna letters, used imperfect verbs in this way as well. If we understand these verses to be a translation, it may be that the translator chose to retain the original verb tense in his translation. On the other hand, passages such as Job 38:7-11 are representative of Classical Biblical Hebrew due to the use of waw + imperfect verbs to indicate past time.

A plural "in" (ין) suffix, as in Aramaic, is in 4:2 and 12:11, though both occurrences are with the same noun.

The spelling associated with the root word laugh (שחק) in 5:22, 8:21, 12:4, 30:1, 40:20, etc. is later than the spelling used in the

Torah (צחק), indicating that Job was placed in final form after the Torah.

5.2.4 Oldest Texts

The oldest manuscripts of Job are three Dead Sea Scrolls. Portions of seven chapters are represented. Also, fragments of a Targum (Aramaic translation) of Job containing Job 3:5-9 and 4:16-5:4 dating to the last half of the first century B.C. have been found.[13] Scroll 4Q101 is written in the paleo-Hebrew script used before the exile. This does not mean the scroll itself is pre-exilic; use of the earlier script continued intermittently afterward.

5.2.5 Conclusion

Job is a translation of an early patriarchal era writing. The original writing in an early Semitic language dates to around 1600 B.C. The Hebrew translation, which is the book of Job essentially as it exists today, was performed around 700 B.C.

5.3 Proverbs

The book of Proverbs is the second book in the Bible to present itself as an anthology, though with less diversity than Psalms. The Proverbs are attributed as follows:

1:1	"The proverbs of Solomon" – probably this is a header for the whole book
1:2-9:18	Introduction
10:1-22:16	"The proverbs of Solomon"
22:17–24:34	"The words of the wise"
25:1-29:27	"The proverbs of Solomon which the men of Hezekiah, king of Judah, transcribed"
30:1–33	"The words of Agur the son of Jakeh"
31:1-31	"The words of King Lemuel, the oracle which his mother taught him"

---

[13] VanderKam, *The Dead Sea Scroll Today*, p. 33

The different sections can be shown to be clearly distinct. The longest section is 10:1-22:16, assigned to Solomon and containing 375 proverbs. All of these proverbs are in the form of short couplets, each one essentially standing alone with no connection to a larger context. The number of these proverbs, 375, exactly matches the numeric value of Solomon's name in Hebrew. 1 Kgs 4:32 says Solomon spoke 3000 proverbs, so this collection of 375 might be a subset selected from an older, larger collection that is now lost. Authorship of these proverbs by Solomon would place them at about 950 B.C. What little internal evidence there is tends to be supportive of this date. The verses which talk of kings or a king are mostly favorable and stated in such a way as to be consistent with an Israelite king (Prov 16:10-15, 20:2, 20:8, 20:26, 20:28 and 22:11). It would be difficult to imagine an Israelite writer applying words like "loyalty," "truth," and "righteousness" (20:28) to a king of Babylon or Persia. The references to sacrifice (15:8, 21:3 and 21:27) rule out a time during the Babylonian exile. Prov 14:12 is repeated in 16:25.

The second collection of proverbs by Solomon is in chapters 25-29. These proverbs were apparently copied from an older text by the "men of Hezekiah" (25:1). The mention of Hezekiah also provides the earliest possible date for compilation of the book – during the reign of Hezekiah (716-687 B.C.). This collection of proverbs again shows marks of pre-exilic origin in the favorable way it speaks of kings (25:1-6, 29:4 and 29:14). Unlike the first collection from Solomon, some of these proverbs span multiple verses (25:4-5). Prov 25:24 is a duplicate of Prov 21:9, from the first collection of Solomon. It is possible that the number of Proverbs in this collection is based on the numeric value of Hezekiah's name in Hebrew – 130 or 136, depending on which spelling of Hezekiah (חזקיה or חזקיהו) is used.

The "words of the wise" collection in 22:17-24:34 is different from the collection of Solomon's proverbs in that most of these proverbs span multiple verses (23:1-3, etc.). It has become popular in recent years to identify this collection as dependent on the "Instruction of Amenemope," an Egyptian wise man who lived about 1100 B.C. This idea is strengthened by the division of the instruction of Amenemope into 30 sections, a number which is reflected in the Hebrew *qire* reading[14] of Prov 22:20. It is possible to divide 22:17-24:34 into 30 sayings. Weakening the case for dependence on Amenemope is the fact that only a few of the biblical proverbs are similar to the Egyptian text. Also, certain of the biblical proverbs are Yahwistic (22:19, 22:23, etc.), showing a distinctly Israelite identity. Some of the proverbs in this collection reflect the ideas and even the wording of the first Solomon collection, such as Prov 24:6b, which matches Prov 11:14b, "in abundance of counselors there is victory." Since Amenemope predated Solomon, however, it would not be surprising if Solomon borrowed at least the *genre* of Egyptian proverbs for his work. Egypt and Israel were at peace during Solomon's reign, and Solomon and Pharaoh had formed a marriage alliance (1 Kgs 3:1 and 9:16). These factors support a date during Solomon's reign for Prov 22:17-24:34.

To date the introductory section of Proverbs 1-9, it is necessary to first consider the drawback of publishing in Hezekiah's time a new collection of proverbs by Solomon. The advantage is obvious – Solomon's wisdom is legendary and his reign represented the golden age of Israel. However, his worship of foreign gods late in his life is troublesome, and the enormous number of his wives and concubines is embarrassing. Proverbs 1-9 address these concerns by focusing on the fear of YHWH (3:5-6) and providing numerous warnings about the dangers of adultery. This section could also reasonably be assigned to Hezekiah's time.

To date Prov 30-31, it is best first to try to identify Agur the son of Jakeh (30:1) and King Lemuel (31:1). Agur might be a genuine

---

[14] The *qire* is a note in the margin of the Hebrew Bible provided by the Masoretic scribes, indicating how a passage should be read and deviating from the *kethiv*, the written text.

personal name of an individual unknown to us. On the other hand, it might be a pen name. Agur means "gatherer" and Jakeh means "pious," perhaps pointing to the individual who gathered the collection of Proverbs together. This then would also be an individual working in Hezekiah's time. There are some clues, discussed below, indicating that this individual may have been Isaiah.

We know the name of all the Israelite kings, and Lemuel is not one of them. It is possible, but it seems unlikely, that Lemuel was king of a non-Israelite country. More likely is that Lemuel is also a pen name. Some scholars have suggested Solomon is Lemuel, bringing Bathsheba into the picture as Solomon's mother (31:1). However, it is not clear why Solomon would have needed a pen name – having already been named three times earlier in the book. Also, the praise of one excellent and apparently non-royal wife in 31:10-31 does not naturally flow from the lips of a man with 700 of them. One king who may have needed a pen name is Hezekiah, if the book was put in final form just after his reign. Hezekiah's son Manasseh turned dramatically against his father's policies, so Hezekiah's name might have been an issue on a newly published book. Likewise, Isaiah, Hezekiah's right-hand man, might have needed a pen name. If tradition is correct, Isaiah was executed by Manasseh.

There are additional reasons to believe Isaiah may be the author of Proverbs 30, and even the introductory section of Proverbs 1:2-9:18.

1. Emphatic duplication, so characteristic of Isaiah's style (see section 4.2.1.2.9) but largely absent elsewhere in the Bible, makes a prominent appearance in chapter 30. Prov 30:9-10 repeats "lest" three times, 30:11-14 repeats four times "There is a generation...," 30:15 says "give, give," 30:19 says "the way" four times, and the Hebrew of 30:21-23 has "under" (תחת) repeated four times.

2. Prov 1:16 essentially equals Isa 59:7, "Their feet run to evil, and they hasten to shed blood."

3. The Prov 30:4 string of rhetorical questions is similar to the string of rhetorical questions in Job 38-41, Isa 10:8-11, 40:12-14, 40:21, etc.

4. "Righteous One" is a designation for God only in Isa 24:16, 53:11 and Prov 21:12.[15]

5. Personification, like the personification of wisdom in Proverbs, was a literary technique of Isaiah also (Isa 24:23, 35:1, 44:23, 55:12, etc.).

6. Isaiah was the only prophet to use the phrase "fear of the LORD" (Isa 11:2-3 and 33:6), a phrase which occurs 24 times in the Bible, including 14 times in Proverbs, and also in Job 28:28.

7. Prov 7:6 indicates that the author's house had a lattice. Only the more affluent homes in Jerusalem had lattices.[16] Isaiah was a favorite of the king, and likely had such a home.

These are verbal connections between Job and Proverbs:

1. Eloah is used for God (41 times in Job, also in Isa 44:8, Prov 30:5 and Psalm 114)

2. "Fear of the LORD is wisdom" (Job 28:28, Prov 1:7 and 9:10)

3. "Hidden treasures" (Job 3:21, Prov 2:4 and Isa 45:3)

4. God "your confidence" (Job 4:6 and Prov 3:26)

5. The search for wisdom in Job 28:12-28 matches the Proverbs introduction, particularly the Prov 8:10, 8:11 and 8:19 comparisons valuing wisdom above gold and jewels.

6. Prov 9:10 and 30:3 refer to God as "Holy One," a phrase from Job 6:10 and one of Isaiah's favorites.

---

[15] The term "Righteous One" in Isa 53:11 applies to the Suffering Servant, an individual identified with Christ in Christian theology.

[16] Jones, *The Complete Guide to the Book of Proverbs*, p. 67

7. Prov 6:16 and Job 5:19 both use the literary device of saying "six…even seven."

Our earlier identification of Isaiah as being the translator of Job means that the ties between Job and Proverbs 1-9 and 30 provide evidence that Isaiah was also involved with these sections of Proverbs.

Contrary arguments can be made. Since Agur's father is also named (Jakeh), this makes it less likely that Agur is a pen name. Isaiah's father was named Amoz (Isa 1:1). Also, in the section by King Lemuel, "bar" is used three times for "son" (Prov 31:2), and this is a significant Aramaism (Hebrew for son would be "ben"). This may in fact point to a non-Israelite king. The Aramaism may also point to Bathsheba, Solomon's mother, who was married to a non-Israelite, Uriah the Hittite.

5.3.1 External Dependencies

Proverbs has few dependencies other than the connections with Job and Isaiah noted earlier. Proverbs does speak about the importance of the Torah in 28:4, 28:7, 28:9 and 29:18. Allusions to the tree of life, from Genesis 2-3, are in Prov 3:18, 11:30 and 15:4. Ecclesiastes seems to draw from Proverbs, as described in section 5.6.1.

5.3.2 Linguistic Analysis

Verbs describing completed past events in Proverbs chapters 1-9 and 30 reflect Classical rather than Early Biblical Hebrew, with a combination of perfect tense and waw + imperfect tense verbs. Examples include the verbs in 3:19-20, 6:1-2, 8:24-30, 9:1-2 and 30:4.[17] The main sections of Proverbs in chapters 10-29 consist mostly of couplets with no references to completed past events, so they cannot be checked to see if the verb usage matches Classical or Early Biblical Hebrew.

---

[17] In 8:29, לא יעברו is a command, not a past event

Older vocabulary includes "she'er" (שאר) for "flesh" in 5:11 and 11:17, "ak" (אך) in 22:16 for "yet" or "surely," "bal" (בל) for "not" in 9:13, 10:30, 12:3, 14:7, 19:23, 22:29, 23:7, 23:35 and 24:23, "zeh" (זה), used as a relative pronoun in 23:22, orakh (ארח) for "way, path" in 2:15, 4:18 and 9:15, "omer" (אמר) for "speech, word" in 1:21, 2:1, 4:5, 5:7, 7:24, 8:8, 15:26, 16:24, 17:27, 19:7, 19:27, 22:21 and 23:12. "Pen" (פן), meaning "lest," appears ten times in Proverbs and appears elsewhere almost exclusively in earlier texts. The older pronoun "anoki" is used two times (24:32 and 30:2), along with the companion "ani," used seven times.

The Septuagint version of the virtuous woman passage of Prov 31:10-31 has verses 25-26 switched. Since this is an acrostic, the verse 25-26 switch is a *pe-ayin* switch, just as is present in Lamentations 2-4. This fact points to the use of an older alphabetical order, making it unlikely that the passage could be post-exilic, since the modern alphabetical order was well-established in the post-exilic era.

The spelling in Proverbs is one of the most modern in the Bible. This is probably due to the activity of the scribes (see Appendix B, section B.1.1).

5.3.3 Oldest Texts
The oldest texts of Proverbs are two Dead Sea Scrolls. Portions of seven chapters are represented.

5.3.4 Conclusion
Proverbs was put into final form around the time of Hezekiah or shortly afterward, around 720-680 B.C. The older core of the book, Proverbs 10-29, consists of selected proverbs from Solomon's time, around 950 B.C. The introduction, Proverbs 1-9, and conclusion, Proverbs 30-31, were added in Hezekiah and Isaiah's time.

5.4 Ruth

The book of Ruth is a short story set during the period of the judges. It describes the struggles and faith of two widows, Naomi and Ruth, Ruth's eventual marriage to Boaz, and how they became ancestors to King David.

Ruth 1:1, setting the story in the days of the judges, indicates that the book post-dates that period. The genealogy reaching to David in 4:17 and 4:22 confirms this.

Jewish tradition expressed in the Talmud assigns authorship of Ruth to Samuel.[18] Although this is not impossible, Ruth 1:1 and 4:7 seem to look back too far for Samuel, who lived close to the time of the events in Ruth. Many modern writers tend to date Ruth in the post-exilic period, where the book is seen as an argument against the policies of Ezra and Nehemiah. The intermarriage of Boaz, a Jewish man, with Ruth, a Moabite woman, is presented favorably in Ruth, whereas in Ezra-Nehemiah it would probably have been forbidden. Also arguing for a later date is the sandal custom (4:7), which is described as being a custom in "former times" in Israel, implying that the book was written so much later that this forgotten custom needed to be explained.

Still, the weight of the evidence favors a composition in the pre-exilic kingdom period. Actually, the mixed marriage argument probably should work in reverse of the way it is described above. The viewpoint of Ezra and Nehemiah came to predominate in post-exilic Israel, which would make it almost impossible for a mixed marriage book like Ruth to make it into the canon of scripture, unless it had already been well established before Ezra-Nehemiah. On the matter of historical accuracy, David sent his parents to Moab (1 Sam 22:3-4) when Saul was trying to kill him, a decision perhaps influenced by his Moabite roots. Ruth and Orpah are apparently not originally Hebrew names, and 1 Chron 2:11 lists Boaz as an ancestor of David. The author of Ruth does

---

[18] Baba Bathra 14b

not seem to invent things he does not know; thus he leaves out the city or location within Moab where Naomi lived. These features favor a historical account rather than a historical novel with a message, and are mildly supportive of an early date.

The sandal handover in 4:7 is clearly related to the levirate marriage law in Deuteronomy 25. Yet the situation in Ruth is different from Deuteronomy in three ways: (1) Ruth's standing is doubtful, since she is a foreigner, (2) Ruth doesn't want to marry the anonymous in-law – she wants to marry Boaz, (3) The anonymous in-law is not a brother-in-law, so the levirate marriage law doesn't apply. Therefore, it was not mandatory for the Israelites to observe the custom in Ruth 4; it was not part of the law, and could have become obsolete at an early date.

5.4.1 Linguistic Analysis

There are a few later Hebrew affinities in Ruth. "Lahen" (להן) in 1:13 means "therefore" in Aramaic, as also in Dan 2:6 and 2:9. The spelling of "Mara" (מרא) in 1:20 matches the Aramaic spelling. The word קום with the meaning "to raise up" or "establish" is used in the piel stem in 4:7, and this appears only elsewhere in exilic or post-exilic texts (Ezek 13:6, Ps 119:28, 119:106; Esth 9:21, 9:27, 9:29, 9:31 and 9:32, although the date of Psalm119 is not certain). The weight of this argument is counterbalanced by the appearance of קום in the hiphil stem in 4:5 and 4:10 with the same meaning. This is the earlier Biblical Hebrew usage (as in Deut 25:7) and the word does not occur with this meaning in later books.

Overall, the weight of linguistic evidence points to a pre-exilic date. The oath form "May YHWH do to me and worse if..." (1:17) is found elsewhere only in Samuel and Kings (2 Sam 3:35; 19:13, 1 Kgs 2:23, 19:2, 20:10 and 2 Kgs 6:31). Other older idioms include "all the city was stirred" (1:19), only elsewhere in 1 Kgs 1:45, Hebrew "ad im" (עד עם) for "until" (2:21), only elsewhere in Gen 24:19 and Isa 30:17, Hebrew "egleh azneka" (אגלה אזנך), literally "uncover the ears" meaning "inform you" in 4:4, elsewhere only 1 Sam 9:15, 20:2, 20:12, 20:13; 22:8, 22:17 and 2 Sam 7:27, and Hebrew "coh" (כה), meaning "here" in 2:8, elsewhere only in Gen 22:5, 31:37, Exod 2:12, Num 11:31, 23:15 and 2 Sam 18:30. The early pronoun "anoki" is used four times (2:10, 2:13, 3:9 and 3:12). The book of Ruth begins (1:1) with a circumstantial clause introduced by ויהי and followed by a waw + imperfect verb, a formulation which is common in Classical Biblical Hebrew but rare in Late Biblical Hebrew. The adverb "bterem" (בטרם), meaning "before" in 3:14, "zulah" (זולה), meaning "except" in 4:4, and the particle "lbilti" (לבלתי), used to negate infinitive verbs (1:13, 2:9 and 3:10), appear almost exclusively in pre-exilic texts. "Pen" (פן), meaning "lest" in 4:6, is also concentrated almost entirely in early texts. Finally, Ruth has one of the oldest spelling patterns in the Bible outside the Torah, with less than 40% of the Hebrew words with a long 'o' sound spelled with a "waw" serving as a vowel letter.[19] David's name is spelled in the early form דוד (4:17 and 4:22), instead of the later form דויד, which is used more than 200 times without exception in the post-exilic books of Chronicles, Ezra, Nehemiah and Zechariah. The linguistic evidence is sufficient for Driver to break from the ranks of the critics and date Ruth before the exile, saying "It seems to the writer that the general beauty and purity of the style of Ruth point more decidedly to the pre-exilic period."[20]

5.4.2 Oldest Texts

The oldest texts of Ruth are four Dead Sea Scrolls: 2Q16, 2Q17, 4Q104 and 4Q105. Portions of all four chapters are represented.

---

[19] Anderson and Forbes, *Spelling in the Hebrew Bible*, p. 161
[20] Driver, *An Introduction to the Literature of the Old Testament*, p. 455

5.4.3 Conclusion

Ruth was probably written early in the days of the united monarchy, around 950 B.C.

5.5 Song of Solomon

Song of Solomon is a love poem. After a one verse introduction, it consists entirely of direct speech, with lines spoken by both the male and female lovers and by a chorus, the "daughters of Jerusalem." Many publications refer to Song of Solomon by the name "Song of Songs," or "Canticles."

Traditionally, authorship of Song of Solomon is attributed to Solomon, mainly due to the introductory verse, "The Song of Songs, which is Solomon's" (1:1). Deviating somewhat is the Talmud, which assigns it to Hezekiah and his company.[21] Most modern scholars date Song of Solomon to the late post-exilic era, primarily due to linguistics.

We believe Song of Solomon falls into the class of an early book that was heavily reworked in the post-exilic period. Other texts in this class are Ecclesiastes and a few of the Book 4 and 5 Psalms. This class of early text with late rewrite is described in Appendix B, section B.1.1. Song of Solomon is assigned to this class because the internal evidence favors an early date, but the linguistic features point to a late date.

Song of Solomon is attributed to Solomon in 1:1. He is mentioned again in 1:5, 3:7, 3:9, 3:11 and 8:11-12. The picture of easy wealth (1:16-17, 3:9-10, 5:13-15 and 8:12) matches Solomon's time. The mention of 60 queens and 80 concubines (6:8) seems to pose no moral or romantic issue for the author – a state of affairs that would seem impossible after Solomon.

The female lover is dark-skinned (1:5-6) and apparently should be identified with the daughter of Pharaoh, with whom Solomon

---

[21] Baba Bathra 15A

formed a marriage alliance (1 Kgs 3:1). Egyptian connections are apparent in Song of Solomon with favorable references to Pharaoh's chariots (1:9). 1 Kgs 10:28-29 says Solomon imported horses and chariots from Egypt. Song 2:13 uses "khanat" (חנט) to describe figs. "Khanat" is an Egyptian term usually applied to embalming and only elsewhere in the Bible when Jacob and Joseph are embalmed in Gen 50:2-3 and 50:26.

Song of Solomon includes 12 place names apparently known by both lovers: En Gedi (1:14), mountains of Bether (2:17), Gilead (4:1), Lebanon (3:9, etc.), Senir and Mount Hermon (4:8), Amana (4:8), Jerusalem (6:14), Tirzah (6:4), Heshbon (7:4), Damascus (7:4), Carmel (7:5) and Baal-hamon (8:11). The northern Israel sites (Gilead, Tirzah, Mount Hermon, Amana and Carmel) were not under Judah's dominion after Solomon, and Damascus was usually the capital of a hostile country. Travel to these sites would have been difficult after Solomon's day. Notably absent from the list is Samaria, which had not been founded in Solomon's day.

Song of Solomon lists numerous trees and plants: henna blossoms (1:14), rose, lily (2:1), apple tree (2:3), fig tree (2:13), an orchard with pomegranates, nard plants, saffron, calamus, cinnamon, trees of frankincense, myrrh and aloes (4:13-14), balsam (5:1), dates (5:11), cedar trees (5:15), nut trees (6:11) and palm trees (7:7). This is a reflection of Solomon's reputation as a naturalist (1 Kgs 4:33).

5.5.1 External Dependencies

Song of Solomon stands largely alone in the Old Testament, with no major dependencies on other books and without lending information to other books. The setting is clearly Solomon's Israel, as described in 1 Kings. Some verbal ties to Proverbs can be seen, as in Song 4:11 with Prov 5:3 saying "lips drip honey," and Song 7:9 with Prov 23:31 saying "wine goes down smoothly." These verbal ties do not seem long enough or numerous enough to draw major conclusions. Ben Sirach says Solomon developed "songs and proverbs and parables" (Sir 47:17), which may refer to Song of Solomon.

5.5.2 Linguistic Analysis

The two most striking features of the linguistics in Song of Solomon are the absence of waw + imperfect conversive verb forms and the repeated use of "shin" as a relative pronoun. Waw + imperfect verb forms occur 14,972 times in the Bible, but are absent in Song of Solomon. This is despite the fact that certain passages in Song of Solomon are past tense narratives (3:1-4, 5:3-7, etc.) that would normally call for the use of waw + imperfect verbs. The "shin" relative pronoun occurs 32 times in Song of Solomon, all in places where Classical Biblical Hebrew usually uses "asher." "Asher," which appears more than 5000 times in the Bible, is in Song of Solomon only once, in the introductory first verse. These linguistic features match the practice of later Hebrew, as the Mishna (200 A.D.) and later writings also avoid the waw + imperfect and replace "asher" with "shin." The Dead Sea Scroll Copper Scroll (3Q15) also shows this use of "shin." However, although these features of Song of Solomon support a post-exilic date of writing, they cannot be used to pin down the date with any precision. This is because the later practice (the common use of "shin" and avoiding waw + imperfect) began as early as the exile (as in Ps 137:8-9), and the earlier practice was still in use when the Dead Sea Scroll Damascus document was written. In other words, between at least a span of 586 – 100 B.C., both practices were in use by some Hebrew writers.

Song of Solomon contains a number of foreign words, including Persian words. Persian words indicate a date after Judea became a province of Persia, after 538 B.C. Persian words include:

1. "Egoz" (אגוז) for "nuts" in 6:11
2. "Nerd" (נרד) for "spikenard" in 1:12 and 4:13-14, a plant from India, probably via Persia

3. "Pardes" (פרדס) for "orchard" (4:13). Some foreign words that name an object can travel with the object, but this doesn't seem to be possible with this word.

Several other foreign words of questionable origin are "carcom" (כרכם) for saffron (4:14), "appiryon" (אפריון) in 3:9 for "portable chair," and "copher" (כפר) for henna in 1:14 and 4:13. Other words only present in other late Hebrew books are "eykakah" (איככה) for "how" in 5:3 (compare Esth 8:6), "gelil" (גליל) for "rod" in 5:14 (compare Esth 1:6), and "shesh" (שש) for "marble" in 5:15 (compare Esth 1:6 and 1 Chron 29:2).

Additional linguistic evidence supports a post-exilic date for Song of Solomon. "Ani" is used ten times in Song of Solomon as a first person singular pronoun, and the older form "anoki" is not used. Use of "ani" includes passages like "I am dark, but lovely" (1:5), a phrase in which earlier Biblical Hebrew would favor "anoki" ("I am <adjective>," as in Gen 3:10). Song 4:4 spells David's name דויד, the longer form used always in post-exilic writing, but almost absent in earlier writing. The particle "shel" (של) is used in 1:6 and 3:7 (only elsewhere in Ecc 8:17). This rare biblical word is common in post-biblical Hebrew and supports a late date.

The spelling in Song of Solomon is generally late, but still shows the early influence of a frequent absence of vowel letters. This is unlike the extra-biblical Dead Sea Scrolls, which use vowel letters whenever possible. An example is the spelling of Jerusalem: ירשלם in Song of Solomon and ירושלים in most of the Dead Sea Scrolls and later Hebrew. This indicates that Song of Solomon is not so late as the Maccabean era.

5.5.3 Oldest Texts

The oldest texts of Song of Solomon are four Dead Sea Scrolls: 4Q106, 4Q107, 4Q108 and 6Q6. Portions of seven chapters are represented. In 4Q106, Song 4:8-6:11 is not missing but absent (apparently intentionally skipped), and in 4Q107, Song 3:5-9 is also not missing but absent.

5.5.4 Conclusion

Song of Solomon was probably originally written at the time of Solomon, around 950 B.C. The language of the book was thoroughly revised in the post-exilic period, around 400 B.C., to reflect the spoken vernacular Hebrew of the time.

5.6 Ecclesiastes

Ecclesiastes is a philosophical wisdom book dealing with the troubles and futility of life. Some publications refer to Ecclesiastes as "Qohelet," for the Hebrew word for "preacher." Traditionally, authorship of Ecclesiastes is attributed to Solomon. The Talmud attributes it to Solomon (Megilla 7a, Shabbat 30) or Hezekiah (Baba Bathra 15a).

Ecc 1:1 and 1:12 identify the author as king in Jerusalem. The reference in 1:1 to "the son of David" could technically apply to any of David's descendents, but it seems likely that Solomon is the king in view, although Solomon is never mentioned by name in the book.

Ecc 2:4-8 speaks of the author's vast wealth, with gold gardens, livestock, slaves and concubines. The picture of wealth is a good fit for Solomon. The author considers himself to be a man of great wisdom (1:16), also a good fit for Solomon. The proverb in Ecc 11:1 takes an analogy from maritime trade, something rare in Israel's history but practiced in Solomon's day (1 Kgs 9:26-28). If the author is Solomon, his words about labor and inheritance may reflect a premonition that his son Rehoboam is likely to squander things (Ecc 2:18-21 and 1 Kgs 12:1-19). Ecc 12:9 says the preacher arranged many proverbs, which certainly could apply to Solomon. We would not assign any significance for dating to the phrase "all who were over Jerusalem before me" (1:16), since if Jebusite kings are included, the list of kings in Jerusalem before Solomon could be very long. Also, a similar phrase is used about Jeroboam (1 Kgs 14:9), who ruled northern Israel immediately after Solomon.

Ecc 3:19-20, 9:5 and 9:10 reflect an absence of theology dealing with resurrection or life after death, a situation consistent with early Old Testament writings but not with later writings (Dan 12:2).

The temple appears to be standing, with sacrificial practices in place when the book was written (5:1 and 8:10). This rules out an exilic date.

Not all the sayings in Ecclesiastes sound natural in Solomon's mouth. The author sometimes speaks of injustice as if he is unable to do anything about it (3:16, 4:1, 5:8, 8:9 and 10:5-7). In places, he speaks about kings as if he were not one of them (4:13 and 8:2-4). Ecc 9:9 has a monogamous ring to it. However, all this may reflect Solomon's attitude toward the end of his life, when he has grown disillusioned and recognizes the limits of power.

Ecc 12:9-14 speaks of the preacher in third person, switching from the first person voice used for most of the book. This may indicate that the passage is an epilogue, but on the other hand, switching voice is not unusual in Biblical poetry.

Overall, the balance of internal evidence favors authorship by Solomon, toward the end of his life, when a certain level of disillusionment had set in.

5.6.1 External Dependencies

There are connections between Proverbs and Ecclesiastes. A "fool" is mentioned 23 times in Ecclesiastes, 76 times in Proverbs, and 46 times elsewhere in the Bible – clearly a disproportionate percentage in these two books by Solomon. Things are compared with one "better" than the other 21 times in Proverbs, 21 times in Ecclesiastes, 2 times in Song of Solomon and 31 times in the rest of the Old Testament. This is also a prominent feature of Solomon's style. Most of the connections between Ecclesiastes and Proverbs are not linguistic, but connections in thought. Some of these are shown below.

1. "Eye satisfied" (Ecc 1:8, 4:8 and Prov 27:20)
2. Laughter and joy (שמחה and שחוק) come to a bad end (Ecc 2:2 and Prov 14:13)
3. Inheritance concerns (Ecc 2:26 and Prov 13:22)
4. Hate as a virtue (Ecc 3:8 and Prov 13:5)
5. Sacrifice of wicked/fools (Ecc 5:1 and Prov 15:8)
6. Hasty before good (Ecc 5:2 and Prov 20:25)
7. Virtue of few words (Ecc 5:2 and Prov 10:19)
8. Many words of a fool (Ecc 5:3 and Prov 15:2)
9. Hasty vows (Ecc 5:5 and Prov 20:25)
10. Working for appetite (Ecc 6:7 and Prov 16:26)
11. Value of a "good name" (Ecc 7:1 and Prov 22:1)
12. Rebuke of the wise (Ecc 7:5, Prov 15:31-32 and 25:12)
13. Bribes (Ecc 7:7, Prov 17:8 and 17:23)
14. Be slow to anger (Ecc 7:9, Prov 14:29 and 16:32)
15. Moderation in good things (Ecc 7:16 and Prov 25:16)
16. Bitterness of being ensnared by an evil woman (Ecc 7:26 and Prov 22:14)
17. Wisdom better than strength (Ecc 9:16, 9:18 and Prov 21:22)
18. Persuading a ruler (Ecc 10:4 and Prov 25:15)
19. Slaves over princes (Ecc 10:7 and Prov 19:10)
20. He who digs a pit may fall into it (Ecc 10:8 and Prov 26:27)
21. Words/lips/mouth of righteous/wise/fools (Ecc 10:12-14, Prov 10:14, 10:31-32 and 18:6-7)

Overall, Ecclesiastes shows no major connection with Old Testament books other than Proverbs, and none show dependencies on it. Ecc 9:14-15, about a great king laying siege to a small city, may be an allusion to 2 Sam 20:16-22. However, the Samuel account, set in David's time, mentions a wise woman, while the Ecclesiastes reference is to a poor wise man. Likewise, Ecc 4:13-16 is reminiscent of the story of Joseph, but the details do not match.

The phrase "under the sun," which occurs 27 times in Ecclesiastes only appears elsewhere in 2 Sam 12:12.

5.6.2 Linguistic Analysis

The linguistic characteristics of Ecclesiastes are quite different from Classical Biblical Hebrew. Some scholars suggest that the linguistics of Ecclesiastes are not necessarily late, but instead are just different from the rest of the Old Testament. Archer states, "The text of Ecclesiastes fits into no known period in the history of the Hebrew language."[22] Most writers, however, understand the linguistics of Ecclesiastes to support a late date of writing.

Ecclesiastes shares the two striking linguistic features of Song of Solomon: the non-use of waw + imperfect verbs and the frequent use of "shin" as a relative pronoun. In Ecclesiastes, there are only three occurrences of waw + imperfect verbs (1:17, 4:1 and 4:7). Instead, Ecclesiastes uses waw + perfect verbs repeatedly to indicate past tense (1:13, 2:5, 2:9, 2:11, 2:12, etc.). This practice matches the later Talmud. Ecclesiastes uses "asher" 67 times and "shin" 51 times, so the replacement of "asher" with "shin" is only partial, unlike Song of Solomon. The name YHWH does not appear in Ecclesiastes.

There are no Greek words in Ecclesiastes. There are two Persian words: Pardes (פרדס) in 2:5 for "park" or "orchard," and pitgam (פתגם) in 8:11 for "sentence" in a legal sense. This argues for a date of writing in the Persian period (538-333 B.C.).

The older pronoun "anoki" is not used, while its companion "ani" appears 28 times. This may hint at a late date. However, the use of "ani" in Ecclesiastes is mostly unique, in that it is used repeatedly in places where it seems unnecessary. In Hebrew, the form of the verb can indicate a first person subject, so using a pronoun with a verb is usually only done for emphasis. Ecc 2:1, for instance, uses "ani" to say "I said..." (אמרתי אני). This use of

---

[22] Archer, *A Survey of the Old Testament Introduction*, p. 465

"ani" would normally indicate that the subject is emphatic ("I myself said…"), but this does not seem to be the intent in Ecclesiastes. The later word for kingdom, "malkut," is used once, in 4:14. Additional linguistic features exist in Ecclesiastes which are unusual, but do not necessarily have anything to say about its date of writing. These include "zoh" (זה) used as a feminine demonstrative pronoun rather than "zot" (זאת) in 2:2, 2:24, 5:15, 5:18, 7:23 and 9:13. Also, masculine plural pronominal suffixes used for feminine nouns occasionally appear, as in 2:6 and 2:10.

Ecclesiastes has many connections to late or post-biblical Hebrew. "Shel" (של), in 8:17 meaning "of the," appears elsewhere in the Bible only in Song of Solomon, but is common in post-biblical Hebrew. Expressions which are in the Bible only in Ecclesiastes, but are present in Aramaic or the Mishna include:

1. "Iy" (אי) meaning "alas" in 10:16
2. "Batal" (בטל) meaning "stand idle" in 12:3
3. "Gumats" (גומץ) meaning "pit" in 10:8
4. "Ben khorim" (בן־חורים) meaning "of nobility" in 10:17
5. "Khush" (יחוש) meaning "enjoy" in 2:25
6. "Khesron" (חסרון) meaning "what is lacking" in 1:15
7. "Yithron" (יתרון) meaning "advantage" or "profit" in 1:3, 2:11, 2:13, 3:9, 5:8, 5:15, 7:12 and 10:10-11
8. "Cavar" (כבר) meaning "already" in 1:10, 2:12, 2:16, 3:15, 4:2, 6:10 and 9:6-7
9. "Milah" (מלאה) meaning "pregnant" in 11:5
10. "Mashak" (משוך) meaning "indulge" in 2:3
11. "Nisken" (יסכן) meaning "be endangered" in 10:9
12. "Ahdenah" (עדנה) meaning "still" in 4:2-3
13. "Ahnin" (ענין) meaning "task" in 2:23, 2:26, 3:10, 4:8, 5:2, 5:13 and 8:16
14. "Pesher" (פשר) meaning "interpretation" in 8:1 (פתרון is used in older Hebrew, as in Gen 40:5)
15. "Teqiph" (תקיף) meaning "the one stronger" in 6:10

16. "Taqan" (תקן) meaning "be straightened" in 1:15, 7:13 and 12:9

Additional expressions in Ecclesiastes matching Late Biblical Hebrew include:

1. "Illu" (אלו) meaning "if even" in 6:6 and Esth 7:4

2. "Bihal" (בהל) meaning "be hasty" in 5:1, 7:9, Esth 2:9 and 2 Chron 35:21

3. "Biken" (בכן) meaning "so then" or "in this" in 8:10 and Esth 4:16

4. "Zeman" (זמן) meaning "appointed time" in 3:1, Neh 2:6, Esth 9:27 and 9:31. Earlier Hebrew usage would have preferred "mo'ehd" (מועד)

5. "Shalat" (שלט) meaning "exercised authority over" or "empower" in 2:19, 5:18, 6:2, 8:9, Ezra 4:20 (Aramaic), 7:24 (Aramaic), Neh 5:15, Esth 9:1 and Ps 119:133 (although Psalm 119 may not be especially late). This word is linked with Aramaic legal documents of the Persian era.

6. "Shavakh" (שבח), meaning "laud" or "praise" is in 4:2, 8:15 and a number of later Psalms.

7. Usage of the qal stem of "ka'as" (כעס) meaning "be angry" in 5:16, 7:9, 2 Chron 16:10, Neh 3:33 and Ezek 16:42.

8. "Natan lev" (נתן with לב) in 7:2, 8:16 and 9:1 is a Late Biblical Hebrew expression for the way a person sets his own heart (1 Chron 22:19, 2 Chron 11:16 and Dan 10:12).

The spelling in Ecclesiastes is, along with Song of Solomon and Esther, among the most modern in the Bible, though not as modern as the Hebrew of the Dead Sea Scrolls.[23] Going against the trend, Ecc 1:1 spells David's name in the older form דוד used primarily in pre-exilic texts. Also, the dual form noun for "two times" is used in 6:6. These are perhaps vestiges of an earlier text of Ecclesiastes.

---

[23] Anderson and Forbes, *Spelling in the Hebrew Bible*, p. 316

5.6.3 Oldest Texts

The oldest texts of Ecclesiastes are two Dead Sea Scrolls: 4Q109 and 4Q110. Portions of four chapters are represented. Scroll 4Q109 has been dated to 175-150 B.C., ruling out any possibility of an exceptionally late date for Ecclesiastes.[24]

5.6.4 Conclusion

Ecclesiastes was probably originally written at the time of Solomon, around 950 B.C. The language of the book was thoroughly revised in the post-exilic period, around 400 B.C., to reflect the spoken vernacular Hebrew of the time.

5.7 Lamentations

Lamentations is a dirge written on the occasion of the destruction of Jerusalem in 586 B.C. The first four chapters take the form of an acrostic, with the first letter of each verse in chapters 1, 2 and 4 using a different letter of the 22-letter Hebrew Alphabet, in alphabetical order. Chapter 3 triples the pattern, using each letter on three consecutive verses, to make 66 verses in the chapter.

5.7.1 Authorship

The traditional understanding of Lamentations is that it was written by Jeremiah shortly after the fall of Jerusalem. An alternate view is that Lamentations was written much later as an imaginative reflection on the fall of Jerusalem for theological purposes.

The Septuagint prefaces the book of Lamentations with the words "And it came to pass, after Israel was lead into captivity, and Jerusalem laid waste, that Jeremiah sat weeping, and lamented this lamentation over Jerusalem and said…". The Vulgate says the same and adds "with a bitter spirit sighing and wailing." The Talmud and Targums also follow this understanding. The

---

[24] Seow, *Ecclesiastes*, p. 6

tradition of Jeremiah's authorship seems probable; the link between Jeremiah and Lamentations is strong. Jeremiah has the sensitive and emotional temperament reflected in Lamentations, and Lam 3:14 and 3:53-55 may refer to events in Jeremiah's life (compare Jer 20:7 and 38:6). Connections between Lamentations and Jeremiah involving ideas include:

1. Allusions to national sin (1:5, 1:8, 3:42, 4:6, 4:22, 5:7 and 5:16), compares with Jer 14:7, 16:10-12, 17:1-3, etc.
2. Guilt specifically of prophets and priests (2:14 and 4:13-15), compares with Jer 2:7-8, 5:31, 14:13 and 23:9-40. The guilt of the prophets works better coming from Jeremiah's mouth than if spoken by anyone else, who would have known of the prophet Jeremiah, a person seemingly innocent.
3. False confidence in allies, sometimes called "lovers" (1:2, 1:19 and 4:17), compares with Jer 2:18, 2:36; 30:14 and 37:5-10.

Additional connections exist in vocabulary and figures of speech:

1. Calling Judah "virgin daughter" or "daughter" (1:15 and 2:13) as in Jer 6:2, 8:21 and 14:7, also "daughter of my people" (2:11, 3:48, 4:3, 4:6 and 4:10) as nine times in Jeremiah (8:11, etc.)
2. Tears in the prophet's eyes (1:16, 2:11, 2:18 and 3:48-49) as in Jer 9:1, 9:18, 13:17 and 14:17
3. "Terror on every side" (2:22) as in Jer 6:25, 20:10, 46:5 and 49:29
4. Women eating their children (2:20 and 4:10) as in Jer 19:9
5. Wormwood (3:15 and 3:19) as in Jer 9:15 and 23:15
6. "Fear and the snare" (3:47) as in Jer 48:43
7. "Kindled a fire" (4:11) as in Jer 11:16, 15:14 and 17:4
8. "Potter's hands" (4:2) as in Jer 18:6

The earlier part of Jeremiah's life was during the time of the Assyrian Empire. The book would likely have been written by someone who had lived during the existence of the Assyrian

Empire, which fell in 612 B.C., because the author of Lamentations remembers it (Lam 5:6). Hostility toward Edom due to their behavior during Jerusalem's fall is also fresh on the author's mind (Lam 4:21-22, see also Ps 137:7).

In opposition to the idea of authorship by Jeremiah, certain words are used repeatedly in Lamentations but not in Jeremiah, such as "Adonai" (אדני), used by itself for "Lord" (1:14, 1:15, 2:1, 2:2, 2:5, 2:18-20, 3:31, 3:36-37 and 3:58), "ahni" (עני) for "affliction" (1:3, 1:7, 1:9, 3:1 and 3:19), "shomem" (שמם) for "desolate" (1:4, 1:13, 1:16, 3:11 and 5:18), "lamo" (למו) for "to them" (1:19, 1:22, 4:10 and 4:15), and the "shin" relative pronoun (2:15-16, 4:9 and 5:18). Also, some of the statements in Lamentations seem to not represent Jeremiah's viewpoint, such as 4:17, hoping for help from Egypt (which Jeremiah never did), or speaking well of the king (4:20). However, in these respects the author of Lamentations is speaking in the plural and representing the view of his people as a whole and not just himself. The vocabulary differences may be due to the fact that Lamentations is a different type of literature than the book of Jeremiah.

5.7.2 External Dependencies

Lamentations is dependent on Deuteronomy, as the following table comparing it with Deuteronomy 28 shows:

1:3 She dwells among the nations, but she has found no rest;	28:65 Among those nations you shall find no rest
1:5a Her adversaries have become her masters	28:44b he shall be the head, and you will be the tail
1:5c Her little ones have gone away as captives before the adversary.	28:32 Your sons and your daughters shall be given to another people
1:6c And they have fled without strength	28:25 you will flee seven ways before them

Before the pursuer.	
1:18c My virgins and my young men have gone into captivity.	28:41 You shall have sons and daughters but they will not be yours, for they will go into captivity.
2:15 All who pass along the way clap their hands in derision at you	28:37 You shall become a horror, a proverb, and a taunt among all the people where the LORD drives you.
2:20b Should women eat their offspring?	28:53 Then you shall eat the offspring of your own body
2:21 On the ground in the streets lie young and old;	28:50b ...who will have no respect for the old, nor show favor to the young.
4:10 The hands of compassionate women boiled their own children;	28:56-57 The refined and delicate woman among you...she will eat them secretly [her children] for lack of anything else
5:2 Our inheritance has been turned over to strangers, our houses to aliens.	28:30b you shall build a house, but you will not live in it
5:5b ...there is no rest for us.	28:65 Among those nations you shall find no rest
5:12b Elders were not respected	28:50b ...who will have no respect for the old

Lam 2:15 appears to be dependent on Ps 48:2 and 50:2. Lam 5:19 is similar to Ps 102:12. We have dated Psalms 48 and 50 prior to Lamentations, and placed Psalm 102 during the exile.

5.7.3 Linguistic Analysis

The acrostic in Lamentations is unusual, because in chapter 1, the letters are in the Modern Hebrew alphabetical order. However, in chapters 2-4, the sixteenth and seventeenth letters, ay*in* and *pe*, are reversed. This reflects an older alphabetical order and makes it unlikely that the book is post-exilic. (See Appendix B, section B.3.2 on the Hebrew alphabet).

The first four chapters of Lamentations are written in the "qinah," or limping meter. This is a rhythm used for dirges in which the second clause, or second part of each line, is shorter than the first. The qinah meter was popular during the exile (Ezek 19:1-7, 26:17-18 and 32:2).

Lamentations and Jeremiah both use "mamlakah" for kingdom rather than the later "melukah." Lam 3:42 uses the form "nakhnu" (נחנו) for "we," rather than the usual "anakhnu" (אנחנו). This is for purposes of the acrostic, since it is the first word of the verse that needs to begin with the Hebrew letter *nun*, but "nakhnu" also appears in the Lachish letters written at almost the same time as Lamentations.[25] Lamentations uses an Aramaic form plural (שוממין) for "desolate" in 1:4, then uses the Hebrew form plural (שוממים) to say the same thing in 1:16.

5.7.4 Oldest Texts

There are four Dead Sea Scrolls of Lamentations: 3Q3, 4Q111, 5Q6 and 5Q7. Portions of all five chapters are represented.

5.7.5 Conclusion

The preponderance of the evidence points to Jeremiah being the author of Lamentations. In the unlikely event Jeremiah is not the author, the same environment and context remain for the book, so in either case the book should be dated shortly after the fall of Jerusalem in 586 B.C.

---

[25] Lachish letter #4 line 10

5.8 Esther

The book of Esther is a short story set during the reign of Ahasuerus, King of Persia. It describes the activities of Esther and Mordechai in saving the Jewish people from a plot to destroy them.

Ahasuerus is usually identified with Xerxes 1 (486-465 B.C.). However, the Septuagint translates Ahasuerus as Artaxerxes, which would make him one of the Persian kings of that name, probably Artaxerxes I (465-424) or Artaxerxes II (404-359). Xerxes 1 is more likely, since the Hebrew spelling for Ahasuerus is closer to the Persian for Xerxes, and because the background for Esther has the Jews in a weak position. After Artaxerxes 1 and Nehemiah, they were substantially stronger. Most of the events in Esther take place in the twelfth year of Xerxes, or about 475 B.C. Esth 1:1 indicates that the book was written after the reign of Xerxes was completed, so the earliest possible date of writing would be 464 B.C.

The author is anonymous. The Talmud attributes authorship to "the men of the Great Synagogue," a group associated with Ezra.[26] This is possible. Less likely is the suggestion of some that Mordechai was the author, probably based on Esth 9:20. The end of the book, Esth 10:2-3, sounds as if it was written after the death of Mordechai. The author of Esther apparently accessed Persian court records (2:23, 6:1 and 10:2). This would make Nehemiah a possible author, since he served the immediate successor to Xerxes.

There are no obvious anachronisms in Esther. Esther is thoroughly Persian in nature, and this argues for a date in the Persian period (538-333 B.C.) rather than the following Greek period.

---

[26] Baba Bathra 15a

5.8.1 External Dependencies

Ben Sirach, written about 185 B.C., provides a list of many notable Old Testament figures, but does not mention anyone from the book of Esther. This argument for a late date, an argument from silence, is not particularly noteworthy, since Ben Sirach also doesn't mention Ezra, Daniel, or a number of other prominent figures.

The earliest clear reference to Esther is 2 Macc 15:37, which mentions the "day of Mordechai." 2 Maccabees was written around 40 B.C.

5.8.2 Linguistic Analysis

The linguistic features in Esther firmly support a date deep within the Persian period. Esther contains at least 10 words of Persian origin, not including proper names. Some of these words were chosen by the author instead of earlier Hebrew synonyms. These words are:

1. "Ahashdarpenim" (אחשדרפנם), meaning "Satraps," a government official, in 3:12, 8:9 and 9:3
2. "Akshtarnim" (אחשתרנים), meaning "royal," in 8:10 and 8:14
3. "Birah" (בירה), meaning "palace" or "fortress," in 1:2, 1:5, 2:3, 2:5, 2:8, 3:15, 8:14, 9:6, 9:11 and 9:12.
3. "Genez" (גנז), meaning "treasury," in 3:9 and 4:7. Earlier Hebrew might have used "otzer" (אצר)
4. "Dat" (דת), meaning "law" in 1:8
5. "Karpas" (כרפס), meaning "cotton" or "fine linen" in 1:6
6. "Kasher" (כשר), meaning "be proper, suitable" in 8:5
7. "Parthmim" (פרתמים), meaning "nobles," in 1:3 and 6:9
8. "Pitgam" (פתגם), meaning "edict," in 1:20
9. "Patshegen" (פתשגן), meaning "copy," in 3:14, 4:8 and 8:13
10. "Ramkim" (רמכים), perhaps meaning "mares," in 8:10.

The Hebrew vocabulary for Esther is also late. The older first person pronoun "anoki" does not appear in Esther, while its companion "ani" appears five times. One of those instances is in Esth 8:5, a usage of the form: "<adjective> ani," a form in which earlier Hebrew prefers "anoki." The older word for kingdom, "mamlakah," is not used, while the newer word, "malkut" appears 26 times. "Zeman" (זמן) is used in place of the earlier "mo'ehd" (מועד) for "appointed time" in Esth 9:27 and 9:31.

Late Akkadian words in Esther are:

1. "Bitan" (ביתן) meaning "palace" in 1:5 and 7:7-8 - earlier Hebrew might have used "heykal" (היכל)
2. "Sharbyt" (שרביט) meaning "scepter" in 4:11, 5:2 and 8:4
3. "Igeret" (אגרת) meaning "letter" in 9:26 and 9:29.

Esther has no Greek words. Esther uses the Babylonian month names adopted after the exile. (Esth 2:16 and 8:9).

The spelling in Esther is late. The only time "Jerusalem" is mentioned in Esther it is with the modern spelling, ירושלים (2:6). This spelling is used only three times out of 667 occurrences in the Bible, but is the usual later spelling in the Dead Sea Scrolls and all post-biblical Hebrew. This is evidence of a late date.

Several linguistic features of Esther reflect Classical Biblical Hebrew rather than Late Biblical Hebrew. These include:

1. Esther always places a cardinal number before the noun (1:1), as in earlier Hebrew. Some Late Biblical Hebrew texts place cardinal numbers after nouns.
2. Esther uses infinitive absolute verbs in an intensifying sense (4:14), a common feature of Classical Biblical Hebrew
3. Leaving the preposition "min" (מן) unassimilated before a noun without an article is sometimes suggested to be a Late Biblical Hebrew feature, but is absent in Esther.
4. Esther uses the waw + imperfect verb form to represent past events, a feature of Classical Biblical Hebrew. The waw + imperfect use includes ויהי to introduce narratives (Esth 1:1).

The Classical Biblical Hebrew features indicate that the linguistic features of Esther, though late, are not uniformly or exceptionally late.

5.8.3 Oldest Texts

There are no copies of Esther in the Dead Sea Scrolls. There are three possible reasons for this: (1) Esther was written too late to be copied at Qumran, (2) Esther was not accepted as canonical by the Qumran community and (3) coincidence. Explanations (2) and (3) seem more likely than (1). In support of (2), Esther never mentions God directly, and may have been perceived as less spiritual than the other Old Testament books. Also, The Qumran Essene community did not list Purim as one of their annual holidays, though they listed all the other biblical holidays, plus three not found in the Bible.[27] In support of (3), several other Old Testament books are attested by just one Dead Sea Scroll, so the fact that one book is not present at all is not surprising – it just happened to be Esther.

Greek translations of Esther are present in the Scheide Papyrii 1 from the third century A.D., Codex Vaticanus (325-350 A.D.) and Codex Sinaiticus (340-350 A.D.). The oldest Hebrew language copy of Esther is in the Aleppo Codex, dated to approximately 925 A.D.

5.8.4 Conclusion

The most likely date for Esther is around 430 B.C., during the governorship of Nehemiah. This date allows time for the death of all the principal characters in Esther, while still retaining the fresh knowledge of the Persian capital and customs, along with the events described in the book. This would also be consistent with

---

[27] VanderKam, *The Dead Sea Scrolls Today*, p. 115

the statement of Josephus that no Old Testament books were written after Artaxerxes.[28]

5.9 Daniel

The story of Daniel is set during the Babylonian exile. It begins with Daniel's introduction to Nebuchadnezzar's court with the first wave of Jewish exiles deported to Babylon in 606 B.C (Dan 1:1), and follows his adventures until shortly after the Persian conquest of 538 B.C. The traditional view of the book assigns authorship to Daniel himself, near in time to the events described. However, the dating of Daniel is very controversial, with the conventional view now being that Daniel was written during the Maccabean period around 165 B.C. This is a discrepancy of over 350 years, and a remarkably late date for an Old Testament book. We will refer to the proposal of a Maccabean date for Daniel as the "Maccabean Hypothesis."

5.9.1 Traditional View

Dan 7:1 can be used to indicate that Daniel wrote at least a portion of the book: "In the first year of Belshazzar king of Babylon Daniel saw a dream and visions in his mind as he lay on his bed; then he wrote the dream down and related the following summary of it." In addition, certain passages from Daniel are written in first person (Dan 8:1, 9:2, 12:4-5, etc.). The internal witness of the book supplies the reasoning behind the traditional understanding that Daniel was written by Daniel toward the end of his life, around 530 B.C.

We believe that the traditional early date for Daniel is correct. Because the alternate view, the Maccabean Hypothesis, is widely accepted today, we will evaluate it closely.

---

[28] Flavius Josephus, *Against Appion*, 1:8. The Artaxerxes mentioned by Josephus is the son of Xerxes, whose reign ended in 424 B.C. We have dated Chronicles, Ezra, and Nehemiah a little later than that.

5.9.2 Evidence for Maccabean Era Authorship of Daniel
Criticism of Daniel began very early. Porphyry, around 300 A.D., wrote *Against the Christians*, alleging Maccabean authorship and a case of "inverted plagiarism" – an obscure author assigning his writing to someone famous. His views were not widely embraced until the 19th century.

English cleric and Hebrew scholar Samuel Driver was influential in support of the Maccabean Hypothesis, and his list of evidence for a late date has been heavily used by subsequent writers. Driver's evidence for the Maccabean Hypothesis includes:[29]

1. In the canon of the Hebrew Bible, Daniel is not included in the prophets, but rather in the writings. The writings are generally assumed to be a later collection than the prophets.

2. Ben Sirach wrote his book around 185 B.C., before the date of Daniel, according to the Maccabean Hypothesis. Ben Sirach chapters 44-50 list a number of famous characters from the Bible, but exclude Daniel. The implication is that Ben Sirach did not include Daniel because he did not know about him.

3. In Daniel, the Chaldeans are synonymous with a caste of wise men, a usage unknown until the post-exilic period.

4. The theology of resurrection, ranks of angels, judgment and Messiah presented in Daniel are late developments in Old Testament history.

5. Daniel suffers from points of historical inaccuracy: Belshazzar is represented as Nebuchadnezzar's son, when in fact they were not blood related. Darius the Mede did not immediately follow on the throne after the fall of Babylon - Cyrus was the ruler.

---

[29] Driver, *An Introduction to the Literature of the Old Testament*, pp. 497ff

6. Dan 9:2 refers specifically to "Jeremiah the prophet" in a collection of books, and cites Jeremiah's prophecy that the exile would last 70 years (Jer 25:11-12 and 29:10). Driver is assuming that it would not be possible for Jeremiah to achieve status as an authoritative book at the time this event occurred, around 538 B.C.

7. The interest of the book culminates in relation to the Jews and the Seleucid ruler Antiochus Epiphanes, who lived in the Maccabean era.

8. Daniel uses many Persian words, even when the setting is in Babylon. Babylonian inscriptions in archeology show no Persian influence.

9. The Aramaic of Daniel is all but identical with Ezra, and is a western Semitic dialect of the type spoken in Palestine. For example, the relative particle in Nineveh and Babylonian inscriptions is "zi," not "di" as in Daniel.

10. The Hebrew of Daniel resembles work not contemporary with Ezekiel, Haggai and Zechariah, but subsequent to Nehemiah - more like Ezra, Chronicles and Esther.

11. Daniel contains three Greek words, implying that the book was written after Alexander the Great conquered the Middle East. Driver sums up the linguistic evidence: "The Persian words presuppose a period after the Persian Empire had been well established: the Greek words *demand*, the Hebrew *supports*, and the Aramaic *permits*, a date *after the conquest of Palestine by Alexander the Great* (332 B.C.)."[30]

The first four points above need only to be addressed briefly, while most of the rest of the evidence can be covered in more depth in the rest of this section. Daniel's exclusion from the prophets may be due to the fact that he did not serve in the normal role of a prophet; he did not speak to the Jewish people as a prophet, but instead spoke to gentiles. Also, the fact that Daniel

---

[30] Driver, *An Introduction to the Literature of the Old Testament*, p. 508

is not now numbered among the prophets does not mean that it was always this way. Jesus refers to him as "Daniel the prophet" (Matt 24:15), as does the Florilegium, a Dead Sea Scroll.[31] Ben Sirach's list of notables also excludes Ezra, Job, Mordechai, Jonathan, most of the good kings and all the Judges except Samuel, so Daniel's absence from this list is a less than compelling argument. As to using the term "Chaldeans" to describe wise men, Dan 1:4 and 9:1 also use Chaldeans in a broader sense. The later books of Baruch (1:2, 6:40), and Judith 5:6-7 do not use Chaldeans in the "wise men" sense either, so there is no real point in saying that the Chaldeans as wise men usage is "late." On the idea that Daniel's theology is late, Isa 26:19 speaks of the resurrection, Zechariah begins with multiple visions and discussions between the author and angels, and certainly neither the Messiah nor the judgment concept is new in Daniel.

5.9.3 Setting for the Book of Daniel

Some aspects of the setting for Daniel argue against the Maccabean Hypothesis. Daniel 1-6 describes a mostly positive relationship between gentile rulers and their Jewish subjects. Daniel and his three friends prosper and are honored by the foreign kings Nebuchadnezzar, Belshazzar and Darius. Daniel expresses respect and affection for two of these foreign kings (Dan 4:19 and 6:21-22). This theme is contrary to the setting for the Maccabean War, in which Jewish subjects violently rebel against oppressive gentile rule.

Daniel and his three friends all received new names in Babylon from their captors, and these names contain the names of pagan deities (Dan 1:7), as shown in Table 5-1.

---

[31] Scroll 4Q174, fragment 1, column 2, line 3

Table 5-1 Pagan Names in Daniel

Hebrew Name	Meaning	Babylonian Name	Meaning
Daniel	My Judge is El	Belteshazzar	Bel protect his life
Hananiah	Grace of YHWH	Shadrach	The command of Aku
Mishael	Who is what El is?	Meshach	Who is what Aku is?
Azariah	YHWH has helped	Abednego	Servant of Nego

Furthermore, the book of Daniel proceeds to use the pagan names of Shadrach, Meshach and Abednego rather than their Hebrew counterparts. It is unlikely that a Jew writing in the midst of the Maccabean war would introduce names containing pagan deities for the heroes of his story. Daniel and his three friends are mentioned in 1 Macc 2:59-60, a Maccabean era work, and in that passage only the Hebrew names are used.

The chief villain of the Maccabean era, Antiochus Epiphanes, is allegedly described in Dan 8:8-12, 9:26-27 and Daniel 11, but he does not destroy the temple, as described in Dan 9:26, and his career does not fit with anything described in Dan 11:39-45. If second century B.C. Jews read Antiochus into these passages of Daniel, they would also realize that Daniel's prophecy was not fulfilled, making Daniel a false prophet. These are elements that would hinder Daniel's acceptance as a book of scripture in the second century B.C.

Daniel repeatedly writes in first person, saying "I, Daniel" in 8:15, 8:27, 9:2, 10:2, 10:7 and 12:5. The sudden emergence of an ancient autobiography would also have aroused suspicion.

5.9.4 What the Author Knew

Contrary to the charge that the author of Daniel knew little about the actual history of the time, the author actually possessed obscure knowledge about Babylonian and Persian geography, politics and culture. This knowledge includes:

1. The knowledge that Babylonian kings could arbitrarily change laws (2:12, 2:46, 3:4-7 and 3:29), but Persian kings could not (6:8, 6:12 and 6:15, compare Esth 1:19 and 8:8).

2. The knowledge that during the Babylonian period Shushan was in the province of Elam and on bank of the river Ulai (8:2). In the later Persian and Greek periods it was in its own province, Susiana.[32]

3. The knowledge that women came to Babylonian royal parties (5:2), unlike in Persia where this was taboo (Esth 1:10-12).

4. The knowledge that Belshazzar (5:1) was co-regent at the time of the fall of Babylon. Belshazzar was co-regent with his father, Nabonidus, which is why he offered to make Daniel *third* ruler in the kingdom (5:29) – third behind him and his father. Herodotus, writing around 450 B.C., did not mention Belshazzar, and 19th century critics did not know about him until the discovery of the Nabonidus Chronicle in 1881. Prior to that discovery, Daniel had been charged with a historical error on this point.

5. The knowledge that Nebuchadnezzar was the builder of new Babylon, as he truthfully brags (4:30).

---

[32] Archer, *A Survey of the Old Testament Introduction*, p. 386, citing Strabo XV:3, 12; XVI:1, 17; Pliny, Natural History VI:27

6. The knowledge that the walls of the palace in Babylon were plastered (Dan 5:5).

7. The method of execution in Dan 3:11 (fire) and Daniel 6 (lions) is appropriate to the cultures. Fire would not have been appropriate in Persia, because fire was sacred in the Zoroastrian religion.

8. In Daniel, reference is made to the "Medes and Persians" (Dan 6:8, 6:12 and 6:15), reflecting the fact that the Median Empire was the older of the two. Later, as the Persians dominated, the order changed to put Persians first, as in Esth 1:3, 1:14, 1:18 and 1:19, (but not 10:2), and in 1 Macc 6:56.

9. The dimensions of the statue in Dan 3:1 (60 cubits by six cubits) hint that the author knew about the Babylonian number system. The Babylonians used a base 60 number system, unlike the modern base 10 number system. See also Ezek 40:5 and 40:14 for perhaps another Babylonian era use of these numbers.

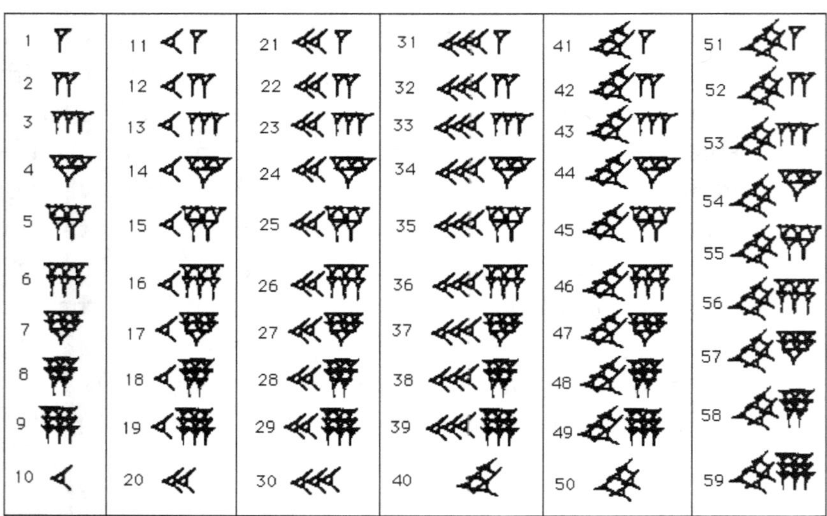

Figure 5-1 Babylonian Base 60 Number System

The fact that the author of Daniel knew these things argues against the Maccabean theory. It is unlikely that a Jew in Israel in 165 B.C. could write accurate history about a situation 1000 miles away and 350 years in the past. The setting in Daniel would be far removed from his culture, an Israelite culture with strong Hellenistic influence. It is more likely that the author lived in the culture about which he wrote.

One point needs to be made to address the critic's contention about Darius the Mede (from #5 on Driver's list above in 5.9.2). When someone wins a military victory he is qualified to become king, and an active tense Hebrew verb (qal stem) is used to indicate that he became king (as in 1 Kgs 16:22). Dan 9:1 says Darius "was made king over the kingdom of the Chaldeans." The verb "was made king" is a Hebrew causative (hophal stem) form, indicating that someone else made him king. Causative forms for making someone king occur in Judg 9:6, 1 Sam 15:35, 1 Kgs 3:7, 2 Kgs 23:34, , Isa 7:6, Jer 37:1, Ezek 17:16 and other passages,[33] all indicating that the individual in question did not have the authority or strength to make himself king, but that he was set on the throne by another. The "another" of Dan 9:1 would by Cyrus, the conqueror of Babylon, who set Darius up as king, or governor, under him. Note that Daniel is familiar with Cyrus as well as Darius (1:21, 6:28 and 10:1). Therefore, the Darius of Daniel is not a confusion with the later Darius 1 of Persia (521-486 B.C.), but an earlier royal person by the same name, serving under Cyrus.

5.9.5 Interpretive Difficulties

The central interpretation of the prophetic passages in Daniel depends on the date the book was written. The book of Daniel repeats a motif of a succession of four great gentile kingdoms. This motif is presented first in Nebuchadnezzar's dream of the statue (2:31-35), then repeated again in Daniel's vision of the four

---

[33] The causative forms in these passages are all hiphil rather than hophal, indicating an active rather than passive verb.

beasts (7:1-14). Each passage explains that the dream/vision represents four successive kingdoms. Nebuchadnezzar's Babylon is explicitly identified as the first kingdom (2:36-38). A casual comparison to secular history quickly suggests the complete sequence: Babylon, Persia, Greece, Rome.

The Maccabean hypothesis requires a different sequence. It requires a climax of evil in the character of Antiochus Epiphanes, the adversary of the Jews in the 170-165 A.D. time frame. He is identified as the "little horn" of Dan 7:8, along with the "little horn" of 8:9, the defiler of the temple in 9:26-27, and he must play some role in the conflicts of chapter 11. Antiochus was the product of the Hellenistic Greek culture, prior to significant Roman influence in the Middle East. Therefore, with a Maccabean era date for Daniel, the four kingdom sequence must end with Greece. No sequence of four major kingdoms beginning with Babylon and ending with Greece is historically possible, but it has been suggested that the author of Daniel did not know his history very well, and was thinking in terms of the sequence: Babylon, Media, Persia, Greece.

The Maccabean Hypothesis sequence of Babylon to Greece has the following problems:

1. Dan 5:28 indicates that Babylon would fall to the Medes and the Persians – not just the Medes – and the word written on the wall, "peres," emphasizes in a historically correct manner the leading role of the Persians.

2. Dan 6:8 and 6:15 indicate that the law in force after the fall of Babylon is the law of the Medes and Persians together. There is no indication that Daniel ever understood there to be a separate Median kingdom after the fall of Babylon.

3. The imagery of the statue supports the Babylon-Rome sequence rather than the Babylon-Greece sequence. The second part of the statue consists of a silver chest and arms (2:32). The two arms can be understood to represent the Medes on one side and the Persians on the other. The

fourth part of the statue consists of iron legs (2:33). The fourth kingdom, "strong as iron," fits well with Rome, which eventually broke into two parts (two legs): an Eastern and a Western Roman Empire. Also, Greek soldiers wore bronze armor and Roman soldiers wore iron armor, matching the metals on the statue (Dan 2:32-33).

4. The imagery of the four beasts supports the Babylon-Rome sequence rather than the Babylon-Greece sequence. The second beast resembles a bear, and it rises up on one side (7:5). This could match the Medo-Persian Empire in which the Persians eventually played the dominant role. The third beast is a winged leopard with four heads (7:6). This could represent Greece, showing the speed with which Greece conquered the known world, and with the four heads indicating how the kingdom of Alexander the Great split into four parts after his death. The fourth beast, "dreadful and terrifying and exceedingly strong," again is a good match with Rome.

5. Daniel's vision of the two beasts in chapter 8 is explained to him: the first beast, a ram with two horns, represents the kings of Media and Persia (8:20). This is just one beast – one kingdom, with the two parts represented by the two horns. This matches the imagery of the second part of the statue in Daniel 2 and the second of the four beasts in Daniel 7. In Dan 8:21-22, the second of the two beasts, the shaggy goat, is interpreted to be Greece. The large horn which is broken is the first king (obviously Alexander the Great), and the four horns which spring up after the first represent the four-fold division of the Greek empire after Alexander. Again, the division into four matches the imagery of the third beast in Dan 7, the winged leopard with four heads. This indicates that Greece is the third kingdom, not the fourth.

6. The Messiah comes to set up God's kingdom in a time associated with the fourth kingdom (2:44 and 7:13-14). For Christians, this idea fits well if the fourth kingdom is Rome. It doesn't work if the fourth kingdom is Greece.

7. Antiochus Epiphanes is identified as the character in Dan 8:23-26 with either sequence of kingdoms, since he is described as arising during the Greek period. However, Antiochus does not fit well the role of lead villain in 9:26-27, because those verses say the "people of the prince who is to come" will destroy Jerusalem and the temple, something neither Antiochus nor any of the Greeks did. The Romans did do this in 70 A.D. Antiochus also does not fit well the role of the little horn of 7:8, because that individual's downfall ushers in the coming of the Messiah (7:13-14), something that did not happen when Antiochus died.

5.9.6 External Dependencies - Inputs

The prayer in Daniel 9 shows that Daniel is familiar with the Law of Moses and the pre-exilic prophets who warned Israel of the consequences of sin. The prayer is reminiscent of the tone and language of Jeremiah. Most specifically, Daniel 9:2 is dependent on Jer 25:11-12 or 29:10. These passages reference the prophecy of Jeremiah that the exile would last for 70 years. Jeremiah wrote letters to the exilic community (Jeremiah 29 contains a letter), so it is not necessary to think that Daniel had before him a full scroll of Jeremiah like we have it today.

5.9.7 External Dependencies - Outputs

Daniel is used by the following external sources:

1. Neh 1:5 is likely borrowed from Dan 9:4, as the phrase "the great and awesome God, who keeps His covenant and lovingkindness for those who love Him and keep His commandments," is repeated exactly. The direction of borrowing is likely Nehemiah borrowing from Daniel, as

Nehemiah's prayer is more advanced in time, since he mentions regathering the redeemed remnant (Neh 1:9-10). Daniel's prayer is one only of confession and request for mercy.

2. Mattathias mentions Daniel and his three friends, Hananiah, Mishael and Azariah in 1 Macc 2:59-60. If this story in 1 Maccabees is true, these words were spoken by Mattathias before the alleged date of writing for Daniel, according to the Maccabean Hypothesis.

3. 1 Macc 1:54 alludes to Dan 9:27. Significantly, Maccabees uses the same wording for "abomination of desolation" as the Septuagint translation of Daniel. 1 Macc 1:54 says "βδέλυγμα ἐρημώσεως," and Dan 9:27 says "βδέλυγμα τῶν ἐρημώσεων". Maccabees is believed to have been written originally in Greek between 135 and 63 B.C. This implies that the Septuagint translation of Daniel may have been available to the author of Maccabees.

4. 1 Enoch 14:18-22 is dependent on the vision of God's throne room in Dan 7:9-10.

5. Jesus cites "the abomination of desolation which was spoken of through Daniel the prophet" in Matt 24:15.

6. The Septuagint translation of Deut 32:8 exhibits a doctrine of national guardian angels found elsewhere only in Daniel 10. It reads, "When the Most High divided the nations, when he separated the sons of Adam, he set the bounds of the nations according to the number of the angels of God."[34] This indicates that it is possible the Septuagint translator of Deuteronomy already was familiar with the text of Daniel.

7. Josephus says that Alexander the Great was shown the prophecies of Daniel: "And when the book of Daniel was showed him, wherein Daniel declared that one of the

---

[34] English translation of the Septuagint by Sir Lancelot C. L. Brenton, 1851

Greeks would destroy the empire of the Persians, he supposed that himself was the person intended."[35] If the account of Josephus is true, it would falsify the Maccabean Hypothesis, since Alexander defeated the Persians in 332 B.C.

8.   Ezekiel, a contemporary of Daniel, mentions him by name in Ezek 14:14, 14:20 and 28:3. Ezekiel's reference to Daniel is likely due to Daniel's high reputation among the exilic Jewish community. It would not, however, be based on the written book of Daniel, since Ezekiel was too soon for that. Some have suggested that Ezekiel would not have placed a contemporary like Daniel in the same company with ancients like Noah and Job, pointing instead to the discovery of an ancient Ugaritic epic involving a man named Daniel. No convincing case can be made, however, and it is not even certain that the Jews knew this Ugaritic epic.

9.   The verbal similarity between the prayers in Baruch 1:15-2:19 and Dan 9:4-19 is strong. The date of Baruch is disputed, with opinions ranging from the sixth century B.C. to the Maccabean period, much like Daniel.

5.9.8 Linguistic Analysis

Daniel is written in Hebrew and Aramaic, with 2:4 – 7:28 in Aramaic. There is no question that the Hebrew linguistic features of Daniel are consistent with other Late Biblical Hebrew. The question is how late – just after the exile, as suggested by the traditional date for Daniel, or in the early Maccabean period, as suggested by the Maccabean Hypothesis? In order to address the Maccabean theory of the authorship of Daniel, we will compare the linguistics of Daniel not just with other biblical books, but also with the non-biblical Dead Sea Scroll writings from Qumran, many of which were written in the Maccabean period. Because the

---

[35] Josephus, *Antiquities of the Jews*, 11:8:5

Qumran scrolls are eccentric in some ways, reflecting scribal practices not present elsewhere, we will also compare Daniel with the later Mishna, which dates to about 200 A.D.

Daniel uses cardinal numbers after the subject (1:5, 1:12, 1:14, 1:15; 9:24-26 and 12:12). Daniel often uses the verb form "waw + cohortative" to indicate past tense action (9:4, 12:8, etc.). These are features associated with Late Biblical Hebrew.

Examples of Late Biblical Hebrew vocabulary in Daniel include:

1. "Hatamid" (התמיד) for "regular sacrifice" in 8:11-13, 11:31 and 12:11, as in the Mishna. Older Hebrew uses "olah hatamid" (עולה התמיד) as in Num 28:10 and even Neh 10:34.

2. "Ahmad" (עמד) meaning "arise, appear, come on the scene" in 8:22-23, 11:2-4, 11:7, 11:20 and 11:31, where earlier Heb would use "qum" (קום). This usage is also in Ps 106:30 and Ezra 2:63 = Neh 7:65.

3. "Ha'ahmid" (העמיד) meaning "appoint, establish" in 11:11 and 11:13-14, as in Neh 7:3 and 1 Chron 15:17.

4. "Abel" (אבל) meaning "however" in 10:7 and 10:21 with adversative force, as in Ezra 10:13, 2 Chron 1:4, etc. In earlier Hebrew it means "surely" (Gen 42:21, 2 Sam 14:5, etc.).

5. "Tsaphir" (צפיר) meaning "he-goat" in 8:5, 8:8 and 8:21, as in 2 Chron 29:21 and Ezra 8:35.

6. "Taqaph" (תקף) meaning "strength" in 11:17, as in Esth 9:23.

7. "Bazah" (בזה) meaning "booty" in 11:24, as in 2 Chron 14:13, Esth 9:10, Neh 3:36 and Ezra 9:7. The older spelling is בז.

8. "Natan lev" (נתן with לב), in Dan 10:12, is a Late Biblical Hebrew expression for the way a person sets his own heart (1 Chron 22:19, 2 Chron 11:16, Ecc 7:2, 8:16 and 9:1).

Daniel uses the older first person pronoun "anoki" once (10:11), as opposed to 23 uses of "ani." "Anoki" was passing out of use in

Daniel's time. Daniel uses only the later "malkut" for "kingdom" and for "reign," in 15 occurrences.

In addition to Late Biblical Hebrew vocabulary, 18 Persian loan-words are present in Daniel, as follows:

1. "Partmim" (פרתמים), meaning "nobles," in 1:3
2. "Patbag" (פתבג), meaning "dainty food," in 1:5, 1:8, 1:13, 1:15, 1:16 and 11:26
3. "Azda" (אזדא), meaning "certainly," in 2:5
4. "Hadam" (הדם), meaning "limb," in 2:5 and 3:29
5. "Dat" (דת), meaning "law," in 2:9, 2:13, 2:15, 6:5 (Aramaic 6:6), 6:8 (Aramaic 6:9), 6:12 (Aramaic 6:13), 6:15 (Aramaic 6:16) and 7:25
6. "Raz" (רז), meaning "secret," in 2:18
7. "Akhashdarpnaya" (אחשדרפניא), meaning government officials or "satraps," in 3:2-3, 3:27 and 6:1-7 (Aramaic 6:2-8)
8. "Adargazra" (אדרגזר), meaning "counselor," in 3:2-3
9. "Detabar" (דתבר), meaning "law-bearer" or "judge," in 3:2
10. "Pitgam" (פתגם), meaning "message" or "order," in 3:16 and 4:14
11. "Hadavar" (הדבר), meaning "lawyer," in 3:24, 3:27, 4:36 (Aramaic 4:33) and 6:7 (Aramaic 6:8)
12. "Sarak" (סרך), meaning "commissioner," in 6:3 (Aramaic 6:4)
13. "Neden" (נדוה), meaning "holder" or "sheath," in 7:15
14. "Apdan" (אפדן), meaning "palace," in 11:45
15. "Sarbel" (סרבל), meaning "mantle," in 3:21 and 3:27
16. "Nebizbah" (נבזבה), meaning "reward," in 2:6 and 5:17
17. "Hamnika" (המניכא), meaning "chain" or "necklace," in 5:7, 5:16 and 5:29
18. "Birah" (בירה), meaning "fortress," in 8:2.

Three Greek words are present in Daniel, the only three indisputably Greek words that appear in the Old Testament:

1. "Qitharos" (קיתרוס), meaning "harp" or "lyre," in 3:5, 3:7, 3:10 and 3:15

2. "Psanterin" (פסנתרין), meaning "psaltery," in 3:5, 3:7, 3:10 and 3:15

3. "Sumponyah" (סומפניה), meaning "bagpipe," in 3:5 and 3:15.

Evaluation of the Greek words is important, since they are often cited as evidence that Daniel was written in or after the Greek period, supporting the Maccabean Hypothesis. However, the level of support is tenuous at best. Note that all three Greek words are names of musical instruments. Since these words are nouns representing objects which travel, they do not necessary imply Greek sovereignty before or during the time of the writer. This is much like an American writer mentioning a pizza – it doesn't imply Italian sovereignty in the writer's home. What it does demonstrate is the existence of cultural interaction between Babylon, Persia and Greece. Greek mercenaries are known to have served in Nebuchadnezzar's army, so connection with the Greek culture existed in sixth century Babylon. Connection of cultures between Greece and Persia was stronger still.

In fact, one could observe that the ratio of Persian to Greek words, 18-3, more strongly argues that the book was written under Persian sovereignty, especially since Daniel uses Persian rather than Greek terms in dealing with government. The book of Ben Sirach and the Dead Sea Scrolls, written under Greek, Maccabean, and Roman sovereignty, seem to leave behind many of the Persian words used in the Persian period. Ben Sirach uses only one of the Persian words found in Late Biblical Hebrew, as noted in Table B-1 in Appendix B (the word רז in Sir 8:18). Some of the Persian words listed above seem to have been unknown to the translator of the Septuagint, who attempted transliterations rather than translations for "partmim" (1:3), "sarbel" (3:21) and "apdan" (11:45). The Septuagint was translated near in time to the Maccabean age. The fact that the translator did not know these words suggests a separation in time somewhat greater than that supported by the Maccabean Hypothesis – the words may have already passed out of use when the translation was made.

In some ways, the Hebrew linguistic features of Daniel point to an older book than the other post-exilic books of Ezra-Nehemiah, Chronicles, Esther, Ecclesiastes and Song of Solomon. Examples include:

1. Daniel uses "mo'ehd" (מועד) for appointed time (8:19, 11:27, 11:29 and 11:35) rather than the later "zeman" (זמן) used in Esther, Nehemiah and Ecclesiastes.

2. Dan 10:4 refers to the month by its number, "first month," rather than its name. This practice of referring to a month by its number starts in Genesis and continues through the exile, including Chronicles and Ezra. Nehemiah, Esther and (usually) Zechariah began a practice of referring to a month by both number and name, and by the time of the Maccabees the name of the month is usually given (16 times out of 21 in the Apocrypha), and the number of the month usually is not. The Elephantine papyri Passover Letter of 419-418 B.C. also names the months.[36] Thus, Daniel's practice is more consistent with the bulk of the Old Testament period than with the Maccabean period.

3. Daniel follows the practice of Classical Biblical Hebrew in using the waw + imperfect verb form to represent past tense action. This is true throughout the Hebrew section of the book. For example, in the first chapter of Daniel, there are 21 waw + imperfect verb forms. In Ecclesiastes and Qumran Hebrew, waw + imperfect verbs serving a past tense function are not as common, and in Song of Solomon and some of the Qumran scrolls they are non-existent. Daniel also uses the common Classical Biblical Hebrew practice of starting what in English would be considered a narrative paragraph with the word ויהי (8:15), meaning

---

[36] Elephantine Papyri Passover Letter, Lines 5 and 8, Quit Claim after Divorce Letter, line 1, Petition to Authorize Temple Reconstruction letter, Lines 4 and 30

"and it was." This is rare in Late Biblical Hebrew, non-existent in Ben Sirach and nearly non-existent in Qumran Hebrew. In this respect, Daniel is linguistically earlier than most Late Biblical Hebrew. Waw + imperfect verbs representing past tense actions pass out of usage by the time of the writing of the Mishna.

4. The particle "lbilti" (לבלתי), used to negate infinitive verbs (Dan 9:11), is rare in post-exilic texts. Later biblical texts adopt "eyn" (אין) for this usage, a practice that continues in Ben Sirach and in the Dead Sea Scrolls.

5. The relative pronoun "asher" (אשר), meaning "that," "which," or "where," is used 47 times in the Hebrew portion of Daniel. 47 uses in 6 chapters are not unusual, as אשר is one of the most common words in Biblical Hebrew. By the time the Mishna was written, "asher" is rarely used, being almost completely replaced by the short form of the "shin" (ש) relative pronoun prefixed to the following word. The beginning of this trend is again present in Ecclesiastes and Song of Solomon, but not Daniel. The non-biblical Qumran scrolls do use "asher," though none so frequently as Daniel. The Qumran copper scroll (3Q15) uses "shin" for a relative pronoun like the Mishna.

6. Daniel's phrasing is similar in places to that of his contemporary, Ezekiel. Daniel is addressed with the phrase "son of man" (בן־אדם) in 8:17. This phrase is applied to a specific person in the Old Testament only in the case of Ezekiel, who uses it 93 times, and in Daniel. Daniel and Ezekiel both use variations on "the time of the end" (עת קץ) in Dan 8:17, 11:35, 11:40 and 12:4, and Ezek 21:25 (Heb 21:30), 21:29 (Heb 21:34) and 35:5. Daniel calls Israel "the beauteous land" (8:9 and 11:41), while Ezekiel calls it "the beauty of all lands" (Ezek 20:6). Both phrases have the ring of an exile longing for home.

Evaluating the Aramaic of Daniel is difficult, since Ezra is the only other biblical book with significant Aramaic content for comparison. One helpful source for comparison is the Elephantine papyri, several archives of Aramaic documents from a Jewish community living in Egypt between 495 and 399 B.C. The Aramaic of Daniel can also be compared with the Aramaic from some Dead Sea Scrolls that are written in that language.

The Aramaic sections of Daniel do show some connections with the Dead Sea Scrolls. Several of the Dead Sea Scrolls match Daniel in the frequent use of I, <name>, which appears in the Aramaic portion of Daniel in 7:15, and then more frequently in the Hebrew sections of Daniel.[37] The Genesis Apocryphon and the book of Enoch, written in Aramaic, also have "watchers" (עירין), as in Dan 4:17 (Aramaic 4:14).[38]

In general, the Aramaic of Daniel is similar to the Aramaic of Ezra, a book written near 400 B.C. Daniel's Aramaic has also been judged to be close to that of the Elephantine papyri. In fairness to Driver, his widely quoted views on Daniel were written before the publication of the Elephantine papyri, and he did not live to see the discovery of the Dead Sea Scrolls. After the discovery of the Elephantine papyri, Driver may have softened his view on the Aramaic of Daniel. In a letter to the *Guardian* on Nov 6, 1907, he admits that the Aramaic spoken in Egypt in 408 B.C. "bears many points of resemblance to that found in the Old Testament – in Ezra, Daniel and Jer 10:11."[39] Kitchen also indicates that the Aramaic of Daniel is similar to the Aramaic of the Elephantine papyri.[40]

---

[37] As in 1QApGen, Genesis Apocryphon, column 5 line 26 and many other instances.

[38] 1QApGen, Genesis Apocryphon, column 7 line 2. Also in 4Q202 Aramaic Enoch, column 4 line 6

[39] McDowell, *Daniel in the Critics Den*, p. 88

[40] Patterson, *Introduction of the Old Testament*, p. 1125, citing K. A. Kitchen, *Notes on Some Problems in the Book of Daniel*, pp. 35ff

One way in which the Aramaic of Daniel stands apart is in the usage of a "hophal" stem for passive, causative verbs in 4:36 (Aramaic 4:33), 5:13, 5:15, 5:20, 6:24, 7:4 and 7:11. This stem is not present in the Aramaic of Ezra, and is rare or non-existent in Qumran. The "hophal" stem occurs in Hebrew also with the same sense, and is used by the author of Daniel in 9:1 and 12:11. This is an unsurprising indication that the Aramaic of Daniel is Hebrew-influenced.

There are some evidences that the Aramaic of Daniel is old. The preposition ל before a king's name to indicate dates (Dan 7:1) may not have survived past the fifth century B.C. This convention is not used in the Elephantine papyri.[41] Dan 5:3 spells "drank" ואשתיו. The Genesis Apocryphon does not use this spelling, deleting the א.[42] This choice of spelling of this word in Daniel is identified as a mark of eastern Aramaic (written from Mesopotamia), while the spelling from the Genesis Apocryphon is identified with western Aramaic (written in Israel). Rosenthal contends that the kind of Aramaic used in Daniel was that which grew up in the courts and chancelleries from the seventh century B.C. and later, and subsequently became widespread in the Middle East.[43]

We have indicated elsewhere that spelling practices in general do not comprise a strong argument for dating books of the Bible. However, the reason for the weakness of the argument is the likelihood that scribes who copied the Bible, at least up until some point around the exile, updated the older spellings to add vowel

---

[41] Elephantine Papyri Passover Letter says in line 5, "the fifth year of King Darius". The Quit Claim after Divorce Letter says in line 1, "the 25th year of King Artaxerxes". The Petition to Authorize Temple Reconstruction letter has similar wording in line 4, 19, 21 and 30. A four line Aramaic tax receipt on a potsherd dated 355 B.C. has similar wording. Aramaic readings are from K.C. Hanson's collection of West Semitic Documents at
http://www.kchanson.com/ANCDOCS/westsem/westsem.html, June 7, 2005.
[42] 1QGenApp, Genesis Apocryphon, column 12 line 15
[43] Patterson, *Introduction of the Old Testament*, p. 1125, citing Rosenthal, *Die Aramaistische Forschung* (1939) pp. 66ff

letters. In doing this, they masked any evidence for an early date. In the case of Daniel, the spelling patterns provide an entirely opposite problem for the Maccabean Hypothesis. The problem is that the spelling practice of Daniel appears to be older than was current in the Maccabean era. This leaves scribal practice completely out of the argument (unless one makes the supposition that the scribes actually went in reverse, taking modern spellings and replacing them with ancient ones – an idea we believe it is safe to discount).

The difference between the spelling in Daniel and the spelling prevalent in the Maccabean era can be shown by comparing Daniel with the non-biblical Dead Sea Scrolls. Daniel exhibits a relatively old spelling pattern, with 49.2% of the Hebrew words with a long 'o' sound using the vowel letter "waw" (ו).[44] The Dead Sea Scroll spelling practice is consistently later. These are differences in the spellings of certain important words:

1. Daniel spells the title of God, "Elohim," as אלהים, consistent with other Old Testament practice. The non-biblical Dead Sea Scrolls prefer the short form "El" (אל) for God, but when they do use "Elohim" the spelling is usually different: אלוהים.

2. Daniel spells "Jerusalem" as ירושלם (Dan 1:1, 9:2, etc.), consistent with Old Testament practice, which uses that spelling 664 out of 667 times. Three times, in mostly late texts (Jer 26:18, Esth 2:6 and 2 Chron 25:1) the spelling is ירושלים. This later spelling is usually used in the Dead Sea Scrolls, and is used consistently in the Mishna and in later Hebrew.

3. Daniel spells "Moses" as משא (Dan 9:11 and 9:13), consistent with the rest of the Old Testament, while the Dead Sea Scrolls usually use מושא.

---

[44] Anderson and Forbes, *Spelling in the Hebrew Bible*, p. 162

4. Daniel spells "sanctuary" as קדש (Dan 9:26), while the Dead Sea Scrolls usually use קודש.

Spelling differences extend beyond just important words into common everyday words. For example:

1. Daniel spells the word for "all" as כל (1:15, 1:17, etc.), while the Dead Sea Scrolls use both כל and כול with roughly equal frequency.
2. Daniel usually spells "and he came" as ויבא (Dan 8:6, 8:17), while the Dead Sea Scrolls usually use ויבוא.
3. Daniel spells the word for "to stand" as לעמד (1:4, etc.), while the Dead Sea Scrolls usually use לעמוד.

Many more examples could be provided, since most words with a long 'o' sound are affected. Of course, the non-biblical Dead Sea Scrolls are an eclectic group, and some of the scrolls use older spelling patterns than others. However, Daniel appears to have an older spelling pattern than any of the Dead Sea Scrolls that are long enough to evaluate.[45]

Ben Sirach can be reliably dated close to 185 B.C., and it is unusual in that it exhibits an earlier spelling practice than some biblical books, and certainly shows an earlier spelling practice than the Dead Sea Scrolls. However, Daniel appears to have an older spelling practice than Ben Sirach as well. For example:

1. Daniel spells the participle meaning "giving" as נתן (Dan 1:16), while Ben Sirach uses נותן (Sir 7:20, 50:28, 51:26 and 51:30).
2. Daniel spells the word for dreams חלמות (1:17), while Ben Sirach uses חלומות (31:1).
3. Both Daniel and Ben Sirach use the phrase "he will not stand," with Daniel spelling "stand" יעמד (Dan 11:25) and Ben Sirach spelling it יעמוד (Sir 6:8).

---

[45] Some of the Dead Sea Scrolls are fragments containing only a sentence or two, therefore being too short to evaluate. In general, works like the Damascus Document and Jubilees have older spellings than most Dead Sea Scrolls, but still appear to be more modern than Daniel.

Therefore we conclude that the linguistic features of Daniel are consistent with Persian period Late Biblical Hebrew. They are not consistent with Greek or Maccabean era writing as expressed in Ben Sirach, the Dead Sea Scrolls, or later Hebrew.

5.9.9 Oldest Texts

The oldest texts of Daniel are eight Dead Sea Scrolls. Portions of all chapters except for chapter 12 are represented. The scrolls show the transition from Hebrew to Aramaic and back. Table 5-2 lists the Dead Sea Scroll Daniel manuscripts and the date they were copied, if known.

Table 5-2 Dead Sea Scroll Daniel Manuscripts

Item	Number	Content Range	Date Copied
1	1Q71	Portions of 1:10 to 2:6	50-68 A.D.
2	1Q72	3:22-30	50-68 A.D.
3	4Q112	Portions of 1:16 to 11:16	50 B.C.
4	4Q113	Portions of 5:10 to 8:16	50-68 A.D.
5	4Q114	10:5 to 11:29	Late 2nd c. B.C.
6	4Q115	3:5 to 7:23	
7	4Q116	Portions of chapter 9	
8	6Q7	8:16 to 11:38	50-68 A.D.

The Dead Sea Scrolls also contain a work related to Daniel titled the Prayer of Nabonidus (4Q242), dated to 75-50 B.C.[46], along with possibly related scrolls 4Q243-245. Extra-biblical texts from the Dead Sea Scrolls that identify Daniel as an authoritative source are the Florilegium (4Q174), dated to 50 A.D., and the Melchizedek Text (11Q13). The Florilegium refers specifically to "the book of

---

[46] VanderKam, *The Dead Sea Scrolls Today*, p. 43

Daniel the prophet,"[47] and the Melchizedek Text quotes from Dan 9:25.[48]

The Dead Sea Scrolls cannot be used to prove a date of writing in the sixth century B.C. – they are too late for that. However, they are near in time to the proposed Maccabean era date for Daniel, and can offer some evidence against such a date. First, the number of Daniel Dead Sea Scrolls, eight, is higher than all the other Old Testament books outside of the Torah, Psalms and Isaiah. Second, multiple extra-biblical Dead Sea Scrolls, as listed above, treat Daniel as an authoritative source. These facts show that the book of Daniel was considered to be a canonical book of scripture by the Qumran community. Because references to Daniel are present in works developed outside of Qumran, such as 1 Maccabees, written prior to 60 B.C., it is safe to say that Daniel was accepted as a scriptural book by the Jewish community in general in the first century B.C. Third, scroll 4Q114 dates to the late second century B.C., only 50 years or so after the original book was allegedly written. The ramifications are significant: it is almost axiomatic that a certain amount of time is required for a book to be accepted as scripture. By any measure, Daniel would have to have been placed on an extremely fast track to be accepted so quickly. This raises the question: is there anything special about Daniel that would put it on such a fast-track to nation-wide acceptance as scripture? Some may suggest that Daniel's themes conform closely to the Maccabean era, encouraging rapid acceptance, but as we have described in section 5.9.3 above, a number of elements of Daniel would have been problematic in this era.

According to Eugene Ulrich, who published scrolls 4Q112 and 4Q113, these two scrolls are not proto-Masoretic texts; they reflect a different textual tradition.[49] This indicates that at the time these scrolls were written, more than one family of Daniel texts had

---

[47] Scroll 4Q174, fragment 1, column 2, line 3

[48] Scroll 11Q13, column 2 line 17-18

[49] Ulrich, *The Dead Sea Scrolls and the Origins of the Bible*, p. 162

already been established. Time is required for the development of a different textual tradition. Does the Dead Sea Scroll evidence allow sufficient time?

The evidence from the Dead Sea Scrolls argues against the Maccabean Hypothesis.

5.9.10 Conclusion

Daniel was written around 530 B.C. The book was put into its current form near the end or shortly after the end of Daniel's life. The book may have been written entirely by Daniel, or it may have been put into final form after his life using his memoirs, as is suggested by the combination of third person narrative and first person writing that is present in the book.

5.10 Ezra

The books of Ezra and Nehemiah are combined into one book in the Hebrew canon. They were regarded as one book by the Talmud, Josephus and the earlier editions of the Septuagint. The books were divided in later editions of the Septuagint and in the Vulgate. The number of the books in the Hebrew Old Testament at one time was counted as 22, matching the number of letters in the Hebrew alphabet.[50] The desire to make the number of books in the Bible match the number of letters in the alphabet may have played a role in keeping Ezra and Nehemiah together as one book in the Hebrew canon.

Whether the books of Ezra and Nehemiah were originally combined as one book is open to debate. Both books share a

---

[50] Flavius Josephus, *Against Appion*, 1:8. The number 22 consisted of (1) Genesis, (2) Exodus, (3) Leviticus, (4) Numbers, (5) Deuteronomy, (6) Joshua, (7) Judges and Ruth combined, (8) Samuel, (9) Kings, (10) Isaiah, (11) Jeremiah and Lamentations combined, (12) Ezekiel, (13) the twelve minor prophets combined into one book, (14) Psalms, (15) Job, (16) Proverbs, (17) Song of Solomon, (18) Ecclesiastes, (19) Esther, (20) Daniel, (21) Ezra and Nehemiah combined, and (22) Chronicles.

common setting and related themes. Ezra, the priest and scribe, appears in both books. The book of Ezra deals with the return and accomplishments of Zerubbabel and Ezra, while the book of Nehemiah describes Nehemiah's efforts to rebuild the walls of Jerusalem amid regional opposition, and to reform Judean society. Certain possible literary patterns, such as the one shown below, have been discerned that may hint at a unity of the two books.[51]

Ezra 1-2 Zerubbabel's return
Ezra 3-6 Zerubbabel's accomplishments
Ezra 7-8 Ezra's return
Ezra 9-10 Ezra's accomplishments
Neh 1-2 Nehemiah's return
Neh 3:1-7:3 Nehemiah's accomplishments
Neh 7:4-13:31Final reforms and lists.

Some facts argue against the unity of the two books. For one thing, the second chapter of Ezra is duplicated in Neh 7:6-73 – an unlikely occurrence in a single work. Also, parts of Nehemiah are written in first person, as coming from the mouth of Nehemiah himself, while parts of Ezra are also in first person, as coming from the mouth of Ezra. Regardless of whether the two books were originally together or separate, the setting and background of both is so close that they should be dated together.

The careers of Ezra and Nehemiah overlapped (Neh 8:1-13) and the setting for Nehemiah can be reliably dated in reference to the Persian King List provided earlier in Table 2-6. It begins in the 20th year of Artaxerxes I,[52] king of Persia (Neh. 2:1), which was 445 B.C. The story continues at least to the 32nd year of Artaxerxes, 433 B.C. (Neh 5:14 and 13:6), and probably a little past that. This

---

[51] The structure is from Dorsey, *The Literary Structure of the Bible*, p. 160

[52] Artaxerxes II of Persia began his reign in 405 B.C. We can know that the Artaxerxes of Nehemiah is Artaxerxes I (465-424) due to an Elephantine papyrus (Cowley #30) dated to 407 B.C. that mentions the sons of Sanballat, the governor of Samaria, and adversary of Nehemiah. See Yamauchi, *Persia and the Bible*, p. 242

would mean the Artaxerxes of Ezra 7:1-8 and 4:7 is also Artaxerxes 1, and that Ezra's arrival in Jerusalem "in the seventh year of the king" (Ezra 7:8) was in 458 or 457 B.C.. It would also make the Ahasuerus of Ezra 4:6 the same king who appears in Esther, Xerxes I (486-465 B.C.), the immediate predecessor to Artaxerxes I. The Darius mentioned in Ezra 4:5 and 4:24 would be Darius I, who ruled from 521 to 486 B.C. This can be confirmed by the sequence of Ezra 6:14: Cyrus, Darius, Artaxerxes, and the fact that Ezra's journey began "after these things, in the reign of Artaxerxes" (7:1).

The narrative pattern in Ezra is similar to the New Testament book of Acts, in which the earlier part of the book is in third person (Acts 1:1-16:9 and Ezra 1-6), then a switch to first person occurs as the author (Ezra in Ezra, Luke in Acts) joins the story. However, unlike Acts, Ezra continues in first person only for chapters 7-9, then the last chapter of Ezra switches back to third person.

Because the book of Ezra picks up where Chronicles ends, it is possible that the individual who put Ezra in final form intended Ezra to be a continuation of the story. The author of Ezra may also be the same individual who wrote Chronicles.

5.10.1 External Dependencies

Ezra is late enough that it can look back on most of the Old Testament. Ezra makes references to books as late as the post-exilic prophets Haggai and Zechariah (Ezra 5:1). The proclamation of Cyrus that begins the book of Ezra (1:1-4) repeats and expands on the ending of 2 Chron 36:23. Since both books are referencing a specific proclamation of the king, this does not necessarily show a connection between Ezra and Chronicles. However, the same verse (1:1) mentions that this was done to fulfill the prophecy of Jeremiah, a clear reference to Jer 25:12 and 29:10. Specific references are also made to the written Law of Moses (3:2). Ezra 3:11

repeats a common phrase from some of the later Psalms: "For He is good, for His mercy endures forever" (100:5, 106:1, 107:1, etc.).

No other Old Testament books make any clear reference to Ezra, although as mentioned above, Ezra 2 and Nehemiah 7 repeat the same records.

5.10.2 Linguistic Analysis

The Hebrew sections of Ezra are representative of Late Biblical Hebrew. Ezra 8:15 places a cardinal number after a noun, a feature found only in late books. Ezra uses the Babylonian month names which came into use only after the exile (6:15). The phrase "ihr and ihr" (עיר ועיר) in 10:14, meaning "this one and that one" (each city), is a predominately post-exilic usage. Negation of an infinitive verb with "eyn" (אין) rather than "lbilti" (לבלתי), as in 9:15, is a late feature. "Hue" (הוא) precedes a personal name only in post-exilic books and means "the same": הוא עזרא "the same Ezra" (7:6).[53] Ezra uses as one of its names for God, "God of Heaven," a title taken from the proclamation of Cyrus in 2 Chron 36:23, but not used without being prefixed by YHWH in any pre-exilic literature. "God of heaven" appears eight times in Ezra, four times in Nehemiah, four times in Daniel, once in Psalm 136, and also in the apocryphal books of Judith, 1 Maccabees and Tobit.

Ezra's origin in the Persian period can be further demonstrated by the Persian words in the book:

1. "Nishtwan" (נשתון), meaning "letter," in Ezra 4:7 and 7:11
2. "Darics" (דרכמונים), a unit of money, in 2:69
3. "Akhashdarpnim" (אחשדרפני), meaning "satraps," in 8:36
4. "Dat" (דת), for "law" or "precept," in 8:36
5. "Tirshatha" (תרשתא), for "Persian governor," in 2:63
6. "Adrazda" (אדרזדא), for "correctly," in 7:23 (Aramaic section)

---

[53] Waltke and O'Connor, *An Introduction to Biblical Hebrew Syntax*, p. 301

7. "Asparna" (אספרנא), for "thoroughly," in 5:8, 6:8, 6:12, 6:13, 7:17, 7:21, 7:26

Ezra 4:8-6:18 and 7:12-26 are written in Aramaic rather than Hebrew. The Aramaic of Ezra is "the imperial Aramaic characteristic of the age in which the book purported to be written, and consonant with it in matters of language and style."[54]

Spelling in Ezra is not especially late (see Table B.2 in Appendix B). David's name, however, is spelled in the later form דויד in all three occurrences.

5.10.3 Oldest Texts
One Dead Sea Scroll (4Q117) contains parts of Ezra 4 and 5.

5.10.4 Conclusion
Ezra and Nehemiah were placed in final form by a chronicler who incorporated their memoirs. Ezra's memoirs consist of Ezra 7-9.This was done shortly after Ezra's life, around 390 B.C., and may have been done by the author of Chronicles.

5.11 Nehemiah
The book of Nehemiah focuses on the title character, who is authorized by the king of Persia to return to Jerusalem and rebuild its walls. The book details the efforts to rebuild the walls, amid external opposition, and to execute other reforms. The books of Ezra and Nehemiah are combined into one book in the Hebrew canon (see section 5.10).

The story of Nehemiah begins in the 20th year of Artaxerxes I, king of Persia (Neh. 2:1), which can be reliably dated to 445 B.C. The story continues at least to the 32nd year of Artaxerxes, 433 B.C. (Neh 5:14 and 13:6), and probably a little past that.

Since much of Nehemiah is written in first person in a manner which would seem to exclude the possibility of it being written by

---

[54] Patterson, *Introduction to the Old Testament*, p. 1141, citing W. F. Albright in H. C. Alleman and E. E. Flack, *Old Testament Commentary*, p. 154

anyone else ("remember me, O my God, for good" – Neh. 13:31), the writing of the parts that are in first person can be dated with confidence between 433 B.C. and the end of Nehemiah's life, probably in the range of 433-400 B.C. The end of the book mentions Nehemiah in third person, looking back on his life, so the book apparently consists of the memoirs of Nehemiah, collected and finalized by a later editor. The appearance of Ezra in the book, along with the close connection between the books of Ezra and Nehemiah, indicate that the two books should be dated to the same period.

One dating problem appears in Neh 12:11, where Jaddua, three generations down from Eliashib, is named. Jaddua was high priest from 351-331 B.C., according to Josephus (Antiquities VI, 7, 2; XI, 8, 5). However, Josephus says Jaddua met Sanballat, the governor of Samaria and contemporary of Nehemiah's, but their lives did not overlap in time, so this is not possible. The historicity of Sanballat is confirmed by an Elephantine Papyri letter that mentions his name.[55] There are several possible explanations for the Josephus passage: there could have been more than one Jaddua, or more than one Sanballat, or Josephus could have simply confused the characters. This passage of Josephus should probably be set aside in dating the book.

More meaningful to note is that Eliashib was high priest when Nehemiah began his work (Neh 3:1) in 445 B.C., and that his genealogy is taken down to Jaddua, his great-grandson, and then his genealogy stops. The three generations are mentioned again in 12:22. This fact implies that the book of Nehemiah was written during the life of Jaddua, three generations after 445 B.C. Since Eliashib was likely to be an older man when he was the high priest, this would take the date of writing for the book down to near 400 B.C. This would make the Darius the Persian of Neh 12:22 Darius II, who reigned from 423-405 B.C. Since 11:22 seems

---

[55] Elephantine Papyri Petition to Authorize Temple Reconstruction letter, line 29

to look back on the reign of Darius II, this implies that the book must have been written after 405 B.C. This gives a rather narrow range for the date of writing: after 405 B.C. and during the life of the great-grandson of a man who was not young in 445 B.C. A date around 390 B.C. seems most likely. Persia eventually had a third king named Darius, who lived from 336-330 B.C. The author was unaware of this third (future) Darius, or he would have worded 12:22 to be more specific.

Two additional verses indicate that the book was placed in final form after the life of Nehemiah and Ezra. These are Neh 12:26, which looks back on the "days of Nehemiah the governor and Ezra the priest and scribe," and Neh 12:47 which looks back on the "days of Zerubbabel and Nehemiah." This implies a date of writing after those days had past. Since most of Nehemiah is in first person, the likely conclusion is that an editor collated Nehemiah's memoirs, adding to them a few records to form the book as it exists today.

5.11.1 External Dependencies

Nehemiah is dependent on the Torah. This is true in the case of specific laws that show not just knowledge of the laws but also a verbal connection (Neh 13:1-2 and Deut 23:3-5). The reference to Solomon in Neh 13:26 seems to be dependent on knowledge of the material in 1 Kings. The reference to Kiriath-arba instead of Hebron in Neh 11:25 seems to imply knowledge of the earlier books (Genesis, Numbers, Joshua and Judges) that equated the two. The prayer of confession in Neh 9:5-37 reviews much of the Old Testament.

The second chapter of Ezra is repeated in Neh 7:6-73. Both books were written at essentially the same time, and show a close connection in multiple ways. Excepting Ezra, Nehemiah was written late enough such that no other Old Testament books make any clear reference to it. Ben Sirach (Sir 49:13) mentions Nehemiah and his project in rebuilding the walls of Jerusalem.

5.11.2 Linguistic Analysis

The linguistic features of Nehemiah are representative of Late Biblical Hebrew. Nehemiah sometimes places cardinal numbers after the noun (2:11 and 5:14), a late feature. The phrase "ahm and ahm" (עם ועם), meaning "this one and that one" (each people in 13:24), is a predominately post-exilic usage. The later word "zeman" (זמן) is used in place of the earlier "mo'ehd" (מועד) for "appointed time" in 2:6.

Nehemiah uses the Babylonian month names that were adopted after the exile (1:1, 2:1 and 6:15). Nehemiah uses the following Persian words:

1. "Darics" (דרכמונים), a unit of money, in 7:69 and 7:71
2. "Pardes" (פרדס), for "park" or "paradise," in 2:8
3. "Tirshatha" (תרשתא), for "Persian governor," in 7:65, 7:69, 8:9 and 10:1 (Heb 10:2)
4. "Birah" (בירה), meaning "palace," in 1:1 and 2:8

The older pronoun "anoki" appears once in Nehemiah, while its counterpart "ani" appears eight times. The use of "anoki" in a late book is unexpected. The choice of words in any passage is a function of the individual style of the author, and in Neh 1:6 when "anoki" is used, Nehemiah is praying, echoing the language of the earlier books in the Bible (Exod 20:6, Deut 7:21, etc.).

Nehemiah uses as one of its designations for God, "God of Heaven," a title taken from the proclamation of Cyrus in 2 Chron 36:23, but not used without being prefixed by YHWH in any pre-exilic literature. "God of heaven" appears eight times in Ezra, four times in Nehemiah, four times in Daniel, in Psalm 136, and also in the apocryphal books of Judith, 1 Maccabees and Tobit.

The spelling practice in Nehemiah is not especially late, although David's name is spelled in the later form דויד in all eight occurrences.

5.11.3 Oldest Texts
One Dead Sea Scroll (4Q117) contains parts of Ezra 4 and 5. Nehemiah is not represented. It is likely that this was originally a combined Ezra-Nehemiah scroll and that the portion with Nehemiah has been lost.

5.11.4 Conclusion
Ezra and Nehemiah were both placed in final form by a chronicler who incorporated their memoirs. Nehemiah's memoirs constitute most of the book. This was done shortly after Nehemiah's life, around 390 B.C., and may have been done by the author of Chronicles.

5.12 First and Second Chronicles
The books of 1 and 2 Chronicles are a record of Israel's history from creation through the exile. The original Hebrew Bible treated 1 and 2 Chronicles as one book, the last book in the Old Testament canon.

Chronicles focuses on history mostly as it relates to worship in the Jerusalem temple. Chronicles is not interested in northern kings or prophets (Elijah and Elisha get no mention) except when there is a connection to a king of Judah (as in Micaiah in 2 Chron 18:12). Chronicles is also not interested in rehashing the wrongdoings recorded in the primary history (David and Bathsheba, Solomon's apostasy, etc.). The author's intention is to provide a scrapbook which celebrates God's faithfulness throughout history, up to the current day. The positive emphasis is highlighted by ending the book with the proclamation of Cyrus, which encourages rebuilding the temple.

Chronicles is indisputably a post-exilic book. The traditional view of Chronicles holds that it was written between 450-400 B.C., possibly with Ezra as the author. The Talmud identifies Ezra and

Nehemiah as authors of the book.[56] Because Chronicles retells many stories from Samuel and Kings, an earlier writing, it provides a useful model for comparison of linguistics between a later book and earlier books.

From the standpoint of narrative history, Chronicles ends in 538 B.C. with the decree of Cyrus that authorized rebuilding the temple in Jerusalem (2 Chron 36:22-23). The story is essentially continued in Ezra-Nehemiah. However, Chronicles begins with an extensive list of genealogies which go further in time than 538 B.C. A key genealogy is in 1 Chron 3:17-24, which appears to take the descendants of Zerubbabel, the governor of Judah in 525 B.C., down six generations: Zerubbabel->Hananiah->Shecaniah->Shemaiah->Neariah->Elioenai->seven sons. This would pull the Chronicles history down near 400 B.C.[57]

Chronicles makes extensive use of "the book of the kings of Israel and Judah." The chronicler changes terminology in describing this book:

1. "Book of the kings of Israel and Judah" (2 Chron 27:7, 35:27 and 36:8)
2. "Book of the kings of Judah and Israel" (2 Chron 16:11, 25:26, 28:26 and 32:32)
3. "Book of the kings of Israel" (1 Chron 9:1 and 2 Chron 20:34)
4. "Book of the kings" (2 Chron 24:27)

Probably these are all references to the same book. It is likely that the biblical book of Kings is in view here, although there is a possibility that the chronicler is referring to the same court records used by the author of Kings. 1 Chron 29:29, 2 Chron 12:15 and 2 Chron 32:32 list additional source material that may have been used by the chronicler. This material includes:

---

[56] Baba Bathra 15a

[57] How to read the genealogies in Chronicles is a subject of debate, and the Septuagint reads somewhat differently in 1 Chron 3, taking the genealogy of Zerubbabel down 11 generations.

1. The words of Samuel the seer
2. The words of Nathan the prophet
3. The words of Gad the seer
4. The records of Shemaiah the prophet and Iddo the Seer, according to the genealogical enrollment
5. The vision of Isaiah the prophet, the son of Amoz (the biblical book of Isaiah).

2 Macc 2:13-15 mentions Nehemiah's library, which might have been available to the chronicler and could explain all the sources referenced in Chronicles. Although much of Chronicles repeats the history of Samuel and Kings, the chronicler adds much additional information, indicating that he had access to additional sources. For example, 1 Chron 11:10-41 has a list of David's mighty men that matches the list in 2 Samuel 23, but then 1 Chron 11:42-47 adds a number of different names not found in Samuel. Another example can be seen in how Chronicles preserves the more original "baal" names, Eshbaal and Meribaal (1 Chron 8:33-34), which were substituted out of Kings in favor of Ishbosheth and Mephibosheth. This implies that the chronicler was using more material than just Samuel and Kings for his information – he may have been using the older sources mentioned in 1 Chron 29:29.

Several "to this day" statements appear in Chronicles, indicating conditions that continue to exist at the time of writing of the book. These include:

1. The northern tribes are carried away (1 Chron 5:26)
2. Some Simeonites live in Mount Seir (1 Chron 4:43)
3. Laments for Josiah are practiced (2 Chron 35:25)

Unfortunately, none of these shed much light on a date of writing. Furthermore, several "to this day" statements in Chronicles reflect pre-exilic wording from sources used by Chronicles and describe conditions which were not in place after the exile. For example, 2 Chron 5:9 has the poles of the Ark of the Covenant in the sanctuary "to this day," but this was not the case when Chronicles was written; instead it reflects when 1 Kgs 8:8 was written, with Chronicles using Kings as a source.

5.12.1 External Dependencies

Chronicles repeats much of the primary history from Genesis through Kings. 1 Chronicles 1 uses the genealogies in Genesis. Chronicles is most heavily dependent on Samuel and Kings. The Tables 4-1 and 4-2 in the sections on Samuel and Kings are not repeated here for purposes of brevity.

2 Chron 16:9 may be dependent on Zech 4:10, "the eyes of the LORD range to and fro throughout the earth." If so, this would be a rare example of a literary dependency on a post-exilic prophet.

Chronicles was written at the end of the Old Testament period, so no other books show a clear dependence on it. Ezra and Chronicles may have been written collaboratively, since Ezra picks up where Chronicles leaves off. The apocryphal book of 1 Esdras duplicates 2 Chronicles 35-36, Ezra 1-10 and Nehemiah 8.

5.12.2 Linguistic Analysis

Chronicles provides the largest body of Late Biblical Hebrew literature. Many of the grammatically late characteristics can be shown by comparing the linguistics of Chronicles to the parallel passages in Samuel and Kings. Selected examples of Late Biblical Hebrew features in Chronicles include:

1. 2 Chron 3:3-4, 3:11, 3:12 and 3:13 are examples of placing a cardinal number after a noun. In particular, the temple dimensions in 2 Chronicles reverse the order used in Kings; Chronicles puts the numbers after the nouns, while Kings puts the numbers before the nouns.

2. Chronicles exhibits a decline in the usage of direct object pointers with pronominal suffixes attached. Kings has direct object markers with attached suffixes 122 times while Chronicles has this form only 43 times.

3. Chronicles shows a marked reduction in the use of infinitive absolute verbs, a late feature (compare 2 Sam 24:12 with 1 Chron 21:10, 1 Kgs 8:13 with 2 Chron 6:2, and 1 Kgs 9:6 with 2 Chron 7:19).

4. Chronicles often negates infinitive verbs with אין (1 Chron 23:26, 2 Chron 5:11, 14:10, 20:6, 22:9 and 35:15). Classical Biblical Hebrew uses לבלתי to negate infinitive verbs.

5. Chronicles uses plural forms in places where earlier texts use singular forms (compare 1 Kgs 10:22 with 2 Chron 9:21 and 2 Kgs 8:27 with 2 Chron 22:3).

6. The grammatical construction "<noun> and <noun>" (the same noun used twice), meaning "this one and that one," is a post-exilic usage appearing in 1 Chron 26:13, 28:14-15, 2 Chron 8:14, 11:12 and 19:5.

Chronicles also shows a later selection of vocabulary and other expressions. Examples include:

1. The early pronoun "anoki" is used just once in Chronicles, while its companion "ani" appears 20 times. Usage of "anoki" comes from 1 Chron 17:1, a passage copied from 2 Sam 7:2 dealing with the Davidic covenant. "Anoki" is changed to "ani" in the parallel passages of 2 Sam 24:12 = 1 Chron 21:10 and 2 Sam 24:17 = 1 Chron 21:17.

2. "Ahmad" (עמד) begins to be used for "raise up" in places where earlier usage requires "qum" (קום) (compare 2 Chron 33:19 with Judg 18:30).

3. "Shavak" (שבח), a late word meaning "laud" or "praise," is in 1 Chron 16:35.

4. "Natan lev" (נתן with לב) is a Late Biblical Hebrew expression for the way a person sets his own heart (1 Chron 22:19 and 2 Chron 11:16).

No Greek words are present in Chronicles, but Chronicles does use a selection of Persian words. This is despite the fact that the narratives in Chronicles are set prior to the Persian era. Persian vocabulary in Chronicles includes:

1. "Nadan" (נדן), for "sheath" in 1 Chron 21:27, rather than older "ta'ahr" (תער).
2. "Ganzak" (גנזך), for "treasure chamber" in 1 Chron 28:11 rather than older "otzer" (אוצר).
3. "Adarconim" (אדרכנים) for "darics," a unit of monetary currency, in 1 Chron 29:7. This is an anachronism, since Darics were a Persian coin first minted in 515 B.C.
4. "Karmil" (כרמיל) for "crimson" in 2 Chron 2:6 rather than the older "shani" (שני).
5. "Zan" (זן) for "kind" in 2 Chron 16:14 rather than the older "min" (מין).
6. "Birah" (בירה) for "palace" in 1 Chron 29:1 and 29:19 rather than the older "heykal" (היכל) or "beyt" (בית).

Other vocabulary showing late foreign influence includes:

1. "Igrot" (אגרות) for "letters" (from late Akkadian *egirtu*) in 2 Chron 30:1 and 30:6 rather than the older "sefer" (ספר).
2. 2 Chron 2:6 spells the word for "purple" with the later Aramaic-influenced spelling of ארגון rather than the earlier ארגמן.

Occasionally, Chronicles chooses to use older vocabulary. An example is the early "bal" for "not" in 1 Ch 16:30. The reason for this usage is that the passage borrows from Ps 96:10. "Zulah" (זולה), meaning "except" in 1 Chron 17:20 appears almost exclusively in pre-exilic texts, but this verse is borrowed from 2 Sam 7:22. Chronicles makes frequent use of both the earlier "mamlakah" and the later "malkut" for "kingdom."

The spelling pattern of Chronicles in general is not unusually late, with a few telling exceptions. Chronicles always spells David's name in the longer late form דויד (Samuel and Kings use the earlier דוד), and 2 Chron 25:1 uses the exceptionally late spelling ירושלים for Jerusalem, a spelling only occurring three times in scripture.

5.12.3 Oldest Texts

Chronicles is represented by only one Dead Sea Scroll, 4Q118, containing portions of 2 Chronicles 28 and 29.

5.12.4 Conclusion

Because Chronicles seems to bring its genealogies up to date around 400 B.C., this is the most likely date of writing for the book. The relationship between Chronicles and Ezra-Nehemiah also supports a date around this time.

CHAPTER 6

Consequences

6.1 Consequences in Biblical Interpretation

One key principle of biblical interpretation is that it is necessary to understand a passage in its historical context. Therefore, if we date a passage incorrectly, we will have the wrong historical context, and this can lead to a misinterpretation of the passage. The chapter 5 discussion on Daniel gives one such example, describing how an incorrect date for Daniel leads to the wrong interpretation of the four-kingdom prophecies in the book. In another example, Blenkinsopp, operating outside of the conventional framework and having moved the J source down in time to the Babylonian exile, proceeds to interpret all the J stories through the lens of exile: God's covenant with Noah after the flood is a response to the collapse of the state, the fall of Jerusalem, and the exile;[1] the story of the exodus generation despoiling the Egyptians relates to the wealth of the returning remnant in the Persian period, etc.[2] Wellhausen, dating the P source after the exile, wipes away any significance for the tabernacle other than the belief that it was modeled retroactively on the temple. Many such examples can be given. To show how an incorrect date of writing can produce a wildly incorrect interpretation, we will expand briefly on just one example: the scapegoat ritual.

Leviticus 16 describes a ritual for Yom Kippur, the Day of Atonement. Two goats are selected. The first goat is presented as an offering to the LORD, and the second goat, the scapegoat, is released alive in the wilderness. Lev 16:8 indicates that lots are

---

[1] Blenkinsopp, *The Pentateuch, An Introduction to the First Five Books of the Bible*, p. 86

[2] Blenkinsopp, *The Pentateuch, An Introduction to the First Five Books of the Bible*, p. 155

drawn, one for the LORD (ליהוה) and one for the scapegoat (לעזאזל). Some modern translations now leave "scapegoat" untranslated, using instead a transliteration of the Hebrew "to Azazel." "Azazel" does not appear in scripture outside Leviticus 16, and its meaning is obscure. Many modern scholars now believe that the "azazel" of Leviticus 16 is actually the name of a desert demon, or goat-god.[3] "Azazel" was indeed the name of a demon in the late first millennium B.C., and it is mentioned in works of the time such as the book of Enoch (8:1, 9:6, 10:4, etc.) and the apocalypse of Abraham (13, 14, 28, etc.). Therefore, the Yom Kippur ritual, so the interpretation goes, actually consisted of two sacrifices: one to the LORD and one to a demon.

The reader may instinctively recoil at the notion that the Bible commands an offering to a demon, and that instinct would be correct. The Torah places tremendous stress on worshipping YHWH only. The Torah repeatedly forbids any worship of foreign gods and any sacrifices to foreign gods, with the death penalty mandated for such behavior. Israel's rejection of other gods was to be so thorough as to even avoid the geographic places where Canaanites worshipped and the rituals associated with them. The desert demon idea is simply impossible - that in the midst of such a fierce emphasis on YHWH, the Torah would command giving a sacrifice to a demon. Yet if this is the case, how can we explain the belief in the Azazel demon?

What has happened here is that dating Leviticus incorrectly has led some modern scholars to reverse cause and effect. The Yom Kippur ritual is not a sacrifice to an existing demon, but rather the Yom Kippur ritual gave rise to the demon myth many years after the Torah was written. "Azazel" was an obscure word used in one Torah passage, written around 1400 B.C. and never used again in the Bible. A thousand years later, the meaning of "azazel" was

---

[3] The Contemporary English Version even translates this phrase as "the demon Azazel" in Lev 16:8 and 16:26

unknown to the common people, but they knew that this "azazel" goat was part of a most solemn religious ritual. It is only natural that superstition gave rise to the belief that there must be some powerful god or demon by that name. It is interesting to note that the Dead Sea Scrolls copy of the book of Enoch and the Temple Scroll both mention "azazel," but with an altered spelling (עזזאל)[4], which is close to "goat god," unlike the spelling in Leviticus. This is evidence of how a legend developed from something that was originally quite different.

The real meaning of "azazel" is probably lost in antiquity, but if we substitute "release" or a near synonym for "atonement," the meaning of the passage is consistent and clear. The popular translation "scapegoat" also works well. It can also be noted that the scapegoat ritual is similar to a Hittite substitution ritual, and "azazel" may be derived from a Hurrian offering term, "azaz-hiya," a term representing the benefit being sought by an offering.[5] The Hurrians played a substantial role in the history of the Hittites, and the Hurrian kingdom of Mitanni was present in Syria from 1500-1300, a likely time range for the exodus and the writing of Leviticus 16.

6.2 Consequences in Faith and Life
6.2.1 Darwinian Evolution and Christian Doctrine
Charles Darwin's *Origin of Species* was published in 1859, leading to rapid acceptance, at least in some elite circles, of biological evolution as the explanation for the origin of life. The development of the Documentary Hypothesis began before 1859 and was essentially completed in 1878 with the publication of Wellhausen's *Prolegomena to the History of Ancient Israel*. The two theories, evolution in the field of science and the Documentary Hypothesis

---

[4] Scrolls 4Q180 fragment 1 line 7-8 and 11Q19 column 26 line 13
[5] Harry A. Hoffner Jr., in Hallo, *The Context of Scripture*, Vol. III, p. xxxii.

in the field of theology, complemented each other with a synergistic effect which continues to this day.

Darwinian evolution produced an intellectual environment in the late 19th century in which evolutionary explanations for everything became popular. These included the idea of an evolutionary history of religion, an idea with which the Documentary Hypothesis is laced. Ancient Israel supposedly evolved from polytheism to henotheism (one god over others) to monotheism, with informal religious practices evolving into highly structured religious rituals and observances.

The Documentary Hypothesis, for its part, undercuts the historicity of the Old Testament and particularly the creation account. Separating Genesis 1-3 into two separate and contradictory creation stories produces a situation in which the Genesis account cannot be understood to be historical.

Abandoning the historicity of Genesis 1-3 produces a ripple effect, undermining not just the Old Testament, but central Christian doctrine as well. The New Testament teaches that death entered the world as a result of human sin (Rom 5:12-14 based on Genesis 2-3, particularly Gen 3:17-19). If Genesis 1-3 is false and evolution is true, history is filled with millions of years of suffering and death before there was any human sin. Not all Christian denominations handle the doctrine of original sin in the same way, but all agree, or at least agreed 150 years ago, that all men inherit a tendency to sin as a result of Adam's fall. Changing the Christian doctrine of sin producing death to an evolutionary doctrine of death before sin undermines the Christian idea of original sin. With no original sin, no sinful inclination, and death not the result of sin, the need for a Savior begins to fade. What exactly is it we need to be saved from anyway? The importance of the doctrine of creation has been noted by more than just evangelical groups. Cardinal Joseph Ratzinger, writing in 1989, said "The main reason for the crisis of Faith is the almost complete disappearance, in theology, of the doctrine of creation."[6] Ratzinger later became Pope Benedict XVI.

6.2.2 Impact on the Church

In 1882, Julius Wellhausen resigned as professor of theology at Greifswald for reasons of conscience. In his resignation letter he wrote: "I became a theologian because I was interested in the scientific treatment of the Bible; it has only gradually dawned on me that a professor of theology likewise has the practical task of preparing students for service in the Evangelical Church, and that I was not fulfilling this practical task, but rather, in spite of all reserve on my part, was incapacitating my hearers from their office."[7] Richard Friedman, referring to the above, wrote "but the threat to religion never really materialized...the experience of subsequent generations has apparently proved him wrong. Many – probably most – Protestant, Catholic and Jewish clergy have now been learning and teaching this subject for over a century and have managed to reconcile it with their beliefs and traditions." Unfortunately, on this matter Wellhausen appears to have been insightful while Friedman appears to be overly sanguine. It is true that most Protestant, Catholic and Jewish clergy have learned and taught this subject, but what are the results?

One of the results of late-dating the books of the Bible is that a great separation in time is created between when the events occurred and when they were written down. Such a separation in time inevitably increases the likelihood that the events are not historical. This conclusion has been embraced by source critics. Blenkinsopp writes: "The origins of Passover are, as the saying goes, lost in the mists of time and need concern us no further

---

[6] *Osservatore Romano*, 11 July 1989

[7] From R.J. Thompson, *Moses and the Law in a Century of Criticism*, pp. 42ff cited in Friedman, *Who Wrote the Bible?*, p. 165

here,"[8] and "As the philosopher and historian Robin George Collingwood reminded us years ago, the first question to ask when reading such texts is not 'Did it really happen?' but 'What does it mean?'"[9] The problem with this perspective is that if the events in the Bible did not really happen, then practically nobody is going to care what they mean. A few academics who love old literature may care, but the great majority of people will simply abandon the Bible and the beliefs formerly held by their culture. This is in fact something that has happened in much of the western world.

The Catholic Church was slow to embrace higher criticism of the Bible. In 1893, as biblical criticism was coming into full bloom, the Catholic Church condemned it. In his Encyclical letter of November 18, 1893, Pope Leo XIII labeled the critics as "rationalists" and described higher criticism as an "inept method." He asserted that "it is absolutely wrong and forbidden, either to narrow inspiration to certain parts only of Holy Scripture, or to admit that the sacred writer has erred. For the system of those who, in order to rid themselves of these difficulties, do not hesitate to concede that divine inspiration regards the things of faith and morals, and nothing beyond, because (as they wrongly think) in a question of the truth or falsehood of a passage, we should consider not so much what God has said as the reason and purpose which He had in mind in saying it - this system cannot be tolerated. For all the books which the Church receives as sacred and canonical, are written wholly and entirely, with all their parts, at the dictation of the Holy Ghost; and so far is it from being possible that any error can co-exist with inspiration, that inspiration not only is essentially incompatible with error, but excludes and rejects it as absolutely and necessarily as it is impossible that

---

[8] Blenkinsopp, *The Pentateuch, An Introduction to the First Five Books of the Bible* p. 156

[9] Blenkinsopp, *The Pentateuch, An Introduction to the First Five Books of the Bible* p. 126

God Himself, the supreme Truth, can utter that which is not true. This is the ancient and unchanging faith of the Church."[10] He further enlists all Catholics with any learning whatsoever to oppose the critical trend. The attitude of the Catholic Church began to change fifty years later, when Pope Pius XII released a new Encyclical letter on the same topic.[11] This letter, though reaffirming Pope Leo's encyclical, encouraged biblical studies in original languages, textual criticism, literary criticism, and the application of "profane sciences" to biblical study. This Encyclical reaffirmed the Bible as "having freedom from any error whatsoever," but the door was apparently cracked and the critics rushed in. Within a generation, Catholic publications began to reflect the critical approach to the Bible. The Jerusalem Bible[12] and the church-sponsored New American Bible[13] now both reflect critical theories like the Documentary Hypothesis and a second century B.C. date for Daniel.

The mainline Protestant denominations were quicker to embrace the theories of source critics. The tendency in Protestant circles, which continues to this day, is to agree with the critics on dates and sources, but to "spin" conclusions in a more favorable manner. While Wellhausen harshly states: (The numbers and names in the Hexateuch) "…are not drawn from contemporary records, but are the fruit solely of late Jewish fantasy, a fancy which, it is well known, does not design nor sketch, but counts and constructs, and produces nothing more than barren plans"[14], Guthrie softens the blow: "This process does not devalue or discredit the biblical narrative properly understood. Rather, it

---

[10] Pope Leo XIII, *Providentissimus Deus*, Encyclical Letter of Nov 18, 1893

[11] Pope Pius XII, *Divino Afflante Spiritu*, Encyclical Letter of September 30, 1943.

[12] Text of Jerusalem Bible, copyright 1966

[13] Text of New American Bible, copyright 1970

[14] Wellhausen, *Prolegomena to the History of Ancient Israel*, p. 348

leads to an understanding of the real nature of Numbers and what Israel's tradition meant to her."[15]

The Jewish community was initially hostile to biblical criticism, no doubt being repelled partly by the anti-Semitic tone of some of the early critics. Furthermore, within Judaism, the Orthodox community has never been receptive to biblical criticism, and to this day largely ignores the topic. However, outside of the observant Orthodox community, the views of the source critics have been widely adopted in Israel and elsewhere, with many Jewish scholars now leaders in this field.

The consequences of all this are telling. The Jewish population outside of Israel is declining due to intermarriage, assimilation and other factors. Outside of Israel, only the Orthodox Jewish community, which teaches the Torah but not the Documentary Hypothesis, is growing. In 1960, total mainline Protestant church membership in the United States was over 29 million. By 2000 this number had fallen to 22 million.[16] By 2004, more people in England were attending mosques on the weekend than were attending Anglican Church services.[17] The growth that has occurred in Protestant Christianity has been in evangelical, fundamentalist, and non-denominational groups that teach the Bible, but do not teach higher criticism of it. The Catholic Church in the western world is developing a shortage of priests. Europe, which was the bulwark of Christianity for more than a thousand years, is now predominately a post-Christian continent. The community of faith has taken a critical and misguided approach to the Bible, and that approach is one of the factors producing these results.

---

[15] Harvey H. Guthrie, Jr., The Book of Numbers, *The Interpreter's One Volume Commentary on the Bible*, p. 85

[16] Michael S. Hamilton and Jennifer McKinney, "Turning the Mainline Around", article in *Christianity Today*, August 1, 2003

[17] Intissar Khreeji Ghannounchi, "Mosque Attendance to Double Churchgoers", article in *The iWitness* (Scotland's Muslim newspaper), 9/24/2005

6.3 An Analogy

In the 14th century A.D., The University of Paris was the undisputed center of scholarship in the western world. There lived, worked and studied the most intelligent and best educated men in Europe. With the black plague ravaging Europe, Philip VI, king of France, asked the University for a report on the cause of the plague. With careful thesis, antithesis, and proofs, the medical faculty at the university ascribed it to a triple conjunction of Saturn, Jupiter, and Mars in the 40th degree of Aquarius said to have occurred on March 20, 1345.[18] This verdict became the official scientific understanding of the black plague, everywhere accepted, even by Arab physicians in Cordova and Granada. A curious facet of this diagnosis is that the church, seemingly so influential in the middle ages, detested astrology. If the medical faculty at the University of Paris had been guided even slightly by the teachings of the church, they would never have reached such a foolish conclusion, which was the product of neither faith nor reason.

The scholars who produced and continue to teach the Documentary Hypothesis and much of the other higher criticism of the Old Testament are not ignorant men. Like the medical faculty at the University of Paris, they are often the most intelligent and best educated scholars in the world today. Their work has at times produced brilliant insight in many areas of biblical study. However, their conclusions have often landed far from the truth. Working from presuppositions such as anti-supernaturalism and the evolution of religion and looking in dark corners for the tiniest clues, they ignore the heavy weight of evidence that argues against their position. Some of that evidence has been presented in this book. Even if that evidence were not in itself convincing enough, they still would have been saved from error if they had

---

[18] This paragraph quotes freely from Barbara Tuchman, *A Distant Mirror*, pp. 102-103

followed the tradition of their Christian or Jewish faith, as understood down through the ages. Reason could have corrected them, and faith could have corrected them. They abandoned both.

6.4 Conclusion

The computer industry has a saying: "garbage in, garbage out." The idea is that if the data used as input to a computer program is flawed, even a good computer program will produce a bad result. To a certain extent, that is what has happened in the field of biblical criticism. The critical method (the computer program) is not necessarily flawed – this book also practices biblical criticism. However, modern source critics have provided flawed inputs to the practice of biblical criticism. These include an evolutionary view of the history of religion, along with anti-supernatural presuppositions. These flawed inputs were key to the establishment of the Documentary Hypothesis. Once the framework of the Documentary Hypothesis was established, most scholars have been content to stay within or near to this framework, rather than doing what should have been done – scrapping it and starting anew. This book does that, and attempts to blaze a different path. The conclusions in this book should in no way be considered as final and definitive; better scholarship and future discoveries will hopefully lead to better understanding.

This work has dated the writing of most of the Old Testament books near their traditional dates, and much earlier than the dates favored by modern critics. The work of the modern critics in this area has been, though often well-intentioned, harmful to the Christian and Jewish faiths. It is the modest hope of the author that this book may contribute in some small measure to the undoing of this harm.

APPENDIX A

Documentary Hypothesis

The list below contains an identification of sources based on the Documentary Hypothesis. The list in Genesis and Exodus is based on the list in the *Interpreter's One Volume Commentary on the Bible*, introductions to Genesis and Exodus. The list from Leviticus, Numbers and Deuteronomy is taken from Friedman's *The Bible with Sources Revealed*.[1] Among modern authors, Friedman is the most thorough in supplying a comprehensive list for Genesis through Deuteronomy, but we chose not to use it as a primary source for Genesis and Exodus since he deviates some from the standard understanding of the Documentary Hypothesis. The list for Joshua is derived from Driver's *Introduction to the Literature of the Old Testament*.[2] Driver provided a nearly complete list for Genesis through Joshua. A sampling of some of the differences of opinion among these scholars is provided in the notes column. The reader will observe that considerable differences of opinion exist on how to divide the text into sources. These divergences of opinion show what Cassuto calls "a certain inner weakness of the theory as a whole."[3]

Abbreviations:
J = Jehovist – 850 B.C.
E = Elohist – 750 B.C.
JE = Either J or E
D = Deuteronomist – 621 B.C.

---

[1] The many references to Friedman in the notes throughout this Appendix are also from Friedman, *The Bible with Sources Revealed*

[2] The many references to Driver in the notes throughout this Appendix are also from Driver, *An Introduction to the Literature of the Old Testament*

[3] Cassuto, *The Documentary Hypothesis*, p. 6

D2 = Exilic Deuteronomist – 580 B.C.
P = Priestly – 500-450 B.C.
R = Redactor (editor) – 450 B.C.

Topic	Scripture Reference	Source	Notes
Creation	Gen 1-2:4a	P	
Eden, the Fall, Cain and Abel	Gen 2:4b – 4:26	J	Friedman assigns 4:25-26a to R. Wellhausen says 4:1-15 is an interpolation.[4]
Genealogies	Gen 5:1-32	P	Friedman assigns this and all other P genealogies to a separate source he calls the book of records. He assigns 5:29 to R. Driver assigns 5:29 to J. 5:29 is problematic for the Documentary Hypothesis, since it uses YHWH in the middle of a P passage and it looks back at Gen 3:17-19 (J).
Wickedness and Judgment	Gen 6:1-8	J	
Preparing the ark	Gen 6:9-22	P	
The flood	Gen 7:1-5	J	
	Gen 7:6	P	Friedman assigns 7:6 to the book of records

---

[4] Wellhausen, *Prolegomena to the History of Ancient Israel*, p. 324

Topic	Scripture Reference	Source	Notes
The Flood	Gen 7:7	J	
	Gen 7:8-9	JR and PR	Wellhausen says 7:6-9 is from R. Friedman assigns 7:8-16a to P. Von Rad assigns 8-10 to J.[5] Driver assigns to J "in the main."
	Gen 7:10	J	
	Gen 7:11	P	
	Gen 7:12	J	
	Gen 7:13-16a	P	
	Gen 7:16b	J	YHWH in 16b
	Gen 7:17a	P	
	Gen 7:17b	J	
	Gen 7:18-21	P	Friedman assigns 7:17-20 to J
	Gen 7:22-23	J	
	Gen 7:24	P	
	Gen 8:1-2a	P	
	Gen 8:2b-3a	J	
	Gen 8:3b-5	P	
	Gen 8:6-12	J	Friedman and Von Rad[6] assign 8:7 to P
	Gen 8:13a	P	
	Gen 8:13b	J	
	Gen 8:14-19	P	

[5] Von Rad, *Genesis, A Commentary*, p. 118
[6] Von Rad, *Genesis, A Commentary*, p.125

Topic	Scripture Reference	Source	Notes
Covenant after the flood	Gen 8:20-22	J	
	Gen 9:1-17	P	
Noah drunk	Gen 9:18-27	J	
Table of nations descended from Noah	Gen 9:28-10:1a	P	Friedman assigns 9:28-29 to the book of records, 10:1a to R, and 10:1b to P
	Gen 10:1b	J	Driver assigns all 10:1-7 to P
	Gen 10:2-7	P	
	Gen 10:8-19	J	
	Gen 10:20	P	
	Gen 10:21	J	
	Gen 10:22-23	P	
	Gen 10:24-30	J	
	Gen 10:31-32	P	
Tower of Babel	Gen 11:1-9	J	
Shem's descendants	Gen 11:10-27	P	Friedman assigns 11:10a and 27a to R, with 11:10b-26 to the book of records.
Abram story begins	Gen 11:28-30	J	Friedman assigns 11:31b and 32b to R.
	Gen 11:31-32	P	
	Gen 12:1-4a	J	

Topic	Scripture Reference	Source	Notes
	Gen 12:4b-5	P	Von Rad assigns all of chapter 12 and 13 to J.[7]
Abram in Egypt and Canaan	Gen 12:6-13:5	J	
Abram and Lot separate	Gen 13:6	P	P likes "possessions"
	Gen 13:7-11a	J	
	Gen 13:11b-12a	P	
	Gen 13:12b-18	J	Wellhausen considered 13:14-17 a later addition[8]
War, Lot's captivity and rescue, Melchizedek	Gen 14	??	Genesis 14 is considered a later addition, not belonging to J, E, P, or D
God's covenant of parts with Abram	Gen 15:1	J?	Verse is questionable because it has both YHWH (J) and a vision (E). Driver assigns all of chapter 15 to E. Blenkinsopp assigns chapter 15 to D.[9]
	Gen 15:2	E?	Friedman assigns 15:1-7a to J
	Gen 15:3-4	J?	
	Gen 15:5-6	E?	

[7] Von Rad, *Genesis, A Commentary*, p.161

[8] Von Rad, *Genesis, A Commentary*, p.172

[9] Blenkinsopp, *The Pentateuch, An Introduction to the First Five Books of the Bible*, p. 123

Topic	Scripture Reference	Source	Notes
God's covenant of parts with Abram	Gen 15:7-12	J	Friedman assigns 15:7b to R
	Gen 15:13-16	E	"Amorite" in E. Friedman assigns 15:13-17a to R
	Gen 15:17-18	J	
	Gen 15:19-21	??	Uncertainty is because both Canaanites and Amorites are mentioned. Friedman assigns 15:17b-21 to J
Sarai, Hagar and Ishmael	Gen 16:1a	P	Friedman, Wellhausen assign 16:1-2 to J. Von Rad assigns 16:1-14 to J[10]
	Gen 16:1b-2	J	"Shifkah" is purportedly used for maidservant in J
	Gen 16:3	P	
	Gen 16:4-8	J	
	Gen 16:9-10	??	Friedman, Driver assign 16:9-10 to J
	Gen 16:11-14	J	
Circumcision covenant	Gen 16:15-17:27	P	El Shaddai
Promise of Isaac	Gen 18:1-16	J	
Sodom	Gen 18:17-19	??	Friedman, Driver assign 18:17-19 to J

---

[10] Von Rad, *Genesis, A Commentary*, p. 194

Topic	Scripture Reference	Source	Notes
Sodom	Gen 18:20-19:16	J	
	Gen 19:17-22	??	Friedman, Driver assign 19:17-22 to J
	Gen 19:23-28	J	
	Gen 19:29	P	
	Gen 19:30a	??	Friedman, Driver assigns 19:30a to J
Lot's daughters' descendants	Gen 19:30b-38	J	
Abraham and Abimelech	Gen 20:1-17	E	Friedman assigns 20:1a to R
	Gen 20:18	??	Friedman assigns 20:18 to E. YHWH appears in this verse, which is the reason for the uncertainty
Isaac born	Gen 21:1a	J	
	Gen 21:1b	P	YHWH occurs in P here.
	Gen 21:2a	J	
	Gen 21:2b-5	P	
Hagar and Ishmael depart	Gen 21:6a	E	This phrase snipped out of J due to Elohim. Driver assigns 6-32 to E.
	Gen 21:6b-7	J	
	Gen 21:8-24	E	"amah" used for

Topic	Scripture Reference	Source	Notes
			maidservant
Abraham and Abimelech	Gen 21:25-26	J	Friedman assigns 21:25-26 to E
	Gen 21:27	E	
	Gen 21:28-30	J	Friedman assigns 21:28-30 to E
	Gen 21:31	E	
	Gen 21:32-33	J	Friedman assigns 21:32-33 to E. 33 has YHWH
Abraham and binding of Isaac	Gen 21:34 – 22:14	E	
	Gen 22:15-19	??	Friedman assigns 22:11-15 to R, along with the phrase "word of YHWH" in 16. Driver assigns 15-18 to J and 19 to E. Von Rad assigns 15-19 to E.[11] The problem is that this is the ending of an "E" story, but it uses YHWH four times.
Nahor's family	Gen 22:20-24	J	
Sarah's burial	Gen 23:1-20	P	
Finding a bride for Isaac - Rebekah; Abraham and Keturah	Gen 24:1-25:6	J	Friedman assigns 25:1-4 to E and 5-6 to R

---

[11] Von Rad, *Genesis, A Commentary*, p. 26

Topic	Scripture Reference	Source	Notes
Abraham's death	Gen 25:7-11a	P	
Ishmael's family	Gen 25:11b	J	
	Gen 25:12-17	P	Friedman assigns 25:12 to R, 25:18 to P
Jacob and Esau	Gen 25:18	J	
	Gen 25:19-20	P	Friedman assigns 25:19 to R
	Gen 25:21-26c	J	
	Gen 25:26d	P	Friedman assigns 26d to J
Esau sells his birthright; Isaac and Abimelech	Gen 25:27-26:33	J	
Esau's wives	Gen 26:34-35	P	
Jacob steals Esau's blessing	Gen 27:1-27:45	J or E	Friedman, Driver assign 27:1-45 to J. Gunkel weaves both J and E together in this passage.[12] Isaac's blessing in 27:27-28 uses both YHWH and Elohim.
Jacob departs, Esau marries	Gen 27:46-28:9	P	El Shaddai in 28:3

---

[12] Cassuto, *The Documentary Hypothesis*, p. 85

Topic	Scripture Reference	Source	Notes
Jacob at Bethel	Gen 28:10	J	Genesis 28 is cut up to keep YHWH in J and the dream in E. Von Rad assigns 10-12 to E.[13]
	Gen 28:11-12	E	Friedman assigns 28:11a to J
	Gen 28:13-16	J	
	Gen 28:17-18	E	
	Gen 28:19	J	
	Gen 28:20-29:1	E	Friedman assigns all of Genesis 29 to J
Jacob meets Rachel	Gen 29:2-14	J	
Jacob marries Leah and Rachel	Gen 29:15-23	E	
	Gen 29:24	P	
	Gen 29:25-28	E	Wellhausen assigns 29:28b to P[14]
	Gen 29:29	P	
	Gen 29:30	E	
Jacob's children	Gen 29:31-35	J	
Jacob's deal with Laban	Gen 30:1-43	J or E	Friedman assigns 30:1b-24a to E and 1a, 24b-43 to J. Driver assigns 30:1-3a, 6, 8, 17-

---

[13] Von Rad, *Genesis, A Commentary*, p.283
[14] Wellhausen, *Prolegomena to the History of Ancient Israel*, p. 329

Topic	Scripture Reference	Source	Notes
			20a, 20c-22b and 23 to E, the rest to J.
Jacob flees Laban	Gen 31:1	J	Friedman assigns to E
	Gen 31:2	E	
	Gen 31:3	J	
	Gen 31:4-16	E	
	Gen 31:17-18a	J	Von Rad assigns 4-18 to E.[15] Friedman assigns 31:18 to P. Driver assigns 31:17-18a to E.
	Gen 31:18b-d	P	Keeping "Paddan-Aram" in P.
Laban pursues Jacob	Gen 31:19-42	E	Household gods in 31:19, so cannot be in P
	Gen 31:43-44	J	Friedman assigns 31:43-54 to E
Laban's covenant With Jacob	Gen 31:45	E	
	Gen 31:46	J	
	Gen 31:47	??	Driver assigns 47 to E
	Gen 31:48	J	
	Gen 31:49	E	Driver assigns 49 to J
	Gen 31:50	J	
	Gen 31:51-32:2	E	
Jacob prepares to meet Esau	Gen 32:3-13a	J	32:9 has YHWH and Elohim both
Jacob wrestles with God; Jacob and Esau meet	Gen 32:13b-23	E	Driver assigns 22 to J. Von Rad assigns 22-32 to J[16]

[15] Von Rad, *Genesis, A Commentary*, p.305

[16] Von Rad, *Genesis, A Commentary*, p. 319

Topic	Scripture Reference	Source	Notes
	Gen 32:24-33:17	J	Friedman assigns this section to E, and assigns special significance to Peniel in 32:30-31, which Jeroboam rebuilt (1 Kgs 12:25)[17]
Jacob in Canaan	Gen 33:18a	E	
	Gen 33:18b	P	P because of "Paddan-Aram." Friedman assigns to the Redactor
	Gen 33:18c-20	E	E likes altars. P does not.
Rape of Dinah and slaughter at Shechem	Gen 34:1-31	J or E	Friedman assigns to J. Driver assigns 34:1-2a, 4, 6, 8-10, 13-18, 20-24, 25(partly) and 27-29 to P, the rest to J. One reason for uncertainty is 35:1-8 in E is not explainable without chapter 34, but the J passage of Gen 49:5-8 condemns Simeon and Levi for what happened in Genesis 34. Also, some source critics prefer to exclude the word "Canaanite" (34:30) from E (E prefers "Amorite")

[17] Friedman, *Who Wrote the Bible*, p. 62

Topic	Scripture Reference	Source	Notes
Jacob at Bethel	Gen 35:1-8	E	Assigned to E because of the altar and repeated use of Elohim
	Gen 35:9-13	P	El Shaddai
Rachel's death	Gen 35:14-20	E	Wellhausen[18] assigns v. 15-16a and 19 to P. Friedman assigns 14 and 15 to P, surprisingly, since 14 contains a stone pillar and a drink offering. Driver assigns 14 to J and 15 to P.
Reuben and Bilhah	Gen 35:21-22a	J	
Jacob's sons; Isaac's death; Esau's family	Gen 35:22b-36:19	P	Friedman assigns 36:1 to R, 36:2-30 to P, and 31-43 to J
Sons of Seir and kings of Edom	Gen 36:20-39	J?	Von Rad assigns to J[19]
Chiefs of Esau	Gen 36:40-43	P	
Joseph's dreams	Gen 37:1-2	P	Friedman assigns 2a to R and 2b to J. Driver assigns 2b to 11 to E.
	Gen 37:3-4	J or E	Friedman assigns 3a and 4 to E, 3b to J
	Gen 37:5-11	E	

---

[18] Wellhausen, *Prolegomena to the History of Ancient Israel*, p. 330
[19] Von Rad, *Genesis, A Commentary*, p. 346

Topic	Scripture Reference	Source	Notes
Joseph sold as a slave	Gen 37:12-20	J or E	Friedman assigns 12-18, 21-22 and 24-25a to E, 19-20 and 23 to J. Driver assigns 12-18 to J and 19-20 to E.
	Gen 37:21	J	
	Gen 37:22-25a	E	Driver assigns 25 to J
	Gen 37:25b-27	J	
	Gen 37:28ab	E	This verse is divided to try to make the Midianites and the Ishmaelites separate peoples
	Gen 37:28c	J	
	Gen 37:28d-30	E	
	Gen 37:31-35	J or E	Friedman, Driver assign 31-35 to J
	Gen 37:36	E	
Judah and Tamar; Joseph, Potiphar and Potiphar's wife	Gen 38:1-39:23	J	
Joseph in prison, Pharaoh's dreams	Gen 40:1-41:28	E	Driver finds traces of J in 40:1b, 3b, 15b and 41:14
	Gen 41:29-44	J or E	Friedman, Driver assign 41:29-45 to E
	Gen 41:45	J	
	Gen 41:46a	P	

Topic	Scripture Reference	Source	Notes
Joseph's wife and sons; famine; Joseph's brothers travel to Egypt	Gen 41:46b-42:7	J or E	Friedman assigns 41:46b to R, 41:47-57 and 42:5, 7 to E, 42:1-4, 6, 8-20, 26-34 and 38 to J. Driver assigns 41:47-57 to J and 42:1-37 to E.
Joseph and his brothers	Gen 42:8-26	E	
	Gen 42:27-28a	J	
	Gen 42:28b-37	E	
Joseph's brothers return to Egypt	Gen 42:38-43:13	J	
	Gen 43:14	E	El Shaddai
	Gen 43:15-45:1a	J	Friedman, Driver assign 43:23b to E
Joseph reveals himself to his brothers	Gen 45:1b-3	E	Friedman assigns 45:1-2 and 4-28 to J. Driver assigns 45:1-46:5 to E with "traces" of J.
	Gen 45:4-5a	J	
	Gen 45:5b-8	E	
	Gen 45:9-14	J	
	Gen 45:15-27	E	
Jacob travels to Egypt	Gen 45:28-46:1a	J	Friedman assigns 46:1a to E
	Gen 46:1b-5	E	Friedman assigns 5a to E and 5b to J

Topic	Scripture Reference	Source	Notes
	Gen 46:6-27	P	
Jacob settles in Goshen	Gen 46:28-47:5a	J	
	Gen 47:5b-6b	P	Friedman assigns 47:5-12 to P
Jacob and Pharaoh	Gen 47:6cd	J	Split away from P because of the word "Goshen"
	Gen 47:7-11	P	
	Gen 47:12	J	
Jacob deals with the famine	Gen 47:13-26	J?	Friedman assigns to E. Driver assigns to J
Jacob asks to be buried in Canaan	Gen 47:27a	J	
	Gen 47:27b-28	P	
	Gen 47:29-31	J	
Jacob blesses Joseph's sons	Gen 48:1-2	E	
	Gen 48:3-6	P	
	Gen 48:7	??	Wellhausen, Friedman, Driver and Von Rad[20] assign 48:7 to P
	Gen 48:8-9a	E	
	Gen 48:9b-10a	J	Friedman and Driver assign 48:9-22 to E.
	Gen 48:10b-12	E	
	Gen 48:13-14	J	

---

[20] Von Rad, *Genesis, A Commentary*, p. 412

Topic	Scripture Reference	Source	Notes
Jacob blesses Joseph's sons	Gen 48:15-16	E	
	Gen 48:17-19	J	
	Gen 48:20-22	E	"Amorite" in E
Jacob's last words to his sons	Gen 49:1a	P	
	Gen 49:1b-28a	J	Friedman indicates 49:1-27 is an older song included in J, then assigns 49:28 to R
Jacob's death and burial	Gen 49:28b-33	P	
	Gen 50:1-11	J	
	Gen 50:12-13	P	
	Gen 50:14	J	
Joseph reassures his brothers, death of Joseph	Gen 50:15-26	E	Friedman assigns 50:22 to J
Names of who went to Egypt	Ex 1:1-5	P	Repeating the genealogy from Genesis 47 in P. Friedman assigns 1:1-5 to R.
Oppression in Egypt	Ex 1:6	J	Wellhausen assigns 1:6 to P[21]
	Ex 1:7	P	
	Ex 1:8-12	J	Friedman assigns 1:8-12 to E

[21] Wellhausen, *Prolegomena to the History of Ancient Israel*, p. 332

Topic	Scripture Reference	Source	Notes
Oppression in Egypt	Ex 1:13-14	P	
	Ex 1:15-20a	E	
	Ex 1:20b-21	??	Friedman and Driver assign to E
Birth of Moses	Ex 1:22-2:10	E	Friedman assigns 1:22 and 2:1-23a to J. Driver assigns 2:1-14 to E.
Moses flees to Midian	Ex 2:11-23a	J	J uses Reuel as the name of Moses' father-in-law
Moses at the burning bush	Ex 2:23b-25	P	
	Ex 3:1	E	E uses Jethro as the name of Moses' father-in-law
	Ex 3:2-4a	J	Driver assigns 3:1-6 to E.
	Ex 3:4b	E	
	Ex 3:5	J	
	Ex 3:6	E	
	Ex 3:7-8	J	
	Ex 3:9-15	E	
	Ex 3:16-4:13	J	Friedman assigns 3:16-18 and 4:1-18 to E. Driver assigns 3:21-22 to E.
	Ex 4:14-15	??	Driver assigns 4:1-16 to J.
	Ex 4:17-18	E	

Topic	Scripture Reference	Source	Notes
Moses returns to Egypt	Ex 4:19-20a	J	
	Ex 4:20b-21	E	Friedman assigns 21b to R and 22-23 to E
	Ex 4:22-26	J	Moses' son circumcised
	Ex 4:27-28	E	Friedman assigns 4:27-31 to E. Driver assigns 4:22-6:1 to J.
	Ex 4:29-31	J	
Moses talks to Pharaoh	Ex 5:1-2	E	Friedman assigns 1-2 to J and 5:3-6:1 to E
	Ex 5:3	J	
	Ex 5:4	E	
Bricks without straw	Ex 5:5-6:1	J	
God talks to Moses; the family of Moses and Aaron; Aaron's rod	Ex 6:2-7:13	P	Friedman assigns 6:12-13 and 6:26-29 to R and 6:14-25 to the book of records
Waters become blood	Ex 7:14-15a	J	Friedman assigns 7:14-18 to E, leaving no plagues in the J account
	Ex 7:15b	E	Moses' staff is mostly kept in E. Driver assigns 7:15b to J.
	Ex 7:16-17a	J	Friedman assigns to E
	Ex 7:17b	E	
	Ex 7:18	J	Friedman assigns to E
	Ex 7:19	P	
	Ex 7:20a	J	Friedman, Driver assign to P

Topic	Scripture Reference	Source	Notes
Waters become blood	Ex 7:20b	E	
	Ex 7:21a	J	Friedman, Driver assign to E
	Ex 7:21b	P	Friedman assigns to E
	Ex 7:22	J	Friedman, Driver assign to P
Plague of frogs	Ex 7:23	P	Friedman assigns to E. Driver assigns to J.
	Ex 7:24-8:4	J	Friedman assigns 7:24-28 and 8:3b-11a to E, 8:1-3a to P. Driver assigns 24 to E.
	Ex 8:5-7	P	
	Ex 8:8-15a	J	Friedman assigns 8:11b to R and 12-15 to P
Plague of lice	Ex 8:15b-19	P	Friedman assigns to 8:16-9:7 to E
Plague of flies	Ex 8:20-32	J	
Plague of livestock disease	Ex 9:1-7	??	Driver assigns to J.
Plague of boils	Ex 9:8-12	P	
Plague of hail	Ex 9:13	J	Blenkinsopp assigns to P part of the hail plague story in v.13-35.[22] Friedman assigns 9:13-9:34 to E
	Ex 9:14-16	??	Driver assigns to J.
	Ex 9:17-21	J	
	Ex 9:22-23a	E	

---

[22] Blenkinsopp, *The Pentateuch, An Introduction to the First Five Books of the Bible*, p. 154

Topic	Scripture Reference	Source	Notes
Plague of hail	Ex 9:23b	J	
	Ex 9:24a	E	Driver assigns 23b-34 to J.
	Ex 9:24b-30	J	
	Ex 9:31-32	??	
	Ex 9:33-34	J	
	Ex 9:35ab	E	Friedman assigns 9:35 to R
	Ex 9:35c	P	Driver assigns 35 to E
Plague of locusts	Ex 10:1a	J	Blenkinsopp assigns to P part of the locust plague story in 1-20.[23] Friedman assigns 10:1-19 to E.
	Ex 10:1b-2	??	Driver assigns to J
	Ex 10:3-11	J	Driver assigns 8-13 to E
	Ex 10:12-13a	E	
	Ex 10:13b	J	
	Ex 10:13c	E	Driver assigns 13b-19 to J except 14a to E
	Ex 10:14-15a	J	
	Ex 10:15b	E	
	Ex 10:15c-19	J	

---

[23] Blenkinsopp, *The Pentateuch, An Introduction to the First Five Books of the Bible*, p. 154

Topic	Scripture Reference	Source	Notes
Plague of darkness	Ex 10:20-23	E	Blenkinsopp assigns to P part of the darkness plague story in 21-29.[24] Friedman assigns 10:20 to R and 21-26 to E.
	Ex 10:24-26	J	Driver assigns to E
	Ex 10:27	E	Friedman assigns to R
	Ex 10:28-29	J	
Last plague - death of first-born announced	Ex 11:1	E	Friedman assigns 11:1-8 to E
	Ex 11:2-3	??	Driver assigns to E
	Ex 11:4-8	J	
	Ex 11:9-10	??	Friedman assigns 11:9-10 to R. Driver assigns to P
Passover	Ex 12:1-20	P	
	Ex 12:21-24	J	Friedman assigns to 12:21-27 to E
	Ex 12:25-27a	D	First occurrence of D. Emphasis on remembering. Driver assigns 21-27 to J.
	Ex 12:27b	J	
	Ex 12:28	P	P because Aaron is mentioned with Moses
Death of the firstborn and exodus	Ex 12:29-34	J	Friedman assigns 29-36 to E. Driver assigns 31-36 to E

---

[24] Blenkinsopp, *The Pentateuch, An Introduction to the First Five Books of the Bible*, p. 154

Topic	Scripture Reference	Source	Notes
Death of the firstborn and exodus	Ex 12:35-36	??	
	Ex 12:37	P	Friedman assigns 37a to R and 37b-39 to E. Driver assigns 37b-39 to E.
	Ex 12:38-39	J	
Passover laws	Ex 12:40-13:2	P	Friedman assigns 12:51 to R and 13:1-19 to E.
Feast of Unleavened Bread	Ex 13:3a	J	Wellhausen says 13:1-16 is a product of Deuteronomic redaction.[25]
	Ex 13:3b	??	Driver assigns 3-16 to J
	Ex 13:4	J	
	Ex 13:5	??	Uncertain because both the verse has both Canaanites and Amorites
	Ex 13:6-7	J	
	Ex 13:8-9	D	
Consecration of firstborn	Ex 13:10-13	J	
	Ex 13:14-16	D	
Route out of Egypt	Ex 13:17-19	E	
	Ex 13:20	P	Friedman assigns 13:20 to R
	Ex 13:21-22	J	
Crossing the sea	Ex 14:1-4	P	
	Ex 14:5-7	J	Friedman assigns 5b and 7 to E
	Ex 14:8	P	

---

[25] Wellhausen, *Prolegomena to the History of Ancient Israel*, p. 88

Topic	Scripture Reference	Source	Notes
Crossing the sea	Ex 14:9a	J	Driver assigns to P
	Ex 14:9b	P	
	Ex 14:10-14	J	Friedman assigns 14:10a and 10c to P, with 10b and 13 to J and 11-12 to E. Driver assigns 10b to E.
	Ex 14:15-18	P	
	Ex 14:19a	E	19a assigned to E due to the angel of God. Blenkinsopp assigns 19a to D.[26]
	Ex 14:19b-20a	J	Friedman assigns 20a to E and 20b to J
	Ex 14:20b	E	
	Ex 14:20c-21a	P	
	Ex 14:21b	J	
	Ex 14:22-23	??	Friedman, Driver assign 22-23 to P
	Ex 14:24	J	
	Ex 14:25	??	Friedman assigns 14:25a to E and 25b to J. Driver assigns 25 to J.
	Ex 14:26-27a	P	
	Ex 14:27b	??	Friedman, Driver assign to J
	Ex 14:27cd	J	

---

[26] Blenkinsopp, *The Pentateuch, An Introduction to the First Five Books of the Bible*, p. 169

Topic	Scripture Reference	Source	Notes
Crossing the sea	Ex 14:28-29	P	
Song of Moses	Ex 14:30-15:1-18	J	Driver assigns the song in v. 1-18 to E. Friedman indicates this is an older song included by J.
Song of Miriam	Ex 15:19-21a	??	Friedman assigns 15:19 and 22a to R and 15:20-21 to E. Von Rad assigns 15:20 to E.[27] Driver assigns 15-19 to P and 20-21 to E.
	Ex 15:21bc	J	
Bitter water made sweet	Ex 15:22a	P	Friedman assigns to R. Driver assigns 22-27 to J.
	Ex 15:22b-25a	J	
	Ex 15:25b	E	
	Ex 15:26	??	Friedman assigns to E
	Ex 15:27	P	Friedman assigns to R
Manna	Ex 16:1-3	P	Friedman assigns 16:1 to R
	Ex 16:4-5	J	
	Ex 16:6-7	P	Friedman assigns 16:6-35a to P.
	Ex 16:8	??	Driver assigns 6-24 to P.
	Ex 16:9-13a	P	

---

[27] Von Rad, *Genesis, A Commentary*, p. 27

Topic	Scripture Reference	Source	Notes
Manna	Ex 16:13b-15a	J	
	Ex 16:15b-26	P	Driver assigns 25-30 to J
	Ex 16:27-30	J	
Water from the rock	Ex 16:31-17:1a	P	Friedman assigns 16:35b to J and 17:1 to R
	Ex 17:1b-2b	E	Driver assigns to J
	Ex 17:2c-3	J	Friedman assigns 17:2-18:27 to E
	Ex 17:4-6	E	Horeb in E
	Ex 17:7a	J	
Fighting Amalek	Ex 17:7b	E	Driver assigns all of 7 to J
	Ex 17:7c	J	
	Ex 17:8-8:1	E	
Jethro's advice	Ex 18:1	E	
	Ex 18:2-4	??	Moses' two sons are mentioned
	Ex 18:5-27	E	Jethro in E
At Mount Sinai	Ex 19:1-2a	P	Friedman assigns 19:2a to R
	Ex 19:2b-3a	E	Blenkinsopp assigns 3-9a to D
	Ex 19:3b-6	D	"If you obey…". Friedman assigns 19:2b-9 to E. Driver assigns 3-19 to E "in the main."
	Ex 19:7-8	E	
	Ex 19:9a	J	

Topic	Scripture Reference	Source	Notes
At Mount Sinai	Ex 19:10-11a	E	Friedman assigns 19:10-16a to J
	Ex 19:11b-13a	J	
	Ex 19:13b-14	E	
	Ex 19:15	J	
	Ex 19:16-17	E	
	Ex 19:18	J	
	Ex 19:19	E	
	Ex 19:20-22	J	
	Ex 19:23-24a	??	Friedman, Driver assign 19:20-24a to J
	Ex 19:24b-25	J	
Ten Commandments	Ex 20:1-17	Other	Ten commandments. Friedman assigns 20:1a to R and 1b-17 to an independent document, excepting 20:11, also assigned to R. Driver assigns to E.
People afraid	Ex 20:18-21	E	
Various laws	Ex 20:22-23:33	Other	Usually considered an independent law code. Friedman says this section was woven into E.
Israel accepts the covenant	Ex 24:1	J	Most assign 24:1-2 and 9-11 to J, and vv3-8 to E. Noth and Beyerlin

Topic	Scripture Reference	Source	Notes
			reverse the order.[28] Friedman assigns 24:1-15a to E
	Ex 24:2	??	Driver assigns to J
	Ex 24:3-8	E	
Moses ascends the mountain	Ex 24:9-11	J	
	Ex 24:12ab	E	
	Ex 24:12c	??	24:12c excluded because God wrote. Driver assigns to E.
	Ex 24:13	E	
	Ex 24:15b-18a	P	
	Ex 24:18b	E	Friedman assigns 18b to R and 18c to J
Instructions for building the ark, the tabernacle and its furnishings	Ex 25:1-31:18a	P	
Golden calf	Ex 31:18b-32:6	E	
	Ex 32:7-8a	J	Friedman, Driver assign the entire golden calf episode to E, 32:1-33:23.
	Ex 32:8b	??	Excluded from J perhaps because E prefers to be the one

---

28 Blenkinsopp, *The Pentateuch, An Introduction to the First Five Books of the Bible*, p. 189

Topic	Scripture Reference	Source	Notes
			saying "brought you up" rather than "brought you out" of Egypt
Golden calf	Ex 32:9-12	J	
	Ex 32:13	??	
	Ex 32:14	J	
	Ex 32:15-34a	E	
	Ex 32:34c	E	Blenkinsopp assigns the angel to D.[29]
	Ex 32:35a	E	
Command to leave	Ex 33:1	J	
Moses talks to God	Ex 33:2	??	Uncertain because the verse has both Canaanites and Amorites. Blenkinsopp assigns v. 2 to D.[30] Noth assigns v. 1-6 to D.[31]
	Ex 33:3-4	J	
	Ex 33:5a	??	
	Ex 33:5b-6	E	
	Ex 33:7-17	J	
	Ex 33:18	??	
	Ex 33:19a	J	

[29] Blenkinsopp, *The Pentateuch, An Introduction to the First Five Books of the Bible*, p. 169

[30] Blenkinsopp, *The Pentateuch, An Introduction to the First Five Books of the Bible*, p. 169

[31] Blenkinsopp, *The Pentateuch, An Introduction to the First Five Books of the Bible*, p. 195

Topic	Scripture Reference	Source	Notes
Moses talks to God	Ex 33:19b	??	
	Ex 33:19c-34:1a	J	In 1b God says he will write again. Friedman assigns 34:1b and "like the first ones" in 4b to R, with the rest of 34:1-28 to J
New tablets and a covenant	Ex 34:2-11a	J	
	Ex 34:11b-13	??	These verses don't fit well with any source since J and E tolerate altars and P doesn't mention them.
	Ex 34:14a	J	
	Ex 34:14b-16	D	
	Ex 34:17-28	J	"Second 10 Commandments"
Shining face of Moses	Ex 34:29-33	P	
	Ex 34:34-35	J	Friedman, Driver assign 34:34-35 to P
Building the tabernacle	Ex 35:1-40:38	P	
Laws about offerings, consecration of the priests, food laws, leprosy laws, cleanliness laws	Lev 1:1-16:34	P	

Topic	Scripture Reference	Source	Notes
Laws on sexual morality, holiness, moral laws and punishments, feasts, Sabbaths, year of Jubilee, promises of blessing and punishment	Lev 17:1-26:46	Other	This passage is known as the Holiness Code. Most Documentary Hypothesis proponents consider it an older code of law used by P. Friedman assigns Lev. 23:29-43 and 26:39-45 to R.
Redeeming persons and property	Lev 27:1-34	P	
First census	Num 1:1-2:34	P	
Census and duties of Levites, various laws, Priestly blessing, record of offerings, dedicating Levites, the second Passover	Num 3:1	R	
	Num 3:2-9:14	P	
Cloud by day and fire by night	Num 9:15-23	R	
Silver trumpets	Num 10:1-12	P	
Leaving Sinai	Num 10:13	R	
	Num 10:14-27	P	
	Num 10:28	R	
	Num 10:29-	J	"Reuel" is the name of

Topic	Scripture Reference	Source	Notes
	36		Moses' father-in-law in J
People complain, 70 elders, quail, Aaron and Miriam complain	Num 11:1-12:16	E	Noth assigns to J.[32] Driver does not differentiate between J and E in Numbers, marking these passages instead as "JE"
Spies sent to Canaan	Num 13:1-16	P	
	Num 13:17a	R	Driver assigns to P
	Num 13:17b-24	J	Driver assigns 21 to P
	Num 13:25-26	P	
	Num 13:27-31	J	Joshua excluded from the good spy group – only Caleb is good in J
	Num 13:32	P	Driver assigns Num 13:32b-33 to JE
	Num 13:33	J	
Israel refuses to enter Canaan	Num 14:1-3	P	Driver assigns Num 14:3, 4, 8-9 to JE
	Num 14:4	J	
	Num 14:5-10	P	Driver assigns 8-9 to JE
	Num 14:11-25	J	
	Num 14:26-	P	Driver assigns 31-33 to

---

[32] Noth, *Numbers, A Commentary*, p. 6

Topic	Scripture Reference	Source	Notes
	38		JE
A failed invasion	Num 14:39-45	J	
Various laws	Num 15:1-31	R	
	Num 15:32-16:1a	P	
Rebellion of Korah, Dathan, and Abiram	Num 16:1b-2a	J	
	Num 16:2b-11	P	
	Num 16:12-14	J	
	Num 16:15-24a	P	Driver assigns 15 to JE
	Num 16:24b	R	"Dathan and Abiram" in R. Dathan and Abiram are kept out of P to allow the P and J stories to be separated.
	Num 16:25-26	J	
	Num 16:27a	P	
	Num 16:27b	R	"Dathan and Abiram" in R. Driver assigns 27b-34 to JE
	Num 16:27c-32a	J	
	Num 16:32b	P	"and all the people who were with Korah and

Topic	Scripture Reference	Source	Notes
			all the property" in P
	Num 16:33-34	J	
Budding of Aaron's rod, laws for priests and Levites, purification	Num 16:35-19:22	P	
Moses error striking the rock	Num 20:1a	R	Through "Kadesh" in R. Driver assigns to P.
	Num 20:1b-13	P	Driver assigns 1b, 3a, 5 to JE
Passage through Edom refused	Num 20:14-21	J	Blenkinsopp assigns v. 16 to D because of the angel reference. [33] Noth assigns to E. [34]
Death of Aaron	Num 20:22	R	Driver assigns to P
	Num 20:23-29	P	
Canaanites defeated	Num 21:1-3	J	
Bronze serpent	Num 21:4a	R	Driver assigns to P
	Num 21:4b-9	E	

---

[33] Blenkinsopp, *The Pentateuch, An Introduction to the First Five Books of the Bible*, p. 169

[34] Noth, *Numbers, A Commentary*, p. 8

Topic	Scripture Reference	Source	Notes
Traveling to Moab, defeating Sihon and Og	Num 21:10	R	Driver assigns 10-11 to P
	Num 21:11-35	J	Noth assigns 21:32 to R and 21:33-35 to D[35]
Balak and Balaam	Num 22:1	R	Driver assigns to P
	Num 22:2	J	
	Num 22:3-4a	E	
	Num 22:4b	R	"to the elders of Midian" in R. Friedman keeps the Midian references out of E because it harmonizes the Balaam story with the Baal Peor story in Num 25.
	Num 22:4c-7a	E	
	Num 22:7b	R	"and Midian's elders" in R
	Num 22:7c-14	E	
	Num 22:15a	J	
	Num 22:15b-26a	E	
	Num 22:26b	J	"to turn right or left" in J
Balaam's speeches	Num 22:27-24:25	E	Balaam discourses are considered old. Noth

[35] Noth, *Numbers, A Commentary*, p. 8

Topic	Scripture Reference	Source	Notes
			assigns 24:20-24 to R.
Israel's sin in Moab, second census, inheritance laws, Joshua appointed next leader	Num 25:1-5	J	
	Num 25:6-26:7	P	
	Num 26:8-11	R	This is assigned to the redactor because it mentions Korah, Dathan and Abiram together, and the Documentary Hypothesis needs to keep them apart
	Num 26:12-27:23	P	
Laws on offerings	Num 28:1-30:1	R	Driver assigns all of chapters 26-31 to P
Laws on vows and war	Num 30:2-31:54	P	
Tribes settling east of the Jordan	Num 32:1	J	
	Num 32:2	P	Driver assigns 32:1-17 to JE "in the main"
	Num 32:3	J	
	Num 32:4	P	
	Num 32:5a	J	
	Num 32:5b	P	"Let this land be given to your servants for a possession" in P. This phrase is cut from J to keep the word "possession" in P.

Topic	Scripture Reference	Source	Notes
Tribes settling east of the Jordan	Num 32:5c	J	
	Num 32:6	P	
	Num 32:7-12a	J	
	Num 32:12b	R	"and Joshua son of Nun" in R. This phrase is cut to avoid Joshua being credited with something good in J
	Num 32:12c	J	
	Num 32:13-24	P	Driver assigns 32:20-27 to JE "in the main"
	Num 32:25-27	J	
	Num 32:28-32	P	
	Num 32:33-42	J	Driver assigns 32:33 to P
Israel's journey from Egypt reviewed	Num 33:1-49	R	Friedman assigns 33:1a through the word "armies," and 33:3-49 to the "book of records." He assigns 33:1b-2 to R.
Invasion instructions	Num 33:50-36:13	P	Noth assigns to R[36]
Moses speaks: historical prologue	Deut 1:1-4:24	D	Driver assigns 1:3 to P and 3:14-17 to D2

---

[36] Noth, *Numbers, A Commentary*, p. 10

Topic	Scripture Reference	Source	Notes
Warnings	Deut 4:25-31	D2	Essentially all the passages with warnings about exile and judgment are assigned to D2. Driver assigns 4:25-28 to D.
Review of history and Ten Commandments, laws and blessings	Deut 4:32-8:18	D	Driver assigns 4:41-49 to D2
Warning	Deut 8:19-20	D2	Driver assigns to D
Review of rebellions, laws, love and obedience	Deut 9:1-11:32	D	Wellhausen says Deut 10:6-7 is an interpolation.[37]
Many laws reviewed	Deut 12:1-26:15	D	Friedman considers this to be an older law code used by D
Laws, blessings and curses	Deut 26:16-28:35	D	Driver assigns 27:1-4, 7b-8, 11-26 to D2 and 27:5-7a to JE.
Warnings of exile	Deut 28:36-37	D2	
More curses	Deut 28:38-62	D	
Warnings of exile	Deut 28:63-68	D2	

---

[37] Wellhausen, *Prolegomena to the History of Israel*, p. 371

Topic	Scripture Reference	Source	Notes
Covenant reviewed	Deut 29:1-20	D	Driver assigns 29:9-30:10 to D2
Warnings	Deut 29:21-28	D2	
	Deut 29:29	D	This verse is cut from D2 because it seems to promise good things "forever"
Promise of return	Deut 30:1-10	D2	
Choice of life or death	Deut 30:11-14	D	
	Deut 30:15-20	D2	Driver assigns to D
Joshua appointed, law to be read	Deut 31:1-13	D	
Joshua at the tent of meeting	Deut 31:14-15	E	Removed from D because of a reference to the tent of meeting. Can't be P because it speaks well of Joshua.
Prediction of rebellion	Deut 31:16-22	D2	
Encouraging Joshua	Deut 31:23	E	Positive verse about Joshua
Law in the ark	Deut 31:24-27	D	
Prediction of rebellion	Deut 31:28-30	D2	
Song of Moses	Deut 32:1-43	Other	Considered to be an independent song

Topic	Scripture Reference	Source	Notes
			inserted by D2. Driver assigns to D2.
Moses and Joshua	Deut 32:44-47	D	Friedman assigns 32:44 to D2
Moses to die	Deut 32:48-52	R	Repeat of Num 27:12-14
Moses final blessing	Deut 33:1	D	
	Deut 33:2-29	Other	Considered to be an older song inserted by D.
Moses death	Deut 34:1-4	D	Driver assigns 1a to P and 1b-5a, 6 and 10 to JE
	Deut 34:5-7	J	Driver assigns 5b, 7-9 to P
	Deut 34:8-9	P	Kind words about Joshua not allowed in D or J
	Deut 34:10-12	D	Driver assigns 11-12 to D2.
Joshua and the Jordan	Josh 1:1-18	D2	
Rahab and the spies	Josh 2:1-9	JE	Bloom and Rosenberg do not assign any of Joshua to J[38]
	Josh 2:10-11	D2	
	Josh 2:12-3:1	JE	

[38] Bloom and Rosenberg, *The Book of J*, p. 269

Topic	Scripture Reference	Source	Notes
Crossing the Jordan	Josh 3:2-4	D2	
	Josh 3:5	JE	
	Josh 3:6-9	D2	
	Josh 3:10-4:11a	JE	Driver sees two separate JE sources in this passage
	Josh 4:11b-12	D2	
	Josh 4:13	P	
	Josh 4:14	D2	
	Josh 4:15-18	JE	
	Josh 4:19	P	
	Josh 4:20	JE	
	Josh 4:21-5:1	D2	
Circumcising the next generation	Josh 5:2-3	JE	
	Josh 5:4-7	D2	
Gilgal	Josh 5:8-9	JE	
Passover and end of manna	Josh 5:10-12	P	
The Jericho campaign	Josh 5:13-6:27	JE	
Achan and the Ai campaign	Josh 7:1	P	
	Josh 7:2 – 8:29	JE	
Renewing the covenant	Josh 8:30-9:2	D2	
Treaty with the Gibeonites	Josh 9:3-9a	JE	
	Josh 9:9b-	D2	

Topic	Scripture Reference	Source	Notes
	10		
Treaty with the Gibeonites	Josh 9:11-15a	JE	
	Josh 9:15b	P	
	Josh 9:16	JE	
	Josh 9:17-21	P	
	Josh 9:22-23	JE	
	Josh 9:24-25	D2	
	Josh 9:26-27a	JE	
	Josh 9:27b	D2	
Sun stands still, southern kings defeated	Josh 10:1-7	JE	
	Josh 10:8	D2	
	Josh 10:9-11	JE	
	Josh 10:12a	D2	
	Josh 10:12b-14a	JE	
Killing the southern kings, victory over south Canaan	Josh 10:14b	D2	
	Josh 10:15-24	JE	
	Josh 10:25	D2	
	Josh 10:26-27	JE	
	Josh 10:28-43	D2	
Victory over north Canaan	Josh 11:1-9	JE	Driver says "amplified by D2 in parts of 2, 3, 6,

Topic	Scripture Reference	Source	Notes
			7, 8b"
Summary of victories, dividing the land	Josh 11:10-13:12	D2	
	Josh 13:13	JE	
	Josh 13:14	D2	
	Josh 13:15-32	P	
	Josh 13:33	D2	
	Josh 14:1-5	P	
Caleb's victory	Josh 14:6-15	JE	
Judah's land	Josh 15:1-13	P	
Caleb's land	Josh 15:14-19	JE	
Judah's cities	Josh 15:20-62	P	
Ephraim's land	Josh 15:63-16:3	JE	
	Josh 16:4-8	P	
	Josh 16:9-10	JE	
West Manasseh's land, additional land for Ephraim and Manasseh	Josh 17:1a	P	
	Josh 17:1b-2	JE	
	Josh 17:3-4	P	
	Josh 17:5-6	JE	
	Josh 17:7	P	
	Josh 17:8	JE	
	Josh 17:9a	P	

Topic	Scripture Reference	Source	Notes
	Josh 17:9b	JE	
	Josh 17:9c-10a	P	
	Josh 17:10b-18	JE	
Dividing the rest of the land	Josh 18:1	P	
	Josh 18:2-6	JE	
	Josh 18:7	D2	
	Josh 18:8-10	JE	
Land for Benjamin and Simeon	Josh 18:11-19:8	P	
	Josh 19:9	JE	
Land for Zebulun, Issachar, Asher, Naphtali, Dan	Josh 19:10-46	P	
	Josh 19:47	JE	
	Josh 19:48	P	
Land for Joshua	Josh 19:49-50	JE	
Cities of refuge, cities for Levites	Josh 19:51-20:3	P	
	Josh 20:4-5	D2	
	Josh 20:6a	P	
	Josh 20:6b	D2	
	Josh 20:7-21:42	P	
Eastern tribes return	Josh 21:43-22:8	D2	
Altar by the Jordan	Josh 22:9-34	P	

Topic	Scripture Reference	Source	Notes
Joshua's final address	Josh 23:1-16	D2	
The covenant at Shechem	Josh 24:1-11a	E	
	Josh 24:11b	D2	To "Jebusite"
	Josh 24:11c-12	E	
	Josh 24:13	D2	
Death of Joshua and Eleazar, bones of Joseph	Josh 24:14-30	E	
	Josh 24:31	D2	
	Josh 24:32-33	E	

APPENDIX B

Development of the Hebrew Language During the Old Testament Period

During the writing of this book it became apparent that a model was needed to describe the development of the Hebrew language during the Old Testament period. The Hebrew language changed over time, as any language will do, but the nature of the changes that took place during the biblical period are not necessarily well understood. The reasons for this are:

1. The relative scarcity of ancient Hebrew texts other than the Bible

2. The fact that the biblical texts have been dated incorrectly, as described in this book. Noteworthy problems include the way archaic features in the Torah have been ignored – this due to the fact that much of the Torah is presumed to be post-exilic.

3. The evidence of sectarian (non-biblical) texts from Qumran has not been widely evaluated.

4. The activity of the scribes who copied the Biblical Hebrew texts is not well understood.

This appendix draws heavily on examples from *A History of the Hebrew Language*, by Angel Saenz-Badillos, *Introduction to Biblical Hebrew Syntax*, by Waltke and O'Connor, along with studies by Avi Hurvitz and others. However, the conclusions and overall model in this appendix are those of this author.

B.1 Activity of the Scribes

Before discussing how the Hebrew language changed over time, it is necessary to discuss how the Biblical texts were copied by scribes to produce the texts we have today. The best way to describe the work of the scribes is to begin from the present time and work backwards.

It is self-evident that the Biblical Hebrew text used today has remained essentially unchanged for a thousand years. The Hebrew text used today is called the Masoretic Text. This is the text on which modern translations are based, and it is the text used in synagogues worldwide. The Leningrad Codex, written about 1010 A.D., is the oldest complete Hebrew Bible in existence today, and it is a Masoretic Text. This takes us back to about 1000 A.D.

The Masoretic Text is named for the Masoretes, a group of Jewish scribes who copied the Bible beginning around 550 A.D. The Masoretes worked to standardize the text, adding a system of dots and dashes as vowel sounds and pronunciation aids around the original text, which consisted of all consonants. They compiled numerous statistics on the scriptures, counting words and letters, calculating middle words in each book, etc. The work of the Masoretes in copying the Bible was done with fanatical care, and we can be confident that from the time the Masoretes began their work, the text was extremely well preserved. This takes us back to about 500 A.D.

A more problematic issue is what text the Masoretes chose as their starting point. The text used as an input by the Masoretes can be called a "proto-Masoretic text." Until the discovery of the Dead Sea Scrolls at Qumran, no Hebrew texts existed that were old enough (before 550 A.D.) to be called proto-Masoretic texts. However, the Dead Sea Scrolls included fragments from 202 Biblical scrolls. Emmanuel Tov, the Dead Sea Scrolls Project Editor-in-Chief, has identified five groups of biblical Qumran texts:[1]

1. Texts written in the special Qumran practice (that is, ones with the types of spelling, grammatical formation, and writing characteristics of the Qumran texts and no other

---

[1] Tov, *Textual Criticism of the Hebrew Bible*, pp. 114-117

group). These texts tend to have numerous errors and corrections and may have been copied from texts that resemble the later Masoretic Text. The manuscripts in this category constitute 20% of the Qumran biblical copies.

2. Proto-Masoretic texts, which resemble very closely the consonants of the later Masoretic Text. The manuscripts in this category constitute 35% of the Qumran biblical copies.

3. Pre-Samaritan texts, which are similar to the later Samaritan Pentateuch. The manuscripts in this category constitute 5% of the Qumran biblical copies.

4. Texts close to the presumed Hebrew source for the Septuagint. Tov finds the manuscripts here to be a less closely knit collection constituting about 5% of the biblical copies.

5. Nonaligned texts, which exhibit no consistent pattern of agreement or disagreement with other witnesses – the remaining 35%.

Of the five types of texts found at Qumran, the proto-Masoretic texts are in general the most conservative, showing the least evidence of scribal alterations. It is understandable that the Masoretes used a proto-Masoretic text as their starting point.

Many of the Dead Sea Scrolls are dated near 100 B.C., and since the Proto-Masoretic Dead Sea Scrolls are so close to later Masoretic texts, we can say that this brings us back to about 100 B.C. with a proto-Masoretic text essentially the same as the consonants in the Hebrew text used today. None of this is highly disputed. It is only when we move back in time prior to 100 B.C., before the Maccabean period, that the subject becomes more difficult.

Although we can assert that there has been little change going forward from the proto-Masoretic texts of 100 B.C. to the consonantal Hebrew text of today, no such assertion can be definitively made going backward from the texts of 100 B.C. to the original texts. For one thing, the very existence of different textual groups (proto-Masoretic, pre-Samaritan, Septuagint source and others) introduces a question as to which tradition is closer to the original. However, in order to proceed, let us assume that the proto-Masoretic texts are closer to the originals than the other textual traditions.[2] We will now address the question of the extent to which the proto-Masoretic texts differ from the original texts. Since we no longer have the original texts, the question obviously cannot be answered in all details. Nevertheless, certain conclusions can be made.

First, we will address the change that is most obvious and least significant: spelling. We can be confident that the scribes made widespread changes in spelling words with medial vowels in all pre-exilic texts. Just before the time of the exile, the Hebrew language began to use the letter "waw" (ו) to represent long 'o' and 'u' sounds and the letter "yodh" (י) to represent long "e" sounds in the middle of words. This practice was absent as late as 700 B.C., and medial "waw" begins to appear only just before the exile in 586 B.C.[3] The use of medial waw and yodh was optional for a time, but by 100 B.C., at Qumran, they seem to be used whenever possible. Therefore, around the time of the exile, the scribes who produced the proto-Masoretic texts began to introduce medial vowels into the text, with the result that all the books of the Bible have at least some medial vowels, thereby showing a spelling pattern later than 700 B.C. This is true not just of whole books, but also of isolated passages, including early poetry. For example, Exod 15:1, the first verse of the song of Moses, has a medial yodh in the first word of the song, אשירה, "I will sing," and a medial vowel in סוס, "horse." However, the process was no sooner introduced than it was quickly aborted. Perhaps out of

----

[2] This assumption is not acceptable to all writers, but a full discussion of the different textual traditions is outside the scope of this book.

[3] Hebrew language usage around 700 B.C. can be represented by the Siloam inscription, celebrating the completion of Hezekiah's tunnel. It has no medial vowels, nor do any earlier Hebrew inscriptions have medial vowels. The Lachish letters of 587 B.C. have some medial waw vowels.

reverence for the sanctity of the scriptures, or out of a desire to preserve unchanged all that had been salvaged from the catastrophe of exile, the scribes began the practice of preserving the scriptures letter for letter, instead of bringing the spelling up to date. This produced a situation in the proto-Masoretic texts in which the older books often show a different spelling pattern than the later books. As an example, the older book of Samuel always spells David's name דוד, without a medial vowel, but the later book of Chronicles spells it דויד, with a medial yodh representing a long "e" sound in the second syllable. The scribes apparently copied the later books, such as Chronicles, without adding any medial vowels other than the ones in the original text. This can be demonstrated by the fact that all proto-Masoretic texts of every book in the Bible have an earlier spelling pattern than the spelling found in non-Biblical Qumran texts. For example, all Biblical texts, including late books, spell Elohim אלהים, while non-Biblical Qumran texts almost always insert a medial waw for the long 'o' sound, אלוהים, which is the modern spelling.[4] The activity of the scribes in the area of spelling did nothing to alter the meaning of any text or even the sound of the text. It was just an effort to bring spelling practices up to date.

From our study of spelling, we have learned one additional thing that is important. The scribes who produced the proto-Masoretic texts froze the practice of updating spelling shortly after the exile, instead making a letter by letter copy of the text, even though this meant preserving archaic spellings. Since the scribes were so conservative in an area where neither the meaning nor even the pronunciation could be affected, it is probable that the scribes tolerated no changes whatsoever in the texts from this

---

[4] The example of אלהים raises the question as to whether or not the yodh is a medial vowel representing a long 'e' sound, but it may not have been. The early pronunciation may have been "Elohiyim", with the yodh acting as a consonant and not a vowel. This may be true for all Hebrew ים plural endings – the pronunciation may have been "iyim".

point on. Changes may still have crept in due to scribal errors, but the intent of the scribes from around 500 B.C. onward seems to have been to produce, letter for letter, an exact copy of the text they had received.

We can verify the thesis that the post-exilic scribes who copied the Masoretic Text were very conservative by making a comparison of Psalms 105:1-15 and 1 Chron 16:8-22. Both passages were originally written after the exile, so the only scribes involved would be post-exilic scribes. The passage from Chronicles is a copy of the passage from Psalms, but being in different books, the two texts would have been copied independently for hundreds of years. A comparison shows that the two passages are extremely close:

1. Six out of 15 verses match letter for letter
2. Six out of 15 verses differ by one letter
3. One verse changes "adam" (אדם) to "ish" (איש), both words meaning "man"
4. One verse drops the direct object marker, an optional feature in Hebrew poetry
5. One verse changed "seed of Abraham" to "seed of Israel."

In summary, the two passages are essentially identical. Different sets of scribes, copying two different texts for hundreds of years, still came up with an essentially identical output.

Understanding that the scribes who produced the proto-Masoretic texts were very conservative copiers in the post-exilic era leads to several conclusions. First, scribal alterations in proto-Masoretic texts are not a significant factor in books originally written in the post-exilic era. These books include Chronicles, Ezra, Nehemiah, Esther, Daniel, Joel, Haggai, Zechariah, Malachi and some Psalms. Second, no scribal alterations from very late periods, such as the Greek or Maccabean period (332 B.C. and later) should be expected in any book, regardless of when it was originally written. There are no Greek words in the Old Testament except for the names of three musical instruments in Daniel 3, a fact that supports this conclusion. Looking for the fingerprint of the scribes, we therefore must narrow our search to pre-exilic texts, and here the picture is somewhat different.

B.1.1 Scribal Update of Language

To discuss the activity of the pre-exilic scribes, let us consider first a comparison between the Hebrew language and the English language. The King James Version (KJV) of the Bible was translated in 1611. 384 years later, the 1995 edition of the New American Standard Version of the Bible (NASB), the English version used in this book, was translated. Both the KJV and the NASB are highly literal translations from the same Hebrew original, and the NASB translators were familiar with the KJV when they did their work. As a result, the differences between the two translations are due primarily to chronology. Notice the differences in Ps 23:4-6:

King James Version	New American Standard Version
4 Yea, though I walk through the valley of the shadow of death, I will fear no evil: for thou art with me; thy rod and thy staff they comfort me.	4 Even though I walk through the valley of the shadow of death, I fear no evil, for You are with me; Your rod and Your staff, they comfort me.
5 Thou preparest a table before me in the presence of mine enemies: thou anointest my head with oil; my cup runneth over.	5 You prepare a table before me in the presence of my enemies; You have anointed my head with oil; My cup overflows.
6 Surely goodness and mercy shall follow me all the days of my life: and I will dwell in the house of the LORD for ever.	6 Surely goodness and lovingkindness will follow me all the days of my life, and I will dwell in the house of the LORD forever.

The time span separating the kingdom of David and Solomon from the exile is roughly the same as the time between the KJV and the 1995 NASB. Use of the KJV in modern churches is problematic – it may be the great masterpiece of the English language, but the language is so out of date that it is awkward, unfamiliar and difficult to understand for modern churchgoers in the English-speaking world. Consequently, modern translations are generally preferred over the KJV. It is possible that the Hebrew language did not change as much from 950 B.C. to 550 B.C. as the English language did over a similar time interval. However, it is certain that changes did occur, and these changes would have had the effect of rendering some of the ancient texts obscure to the later Jewish community in the same way that the KJV is obscure to modern English speakers. The scribes apparently dealt with this problem in three different ways.

The first way the scribes dealt with the problem was to update the language when they copied a text. We believe that the scribes who copied pre-exilic texts took steps to bring the language up to date as they did their work. This would involve replacing archaic vocabulary if that vocabulary had dropped out of use, and altering grammar if necessary to conform to the practices used in their own time. The result of this effort is what is called Standard Biblical Hebrew, or Classical Biblical Hebrew. This Classical Biblical Hebrew is consistent throughout most of the Bible. Multiple lines of evidence can be brought to bear to support the idea that the scribes performed this type of language update.

First, Biblical Hebrew can be learned as one language, despite the fact that the time frame for Old Testament writings stretches across 1000 years. Scholars today usually categorize Biblical Hebrew as being either late (some of the post-exilic books) or classical (most everything else), with the difference between the two being relatively minor. The Hebrew of Exodus 3 and Daniel 1 is different, but only a little different. Yet in this book we have dated Exodus 900 years before Daniel.[5] There are three possible explanations for this: (1) Hebrew changed very little over 1000 years, (2) the later books of the Bible were deliberately written in an earlier style, or (3) the scribes updated the language of the earlier books. Explanation (1) is contrary to our experience with other languages that can be examined over a 1000 year period. Explanation (2) requires a conspiracy, and in any case is falsified by archeology.[6] This leaves (3) as the most likely explanation.

As a result of the scribes' work, when we read very old biblical prose, we see only occasional snippets that show its age, and those snippets would mostly reflect Hebrew that, though it was old, was still understood by the post-exilic community. For example, the common spelling of "laugh" had long since changed from צחק to שחק, but the older צחק was still recognized due to its being a part of Isaac's name, יצחק, so the scribes who copied this word in the Torah didn't change the spelling.

Although the line of reasoning above is suggestive, in order to conclusively prove the contention that pre-exilic scribes updated the language as they did their work, we would need to find a pre-exilic manuscript dating back to about 1000 B.C., so we could compare it against our later proto-Masoretic text. Unfortunately, this is unlikely ever to happen. However, there is another way to get partially at the problem, and it involves comparing separate copies of the same text, much like we compared Psalm 105 and 1 Chronicles 16 above. A similar comparison of older texts is possible in the case of 2 Samuel 22 and Psalm 18. These two passages repeat the same Psalm recorded in two different places.

---

[5] Most source critics would use different dates from those in this book, but this does not evade the problem. The J passages in Exodus 3 would be dated to 900 B.C., while Daniel would be dated around 170 B.C. – still a difference of 730 years.

[6] Some writers will occasionally archaize – that is, adopt certain features of a writing style older than their own time. However, it is doubtful whether any writer, either intentionally or unintentionally, would write in a style that matches an earlier era in all respects.

They are attributed to David, which would place them around 1000 B.C. Although they are essentially the same, there are numerous minor differences, and the extent of the differences is large enough that it does not look as though either text is a late copy of the other. It looks instead as though the two Psalms diverged at an early stage - a not unexpected development, since they are in two different books. If, as we suppose, the pre-exilic scribes were inclined to update the language, we might expect to see cases in these two texts where one scribe (say, the scribe copying Psalm 18) made an update, while the other (the scribe copying 2 Samuel 22) left the text unchanged. Our test is imperfect, since if any word or phrase was really archaic, both scribes might change it. Also, this Psalm is poetry, and the scribes in general would be inclined to change poetry less than prose – changing the words in a poem can detract from its style. Therefore, our hunt for language updates might be difficult. Still, a close look at these two passages supports our theory.

Looking at the Psalm overall, we see numerous marks of antiquity (see the write-up on Psalm 18 in section 5.1 for more on this). In general, the scribes who copied Psalm 18 seem to have been a little more conservative than the ones who copied 2 Samuel 22, but updates have been made in both texts. Some of the differences are:

1. Ps 18:31 (Heb 18:32) uses a rare and predominately early word for God, "Eloah" (אלוה), while Samuel changes it to the more common "El" (אל).

2. Also in Ps 18:31 (Heb 18:32), Psalms uses "mibbaladey" (מבלעדי) for "except" in its first occurrence and "zulah" (זולה) in its second occurrence. זולה appears to be an old word, and Samuel replaces it, using מבלעדי for both occurrences.

3. In 18:45 (Heb 18:46), Psalms uses a rare word, "kharag" חרג, for "come trembling." This word shows up otherwise only in the very old poem of Deut 32:25, and the scribe

who copied Samuel may not have known this word. Samuel inverts the letters to "khagar" (חגר), which means "clothed," and is probably not correct (and not used in most translations of this verse).

4. The first verse in Psalms 18 is significant. In English it starts with "I love you, O LORD, my strength," but the Hebrew word for "love" used here is "rakham" (רחם), as opposed to the normal "ahav" (אהב). The problem with רחם is that elsewhere it is always used in the sense of showing compassion, as from a greater being showing compassion to a lesser (see for example Ps 103:13 and Isa 13:18). This could be considered an inappropriate attitude toward God, and as a result the Samuel passage leaves this phrase out, possibly because a scribe felt it was irreverent. However, there is a good possibility that in the period of 1000 B.C., רחם was an acceptable word to use to express love for God, but that the passage of time modified the meaning of the word in such a way as to render it unsuitable.

5. There are 18 cases in this Psalm where an imperfect verb is used to describe past tense action. This is not the Classical Biblical Hebrew practice, but it was a common practice in early poetry. In verses 6 and 11 (Heb verses 7 and 12) the Psalms text has an imperfect verb and the Samuel text has apparently changed it to a waw + imperfect verb - that is the Classical Biblical Hebrew practice. In verses 14 and 16 the Samuel text has an imperfect verb and the Psalms text has apparently changed it to a waw + imperfect verb. It is likely that in the original for this Psalm, all four of these verses reflected the early practice of using an imperfect verb for past tense, but that each text was slightly updated to reflect the later practice of using waw + imperfect verbs for past tense.

6. Thirteen words are spelled differently between the two passages, with Samuel having the older spelling ten of the thirteen times. Spelling differences are in 2 Sam 22:2, 6 (three words), 14, 19, 29, 30, 35, 42, 47 and 48 (two words). Again, it is likely that in the original, the older spelling was present in all thirteen words in both passages.

These are only a few of the differences between 2 Samuel 22 and Psalm 18, which are much greater and of a different nature than the miniscule differences between the post-exilic texts of 1 Chronicles 16 and Psalm 105. Further, we have shown that many of the differences here relate to cases where one passage has an archaic reading and the other has updated the reading. These differences support the conclusion that the early scribes in the pre-exilic period took steps to update the language when they copied the text.

These are some of the areas where scribal updates were apparently made during the pre-exilic period:

1. Spelling. The manner in which Hebrew words were spelled changed over time, especially with regard to vowel letters (see section B.16 below for more on spelling).

2. Vocabulary. Rare or archaic words were probably replaced by more current words. The fact that older poetry is strewn with archaic words that survived the scribal process is evidence that older prose once had many of those words as well.

3. In some cases in poetry, scribes made imperfect tense verbs acting as past tense into waw-conversive (waw + imperfects) verbs. If the older usage was ever part of early Hebrew prose is uncertain. If it was, the scribes have switched the tenses so thoroughly as to eliminate any evidence of such usage. Examples of this change were shown in our comparison of Psalm 18 with 2 Samuel 22, above.

4. The Hebrew alphabetical order apparently changed during the Old Testament period, and scribes may have switched

the verse order on older acrostics to keep the acrostics in alphabetical order (as examples, verses 15 and 16 in Ps 34 and verses 25 and 26 in Prov 31 are probably reversed). See section B.3.2 below on the Hebrew alphabet.

5. Scribes updated geographic references (as in the Gen 14:14 reference to "Dan," a location in northern Israel named after the founder of the Dan tribe, since the Genesis 14 account was before Dan was born). The tendency to update geographic locations did not continue after the exile, and as a result there are no Greek place names in the Old Testament. The older names are used – in Hebrew the text always says "Aram" and never "Syria."

6. Scribes occasionally brought family records up to date, as in the Esau genealogy in Genesis 36 or the Jair verses in Num 32:41, Deut 3:14 and Josh 13:30 (Jair's story is set later in Judg 10:3-4).

7. The attributions on the Psalms and the first verse or so on most of the prophets may be identifiers added by the scribes.

We can conclude then, that the activity of the earlier scribes produced a large volume of Biblical texts that represent the Hebrew language the way it was written around the time of the exile (586 B.C.). By bringing language up to date, scribes have masked out some of the earlier archaic vocabulary and grammar, making it difficult to date earlier Biblical texts by linguistics. The texts we have today appear to show a situation where most of the pre-exilic biblical literature was essentially frozen in the form in which it existed at the time of the exile. The reason for the "freeze" should be readily apparent. The shock of the exile was very great. Everything central to the Jewish religion – temple, sacrifice, land, the Davidic monarchy – was lost. All that remained were the sacred writings of their faith and history. These writings were saved like family pictures snatched from a burning house, treasured in the extreme, and thereafter every effort was made to preserve them unchanged for all time. Because the tendency to update the language ceased around the time of the exile, books written later do show some variance from Classical Biblical Hebrew. As a result, most of the post-exilic books are considered to represent Late Biblical Hebrew as opposed to Classical Biblical Hebrew.

The second way the scribes dealt with archaic language was, in certain cases, to leave it alone. This was particularly true in the case of older poems. In fact, some of this tendency was probably in place in the example of Psalms 18 / 1 Samuel 22 that we evaluated above. The problem with updating the language of a poem is that changing a poem will often damage it. If the poem is a well-known song, like the Song of Moses in Exodus 15, the community would be inclined to reject any changes. As a result, much of the early poetry in the Bible largely escaped the scribal update process. Therefore, these early poems represent an older form of Hebrew than the Classical Biblical Hebrew that makes up the bulk of the Bible. For example, the Song of Moses in Exodus 15 exhibits the following features that are not consistent with Classical Biblical Hebrew:

1. Absence of waw + imperfect verb forms
2. Use of imperfect tense verbs for actions that occurred in the past
3. Absence of definite article and direct object pointer
4. Use of rare and/or archaic vocabulary

A second example can be used to introduce this concept. Scholars of all persuasions agree that the Song of Deborah in Judges 5 represents an early poem, and generally date it around 1100-1200 B.C. The Song of Deborah is for a Hebrew reader an extremely difficult passage to understand – the grammar is unusual and the vocabulary is often obscure. This is the situation in Judges 5. Judges 4 and 6, on the other hand are not difficult to read. These facts suggest that the scribes who copied Judges 4 and 6 updated to some extent the vocabulary and grammar, to make these passages more understandable by their contemporaries. Why would the vocabulary and grammar be updated for Judges 4 and 6, but not Judges 5? The answer again is that Judges 5 is a song, a poem. Even today we commonly sing English language songs with archaic wording, and this is especially true when the songs are religious. Thus, the Hebrew of Judges 5 may represent Hebrew as it existed in 1100-1200 B.C., while the Hebrew in Judges 4 and 6 more closely represents Hebrew as it existed in 600 B.C.

There may have been yet a third way in which the scribes dealt with the problem of archaic language. The linguistics of Ecclesiastes and Song of Solomon are in a somewhat different category from the rest of the Bible. They appear to reflect Late Biblical Hebrew in numerous ways, but contain several additional features not found in any book of the Bible. Some of those features, like the prolific use of the letter "shin" (ש) as a relative pronoun, became common in post-biblical Hebrew. In short, Ecclesiastes and Song of Solomon seem to reflect the vernacular spoken language of the Late Biblical Hebrew period, with no effort made to imitate the earlier literary style of the Bible. At the same time, both Ecclesiastes and Song of Solomon are traditionally understood to have Solomon himself as their author, and we have found reasonable internal evidence in each book that indicates that they did originate in Solomon's lifetime (see section 5.5 and 5.6). The dilemma is sharp – internal evidence of an early date contrasted with linguistic evidence pointing to possibly the latest literature in the entire Old Testament. Most critics have assumed that these books were written in the Late Biblical Hebrew period by an author who wrote from the perspective of Solomon, in a kind of reverse plagiarism. However, there is another possibility, and it is again analogous to what has happened with English Bible translations. Just as the King James Version of the English Bible remained unchanged for some time, these archaic Hebrew texts remained unchanged for a long period of time. Then in the post-exilic period, a decision was made to essentially rewrite these texts in the Late Biblical Hebrew commonly spoken by the community of that day. The result is language that differs from the original as much as say, the Contemporary English Version differs from the KJV:

King James Version (Ps 23:4-6)	Contemporary English Version (Ps 23:4-6)
4 Yea, though I walk through the valley of the shadow of death, I will fear no evil: for thou art with me; thy rod and thy staff they comfort me.	**4** I may walk through valleys as dark as death, but I won't be afraid. You are with me, and your shepherd's rod makes me feel safe.
5 Thou preparest a table before me in the presence of mine enemies: thou anointest my head with oil; my cup runneth over.	**5** You treat me to a feast, while my enemies watch. You honor me as your guest, and you fill my cup until it overflows.
6 Surely goodness and mercy shall follow me all the days of my life: and I will dwell in the house of the LORD for ever.	**6** Your kindness and love will always be with me each day of my life, and I will live forever in your house, LORD.

In addition to Ecclesiastes and Song of Solomon, this "reworked" category may include some of the Davidic Psalms towards the end of the Psalter: 103, 122, 124, 131, 133, 144 and 145. It should be emphasized that the end products of these "reworked" texts are much different from the Classical Biblical Hebrew texts produced by the first scribal method of updating texts to bring the language up to date. The first method was conservative, making only the changes needed to keep the language understandable. It also did not go so far forward in time – reaching only the Classical Biblical

Hebrew phase as it was understood in the late pre-exilic period. By contrast, the "reworked" texts leaped all the way down in time to the post-exilic period, leaving behind the Classical Biblical Hebrew phase and any effort to emulate the earlier literary style to arrive in the spoken form of Late Biblical Hebrew.

Ecclesiastes and Song of Solomon are more unlike the rest of the Old Testament than any other two books – Song of Solomon is a romantic love poem, and Ecclesiastes is a philosophical treatise with conclusions that are challenging to reconcile with the rest of a biblical world-view. YHWH is mentioned only once in the two books. In the early post-exilic period, these books may not have attained the sacred status of the other writings, and this would explain why the scribes felt comfortable reworking them for a popular audience.

B.2 Old Testament Language Categories

In this book, the languages of the Old Testament are categorized as follows:

1. Proto-Aramaic/Proto-Hebrew – It is likely that the language of the patriarchs was substantially different from the Hebrew of any known biblical period. Educated guesses can be made as to the nature of these languages, but they are not preserved in the Bible as we have it today, except perhaps in some of the names in Genesis. Therefore, we will not address these languages in this appendix.

2. Early Biblical Hebrew – This was the language used from the exodus through the united monarchy period, around 1450 – 850 B.C. It is preserved in the names of the Bible from Exodus through Samuel and through a number of early poems in the Bible. The early prose sections of the Bible (Genesis through Samuel) retain only vestiges of Early Biblical Hebrew, due to the activity of the scribes, who succeeded in updating the language into Classical Biblical Hebrew as described in section B.1.1 above. Some

critics have suggested that Hebrew was not developed until as late as 1000 B.C., since the oldest Hebrew inscription (The Gezer calendar) discovered to date belongs to the 10th century B.C. However, this is an argument from silence, an inherently unreliable thing. In the 19th century some critics argued that Moses could not have written the Torah because man hadn't invented writing that early – an argument based on silence at that time, which was thoroughly refuted by later archeology. Ancient Hebrew inscriptions prior to the Dead Sea Scrolls are rare in general. Since the ancient Israelites primarily wrote on soft material such as scrolls, it should not be expected that much of their writing would survive 3000 years of weathering.

3. Classical Biblical Hebrew – This is the language used from the divided monarchy period until the Babylonian exile, around 850-550 B.C., and it constitutes most of the language of the Bible. It includes most of the primary history running from Genesis through Kings, most of the prophets, and much of the Writings. Early and Late Biblical Hebrew are described in terms of the way they differ from Classical Biblical Hebrew.

4. Late Biblical Hebrew – This is the language used by most biblical books written after the exile, around 550-350 B.C. The extent to which Late Biblical Hebrew differs from Classical Biblical Hebrew depends on two factors: (1) chronology - how late the text was written, and (2) influence of the exile – how much the author was influenced by the surrounding gentile culture. Therefore, texts like Ezekiel show more marks of Late Biblical Hebrew than Haggai and Zechariah, even though those books were written a little later than Ezekiel, because Ezekiel was living in Babylon when he wrote and was more influenced by the culture there. Likewise, Esther and Daniel show the heaviest marks of Late Biblical Hebrew, because they were written

by exiles intimately involved in the Persian culture and political system. In this book, we categorize the following
texts as representative of Late Biblical Hebrew: Song of
Solomon, Ecclesiastes, Esther, Daniel, Ezra, Nehemiah,
Chronicles and some Psalms. Ezekiel is a transitional book
showing some signs of Late Biblical Hebrew. In addition,
we have categorized Joel, Haggai, Zechariah and Malachi
as post-exilic books, and in these we can occasionally find
traces of Late Biblical Hebrew, although they more nearly
reflect the Classical Biblical Hebrew of the earlier era.

5.   Late Biblical Hebrew Vernacular – Ecclesiastes and Song of
     Solomon, perhaps along with a few Psalms, are in their
     own sub-category within Late Biblical Hebrew. These texts
     seem to reflect the spoken marketplace language of the
     Late Biblical Hebrew period, with certain elements of post-
     biblical Hebrew.

6.   Post-Biblical Hebrew – This includes the language of Ben
     Sirach (200 B.C.), the Dead Sea Scrolls (100 B.C. to 68 A.D),
     and then Rabbinic and Modern Hebrew (200 A.D. to the
     present). Post-biblical Hebrew is outside the scope of this
     book but is sometimes referenced for purposes of compari-
     son.

Of course, these categories are generalizations, and certain
books will show characteristics of more then one category. Ezekiel, for instance, straddles the line between Classical and Late
Biblical Hebrew.

From a modern perspective, looking at the Old Testament as a
whole, we should note that information can flow forward in time
from the early categories to the later categories: the vocabulary of
an Early Biblical Hebrew poem may be picked up and used again
in a much later book. This tendency makes it harder to identify an
early writing than a late writing; when a late writing reuses an
early feature, it makes it difficult for a modern reader to identify
that feature as being early. On the other hand, information does

not tend to flow backward in time across the categories. Unless a scribe changes the text, there is no way for a Persian word to get into an early poem, as the early poets had no exposure to any Persian culture.

Another factor that can make dating texts based on linguistics difficult is "archaizing." This is the tendency of some writers to use an older style of writing than the style of their day. For example, a modern English writer who writes using "thee" and "thou" would be archaizing. This sometimes occurs in the Bible, particularly when a later writer is trying to echo language from an older text. A Biblical example can be shown from the Torah phrase "gathered to his people," which is repeatedly used as a euphemism for death. This phrase passes out of use until Josiah's time in 2 Kings 22, when the "book of the law" is found and Huldah the prophetess reflects its usage by informing Josiah that he would be "gathered to your grave in peace" (2 Kgs 22:20).

B.3 Development of the Hebrew Language
B.3.1 Script

The original Hebrew script (the way the letters were formed) was different from the script in which the text is preserved today. The original angular script was more pictorial, with the first letter representing an ox head and yoke, etc. This script was used throughout the periods of Early Biblical Hebrew and Classical Biblical Hebrew, and is attested in all pre-exilic Hebrew inscriptions. A few of the Dead Sea Scrolls retained the use of the angular script. This script is shown below, with letters counted right to left.

Figure B-1 Early Hebrew Script[7]

The modern script used in this text, sometimes called the "square script," was adopted from Aramaic shortly after the Babylonian exile. This script has remained essentially unchanged since around 500 B.C. except for variations in style.

B.3.2 Alphabet

Any material written in the patriarchal time would probably have been written in cuneiform, with an alphabet not classified as Hebrew. By the time of the exodus, the Israelites may have been using the Phoenician/Canaanite alphabet which would eventually become the Hebrew alphabet known today. It is possible that this early alphabet had more than the 22 letters currently in the biblical text, as early cognate languages such as Ugaritic had a 30 letter alphabet at about the time of the exodus. It is also possible that the earliest Hebrew writing was left to right, as is evidenced by the 22 letter alphabet in the Izbet Sartah ostracon, a Canaanite or Hebrew relic from about 1200 B.C.[8] No Hebrew inscriptions exist before 1200 B.C., but all inscriptions since that time indicate that the modern 22 letter alphabet was in use.

The Hebrew alphabet may have originally had a different alphabetical order. A possible older order is given by the Tel Zayit

---

[7] Early Hebrew Script drawn by Ager, Simor, "Omniglot - writing systems and languages of the world", 10-30-2006, www.omniglot.com

[8] Dembski in Hallo, *The Context of Scripture*, Vol. I, p. 363

inscription from the tenth century B.C., which reverses the fifth and sixth letters (*waw* and *he*), the seventh and eighth letters (*zayin* and *heth*), the eleventh and twelfth letters (*kaf* and *lamedh*), and the sixteenth and seventeenth letters (*ayin* and *pe*). This order was (letters written right to left):

א ב ג ד ו ה ה ז ח ח ט י ל כ כ מ נ ס פ ע צ ק ר ש ת

The current order and the one used later in the Old Testament period is:

א ב ג ד ה ו ז ח ט י כ ל מ נ ס ע פ צ ק ר ש ת

The *ayin-pe* and *zayin-heth* reversals are also present in the Izbet Sartah ostracon, while the *ayin-pe* reversal persists into the exilic period, sometimes showing up in biblical literature as late as the acrostics of Lamentations 2, 3 and 4.

There is evidence that the scribes may have struggled with how to deal with an older alphabetical order. Certain passages in the Bible are acrostics, that is, each verse begins with a different letter starting with the first letter of the Hebrew alphabet and ending with the last. Lamentations 1-4, the virtuous woman passage in Prov 31:10-31, and Psalms 9-10, 25, 34, 37, 111, 112, 119 and 145 are acrostics. In Lamentations chapters 2, 3 and 4 (but not chapter 1), *ayin* and *pe* are switched. They are also switched in the Septuagint version of Proverbs 31. They are not switched in any of the acrostic Psalms. Only Psalms 111, 112 and 119 are letter perfect acrostics, with all letters of the Hebrew alphabet represented in their current alphabetical order. Those were all likely written late in the Old Testament period. The other acrostic Psalms, 9-10, 25, 34, 37 and 145, are all Psalms of David and have some features (letters missing, etc.) which prevent them from being perfect acrostics. This may be an argument for antiquity of those Psalms. Any language updates may have altered what was originally a complete acrostic. The situation would be more pronounced if David was working with a different alphabetical order, like the one in the Tel Zayit inscription. In that case, a scribe would not only be confronted with the difficulty of archaic language, but also might be tempted to think the text before him was corrupt to begin with, and might himself reverse some of the verses. Trying to determine whether a scribe switched verse order is difficult, because the verses in most acrostic Psalms stand alone, not showing a progression of thought, and thus any order would work equally well. However, Psalms 34 gives one example of a case where a scribe apparently did switch verses with the *ayin* and *pe* letters. In the table below, the first part of verse 17 is retranslated to change the words "The righteous" to "they." "The righteous" is not present in the original Hebrew – modern translators correctly perceive that there is a point of confusion there and had to insert it.

Psalm 34 Current Verse Order	Psalm 34 Proposed Original Verse Order
[15]The eyes of the LORD are toward the righteous, and His ears are open to their cry.	[16]The face of the LORD is against evildoers, to cut off the memory of them from the earth.
[16]The face of the LORD is against evildoers, to cut off the memory of them from the earth.	[15]The eyes of the LORD are toward the righteous, and His ears are open to their cry.
[17]They cry out, and the LORD hears, and delivers them out of all their troubles.	[17]They cry out, and the LORD hears, and delivers them out of all their troubles.

The "Proposed Original Verse Order" on the right half of the table is probably the original, rather than what is in the text today. Otherwise, we would have the evildoers crying out for help to the LORD, rather than the righteous. Psalm 34 is also missing a verse that begins with a *waw*, the fifth letter of the alphabet. *Waw* is one of the reversed letters in the Tel Zayit inscription. We can perhaps appreciate the dilemma of an ancient scribe who was copying this Psalm, and knew that it was an alphabetic Psalm, but saw that the verses were (in his mind) out of order. He switched verses 16 and 17. He also may have switched verses seven and six, and verses ten and eleven, but couldn't do that with verses four and five because the meaning would somehow be ruined – so he moved what would have been verse 5, the *waw* verse, to the end of the Psalm. The absence of a verse can be seen by the fact that the current verse 5 has a pronoun "they," but there is no indication who "they" are. The original verse ordering for the Psalm may have been as follows:

1-4,

22 with *waw* inserted before the first word. By making this a waw consecutive, the verb tense of the first part of the verse matches the verb tense of the second part of the verse (otherwise, it doesn't match)

5, 7, 6, 8-9, 11, 10, 12-14, 16, 15, 17-21.

Psalm 37, a second Davidic acrostic Psalm also shows an interesting pattern on the *ayin* and *pe* letters. In this Psalm, the *ayin* verse is missing, or replaced by the second part of verse 28, which at least has an *ayin* as its second letter. It is possible that verses 8 and 10 could be switched, as could the pair of verses 12-13 with verses 14-15.

These are indications that the Hebrew language alphabetical order has changed during the Old Testament period, and that only near the end of the Old Testament period did it solidify into the order used today.

B.3.3 Names

Names can be useful clues to the development of a language, because names will tend not to be changed during scribal activity. Thus, the language of the patriarchs may at one time have had a word "esau" which meant "red" (Gen 25:25), though no such word is known in Biblical Hebrew.

The name for God, YHWH, entered the language at the beginning of the Early Biblical Hebrew period (Exod 6:3). The fact that YHWH entered the language at this time and not before can be demonstrated by Exod 3:13 and 6:3, as well as the absence of Yahwistic names in the early part of the Bible. (For an explanation of the many uses of the name YHWH in Genesis, see section 3.3.9.2.2). Yahwistic names are names which contain part of the divine name YHWH. They can be easily identified in English, because the most common form involved a YH ending, which is translated "iah" or "jah," as in Isaiah or Elijah. Names that in English start with "Jeh," such as Jehoshaphat and Jehoiachin, are also Yahwistic names. Early Biblical Hebrew literature (Torah and Joshua) contains no Yahwistic names (discounting Joshua, who was born as "Hoshea" – Num 13:16). Judges 17:1, Micah (מיכיהו), is the next clearly Yahwistic name to appear in the Bible. Yahwistic names came into common use early in the monarchy (about 1000 B.C.) and became so popular that most of the kings of Judah had a Yahwistic name. Use of Yahwistic names remained heavy throughout the Old Testament period but began to decline by the New Testament period due to reverence for and reluctance to use the divine name.

The early designations used for God are El, Elohim, Eloah and El Shaddai. "Eloah" is apparently a singular form for Elohim which appears early and is used sparingly throughout the Old Testament period (Deut 32:15, Neh 9:17, etc.), but with somewhat more frequency in early texts. Note that Shaddai names are present in the Torah (Num 1:5-6 and 1:12), along with numerous El/Elohim names (Israel, Ishmael, etc.). The designation "LORD of Hosts" enters the Bible towards the end of the period of the Judges (1 Sam 1:3, 1:11, etc.) and goes on to be used 229 times throughout the rest of the Old Testament period. "Tsur" (צור), meaning "rock" was a common early designation for God, going a little beyond just its use as a metaphor. "Rock" appears as a designation for God five times in Deuteronomy 32, including unusual phrases like "our Rock is not like their rock" (Deut 32:31). It also appears in names, such as Zuriel (Num 3:35), meaning "God is my Rock," Elizur (Num 1:5), meaning "my God is a Rock," Pedahzur (Num 1:10), and "Zur," a Midianite (Num 31:8). The distribution of this metaphor shows that it is linked primarily to earlier texts (1 Samuel 2, 22, Isaiah 17, 26, 44, 51, Habakkuk 1, Psalms 28, 31, 42, 62, 71, 78, 89, 92, 94, 95 and 144). The metaphor of God as a rock provides an interesting example of how a figure of speech can go in and out of vogue and then come back in again. This metaphor was popular in the early Old Testament period and then declined in use. By around 200 B.C., the Septuagint translators found something about this metaphor to be improper, such that they never translate "rock" literally in relationship to God, instead substituting "God" or some other suitable alternative. This is reflected in many different Old Testament books, so multiple Septuagint translators all felt the same about it. Yet by the end of the first century A.D., the New Testament writers loved to apply the rock metaphor to Christ (Acts 4:11, Rom 9:32-33, 1 Cor 10:4, Eph 2:20 and 1 Pet 2:4-8).

One designation for God is entirely post-exilic: "God of Heaven," without being prefixed by YHWH. This term appears 18 times, but only in Chronicles, Ezra, Nehemiah and Daniel.

An interesting name in Judges is Anath, the father of Shamgar (Judg 3:31 and 5:6). He was probably named after Anat, an ancient Canaanite war-goddess. The cities of Anathoth (Jer 1:1, etc.) and Beth-anath (Josh 19:38, etc.) may also have been named after Anat. This name is a mark of antiquity.

B.3.4 Nouns

Other old Semitic languages used case endings on nouns for nominative, genitive and accusative cases. Very early Hebrew may have used these case endings, but if so, they were almost completely lost by the time the Bible was written, as Biblical Hebrew has no case endings. There may be instances where remnants of the old case endings can be seen in the Biblical text, although these are not undisputed. The case endings in other Semitic languages are 'u' (ו) = nominative, 'i' (י) = genitive, and 'ah' (ה) = accusative. Case endings in the Bible are most likely reflected in older names and a few other phrases. These would include the name "Methuselah" (מתושלח) as a nominative example (Gen 5:21), and "Melchizedek" (מלכי־צדק), "king of righteousness" (Gen 14:18) and "Adoni-zedek" (אדני־צדק), "lord of righteousness" (Josh 10:1) as genitive examples. The accusative case ending is likely preserved in the common practice of affixing a ה to the end of a noun to indicate direction, as in "to Egypt" (מצרימה) in Gen 12:10.

Hebrew nouns can be singular, plural, or dual. The dual form is used throughout the biblical period to denote items that naturally come in pairs, such as hands or wings. Normally when two separate items are enumerated, as in "two sons," the dual is not used, but rather the Hebrew number two is used along with a plural form of the noun. However, in earlier Hebrew, certain nouns, especially measurements, appear in dual form rather than the "two + plural" form. Examples are two cubits (Exod 25:10, 25:17, 25:23, 30:2, 37:1, 37:6 and 37:10), two years (Gen 11:10, 45:6, 1 Kgs 15:25, 1 Kgs 16:8, 2 Kgs 15:23, Jer 28:3, 28:11 and Amos 1:1), two weeks (Lev 12:5), two days (Exod 16:29, Num 9:22, 11:19 and Hos 6:2), two times (Gen 27:36, 41:32, 43:10, Num 20:11, 1 Sam 18:11 and 1 Kgs 11:9), two talents (1 Kgs 16:24 and 2 Kgs 5:23), two measures" (2 Kgs 7:1, 7:16 and 7:18) and two kinds (Lev 19:19 and Deut 22:9). This usage of the dual begins to drop out of Hebrew even in the pre-exilic era, as the "two + plural" form appears for "two years" in 1 Sam 13:1, 2 Sam 2:10, 2 Kgs 21:19 and 2 Chron 33:21. The two + plural form is used for "two days" in 2 Sam 1:1, Ezra 10:13 and Esth 9:27, and for "two cubits" in Ezek 40:9, 41:3,

41:22 and 43:14. The late passage Neh 13:20 also avoids the dual for "two times."

Classical Biblical Hebrew texts sometimes use a singular expression for plural entities, while Late Biblical Hebrew texts are more likely to insist on a plural expression in such cases. For example, 1 Kgs 10:22 uses a singular (אני) for "ships," while the parallel passage of 2 Chron 9:21 makes it plural (אניות). Likewise, 2 Kgs 8:27 has Ahaziah walking in "the way of" (דרך) Ahab, while 2 Chron 22:3 has him walking in "the ways of" (דרכי) Ahab. The movement toward more plurals is irregular, with late books like Chronicles sometimes adopting the earlier usage (as in 2 Chron 21:13, which uses a singular "the way of").

B.3.5 Calendar

In the Bible, months are usually designated by their number, but they did have names. The names of months changed during the Old Testament period. Four of the earlier names are mentioned: Abib – first month (Exod 13:4), Ziv – second month (1 Kgs 6:1), Bul – eighth month (1 Kgs 6:38) and Ethanim – seventh month (1 Kgs 8:2). Ziv, Bul and Ethanim are known from the Phoenician language, making it likely that this early Hebrew calendar reflected Canaanite month names. Later Biblical texts used the modern Jewish calendar month names, which were borrowed from the Babylonian names. The switchover took place during the Babylonian exile. The following names all appear in later Biblical texts: Nisan (Neh 2:1), Sivan (Esth 8:9), Elul (Neh 6:15), Tevet (Esth 2:16), Kislev (Neh 1:1), Shebat (Zech 1:7) and Adar (Ezra 6:15). The distribution of month names shows that Exodus and most of Kings were written before the exile, with Zechariah, Ezra, Nehemiah and Esther written after the exile.

B.3.6 Numbers

Biblical Hebrew uses numbers in a variety of different ways. Cardinal numbers can be used before the noun (Ruth 3:15) or after the noun (Hag 2:16). Sometimes the number will be in construct form before the noun, with the noun in plural form (Deut 5:13). Sometimes the number will be in construct form before the noun, but with the noun in singular form (Esth 1:4). Sometimes cardinal numbers can be in front of a noun in singular form (Gen 7:12). Of these combinations, only one shows evidence of being related to chronology - placement of the number after the noun. This occurs in late writings (2 Chron 3:3-4, 3:11-13, Ezra 8:15, Neh 2:11, 5:14, Dan 1:12, 1:14; 12:11, Hag 2:16, etc.).[9] In particular, the temple dimensions in 2 Chronicles reverse the order used in Kings; Chronicles puts the numbers after the nouns, while Kings puts the numbers before the nouns. However, this switch in usage over time was not an absolute number-before to number-after switch, rather it was number-before to optional. The late book of Esther continues the older practice of number before noun (Esth 1:4 and 5:14) while Ezra and Chronicles go both ways (Ezra 6:22 and 1 Chron 11:23 are examples of the old number-before usage). Therefore, the presence of a number after the noun is evidence of a late date. Any of the other combinations cannot be used as evidence for any date, since they were apparently all used throughout the Biblical period. The mixed usage continued through the time of the Dead Sea Scrolls.[10]

B.3.7 Pronouns

The relative pronoun "asher" (אשר) enters the Hebrew language during the Early Biblical Hebrew period and becomes one of the most frequently used words in the Bible, appearing 5503 times. It is possible that this word was not in the language at the beginning

---

[9] An outlier is 2 Sam 1:1, an early writing with the number after the noun.

[10] An example of number before noun would be scroll 4Q365a, fragment 2 column 2 verse 2. An example of number after noun would be scroll 4Q390, fragment 2 column 1 verse 6. Also noteworthy on this subject is the fact that one of the Arad inscriptions from just before the exile shows the *late* usage of number after the noun.

of this early period, as it is absent in the Song of Moses, which substitutes the much rarer "zu" (זו) as a relative pronoun (Exod 15:13) and Psalm 90, attributed to Moses. The Song of Deborah substitutes the attached particle שׁ as a relative pronoun in Judg 5:7, but then uses אשר in 5:27. Davidic Psalms, by comparison, use אשר with some frequency (Ps 3:7, etc.). Because אשר is not found in the closely related Ugaritic language tablets, and those tablets represent literature prior to 1200 B.C., it seems reasonable to believe that אשר was not part of the Hebrew language at the time of Moses, but entered the language prior to David, by 1000 B.C. Of the two relative pronoun variants, זו occurs only 14 times and passes out of usage prior to the exile, with the last occurrence in time in the Bible in Hab 1:11. The other pronoun, שׁ, goes on to become common in Late Biblical Hebrew and becomes the preferred form in post-biblical Hebrew. The use of the particle שׁ in place of the full relative pronoun אשר has an unusual history. In Psalms, שׁ appears 17 times, but all those appearances are in the fifth and latest section of the Psalms, beginning in chapter 122. In later Rabbinic Hebrew, שׁ is commonly used as a relative pronoun. This would seem to indicate that שׁ is a marker for a late date. However, שׁ makes occasional appearances in indisputably very early Hebrew, as in Judg 5:7, 7:12 and 8:26. It sees only occasional use throughout the Old Testament, until Song of Solomon and Ecclesiastes are reached, and there it is used 68 times in Ecclesiastes and 32 times in Song of Solomon. In the Dead Sea Scrolls, it is rarely used, except in the 3Q15 Copper Scroll, where it is used throughout. The uneven concentration of usage of שׁ is thought provoking. However, since it sometimes appears in Early, Classical, and Late Biblical Hebrew, and since other lengthy Early, Classical and Late Biblical Hebrew passages do not use it at all, it is not an especially good indicator of the date of a passage.

The use of "zu" as a relative pronoun can be used as an indication of a pre-exilic date for biblical texts, prior to 600 B.C. This is a useful clue, especially for Psalms. "Zu" pronouns appear, along with a variant, "zo," in Exod 15:13, 15:16, Ps 9:15 (Heb 9:16), 10:2, 12:7 (Heb 12:8), 17:9, 31:4 (Heb 31:5), 32:8, 62:11 (Heb 62:12), 68:28 (Heb 68:29), 132:12, 142:3 (Heb 142:4), 143:8, Isa 42:24, 43:21 and Hos 7:16.

The relative pronoun used to mean "these" in Hebrew is "eleh" (אלה), or with a definite article, "ha'eleh" (האלה). In the Torah only, the shortened form "ha'el" (האל) is sometimes used (Gen 19:8, 19:25, 26:3, 26:4, Lev 18:27, Deut 4:42, 7:22 and 19:11), along with the later form (Gen 15:1, 22:1, etc.).

Hebrew literature from the earliest period uses both "ani" (אני) and "anoki" (אנכי) as a first person singular pronoun ("I"), with the choice between the two based on subtle guidelines. These guidelines include:[11]

    1a. In a clause that says "I am <name>," use "ani" when emphasis is on <name>, as it almost always is. Examples are "I am YHWH" (Lev 19:14 and many more times) and "I am Joseph" (Gen 45:3).

    1b. In a clause that says "I am <name>," use "anoki" when the emphasis is on "I," which is rare. Examples are Exod 20:2-3, "*I* am the LORD your God who brought you out from the land of Egypt, from the house of bondage; you shall have no other gods before *Me*." This is also a chiasm:

        A I am
        B   YHWH your God
        C   who brought out you
        D   from the land of Egypt
        D'   from the house of bondage
        C'   there shall not be to you
        B'   other gods
        A' before Me.

---

[11] Umberto Cassuto, in *The Documentary Hypothesis, Eight Lectures*, pp. 50-51, develops a more detailed set of guidelines covering all instances of anoki and ani in the book of Genesis.

Notice the contrast when Esau says "I am *Esau*" (Gen 27:32). Esau's statement is a normal sentence using "ani," but when Jacob says "*I* am Esau" (Gen 27:19), he is lying, the emphasis falls awkwardly on the pronoun, and "anoki" is used.

2. Use "anoki" when the pronoun equates to a modifying adjective. Examples are "I was naked" (Gen 3:10) and "I am a Hebrew" (Jonah 1:9). Examples are numerous - see Ruth 3:12, 1 Sam 1:15, Isa 6:5, Jer 1:6, Amos 7:14, etc. However, this usage is only a tendency, and in certain phrases is reversed: all five occurrences of "I am your servant" that include a pronoun use "ani."

3a. Use "anoki" after the long form of "behold" (הנה), as in Gen 24:13, Exod 3:13, Num 22:32, etc. This usage occurs 30 times in the Bible.

3b. Use "ani" after the short form of behold (הן), as in Exod 6:30, Job 33:6, Isa 49:21 and 56:3.

During the Babylonian exile, usage of "anoki" began to decline, and the latest Old Testament books rarely use it at all. There are no occurrences of "anoki" in Ezekiel (where we can see the beginning of the trend), Ezra, Esther, Joel, Ecclesiastes, Song of Solomon, Zechariah 1-8, or Haggai. Chronicles uses it once, in a quotation from Samuel. Daniel and Malachi also use it exactly once. In all 349 occurrences in the Bible, "anoki" is never spelled with a vowel letter ו in the second syllable (אנכי), even though by all indications it has a long 'o' sound. There are a few instances in the Dead Sea Scrolls in which this word appears, and when it does, the spelling is אנוכי. It is not used in rabbinic literature except when quoting scripture.

Some source critics have suggested that because the P source uses "ani" almost exclusively, this is evidence that P is a late text. However, the passages assigned to P are still following the guidelines of Classical Biblical Hebrew. The phrase, "I am YHWH," repeated 72 times in the Torah, mostly in passages assigned to P, requires the use of "ani," as defined in guideline 1a. When P does need to use a phrase of the form "I am <adjective>," it uses "anoki," in accordance with guideline 2, as in the P passage of Gen 23:4, "I am a foreigner." Truly late texts such as Mal 1:6, "If I am a father…," use "ani," thereby breaking the rule and showing that they are late.

The phasing out of "anoki" can also be seen in the phrase "Who am I?" which uses "anoki" in the earlier passages of Exod 3:11, 1 Sam 18:18 and 2 Sam 7:18, then switches to "ani" in 1 Chron 17:16, 29:14 and 2 Chron 2:5 (Heb 2:6). Note that 1 Chron 17:16 is a quote from 2 Sam 7:18, yet even here the pronoun changes.

In general, the presence of "anoki" indicates antiquity, while the presence of "ani" indicates nothing, except when it is used in a phrase where older grammatical guidelines require "anoki" – in that case "ani" indicates a later text.

The Torah commonly uses a single pronoun, "hue" (הוא) for third person singular masculine or feminine (meaning "he/she/it"), without distinction for gender. The usual "hie" (היא) to represent third person feminine singular ("she") also appears in the Torah, but only 11 times, much less than the 168 times הוא is used in that role. However, the split usage quickly took hold, with הוא masculine and היא feminine, so that no literature after the Torah ever uses הוא for feminine. This includes very old songs, such as the song of Deborah, which uses היא as a feminine pronoun. This is an argument for the unity of the Torah, and for its separation from Joshua (the first six books are not a "hexateuch"). However, because the difference in הוא and היא is a vowel letter, it is best to not treat this as an argument for the antiquity of the Torah. The use of vowel letters likely did not begin until after the Torah had been written, indicating that the original writing was likely just הא for either pronoun, with scribes adding the middle vowel later.

B.3.8 Pronominal Suffixes

In Biblical Hebrew it is possible to make a pronoun a direct object by either using a direct object marker with a suffix attached, or by attaching a pronominal suffix directly to the verb. Both uses appear throughout the Bible. It has been suggested that in Late Biblical Hebrew, the use of the direct object marker with attached pronominal suffixes declined. The observation is true; Kings has this form 122 times while the later Chronicles has this form only 43 times. However, it is unlikely this can be used as an argument for dating Biblical texts. The texts in question are usually much shorter than Chronicles, and the 43 occurrences in Chronicles hardly mark it as rare. Also, although the use of the direct object marker with suffixes declined, it never passed out of use completely, and was still present in the extra-Biblical Dead Sea Scrolls.[12] Factors other than chronology, such as subject matter, poetic considerations, and an author's individual style can also suppress the usage, as it only occurs four times in Psalms, not at all in Lamentations, Ruth, or Daniel, four times in Esther, once in Ezra, four times in Nehemiah, once in Ecclesiastes, four times in Song of Solomon, seven times in Job and four times in Proverbs. It is doubtful that this distribution can be used as a meaningful measure for dating Biblical texts.

The third person masculine plural pronominal suffix "mo" (מו) was present in Early Biblical Hebrew. Like all pronominal suffixes, it can be attached to nouns (Ps 2:3), verbs (Exod 15:5, 15:7) and prepositions (Ps 2:5). This usage continued through the period of the older Psalms (Ps 17:10, 21:9 [Heb 21:10], etc.). The usual form of the third person masculine plural suffix "hem" (הם) and the earlier form can appear in the same passage (Exod 15:16 and 15:19 have "hem"). By the time of the prophets, the early form is completely absent except for a few cases in Isaiah, Habakkuk

---

[12] As in the Damascus Document, CD-A column 1 line 6

and Lamentations where it is attached to a preposition. There are no occurrences of the early suffix "mo" attached to nouns or verbs in the prophets or later writings. Therefore, the use of this pronominal suffix can be used as a clue indicating an early date as follows:

1. "Mo" pronominal suffixes on nouns and verbs as well as on the prepositions אל and על are not later than 700 B.C. (Exodus 15, Deuteronomy 32, 33, Psalms 2, 5, 11, 17, 21, 22, 35, 45, 49, 55, 58, 59, 64, 73, 80, 83, 89, 140 and Job 27).
2. "Mo" pronominal suffixes attached to the preposition ל are not post-exilic; not later than 538 B.C.: (Gen 9:26-27, Deuteronomy 32, Isa 16:4, 23:1, 26:14, 26:16; 30:5, 35:8, 43:8, 44:7, 48:21, 53:8, Hab 2:7, Lam 1:19, 1:22; 4:10, 4:15, Psalms 2, 28, 44, 49, 55, 56, 58, 59, 64, 66, 73, 78, 80, 88, 99, 119:165, Job 3, 6, 14, 15, 22, 24, 30, 39 and Prov 23:20).

The second person singular masculine pronominal suffix, "ki" (כי) is irregular, probably based on Aramaic, and appearing only in 2 Kgs 4:2-7, Jer 11:15 and the late Psalms 103, 116, 135 and 137.

The "energic nun" is an additional nun (נ) appearing in a pronominal suffix, as in תשופנו, "you will bruise him" (Gen 3:15). The occurrences of the energic nun are distributed as follows:

Genesis	35	Song of Solomon	3
Exodus	25	Isaiah	45
Leviticus	39	Jeremiah	27
Numbers	25	Lamentations	3
Deuteronomy	60	Ezekiel	12
Joshua	7	Hosea	4
Judges	12	Joel	1
Ruth	0	Amos	8
Samuel	19	Obadiah	0
Kings	19	Jonah	0
Chronicles	6	Micah	3
Ezra	0	Nahum	0
Nehemiah	4	Habukkuk	3

Esther	0	Zephaniah	0
Job	72	Haggai	0
Psalms	55	Zechariah	2
Proverbs	39	Malachi	1
Ecclesiastes	11		

The distribution indicates that there is a higher concentration of the energic nun in the earlier books. It appears frequently in the Torah and Job. It appears more in Isaiah than Jeremiah and more in Jeremiah than Ezekiel (working from oldest to newest Major Prophets). Among Minor Prophets, it appears most in the oldest books of Amos and Hosea. Still, the energic nun appears with some frequency in every era of Biblical Hebrew, so its decreasing use over time is only a generality.

B.3.9 Verbs and Adverbs

The way Biblical Hebrew verb tenses work is not intuitive to modern readers, since Biblical Hebrew does not have an exact equivalent for past, present and future tenses. Instead, Biblical Hebrew uses two finite verb forms, the perfect tense (sometimes called the suffix form) and the imperfect tense (sometimes called the prefix form). Each of these verb tenses can be preceded by a connected letter *waw* (ו) in such a way as to alter the meaning of the verb tense.[13] The result is four finite verb forms, with a distribution in the Bible as shown below:

1. Perfect – 13, 874 occurrences
2. Imperfect - 14, 299 occurrences
3. Waw + perfect – 6,378 occurrences
4. Waw + imperfect - 14,972 occurrences (conversive form).[14]

It is important to remember that perfect and waw + perfect are not the same; the meaning is entirely different. Likewise, imperfect and waw + imperfect are not the same.

---

[13] This discussion is a generalization. An in-depth treatment of Hebrew verbs is beyond the scope of this book.

[14] Word counts taken from Waltke and O'Connor, *Biblical Hebrew Syntax*, p. 456

Past tense narratives in Classical Biblical Hebrew use a combination of perfect and waw + imperfect verb forms. Genesis 1 provides a textbook example, with "In the beginning God *created* [perfect tense verb ברא] the heavens and the earth." It then follows with a long series of waw + imperfect verbs beginning in Gen 1:3 "Then God *said* [waw + imperfect verb ויאמר]…" This is the standard form for past tense narratives throughout the Bible. The only time the imperfect verb tense is used for past action is to describe a past action that occurred habitually or repeatedly. This standard usage also applies to Hebrew poetry from the prophetic period, from at least 750 B.C. onward. Isa 5:1-2 provides an early prophetic example: "…My beloved *had* [perfect tense verb היה] a vineyard on a fertile hill. He *dug it all around* [waw + imperfect verb ויעזקהו], *removed its stones* [waw + imperfect verb ויסקלהו]…" This practice appears in all the writing prophets beginning with Hosea, Amos and Isaiah and continuing through Malachi.

In early Hebrew poetry the use of verb tenses is different, in that imperfect tense verbs are used along with perfect tense verbs to indicate past time. This is similar to the Ugaritic language of the second millennium B.C.[15] An example of the early usage is in Exod 15:5, where יכסימו is an imperfect tense verb used to say the water *"covered them"* (Pharaoh's army), describing a one time, completed action in the past. Therefore, poetry showing this use of imperfect verb tenses for past action is likely to have originated prior to the eighth century B.C. (Deut 32:8, 32:10, Judg 5:26, Ps 18:4 [Heb 18:5], 18:6 [Heb 18:7], etc.). Using this convention to date poetry puts passages in one of four categories:

1. Lengthy poems recounting past events, such as Exodus 15, Deuteronomy 32, Judges 5 and Psalm 18 can be dated early based on this criterion, because many verbs with a past tense sense can be checked. Likewise, lengthy poems like Psalm 136 can be dated as not early, because many verbs

---

[15] Robertson, *Linguistic Evidence in Dating Early Hebrew Poetry*, p. 14

are present with a past tense sense, but none are imperfect forms.

2. Short poems can also be categorized as early, if imperfect verbs can be unambiguously determined to mean past tense. This can be done especially when a perfect and an imperfect verb are used in parallel (Ps 24:2).

3. A number of passages might be showing this early usage of imperfect verbs for past tense, but it is difficult to be certain that the tense is not supposed to be present rather than past. This is true of a number of Psalms (Ps 21:3 [Heb 21:4], 21:6 [Heb 21:7]; Ps 22:15 [Heb 22:16], 40:3 [Heb 40:4], 44:9 [Heb 44:10], 48:7 [Heb 48:8], etc.). In some cases, it is not even clear if the tense is supposed to be past or future, as in Ps 40:3b (Heb 40:4b).

4. A number of passages look to be not early based on absence of this usage. However, the number of verbs to consider is too small for this line of evidence alone, which is an argument from silence, to be convincing. In this category, Psalm 137 is an example we believe is late (exilic), while Psalm 51 we believe to be early.

5. Some poetic passages cannot be dated using this criterion, because they do not recount past events (Psalm 23).

Because the identification of imperfect verbs acting as past tense is one of the better markers of Early Biblical Hebrew, we should comment on its distribution within the Bible. This feature is absent from all prose. It is present in some of the old poems in the primary history (Exodus 15, Deuteronomy 32, Judges 5, 2 Sam 1:22, 2 Samuel 22). This feature is absent from all the writing prophets, with the exception of the prayer of Habakkuk in Habakkuk 3. It is present in Job, a number of older Psalms (18, 24, 44, 68, 77, 80, 81, 104, 114, 138 and 139) and some Psalms we have dated around the time of Isaiah (Psalms 44, 66 and 78). There are a few isolated occurrences in Psalms we have dated after the time of

Isaiah (Psalm 74, 105 and 106). It is not present in the poetry of Proverbs, Lamentations, Ecclesiastes, or Song of Solomon.

It is possible that the earliest Hebrew poetry made no use of the waw + imperfect (waw-consecutive or waw-conversive) verb conjugation. This verb conjugation is the most common in the Bible, yet it is absent from the Song of Deborah and occurs only once in the Exodus 15 Song of Moses.[16] However, scribal activity has probably masked this feature in much of the Bible. If a scribe saw an imperfect form verb clearly describing a completed past tense action, he would be strongly tempted to add the letter waw to the verb; this would create a waw + imperfect verb, bringing the language up to date so as to be understandable to his readers, who might otherwise misunderstand the text.

While the waw + imperfect verb conjugation entered the Hebrew language early in the Old Testament period, it also began to leave it at the end of the Old Testament period. Waw + imperfect verb forms occur only three times in Ecclesiastes, being replaced by waw-connective + perfect, and not at all in Song of Solomon. Although the waw + imperfect conjugation is still present in some Dead Sea Scrolls, it seems to have left the language completely shortly after that, being essentially unused in Rabbinic and Modern Hebrew.

One use of the waw + imperfect verb conjugation in Classical Biblical Hebrew is to write ויהי (literally "and it was") to introduce the equivalent of an English narrative paragraph (Gen 22:20, Judg 17:1, 1 Sam 9:1, Jonah 1:1, etc.). This usage is common until the Late Biblical Hebrew period, when it decreases sharply.

Late Biblical Hebrew sometimes uses the form waw + cohortative verb for past tense, as in Neh 2:13, 5:8, Dan 9:4, 12:8, etc. This also occurs in Ben Sirach, as in Sir 51:8.

---

[16] The one time is in Exod 15:19. Exod 15:2 may be a second example, but an alternate reading is possible.

The frequency of use of infinitive absolute verbs declines considerably in Late Biblical Hebrew. There are parallel passages in which the later Chronicles avoids the infinitive absolute used in the earlier passage (2 Sam 24:12 = 1 Chron 21:10, 1 Kgs 8:13 = 2 Chron 6:2, 1 Kgs 9:6 = 2 Chron 7:19). Still, occasional occurrences of the infinitive absolute remain present in later books (Zech 6:10, Esth 4:14).

Classical Biblical Hebrew uses the adverbs "terem" (טרם) to mean "not yet" (Gen 2:5) and "bterem" (בטרם) to mean "before" in the temporal sense (Gen 27:33), with a total of 56 occurrences in the Bible. Neither of these words appears in Late Biblical Hebrew, other than a variation "mterem" (מטרם) once in Hag 2:15. Both early and late texts sometimes use "lifne" (לפני) in the same sense (Gen 36:31, 1 Chron 1:43, 1 Chron 24:2), so the two words, בטרם and לפני exist in parallel until בטרם drops out of usage. Disputed texts therefore marked as not late are Prov 8:25 (which uses both words in parallel), 18:13, 30:7, Ruth 3:14, Ps 90:2, Isa 42:9, 48:5 and 66:7. "Terem" returns in the Dead Sea Scrolls, but the usage is different: Qumran Hebrew uses "terem" before a perfect tense verb, while Biblical Hebrew places it before an imperfect tense verb.

"Be'ohd" (בעוד), meaning "while still" is concentrated in Early and Classical Biblical Hebrew (Gen 25:6, 40:13, 40:19, 48:7, Deut 31:27, Josh 1:11, 2 Sam 3:35, 12:22, Isa 7:8, 21:16, 28:4, Jer 28:3, 28:11, Amos 4:7, Ps 104:33, 146:2, Prov 31:15, Job 29:5 and in the Siloam tunnel inscription of 700 B.C.). Late Biblical Hebrew prefers just "ohd" (עוד) for this meaning, in a usage present in both early and late passages (Gen 29:9, 1 Chron 12:1, etc.).

B.3.10 Prepositions

The expressions "bizeh" (בזה) or "mizeh" (מזה) meaning "in this place" or "from this place" are not in Late Biblical Hebrew. They appear in earlier texts in Gen 37:17, 42:15, 50:25, Exod 11:1, 13:3, 33:1, 33:15, Deut 9:12, Josh 4:3, Judg 6:18, Judg 18:3, 1 Kgs 17:3, Jer

38:10 and the Lachish Letters of 587 B.C. (Lachish 3.18). Later usage requires the word "maqom" (מקום), which is also present earlier, to say "this place," as in Hag 2:9 and 2 Chron 7:15.

"Zulah" (זולה), meaning "except" or "beside," appears 16 times in the Bible. None of the occurrences are in Late Biblical Hebrew passages except for 1 Chron 17:20, which is copied from 2 Sam 7:22. The equivalent of "zulah" is "mibbaladey" (מבלעדי), which is used in both early and late texts.

There is some replacement of "el" (אל), usually meaning "to," with "ahl" (על) or the attached preposition ל in Late Biblical Hebrew. For example, "if it please" uses אל in 1 Sam 20:13 and על in Neh 2:5, 2:7. Sometimes, Late Biblical Hebrew uses על where ל would have been used earlier, as in אם־עליכם טוב, "If it seems good to you" (1 Chron 13:2). However, all three prepositions, אל, על and ל, remain extremely common in all periods of Biblical Hebrew.

B.3.11 Particles

Several particles can be used to date biblical texts, as described below.

1. The use of "bal" (בל) as an alternate way of saying "not" appears for the first time in older Psalms (10, 16, 17, 21, 30, 32, 46, 49, 58, 68, 93, 96, 104, 140, 141, 147 and 149). Its use in time extends to only the eighth century B.C. prophets Hosea (7:2 and 9:16) and Isaiah (who uses it 20 times). It occurs in Job 41:15 and ten times in Proverbs. It does not occur in any of the later prophets or writings except for 1 Chron 16:30, which is quoting Ps 96:10. It appears twice in late Psalms, Ps 147:20 and 149:7, which are probably postexilic texts, making them likely instances of archaizing.

2. Classical Biblical Hebrew uses "lbilti" (לבלתי) to negate infinitive verbs (Gen 4:15, etc.). This is a common usage continuing through the time of Ezekiel and Daniel (Dan 9:11). In Late Biblical Hebrew after Daniel it becomes rare, ap-

pearing only in 1 Chron 4:10 and 2 Chron 16:1 (quoting 1 Kgs 15:17). It is not present at all in the post-exilic books of Joel, Haggai, Zechariah, Malachi, Ezra, Nehemiah, Esther, Ecclesiastes, or Song of Solomon. In Late Biblical Hebrew, the particle "eyn" (אין), usually translated "there is not" and applied to nouns, is used to negate infinitive verbs (1 Chron 23:26, 2 Chron 5:11, 14:10, 20:6, 22:9, 35:15, Ezra 9:15, Ecc 3:14, Esth 4:2 and 8:8). This late usage continues in Ben Sirach (10:23, 39:21 and 40:26) and the Dead Sea Scrolls. Note that the late usage appears twice in early texts (1 Sam 9:7, Ps 40:5 [Heb 40:6]).

3. "Pen" (פן), meaning "lest," occurs 133 times in the Bible, but its use is concentrated in early texts. It is rare in Late Biblical Hebrew, not appearing in Ezekiel, Ezra, Nehemiah, Esther, Daniel, Ecclesiastes or Song of Solomon. Its only appearance in Chronicles is in 1 Chron 10:4, a copy of 1 Sam 31:4. It is also rare in Kings, with only two occurrences (2 Kgs 2:16 and 10:23), both of which come from an older northern Israelite source. Note that while Isa 36:18 has it, the duplicate 2 Kgs 18:32 substitutes כי.

4. The common particle "na" (נא), which has several meanings and is used 401 times in the Bible, appears less frequently in Late Biblical Hebrew, but still occurs eight times in Chronicles, seven times in Ezra and Neh, and twice in Daniel. Note how the earlier 2 Sam 7:2 uses "na," while the later parallel 1 Chron 17:1 avoids it.

5. The particle "ak" (אך), meaning "only, surely" appears 160 times in the Bible. It is in early Hebrew and continues to the time of Ezekiel (Ezek 45:17), but doesn't make it into any post-exilic text.

6. The definite article and the direct object marker are not present in Ugaritic and Egyptian, and may not have been present in earliest Hebrew. They are rare in early poetry. The direct object marker occurs 10,978 in the Bible, but it is

absent in the Song of Deborah (Judges 5), the Song of Moses (Exodus 15), the Song of Moses in Deuteronomy 32 and the one Psalm attributed to Moses, Psalm 90. It occurs once in the blessing of Jacob (Gen 49:15) and twice in the blessing of Moses (Deut 33:9).[17] The direct object marker occurs in poetry of any date with less frequency than in prose, so the significance of its absence in early poetry may not be that great. The same comments can be made about the definite article – it is rare in early poetry, yet appears in Gen 49:14-15 and a few times in the song of Moses in Deuteronomy 32 and the blessing of Moses in Deuteronomy 33. Its omission in early poetry appears not to be coincidental. For example, Exod 15:6 looks like it needs an article before "enemy" – "*the* enemy" – but no article is there. Definite articles do not appear in Psalm 90, but do appear in Judges 5. Both the direct object marker and the definite article appear with some frequency in Davidic Psalms, so they must have been part of the language by 1000 B.C.

B.3.12 Aramaic Influence

The Hebrew and Aramaic languages existed side by side in the Middle East throughout most of the Old Testament period. Aramaic influenced the language of the Old Testament, with the level of influence increasing greatly after the Babylonian exile.

The first hint of interaction between Hebrew and Aramaic is in Gen 31:47, where Jacob and Laban name the same monument, with Jacob naming it in Hebrew and Laban in Aramaic. Around 700 B.C., Hezekiah's royal officials tried to persuade the Assyrian king's representatives to speak to them in Aramaic (2 Kgs 18:26),

---

[17] Gen 49:15 and Deut 33:9 may be verses that have been updated from their early form by the scribes. Gen 49:15 has not only a direct object marker, but two definite articles, while Deut 33:9 has two direct object markers and a definite article. This would be normal in Classical Biblical Hebrew, but in early poetry these are abnormal concentrations of these features.

in a story which indicates that at this time the elites in Judah could speak Aramaic, while the common people could not. Aramaic became ascendant in the Middle East during the Babylonian period (586-538 B.C.) and afterward. Around 440 B.C., Neh 13:24 shows that not all the Jews in Judah could speak Hebrew. Hebrew was still the primary written language in Qumran in the Maccabean period (beginning around 170 B.C.), though Aramaic was used as well. By the time of the New Testament, Aramaic had become the primary spoken language by Jews in the province of Judea.[18]

Three blocks of post-exilic scripture are written in Aramaic rather than Hebrew: Ezra 4:8-6:18, Ezra 7:12-26 and Dan 2:4-7:28. Earlier uses of Aramaic include Jer 10:11, a verse entirely in Aramaic, and the name mentioned above in Gen 31:47.

Aside from texts written in Aramaic, there are some Hebrew texts that show an Aramaic influence. "Aramaisms" in a Hebrew text are words, grammar, or figures of speech considered common to Aramaic but not intrinsically part of Biblical Hebrew. Because the influence of Aramaic became so great after the exile, Hebrew texts with many Aramaisms are usually considered to be written after the exile. As Hurvitz puts it: "…the *critical* meeting point of these two languages is assigned to the sixth century BCE, even though sporadic contacts are documented in the Biblical tradition prior to this date."[19] However, the presence of Aramaisms as a criterion for dating a Hebrew text can be misleading and must be done cautiously, for the following reasons:

1. Hebrew and Aramaic are closely related languages. What appears to be an Aramaism may instead be a valid Hebrew expression, just one that is rarer in Hebrew than Aramaic.

---

[18] The New Testament, written in Greek, preserves a number of original language quotes, and these quotes are in Aramaic. Examples are "Eli, Eli, lama sabachthani?" (Matt 27:46) and Talitha kum" (Mark 5:41).

[19] Hurvitz, Avi, "Hebrew and Aramaic in the Biblical Period", in Young, *Biblical Hebrew Studies in Chronology and Typology*, p. 34

2. Aramaic was spoken by nations interacting with Israel in very early periods, and some expressions may have passed into Hebrew early.

3. Northern Israel had more interaction with Aramaic speaking cultures than the southern Kingdom of Judah. As a result, more early Aramaisms appear in passages with a northern Israelite origin. For example, 2 Kgs 4:2-7 has the northern Israelite prophet Elisha speaking, and four times he uses the Aramaic pronominal suffix כי. These are the only four occurrences of כי in the primary history of Genesis-Kings. Because it is not always possible to determine the geographic origin of a Hebrew text, this can lead to uncertainty as to whether the text is late, or whether it is just northern.

4. Sometimes, a Biblical writer will place Aramaisms in the mouth of gentile speakers or increase the use of Aramaisms in a gentile setting. For example, 2 Kgs 6:8-19 describes a war council held by the king of Syria (Aram) and this passage has multiple Aramaisms.[20] In Jonah 1:7, "beshelmi" (בשלמי), is an Aramaism meaning "on whose account," used when gentile sailors are speaking to one another. When they speak to Jonah, they say the same thing with the more Hebraic form of the same idiom in 1:8 "ba'asher lemi" (באשר למי). Note also that both these examples appear to have a northern Israelite origin.

In conclusion, sporadic Aramaisms can occur in a Biblical Hebrew text for a number of reasons, not all of which are knowable. These, therefore, are not very useful in dating Biblical Hebrew texts. The presence of a few Aramaic expressions in a Hebrew text cannot by itself be used as meaningful information for dating a text. Samuel Driver, a renowned Hebrew scholar who generally supports a

---

[20] Aramaisms in 2 Kgs 6:8-19 include words translated as "encamped" (תחנות in v8), "of us" (משלנו in v11), and "that" (זה in v19)

modern critical analysis of the Old Testament, agrees: "words, with Aramaic or late Hebrew affinities, occur, at least sporadically, in passages admittedly of early date."[21] A heavy concentration of Aramaisms, on the other hand, is a good indication of an exilic or post-exilic date.

B.3.13 Vocabulary

Early Biblical Hebrew vocabulary can be attested by the words in early poems. It is difficult to definitively classify words as early, because once the word is written down in a poem it is available to later generations and can be used even in a very late writing. This detracts from the usefulness of early vocabulary as a marker for dating other texts. However, there are some cases where a word is used in an early poem, then goes on to appear in considerable concentration in other early texts, and then nearly disappears from late texts in favor of a more common synonym. These words can be classified as early with some confidence, and then be used to evaluate other texts of unknown date. Examples are listed below.

1. "Orakh" (ארח) for "way, path" appears in early poetry (Gen 49:17 and Judg 5:6) and goes on to be used 57 times, with no occurrence chronologically later than about 700 B.C. except for Psalm 119 and the difficult to date Joel 2:7. The much more common synonym is Derek (דרך).

2. "Omer" or "amer" (אמר) for "speech, word," instead of the more common "davar" (דבר), is in early poetry (Gen 49:21, Num 24:4, Deut 33:9 and Judg 5:29), and goes on to be used 49 times, concentrated mostly in other early passages.

3. "Makhatz" (מחץ) for "strike" appears 14 times, entirely in early poetry (Deut 32:39, Judg 5:26, Ps 68:21 [Heb 68:22], etc.).

---

[21] Driver, *An Introduction to the Literature of the Old Testament*, p. 455

Some additional Hebrew words such as "pa'al" (פעל) for "do, make," and "khavah" (חוה) for "say" appear in early poetry and may well reflect common early vocabulary, since they are largely replaced later by more common synonyms. However, these are difficult to use as chronological markers because they have a limited number of occurrences, and their use seems to persist, though with decreasing frequency, through most of the Classical Biblical Hebrew period.

Some additional words that can be used as chronological markers are listed below:

1. Earlier prose uses "makar" (מכר), usually translated as "sold," in a sense that has nothing to do with money, but refers instead to giving someone into the power of their enemies (Deut 32:30, Judg 2:14, 3:8, 4:2, 10:7 and 1 Sam 12:9). Later Hebrew uses "natan" (נתן), meaning "give" (Jer 20:4, Dan 1:2, etc.), to produce the same meaning.

2. "Ehdah" (עדה), meaning "congregation," appears 149 times in the Bible, 113 of those occurrences being in the Torah. It occurs only once in an unambiguously exilic or post-exilic biblical passage, 2 Chron 5:6, which is quoting the earlier 1 Kgs 8:5. Late texts are more likely to use "qahal" (קהל) for congregation. "Qahal" appears in both early and late texts (Gen 49:6, 2 Chron 20:5, etc.), but it is heavily used in late texts, appearing 33 times in Chronicles, and multiple times in Ezekiel, Ezra and Nehemiah.

3. "Enosh" (אנוש), meaning "man" or "men," appears 42 times in the Bible, but only once in a post-exilic book, in the mouth of Asa in 2 Chron 14:10, a passage that may have an older origin. "Enosh" appears first in the old poem of Deut 32:26, then frequently in Job, Isaiah and early Psalms.

4. "Shesh" (שש) is earlier than "butz" (בוץ), both words meaning "linen." "Shesh" occurs in the Torah 34 times, then five

times afterwards. "Butz" appears eight times, beginning with Ezekiel.

5. In Psalms, "selah" (סלה), usually understood to denote some sort of musical pause, appears predominately in the earlier Psalms (Ps 3:2 [Heb 3:3], 4:2 [Heb 4:3], 7:5 [Heb 7:6], etc.).

6. "Isheh" (אשה), meaning "offering by fire," is used 65 times in the Bible, 63 times in the Torah and also in Josh 13:14 and 1 Sam 2:28. "Isheh" seems to be phased out in favor of a combination of related words, including "ohlah" (עלה), usually translated as "burnt offering," "minkhah" (מנחה), usually translated as "gift offering," or "zavakh" (זבח), usually translated as "sacrifice" (see for example 2 Chron 7:1). It does however appear in the very late text of Ben Sirach 45:21-22.

7. "Makhtah" (מחתה) for "firing pan" or "censer" is used 22 times in the Bible, 18 occurrences being in the Torah (Exod 25:38, Num 16:39 [Heb 17:4], etc). "Miqteret" (מקטרת) is a synonym that seems to be used in later texts (Ezek 8:11 and 2 Chron 26:19).

8. "She'er" (שאר) for "flesh" is early, with 17 occurrences, ranging in time from the Torah to Jeremiah (Lev 2:11, Jer 51:35, etc.) but not making it into Ezekiel or any post-exilic books.

9. The words "mamlakah" (ממלכה) and "malkut" (מלכות) are both used to mean "kingdom." Of the two, ממלכה is preferred in earlier texts (all five occurrences in Joshua, for example) and מלכות is preferred in later texts (many occurrences in Daniel). However, both words appear at least intermittently in both early and late texts, so this word selection only provides a hint at dates.

10. Both "khodesh" (חדש) and "yareakh" (ירח) are used for "month" in earlier literature, but "yareakh" drops out of use after Zech 11:8.

11. "Shavakh" (שבח), meaning "laud" or "praise" (Ps 63:3 [Heb 63:4], 117:1, 145:4, 147:12, 106:47 = 1 Chron 16:35, Ecc 4:2 and 8:15) appears mostly in late texts and in post-biblical Hebrew. Ps 63:4, a Davidic psalm, is an exception.

12. "Hallel" (הלל), meaning praise, is used as an imperative much more frequently in late passages (Ps 111:1, 112:1, 113:1, etc.) than early passages. Early passages are more likely to use the hiphil form of "yadah" (ידה), sometimes translated as "give thanks" (Ps 30:4 [Heb 30:5], 33:2, etc.).

13. In Late Biblical Hebrew, "Ahmad" (עמד) which usually means "stand," begins to be used in place of "qum" (קום), which usually means "raise up." This occurs when the meaning of "raise up, establish" is needed. Early examples with "qum" are Gen 26:3, Exod 1:8, Lev 26:9, Num 30:13-15, Deut 19:15, Judg 10:1, etc. Late examples with "ahmad" are Ezek 17:14, Esth 3:4, Dan 8:23, etc. Compare especially the early Judg 18:30 with the late 2 Chron 33:19. The late usage can also be seen in Ben Sirach 47:1 and the Dead Sea Scroll, Florilegium.[22]

14. Beginning in the time of Isaiah and continuing into the Late Biblical Hebrew period, the hiphil stem of "bin" (בין), meaning "understand," is used to mean "teach," (Job 6:24, 32:8, Isa 28:9, 40:14, Ps 119:27, 119:34, 119:73, 119:125, 119:130, 119:144, 119:169, Dan 1:17, 8:16, 8:27, 9:22, 10:14, 11:33, Ezra 8:16, Neh 8:7-9, 1 Chron 15:22, 25:7-8, 27:32 and 2 Chron 35:3). The other word for teach, "lamad," (למד), is used throughout the biblical period.

15. "Kithav" (כתב), a noun meaning "a writing," is derived from a common verb and appears 17 times exclusively in exilic and post-exilic texts (Ezek 13:9, Dan 10:21, 1 Chron 28:19, Esth 1:22, Ezra 2:62 = Neh 7:64, etc.). Earlier texts have the more common "sepher" (ספר), usually translated

---

[22] Dead Sea Scroll 4Q174, fragment 1 column 1 line 13.

as "book" or "letter," which is used throughout the biblical period.

This list is far from complete. Some additional Hebrew words can be categorized as either early or late, but have been omitted in this section due to a small number of occurrences. For example, "Jeshurun" (ישרון) as a name for Israel could probably be considered as early, but with only four occurrences (Deut 32:15, 33:5, 33:26 and Isa 44:2) both our level of confidence in its earliness and its value as a dating marker must necessarily be low. We have also omitted other words which could probably be categorized as early or late, but a few stray appearances in unexpected places lend an air of doubt to any conclusion. An example is the probably late "shallat" (שלט) and its variants, which appear in Gen 42:6, Ps 119:133, Ecc 2:19, 5:18, 6:2, 7:19, 8:4, 8:8, 8:9, Esth 9:1 and Neh 5:15 in reference to control of inheritance and assets. The Genesis 42:6 reference is an early outlier, and some suggest it is a late scribe's substitution for the original word, now lost.[23] However, it is impossible to be sure – a word long in the language might have become popular at a late date.

B.3.13.1 Vocabulary - Persian Words

Persian words entered the Hebrew language after 538 B.C. when Judah became a Persian province. Because the Persian culture had little direct contact with Israel before then, Persian words are absent from all pre-exilic and exilic books (Genesis through Kings and most of the prophets). Persian words are heavily present in the books set outside of Israel, Daniel and Esther, and rarer in Ezra, Nehemiah, Chronicles, Song of Solomon and Ecclesiastes. Not all the Persian words used in the Old Testament remained in the language after the time of Alexander the Great; they were replaced by Greek words or other equivalents. Only one of these

---

[23] Brown, Driver, and Briggs, *Hebrew and English Lexicon of the Old Testament*, p. 1020

words is in Ben Sirach (the word רז in Sir 8:18). Most Persian words seem to have washed out of the language when Persia fell to Greece. The Septuagint translator of Daniel, working around 200-100 B.C., apparently did not know how to translate 3 of the 17 Persian words in the book. Therefore, Persian words are an especially good indicator that a text was written after 538 B.C., and the use of many Persian words favors a date prior to the Greek period which began in 332 B.C. Table B-1 below lists Persian loan-words found in the Old Testament. Some of these are in the Aramaic sections of Daniel and Ezra.

Table B-1 Persian Loan-words

Persian Word	Translation	Example Verse	Total # of Occurrences	Distribution
אגוז	nuts	Song 6:11	1	Song
אדרזדא	correctly	Ezra 7:23 (Aramaic)	1	Ezra
אדרגזר	counselor	Dan 3:2 (Aramaic)	2	Dan
אדרכנים דרכמון	darics, a unit of money	1 Chron 29:7	6	Ezra, Neh, Chron
אזדא	certainly	Dan 2:5 (Aramaic)	2	Dan
אחשתרנים	royal	Esth 8:10	2	Esth
אחשדרפנים	satraps	Esth 3:12	13	Dan, Esth, Ezra
אספרנא	thoroughly	Ezra 5:8 (Aramaic)	1	Ezra
אפדן	palace	Dan 11:45	1	Dan
בירה	fortress, palace, temple	Neh 2:8	18	Chron, Neh, Esth, Dan
גנז	treasury	Esth 3:9	2	Esth
גנזך	treasure	1 Chron	1	Chron

Persian Word	Translation	Example Verse	Total # of Occurrences	Distribution
	chamber	28:11		
דנה	unless, indeed	Dan 2:12 (Aramaic)	1	Dan
דת	law	Ezra 8:36	22	Esth, Dan, Ezra
דתבר	judge	Dan 3:2 (Aramaic)	2	Dan
הדבר	counselor	Dan 3:24 (Aramaic)	4	Dan
הדם	limb	Dan 2:5 (Aramaic)	2	Dan
המניכא	chain, necklace	Dan 5:7 (Aramaic)	3	Dan
כרמיל	crimson	2 Chron 2:6	3	Chron
כרפס	cotton or fine linen	Esth 1:6	1	Esth
כשר	be proper, suitable	Esth 8:5	3	Esth
נבזבה	reward	Dan 2:6 (Aramaic)	2	Dan
נדן	sheath	1 Chron 21:27	2	Chron
נרד	spikenard	Song 1:12	3	Song
נשתון	letter	Ezra 4:7	2	Ezra
סרבל	mantel or trousers	Dan 3:21 (Aramaic)	2	Dan
סרך	commissioner	Dan 6:3 (Aramaic)	3	Dan
פרדס	park, paradise	Ecc 2:5	3	Song, Ecc, Neh

Persian Word	Translation	Example Verse	Total # of Occurrences	Distribution
פרתמים	nobles	Esth 1:3	3	Esth, Dan
פת־בג	dainty food	Dan 1:5	6	Dan
פתגם	edict	Ecc 8:11	2	Esth, Dan
פתשגן	copy	Esth 3:14	3	Esth
רז	secret	Dan 2:18 (Aramaic)	9	Dan
רמכים	mares?	Esth 8:10	1	Esth
תרשתא	title of Persian governor	Neh 7:65	5	Ezra, Neh

It has been suggested that several Persian loan-words appear in Classical Biblical Hebrew texts we have marked as pre-exilic. These are all disputed, and we have not included them in Table B-1. They include:

1. פרורים for "precincts" in 2 Kgs 23:11. This is the only occurrence of this word in the Bible. It may be the plural form of פרבר in 1 Chron 26:18, which may mean something like "open kiosk," but is usually left untranslated as "parbar." In any case, the word is not well understood.

2. פלדות for "steel" in Nah 2:3 (Heb 2:4). This is the only occurrence of this word in the Bible.

3. אשדת for "law of fire" in Deut 33:2. Although this reading was favored by the Masoretes and is used in most translations, it is a doubtful reading. It requires splitting the word into אש and דת, with דת then being the word for law listed in the table above. However, besides being a Persian word, דת usually means an individual law, which does not fit the context of Deuteronomy 33. Also, see Deut 3:17 and 4:49 for another reading of אשדת, meaning "mountain slopes," a reading we believe should be preferred in Deut 33:2.

B.3.14 Figures of Speech

Anthropomorphisms applied to God are indicative of early writing, and they are avoided in later texts. For example, the early Lev 26:11-12 contains the anthropomorphism of God "walking": "I will make My dwelling among you, and My soul will not reject you. I will also walk among you and be your God, and you shall be My people," while Ezek 37:27 says the same thing differently: "My dwelling place also will be with them; and I will be their God, and they will be My people." Other passages where God walks (התהלך) are in Gen 3:8, Deut 23:14 (Heb 23:15) and 2 Sam 7:6 (compare the later 1 Chron 17:5). God *smells* an offering early (Gen 8:21, Lev 26:31, Num 28:6, 28:13, 28:24, Deut 33:10, 1 Sam 26:19 and Amos 5:21). This terminology is avoided in late writings. Even the common expression of the "face" of God is mentioned only once in a post-exilic text (2 Chron 7:14).

The phrase, "Gathered to his people" is a figure of speech used in Early Biblical Hebrew as a euphemism for death, with "people" meaning kinsmen (Gen 25:8, 25:17, 35:29, 49:29, 49:33, Num 20:24, 20:26, 27:13, 31:2 and Deut 32:50). The usage in general of "ahm" (עם), people, to mean "kinsmen" is also early, and is preserved in the name "Ammiel" (God is my kinsman) in Num 13:12 and 2 Sam 9:4-5. Judg 2:10, "gathered to their fathers," is a parallel which may be later by comparison. This figure of speech for death passed out of use during the Early Biblical Hebrew period.

"Natan lev" (נתן with לב) is a Late Biblical Hebrew expression for the way a person sets his own heart (1 Chron 22:19, 2 Chron 11:16, Dan 10:12, Ecc 7:2, 8:16 and 9:1). "Sam lev" or "sat lev" (שים or שית with לב) is the Classical Biblical Hebrew equivalent (Deut 32:46, 2 Sam 13:33, 19:19, Ps 62:10 [Heb 62:11], Isa 57:1, Jer 12:11 and Zech 7:12).

B.3.15 Meter

Dirges in Classical Biblical Hebrew have their own distinctive meter. Dirges are present in Amos 5:1-3, Lamentations 1-4, Ezek 19:1-14, 26:17-18, 27:3-10, 27:28-32 and 27:34-36. They all use the "limping meter" in which the second part of a line is shorter than the first part, usually with three beats in the first part of the line and two beats in the second part. The "Song of the Bow" in 2 Sam 1:19-27 is a dirge composed by David to mourn the death of Saul and Jonathan, but it does not use the limping meter, probably because it had not yet been developed. Likewise, the short dirge David composed for Abner in 2 Sam 3:33-34 does not use the limping meter.

B.3.16 Spelling

Modern spelling practice in most languages requires one correct spelling for each word, and with rare exceptions, all other spellings are incorrect. In Classical Biblical Hebrew this is not the case. The Hebrew alphabet consists of 22 consonants and no vowels. During the biblical period, Hebrew writers began letting some of the consonants double as vowels. These letters were "he" (ה), "waw" (ו) and "yodh" (י), which are sometimes called "matres lectiones" (mothers of reading), and which we will call "vowel letters."

It is likely that the earliest Hebrew writing made no use of vowel letters. This understanding is based on the fact that closely related ancient Semitic languages did not use vowel letters, and the few surviving early Hebrew inscriptions do not appear to use them either. During the Classical Biblical Hebrew period, scribes began using a vowel letter "he" (ה) on the end of words to indicate when it ended in a vowel. A little later, beginning shortly before the Babylonian exile, scribes began using the letter "waw" (ו) to indicate a long "u" or long "o" sound and the letter "yodh" (י) to indicate a long "e" sound. The letter "he" on the end of a word was relegated to representing an "ah" sound. Because the letter "he" on the end of words had for a while been used to represent any vowel, this required changing the spelling of some words ending in other vowel sounds. In almost all cases, the scribes who copied the Bible made this change to represent the newer spelling, but in some places in the Torah, the old pattern remains. For example, Gen 9:21 spells "his tent," ending in a long "o" sound, אהלה. This archaic spelling pattern with "he" representing a long 'o' sound is present in the following verses: Gen 9:21, 12:8, 35:21 and 49:11. The archaic spelling of a word ending in an "ah" sound but leaving the final "he" off is present in the word for young woman, "na'arah" (נערה, or in this case נער), in Gen 24:14, 24:16, 24:28, 24:55, 24:57, 34:3, 34:12, Deut 22:15, 22:20, 22:21, 22:23, 22:24, 22:25, 22:26, 22:27, 22:28 and 22:29. The vowel letter "he" remained restricted to the end of words, but "waw" and "yodh" began to be used in increasing measure in medial positions within words. It was during this time of transition that Judah was conquered by Babylon, and the scribal practice was soon modified to preserve the scriptures letter for letter. This practice therefore petrified the older books of the Bible in a situation where vowel letters are sometimes used and sometimes not used, even in the spelling of the same word within the same verse. (Instances of the same word spelled different ways in the same verse are numerous – for example, 2 Chron 4:4 and the spelling of "three" - שלושה and שלשה). Books written after the exile tend to reflect a further development of the process of adding vowel letters, and therefore are likely to use the vowel letters more.

Therefore, over time a clear trend can be discerned: the earlier writings are less likely to use vowel letters, and the later writings are more likely to use vowel letters. This can be illustrated by looking at the spelling of David's name. The short form spelling is דוד, with no vowel letters, and the long form is דויד, with a vowel letter "yodh." Below is a breakdown of how David's name is spelled in different books of the Bible:

דוד – Ruth, 1&2 Samuel, 1&2 Kings, Psalms, Proverbs, Ecclesiastes, Isaiah, Jeremiah, Ezek 34:24, 37:24, 37:25 and Hosea

דויד – 1&2 Chronicles, Ezra, Nehemiah, Zechariah, Song of Solomon, Amos and Ezek 34:23

The five books which were indisputably written after the exile (1&2 Chronicles, Ezra, Nehemiah and Zechariah) always use the long form spelling דויד, 279 times in all.[24] The earlier books of Samuel and Kings, which are parallel to Chronicles, use the short form spelling דוד 669 out of 672 times. This practice goes beyond just the spelling of David's name. Even in passages where Chronicles is quoting from Samuel or Kings, the Masoretic Text often shows short form spellings in Samuel-Kings and long form spellings in Chronicles. Working with a date of 600 B.C. for the writing of Kings and 400 B.C. for Chronicles, we can get a fair idea of spelling practices at those times by a comparison of those books. The general conclusion is clear: short form = early, long form = late. Table B-2 gives a statistical breakdown of how the long "o" sound is spelled in the Hebrew Bible, provided by Anderson and Forbes.[25]

Table B-2 Spelling of Long "o"

Book	Short	Long	Total	% Long
Genesis	3147	1982	5129	38.6
Exodus	3181	1240	4421	28.0
Leviticus	1925	1250	3175	39.4
Numbers	2541	1266	3807	33.3
Deuteronomy	2286	1280	3566	35.9
Joshua-Judges	2191	2340	4531	51.6
Samuel	3047	2564	5611	45.7

---

[24] Interestingly, Ben Sirach, written around 200 B.C., uses a mostly early spelling practice, including the older spelling of David's name in all but one occurrence (Sirach 47:2).

[25] Anderson and Forbes, *Spelling in the Hebrew Bible*, p. 162

Book	Short	Long	Total	% Long
Kings	3570	2275	5845	38.9
Isaiah	2086	2315	4401	52.6
Jeremiah	2553	2297	4850	47.4
Ezekiel	2202	2392	4594	52.1
Minor Prophets	1747	1950	3697	52.7
Psalms	2220	3011	5231	57.6
Job	1054	1112	2166	51.3
Proverbs	684	1019	1703	59.8
Megillot[26]	1055	1344	2399	56.0
Daniel	291	282	573	49.2
Ezra-Neh	955	948	1903	49.8
Chronicles	2674	3195	5869	54.4

Table B-2 supports the generalization that fewer vowel letters (represented by a smaller percentage in the right-most column) imply an early text and more vowel letters imply a later text. The Torah has the earliest spelling pattern in the Bible. Still, some of the data is problematic – for example, based on this table, Proverbs has the latest spelling pattern in the table, but it is almost surely not the latest book written.

The use of spelling to determine age must be used with caution. As an example of how spelling can vary without any significance, consider the Hebrew word "toledot," which has two long "o" sounds and is translated "generations" in the important Genesis phrase "These are the generations." Those who understand Genesis to be written by one author will see that verses from the one author spell this word four different ways in Hebrew.

---

[26] Megillot" is Hebrew for "scrolls", and includes the collection of Ruth, Lamentations, Song of Solomon, Ecclesiastes, and Esther. This is an unfortunate combination for this table. Ruth's spelling pattern is old, while Song of Solomon, Ecclesiastes, and Esther are young.

Those who follow the Documentary Hypothesis are no better off, because all these verses are assigned to the "P" author, so they also are stuck with verses from one author spelling the word four different ways, as shown below:

TLDT (תלדת) – Gen 25:12, Exod 6:16

TOLDT (תולדת) – Gen 5:1, 6:9, 10:1, 11:10, 11:27, 25:19

TLDOT (תלדות) – Gen 36:1, 36:9, 37:2

TOLDOT (תולדות) – Gen 2:4, also Ruth 4:18.

There are further reasons for caution when evaluating spelling:

1. It is helpful to compare the spelling in biblical texts to extra-biblical Hebrew inscriptions, but the sum total of all such inscriptions which are pre-exilic does not equal more than a few pages of biblical text. At least in the earlier years, there is not much to work with.

2. A review of the pre-exilic inscriptions we do have leads to the conclusion that spelling patterns in the Bible cannot be used to differentiate the dates of different pre-exilic material. The reason for this is that pre-exilic Hebrew inscriptions show an older spelling pattern than any biblical text. This is not an argument to date any pre-exilic book late, since even those passages that scholars of every persuasion date early, such as the Song of Deborah in Judges 5, show later spelling patterns than any pre-exilic inscriptions. Instead, this is due to the activity of the scribes, who for a time were in the habit of bringing spelling up to date when they copied a scroll. The Torah, which has the oldest spelling pattern in the Bible, still looks newer than the Siloam inscription on Hezekiah's tunnel (700 B.C.), and for the most part looks newer than the Lachish letters (587 B.C.). The Siloam inscription was cut into stone to mark the completion of Hezekiah's tunnel (2 Chron 32:30), and would have been made during the life of Isaiah. However, the Masoretic Text of Isaiah spells "voice" קול, while the Siloam inscription spells it in the short form קל (inscription

line 2), without the vowel letter *waw* (ו). Likewise, Masoretic Text Isaiah spells "rock" צור, while the Siloam inscription has a shorter form צר (line 6), and Masoretic Text Isaiah uses ים for the masculine plural suffix, while the Siloam inscription just uses ם (line 4). The general picture as far as spelling is concerned is that all the pre-exilic inscriptions look older than the Torah, and the Torah looks older than everything else in the Bible. The reason the Torah has an older spelling pattern than other pre-exilic books is probably due to the special reverence with which it was held by the scribes, who copied it more conservatively than other books of the Bible. Therefore, spelling can only be used to date books written after about 600, with anything written before that time simply placed in a large category called "pre-exilic." We cannot have any success using spelling to distinguish between a text written in 700 B.C. and one written in 1000 B.C.; the scribes have apparently erased the distinctions.

3. In the area of spelling, we are at the mercy of the scribes who produced the Masoretic Text. Translations such as the Septuagint, of course, cannot help. Other Hebrew texts, such as the Samaritan Pentateuch and most of the Dead Sea Scrolls, have updated their spelling to such an extent that they have wiped away all the evidence. Spelling analysis to date books in the Bible would not be possible at all were it not for the very conservative habits of the scribes who produced the Masoretic Text. For example, the name of David is spelled in the older short form דוד ten times out of ten in Isaiah in the Masoretic Text, but in the Qumran Great Isaiah Scroll (which is not a proto-Masoretic text) the scribes have updated the spelling so that all ten times the newer long form דויד is used. This is characteristic of the practice of the scrolls copied at Qumran. Even a Dead Sea Scroll like 4QExod-Lev^f (4Q17), dated prior to

200 B.C. (therefore carried to Qumran rather than copied there), shows 13 instances where long form spelling is used in passages where the Masoretic Text uses the short form.[27] An interesting example of how spelling can be changed based on the work of the scribes is seen in Jer 26:18, which quotes Mic 3:12. Jeremiah as we have it today in the Masoretic Text has in general the oldest spelling pattern of the latter prophets. However, in Jer 26:18 Jerusalem is spelled ירושלים, a very late spelling which does not appear in the Bible except for the late post-exilic passages of Esther (2:6) and 2 Chron 25:1. This later spelling came to predominate by the time of the Dead Sea Scrolls, but it is not used elsewhere in Jeremiah, nor is it in Micah, the book from which he is quoting. We can only speculate that some scribe who was copying Jeremiah wanted to ensure he got the Micah quotation right, so he read from a Micah scroll that used a later spelling than what made it into the Masoretic Text.

4. Finally, we are attempting to look systematically at an area in which neither the earlier scribes, nor in all probability the original writers, were very systematic.

Our conclusion is that comparisons of long and short form spelling can be useful when large numbers of words are used, but when small numbers are used, any conclusions must be tentative. This is typical of any argument which is inherently statistical in nature. Statistics work well with large sampling, but poorly with small sampling. With smaller subsets, pronounced deviation from the statistical trend can be present. To give one final example, we have already noted that the spelling pattern in Chronicles is later than that of Samuel. However, "is not?" is spelled in the short form הלא 18 times and long form הלוא zero times in Chronicles, but in Samuel, the long form is used 34 times and the short form is

---

[27] Anderson and Forbes, *Spelling in the Hebrew Bible*, p. 191

not used at all, a practice going completely opposite the larger trend. In this book we have occasionally pointed out spelling in small samples. It should be understood that when this is done, it constitutes a *weak* argument.

The preceding discussion deals with spelling as it involves the use or lack of use of vowel letters. There are several additional spelling changes in the Bible that are unrelated to the subject of vowel letters. These include:

1. The original spelling of "laugh" was צחק, and this spelling has been preserved in Isaac's name (יצחק). This spelling is used throughout the Torah (Gen 17:17, 18:12, 21:9, etc) and only twice afterward. The later spelling is שחק, which is never used in the Torah, but is used in Classical Biblical Hebrew and afterwards. Judg 16:25, a writing we date around 950 B.C., uses both spellings in the same verse.

2. "Kesev" (כשב), the word for lamb, and "kisbah" (כשבה), for ewe lamb, are used 14 times in the Torah (Gen 30:32-40, Lev 1:10, Deut 14:4, etc.). These words do not appear outside the Torah. The more common word for lamb with transposed consonants "keves" (כבש) appears 115 times in the Bible. The later spelling also appears multiple times in the Torah, in early prophetic texts such as Hos 4:16 and Isa 11:6, and in earlier writings such as Job 31:20 and Prov 27:26. This indicates that the transitional period for the spelling of this word was very early, at about the time the Torah was being written, around 1400 B.C.

3. The third masculine singular form of "khayah" (חיה), the word for "live," loses its final letter in early texts, so as to be spelled חי in Gen 5:5, Lev 18:5, Ezek 20:11 etc. Later writings include the final letter "he" (חיה): Ezek 18:23, Ecc 6:6, Esth 4:11 and Neh 9:29. This later spelling is used in post-biblical Hebrew and Aramaic. Note that Ezekiel is transitional, and uses both spellings.

Selected Bibliography

Alter, Robert and Kermode, Frank, *The Literary Guide to the Bible*, The Belknap Press of Harvard University Press, Cambridge Massachusetts, 1987

Anderson, Francis I. and Forbes, A. Dean, *Spelling in the Hebrew Bible*, Dahood Memorial Lecture, Rome, Biblical Institute Press, 1986

Archer, Gleason, *A Survey of Old Testament Introduction*, Chicago: Moody Press, 1964, 1974

Armstrong, Terry A, Busby, Douglas L. and Carr, Cyril F., *A Reader's Hebrew-English Lexicon of the Old Testament*, Zondervan Publishing House, Grand Rapids MI, 1989

Arnold, Bill T. and Beyer, Bryan E., *Encountering the Old Testament*, Baker Book House Company, PO Box 6287, Grand Rapids Michigan 49516-6287, 1999

Blenkinsopp, Joseph, *The Pentateuch, An Introduction to the First Five Books of the Bible*, Doubleday, 666 Fifth Avenue, New York, N.Y 10103, 2000

Bloom, Harold and Rosenberg, David, *The Book of J*, Published by Grove Weidenfeld, NY, NY 1990

Butterick, George A., *Interpreter's One Volume Commentary on the Bible*, Abingdon Press, 1971

Cassuto, Umberto, A *Commentary on the Book of Genesis, Part I*, The Magnes Press, The Hebrew University, 1989 edition. First published in Hebrew in Jerusalem 1944, First English Edition 1961

Cassuto, Umberto, *A Commentary on the Book of Genesis*, Part II, The Magnes Press, The Hebrew University, 1984 edition. First published in Hebrew in Jerusalem 1949, First English Edition 1964

Cassuto, Umberto, *The Documentary Hypothesis and the Composition of the Pentateuch, Eight Lectures*, Translated from Hebrew by Israel Abrahams, Magnus Press, The Hebrew University of Jerusalem, 1961. English edition distributed by Oxford University Press

Currid, John D., *Ancient Egypt and the Old Testament*, Baker Book House Company, P.O. Box 6287, Grand Rapids Michigan 49516-6287, 1997

Dorsey, David, *The Literary Structure of the Old Testament*, a Commentary on Genesis to Malachi, Baker Books, Grand Rapids MI, 1999

Driver, Samuel Rolles, *An Introduction to the Literature of the Old Testament*, Charles Scribner's Sons, NY 1900

Eiselen, Frederick Carl, "The Pentateuch – Its Origin and Development," article in *The Abingdon Bible Commentary*, The Abingdon Press, 1929

Friedman, Richard, *The Bible with Sources Revealed*, HarperCollins Publishers Inc., NY 2003

Friedman, Richard, *Who Wrote the Bible?*, Summit Books, New York NY, 1987

Garrett, Duane, *Rethinking Genesis, The Sources and Authorship of the First Book of the Pentateuch*, Christian Focus Publications, Geanies House, Fearn, Ross-Shire, IV20 1TW, Great Britain, 2000

Hallo, William W. (Editor), *The Context of Scripture, Volumes I-III*, Koninklijke Brill NV, Leiden, The Netherlands, 2000

Harrison, R. K., *Introduction to the Old Testament*, William B. Eerdmans Publishing Company, Grand Rapids, Michigan, 1969

Hurvitz, Avi, *A Linguistic Study of the Relationship between the Priestly Source and the Book of Ezekiel*, J. Gabalda and Committee, Editors, Rue Bonaparte 90, Paris, 1982

Hurvitz, Avi, *The Transition Period in Hebrew, A Study in Post-Exilic Hebrew and its Implications for the Dating of Psalms*, Bialik Institute, Jerusalem 1972 (book is in Hebrew)

Jerusalem Bible, Readers Edition, Doubleday & Company, Inc., Garden City New York, copyright 1966

Jobes, Karen H. and Silva, Moises, *Invitation to the Septuagint*, Published by Baker Academic, a Division of Baker Book House Company, P.O. Box 6287, Grand Rapids, MI 49516-6287, 2000

Jones, Cody, *The Complete Guide to the Book of Proverbs*, Quinten Publishing, Union Lake MI, 2000

Josephus, Flavius, *Josephus, Complete Works*, translated by William Whiston, Kregel Publications, Grand Rapids Michigan 49501, 1985

Kikawada, Isaac M. and Quinn, Arthur, *Before Abraham Was*, Abingdon Press, Nashville, 1985

Kitchen, K. A., *On the Reliability of the Old Testament*, William B. Eerdmans Publishing Company, Grand Rapids, Michigan /Cambridge, UK, 2003

Leo XIII (Pope), *Providentissimus Deus, Encyclical Letter*, Nov 18, 1893

Margalioth, Rachel, *The Indivisible Isaiah*, Sura Institute for Research, Jerusalem, and Yeshiva University, New York, 1964. Translated from Hebrew

Martinez, Florentino Garcia and Tigchelaar, Eibert J. C., *The Dead Sea Scrolls Study Edition*, 1997 (Vol. 1) and 1998 (Vol. 2), William B. Eerdmans Publishing Company, 255 Jefferson Ave. SE, Grand Rapids MI 49503

McDowell, Josh, *Daniel in the Critic's Den*, "A Campus Crusade for Christ Book," Here's Life Publishers, Inc., P.O. Box 1576, San Bernardino CA, 1979

McDowell, Josh, *The New Evidence that Demands a Verdict*, Thomas Nelson Publishers, Nashville, 1999

New American Bible, Confraternity of Christian Doctrine, Washington D.C., copyright 1970

New American Standard Bible, The Lockman Foundation, 1995 edition

Noth, Martin, *The Laws in the Pentateuch and Other Studies*, translated by D.R. AP-Thomas, Fortress Press, Philadelphia PA, 1967

Noth, Martin, *Numbers, A Commentary*, Translated by James D. Martin, Westminster Press, Philadelphia PA, 1966

Orr, James (General Editor), *International Standard Bible Encyclopedia*, 1915

Pettinato, Giovanni, *The Archives of Ebla, an Empire Inscribed in Clay*, Doubleday & Company, Inc, Garden City, New York, 1981. Originally published in Italian under the title of *Ebla, Un Impero Inciso nell'Argilla,* copyright 1979 Arnoldo Monadori, with some parts omitted, Editore S.p.A., Milano.

Pius XII (Pope), *Divino Afflante Spiritu,* Encyclical Letter of September 30, 1943

Robertson, David A., *Linguistic Evidence in Dating Early Hebrew Poetry,* published by the Society of Biblical Literature. Printed by University of Montana, Missoula, Montana 59801, 1972

Rogerson, John, *Chronicle of the Old Testament Kings,* Thames and Hudson Ltd, London, 1999

Saenz-Badillos, Angel, *A History of the Hebrew Language,* translated from Spanish by John Elwolde, Cambridge University Press, 1993

Sailhamer, John H., *Introduction to Old Testament Theology,* Zondervan Publishing House, Grand Rapids, MI 49530, 1995

Scarre, Christopher and Fagan, Brian M., *Ancient Civilizations,* Prentice Hall, Pearson Education Inc., Upper Saddle River New Jersey 07458, 2002

Seitz, Christopher R., *Zion's Final Destiny, The Development of the Book of Isaiah*, A Reassessment of Isaiah 36-39, 1991, Augsburg Fortress, 426 S. Fifth St., Box 1209, Minneapolis, MN 55440

Seow, C.L., *Ecclesiastes,* Doubleday, 1540 Broadway, New York New York 10036, 1997

Simpson, Cuthbert, "The Growth of the Hexateuch," article in *The Interpreter's Bible Commentary*, Abingdon Press, NY 1952.

Tuchman, Barbara, *A Distant Mirror*, The Ballantine Publishing Group, New York NY, 1978

VanderKam, James C., *The Dead Sea Scrolls Today*, William B. Eerdmans Publishing Co., 225 Jefferson Ave. S.E., Grand Rapids MI 49503, 1994

Von Rad, Gerhard, *Genesis, A Commentary*, Revised Edition, translated by John H. Marks, Westminster Press, Philadelphia Pennsylvania, 1972

Waltke, Bruce K. and O'Connor, M., An *Introduction to Biblical Hebrew Syntax*, Eisenbrauns, Winona Lake, Indiana, 1990

Wellhausen, Julius, *Prolegomena to the History of Ancient Israel*, Meridian Books, The World Publishing Company, Cleveland Ohio, 1957, translated from the German edition of 1883 by J. Sutherland Black and Allan Menzies

Wiseman, P. J., *Ancient Records and the Structure of Genesis*, Thomas Nelson Publishers, Nashville, 1985

Pfieffer, Charles F., Rhea, John and Vos, Howard F., *Wycliffe Bible Encyclopedia*, Moody Press, 1975

Yahuda, Abraham S., *The Language of the Pentateuch in its Relation to Egyptian*, Volume 1, Oxford University Press, 1933.

Yamauchi, Edwin M., *Persia and the Bible*, Baker Books, P.O. Box 6287, Grand Rapids, MI 49516-6287, 1990

Young, Ian, Editor, *Biblical Hebrew Studies in Chronology and Typology*, T&T Clark International, 15 East 26th Street, Suite 1703, New York, NY 10010, 2003

Index of Scriptures

Scriptures are indexed according to their section number within the book, rather than the page number. Scriptures are ordered in English Bible order, with New Testament and apocryphal books included.

Genesis

1:1	3.3.9.2
1:2	3.2.2.1.2, 3
	.3.11.2.3,
	4.2.2.2, 5.2.1.3
1:3	3.3.5.2, B.3.9
1:16	3.3.5.2
1:22	3.2.3.2
1:24	3.3.11.2.2
1:26	3.2.1.9.1
1:28	3.2.3.2
2:4	3.2.1.1,
	3.2.1.9.1,
	3.2.3.1, 3.3.9.2,
	B.3.16
2:5	3.2.1.1, B.3.9
2:7	3.2.1.1, 3.3.9.2
2:9	3.2.1.1
2:10-14	3.3.9.1
2:12	3.3.9.1
2:14	3.3.12.2.3
2:19	3.2.1.1
2:21	3.2.1.1
2:23	3.2.1.10,
	3.2.3.1,
	3.3.11.2.2
3:1	3.2.1.1
3:3	3.2.1.1
3:5	3.2.1.1
3:8	3.3.11.3, B.3.14
3:10	3.3.11.3, 5.5.2,
	B.3.7
3:15	B.3.8
3:17-19	6.2.1
3:20	3.2.1.10,
	3.2.3.2,
	3.3.9.2.1,
	3.3.11.3
3:22	3.2.1.1,
	3.2.1.9.1
4:1	3.2.1.1
4:4	3.2.1.1
4:16-22	3.2.1.7
4:6	3.2.1.1
4:9	3.2.1.1
4:11	3.3.11.2.2
4:15	3.2.1.1, B.3.11
4:22	3.3.11.2.3
4:26	3.2.1.1, 3.2.3.2
5:1	3.2.2.4.4,
	3.3.9.2, B.3.16
5:2	3.3.9.2
5:5	B.3.16
5:21	B.3.4
5:27	3.2.1.7
5:29	3.2.1.1,
	3.3.9.2.1
6:2-6	3.2.3.2
6:3	3.2.1.1
6:3	3.3.11.3
6:5	3.2.1.1
6:6	4.2.9.2
6:7	3.3.11.2.2
6:8	3.2.1.1
6:8-9	3.2.3.1
6:9	3.3.9.2, B.3.16
6:10	3.2.3.1, 3.3.9.2
6:11-12	3.3.9.2
6:12	3.2.1.1
6:14	3.3.11.2.3
6:14-16	3.2.3.1
6:17	3.2.3.1
6:18-20	3.2.3.1
6:21	3.2.3.1
6:22	3.2.1.1
7:1	3.2.1.1
7:1-3	3.2.3.1
7:4	3.3.11.2.2
7:4-5	3.2.3.1
7:5	3.2.1.1
7:7-10	3.2.3.1
7:9	3.2.1.1
7:11	3.3.11.2.3,
	4.2.7
7:11-15	3.2.3.1
7:12	3.3.11.2.2,
	B.3.6
7:16	3.2.1.1, 3.2.3.1
7:17	3.2.3.1
7:17-18	3.2.3.1
7:17-23	3.2.1.8
7:18-20	3.2.3.1
7:21-24	3.2.3.1
8:1	3.2.3.1
8:2	3.3.11.2.3
8:3	3.2.3.1
8:4	3.3.9.1
8:4-5	3.2.3.1
8:6	3.2.3.1
8:7-9	3.2.3.1
8:10-11	3.2.3.1
8:12-13	3.2.3.1
8:15	3.2.1.1
8:15-17	3.2.3.1

21:33	3.2.1.1	25:18	3.3.9.2	28:4	3.2.1.1
21:34	3.3.10	25:19	3.3.9.2, B.3.16	28:7	3.2.1.9.4
22:1	B.3.7	25:21	3.2.1.10,	28:11-12	3.2.2.4.9
22:1-14	3.2.3.1		3.2.3.2	28:13-14	3.2.3.2
22:5	5.4.1	25:24-26	3.2.1.10	28:19	3.2.1.9.9,
22:9	3.2.1.3	25:25	3.3.9.2.1, B.3.3		3.3.9.1
22:11	3.2.1.1	25:26	3.2.2.4.9	28:20	3.2.1.1
22:11-15	3.2.1.1	25:28	3.2.3.2	28:21	3.2.1.1
22:14	3.2.1.1, 3.2.3.2	25:29-34	3.2.1.10,	29:1	3.2.1.2.1
22:15-19	3.2.3.1		3.3.9.1	29:1-14	3.2.1.10
22:16	3.2.1.1,	25:30	3.3.9.2.1	29:9	B.3.9
	3.3.11.1	26:1	3.3.10	29:15-25	3.2.2.4.9
22:17	3.2.1.9.2,	26:1-11	3.2.1.10	29:24-25	3.2.1.10
	3.2.3.2	26:3	3.3.11.3, B.3.7,	29:26	3.2.3.2
22:18	3.2.2.2.3		B.3.13	29:31	3.2.1.10,
22:19	3.2.1.9.8	26:4	3.3.11.3, B.3.7		3.2.2.4.9
22:20	B.3.9	26:7	3.3.9.1	30:1-2	3.2.1.10
22:20-24	3.2.3.1	26:8	3.2.1.9.3,	30:3-4	3.3.9.1
23:1	3.9.9.2		3.3.10	30:3-5	3.2.1.10
23:2	3.3.2, 3.3.9.1	26:14	3.3.10	30:9	3.3.9.1
23:3	B.3.16	26:15	3.3.10	30:9-10	3.2.1.10
23:4	B.3.7	26:15-31	3.2.1.10	30:22-23	3.2.3.2
24:2	3.3.11.1	26:18	3.3.10	30:27	3.2.1.1
24:2-3	3.3.9.1	26:33	3.2.1.9.8	30:32-40	3.3.11.3, B.3.16
24:3	3.2.3.2	26:34-35	3.2.1.9.4	31:7	3.2.1.1
24:9	3.3.9.1	27:1-5	3.2.3.1	31:16	3.2.1.1
24:11-25	3.2.1.10	27:1-45	3.2.1.9.4	31:18	3.2.1.2.1
24:13	B.3.6	27:6-17	3.2.3.1	31:19	3.2.1.2.1,
24:14	B.3.16	27:8-13	3.2.1.9.4		3.3.9.1
24:16	B.3.16	27:11	4.2.6	31:30	3.3.9.1
24:19	5.4.1	27:18-29	3.2.3.1	31:32	3.3.9.1
24:28	B.3.16	27:19	3.3.9.2.1, B.3.7	31:37	5.4.1
24:55	B.3.16	27:30-40	3.2.3.1	31:42	3.2.3.2
24:57	B.3.16	27:32	3.3.9.2.1, B.3.7	31:44	3.2.1.1
24:62	3.3.9.1	27:33	B.3.9	31:47	3.3.9.2.1,
24:65	3.3.11.3	27:36	3.3.11.3, B.3.4		B.3.12
25:6	3.3.9.1, B.3.9	27:41-45	3.2.3.1	31:50	3.2.1.1
25:8	B.3.14	27:43-35	3.2.1.9.4	32:13-23	3.2.2.4.9
25:9	3.3.9.2	27:46	3.2.1.9.4	33:5	3.2.1.1
25:11	3.3.9.2	27:46-28:5	3.2.3.1	33:11	3.2.1.1,
25:12	3.3.9.2, B.3.16	27:46–28:9	3.2.1.9.4		3.3.11.2.2
25:17	B.3.14	28:3	3.3.9.2.2	33:18	3.2.1.2.1, 3.3.2

33:19	5.2.1.1	38:7-10	3.2.1.10	45:6	3.3.11.3, B.3.4
33:20	3.2.1.2.1,	38:9-10	3.2.3.2	45:8	3.3.11.2.2
	3.2.1.3	38:10	3.2.1.1	45:21	3.3.11.2.2
34:12	B.3.16	38:14-20	3.2.3.2	46:2	3.2.1.2,
35:4	3.2.2.3	38:16	3.2.1.10		3.2.1.2.5
35:6	3.3.9.1	38:17-18	3.3.11.3	46:8-27	3.2.1.10,
35:8	3.3.9.2	38:27-30	3.2.1.10		3.3.9.2
35:11	3.2.2.4.5,	39:1	3.2.1.2.4,	46:34	3.3.5
	3.2.3.2,		3.3.11.2.2	47:9	3.3.11.2.2
	3.3.9.2.2	39:12-13	3.2.1.10	47:26	3.3.5
35:15	3.2.1.9.9	39:15	3.2.1.10	47:29	3.3.9.1,
35:21	B.3.16	39:18	3.2.1.10		3.3.11.1
35:27	3.3.9.1	40:1	3.3.11.2.2	48:3	3.3.9.1,
35:29	3.3.9.2, B.3.14	40:2	3.3.11.2.2		3.3.9.2.2
36:1	3.3.9.2, B.3.16	40:3	3.3.11.2.2	48:7	3.3.11.3, B.3.9
36:8	3.3.9.2	40:5	5.6.2	48:10	3.3.11.2.2
36:9	B.3.16	40:13	3.3.11.2.2,	48:18	3.2.3.2
36:31	3.3.10, B.3.9		B.3.9	48:22	3.3.9.2
36:33	5.2.1.1	40:19	B.3.9	49:2	3.2.1.2.5
36:43	3.3.9.2	41:1-4	3.3.5	49:2-27	3.3.9.2.1
37:1	3.3.9.2	41:1-7	3.2.1.10	49:6	B.3.13
37:1-2	3.2.2.4.8	41:29	3.2.2.4.8	49:10	3.2.2.4.5
37:2	3.3.9.2,	41:29-44	3.2.2.4.8	49:10-11	3.3.11.3 (note)
	3.3.9.2.1,	41:32	3.3.11.3, B.3.4	49:11	B.3.16
	B.3.16	41:40	3.3.11.2.2	49:14-15	B.3.11
37:3	3.2.1.10	41:42	3.3.11.2.2	49:15	B.3.11
37:3-4	3.2.2.4.8	41:45	3.2.2.4.8	49:16	4.2.1.3
37:5-8	3.2.1.10	42:6	B.3.13	49:17	B.3.13
37:5-11	3.2.2.4.8	42:15	B.3.10	49:21	B.3.13
37:9-11	3.2.1.10	42:21	5.9.8	49:24	3.2.1.2.5, 5.1.8
37:12-20	3.2.2.4.8	42:30	3.3.11.2.2	49:25	3.3.11.4
37:17	B.3.10	42:33	3.3.11.2.2	49:29	B.3.14
37:19	3.3.11.3	43:10	3.3.11.2.2,	49:31	3.3.9.2
37:21	3.2.2.4.8		3.3.11.3, B.3.4	49:33	B.3.14
37:22	3.2.2.4.8	43:14	3.3.9.2.2	50:2	3.3.5
37:23	3.2.1.10	43:16	3.3.11.2.2	50:2-3	5.5
37:25	3.3.11.3	43:28	3.2.1.1	50:15-21	3.2.2.4.9
37:25-27	3.2.1.2.4	43:32	3.3.5	50:20	3.2.2.4.8
37:28	3.2.1.2.4	44:1	3.3.11.2.2	50:25	B.3.10
37:31-32	3.2.1.10	44:4	3.3.11.2.2	50:26	3.3.5, 5.5
38:2	3.3.11.3 (note)	44:8	3.3.11.2.2		
38:7	3.2.1.1	45:3	B.3.7		

Exodus

1:1	3.3.9.2
1:1-5	3.2.1.10, 3.3.9.2
1:6	3.3.9.2
1:7-2:10	3.2.3.2
1:8	3.3.5, B.3.13
1:8-10	3.3.5
1:11	2.1.1
1:19	3.3.11.2.2
2:3	3.3.2
2:10	3.3.6
2:11	3.2.2.4.9
2:12	5.4.1
2:15-21	3.2.1.10
2:16	3.3.6
2:18	3.2.1.2.3
2:21	3.3.6
3:1	3.2.1.2.3
3:4	3.2.1.1
3:6	3.2.1.1, 3.2.3.2
3:11	B.3.7
3:13	B.3.3, B.3.6
3:13-15	3.3.9.2.2
3:14	3.2.1.1, 3.2.2.3, 3.2.3.2
3:18	3.2.1.1
4:1	3.2.1.1
4:11	3.2.1.1
4:17	3.2.2.4.9
4:18	3.2.1.2.3
4:24-26	3.2.2.4.9
4:30	3.2.1.1
4:31	3.2.1.1
5:6-12	3.3.5
5:21	3.2.1.1, 3.3.5, 3.3.11.2.2
6:2	3.2.2.4.9
6:2-3	3.3.9.2.2
6:3	3.2.1.1, B.3.3
6:16	B.3.16
6:16-20	2.1.1
6:30	B.3.6
7:1	3.2.1.1
7:8-12	3.3.5.1
7:10-12	3.2.2.4.8
7:13	3.3.11.2.2
7:15-25	3.3.5.1
8:1-6	3.3.5.1
8:16-24	3.3.5.1
8:19	3.3.11.2.2
8:29-30	3.2.1.1
9:1-7	3.2.2.4.8, 3.3.5.1
9:5	3.2.1.1
9:7	3.3.11.2.2
9:8-12	3.3.5.1
9:13-35	3.3.5.1
9:28	3.3.11.2.2
10:1-20	3.3.5.1
10:5	3.3.11.2.2
10:10	3.3.5.1
10:15	3.3.11.2.2
10:18	3.2.1.1
10:21-29	3.3.5.1
11:1	B.3.10
11:1-10	3.3.5.1
11:5	3.3.11.2.2
11:7	3.3.5.1
12:1-13	3.2.1.10
12:12	3.2.2.4.8, 3.3.5.1
12:13	4.2.1.2.9.12
12:17	3.3.11.2.2
12:29-30	3.3.5.1
12:37	3.3.2
12:39	3.3.11.2.2
12:41	3.3.11.2.2
12:51	3.3.11.2.2
13:3	3.3.4, B.3.10
13:4	3.2.2.1.5, B.3.5
13:17	3.3.10
13:18	3.3.11.2.2
13:20	3.3.2
13:21	3.2.1.1
14:2	3.3.2
14:11	3.3.5
14:13	3.2.1.1
14:16	3.2.2.4.8
14:19	3.3.3
14:27	3.3.11.2.2
14:31	3.2.1.1
15:1	3.2.1.1, B.1
15:1-17	3.3.9.2.1
15:2	5.1.8
15:5	3.3.11.4, B.3.8, B.3.9
15:6	B.3.11
15:7	3.3.11.4, B.3.8
15:11	5.1.6, 5.1.8
15:12	3.3.11.4, B.3.9
15:13	3.3.11.4, B.3.7
15:16	3.3.11.4, B.3.7, B.3.8
15:19	B.3.8, B.3.9
15:21	3.3.9.2.1
15:27	3.3.4
16:1	3.2.1.2.2
16:29	3.3.11.3, B.3.4
17:6	3.2.1.2.2
17:2-7	3.2.1.9.6
18:1-12	3.2.1.2.3
19:5	4.2.2.2
19:16	3.3.3
19:18	3.2.1.1, 3.2.2.3, 5.1.5
19:21	3.2.1.1
19:22	3.2.1.1
19:23	3.2.1.1
19:24	3.2.1.1
20:1	5.1.6
20:1-17	3.2.1.9.7
20:2	3.2.3.2
20:2-3	B.3.7
20:6	5.11.2

9:12	B.3.10	18:11	3.3.5.2	28:2	3.3.8
9:18	3.3.5.1	19:11	3.3.11.3, B.3.7	28:15	3.3.8
10:6	3.2.1.4	19:14	3.2.2.2.4	28:17	3.3.11.2.2
10:12	3.2.2.2.4,	19:15	B.3.13	28:25	5.7.2
	3.2.2.4.3	19:17	3.3.7	28:30	5.7.2
10:22	3.2.3.2	20:16-18	3.2.2.2.5	28:32	5.7.2
11:6	3.2.1.9.10	21:5	3.2.1.4	28:37	5.7.2
11:10-11	3.3.5	21:17	3.2.3.2	28:38-40	3.2.2.4.3
11:14	3.2.2.2.4	22:9	3.3.11.3, B.3.4	28:41	5.7.2
11:16	3.2.1.10	22:15	B.3.16	28:44	5.7.2
11:30	3.2.1.6	22:19	3.3.11.3 (note)	28:50	5.7.2
12:2-4	3.2.1.3	22:20	B.3.16	28:51	3.2.2.2.4
12:5-6	3.2.1.3	22:21	B.3.16	28:53	5.7.2
12:17	3.2.2.2.4	22:23	B.3.16	28:56-57	5.7.2
13:1-5	3.2.2.2.5	22:24	B.3.16	28:62	3.2.3.2
13:1-16	3.2.1.10	22:25	B.3.16	28:64	3.2.1.10
14:1	3.3.5.2	22:26	B.3.16	28:65	5.7.2
14:4	3.3.11.3, B.3.16	22:27	B.3.16	29:24-28	4.1.4.2
14:5	3.3.2	22:28	B.3.16	30:19	3.2.2.2.4,
14:21	3.3.5.2	22:29	B.3.16		3.3.5.2, 3.3.8
14:23	3.2.2.2.4	23:3-4	3.2.2.2.3	31:6	4.1.1.2
14:28	3.2.2.2.4	23:3-5	5.11	31:7	4.1.1.2
15:12	4.2.2.2	23:7-8	3.2.2.2.3	31:9	3.2.1.4, 3.3.1.1,
15:15	3.3.4	23:10	3.2.2.1.2		3.3.8
16:1	3.2.2.1.5	23:10-12	3.3.3	31:22	3.3.1.1
16:3	3.3.4	23:14	3.3.11.3, B.3.14	31:23	4.1.1.2
16:7	3.3.3	24:1-4	3.3.1.3	31:24-26	3.3.1.1
16:12	3.3.4	24:9	3.2.1.4,	31:25	3.2.1.4
16:13	3.2.2.1.2		3.2.2.1.2, 3.3.4	31:27	B.3.9
16:18	3.3.7	24:16	3.2.3.2	31:28	3.2.2.2.4
16:21-22	3.2.1.3	24:18	3.3.4	32:1	3.2.2.2.4
17:1-7	3.2.1.10	24:22	3.3.4	32:1-43	3.3.9.2.1
17:2-5	3.3.5.2	25:7	5.4.1	32:4	3.3.11.4
17:2-7	3.2.2.2.5	25:13-15	3.2.2.2.4	32:7	33.11.4
17:9	3.2.1.4	25:17	3.3.4	32:8	3.3.11.4, 5.9.7,
17:12	3.3.7	25:17-19	3.2.2.2.5		B.3.9
17:14-20	3.3.7	26:12	3.2.2.2.4	32:10	3.3.11.4, B.3.9
17:15	3.2.2.2.5	26:14	3.3.5.2	32:13	3.3.11.4
17:16	3.2.2.2.5, 3.3.5	27:4-7	3.2.2.2.5	32:15	3.3.11.4, B.3.2,
17:18	3.2.1.4	27:4-8	4.1.1.2		B.3.13
18:1	3.2.1.4	27:5-7	3.2.1.3	32:16-17	3.3.11.4
18:4	3.2.2.2.4	27:9	3.2.1.4	32:17	3.3.11.4

Ref	Code	Ref	Code	Ref	Code
2:6	4.1.2.1.2, 4.1.2.1.3, 4.1.2.1.4	8:14	4.1.2.6	16:7	3.2.2.1.2
		8:17	4.1.2.1.2	16:25	3.3.11.3, 4.1.2.4, B.3.16
2:6-9	4.1.1.3, 4.1.2.2	8:19	3.3.11.1, 4.1.2.4	16:31	2.1.1
2:7	2.1.1	8:22-28	4.1.2.1.2	17:1	4.1.2.4, B.3.2, B.3.9
2:10	2.2.1, 4.1.2.4, B.3.14	8:24	3.2.1.2.4	17:5	3.2.2.1.2
		8:26	4.1.2.4, B.3.7	17:6	4.1.2.1.1
2:11	4.1.2.1.2	8:27	3.2.2.1.2	18:1	4.1.2.1.1
2:14	4.1.2.4, B.3.13	8:28	2.1.1	18:3	B.3.10
3:7	4.1.2.1.2	8:33	4.1.2.1.2	18:12	4.1.2.1.3
3:8	2.1.1, 4.1.1.1, 4.1.2.4, 4.2.12, B.3.13	9:1	4.1.3.4	18:30	4.1.2.1.1, 5.12.2, B.3.13
		9:6	5.9.4		
3:9	4.1.1.1	9:8-15	4.2.9.1	18:31	4.1.2.1.1
3:11	2.1.1	9:22	2.1.1	19:1	4.1.2.1.1
3:12-14	4.1.2.1.2	9:46-49	4.1.2.1.2	19:20-24	3.2.1.10, 4.1.2.2
3:14	2.1.1	9:50-54	4.1.2.3		
3:30	2.1.1	9:53	4.1.2.1.2	20:1	4.1.2.4
3:31	4.1.2.1.2, B.3.3	10:1	B.3.13	20:27	4.1.2.1.1
4:2	4.1.2.4, B.3.13	10:2	2.1.1	20:28	4.1.2.1.1
4:3	2.1.1	10:3	2.1.1	20:29-35	4.1.2.2
4:21	4.1.2.1.2	10:3-4	4.1.1.1, B.1.1	21:10	4.1.2.4
5:2	4.1.2.1.2	10:4	3.3.10, 4.1.2.1.3	21:13	4.1.2.4
5:4	4.1.2.1.2			21:16	4.1.2.4
5:4-5	5.1.5	10:6	4.1.2.1.2	21:25	4.1.2.1.1
5:6	B.3.3, B.3.13	10:6-9	4.1.2.1.2		
5:7	4.1.2.4, B.3.7	10:7	4.1.2.4, B.3.13	**Ruth**	
5:17	4.1.2.1.2	10:8	2.1.1	1:1	5.4, 5.4.1
5:26	4.1.2.4, B.3.9, B.3.13	10:10	4.1.2.1.2	1:13	5.4.1
		11:15-27	4.1.2.2	1:17	3.3.11.1, 5.4.1
5:27	B.3.7	11:26	2.1.1	1:19	5.4.1
5:29	B.3.13	12:1	4.1.2.1.2, 4.1.2.4	1:20	5.4.1
5:31	2.1.1			1:20-21	3.3.9.2.2, 5.2.1.2
6:1	2.1.1	12:7	2.1.1		
6:18	4.1.2.4, B.3.10	12:9	2.1.1	2:8	5.4.1
6:24	4.1.2.1.3	12:11	2.1.1	2:9	5.4.1
6:25-26	3.2.1.3	12:14	2.1.1	2:10	5.4.1
7:8	4.1.2.4	13:1	2.1.1	2:13	3.2.1.2.6, 5.4.1
7:12	4.1.2.4, B.3.7	13:5-7	3.2.2.1.2	2:21	5.4.1
7:24	4.1.2.4	13:16-20	3.2.1.3	3:9	3.2.1.2.6, 5.4.1
8:1	4.1.2.1.2, 4.1.2.4	15:10	4.1.2.4	3:10	5.4.1
		15:15-17	4.1.2.1.2	3:12	5.4.1, B.3.7
		15:19	4.1.2.1.3		

7:22	4.1.3.1.2,	23:1-7	4.1.3.1.1,	6:23-27	4.1.4.3
	5.12.2, B.3.10		4.1.3.1.2,	6:38	4.1.4.4, B.3.4
7:27	5.4.1		4.1.3.5, 5.1.1	7:21	4.1.4.3
8:1-8	4.1.3.3	23:3	5.1.1	7:23-26	4.1.4.3
8:3	5.1.1	23:8-29	4.1.3.3	7:38-39	4.1.4.3
8:13	5.1.1	23:8-39	4.1.3.1.1	7:40-51	4.1.4.3
9:4-5	B.3.14	24:1	4.2.9.2	8:1-66	4.1.4.3
10:1-19	4.1.3.3	24:1-25	4.1.3.3	8:2	4.1.4.4, B.3.5
11:1	4.1.3.3	24:12	5.12.2, B.3.9	8:4	3.2.2.1.2,
11:21	4.1.2.3, 4.1.3.4	24:17	5.12.2		3.2.2.4.11
12:1-4	4.2.9.1	24:25	3.2.1.3	8:5	B.3.13
12:12	5.6.1			8:8	4.1.4.1, 5.12
12:22	5.1.1, B.3.9	**1 Kings**		8:13	4.2.1.3, 5.12.2,
12:30-31	4.1.3.3	1:28-53	2.1.1		B.3.9
13:33	B.3.14	1:39	3.2.2.1.2	9:1-11	4.1.4.3
14:5	5.9.8	1:45	5.4.1	9:4-7	4.1.4.2
16:5	5.1.4	1:50	3.2.1.3,	9:6	5.12.2, B.3.9
18:18	4.1.3.1.2		3.2.2.1.2	9:13	4.1.4.1
18:30	5.4.1	2:3	3.2.3.2, 3.3.1.2	9:16	3.2.1.5, 4.1.1.1,
19:13	5.4.1	2:11	4.1.4.3		4.1.2.1.3, 5.3
19:19	B.3.14	2:23	5.4.1	9:17-25	4.1.4.3
20:16-22	5.6.1	2:28	3.2.1.3	9:20-21	4.1.4.1
20:23-26	4.1.3.1.1	2:28-30	3.2.2.1.2	9:26-28	4.1.4.3, 5.6
20:24	4.1.3.1.1	3:1	5.3, 5.5	9:28	5.1.5
21:1	4.1.1.1, 4.1.1.3	3:4	4.1.4.3	10:1-27	4.1.4.3
21:7-8	4.1.3.4	3:5-13	4.1.4.3	10:12	4.1.4.1
22:2	5.1.1, B.1.1	3:6-9	4.1.4.3	10:22	5.12.2, B.3.4
22:5	5.1.1	3:7	5.9.4	10:28-29	4.1.4.3, 5.5
22:6	B.1.1	3:18	4.1.4.4	11:9	4.1.4.4, B.3.4
22:14	4.1.3.4, B.1.1	4:31	5.1.1	11:40	2.1.1
22:16	4.1.3.4, B.1.1	4:32	5.3	11:41	4.1.4.1
22:19	B.1.1	4:33	5.5	11:41-43	4.1.4.3
22:29	B.1.1	5:2-5	4.1.4.3	12:1-19	4.1.4.3, 5.6
22:30	B.1.1	5:6	4.1.4.3	12:19	4.1.4.1
22:34	4.1.3.4	5:7-8	4.1.4.3	12:20	4.1.4.4
22:35	B.1.1	5:9	4.1.4.3	12:21-24	4.1.4.3
22:42	B.1.1	5:15	4.1.4.3	12:25	App. A
22:47	B.1.1	6:1	2.1.1, 4.1.4.4,	12:26-33	3.2.1.3
22:49	B.1.1		B.3.5	12:28	3.2.2.1.2
22:39	4.2.1.2.9.10	6:1-3	4.1.4.3	12:32-33	3.2.2.1.2
		6:20-21	4.1.4.3	13:2	4.1.4.1
		6:20-22	3.2.1.3	14:1-17	3.2.2.1.2

19:36	2.1.1	24:5	4.1.4.3	14:1-17	4.1.3.3
19:37	2.1.1	24:8-10	4.1.4.3	15:2	3.2.1.4
20:4-6	4.2.1.2.12	24:14	4.1.4.4	15:17	5.9.8
20:12	2.1.1	24:17-20	4.1.4.3	15:19	5.1.1
20:20-21	4.1.4.3	24:18-25:30	4.1.4.3,	15:22	B.3.13
21:1	4.2.1.2.5		4.2.2.2	15:25-29	4.1.3.3
21:1-9	4.1.4.3	25:1	4.1.4.3	16:1-3	4.1.3.3
21:17	4.1.4.3	25:13-14	4.1.4.3	16:5-7	5.1.6
21:18-24	4.1.4.3	25:18-19	4.1.4.3	16:8-22	5.1.7, B.1
21:19	4.1.4.4, B.3.4	25:27	2.1.1	16:8-36	5.1.7, 5.1.8
22:1-2	4.1.4.3			16:23-33	5.1.7
22:3-20	4.1.4.3	**1 Chronicles**		16:30	5.1.7, 5.12.2,
22:4	3.2.2.1.2	1:29	3.3.9.2		B.3.11
22:8	3.2.2.1.2,	1:43	B.3.9	16:34	4.2.2.3, 5.1.8
	3.2.2.2	2:1	2.1.1	16:34-36	5.1.7
22:10	3.2.2.2.2	2:4	2.1.1	16:35	5.12.2, B.3.13
22:16-17	4.1.4.2	2:5	2.1.1	17:1	5.12.2, B.3.11
22:19	3.3.11.1	2:9	2.1.1	17:1-27	4.1.3.3
22:20	2.2.1, 4.1.2.4,	2:11	5.4	17:5	4.1.3.4, B.3.14
	B.2	2:18-21	2.1.1	17:16	B.3.7
23:1-4	4.1.4.3	3:17-24	5.12	17:20	5.12.2, B.3.10
23:2	3.2.2.2.2	3:19-21	2.0	18:1-17	4.1.3.3
23:4	3.2.2.1.2	4:10	B.3.11	18:9-12	5.1.1
23:4-5	4.1.3.4	4:43	5.12	19:1-19	4.1.3.3
23:6-10	4.1.4.3	5:6	2.1.1	20:1	4.1.3.3
23:8-19	3.2.2.2,	5:26	2.1.1, 5.12	20:2-3	4.1.3.3
	3.2.2.2.2	6:39	5.1.1	21:1	4.2.9.2
23:11	B.3.13.1	7:22-27	2.1.1	21:1-26	4.1.3.3
23:21	3.2.2.2.2,	8:33	4.1.3.4	21:1-22:1	5.1.1
	4.1.4.3	8:33-34	5.12	21:10	5.12, 5.12.2,
23:22-23	4.1.4.3	8:34	4.1.3.4		B.3.9
23:25	3.2.2.2.2,	9:1	5.12	21:16	3.2.3.1
	3.3.1.1	10:1-12	4.1.3.3	21:17	5.12.2
23:26	4.1.4.1	10:4	B.3.11	21:26	3.2.1.3
23:29	3.3.5	11:1-9	4.1.3.3	21:27	5.12.2, B.3.13.1
23:29-30	4.1.4.3	11:10-41	5.12	22:19	5.6.2, 5.9.8,
23:29-35	2.1.1	11:11-41	4.1.3.3		5.12.2,
23:30-31	4.1.4.3	11:23	B.3.6		B.3.14
23:33-34	4.1.4.3	11:42-47	5.12	23:26	5.12.2, B.3.11
23:34	5.9.4	12:1	B.3.9	24:2	B.3.9
23:36	4.1.4.3	13:2	B.3.10	25:5	5.2.2
24:1	2.1.1, 4.1.4.3	13:5-14	4.1.3.3	25:7-8	B.3.13

Reference	Section
27:7-9	4.1.4.3
28:1-6	4.1.4.3
28:16	4.1.4.3
28:21	4.1.4.3
28:26	5.12
28:26-27	4.1.4.3
29:1-2	4.1.4.3
29:21	5.9.8
29:32-33	4.2.10
30:1	5.12.2
30:6	5.12.2
30:27	3.2.1.4
32:1-2	2.1.1
32:9-10	2.1.1
32:22	2.1.1
32:30	B.3.16
32:32	5.12
32:32-33	4.1.4.3
32:32	5.12
33:1-10	4.1.4.3
33:18	4.1.4.3
33:19	5.12.2, B.3.13
33:20-25	4.1.4.3
33:21	B.3.4
34:1-2	4.1.4.3
34:3-7	4.1.4.3
34:8-28	4.1.4.3
34:18	3.2.2.2.2
34:27	3.3.11.1
34:28	2.2.1
34:29-33	4.1.4.3
35:1	4.1.4.3
35:3	B.3.13
35:10-14	3.2.2.2.2
35:12	3.3.1.1
35:15	5.12.2, B.3.11
35:18-19	4.1.4.3
35:20-22	2.1.1
35:20-24	4.1.4.3
35:21	5.6.2
35:25	4.2.2.1, 5.12
35:27	5.12
36:1-2	4.1.4.3
36:3-4	4.1.4.3
36:4	2.1.1
36:5	4.1.4.3
36:6	2.1.1, 4.1.4.3
36:8	4.1.4.3, 5.12
36:9-10	4.1.4.3
36:10-13	4.1.4.3
36:12	4.2.2.1
36:17	4.1.4.3
36:18-19	4.1.4.3
36:20-21	4.1.4.3
36:21-22	4.2.2.1, 4.2.2.3
36:22-23	2.1.1, 4.2.1.1, 5.12
36:23	5.1.8, 5.10.1, 5.10.2, 5.11.2

Ezra

Reference	Section
1:1	2.1.1, 4.2.2.1, 5.10.1
1:1-4	5.10.1
1:2	5.1.8
1:7	2.1.1
1:8	2.1.1
2:2	2.1.1
2:62	B.3.13
2:63	5.9.8, 5.10.2
2:64	4.2.1.3
2:69	5.10.2
3:2	3.3.1.2, 5.10.1
3:9	4.2.1.3
3:10	5.1.1
3:11	4.2.2.3, 5.10.1
4:2	2.1.1
4:3	2.1.1
4:5	2.1.1, 5.10
4:6	5.10
4:7	2.1.1, 5.10, 5.10.2, B.3.13.1
4:8-6:18	5.10.2, B.3.12
4:20	5.6.2
4:24	5.10
5:1	4.2.1.2.8, 4.2.14, 4.2.15.1, 5.10.1
5:8	5.10.2, B.3.13.1
5:11	5.1.8
5:14	2.1.1
5:16	2.1.1
6:8	5.10.2
6:12	5.10.2
6:13	5.10.2
6:14	4.2.1.2.8, 4.2.14, 4.2.15.1, 5.10
6:15	3.2.2.1.5, 5.10.2, B.3.5
6:18	3.3.1.1
6:20	4.2.1.3
6:22	B.3.6
7:1	5.10
7:1-8	5.10, 2.1.1
7:6	5.10.2
7:8	5.10
7:11	5.10.2
7:12-26	5.10.2, B.3.12
7:17	5.10.2
7:21	5.10.2
7:23	5.10.2, B.3.13.1
7:24	5.6.2
7:26	5.10.2
8:15	5.10.2, B.3.6
8:16	B.3.13
8:35	5.9.8
8:36	5.10.2, B.3.13.1
9:1	3.2.1.5
9:2	4.2.16
9:7	5.9.8
9:15	5.10.2, B.3.11
10:3	4.2.16
10:13	5.9.8, B.3.4
10:14	5.1.6, 5.10.2
10:16-44	4.2.16

24:2	5.1.4, B.3.9	33:12	5.1.4	39:8	5.1.4
24:6	5.1.4	33:16	5.1.4	39:9	5.1.4
24:10	5.1.4	34:1-4	B.3.2	39:12	5.1.4
25:2	5.1.4	34:5	B.3.2	40:5	B.3.11
25:3	5.1.4	34:6	B.3.2	40:13	5.1.4
25:4	5.1.4	34:7	B.3.2	40:13-17	5.1.4
25:5	5.1.4	34:8-9	B.3.2	40:14-15	5.1.4
25:19	5.1.4	34:10	B.3.2	40:15	5.1.4
25:20	5.1.4	34:11	B.3.2	40:17	5.1.4
26:11	5.1.4	34:12-14	B.3.2	41:4	5.1.4
27:2-3	5.1.4	34:15	5.1.4, B.1.1,	41:8	4.2.1.2.9.10
27:5-6	5.1.4		B.3.2	41:9	5.1.1
27:6	5.1.4	34:16	5.1.4, B.1.1,	41:10	5.1.4
27:7	5.1.4		B.3.2	41:13	5.1.4
27:11-12	5.1.4	34:17	B.3.2	42:5	5.1.5
27:12	5.1.4	34:17-21	B.3.2	42:9	5.1.5
28:1	5.1.4	34:20	5.1.4	42:11	5.1.5
28:2	5.1.4	34:22	B.3.2	43:5	5.1.5
28:6	5.1.4	35:3	5.1.4	44:2	5.1.5
28:8	5.1.4	35:6	5.1.4	44:8	5.1.5
29:6	5.1.4	35:10	5.1.4	44:9	5.1.5
29:10	3.3.11.3, 5.1.4	35:13-14	5.1.4	44:11	5.1.5
30:4	B.3.13	35:16	5.1.4, 5.1.8	44:18	5.1.5
30:6	5.1.4	35:21	5.1.4	44:20-21	5.1.5
30:10	5.1.4	36:5	5.1.4	44:22	5.1.5
31:1	5.1.4	36:7	5.1.4	45:6	5.1.5
31:2	5.1.4	36:10	5.1.8	45:9	5.1.5
31:4	B.3.7	37:8	B.3.2	45:12	5.1.5
31:5	5.1.4	37:10	B.3.2	45:16	5.1.5
31:9	5.1.4	37:12	5.1.8	46:3	5.1.5
31:13	4.2.2.2, 5.1.4	37:12-13	B.3.2	46:5	5.1.8
31:15	5.1.4	37:14-15	B.3.2	46:6	5.1.5
31:22	5.1.4	37:25	5.1.4	46:7	5.1.5
32:1-2	5.1.1	37:26	5.1.8	46:10	5.1.5
32:3	5.1.4	37:28	B.3.2	46:11	5.1.5
32:4-5	5.1.4	38:3	5.1.4	47:3	5.1.5
32:7	5.1.4	38:12	5.1.4	47:4	5.1.5
32:8	5.1.4, B.3.7	38:13	5.1.4	47:6-7	5.1.5
32:9	5.1.4	38:16	5.1.4	48:2	5.1.5, 5.7.2
32:11	5.1.8	38:19	5.1.4	48:4-6	5.1.5
33:2	B.3.13	38:20	5.1.4	48:7	5.1.5
33:10	5.1.4	38:22	5.1.4	48:8	5.1.5

Ref	Section	Ref	Section	Ref	Section
77:20	5.1.6	83:8	5.1.6	92:15	5.1.7
78:9-11	5.1.6	83:9-11	4.1.2.3	93:1	5.1.7, 5.1.8
78:12	5.1.6	83:11	5.1.6	93:3	5.1.7
78:15	5.1.6	83:13	5.1.6	94:15	5.1.8
78:20	5.1.6	84:4	5.1.6	94:22	5.1.7
78:26	5.1.6	84:5	5.1.6	95:1	5.1.7
78:29	5.1.6	84:8	5.1.6	95:7	5.1.7
78:35	5.1.6	84:12	5.1.6	96:1-2	5.1.7
78:36	5.1.6	85:2-4	5.1.6	96:1-13	5.1.7
78:41	5.1.6	86:3	5.1.6	96:7-8	5.1.7
78:43	5.1.6	86:5	5.1.6	96:10	5.1.7, 5.1.8,
78:44	5.1.6	86:6	5.1.6		B.3.11
78:45	5.1.6	86:8	5.1.6	97:1	5.1.7
78:50	5.1.6	86:14	5.1.6	97:6	5.1.7
78:52	5.1.6	86:15	4.2.6, 5.1.6	97:8	5.1.7
78:58	5.1.6	86:16	5.1.6	97:12	5.1.7
78:60	4.1, 5.1.6	87:3	5.1.6	98:1	5.1.7
78:64	5.1.6	87:4	5.1.6	98:3	5.1.7
78:67-68	5.1.6	87:5	5.1.6	98:4	5.1.5, 5.1.7
78:72	5.1.6	88:7	5.1.6	98:9	5.1.7
79:1	5.1.6	88:10	5.1.6	99:1	5.1.7
79:2-3	5.1.6	88:15	5.1.6	99:4	5.1.7
79:6-7	5.1.6	89:2	5.1.6	99:6	4.1.3.3
79:7	5.1.6	89:3-4	5.1.6	99:9	5.1.7
79:10	5.1.8	89:10	5.1.6	100:1	5.1.5, 5.1.7
79:13	5.1.6	89:12	5.1.6	100:3	5.1.7
80:1	5.1.6	89:14	5.1.6	100:5	4.2.2.3, 5.1.7,
80:1-2	5.1.6	89:17	5.1.6		5.10.1
80:5	5.1.6	89:18	5.1.6	101:8	5.1.7
80:7	5.1.6	89:24	5.1.6	102:3	5.1.7
80:8	5.1.6	89:26	5.1.6	102:5	5.1.7
80:11	5.1.6	89:33	5.1.6	102:6	5.1.7
80:14	5.1.6	89:37	5.1.6	102:8	5.1.7
81:4-5	5.1.6	89:49	5.1.6	102:12	5.7.2
81:5	5.1.6	90:2	5.1.7, B.3.9	102:16	5.1.7
81:6-7	5.1.6	90:3	5.1.7	102:22	5.1.7
81:7	5.1.6	91:1	3.3.9.2.2, 5.1.7	102:26	5.1.7
81:10	5.1.6	91:12	5.1.7	103:1	5.1.7
81:12	5.1.6	91:15	5.1.7	103:2	5.1.7
82:2	5.1.6	92:5	5.1.8	103:3	5.1.7
82:8	5.1.6	92:10-11	5.1.7	103:4	5.1.7
83:7	5.1.6	92:11	5.1.7	103:5	5.1.7

Reference	Section		Reference	Section		Reference	Section
124:8	4.2.1.2.9.1, 5.1.8		137:8-9	5.1.8, 5.5.2		145:13	4.2.1.3, 5.1.8
125:1-2	5.1.8		138:1	5.1.8		145:17-21	5.1.8
125:4	5.1.8		138:3	5.1.8		146:2	B.3.9
125:5	5.1.8		138:4	5.1.8		146:3	5.1.8
126:1	5.1.8		138:7	5.1.8		146:5	5.1.8
126:4	5.1.8		139:3	5.1.8		146:6	5.1.8
128:1	5.1.8		139:8-10	4.2.7		147:2	5.1.8
128:5	5.1.8		139:11	5.1.8		147:4	5.1.8
128:6	5.1.8		139:13	5.1.8		147:12	B.3.13
129:6	5.1.8		139:16	5.1.8		147:20	5.1.8, B.3.11
129:7	5.1.8		139:19	5.1.8		149:7	B.3.11
130:7	5.1.8		139:19-22	5.1.8			
131:3	5.1.8		140:3	5.1.8		**Proverbs**	
132:1	5.1.8		140:4	5.1.8		1:1	5.3
132:2	5.1.8		140:6	5.1.8		1:2-9:18	5.3
132:5	5.1.8		140:9	5.1.8		1:7	5.1.8, 5.2.2, 5.3
132:12	5.1.8, B.3.7		140:10	5.1.8		1:16	5.3
133:2	5.1.8		140:11	4.2.1.2.9.10, 5.1.8		1:21	5.3.2
133:3	5.1.8		141:4	5.1.8		2:1	5.3.2
134:3	5.1.8		141:7	5.1.8		2:4	5.2.1.3
135:1	5.1.8		141:9-10	5.1.8		2:15	5.3.2
135:2	5.1.8		141:10	5.1.8		3:5-6	5.3
135:3	5.1.8		142:3	5.1.8, B.3.7		3:18	5.3.1
135:6	5.1.8		142:6	5.1.8		3:19-20	5.3.2
135:8	5.1.8		143:1	5.1.8		3:26	5.3
135:9	5.1.8		143:3	5.1.8		4:5	5.3.2
135:10	5.1.8		143:6	5.1.8		4:18	5.3.2
135:11	5.1.8		143:8	5.1.8, B.3.7		5:3	5.5.1
135:15-18	5.1.8		143:9	5.1.8		5:7	5.3.2
135:18	5.1.8		143:12	5.1.8		5:11	5.3.2
135:19-20	5.1.8		144:1	5.1.8		6:1-2	5.3.2
135:21	5.1.8		144:3	5.1.8		6:16	5.3
136:1	4.2.2.3		144:9	5.1.8		7:6	5.3
136:23	5.1.8		144:10	5.1.8		7:24	5.3.2
136:26	5.1.8		144:12-15	5.1.8		8:8	5.3.2
137:1	5.1.8		144:15	5.1.8		8:10	5.3
137:3	5.1.8		145:1-16	5.1.8		8:11	5.3
137:3-4	5.1.3		145:4	5.1.8, B.3.13		8:19	5.3
137:7	4.2.2.3, 4.2.8, 5.2.1.2, 5.7.1		145:8	4.2.6		8:24-30	5.3.2
			145:11	5.1.8		8:25	B.3.9
137:6	5.1.8		145:12	5.1.8		9:1-2	5.3.2
						9:10	5.2.2, 5.3

2:19	5.6.2, B.3.13	7:23	5.6.2	**Song of Solomon**	
2:23	5.6.2	7:26	5.6.1	1:1	5.5
2:24	5.6.2	8:1	5.6.2	1:5	3.3.11.3, 5.5,
2:26	5.6.1, 5.6.2	8:2-4	5.6		5.5.2
3:1	5.6.2	8:4	B.3.13	1:5-6	5.5
3:8	5.6.1	8:8	B.3.13	1:6	5.5.2
3:9	5.6.2	8:9	5.6, 5.6.2,	1:9	5.5
3:10	5.6.2		B.3.13	1:12	5.5.2, B.3.13.1
3:14	B.3.11	8:10	5.6, 5.6.2	1:14	5.5, 5.5.2
3:15	5.6.2	8:11	5.6.2, B.3.13.1	1:16-17	5.5
3:16	5.6	8:15	5.6.2, B.3.13	2:1	5.5
3:19-20	5.6	8:16	5.6.2, 5.9.8,	2:3	5.5
4:1	5.6, 5.6.2		B.3.14	2:13	5.5
4:2	5.6.2, B.3.13	8:17	5.5.2, 5.6.2	2:17	5.5
4:2-3	5.6.2	9:1	5.6.2, 5.9.8,	3:1-4	5.5.2
4:7	5.6.2		B.3.14	3:5-9	5.5.2
4:8	5.6.1, 5.6.2	9:5	5.6	3:7	5.5, 5.5.2
4:13	5.6	9:6-7	5.6.2	3:9	5.5, 5.5.2
4:13-16	5.6.1	9:9	5.6	3:9-10	5.5
4:14	5.6.2	9:10	5.6	3:11	5.5
5:1	5.6, 5.6.1, 5.6.2	9:13	5.6.2	4:1	5.5
5:2	5.6.1, 5.6.2	9:14-15	5.6.1	4:4	5.5.2
5:5	5.6.1	9:16	5.6.1	4:8	5.5
5:8	5.6, 5.6.2	9:18	5.6.1	4:8-6:11	5.5.3
5:13	5.6.2	10:4	5.6.1	4:11	5.5.1
5:15	5.6.2	10:5-7	5.6	4:13	5.5.2
5:16	5.6.2	10:7	5.6.1	4:13-14	5.5, 5.5.2
5:18	5.6.2, B.3.13	10:8	5.6.1, 5.6.2	4:14	5.5.2
6:2	5.6.2, B.3.13	10:9	5.6.2	5:1	5.5
6:6	5.6.2, B.3.16	10:10-11	5.6.2	5:3	5.5.2, 5.6.1
6:7	5.6.1	10:12-14	5.6.1	5:3-7	5.5.2
6:10	5.6.2	10:16	5.6.2	5:13-15	5.5
7:1	5.6.1	10:17	5.6.2	5:14	5.5.2
7:2	5.6.2, 5.9.8,	11:1	5.6	5:15	5.5, 5.5.2
	B.3.14	11:5	5.6.2	6:4	5.5
7:5	5.6.1	11:6	4.2.1.3	6:8	5.5
7:7	5.6.1	12:2-6	4.2.9.1	6:11	5.5, 5.5.2,
7:9	5.6.1, 5.6.2	12:3	5.6.2		B.3.13.1
7:12	5.6.2	12:9	5.6, 5.6.2	7:4	5.5
7:13	5.6.2	12:9-14	5.6	7:5	5.5, 5.6.1
7:16	5.6.1			7:7	5.5
7:19	B.3.13			7:9	5.5.1

29:13	4.2.1.2.1	31:1	4.2.1.2.9.1	34:16	4.2.1.2.9.13
29:15	4.2.1.2.9.13	31:4	5.2.1.3	35:1	4.2.1.2.9.5, 5.3
29:16	4.2.1.2.9.1, 4.2.1.2.9.9, 4.2.1.2.9.11	31:7	4.2.1.2.4	35:1-10	4.2.1.2.6
		31:9	4.2.1.2.9.4	35:2	4.2.1.2.9.6, 4.2.1.2.9.8
29:18	4.2.1.2.9.2, 4.2.3.1	32:6	4.2.1.2.9.13		
		32:9	4.2.1.2.11	35:5	4.2.1.2.9.2, 4.2.1.2.9.6, 4.2.1.2.9.11, 4.2.3.1
29:19	4.2.1.2.9.1	32:11	4.2.1.2.11		
29:20	4.2.1.2.9.13	32:13	4.2.1.2.9.7		
29:21	4.2.1.2.9.13	32:13-18	4.2.1.2.6	35:6	4.2.1.2.9.5, 4.2.1.2.9.6
29:23	4.2.1.2.9.2	32:14	4.2.1.2.9.7, 5.2.1.3		
30:4	5.1.6			35:7	4.2.1.2.9.5, 5.1.5
30:5	4.2.1.2.9.13, 4.2.1.3, 5.2.3, B.3.8	32:16	4.2.1.2.9.11		
		32:17	4.2.1.2.9.6	35:8	4.2.1.2.9.5, 4.2.1.2.9.6, 4.2.1.2.9.13, 4.2.1.3, 5.2.3, B.3.8
		33:6	4.2.1.2.9.12, 5.3		
30:6	4.2.1.2.9.13				
30:7	4.2.1.2.9.10, 4.2.1.2.9.13, 5.1.6, 5.2.1.3	33:8	4.2.1.2.9.5, 4.2.1.2.9.13, 4.2.1.3		
				35:9	4.2.1.2.9.13
		33:9	4.2.1.2.9.11	35:10	4.2.1.2.9.2, 4.2.1.2.9.5, 4.2.1.2.9.7
30:8	4.2.1.2.14	33:10	4.2.1.2.9.1, 4.2.1.2.9.3, 4.2.1.2.9.12		
30:9	4.2.1.2.9.9				
30:10	4.1.3.1.2				
30:11	4.2.1.2.9.1, 4.2.1.2.9.13, 4.2.1.3	33:15	4.2.1.2.9.13	36:1	2.1.1, 4.2.1.2.8, 5.1.5
		33:18	4.2.1.2.9.13		
		33:20	4.2.1.2.9.4, 4.2.1.2.9.13	36:2	4.2.1.2.9.5
30:12	4.2.1.2.9.1, 4.2.1.2.9.11			36:6	4.2.1.2.9.12
		33:21	4.2.1.2.9.13	36:18	4.2.1.2.12, B.3.11
30:17	5.4.1	33:23	4.2.1.2.9.13		
30:18	4.2.1.2.9.13	33:24	4.2.1.2.9.13	37:3	4.2.1.2.9.11, 4.2.1.2.12
30:19	4.2.1.2.9.4, 4.2.1.2.9.6, 4.2.1.2.9.13	34:1	4.2.1.2.9.3, 4.2.1.2.9.12, 4.2.1.2.9.13		
				37:16	3.2.2.1.2, 5.1.7
		34:4	4.2.1.2.9.10	37:17	2.1.1
30:22	4.2.1.2.4, 4.2.1.2.9.13	34:7	5.2.1.3	37:21	2.1.1
		34:8	4.2.1.2.9.12	37:22	4.2.1.2.9.4
30:23	4.2.1.2.9.12	34:10	4.2.1.2.9.10, 4.2.1.2.9.11	37:23	4.2.1.2.9.1, 4.2.1.2.12
30:25	4.2.1.2.9.11				
30:28	4.2.1.2.9.11, 4.2.1.2.9.13	34:11	3.2.2.1.2, 4.2.1.2.9.13, 5.1.7, 5.2.1.3	37:26	4.2.1.2.9.12
				37:27	4.2.1.2.9.13
30:29	4.2.1.2.9.1, 5.1.3			37:30	4.2.1.2.9.6
		34:13	5.1.5, 5.2.1.3	37:32	4.2.1.2.9.4, 4.2.1.2.12, 4.2.6
30:30	4.2.1.2.9.10				
30:31	4.2.1.2.9.10	34:15	5.2.1.3		

Ref	Code	Ref	Code	Ref	Code
42:23	4.2.1.2.9.3		4.2.1.2.9.13, 5.3	46:3	4.2.1.2.5
42:24	4.2.1.2.9.9, 4.2.1.3, B.3.7	44:9	4.2.1.2.4, 4.2.1.2.9.9, 4.2.1.2.9.13	46:6-7	4.2.1.2.4
43:1	4.2.1.2.9.1	44:12	4.2.1.2.9.10	46:11	4.2.1.2.6, 4.2.1.2.9.12
43:2	4.2.1.2.9.11	44:15	4.2.1.2.4, 4.2.1.2.9.13	47:1	4.2.1.2.9.10
43:3	4.2.1.2.9.1	44:22	4.2.1.2.9.13	47:4	4.2.1.2.9.1
43:4	4.2.1.2.9.13	44:23	4.2.1.2.9.7, 5.1.7	47:5	4.2.1.2.9.4
43:5	4.2.1.3	44:24	4.2.1.2.9.1	47:8	4.2.1.2.11
43:7	4.2.1.2.9.12	44:25	4.2.1.2.14	47:10	4.2.1.2.9.12, 4.2.1.2.11
43:8	4.2.1.2.9.2, 4.2.3.1, B.3.8	44:26	4.2.1.1	48:2	4.2.1.2.13
43:9	4.2.1.2.9.12, 4.2.1.2.9.13, 4.2.1.2.14	44:28	2.1.1, 4.2.1.1	48:3	4.2.1.2.9.3
43:10-11	3.2.2.2.4	45:1	2.1.1, 4.2.1.1	48:3-7	4.2.1.2.14
43:11	4.2.1.2.9, 4.2.5	45:3	5.2.1.3, 5.3	48:5	4.2.1.2.4, 4.2.1.3, B.3.9
43:12	4.2.1.2.9.3, 4.2.1.2.14	45:3-5	4.2.1.2.14	48:6	4.2.1.2.9.13
43:13	4.2.1.2.9.12	45:5	4.2.1.2.9.13, 4.2.1.2.11, 4.2.1.3	48:8	4.2.1.2.9.9, 4.2.1.2.9.11
43:14	4.2.1.2.7, 4.2.1.2.9.1	45:6	4.2.1.2.11, 4.2.1.3	48:11	4.2.1.2.9.13
43:17	4.2.1.2.9.10, 4.2.1.2.9.13			48:15	4.2.1.2.9
43:20	5.1.5, 5.2.1.3	45:8	4.2.1.2.9.6	48:16	4.2.1.2.9.3, 4.2.1.2.9.13
43:21	4.2.1.3, B.3.7	45:9	4.2.1.2.9.1, 4.2.1.2.9.9, 5.2.1.3	48:17	4.2.1.2.9.1, 4.2.1.2.9.13
43:23-24	4.2.1.2.3, 4.2.1.2.9.9	45:11	4.2.1.2.9.1, 4.2.1.2.9.2	48:18	4.2.1.2.9.6
43:25	3.2.2.2.4, 4.2.1.2.9, 4.2.1.2.9.13	45:12	3.2.2.1.2	48:19	4.2.1.2.9.13
		45:14	5.2.1.3	48:20	4.2.1.1, 4.2.1.2.5
43:28	4.2.1.2.3	45:16	4.2.1.2.4	48:21	4.2.1.2.9.13, 4.2.1.3, 5.2.3, B.3.8
44:2	4.2.1.2.9.1, B.3.13	45:17	4.2.1.3		
44:3	4.2.1.2.9.13	45:18	3.2.2.1.2, 4.2.1.2.9.13, 4.2.1.2.11	49:1	4.2.1.2.9.13, 5.1.7
44:3-4	5.2.1.3	45:19	4.2.1.2.9.13	49:4	4.2.1.2.9.10, 4.2.1.2.9.13
44:4	4.2.1.2.9.11, 4.2.1.2.9.13	45:21	4.2.1.2.9.13, 4.2.1.2.14, 4.2.1.3, 4.2.5	49:5	4.2.1.2.9.1, 4.2.1.2.9.3
44:7	B.3.8	45:24	4.2.1.2.9.13	49:6	4.2.1.2.9.13
44:7-8	4.2.1.2.14	46:1	4.2.1.1	49:7	4.2.1.2.9.1
44:8	4.2.1.2.9.1, 4.2.1.2.9.3,			49:8	4.2.1.2.9.6
				49:10	4.2.1.2.9.5
				49:11	4.2.1.2.9.5

59:2-3	4.2.1.2.9.10	61:3	4.2.1.2.9,	65:7	4.2.1.3
59:3	4.2.1.2.9.9,		4.2.1.2.9.2,	65:10	4.2.1.2.9.11
	4.2.1.2.9.13		4.2.1.2.9.6	65:12	4.2.1.2.9.9
59:4	4.2.1.2.9.11,	61:4	4.2.1.1	65:14	4.2.1.2.9.7
	5.2.1.3	61:6	4.2.1.2.9.4	65:17	3.2.2.1.2
59:5	4.2.1.2.9.13,	61:7	4.2.1.2.9.5,	65:18	4.2.1.2.9.7,
	5.2.1.3		4.2.1.2.9.7		4.2.1.2.9.12
59:7	4.2.1.2.9.5, 5.3	61:9	4.2.1.2.9.13	65:19	4.2.1.2.9.4
59:9	4.2.1.2.9.10,	62:1	4.2.1.2.9.4	65:21	4.2.1.2.9.6
	4.2.1.2.9.11	62:3	4.2.1.2.9.2	65:23	4.2.1.2.9.13
59:11	4.2.1.2.9.10,	62:4	4.2.1.2.5,	65:24	4.2.1.2.9.6
	4.2.1.2.9.12		4.2.1.2.9.4,	65:25	4.2.1.2.9.8,
59:14	4.2.1.2.9.11		4.2.1.2.9.11		4.2.1.3
59:19	4.2.1.2.9.8,	62:5	4.2.1.2.9.7	66:3	4.2.1.2.3,
	4.2.1.3	62:6	4.2.1.2.7		4.2.1.2.4,
60:1	4.2.1.2.9.1	62:10	4.2.1.2.9,		4.2.1.2.9.9
60:2	4.2.1.2.9.13		4.2.1.2.9.5,	66:4	4.2.1.2.9.9,
60:6	4.2.1.2.11		4.2.16		4.2.1.2.9.13
60:7	4.2.1.2.3	62:11	4.2.1.2.9.1	66:5	4.2.1.2.9.3
60:8	4.2.1.2.9.13	62:12	4.2.1.2.9.4,	66:6	4.2.1.2.9.10
60:9	4.2.1.2.9.1		4.2.1.2.9.6	66:7	4.2.1.3, B.3.9
60:10-11	4.2.1.2.9.6	63:4	4.2.1.2.9.12	66:7-8	4.2.1.2.9,
60:11	4.2.1.2.9.12	63:6	4.2.1.2.9.10		4.2.1.2.9.11
60:13	4.2.1.2.9.6,	63:18	4.2.1.1	66:8	4.2.1.2.9
	4.2.1.3	63:19	4.2.1.2.9.13	66:9	4.2.1.2.9.3,
60:14	4.2.1.2.9.1,	64:1	4.2.1.2.9.10,		4.2.1.2.9.11,
	4.2.1.2.9.4		4.2.1.2.9.13		4.2.1.2.12
60:15	4.2.1.2.9.7,	64:2	4.2.1.2.9.13	66:10	4.2.1.2.9.7
	4.2.1.2.9.10,	64:3	4.2.1.2.9.13,	66:12	4.2.1.2.9.11
	4.2.1.2.9.11		4.2.1.3	66:15	4.2.1.2.9.10
60:16	4.2.1.2.9.1,	64:5	4.2.1.2.9.10	66:15-16	4.2.1.2.9.10
	5.1.8	64:7	4.2.1.2.9.1,	66:17	4.2.1.2.4,
60:17	4.2.1.2.9,		4.2.1.2.9.2		4.2.1.2.9.9,
	4.2.1.2.9.6,	64:8	4.2.1.2.9.11		4.2.1.3
	4.2.1.2.9.11	64:9	4.2.1.2.9.4	66:18	4.2.1.2.9.8,
60:18	4.2.1.2.9.6	64:9-10	4.2.1.2.9.10		4.2.6
60:19	4.2.1.2.9.1,	64:10	4.2.1.2.9.10	66:20	4.2.1.2.9.5
	4.2.1.2.9.11	64:10-11	4.2.1.1	66:24	4.2.1
60:21	4.2.1.2.9.2,	65:1	4.2.1.2.9		
	4.2.1.2.9.13	65:1-2	4.2.1.2.1	**Jeremiah**	
61:1-2	4.2.1.2.1	65:2-4	4.2.1.2.4	1:1	B.1.1
61:2	4.2.1.2.9.12	65:3	4.2.1.2.9.9	1:2	4.2.2.1

41:9	4.2.2.2
42:10	4.2.1.2.9.11
43:1-7	4.2.2.1
44:30	2.1.1, 3.3.5
45:1	4.2.2.1, 4.2.2.3
45:4	4.2.1.2.9.11
46:2	2.1.1, 4.2.2.1
46:5	4.2.2.2, 5.7.1
46:18	4.2.13.1
48:43	5.7.1
48:45-46	4.2.2.2
48:47	3.2.2.2.3
49:6	3.2.2.2.3
49:7-22	4.2.8
49:9	4.2.2.3
49:14	4.2.2.3
49:16	4.2.2.3
49:17-18	3.2.2.2.3
49:23	4.2.15.2
49:29	4.2.2.2, 5.7.1
50:6	4.2.15.2
50:16	4.2.1.2.11
50:19	4.2.15.2
50:25	4.2.1.2.11
50:29	4.2.1.2.11
50:35-37	4.2.1.2.11
50:39	4.2.1.2.11
50:42	4.2.1.2.11
51:5	4.2.1.2.11
51:11	4.2.1.2.11
51:12	4.2.1.2.11
51:15	4.2.1.2.11, 4.2.15.2
51:20-23	4.2.1.2.11
51:27	4.2.1.2.11
51:35	B.3.13
51:53	4.2.1.2.11
51:58	4.2.1.2.9.13, 4.2.1.2.11, 4.2.2.2, 4.2.12
51:64	4.2.1.2.9.10, 4.2.2.2

| 52:1 | 4.1.4.3, 4.2.2.2 |
| 52:31 | 2.1.1 |

Lamentations

1:2	5.7.1
1:3	5.7.1, 5.7.2
1:4	5.7.1, 5.7.3
1:5	5.7.1, 5.7.2
1:6	5.7.2
1:7	5.7.1
1:8	5.7.1
1:9	5.7.1
1:13	5.7.1
1:14	5.7.1
1:15	5.7.1
1:16	5.7.1, 5.7.3
1:18	5.7.2
1:19	5.7.1, B.3.8
1:22	5.7.1, B.3.8
2:1	5.7.1
2:2	5.7.1
2:5	5.7.1
2:6	3.2.2.1.3
2:11	5.7.1
2:13	5.7.1
2:14	5.7.1
2:15	5.7.2
2:15-16	5.7.1
2:18	5.7.1
2:18-20	5.7.1
2:20	5.7.1, 5.7.2
2:21	5.7.2
2:22	5.7.1
3:1	5.7.1
3:11	5.7.1
3:14	5.7.1
3:15	5.7.1
3:19	5.7.1
3:31	5.7.1
3:36-37	5.7.1
3:42	5.7.1, 5.7.2
3:47	5.7.1

3:48	5.7.1
3:48-49	5.7.1
3:53-55	5.7.1
3:58	5.7.1
4:2	5.7.1
4:3	5.7.1
4:6	5.7.1
4:9	5.7.1
4:10	5.7.1, 5.7.2, B.3.8
4:11	5.7.1
4:13-15	5.7.1
4:15	5.7.1, B.3.8
4:17	5.7.1
4:20	5.7.1
4:21-22	4.2.2.3, 4.2.8, 5.2.1.2, 5.7.1
4:22	5.7.1
5:2	5.7.2
5:5	5.7.2
5:6	5.7.1
5:7	5.7.1
5:12	5.7.2
5:16	5.7.1
5:18	5.7.1
5:19	5.7.2

Baruch

1:2	5.9.2
1:15-2:19	5.9.7
6:40	5.9.2

Ezekiel

1:2	4.2.3.1
1:3	4.2.3.1
1:24	3.3.9.2.2
5:17	4.2.3.1
6:3	4.2.3.2
6:11-12	4.2.3.1
7:15	4.2.3.1
7:26	4.2.3.1
8:3	3.2.3.1

Ref	Sections	Ref	Sections	Ref	Sections
2:20	5.1.8	6:1-7	5.9.8	8:27	5.9.3, B.3.13
2:31-35	5.9.5	6:3	5.9.8, B.3.13.1	9:1	5.9.2, 5.9.4,
2:32	5.9.5	6:5	5.9.8		5.9.8
2:33	5.9.5	6:7	5.9.8	9:2	4.2.2.1, 4.2.2.3,
2:36-38	5.9.5	6:8	5.9.4, 5.9.5,		5.9.1, 5.9.2
2:44	5.9.5		5.9.8		5.9.3, 5.9.6,
2:46	5.9.4	6:12	5.9.4, 5.9.8		5.9.8
3:1	5.9.4	6:15	5.9.4, 5.9.5,	9:4	5.9.7, 5.9.8,
3:2	5.9.8, B.3.13.1		5.9.8		B.3.9
3:2-3	5.9.8	6:21-22	5.9.3	9:4-19	5.9.7
3:2-15	3.2.1.8	6:24	5.9.8	9:11	5.9.8, B.3.11
3:4-7	5.9.4	6:28	5.9.4	9:13	3.3.1.2, 5.9.8
3:5	5.9.8, 5.9.9	7:1	5.9.1, 5.9.8	9:16	4.2.1.2.9.5
3:7	5.9.8	7:1-14	5.9.5	9:22	B.3.13
3:10	5.9.8	7:4	5.9.8	9:24	4.2.1.3
3:11	5.9.4	7:5	5.9.5	9:24-26	5.9.8
3:15	5.9.8	7:6	5.9.5	9:26	5.9.3, 5.9.8
3:16	5.9.8	7:8	5.9.5	9:26-27	5.9.3, 5.9.5
3:21	5.9.8, B.3.13.1	7:9-10	5.9.7	9:27	5.9.7
3:22-30	5.9.9	7:11	5.9.8	10:1	5.9.4
3:24	5.9.8, B.3.13.1	7:13-14	5.9.5	10:2	5.9.3
3:27	5.9.8	7:15	5.9.8	10:4	5.9.8
3:29	5.9.4, 5.9.8	7:23	5.9.9	10:5	5.9.9
4:14	5.9.8	7:25	5.9.8	10:7	5.9.3, 5.9.8
4:17	5.9.8	8:1	5.9.1	10:11	5.9.8
4:19	5.9.3	8:2	5.9.4, 5.9.8	10:12	5.6.2, 5.9.8,
4:30	5.9.4	8:5	5.9.8		B.3.14
4:35	5.1.8	8:6	5.9.8	10:14	B.3.13
4:36	5.9.8	8:8	5.9.8	10:21	5.9.8, B.3.13
5:1	5.9.4	8:8-12	5.9.3	11:2-4	5.9.8
5:2	5.9.4	8:9	5.9.5, 5.9.8	11:7	5.9.8
5:3	5.9.8	8:11-13	5.9.8	11:11	5.9.8
5:5	5.9.4	8:15	5.9.3, 5.9.8	11:13-14	5.9.8
5:7	5.9.8, B.3.13.1	8:16	5.9.9, B.3.13	11:16	5.9.9
5:10	5.9.9	8:17	5.9.8	11:17	5.9.8
5:13	5.9.8	8:19	5.9.8	11:20	5.9.8
5:15	5.9.8	8:20	5.9.5	11:24	5.9.8
5:16	5.9.8	8:21	5.9.8	11:25	5.9.8
5:17	5.9.8	8:21-22	5.9.5	11:26	5.9.8
5:20	5.9.8	8:22-23	5.9.8	11:27	5.9.8
5:28	5.9.5	8:23	B.3.13	11:29	5.9.8, 5.9.9
5:29	5.9.4, 5.9.8	8:23-26	5.9.5	11:31	5.9.8

7:14	B.3.7	3:12	4.2.2.2, 4.2.10, B.3.16	**Habakkuk**	
8:5	3.2.2.2.4			1:2-4	4.2.12
8:14	4.2.1.2.9.10, 4.2.7	4:1-3	4.2.1.2.13, 4.2.1.2.9.8, 4.2.9.2, 4.2.10	1:5	4.2.12
				1:6	4.2.12
9:2-4	4.2.7			1:8	4.2.12
9:11	4.2.7, 4.2.7.1	4:2	3.2.2.2.4, 4.2.10.1, 5.1.5	1:11	4.2.12.1, B.3.7
9:13	4.2.6, 4.2.7			2:3	4.2.12
		4:3	4.2.1.2.11, 4.2.6	2:7	4.2.1.2.9.13, B.3.8
Obadiah		4:4	4.2.10	2:9	4.2.12
1	4.2.2.3	4:8	4.2.10.1	2:13	4.2.1.2.9.13, 4.2.1.2.11, 4.2.2.2, 4.2.12
3	4.2.2.3	4:10	4.2.10		
5	4.2.2.3	4:13	4.2.1.2.13		
10	4.2.8	5:5-7	4.2.10	3:1	4.2.12.1
10-14	4.2.2.3, 4.2.8	6:1-2	3.2.2.4.3	3:2	4.2.12
11	4.2.8	6:4	3.2.2.4.3	3:3	4.2.12, 4.2.12.1
19	4.2.8	6:5	3.2.2.4.3, 4.1.1.3	3:4	4.2.12.1
				3:5	4.2.12.1
Jonah		6:6-7	3.2.2.4.3	3:6	4.2.12
1:1	B.3.9	6:7	4.2.10	3:7	4.2.12, 4.2.12.1
1:7	4.2.9.6, B.3.12	6:8	3.2.2.2.4, 3.2.2.4.3	3:9	4.2.12.1
1:8	4.2.9.6, B.3.12			3:10	4.2.12.1
1:9	B.3.7	6:11	3.2.2.4.3	3:12	4.2.12.1
1:12	4.2.9.6	6:15	3.2.2.4.3	3:13	4.2.12.1
2:4	4.2.9	6:16	3.2.2.4.3, 4.2.10	3:17-18	4.2.12
2:7	4.2.9, 4.2.9.2			3:19	4.2.12, 4.2.12.1, 5.1.4
3:9	4.2.6, 4.2.9.5	7:8	4.2.1.2.9.1		
3:10	4.2.9.2	7:12	4.2.10		
4:2	4.2.6, 4.2.9.5	7:14-15	3.2.2.4.3	**Zephaniah**	
4:5	4.2.9.4	7:17	4.2.1.2.13	1:1	4.2.1.2.11, 4.2.13
4:11	4.2.9.4	7:20	3.2.2.4.3		
				1:4-6	4.2.13
Micah		**Nahum**		1:8	4.2.13
1:1	4.2.10	1:3	4.2.11	1:12	4.2.13
1:5	4.2.10	1:9	4.2.1.2.9.10, 4.2.11.1	2:6	4.2.14
1:6	4.2.10			2:9	4.2.13.1
1:10	4.2.10	1:15	4.2.1.2.11, 4.2.11	2:13	4.2.13
2:13	4.2.1.2.13			2:15	4.2.1.2.11
3:7	4.1.3.1.2	2:3	B.3.13.1	2:22	4.2.14
3:8	4.2.1.2.13, 4.2.10	3:1	4.2.11	3:8	4.2.13.1
		3:5	4.2.11.1		
3:11	4.2.1.2.13	3:8-10	4.2.11		

Matthew

1:23	4.2.15.2
2:15	4.2.15.2
2:23	4.2.15.2
3:3	4.2.1.2.1
3:7-15	4.2.16
4:14-16	4.2.1.2.1
8:4	3.3.1.3
8:17	4.2.1.2.1
11:10	4.2.16
12:17-21	4.2.1.2.1
12:39-41	4.2.9
13:14-15	4.2.1.2.1
15:7-9	4.2.1.2.1
15:22	3.2.1.5
16:4	4.2.9
19:4-5	3.2.1.9.1
19:8	3.3.1.3
22:43	5.1.1
24:15	5.9.2, 5.9.7
27:9-10	4.2.2.1, 4.2.15.2
27:46	B.3.12

Mark

1:1-3	4.2.1.2.1
1:2-3	4.2.16
1:44	3.3.1.3
4:12	4.2.1.2.1
5:41	B.3.12
7:6-7	4.2.1.2.1
7:10	3.3.1.3
12:26	3.3.1.3
12:36	5.1.1

Luke

3:4-6	4.2.1.2.1
4:17-19	4.2.1.2.1
7:27	4.2.16
8:10	4.2.1.2.1
11:29-32	4.2.9
16:29-31	3.3.1.3
20:37	3.3.1.3
20:42	5.1.1
24:27	1.6, 3.3.1.3
24:44	1.6, 3.3.1.3

John

1:17	3.3.1.3
1:23	4.2.1.2.1
5:46	3.3.1.3
7:19	3.3.1.3
7:22	3.3.1.3, 3.3.9.2
12:37-38	4.2.1.2.1
12:39-41	4.2.1.2.1.2.1

Acts

1:1-16:9	5.10
1:16	5.1.1
2:25	5.1.1
4:11	B.3.3
8:28-33	4.2.1.2.1
28:25-27	4.2.12.1.2.1

Romans

4:6	5.1.1
5:12-14	6.2.1
9:29	4.2.1.2.1
9:27-28	4.4.2.1.2.1
9:32-33	B.3.3
10:2	3.3.1.3
10:16	4.2.1.2.1
10:20-21	4.2.1.2.1
11:9	5.1.1
15:12	4.2.1.2.1

1 Corinthians

9:9	3.3.1.3
10:4	B.3.3

Ephesians

2:20	B.3.3

Hebrews

4:7	5.1.7

1 Peter

2:4-8	B.3.3